Scott, Foresman
Spanish Program
Book 2

TEACHER'S ANNOTATED EDITION

PASOS Y PUENTES

Bernadette M. Reynolds
Montbello High School
Denver, Co

Carol Eubanks Rodríguez
Glen Crest Junior High School
Glen Ellyn, Il

Rudolf L. Schonfeld
Parsippany High School
Parsippany, NJ

Scott, Foresman and Company
Editorial Offices: Glenview, Illinois

Regional Offices: Sunnyvale, California · Tucker, Georgia
Glenview, Illinois · Oakland, New Jersey · Dallas, Texas

ISBN: 0-673-20723-4

12345678910 RRC 999897969594939291908988

CONTENTS

COMPONENTS OF THE PROGRAM

PASOS Y PUENTES is the second book in a three-book series. The student text opens with an activity-oriented *Repaso* focusing on basic, high-frequency vocabulary and structures from approximately the first half of VOCES Y VISTAS. This is followed by sixteen chapters and an appendix offering five optional grammar points with exercises, verb charts, Spanish-English and English-Spanish vocabularies covering Books 1 and 2, a grammar index, and maps.

This Teacher's Annotated Edition reproduces the student text with overprinted answers, teaching suggestions, and cross references to the ancillary materials. This front section also includes:

- "Organization of the Text," a description of all chapter elements with suggestions for their use
- "A Teacher's Perspective," a practical view of PASOS Y PUENTES
- "A Guide to Bridging from VOCES Y VISTAS," Book 1 of the series
- "A Guide to Bridging to ARCOS Y ALAMEDAS," Book 3 of the series
- An article, "Paired Practice: Why and How"
- "Teacher Notes," a section of chapter-by-chapter objectives, suggestions for classroom props or materials, cultural information on the photographs and realia, additional teaching, review, and enrichment suggestions, answers to specific sections of the chapter, and oral proficiency tests
- "Index of Cultural References" for use in planning your cultural presentations to the class

Ancillary materials to accompany PASOS Y PUENTES include the following:

- *Cassette Tapes:* A set of 17 cassettes, one for each chapter and a separate listening comprehension testing tape.
- *Workbook / Tape Manual:* A two-part student book. The Workbook section contains material to supplement each book chapter, plus special review sections following Chapters 4, 8, 12, and 16. The Tape Manual section contains all of the printed material necessary for students to do the listening exercises on the tapes.
- *Teacher's Edition: Workbook / Tape Manual:* The student material with overprinted answers and a complete tapescript.
- *Practice Sheet Workbook* (with separate *Teacher's Answer Key):* Worksheets designed to provide the basic-level mechanical practice for all vocabulary and grammar sections of the student text.
- *Teacher's Resource Book* (including *Testing Program):* A three-ring binder containing blackline master quizzes for all vocabulary and grammar sections, chapter tests, and four review tests (all with answers on reduced pages). The *Teacher's Edition: Workbook / Tape Manual* and a classroom wall map are also included.
- *Communicative Activity Blackline Masters:* A set of oral classroom activities for paired and group practice designed to supplement those already in the student text.
- *Overhead Transparencies:* A package of full-color overhead visuals that includes all vocabulary-teaching illustrations (with objects unlabeled), all conversation visuals *(¿Qué pasa?),* and the cartoon-strip illustrations for the *Temas* (without the captions). Also included are suggestions for use of the transparencies and an identification key.
- *Reader:* A graded reader specially designed to be used in conjunction with PASOS Y PUENTES.
- *Computer Software:* A package of computer-assisted instruction designed for use with the Scott, Foresman Spanish Program.
- *Videotape:* A tape designed to acquaint students with aspects of daily life in the Spanish-speaking world. A *Teacher's Guide* with student blackline masters is included.

ORGANIZATION OF THE TEXT

A glance at PASOS Y PUENTES will reveal an efficient predictability of format. All chapters begin with a *Prólogo cultural*. All end with a chapter vocabulary list. In between you will find the following:

Palabras Nuevas I
   Aplicaciones*
Palabras Nuevas II
Explicaciones I
   Aplicaciones
Explicaciones II
   Aplicaciones

Predictability of format, however, in no way implies sameness. There is enormous variety in presentation and practice. But predictability is crucial if a book is to work truly flexibly in the classroom. If you, the teacher, are to plan well for what to emphasize or to omit, you must be able to know the organization of the text.

PASOS Y PUENTES begins with a *Repaso* composed of 26 conversation—or activity—based exercises. These are designed to bring students back to language learning in an enjoyable, interactive way. Emphasis is on what students remember or can quickly recall, with no structural review or teaching *per se*.

Sixteen chapters compose the main body of the text. What follows are some very basic suggestions for using the chapter sections. Next to each section title there are five boxes representing Listening (L), Speaking (S), Reading (R), Writing (W), and Culture (C). These show you the relative emphasis that each text section gives to each of these skills or areas of understanding. Red boxes represent strong emphasis; purple boxes mean some emphasis.

PRÓLOGO CULTURAL   L S R W C

These essays give informative, curiosity-piquing glimpses into Hispanic culture. Each focuses on one of the main themes of the chapter.

* The first *Aplicaciones* section focuses on listening and speaking, the second on speaking and reading, the third on writing.

We recommend that you:

- Assign the *Prólogo* as homework, with or without classroom discussion the following day.
- Help students compare and contrast what they have read with their own culture, encouraging development of a global perspective.
- Ask students to keep a cultural notebook.
- Let students use these as a point of departure for extra-credit cultural reports.
- Make as full use as possible of native speakers who may be in your class or in the school to elaborate on particular topics.
- Begin immediately to use the Teacher Notes for additional cultural information that you can share with the class.

PALABRAS NUEVAS I

Contexto visual   L S R W C

This is new, active vocabulary presented in a visual context.

- Use the overhead transparency as the tape recites the words; have students listen and repeat.
- Identify items affirmatively / negatively (*¿Es un . . . ? / Sí. Es un . . . / No. Es un . . .*); pose either / or or open-ended questions; use gestures and pantomime, synonyms / antonyms / related words / definitions in Spanish.

Contexto comunicativo   L S R W C

This is new active vocabulary that does not lend itself to illustration. These words are presented in the context of mini-dialogues with substitutions. New words are in boldface type and are glossed in the right-hand margin.

- Let students hear the mini-dialogues on tape.
- Let pairs of students read the mini-dialogues aloud (without the substitutions).
- Let volunteers read (or perform) the mini-dialogues for the class.
- Ask for volunteers or assign students to read the

mini-dialogues with you (you might want to assume the role that has longer or more difficult speeches).*

- Redo the mini-dialogues with the class, using the *Variaciones.* With students who are new to the Scott, Foresman Spanish Program, explain how these work: The individual words and phrases in the text should be replaced by those to the right of the arrow. Point out that a red box represents a new *Variación.* When two or more substitutions are shown after a box, all must be made for the mini-dialogue to make sense.
- Ask simple comprehension questions, or use those provided on the tape.
- Avoid grammar discussions at this point. When you get to the *Explicaciones,* you may then want to refer to these mini-dialogues as a point of departure. Cross references appear in the on-page teacher notes.

Even at upper levels the use of props and Total Physical Response (TPR) techniques can be very effective in presenting vocabulary.

En otras partes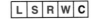

This feature offers examples of how Spanish vocabulary differs from region to region and discourages viewing vocabulary choice as a matter of right or wrong. The words given in this feature are *not active vocabulary.* They are shown as a means of pointing out to students that they might hear variant forms depending on the speaker's native country or region. If you have native speakers in your class, encourage them to add any additional variants that they may use.

Práctica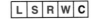

These exercises are designed to help students begin to learn the new material. Many are set up for paired practice, though you may do them in a more traditional way simply by playing one of the roles yourself. (For a discussion of paired practice, see page T17.)

- You do the model and perhaps the first one or two

*One role is often shorter or easier than the other to encourage less verbal or performance-shy students.

numbered items aloud with the class before dividing them into smaller groups.
- Assign more complex exercises as homework, using in-class paired practice the following day.
- Use the *Hablemos de ti* (the final exercise) to clarify for the students the real-life, personal use of the vocabulary they are learning.

Basic vocabulary practice exercises are available in the *Practice Sheet Workbook;* higher level practice plus the written material necessary for doing tape exercises are available in the combination *Workbook / Tape Manual.* There is, in addition, a quiz on every essential chapter section as part of the testing program in the Teacher's Resource Book. This may, if you choose, be used as homework practice instead.

APLICACIONES
Diálogo

Like all of the *Aplicaciones* sections, this is discretionary. The *Diálogo* gives students an example of extended discourse, most often with explicit or underlying cultural information. Some new passive vocabulary is included for reading recognition. Words and expressions that students would not readily understand are glossed. To promote the important skill of informed guessing, cognates and more easily decodable words are not glossed.

- Play the tape as students listen.
- Interrupt the tape to ask simple factual questions (who/what/where/when/how).
- Ask for volunteers to read or perform the *Diálogo* for the class, or divide students into small groups so that they may read together.
- Point out and discuss any cultural information mentioned or implicit in the *Diálogo.*
- Assign the *Preguntas* as written homework and then go over them in class the following day.
- You might instead handle the *Preguntas* in class immediately after reading, then assign students the task of writing a third-person summary of the *Diálogo.*
- Use the additional taped oral questions either immediately after listening to the *Diálogo* the first time or, after a few days, replay the tape and let students answer them then.

Participación

L S R W C

This optional section provides students a controlled opportunity to create their own dialogue. Since the topic is based on the *Diálogo,* students have a model that they can follow closely.

- Assign this as an extra-credit activity for pairs of students.
- Assign the *Participación* as an oral project. In each chapter, assign it to a different pair of students. You might also ask them to prepare a written set of *Preguntas* to hand out as a listening comprehension quiz for their classmates.

PALABRAS NUEVAS II

This is identical in format to *Palabras Nuevas I,* and recommendations for use are the same. One additional optional feature concludes *Palabras Nuevas II:*

Estudio de palabras

L S R W C

This section is designed to promote both linguistic and cultural awareness. Cover it quickly, but emphasize for students that an understanding of the topics discussed will help them immeasurably in their comprehension of both written and spoken Spanish. It will also help them to make educated guesses if they need to "invent" a word when they are speaking.

- Read the section aloud with the class or assign it as homework.
- Explain that any new words discussed or mentioned in this section will not appear on tests, but that students will be expected to recognize them when they read.
- Encourage students to look for these and additional word relationships as they read and study.
- Encourage students to examine their own language's roots, affixes, verb-noun-adjective relationships, and so on.

Actividad

L S R W C

One or the other of the two *Palabras Nuevas* sections includes an optional paired or small group recreational activity designed for open-ended oral practice. For some *Actividades,* props will be needed. These are listed for you in the Teacher Notes under the heading "Suggested Materials."

EXPLICACIONES I

These are student-oriented grammar presentations with examples and charts. Grammatical terminology is kept to a minimum, and when used it is clarified with reference to the students' experience with their native language.

To make learning the grammar easier, most structures are first introduced lexically in the *Palabras Nuevas.* Students then use the new structures in a carefully controlled context as they practice the new words. Thus by the time students come to the formal grammar presentation, they are already familiar with the structures and in many cases even have some active control of them.

To help students see the immediate practicality of what they are learning, a list of objectives appears with each grammar topic. These usually take the form of language notions and/or functions and are derived either from the basic use of the structure being studied or from the contexts and formats of the exercises in the *Práctica.*

- Begin discussion of the grammar topic by reviewing the *Palabras Nuevas* mini-dialogue(s) where the structure was initially presented (on-page notes in this teacher's edition provide cross references).
- Be sure to go over the explanations, but don't let the class get stuck there. The majority of students will learn more from the practice itself (in the book, in the *Practice Sheet Workbook,* and in the *Workbook / Tape Manual)* than from discussion of grammar points. Do not aim for immediate mastery, particularly of the more complex structures. They are continually re-entered, practiced, and reinforced in subsequent chapter elements and in subsequent chapters.
- Ask students to make up additional examples of the target structure.
- Use simple oral pattern drills before doing the text exercises.
- Use the overhead transparencies or other visuals for oral drill (short question / answer or narrative description).

Práctica ☐L☐S☐R☐W☐C

See *Palabras Nuevas I,* above, for recommendations.

Actividad ☐L☐S☐R☐W☐C

A discretionary oral activity follows one of the two *Explicaciones* sections of each chapter. See *Palabras Nuevas II*, above, for recommendations.

APLICACIONES

¿Qué pasa? ☐L☐S☐R☐W☐C

This conversation visual appears in odd-numbered chapters. It comprises an illustration with a few simple identification questions and suggestions for creating a dialogue based on it. Like other *Aplicaciones,* this section is discretionary and should be used as time permits. (Select from among the *Participación,* the *Actividades,* and the *¿Qué pasa?,* doing only one or two of the four.)

- Use the overhead transparency.
- Ask students to identify the objects and situations in the visual by naming, describing, expressing location, ownership, or by making a personal comment or observation.
- Allow students to prepare dialogues or narratives based on the visual either as homework or, as small-group work, in class. Sample dialogues appear in the Teacher Notes.
- Ask for volunteers to role play the situation.
- You may want to let students add new characters to the situation or to alter the situation suggested; encourage spontaneity, gesture, overacting, use of props, and so on; let students prepare scripts for more extended skits based on the visual.
- Emphasize performance, encouraging careful pronunciation, intonation, etc.

Lectura ☐L☐S☐R☐W☐C

This reading appears in even-numbered chapters and, like the *¿Qué pasa?* with which it alternates, is discretionary. It comprises a culturally informative extended dialogue or narration with glossed passive vocabulary followed by a series of questions. A pre-reading feature, *Antes de leer,* helps set the scene and focus the students' attention.

- Go over the *Antes de leer* in class, making sure that students understand the questions being asked.
- Play the tape as students follow along, and then review the *Antes de leer* questions to see if students understood the main idea and some of the basic information.
- Ask students to cover the glosses to see if they can understand the words from context, or go over the glossed words in advance.
- Assign the *Lectura* as homework to be gone over in class the following day (in which case, go over the *Antes de leer* when you make the assignment).
- Play the tape again, this time including the brief oral questions that follow it; stop the tape after each question to allow for student response.
- Point out and discuss cultural information mentioned or implicit in the *Lectura.*
- Assign the *Preguntas* as written homework or do them orally in class.
- Ask students to prepare one or two true / false statements or additional questions to ask a classmate.
- Use visual aids appropriate to the *Lectura* to stimulate additional conversation.
- Ask students to summarize the *Lectura* in their own words, either orally or in writing.

EXPLICACIONES II ☐L☐S☐R☐W☐C

See *Explicaciones I,* above.

APLICACIONES

This is a four-part section designed for review and writing practice. You may choose to do all, none, or only selected portions of this material.

Repaso ☐L☐S☐R☐W☐C

The *Repaso* is a review and writing exercise closely linked to the *Tema* that follows it. It consists of a numbered series of Spanish sentences. Each is followed by English sentences which, when put into Spanish, will mirror the model sentence syntactically. The sentences in the *Repaso* are unrelated in theme and, in English, may differ greatly. But when properly rendered into Spanish, word order and part of speech will have a one-to-one relationship to the Spanish model. (Answers appear in the Teacher Notes.)

To students new to the Scott, Foresman Spanish Program this may at first appear to be a very peculiar exercise. But modeled writing is not translation for its own sake. It is guided writing that aids students in making the transition from the English thought process to the Spanish thought process. They will soon be surprised to discover how much they are learning from it. Above all, it will lead to their encountering an unusual degree of success in writing Spanish. (See suggestions for the *Tema*.)

The *Repaso* also reviews the vocabulary and structures presented in the chapter, as well as those from earlier chapters. The target structures are noted for you in the on-page teacher's notes. In early chapters:

- Do the first substitution in each set for the class, emphasizing the correspondence once the sentence has been rendered into Spanish.
- Let students do the subsequent sentences as a group or working in pairs.
- Let students write what they have done on the board, with corrections being made on the spot.
- Identify areas where additional review is necessary and go over the appropriate page(s) in the text or *Practice Sheet Workbook,* or do the appropriate exercise(s) in the *Comprueba tu progreso.*
- In later chapters, assign the *Repaso* or selected sentences in it as homework to be gone over in class. Make corrections on the board or through answer sheets or transparencies that you prepare.

Tema   L S R W C

The *Tema* is a cartoon strip with English captions. Point out to the students that, syntactically, the Spanish version of each caption will be identical to the similarly numbered Spanish sentence in the *Repaso.* (Even if you choose not to use the *Repaso,* this should be pointed out so that students have a Spanish-language model to work from as they write.) Assign the *Tema* as written homework. (Answers appear in the Teacher Notes.)

You might also enjoy using the overhead transparency of the *Tema* cartoon strip (on which the captions do not appear) as a stimulus for in-class

conversation, story-telling practice, or group composition.

Redacción   L S R W C

This writing exercise gives a choice of two or three additional topics for student compositions. This section is best used as an extra-credit assignment or with better classes.

Comprueba tu progreso   L S R W C

This section is designed for extra practice or as a pre-test before the chapter test. Answers appear in the Teacher Notes. You may want to use them to create an answer key for the students' own use.

- Assign the *Comprueba tu progreso* two days before the chapter test will be given.
- Quickly go over the material the following day, helping students identify areas of weakness either for immediate in-class review or for extra study that evening before the following day's test.
- Point out to the students the *Vocabulario del capítulo* on the following page, reminding them that these are the words they will be responsible for knowing on the test.

PHOTOS / REALIA   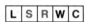 L S R W C

Throughout the program, photographs serve to illustrate the culture. Realia—tickets, menus, ads, schedules, and so forth—are provided to enrich the language-learning experience.

- Encourage students to make cultural inferences about what they see.
- Supplement the material in the student text with the additional information provided in the Teacher Notes.
- Ask students to prepare more extensive captions than those that appear in the book or to make up questions about the pictures or realia that they can ask their classmates.
- Use the photos to stimulate narrative description, or let students use them to create a dialogue.
- Use them for spot evaluation of listening and speaking ability; for suggestions, see the oral proficiency tests in the Teacher Notes.

A TEACHER'S PERSPECTIVE

The Scott, Foresman Spanish Program provides everything you need to face the challenge of today's foreign-language classroom. Growing enrollments, the changing profile of the Spanish class, the emphasis on student communicative ability and on proficiency—all mean new teacher goals and new student expectations. Above all, it means newly designed tools for easier teaching and more active student involvement.

Here is how the Scott, Foresman Spanish Program responds to your needs and concerns and how it will help you bring your students to a realistic and rewarding level of proficiency in their new language.

"How can a book help students talk?"
PASOS Y PUENTES provides for extensive oral practice from the first page, and both the text and special ancillary materials provide abundant opportunity for growth toward oral proficiency:

- *Prácticas,* text exercises based on true-to-life contexts that students will relate to, are set up for paired practice.
- Every *Palabras Nuevas* and every *Explicaciones* section ends with *Hablemos de ti.* This series of related real-life questions practices new vocabulary and structures and reinforces for students that they are learning something practical and useful.
- *Actividades,* two per chapter, allow for paired or small-group oral practice.
- An oral-practice orientation in the *Contexto comunicativo* of each *Palabras Nuevas* section provides slot substitutions *(Variaciones)* to engage students actively in their learning of the new vocabulary.
- A conversation visual, *¿Qué pasa?,* encourages oral description, narration, and dialogue development. This feature appears in all odd-numbered chapters.
- A *Diálogo* in every chapter is followed by a *Participación,* in which students may create their own conversation based on the dialogue. The

Diálogo itself is also on tape, followed by oral questions for oral response.
- *Pronunciación* section on each chapter tape provide necessary engoing practice.
- The Teacher Notes provide an oral proficiency test for each chapter.

"How can we get students to learn how to really listen?"
Practice in the listening skill will occur naturally in paired exercise work and in the *Actividades,* for unless students listen to their partners, they will not be able to respond appropriately. Yet that, of course, is not the same as listening to native speakers. To better develop the listening skills needed for real-world communication, you will find the following in PASOS Y PUENTES:

- Extensive listening practice appears on the tapes. Much of it involves use of the *Tape Manual,* since paper-and-pencil activity helps ensure that attention remains focused on the listening task.
- For each chapter there is a test of listening comprehension on the separate testing tape.
- All of the *Diálogos* and *Lecturas* are on tape. So, too, are all of the visualized words and the mini-dialogues in the *Palabras Nuevas,* which offer students additional pronunciation and intonation models while helping them practice the new words. In addition, the listening skill is sharpened through the brief taped *dictados* (listen-write) and the inclusion of simple comprehension questions that follow the *Diálogo,* the *Lectura,* and the final mini-dialogue of each *Palabras Nuevas.* These have no written apparatus and call for very brief oral response (listen-speak).
- A videotape presents sixty minutes of authentic oral Spanish. Filmed in Spain and Mexico, the tape offers narration as well as unscripted, unrehearsed conversations and interviews in such locations as a department store, a school, a market, and a family home.

"I want to make sure my students learn to read"

All even-numbered chapters include a *Lectura* followed by a series of questions. The task of learning to read in a foreign language is eased through the *Antes de leer* that precedes each reading. This provides clues to a decoding of the reading, suggests things to look for while reading, and/or stimulates students to think about their own experiences in similar situations. This encouragement of basic reading strategies in the foreign language makes the overall decoding task a much less formidable one. In addition:

- The realia included in the text give students multiple opportunities to read "real" things, the types of things that they will have to read if they travel to a Spanish-speaking country. This type of reading brings special rewards as students begin to realice how much they know and can understand.
- All *Práctica* directions are in Spanish. These give a statement of the context plus directions that explain what the student is to do. This also offers important reading practice.
- Few things give students a greater sense of accomplishment than being able to read material outside the basic text. Thus a separate graded reader is available, specially designed for use with PASOS Y PUENTES.

"How can I help my students learn to write?"

Writing well is a problem for many students today even in their native language, so what can we expect in Spanish? With some help, we can expect quite a bit. The unique *Repaso, Tema,* and *Redacción,* found in the third *Aplicaciones* section of every chapter, carefully guide students in acquiring the writing skill.

Practice in writing is also provided in the *Workbook / Tape Manual,* in the taped *dictados,* in the *Practice Sheet Workbook,* and in any of the *Prácticas* or *Preguntas* that you choose to assign as written homework. Many of the *Actividades,* too, though oral in purpose, involve advance written preparation or a post-activity written summary.

"How do you teach the culture?"

Each chapter begins with a *Prólogo cultural,* a cultural overview of one of the main themes of the chapter.

These are in English to make them fully accessible to the students. And on whatever you may open the book you will discover Spanish-language captioned photographs and/or realia. You are provided with additional cultural information on all of these in the Teacher Notes in this front section. In addition:

- An Index of Cultural References cuts the time you need to spend preparing your cultural presentations.
- A videotape offers authentic cultural situations in Spain and Mexico. A *Teacher's Guide* with blackline masters for student use is included with the tape so that students can gain maximum cultural and linguistic benefit.
- Brief tests of the cultural information presented in the *Prólogo cultural* are included on each chapter and review test in the *Teacher's Resource Book.*
- The Spanish language itself, of course, is a reflection of Hispanic culture. This is made evident to the students in the *En otras partes,* where examples are given of how Spanish differs from country to country and region to region.
- In the *Estudio de palabras,* students learn not only vocabulary-acquisition and reading strategies, such as an understanding of word families and affixes, but also the historical-cultural concepts of loanwords, cognates, and language roots. An understanding of how a people's language functions is a basic tool for understanding the people themselves. The Arabic and indigenous American contributions to the Spanish language reflect not only history, but also geography and ethnicity and the various world views that the three combined have fostered to create what we know as Hispanic culture.

"Is there any way to teach a little less so my students can learn a lot more?"

Yes, and to ease your and your students' task, *the scope of each book in the Scott, Foresman Spanish Program provides for a far more even pace than any program previously developed.* Most students just cannot learn and retain the amount of new material that is presented in the typical two-year sequence. This program offers a three-year pacing that students can learn from. Because what is taught is usable and is continually reinforced, your students will almost surely master and retain more than you are accustomed to.

Since language learning is cumulative and gradual, there is strong focus here on regular re-entry and reinforcement. *We would urge you not to teach each vocabulary set and each grammar topic for immediate mastery before moving on.* Individual words and structures are frequently re-entered. Previously taught structures are continually woven into subsequent chapters' vocabulary exercises, giving students reinforcement and giving you a clear opportunity to identify areas that need additional practice. Do not let students get bogged down when they fail to grasp something immediately. Let them continue to watch for its reoccurrence. Let them continue to encounter and say it aloud in mini-dialogues. Give them the basic practice provided in the *Practice Sheet Workbook.* Soon you and they will find that they are using the structure with less hesitancy and, eventually, automatically. Language learning is, after all, a skill-mastering process far more than a data-memorizing one.

Here is how PASOS Y PUENTES will help you and your students avoid overload:

- The book always lets you and the students know what they will be held responsible for. *All structures for which they are responsible are explained and practiced in the* Explicaciones. *All active vocabulary is presented and practiced in the* Palabras Nuevas. *All other material is discretionary.*
- Most structures are presented as vocabulary items before they are taught as grammar points. This gives students an opportunity to use the language naturally and then later to have it codified. For example, the *yo / tú* forms of verbs are taught in the *Palabras Nuevas* and used conversationally in the *Práctica.* Only then, after true-to-life, contextual practice, is the verb paradigm presented and practiced on its own. The fear of grammar is dissipated because so often the irregularities and problem areas have been made a part of the students' active language.

- Five of the more advanced Spanish structures are presented in an optional appendix. Each includes one practice exercise. You may present these if you chosse. Should you elect to do so, each structure has a note suggesting the optimal occasion for presenting it.

"There's never enough practice material!"
The Scott, Foresman Spanish Program offers considerably more practice material than you will need. You shouldn't even have to devise your own practice sheets or quizzes. Here's why:

- There are book exercises to accompany not only the grammar, but also the vocabulary presentations.
- There is a *Practice Sheet Workbook* that offers students mechanical practice for all vocabulary and grammar.
- There is a *Workbook / Tape Manual* that offers higher-level writing practice for vocabulary and grammar, plus listening practice with the tapes.
- Oral practice—particularly communicative practice—is provided through 1) the *Contexto comunicativo* in the *Palabras Nuevas,* 2) the communicatively formatted exercises in the *Prácticas,* 3) the four *Hablemos de ti* sections of each chapter, 4) the *Participaciones* following the *Diálogos,* 5) the *¿Qué pasa?,* 6) the *Actividades,* and 7) the *Communicative Activity Blackline Masters* that accompany the text.
- Though any exercise can also be written, practice in the writing skill is specifically provided for in the *Repaso, Tema,* and *Redacción.*

"Do you really think I can finish this book?
Yes, but you will have to make some choices. The only material that must be covered thoroughly is in the essential chapter elements: *Palabras Nuevas I–II* and *Explicaciones I–II.* These are clearly marked for you in this Teacher's Annotated Edition. All the rest is there for you to choose among as you design lessons around your particular goals and teaching style. You may safely omit any of the three *Aplicaciones* sections knowing that there is nothing new in them that students will be held responsible for. This assurance

gives you freedom and flexibility and puts you in control of the text.

You may want to use the *Aplicaciones* only occasionally (in alternate chapters, for example) or where you feel students particularly need that extra reinforcement. You may elect to omit some entirely from your teaching plans. Every chapter has a *Participación* and two *Actividades.* You might use only one of the three. The *Repaso* and *Tema* may be omitted, or you may assign and go through only a few of tho cubstitution sentences in the *Repaso* and omit lI ie *Tema.* You may use the *Tema* overhead transparency for conversation rather than writing practice. The *Diálogo* and *Lectura* include some unknown vocabulary for one-time use only. No new active material appears in them, so either or both may be skipped as often as you like.

To teach each section for immediate mastery or to follow the book assigning every exercise and activity on every page will certainly prevent your finishing the book. But that, too, is a valid choice, and careful provision has been made for the third-year teacher whose students did not finish PASOS Y PUENTES, just as one has been provided for you in case your second-year students did not finish the first book, VOCES Y VISTAS.

Whatever your choices, enjoy using this program. Above all, enjoy watching your students actively engage themselves in learning Spanish.

A GUIDE TO BRIDGING TO ARCOS Y ALAMEDAS

By allowing mastery of the essential material to come gradually, and by a careful choosing from among both the ancillary practice materials and the discretionary text elements, most classes should have been able to complete the essentials of VOCES Y VISTAS in one school year. If, however, you second-year students did not finish the first book, careful provision has been made for them to move into PASOS Y PUENTES. The bridging plan assumes:

- *Mastery* (i. e., comprehension and a certain level of fluency) of all structures and vocabulary through Chapter 9 of VOCES Y VISTAS.
- *Coverage* (i.e., acquaintance and recognition) through Chapter 13.

All structures taught in Chapters 9–16 of VOCES Y VISTAS are re-presented in PASOS Y PUENTES, as are some of the more difficult concepts taught before Chapter 9 (e. g., *ser* vs. *estar,* object pronouns). In most such re-presentations, some additional new information is taught.

PASOS Y PUENTES begins with a *Repaso* that provides a series of exercises for reviewing the early grammar and lexical fields of VOCES Y VISTAS. If, for whatever reason, your students did not get beyond Chapter 13 of VOCES Y VISTAS, they will need to have the "missed" vocabulary presented as new words. Here is a list of the first occurrence in PASOS Y PUENTES of the vocabulary taught in Chapters 14–16 of VOCES Y VISTAS. Parenthetical numbers refer to the Book 1 chapters in which the words were taught. Book 1 overhead transparencies are excellent for introducing or reviewing vocabulary categories.

Repaso
The following would need to be taught:

el golf (14)	fantástico, -a (15)
el volibol (14)	la aventura (16)
correr (14)	

Capítulo 1
The following would need to be taught:

personal hygiene items (visual, Chap. 14)	el portugués (15)
	la pared (15)
el/la dentista (14)	la tarjeta postal (15)
el despertador (14)	privado, -a (5)
el equipo (14)	por (15)
atlético, -a (14)	el/la escritor(a) (16)
fuerte (14)	el/la médico(a) (16)
hay que (14)	la novela (16)
lo que (14)	algo (16)
describir (15)	algún, alguna (16)
cardinal points (15)	lo siento (16)
la lengua (15)	por eso (16)

Capítulo 2
The following would need to be taught:

acostarse (14)*	furniture items (visual, Chap. 15)
levantar (14)	
la mano (14)	con vista a(l) (15)
el/la atleta (14)	de veras (15)
la pelota (14)	en seguida (15)
débil (14)	descansar (16)
enérgico, -a (14)	estar de acuerdo (16)
perezoso, -a (14)	el/la enfermero(a) (16)
mandar (15)	excelente (16)
saber (15)	adentro (16)
el edificio (15)	afuera (16)

Capítulo 3
The following would need to be taught:

despertarse (14)	conocer (15)
divertirse (14)	quisiera (15)
lavarse las manos (14)	el puente (15)
perder (14)	el río (15)
quitarse (14)	el brazo (16)
el/la aficionado(a) (14)	la cabeza (16)
el/la jugador(a) (14)	el dedo (16)
despacio (14)	formidable (16)
rápidamente (14)	preferido, -a (16)

* Reflexive verbs are re-entered for meaning only. As with all structures re-presented in PASOS Y PUENTES, students are not asked to manipulate reflexives until they have been reviewed in an *Explicaciones* section.

A GUIDE TO BRIDGING TO ARCOS Y ALAMEDAS

The bridging plan between Books 1 and 2 and between Books 2 and 3 is similar. It assumes:

- *Mastery* (i.e., comprehension and a certain level of fluency) of all structures and vocabulary through Chapter 9 of PASOS Y PUENTES.
- Coverage (i.e., acquaintance and recognition) through Chapter 13.

All structures taught in Chapters 9–16 of PASOS Y PUENTES are re-presented in Book 3 (ARCOS Y ALAMEDAS), as are some of the more difficult concepts taught before Chapter 9 (familiar commands, reflexive commands). In most such re-presentations, some additional new information is taught.

ARCOS Y ALAMEDAS begins with a *Repaso* similar to the one in this book. It provides a series of exercises for reviewing the early grammar and lexical fields of VOCES Y VISTAS and PASOS Y PUENTES. If, for whatever reason, students do not get beyond Chapter 13 of PASOS Y PUENTES, Book 3 students will need to have the "missed" vocabulary presented as new words. Here is a list of the first occurrence in ARCOS Y ALAMEDAS of the vocabulary taught in Chapters 14–16 of PASOS Y PUENTES. Parenthetical numbers refer to the Book 2 chapters in which the words are taught.

Repaso
The following would need to be taught:
el artículo (14)   la estatua (14)

Capítulo 1
The following would need to be taught:*
destruir (14)   el sitio (15)
producir (14)   alegrarse de (16)
el oro (14)   enojarse con (16)
muerto, -a (14)   preocuparse (16)
el/la ayudante (15)   continuamente (16)
los consejos (15)   a/en/por todas partes (16)
el resto (15)

Capítulo 2
la lana (14)   el helicóptero (15)
a causa de (14)   el jefe/la jefa (15)
acompañar (15)   probable (16)
aconsejar (15)   supersticioso, -a (16)
la canoa (15)   es cierto (16)
el clima (15)

Capítulo 3
escaparse (14)   propio, -a (15)
volveré (14)   dudar (16)
el ingeniero, la   negar (16)
  ingeniera (14)   sentir (16)
el mundo (14)   sorprender (16)
el robo (14)   temer (16)
el titular (14)   lo lástima (16)
ahorrar (15)   enojado, -a (16)
práctico, -a (15)   extraño, -a (16)

* In addition to the words in the list, the imperfect ending *-ía* (*quería, tenía, parecía, comía*) appears in dialogues and readings of early Book 3 chapters. The imperfect of *-er/-ir* verbs is presented in Chapter 14 of PASOS Y PUENTES. If students have not covered Chapter 14, Book 3 teachers can quickly explain the one form and move on.

PAIRED PRACTICE: WHY AND HOW

Paired practice is the most basic and least threatening way of increasing interaction in the foreign language classroom. Undoubtedly our classrooms have always been interactive in some ways: Teacher asks/student answers, teacher cues/student repeats or responds, students read a dialogue aloud. All of these are examples of person-to-person interaction (though some might call them parallel monologues). Paired practice, however, expands and transforms the nature of the interaction.

Paired practice is, very simply, two students practicing the language together. What are its advantages?

- *It greatly increases opportunities for student involvement and participation.* If 12 or 16 or 20 students are simultaneously saying something in the target language to their partner, that is a significantly larger number than one student at a time responding to the teacher.
- *It greatly increases meaningful, productive use of the textbook.* In paired practice, each student is practicing the entire exercise instead of only the eight or ten students called upon to do the eight or ten exercise items.
- *It promotes a level of realism and relevancy.* Paired practice simulates real-life social contact, with students having the opportunity to ask and answer questions and to initiate and engage in conversational exchanges.
- *It encourages a more natural use of language.* Face-to-face interaction encourages eye contact, proper intonation, emotional tone, rejoinders, exclamations, and so on.
- *It greatly reduces stress and reluctance to participate, thereby improving learning.* Fear of making errors in front of a whole class can be a terribly inhibiting factor, especially among teenagers, while doing so with a sympathetic peer is considerably less so. In paired practice, students can confirm what they already know and find out what they should know through a form of cooperative learning or peer teaching that can greatly help those whom we sometimes seem unable to reach.
- *It provides variety in classroom pace with time devoted to directed skill-getting and practice.* Paired practice is a teacher-directed/student-centered activity that gives students monitored "hands-on" practice with the tools whose use they are acquiring.

Why are we sometimes reluctant to use paired practice? Loss of control and fear of students' getting off track are two major reasons. More general concerns about noise level and the number of student errors are also involved. But there are ways of guaranteeing successful and productive paired practice:

- *Keep the pairing simple.* Starting from a given point in the room, tell students to turn to the person to their left (right, etc.). Proximity is an easy way of pairing, and the different directions ensure that students will have at least four different partners over a period of time. (Periodic absences will increase the number.) If you change the seating plan every grading period, the number of potential partners greatly increases. (In certain situations, it may be best to let students choose their own partners. You will find that individuals are very rarely left out in the cold.)
- *Give clear instructions.* Make sure students understand the context in which the exercise is set and the directions for what they are supposed to do. Always do the model with one of the students. If you like, you can then ask for a volunteer pair to do the first numbered item for the class as a second model.
- *Establish a time limit.* A short question-answer or statement-rejoinder exercise should be given a time limit of no more than two to three minutes, particularly at the beginning of the year.
- *Require feedback.* Ask the whole group the same questions that were just practiced in pairs. For less able students, you would ask the identical

questions. For more able ones, you might pose some variation or extension of the questions. Now you will find students prepared and willing to recite in the large group because they know what is expected of them and they have gained confidence through the less threatening work with a peer.

How do you keep students from using English? Be mobile. Monitor what is going on and, if necessary, make it clear that English is not acceptable. The controlled task and time limit help eliminate the problem. When students find that feedback must be in Spanish, they will realize that using English in paired practice will not help them. Model and re-model carefully rather than correcting errors, and you will almost certainly find most students eager to go along with paired practice and reluctant to jeopardize what they will view as one of the real privileges of the foreign language classroom.

What are the alternatives for the teacher who does not want to use paired practice even though the exercise directions seem to call for it? The teacher takes will role of Student A and calls on a series of students to respond as Student B. Or, in some situations, it will work just as nicely for you to reverse the roles, calling on individuals to act as Student A while you respond or react as Student B.

Different teaching and practice formats should be used depending on the nature of the activity involved. Large-group instruction is superb for initial presentation of new concepts, i.e., for teaching and for the early stages of learning. A small-group format is good for tasks that require differentiated skills—for recombination and multi-skill practice. Individual instruction is best for remediation. Pair work, however, long the most neglected of our options, is the ideal medium for skill-getting practice and for reinforcing learning. It ensures adequate practice for everyone and helps students acquire those interactive skills so crucial to a communicative classroom and a proficiency-based curriculum.

ORAL PROFICIENCY TESTING

In the Teacher Notes for each chapter you will find a suggested oral proficiency test. There are four types of test items.

- *Direct Response,* in which a statement is made in English that directs the student to ask a certain question or to make an appropriate remark.
- *Picture-Cued Response,* in which the student is shown a photograph or illustration and is asked one or more questions in Spanish.
- *Situations,* in which a context is presented in English and, given a choice of three remarks or responses, the student is directed to select the appropriate one. You might either immediately give the three choices orally and ask the student to repeat the correct one or, with better students, you might want to allow an opportunity for the testee to come up with an appropriate response. With weaker students you may want to present the three choices on a 3 × 5 card, allowing the student to read the appropriate choice.
- *Real-Life Questions,* in which the student is asked to reply conversationally to real-life or personalized questions.

The oral proficiency tests provided look for basic, minimum competency, and the suggested answers are to help you guide the student toward what you expect of him or her. Students must be free to answer creatively and spontaneously. If a response communicates correct information, no matter how it differs from what the book suggests, the answer is correct. If students respond well, you should feel free to expand with additional questions or comments to create a brief dialogue with the testee.

In using the Picture-Cued Responses, make use of the overhead transparencies (if they are available to you) instead of the visuals in the book. In those cases, hand the transparency itself to the student as you ask the questions. That will save you the trouble of covering the labels that appear in the book versions of the illustrations.

In using the Directed Response, Situations, and Real-Life Questions, adapt the items to make them as compatible as possible with the student's own experience. Use real names. That will make for real conversation. Provide appropriate props where possible and strive to use them in situations that students can identify with. This will help emphasize that speaking Spanish is not an artificial thing, but rather an important skill that is useful in real life.

Oral proficiency tests should always be administered privately, but in as relaxed and nonthreatening a setting and manner as possible. Always bear in mind that some students are uncomfortable with questions about home and family. Not all have mother, father, brothers, sisters, and pets. Not all have their own room in a single-family dwelling.

Evaluating oral proficiency and communicative progress largely involves attention to the adequacy and appropriateness of an exchange of information. Since an identifiable "perfect" score does not exist, it is simpler to give points than to subtract them from an ideal maximum. A set of three scales provides an effective and easy way to evaluate communication skills. Each scale measures a different aspect: (1) appropriateness and adequacy in carrying out the communicative intent, (2) correctness of grammar, and (3) accuracy of pronunciation. The scales are weighted differently, with the greatest importance given to the first aspect and the least to accuracy of pronunciation (though, of course, incorrect pronunciation can sometimes impede communication). You are free to modify the scale according to your own teaching objectives. You might, for example, increase the emphasis on grammatical correctness so that it matches the 0–4 scale of the communication aspect.

Here are three examples:

COMMUNICATION	GRAMMAR	PRONUNCIATION
Appropriateness *Adequacy*	*Correctness*	*Accuracy*

4 ③ 2 1 0   3 ② 1 0   ② 1 0

PICTURE-CUED RESPONSE: Chapter 8. Pointing to the photograph on p. 269, ask: *¿Qué le va a hacer al joven el policía?* Student response: *Va a poner una multa.*

4 3 2 ① 0   ③ 2 1 0   2 ① 0

REAL-LIFE QUESTION: Chapter 3. *¿Cuántos años tienes?*

Student response: *Tengo seis años.*

④ 3 2 1 0   3 ② 1 0   2 ① 0

DIRECTED RESPONSE: Chapter 2. How would you tell a salesperson that you don't like these pants, that you prefer those over there? Student response: *No me gustan estos pantalones aquí. Prefiero esos pantalones allá.*

Because an exchange of information is the goal, error correction should be delayed in order to avoid interrupting the student's train of thought. It can also be helpful to correct errors by category, rather than student by student, when you find a consistency in the types of errors being made.

TEACHER NOTES

TITLE PAGE

Photo

The door of a typical adobe building in Santa Fe, New Mexico. The capital of New Mexico, Santa Fe was founded in 1609 and is one of the oldest cities in the U.S. Despite rapid growth since 1960, Santa Fe has retained its colonial atmosphere through enactment of a zoning ordinance requiring that construction and remodeling conform to the existing architectural style.

Of all the states, New Mexico has the highest proportion of residents of Hispanic origin (approximately 40%), most of whom are centered in the north central area.

PAGE VI

Photo

A group of students at a school in Mexico City. The hours during which students in Mexico attend classes vary considerably from school to school. For example, some schools hold classes from 8 a.m. until 6 p.m. with a long break for lunch, while others hold classes from 7 a.m. until 3 p.m. Class schedules also vary, and students do not take the same courses every day.

Generally, education in Mexico consists of six years of *educación primaria*, three years of *educación secundaria*, and three years of *preparatoria*. The number of years devoted to higher education depends on the field of study that one chooses.

PAGE IX

Photo

A fair in San Juan, Puerto Rico. Fairs like this one move from town to town throughout the island so that a greater number of people can experience the thrilling rides and attractions associated with them. The young people in the photo are waiting in line to ride the "Super Loop," a ride whose principal attraction is that it allows its passengers to defy the laws of gravity.

PAGE X

Photo

Highway signs from Mexico. In Mexico, as in many other countries throughout the world, efforts have been made to simplify instructions and other information for travelers. The trend internationally is to standardize signs, especially road signs and signs that are commonly used in public places.

Many signs in Mexico use pictures and words to communicate information. The signs shown in the photo direct travelers to various places of interest in Mexico.

PAGES XII-XIII

Photo

Dancing the *flamenco* during the gypsy pilgrimage to El Rocío. Since medieval times, Spaniards have celebrated the *romería*, an annual pilgrimage to the shrine of a patron saint during which the participants sing, dance, have picnics, and generally have a good time. Each region has its own *romería* dedicated to its patron saint. The people in the photo are part of the gypsy pilgrimage to El Rocío, which is southwest of Almonte in the province of Huelva. Note the regional costumes worn by some of the participants.

PAGE XIV

Photo

An Indian woman carrying a small child during the Holy Week procession in the Guatemalan village of Zunil. Guatemala is the only Central American nation that is predominantly Indian, and many of its inhabitants are direct descendants of the Quiché Maya Indians.

The dress and shawl worn by the woman in the photograph are typical of weavings from Guatemala, where textiles are noted for their intricate patterns and vivid colors. Their distinctiveness is due largely to the

Indians' perfection of an ancient Mayan technique called *ikat* (tie-dyeing). This is a method of producing patterns in textile by tying small portions of cotton or silk yarn so tightly with string that the tied parts do not absorb the dye when the treads are dipped. This elaborate process must be repeated for every color in the design. The tie-dyed skirts of Salcajá, shawls from Mazatenango, and silk headbands from Totonicapán are just a few examples of the exceptional garments produced by Guatemalan weavers employing the tie-dyeing technique.

PAGES XVI-XVII
Photo
Masks from the Indian market in Chichicastenango, Guatemala. Chichicastenango is a small highland town that comes alive on Thursdays and Sundays, when hundreds of brilliantly attired local Indians from throughout the region come into town for market days. Although the markets are conducted primarily for the local people, numerous native handicrafts that are intended primarily for tourists are also displayed. Among the latter are carved wooden masks, like the ones shown in the photo, which the Indians use in ceremonial dances. These masks are worn on the *Fiesta de Santo Tomás* (Chichicastenango's patron saint), when farmers, weavers, potters, and other workers dress in unusual costumes and dance to the accompaniment of marimbas, drums, and flutes. One of the most popular dances is *La Conquista* (the Dance of the Conquest), in which Indians wearing masks of the Spanish conquerors reenact the conquest of the native Quiché Maya Indians.

REPASO

PAGE 2

Additions to on-page notes

Notes: Welcome to Level II! This *Repaso* chapter is designed to reintroduce students to grammar points and vocabulary presented through Chapter 7, Level I, thereby easing the transition from one stage of their learning to the next. Each exercise reviews a specific grammar point in conjunction with thematically related vocabulary. We hope that you and your students will profit from and enjoy these activities.

PAGE 12

Photo

A family watching television in Madrid. Television is a popular evening diversion for the whole family in Spain, where it is not uncommon to find several generations living under the same roof. And with only two main channels in most areas, there aren't too many arguments about which show to watch..

PAGE 15

Additions to on-page notes

Notes: Expand the practice with question words by suggesting or eliciting questions with *cuántos(as):* *¿Cuántos estudiantes hay en la biblioteca? ¿Cuántas muchachas hay? ¿Cuántos muchachos hay?*

PAGE 16

Photos

(a) Home computing in Spain. Inexpensive European brands such as Sinclair and Amstrad (both British) have established themselves as the leaders in the Spanish personal computer market. One way to keep the price of computers down is to use cassette recorders rather than disk drives to load and store programs.

(b) Teens resting along the side of a *ciclovía* (bicycle path) in Colombia's capital city of Bogotá.

(c) Three sisters singing and playing the guitar in Madrid. The first guitar was probably made by the Egyptians more than 5,000 years ago. The Moors introduced the instrument to Spain, and from there it spread to the rest of Europe. The guitar has undergone several changes in size and shape, but by the second half of the nineteenth century, the Spaniard Antonio de Torres Jurado had refined it to the instrument we know today.

The guitar has always had its place in popular and folk music, but it was a Spanish guitarist-composer, Francisco Tárrega (1854–1909), who first transcribed the music of Bach, Mozart, and others for the instrument. Andrés Segovia (1894–1987) made classical music popular throughout the world. Portable electronic keyboard synthesizers are becoming very popular in Spain, but the place of the guitar seems assured not only because of tradition but because of the unique quality of its sound.

Additions to on-page notes

Notes: Before students begin Ex. 0, you may want volunteers to model questions and answers with each element in the first two columns.

PAGE 17

Photos

(a) Teenagers setting the table in a kitchen in Santander, located in Spain's northern region of Cantabria. In rural houses, the kitchen, with its large fireplace, traditionally served as a family room as well as a place to cook and to eat. In apartments built in the cities over the past hundred years, kitchens became progressively smaller and less important as gathering places. In recent years, however, the kitchen has begun to regain its status as a family room.

(b) A Spanish teenager listening to music. The availability of high-fidelity stereo equipment in Spain has spurred an interest in classical music. Spanish music in particular has benefited from this renewed interest, and recordings of works that range from the *cantigas,* or ballads, of King Alfonso X (1221–1284) to contemporary pieces by composers such as Luis de Pablo and Tomás Marco are available in record stores.

PAGE 21
Photos
(a) Detail of main entrance ot Mexico City's Palacio de Bellas Artes, or Palace of fine Arts. A combination of theater and exhibition hall, Bellas Artes was begun in 1900 by Italian architect Adamo Boari. Construction was interrupted by the Revolution of 1910 and finally completed in 1934 by Mexican architect Federico Mariscal.
(b) An aerial view of the Palacio de Bellas Artes. The exterior of the building is in the art nouveau style, with floral decoration in white marble.

    The interior's style is quite different: art deco with dark and reddish marble. Bellas Artes houses a collection of modern Mexican art, including murals by José Clemente Orozco, Diego Rivera, David Siqueiros, and Rufino Tamayo.

PAGE 23
Photos
(a) Teens buying ice cream at an outdoor stand in Madrid. RAM is the brand name of the ice cream. The signs on either side of the stand illustrate the variety of ice cream available and list the prices. Here, the average price is 80 pesetas, which is approximately the equivalent of what street-vendor ice creams sell for in the U.S. Note that one ice cream comes with a prize—*premio seguro.*
(b) Friends at a café in Bogotá. The European tradition of the outdoor café is a popular one in many Latin American cities. Students in Latin America will gather in a café after school just as students in the U.S. meet in a fast-food restaurant or a pizza parlor.
(c) A rainy day in the Puerta del Sol (Gate of the Sun), Madrid's major crossroads. Rain is relatively rare in the *meseta* (Castilla's central flatlands), where the threat of drought is a very

real problem. Thus, a shower is enough of a novelty to be amusing to these Spanish teenagers.

PAGE 25
Photo
Students taking a break between classes at the University of Puerto Rico. U.P.R.'s main campus, founded in 1900, is located in the Río Piedras section of the capital city of San Juan; smaller regional branches are scattered throughout the island. The buildings on the beautifully landscaped Río Piedras campus represent a mixture of architectural styles, from colonial to contemporary, and include a museum and the José M. Lázaro Library, the largest on the island.

Additions to on-page notes
Notes: You may want to ask students to write the letter at home. Then go over the assignment in class asking students to correct their own papers as volunteers write the sentences on the board. Or you may prefer to ask students to exchange papers and correct them as you write the completed letter on the board.

PAGE 26
Photo
Two friends in Barcelona, Spain's second largest city and capital of the northeastern region of Cataluña. Barcelona was one of the first Spanish cities to establish a gridlike plan of straight streets and square blocks. Only the areas near the harbor and the outlying districts have the curving streets and irregular blocks characteristic of older Spanish cities. As part of a revitalization project related to the preparations for the 1992 Olympic Games, which Barcelona will host, some neighborhoods are being torn down and rebuilt.

Additions to on-page notes
Notes: Before students begin Ex. Y, make sure they understand which pronoun is represented in each of the drawings.

Photo

Teenagers at an outdoor café in Spain. Before the invention of air conditioning, there was probably no better place to spend a warm summer's day in Madrid than at an outdoor café. It still has its attractions. You can eat a *bocadillo* (sandwich), have a coffee or a cold drink, indulge in a bit of light conversation, and watch the rest of the world go by.

CAPÍTULO 1

OBJECTIVES

Communication
- to identify nationalities
- to identify school-related vocabulary

Grammar
- to use the verbs *ser* and *estar*
- to use the personal *a*
- to use direct object pronouns *(lo, la, los, las)*
- to use the verbs *dar* and *ver*
- to use indirect object pronuns *(le* and *les)*

Culture
- to compare and contrast U.S. schools with those in Latin America
- to discuss course loads, schedules, and types of schools
- to point out the role of local clubs in sports competitions
- to tell about school holidays in South America

SUGGESTED MATERIALS

pp. 30–31 (Palabras nuevas I): wall map(s) showing Mexico, Central America, and the Spanish-speaking Caribbean; a compass

pp. 36 (Diálogo): wall map(s) showing the western and southwestern regions of the U.S. and Mexico

pp. 38–39 (Palabras nuevas II): a dictionary, paper clips, a pencil sharpener, a calculator, a stapler and staples

PAGE 28–29

Photo
High school students in class in Spain. During the 1985–86 school year, 1,238,874 Spanish high-school students prepared for college. College-bound students take the three-year *bachillerato* degree (roughly equivalent to the high-school diploma in the U.S.), which they typically complete at age 16. This degree is followed by the one-year *curso de orientación universitaria* (university orientation course).

Spaniards put a high premium on education, and the Spanish Ministry of Education and Science is considering several reforms of the educational system at the grade-school and high-school levels. If approved, these reforms will begin to be implemented in 1988. Compulsory education, which now applies to students from six to fourteen years old, will be extended for two additional years so that the average graduate will be sixteen years old. After finishing compulsory education, the student will be able to choose between a technical education track or a *bachillerato.* The *bachillerato,* which will last two years, will prepare students for the difficult university entrance exam. The Spanish Ministry of Education and Science is hoping that by the year 2000 (provided the new system is approved), all students will have gone to school until age 16, and approximately 80 percent until age 18.

PAGE 29

Prólogo cultural
You may want to assign the *Prólogo cultural* as homework or for additional outside reading. Or you may base a classroom lesson on the photograph and on specific questions about the selection. For example: What are the major differences between high schools in the U.S. and those in Latin America? Why is there no separate Christmas vacation for students in South America? The *Prólogo* theme may also suggest topics for oral or written research assignments. Students will not be tested on the *Prólogos;* this section, however, provides a useful overview of the chapter theme and a presentation—in English—of information that students will later encounter in Spanish.

For additional suggestions for use, see p. T5.

PAGE 30

Palabras nuevas

Each chapter has two *Palabras nuevas* sections, where new active vocabulary is introduced in visuals or in a written context, or both. Where possible, the contextual presentations are in the form of mini-dialogues, so that students can have additional exposure to communication models.

Each *Palabras nuevas* section has its own set of *Prácticas,* designed to lighten the task of vocabulary acquisition. The types of exercises used include visual, question-answer, open-ended, *cloze* method, which word best fits the context?, which is the logical response?, etc. Special care is given throughout the book to regular re-entry of the vocabulary presented in the *Palabras nuevas.*

For suggestions for use, see p. T5 and the Teacher Notes for T30–31. An alphabetical word list by part of speech is available on the last page of each chapter.

Introduce the words presented in the *Contexto visual* by showing transparency 1. Ask students to listen as you model the words for them, or play the tape. Then ask students to repeat, first as a class and then individually. Stress that errors are a natural and necessary part of second-language learning. And reinforce students' efforts to imitate correct pronunciation and intonation.

Additions to on-page notes

Reteach / Extra Help: You may want to call attention to the *ñ* in *hondureño, salvadoreño,* and *panameño.* Point out the dieresis in *nicaragüense.* Can students give another example of a word with *ü*? *(bilingüe)* Remind students that the dieresis indicates that the *u* is pronounced.

PAGE 31

Additions to on-page notes

Notes: You may want to go over the vocabulary presented in the *Contexto comunicativo* on pp. 31–32 before students open their books. Read each mini-dialogue to the class, or play the tape. Ask students to repeat and offer feedback to help them to

approximate correct rhythm, intonation, and pronunciation.

You may want to ask volunteers to act out the dialogues, or ask students to do choral reading by assigning one role to half the class and the second role to the other half. Encourage students to be enthusiastic since fostering enthusiasm will make their language-learning experience more positive.

Enrichment: In connection with mini-dialogue 1, you may want to assign different countries to pairs of students. Ask them to do research and to substitute the information about their country for that given about Guatemala. Volunteers may present their dialogues to the class.

PAGE 33

Additions to on-page notes

Notes: The exercises in the *Práctica* sections may be used in a variety of ways: as oral work without preparation, as preparation for in-class oral work, as written homework, or as question-and-answer practice with students' books closed. Exercises that include *Estudiantes A* and *B* can be used in class as chain responses or as pair work with role switching.

Whether students work on the *Práctica* in class or as homework, make sure that they understand the directions. You may want to ask volunteers to model the example and the first few items of each exercise.

For additional suggestions for use, see p. T5.

PAGE 35

Photo

A group of students from Oaxaca, a city in southern Mexico and capital of the state of the same name. Although uniforms are not worn at most public schools, they are quite common in Mexico's many private schools. Besides identifying which school students attend, the practice of wearing uniforms removes the pressure of having to keep up with the latest fashions.

Hablemos de ti

These are questions that allow students to talk about themselves—their families, daily lives, interests, opinions, plans, and ambitions. This section re-enters known vocabulary and structures in such a way that students can readily see that Spanish, like their native language, is a tool of self-expression.

The following are some suggestions for presenting the *Hablemos de ti* and other open-ended exercises (whose answers are usually indicated as "Answers will vary.")

1. Draw a grid on the board that lists categories of acceptable responses. Ask one student to act as secretary and keep a tally of responses given to each question. After all answers have been given, the grid will provide a summary of the most frequently occurring responses.

2. Encourage students to offer as wide a variety of answers to the questions as possible. Appoint a secretary to copy all answers on the board. When all answers have been given, ask students to decide which answer was the most unusual, most complex, most inappropriate, funniest, and so on.

3. Set a time limit and see how many possible answers students can give to individual questions within that time limit. This technique encourages fluency because the emphasis is on language production and quickness of thinking.

Additions to on-page notes

Enrichment: You may want to assign preparation for the *Actividad* as homework. Some students may want to draw the uniform they design. You may want to put students' drawings on the bulletin board. The class can then choose the best uniform, the most comfortable, the most attractive, and so on.

Another possibility also practices listening comprehension: ask individuals to describe their uniforms while other students draw the designs. Which drawings fit the descriptions most accurately?

PAGE 36
Diálogo
Each chapter has a teen-oriented *Diálogo* that serves as a situational culmination of *Palabras nuevas I*. The *Diálogo* is a discretionary activity and may be omitted, assigned for extra credit, or used as a classroom activity as time allows. For additional suggestions for use, see p. T6.

Additions to on-page notes

Notes: Model the *Diálogo* for repetition, or play the tape. You may want to have students play the parts of Roberto and Graciela. Begin by asking all the girls to read Graciela's part and all the boys Roberto's. Then ask individuals to play the roles and act out the dialogue. Encourage students to dramatize the conversation.

PAGE 37
Photo
Students talking about books in Spain. After summer vacation, most public schools in Spain resume classes around September 15. However, the school year gets off to a relatively late start for private-school students, many of whom do not go back until the beginning of October.

Additions to on-page notes

Notes: You may want to set aside class time to allow pairs of students to prepare the *Participación*. While students are working, circulate to provide help. Or you may prefer that students prepare the *Participación* as a written homework assignment. Ask volunteers to perform their dialogues for the class.

Enrichment: If your students enjoy using their imaginations, ask them to create a dialogue about a dream, or ideal, school routine.

PAGE 40
Additions to on-page notes

Reteach / Extra Help: Reinforce the meaning and use of *no sé todavía / todavía no sé* in mini-dialogue 3 by asking these questions: *¿Quién va a ser tu profesor de inglés el año próximo? ¿Vas a salir bien en esta clase?*

PAGE 42
Estudio de palabras
Students will not be tested on material in the *Estudio de palabras.* These sections do, however, provide helpful learning tools. They help students develop an

ability to recognize related words and word families. They also help students to recognize the interrelationship of languages.

Additions to on-page notes

Notes: You way want to expand the study of the origin of place names by asking students to research the origin of Bolivia, Colombia, El Salvador, La República Dominicana, Ecuador, Peru, Mexico, and so on.

PAGE 43

Explicaciones

Every chapter has two *Explicaciones* sections, each of which presents one or more grammatical points. In the *Explicaciones,* the various aspects of a given grammar topic are presented in a series of numbered subpoints. The explanations are followed by *Prácticas*, arranged in order of difficulty and generally following the sequence of the subpoints.

For suggestions for use, see p. T7.

PAGE 44

Additions to on-page notes

Enrichment: You may want to expand on Ex. A on p. 44 or B on p. 45 by asking students to give one additional sentence for each item. In Ex. A, students can add what the person in each item does in his or her job. In Ex. B, students can add what the people or animals are doing in the drawing.

PAGE 46

Photo

High-school students in a Buenos Aires classroom. Argentina places a strong emphasis on education and has one of the highest literacy rates in Latin America. A high-school degree, called a *bachillerato,* is required for many jobs and is necessary if a student wants to pursue more advanced studies.

PAGE 48

Photo

A student looking through his notes at a high school in Puerto Rico. The island's educational system more closely resembles that of the U.S. than that of Latin America. Students attend elementary school *(la primaria)* for six years, junior high *(la secundaria inferior)* for two, and high school (*el colegio* or *la secundaria*) for four. The primary language of instruction in Puerto Rico's public schools is Spanish, although students receive classes in ESL, or English as a Second Language, for the full 12 years. Conversely, most classes in the numerous private schools are taught in English, with Spanish being taught as a second language.

PAGE 51

¿Qué pasa?

The *¿Qué pasa?* is intended to help develop conversational skills on three levels. (a) The questions encourage responses at the simplest level, and you may want to supplement these with additional questions based on the art. (b) There is also a suggested situation for role-playing. (c) Finally, at the highest level, you may want to have students create their own dramatizations, improvising playlets or developing scripts for more polished presentations. The use of costumes, props, and sound effects can provide added interest and enjoyment.

Depending on the capabilities of your students, you may want to select among the activities, or make individual assignments according to the varying degrees of difficulty of the activities.

The *¿Qué pasa?* appears in odd-numbered chapters only. Even-numbered chapters have a *Lectura* in which previously learned vocabulary and structures are recombined in a new context. Some new—passive—vocabulary also appears in each *Lectura.*

For additional suggestions for use, see p. T8.

Sample dialogues for *¿Qué pasa?*

Arturo and Mónica are discussing a composition they have to write about a Central American country.

M: Las diapositivas de Guatemala son muy lindas. ¿Por qué no escribimos sobre ese país?

A: ¡Bueno! ¿Tenemos que escribir la composición a máquina?

M: ¡Claro que sí! Y también tenemos que hacer unos dibujos, para explicar mejor la vida de los habitantes.

A: Puedo dibujar un mapa. Tenemos el mapa de Guatemala en uno de los carteles. Lo voy a buscar ahora.

A: Mira, en los carteles los costarricenses están muy contentos.

M: Sí, es verdad. ¿Quieres escribir la composición sobre ese país?

A: Sí. No tenemos que escribirla a máquina, ¿verdad?

M: No, pero hay que hacer un dibujo y un mapa.

A: ¡Bueno! Voy a buscar en el mapa de la América Central dónde está Costa Rica. Y después puedo dibujar el país.

M: Está bien. Yo voy a escribir. Tenemos que explicar por qué casi todos los habitantes de la América Central hablan el mismo idioma.

PAGE 53
Photos
(a) The poster in Bogotá, Colombia, advertises Steven Spielberg's movie *Indiana Jones and the Temple of Doom*

(b) Also shown is the marquee of a Buenos Aires movie theater screening the Academy Award-winning film *The Kiss of the Spider Woman,* based on the novel of the same title by Argentina's Manuel Puig.

(c) The moviegoers at the ticket window (*boletería* or *taquilla,* depending on the country) are at a theater in Costa Rica. Action and adventure films made in the U.S. are extremely popular in the Spanish-speaking world. In most cases, Spanish subtitles are provided so that the audience can follow the English dialogue, although sometimes the English voice track is dubbed in Spanish.

PAGE 54
Realia
The monetary unit of Mexico is the peso, which is divided into 100 centavos. Shown here are various examples of coins and paper money. The 500-peso bill shows the Aztec calendar, also known as *Piedra del Sol* (Sun Stone), set against a background of carved Aztec figures. On the 1,000-peso bill is Mexico's most famous poet, Sor Juana Inés de la Cruz (1648–1695). Born Inés de Asbaje y Ramírez de Santillana, she became a cloistered Catholic nun in 1669 in order to devote herself to writing. The seven-sided 10-peso coin features the image of Father Miguel Hidalgo y Costilla, the priest whose famous *Grito de Dolores* (shout from Dolores) on September 16, 1810 sparked Mexico's war of independence from Spain. Father Hidalgo was shot by a firing squad in 1811, and it was not until September, 1821 that his country became independent.

Additions to on-page notes
Notes: Refer students to mini-dialogue 3 on p. 40 for an example of *le* attached to an infinitive. Elicit the alternate sentence, with *le* before the main verb *(Pero le tienes que dar la composición al profesor esta tarde.)*

PAGE 55
Photo
A girl writing a letter in Spain. In the twentieth century, and particularly since the Spanish Civil War (1936–39), there has been a dramatic population shift from the small towns to the cities. Nearly everyone in Spain's bigger cities has relatives "*en el pueblo.*" As a result, letter-writting has not become a lost art—not even among teenagers.

PAGE 57
Photo
Students reading at the library of a private school in Mexico City. Many private schools in Spanish-speaking countries have well-stocked libraries.

There are three main types of public libraries in

Latin American countries: national, municipal, and university libraries. The main function of national libraries is to keep copies of the books published in each country, and to serve as research centers. National libraries are usually considered important national institutions, even though funds available for these and other public libraries are sometimes limited. The position of Director of the National Library is often given to persons of significant scholarly achievement; for instance, after Jorge Luis Borges of Argentina gained international renown as a writer, he was given the position of Director of the Argentine National Library.

Another kind of public library is the municipal library, which is less prestigious than a national library, and whose main function is to lend to the public. Finally, public universities have their own libraries. Those in larger universities usually have a wide variety of books and periodicals.

PAGE 58
Photos
(a) Spanish students learning computer basics. Computer education has added English words like software and input and the names of popular programs (like IBM's Open Access) to everyday Spanish; this may be the reason the borrowed word *computadora* is more popular than the official Spanish term *ordenador*. There can be no doubt that the computer revolution is one of the factors that encourages the study of English in Spain today.
(b) Students in Madrid. After eight years of *enseñanza general básica,* students who expect to go on to a university take three years of general studies that lead to the *bachillerato* degree, followed by one year of pre-university studies. The alternative is to follow a two-to five-years course of vocational studies. The vocational degree, obtained fater five years, is considered the equivalent of the *bachillerato,* and students with that degree can then switch to pre-university studies.

PAGE 58
Repaso, Tema y Redacción
This section consists of a three-part summary and review of vocabulary and structures.
1. *Repaso:* The student is given a Spanish sentence, followed by English sentences to be put into Spanish. When correctly completed, the sentences are structurally identical to the model. Each sentence is designed to review one or more specific grammar points and chapter vocabulary.
2. *Tema:* This is a cartoon strip of four to six panels. Each panel has one or more English sentences representing the dialogue or describing the scene. The sentences that accompany the cartoon strip are structurally identical to the model sentences in the *Repaso.* Upon rendering them into Spanish, the student will have written a unified dialogue or paragraph.
3. *Redacción:* This section offers suggestions for more open-ended, yet guided, writing practice.

For suggestions for use, see p. T9 and the Teacher Notes for p. T58.

Additions to on-page notes
Notes: You may want to do the *Repaso* orally in class, or you may prefer to cover only the model sentence and the first English sentence as preparation for written homework. Assign the *Repaso* to the whole class, or assign single sentences to individuals or rows of students. Go over the assignment in class. You may want to create additional English cues for further practice or for extra credit.

Answers to *Repaso*
1. M.A. Asturias es un autor guatemalteco. / Son pilotos panameños. / Somos bibliotecarias nicaragüenses.
2. ¿Asistes a un colegio particular ahora? / Asistimos a un concierto interesante hoy. / Asisten a una clase bilingüe ahora.
3. Soy muy generoso(a). Les doy sujetapapeles. / Es muy inteligente. ¿Les enseña lenguas? / La directora es muy aburrida. Les lee biografías.
4. Estamos ocupados(as) porque tenemos mucha tarea. / Luz está aburrida porque no tiene muchos

amigos. / Estoy preocupado(a) porque no tengo muchos apuntes.

5. A menudo vemos al bibliotecario y lo ayudamos en la biblioteca. / Siempre llamas a tus amigas o las ves en el café. / Siempre admiro a esa actriz y la veo en la tele.

PAGE 59

Answers to *Tema*

1. Pablo es un estudiante (alumno) costarricense.
2. Asiste a un colegio público ahora.
3. Los estudiantes (alumnos) son muy simpáticos (amables). Le enseñan inglés.
4. Pablo está contento porque tiene muchos amigos.
5. A menudo llama a sus amigos y los invita a su casa.

PAGE 60

Comprueba tu progreso

You may want to assign the *Comprueba* as written homework. It can also function as a review of or additional practice for specific grammar points or vocabulary. If you prefer, assign the *Comprueba* for at-home preparation and review the exercises orally in class. Other possibilities include using the *Comprueba* as an in-class writing assignment or as a self-test.

For additional suggestions for use, see p. T9.

Answers to *Comprueba tu progreso*

A
1. Es
2. Estoy
3. están
4. está
5. somos
6. es, está
7. está

B
1. Pablo lo pasa en Chile.
2. Daniel la manda.
3. La profesora la explica.
4. Los chicos las escuchan.
5. Los llevan al laboratorio.
6. Mis padres los hacen.

C
1. Sí, voy a practicarlo.
   Sí, lo voy a practicar.
2. Sí, voy a mostrarlas.
   Sí, las voy a mostrar.

3. No, no tengo que llevarlo todos los días.
   No, no lo tengo que llevar todos los días.
4. No, no quiero visitarla mañana.
   No, no la quiero visitar mañana.
5. No, no prefiero comerla.
   No, no la prefiero comer.

D
1. ¿Llamas a Juan?
2. ¿Busca Javier al médico?
3. Admiro a la profesora.
4. ¿Compra Mónica la máquina de escribir?
5. Los estudiantes escuchan al director.
6. ¿Usan Uds. el proyector?
7. Mario invita a todos los estudiantes.
8. Veo al policía.

E
1. dan
2. ves
3. vemos
4. da
5. doy
6. veo
7. Ven
8. damos
9. dan

F
1. ¿Le presta Horacio los diccionarios a su amigo?
   Va a prestarle los diccionarios más tarde.
2. ¿Les das helados a los niños?
   Voy a darles helados más tarde.
3. ¿Les escriben ellos cartas a sus hijos?
   Van a escribirles cartas más tarde.
4. ¿Le explica Ana la historia a su compañera?
   Va a explicarle la historia más tarde.
5. ¿Le dan Uds. la grapadora a Patricia?
   Vamos a darle la grapadora más tarde.
6. ¿Les presta Ud. la grabadora a sus hijas?
   Voy a prestarles la grabadora más tarde.
7. ¿Les mandan ellos comida a los habitantes de esa parte del país?
   Van a mandarles comida más tarde.

PAGE 61

Photo

Three pages of a handwritten Mayan book, or codex. These pages deal with the deeds and powers of a number of Mayan gods. Mayan books were written on bark strips that were smoothed into thin sheets with wooden mallets. The paper was then coated with white plaster.

ORAL PROFICIENCY TEST

Before administering the Oral Proficiency Test, refer to the section called Oral Proficiency Testing (on pp. T19-T21 of this Teacher's Edition), which presents guidelines for evaluating communicative progress.

Directed Response

1. Carlos is watching a movie but doesn't seem very interested in it. Ask him if he is bored. *(¿Estás aburrido?)*
2. Your father wonders whether you've been keeping in touch with your sister, Josefina, who's away at school. How could you tell him that you write to Josefina often? *(Le escribo a Josefina a menudo.)*
3. Your class is collecting money to buy Federico a present, since he's moving. Ask to whom you give the money. *(¿A quién le damos el dinero?)*

Picture-Cued Response

4. Using the visual on p. 45, point to the dog and ask: ''¿Por qué no está contento el perro?'' *(El perro no está contento porque hay un gato en el árbol.)*

Point to the photograph on p. 55 and ask:

5. ¿A quién ves en la foto? *(Veo a una muchacha (a una chica).)*
6. Ella escribe una carta. ¿La escribe a máquina? *(No, no la escribe a máquina.)*

Situations

7. Professor Raimundo is explaining a very difficult scientific concept. How would he tell the students that they have to pay attention?
   a. Tienen que hacer unas preguntas.
   b. Tengo ganas de explicar la lección.
   c. *Hay que prestar atención.*
8. Daniel has asked you to go with him to the football game tomorrow. You can go only if you don't have too much homework. How might you answer him?
   a. Todavía no.　　b. Lo siento.　　c. *Quizás.*

Real-Life Questions

9. ¿Cómo son tus clases este año? ¿Son fáciles o difíciles? ¿Son interesantes o aburridas?
10. ¿Para qué clases tienes que escribir composiciones?
11. Cuando escribes una composición, ¿la escribes a máquina o en la computadora?

CAPÍTULO 2

OBJECTIVES

Communication
- to identify vocabulary related to household chores
- to identify vocabulary related to cooking

Grammar
- to use o → ue stem-changing verbs
- to use the affirmative *tú* command
- to use demonstrative adjectives
- to use demonstrative pronouns
- to use the expression *hace . . . que*

Culture
- to describe the physical layout of a typical home in southern Spain
- to emphasize the importance of the patio to the Spanish family
- to point out the Arabic origin of the inner garden and adobe houses in Spain
- to convey the influence of climate on our lives

SUGGESTED MATERIALS

p. 63 (Prólogo cultural):   a wall map showing southern Spain

pp. 64–65 (Palabras nuevas I):   magazine pictures showing household appliances and chores

pp. 72–73 (Palabras nuevas II):   magazine pictures of kitchen and laundry-room appliances; a frying pan, a saucepan, a pot, a trash can

p. 84 (Actividad):   index cards

pp. 86–87 (Explicaciones):   classroom objects

p. 91 (Actividad):   index cards

PAGES 62–63

Photo
The patio of a house on Gran Canaria, one of seven principal islands known as the Canary Islands. An archipielago located approximately 70 miles off the northwestern coast of Africa, las Canarias have been under Spanish rule since 1496.

The house shown in the photo is typical of many buildings in Spanish-speaking countries with a mild climate. The central patio with its potted plants and flowers serves as a "backyard" for the family (houses are usually built right up to the property line, with no surrounding lawns or gardens). Because it is open to the sky, the patio serves as a cooling system in the warmer months, allowing heat to escape. The surrounding balconies are covered to keep the high summer sun off the interior walls and to protect the balconies from rain. In the cooler months, the flat eaves allow the low winter sun to reach under them to help warm the house.

PAGE 63

Additions to on-page notes
Notes: You may want to present these questions to students before assigning the *Prólogo:* What are some differences between a typical house in southern Spain and one in our area? Who introduced inner gardens? When were these people in Spain? What is the advantage of using adobe to build houses? Where in the U.S. can you see homes made of adobe?

PAGE 65

Additions to on-page notes
Reteach / Review: After presenting the *Contexto comunicativo* on pp. 64–66, you may want to reinforce word order in exclamations with *tan* by asking students to suggest additional sentences with familiar nouns and adjectives. For example: *¡Qué muchacha tan perezosa! ¡Qué ventana tan sucia!*

PAGE 68

Photo
Private house in Marbella, Spain. Marbella, located about halfway between Málaga and Gibraltar, is one

of the more expensive resort centers on the Costa del Sol. Many of the houses belong to wealthy people from around the world who spend a few months there each summer. The traditional roof of curved tiles provides a simple and effective means of waterproofing. The concave tiles serve as channels for rainwater and the convex ones cover the joints of the concave ones.

PAGE 69

Photos

(a) New skyscrapers *(rascacielos)* in Caracas, the capital of Venezuela, one of the world's largest producers of oil. *La Ciudad de las Autopistas* (City of Highways), as Caracas is often called, has grown over 300 percent in the last 40 years.

(b) A primitive hut, called a *choza,* located in Mexico's Yucatán Peninsula. The house is built in the traditional Mayan style with a thatched *palapa* roof made from palm leaves that is able to withstand the torrential downpours of the rainy season.

(c) A house for sale in the town of San Isidro, a popular and luxurious Buenos Aires residential community of 80,000 residents. Located on the Río de la Plata, San Isidro boasts a charming central plaza, as well as recreational facilities for golfing, boating, and swimming.

Additions to on-page notes

Enrichment: After students have completed Ex. D in class, you may want to use the exercise for a written homework assignment. Ask students to write an exclamation using each of the adjectives that they did not use in class.

PAGE 71

Photo

(a) Two sisters listening to records at their home in Bogotá. Music has always been an important part of life in South America, where Indian, Spanish, and African influences have created musical forms that are unique to the continent. The music of Colombia draws predominantly on Iberian

rhythms, but there are regions—especially in the northern coastal area—where the African influence is evident in *el mapalé* and *la cumbia. El bambuco* and *la cumbia* are two lively rhythms appreciated by people of all ages in the Spanish-speaking world.

(b) Two teenagers at a boardinghouse in Sevilla, Spain, accompany each other on mandolin and guitar.

PAGE 74

Photo

Spanish family members frying salted almonds. Almonds are grown in Spain and are commonly served toasted or fried, salted or unsalted. They are also used in such diverse foods as hard or soft nougat candy called *turrón de almendra* and a cold soup called *ajo blanco* that is made with mashed almonds and garlic.

PAGE 76

Photo

A teenage boy washing dishes at home in California. Not so long ago, dishwashing and other household chores were considered to be strictly women's work in Hispanic homes in the U.S. Today, however, as divisions of domestic labor gradually disappear from other North American homes, they are also fading in Hispanic homes.

Additions to on-page notes

Enrichment: Additional questions for Ex. D: *¿The gusta planchar? ¿Planchas a menudo ¿Qué clase de ropa necesitas planchar? ¿Dónde secas la ropa que no puedes poner en la secadora?*

PAGE 77

Additions to on-page notes

Reteach / Extra Help: To facilitate comparing the results of the survey, you may want to ask volunteers to write their group's results on the board. Or students may post their tally sheets on the bulletin board.

PAGE 78

Realia

Advertisements from the classified section of *Presencia,* a newspaper in La Paz, Bolivia. They offer services such as installation, repairs, and maintenance of appliances such as refrigerators and freezers, washing machines, and gas and electric stoves and heaters.

PAGE 80

Additions to on-page notes

Enrichment: You may want to assign Ex. B for written homework. Ask students to decide where Emilia is spending her vacation. Can they name a beach resort in a Spanish-speaking country? (Possible answers include Mar del Plata, Argentina; Costa del Sol, Alicante, Torremolinos, Spain; Acapulco, Mexico; Viña del Mar, Chile; Isla Margarita, Venezuela.)

Tell students to write out the entire paragraph. Check their work for correct spelling, punctuation, and capitalization.

PAGE 81

Photo

Four young Spaniards eating lunch. The midday meal continues to be the most important one of the day in Spain. Most families get together around 2:00 P.M. for a large meal. Even in the largest cities, many small stores and offices close from about 1:00 to 4:00 P.M. each workday. Banks usually close for the day at 2:00 P.M. However, most large offices and businesses remain open during the lunch break.

PAGE 82

Additions to on-page notes

Enrichment: Time permitting, expand on the practice in Ex. B. Ask *Estudiante A* to wind up each of the exchanges by telling *B* to do the second chore. For example: *B: Limpia la sala primero. A: Después, lava el suelo de la cocina.*

PAGE 83

Additions to on-page notes

Enrichment: You may want to use Ex. D for written work. Ask students to write the sentences either in class or at home. They may add instructions for making *flan.* Refer them to mini-dialogue 1 on p. 72 for help with the procedures.

PAGE 84

Photos

(a) Two teens in front of a wrought-iron grille door in Tijuana, located in the northwestern Mexican state of Baja California. Situated just across the U.S.-Mexican border, Tijuana is one of Mexico's major tourist towns. It is visited annually by more U.S. citizens than any other foreign city. It is popularly held that the name Tijuana is a contraction of *Tía Juana* (Aunt Jane), which was the name of a cattle-rearing hacienda established in 1829. Others say, however, that the name was probably derived from *Ticuán* (near water), which was the Indian name for the settlement on the banks of the Tijuana River. Today Tijuana is a bustling city of shopping malls, restaurants, and other tourist attractions.

(b) Teens washing a car in Mexico City's fashionable southern suburb of San Ángel. Mexican teens must wait until their eighteenth birthday before they can apply for a driver's license. Because of high import duties and taxes, new U.S. and foreign cars are extremely expensive for most young Mexicans.

Additions to on-page notes

Notes: In order to save class time for the *Actividad,* you may want to write each of the verbs on an index card. Distribute the cards among the groups and ask students to exchange cards with another group when they have finished.

PAGE 85

Photo

The medieval quarter of Córdoba, an ancient city in Spain's southern region of Andalucía, is famous for its picturesque narrow streets, such as Calle de las Flores shown here. The influence of the Moors (who occupied Spain from 711 until 1492) is evident in the flowers, fountains, hand-painted tiles, and wrought-iron grillwork that adorn the bright whitewashed walls of the city's centuries-old houses. Every spring, during the first half of May, the people of Córdoba celebrate the *Festival de los Patios,* proudly decorating their patios, courtyards, and balconies with newly-planted flowers.

PAGE 86

Additions to on-page notes

Reteach / Extra Help: Clarify the difference between *este, ese* and *aquel* by positioning various objects around the classroom and asking questions: *¿De qué color es aquel basurero en la esquina? ¿Vas a usar ese bolígrafo que está encima de tu escritorio? ¿Te gusta esta pulsera?* Elicit additional examples.

Reinforce noun-adjective agreement by writing *este / ese / aquel, esta / esa / aquella, estos / esos / aquellos, estas / esas / aquellas* on the board. Ask students to provide an appropriate noun for each of the four columns.

Students may work in pairs to ask and answer questions that contrast demonstrative adjectives and pronouns. Ask students to use a hand signal each time they use a demonstrative pronoun that requires an accent mark.

PAGE 87

Realia

This advertisement promotes a "neutral" laundry product called T2000. According to the ad, the product aids in washing collars, cuffs, and baby clothes as well as wool and silk fabrics, curtains, table linen, lingerie, and other delicate items. If the consumer uses a couple of spoonfuls along with detergent and bleach, the wash will turn out cleaner, softer, delicately scented, and brighter. The user of T2000 will not need fabric softener and will save on detergent.

Additions to on-page notes

Reteach / Review: In order to provide more practice with the demonstrative pronouns *esto, eso,* and *aquello,* ask volunteers to draw objects that classmates will have trouble identifying: a plain square that represents a mirror and a circle that represents a rug, for example. Explain that the goal is to have classmates ask *¿Qué es esto / eso / aquello?*

PAGE 89

Photo

Two Barcelona teens reading at home. Barcelona is both an important publishing center and a major market for books. Many books and periodicals produced in Barcelona are printed exclusively in *catalán,* a Romance language that is most closely related to the Provençal of southeastern France.

PAGE 91

Photo

A Venezuelan teenager studying on the balcony of her home. Because the country's climate is tropical year-round, covered balconies—often overlooking a garden—are a practical and attractive feature of many Venezuelan homes.

PAGE 92

Photos

(a) A girl cleaning the house in Spain's northeastern city of Zaragoza. Until fairly recently, floors in new Spanish buildings were covered with tiles, and mops were far more useful than vacuum cleaners.

(b) Teenagers in Zaragoza. Dishwashers are among the most recent additions to the Spanish kitchen. Appliances of all kinds have become increasingly popular, perhaps because families have less time for domestic chores as more and more mothers join the work force.

Answers to *Repaso*

1. Es jueves. Hace dos días que el lavaplatos del restaurante está descompuesto. / Es domingo. Hace un mes que el suelo del sótano está limpio. / Es viernes. Hace diez días que la hermana de Pepe está enferma.
2. Aquella olla está llena, pero ésta está vacía. / Esos hombres (señores) están contentos (felices), pero aquéllos están tristes. / Esta carne está quemada y ésa está fría.
3. No puedo cortar el césped porque Uds. juegan allí (allá) / No pueden pasar la aspiradora porque sus padres duermen ahora. / No podemos barrer el patio porque almuerzas allí (allá).
4. Enchufa esa lavadora, por favor. Voy a lavar la ropa. / Recoge estos cordones, por favor. Voy a barrer el suelo. / Añade aquel limón, por favor. Él va a mezclar la ensalada.

PAGE 93

Answers to *Tema*

1. Es sábado. Hace una semana que el cuarto de Enrique está desordenado.
2. Este armario está ordenado, y ése está desordenado.
3. No puede hacer su cama porque su perro duerme allí (allá).
4. Limpia este cuarto, por favor, Chispa. Voy a tirar la basura.

PAGE 94

Answers to *Comprueba tu progreso*

A
1. hace
2. suelo
3. barre
4. bombilla
5. secadora
6. corta
7. lavaplatos
8. ahora mismo
9. enchufo

B
1. podemos, llueve
2. juega
3. vuelven
4. almorzamos, cuesta
5. puedo, encuentras
6. duerme
7. contamos

C
1. Vuelve temprano.
2. Escoge otro mantel.
3. Almuerza conmigo.
4. Bate los huevos con el azúcar.
5. Seca los cuchillos ahora mismo.
6. Añade leche al café.
7. Enchufa la tostadora.
8. Alquila esa película.

D
1. Esta secadora
2. estos cordones
3. este fregadero
4. esa cacerola
5. esas ollas
6. ese lavaplatos
7. Aquellos basureros
8. aquella lavadora
9. aquellas escobas

E
1. Ésta
2. éstos
3. éste
4. ésa
5. ésas
6. ése
7. Aquéllos
8. aquélla
9. aquéllas

F
1. Hace mucho tiempo que practico el piano.
2. Hace tres meses que viven en esta ciudad.
3. Hace dos semanas que los Ramírez están de vacaciones.
4. Hace media hora que Pablo duerme.
5. Hace quince minutos que ella barre el patio.
6. Hace varios días que mi hermanito está enfermo.

PAGE 95

Photo

A scene on tile in a private home in Toledo, Spain. The costumes shown are typical of the late sixteenth century, when Spain's power and influence were at their peak. The discovery and conquest of America had brought vastly increased prestige and wealth to the country. And Carlos V had succeeded in unifying much of Europe as well as other portions of the known world that were under Spanish influence. Spanish culture was admired, and its prestige was reflected in the world of fashion. Spanish costumes were imitated in much of the known world, especially in Western Europe. These fashions reached their zenith in the third quarter of the sixteenth century and then declined in influence in the seventeenth century.

As the scene on tile illustrates, Spanish costumes

of the time combined austerity with exaggeration. The dark, severe costume of the tall man standing next to the table exemplifies the former, while the ruff, a wide, pleated collar worn by both sexes, is an example of the latter. The ruff was developed after 1560 from the much more moderate ruffle. Beards of varied shapes and sizes were also popular at the time; in fact, shaved chins were infrequent, except among very young men.

Some examples of women's fashions are also shown. A tight-fitting upper garment, with long sleeves and exaggerated shoulder puffs, was the fashion during this time. The skirt, on the other hand, was loosefitting and flared due to the stiff, bell-shaped underskirt that was worn beneath it. The result was the typical cone-shaped Spanish costume. The scene on tile also shows that the women's hairdos resembled a smaller version of the pompadour, with the hair brushed straight back from the forehead and stacked in a roll at the top.

ORAL PROFICIENCY TEST

Directed Response

1. How would you tell a salesperson that you don't like these pants, that you prefer those over there? *(No me gustan estos pantalones; prefiero (me gustan más) aquéllos.)*
2. Tell your little brother to please throw away the garbage. *(Tira la basura, por favor.)*
3. Your friend asks you how long you've had your after-school job. Say that you've been working there for two weeks. *(Hace dos semanas que trabajo allí.)*

Picture-Cued Response

4. Point to the photograph on p. 81 and ask: "¿Come el desayuno esta familia o almuerza?" *(Almuerza.)*

Using the photographs on p. 92, point to the different women and ask:

5. ¿Qué hace la chica que está en la sala? *(Pasa la aspiradora.)*
6. ¿Dónde pone los platos esta chica? *(Pone los platos (Los pone) en el lavaplatos.)*

Situations

7. Your mother wants you to pick up your clothes, which are all over the floor. What would you say to her?
   a. *La recojo ahora mismo.*   b. La tiro ahora.   c. La escojo en seguida.
8. Paco can't get the toaster to work. Elena laughs when she notices why. What might the problem be?
   a. Hay que quemarla.   b. *Hay que enchufarla.*   c. Hay que desenchufarla.
9. Ángela turns fifteen today. What would her friends say to her as she arrives at school?
   a. *¡Feliz cumpleaños!*   b. ¡Qué lástima!   c. ¡Imagínate!

Real-Life Questions

10. ¿En qué ciudad o pueblo vives? ¿Cuánto tiempo hace que vives allí?
11. ¿Qué haces en casa para ayudar a tus padres? ¿Qué puedes hacer para ganar un poco de dinero?
12. Durante la semana, ¿almuerzas solo(a) o almuerzan juntos(as) tú y tus amigos(as)? Y los fines de semana, ¿con quién almuerzas?

CAPÍTULO 3

OBJECTIVES

Communication
- to use vocabulary related to leisure-time activities

Grammar
- to use $e \rightarrow ie$ stem-changing verbs
- to use object pronouns (*lo, la, los, las, le, les*) with affirmative *tú* commands
- to use comparative adverbs and adjectives
- to use superlative adjectives

Culture
- to point out the universality of parks
- to discuss Mexico City's Parque de Chapultepec
- to describe Madrid's Parque del Buen Retiro
- to contrast Chapultepec and El Retiro

SUGGESTED MATERIALS

p. 98 (Palabras nuevas I): magazine pictures showing various leisure-time activities

p. 100 (Práctica A): art book(s) showing reproductions of works by Spanish artists such as Velázquez, Goya, El Greco, Dalí, and Miró

p. 102 (Diálogo): a pair of glasses, a pair of sunglasses, necklaces, bracelets, rings, earrings, a scarf, a hat

pp. 116–117 (Explicaciones II): classroom objects

PAGES 96–97

Photo
El Parque del Buen Retiro, Madrid. A fashionable retreat of Spanish royalty in the seventeenth century, El Retiro is now Madrid's most popular park. Parents bring toddlers for a stroll, the elderly chat and people-watch in outdoor cafés, and groups of young people wander along the shady paths or rent boats and row around *el estanque,* the park's rectangular artificial lake.

El Retiro's major monument celebrates King Alfonso XII, who was called *el Pacificador* (the Peacemaker). The King's equestrian portrait (by Mariano Benlliure) is on the central column. The short-lived Alfonso became king at the age of seventeen and ruled from 1874 to 1885. The monument was initiated by his son, Alfonso XIII, in 1902. Statues representing Peace, Liberty, and Progress stand in front of the main column, and others surrounding it depict Agriculture, the Sciences, the Army, and the Navy.

PAGE 97

Additions to on-page notes
Notes: You may want to give students these questions before assigning the *Prólogo:* In your opinion what is the purpose of public parks? What does the *Prólogo* say about the purpose of parks around the world? Where is Parque de Chapultepec? What is the meaning of its name, and who gave it this name? Describe Parque de Chapultepec. Where is El Retiro? What does *retiro* mean? How is El Retiro different from Chapultepec? Name three things that you can do in El Retiro.

PAGE 100

Photo
An art student copying a painting in Madrid's Prado Museum. Students sometimes come here to copy the work of famous painters in order to learn some of their secrets. Copyists must obtain permission from the museum, and only a limited number of artists are allowed to work at any one time. To avoid problems of counterfeiting or theft, a copy cannot be the same size as the original, and the museum stamps each work to indicate that it is a copy. In the case of this particular work, it is unlikely that the copy would be taken for the original, which was painted on slate. It is a portrait of Christ, *Ecce Homo* (Behold the Man), by the Venetian Renaissance artist Titian (c. 1490–1576), who gave it

to Spanish King Carlos V. The other painting, *Mater Dolorosa* (Suffering Mother), is also by Titian. It was painted on marble.

PAGE 101
Photo
Guitarists in Madrid's Parque del Buen Retiro on a Sunday afternoon. On any day in decent weather, Madrid's two major parks—El Retiro and Casa del Campo—are full of people. El Retiro, the smaller and more central of the two, attracts people who are out to stroll or to get together with friends. La Casa del Campo, formerly the royal hunting grounds, attracts more physically active people: the swimmers, bike riders, joggers, soccer players, and *petanca* fanatics. *Petanca,* or boccie, is a ball game similar to bowling and is popular in parts of Europe and South America.

Additions to on-page notes
Enrichment: If students do Ex. C as written homework, ask them to bring in photographs or magazine pictures of people engaged in leisure-time activities. Students who collect something may want to show their collections to the class.

PAGE 102
Realia
An ancient drawing of a palm used to teach the art of palmistry.

PAGE 103
Photo
A high school student plays fortune teller in Texas. Fortune telling is often associated with the Gypsies. Among the Gypsies, fortune telling is usually a woman's activity. To analyze the future, fortune tellers use devices such as tea leaves, crystal balls, and cards. Above all, Gypsy fortune tellers are experts in palmistry, or the reading of palms, judging a person's character and future by the shape and size of the person's hand and the design of the lines on the palm.

PAGE 108
Photos
(a) A poster for the movie Rocky IV in Costa Rica. Hollywood movies dominate the market in Spanish-speaking countries, even in those with relatively large domestic film businesses like Argentina, Mexico, and Spain.

(b) A movie theater façade in Madrid. Advertising like this commonly appears on first-run movie houses in Spain's major cities. The images are hand-painted on canvas frames that are attached to the front of the building. The film *Superman IV* was also being shown in another theater on one of Madrid's principal avenues, Gran Vía, where it was advertised with an image four times this size and larger-than-life portraits of the major characters.

PAGE 110
Additions on-page notes
Reteach / Extra Help: You may want to reinforce the verb forms with a substitution drill before students begin the *Práctica.* Write *yo, tú, él, ella, Ud., nosotros(as), ellos, ellas* on the board. Then point to a pronoun and call on a volunteer as you say each of the following sentences. Ask the student to repeat the sentence, substituting the form of the verb indicated by the pronoun: *Quiero un millón de dólares. Piensas comprar un coche, ¿verdad? Empezamos la clase a la(s) _____. Uds. cierran el libro a la(s), _____, ¿no?*

PAGE 111
Photo
An outdoor art exhibit in Plaza San Jacinto, located in Mexico City's southern suburb of Villa Obregón, popularly known as San Ángel. Every Saturday a handicraft market called Bazar Sábado is held in a seventeenth-century mansion that flanks the plaza. Another outdoor area where up-and-coming Mexican artists can display their works is the Jardín del Arte in Mexico City's centrally located Parque Sullivan.

PAGE 112
Photo

Rowing is a popular activity among Buenos Aires residents, who are referred to as *porteños.* Shown here is the large central lake in the Parque 3 de Febrero section of the Parque Palermo complex, which is located in the Argentine capital's tree-lined neighborhood of Palermo. The complex contains many recreational facilities including a racetrack, planetarium, bicycle track, zoo, Japanese and botanical gardens, tennis courts, riding paths, and polo and soccer fields.

PAGE 113
Photo

The amusement park located in Mexico City's Parque de Chapultepec. In the background is the famed *montaña rusa* (roller coaster); the exciting *remolino,* or whirly-ride, is in the foreground. The grasshopper symbol in the inset is used to designate the park.

Additions to on-page notes

Reteach / Extra Help: Before students begin the *Práctica* on p. 114, write these lists of verbs and nouns on the board: *cerrar, comprar, despertar, preguntar; las ventanas, el coche, el director.* Then ask students to work in pairs asking and answering questions by combining the lists. For example: *¿Cierro las ventanas? Sí, ciérralas. ¿Compro el coche? Sí, cómpralo.*

Notes: Point out to students that the accent mark is added to the stressed vowel only if the original command has two or more syllables.

PAGE 115
Sample dialogues for *¿Qué pasa?*

Victoria and Antonio are at an amusement park and can't decide which ride to go on next.

A: ¡Qué alivio! ¡Por fin salimos! ¡Qué susto me da la casa de los fantasmas!

V: ¡Ay, Antonio! ¿Damos una vuelta ahora en la montaña rusa?

A: ¿La montaña rusa? ¡Ay, no! Prefiero dar una vuelta en el carrusel.

V: No eres muy valiente. Pero, está bien. Primero el carrusel y después la montaña rusa.

V: ¡Qué maravilla! Me gustaría dar una vuelta en la montaña rusa.

A: ¡Ay, no, Victoria! ¡Qué susto! Eres muy valiente. Prefiero dar una vuelta en el carrusel.

V: ¡Qué lata! Pero, bueno. Vamos.

A: ¡Qué alivio!

PAGE 117
Photos

(a) A juice vendor in Mexico City's Parque de Chapultepec. On Sundays, this park and the Alameda are bustling with people of all ages enjoying a wide range of amusements: musical concerts, organ grinders *(organilleros)* with their monkeys, dance recitals, and poetry readings.

(b) This vendor offers *aguas de fruta natural* to thirsty visitors to Chapultepec Park in Mexico City. Similar to fresh-squeezed lemonade, these *aguas* are a mixture of water, sugar, ice, and fresh fruit pulp, usually *limón* (similar to the Florida key lime), pineapple, or mango. Other sweet snacks include *rebanadas*, slices of fresh fruits such as mango, papaya, and melon sprinkled with chile powder, and ice cream cones and *paletas* (similar to popsicles). Those with a heartier appetite might sample a *gordita*, a thick tortilla split open and filled with various mixtures, including meat, *frijoles* (refried beans), fried eggs, or cheese, and served with *salsa*, a mixture of tomatoes, hot green chiles, and onions. Crisp *chicharrones* (fried pork rinds) are also popular treats sold by park vendors.

PAGE 119
Photo

The entrance to Chapultepec Zoo in Mexico City. In addition to its excellent variety of animals, including giant pandas, the zoo offers rides in goat carts, pony rides, a miniature train, and a daily show featuring trained elephants.

PAGE 122

Photo

A *tómbola* stand at a summer fair in Aranjuez, a town about 29 miles south of Madrid. *Tómbolas* have been a popular form of raffle in Spain for many years and are often used to raise money for charities. Patrons of the game of chance shown in the photo buy paper tickets and tear them open to find out if they have won anything. To the right is the *venta de boletos,* or ticket booth; to the left, the *entrega de premios,* where winners go to pick up their prizes.

PAGE 123

Photo

The *rueda de feria,* or ferris wheel, at an amusement park in Puerto Rico. Although there are few permanent amusement parks on the island, rides are an important part of the *fiestas patronales,* local festivals celebrating a town's patron saint. Temporary parks are also set up for Puerto Rico's major holidays (among them Three Kings' Day on January 6, Columbus Day on October 12, and Discovery of Puerto Rico Day on November 19), as well as for *verbenas,* fund-raising events held to benefit schools, churches, and charity programs.

Additions to on-page notes

Enrichment: Ask students to suggest additional examples to illustrate each of the three grammar points.

You may want to write these adjectives on the board: *poco, lindos, famoso, rica.* Ask students to add the *-ísimo* suffix to each word and to create sentences with the new adjectives.

PAGE 124

Additions to on-page notes

Enrichment: Additional questions for Ex. C: *¿Cuál es la mejor banda de rock de los Estados Unidos? ¿Por qué es la mejor? ¿Quién canta peor, tú o tu mejor amigo(a)?*

PAGE 125

Photo

The main upstairs gallery of the Prado Museum in Madrid. The Prado is home to more than 7,000 of the world's most important works of art from Spain and other European countries. The collection includes works by such Spanish masters as Velázquez, Goya, and El Greco. Carlos III ordered the creation of the building in 1785, but he intended it to be a natural-science museum. Completed after the Napoleonic Wars, the Prado opened as an art museum in 1819. The museum derives its name from the Paseo del Prado, the grand promenade that Carlos III had built along a stream that flowed through a meadow *(prado).*

PAGE 126

Photo

Family members riding in the *carros locos,* or crazy (bumper) cars, in Mexico City's Parque de Chapultepec.

Answers to *Repaso*

1. Esta tarde pienso dar un paseo. / El miércoles queremos hacer un picnic. / Este jueves prefieren ir de excursión.
2. Estos patines (de ruedas) son los mejores de la tienda. Cómpralos. / Ese parque de diversiones es el más grande del suroeste. Visítalo. / Esta exposición de arte es la más interesante del año. Descríbela.
3. Cree que las atracciones son menos emocionantes que esos globos gratis. / Creo que la bolsa es más pequeña que esta canasta vieja. / Creemos que los cacahuates son más caros que esas palomitas calientes.
4. ''¡Qué lástima! Es tan tímido como su papá (padre),'' dice abuelo. / ''¡Qué maravilla! Es tan valiente como un león,'' dice Anita. / ''¡Qué lata! Está tan asustada como yo,'' dice él.
5. Luego (Entonces) vamos al espectáculo. ''Mira a esos niños,'' dice papá. ''Cómprales entradas. Son baratísimas.'' / Antes van a los puestos. ''Mira a tu hija,'' dice mamá. Cómprale una máscara. Son graciosísimas.'' / Ahora vamos al zoológico.

"Mira a esas niñas," dice Luz. "Cómprales unos cacahuates. Están deliciosísimos."

PAGE 127

Answers to *Tema*

1. Este domingo María y Ángela piensan ir a la feria.
2. Esta rueda de feria es la más alta del país. ¡Mírala!
3. Creen que el carrusel es menos emocionante que esta montaña rusa.
4. "¡Caramba! Soy tan fea como tú," dice María.
5. Después van a la heladería. "Mira a ese niño," dice Ángela. "Cómprale un helado. Está buenísimo."

PAGE 128

Answers to *Comprueba tu progreso*

A 1. la montaña rusa   4. bolsa
     2. puesto   5. gratis
     3. tímido   6. Qué lata

B 1. ¿Entienden Uds. la obra de teatro?
     Sí, entendemos la obra de teatro (la entendemos).
     2. ¿Piensa dar un paseo?
     Sí, piensa dar un paseo.
     3. ¿Quieres tomar algo?
     Sí, quiero tomar algo.
     4. ¿Piensas hacer un picnic?
     Sí, pienso hacer un picnic.
     5. ¿Quieren Uds. ir de excursión?
     Sí, queremos ir de excursión.
     6. ¿Prefiere Ud. el invierno?
     Sí, prefiero el invierno (lo prefiero).

C 1. ¿Leo los apuntes?
     Sí, léelos en seguida.
     2. Recojo mis cosas?
     Sí, recógelas por la mañana.
     3. ¿Cierro la puerta?
     Sí, ciérrala ahora mismo.
     4. ¿Visito la exposición de arte?
     Sí, visítala antes de salir.
     5. ¿Invito a mis primos?
     Sí, invítalos esta noche.
     6. ¿Escribo la carta?

Sí, escríbela mañana.
     7. ¿Empiezo la canción?
     Sí, empiézala en unos minutos.
     8. ¿Como las verduras?
     Sí, cómelas todas.

D 1. más bajo qué   4. la mayor de
     2. la más baja de   5. menor (más joven) que
     3. mayor que   6. el menor (el más joven) de

E 1. Sí, es famosísimo.
     2. Sí, es facilísimo.
     3. Sí, son riquísimas.
     4. Sí, es grandísima.
     5. Sí, son baratísimas.
     6. Sí, es rapídisimo.

F 1. tan, como   5. tan, como
     2. tantos, como   6. tantos, como
     3. tanto, como   7. tanto, como
     4. tan, como

PAGE 129

Photo

Polished clay candelabra from Acatlán, Mexico. Located in the state of Puebla, the town of Acatlán is famous for its ceramics. This clay candelabra is a variation of the tree of life motif frequently found in folk art in Mexico. Trees of life usually represented the origin of life in the Garden of Eden, with images of God, the angels, Adam and Eve, and the serpent. In its basic form, the tree of life has religious implications and is often used as a symbolic decoration in weddings. However, trees of life vary greatly not only in size, but also in theme. In some variations it is not life, but death, that is represented, with images of skeletons among the leaves of the tree. The particular variation shown here has lost most of its religious symbolism, and is used mainly for decorative purposes. The tree of life theme originated in the Middle East. The Moors introduced it centuries ago to Spain, where it took on a Christian significance; the Spaniards, in turn, brought it to Mexico.

ORAL PROFICIENCY TEST

Directed Response

1. How would you ask your friend what she thinks of this class? *(¿Qué piensas de esta clase?)*
2. Jorge has not started his homework. Tell him to start it right now. *(Empiézala ahora mismo.)*
3. Mother asks you how you like Ana's sister. Say that she's as amusing as Ana is. *(Ella es tan graciosa como Ana.)*

Picture-Cued Response

4. Pointing to the visual on p. 107, ask questions such as: ¿Cuesta un globo tanto como una bolsa de cacahuates? *(No, un globo no cuesta tanto como una bolsa de cacahuates. OR No, un globo cuesta menos que una bolsa de cacahuates.)*
5. Using the visual on p. 115 or transparency 10, ask: ''¿Qué piensan hacer los jóvenes?'' *(Piensan comprar un helado. OR Piensan ir en la rueda de feria.)*

Situations

6. It took you and your friends twice as long as it usually does to get to the park. What might you say when you arrive?
   a. ¡Qué maravilla!   b ¡Vámonos!
   c. ¡Por fin!
7. Juan has seven dollars and Ana has seven dollars. Which of the following statements is true?
   a. *Ana tiene tanto dinero como Juan.*
   b. Juan tiene más dinero que Ana.
   c. Ana tiene menos dinero que Juan.

Real-Life Questions

8. ¿Cómo se llama tu mejor amigo(a)? ¿Qué prefieres hacer cuando estás con tu amigo(a)?
9. ¿Quién es el (la) mayor de tu familia? ¿Cuántos años tiene?
10. ¿Cómo eres? ¿Eres una persona cómica o seria? ¿Eres valiente o tímido(a)?
11. ¿A qué hora te despiertas cada mañana cuando tienes clases? ¿Te despiertas rápidamente o lentamente?

CAPÍTULO 4

OBJECTIVES
Communication
- to identify vocabulary related to food
- to identify vocabulary related to camping

Grammar
- to use the verbs *decir, oír, hacer, poner, salir, traer*
- to use all the direct and indirect object pronouns
- to use verbs with irregular affirmative *tú* commands

Culture
- to point out the variety in Spanish food
- to describe two classic Spanish soups: *caldo gallego* and *gazpacho*
- to discuss the popularity and abundance of fish in Spain
- to convey the importance of eggs, potatoes, garlic, and olive oil in the Spanish diet

SUGGESTED MATERIALS
p. 131 (Prólogo cultural):   a wall map of Spain

p. 132 (Palabras nuevas I):   magazine pictures of objects or foods associated with a barbecue

p. 136 (Práctica C):   blank restaurant checks

p. 138 (Diálogo):   a wall map of Puerto Rico

p. 140 (Palabras nuevas II):   objects associated with camping (flashlight, batteries, can opener, canned soup)

PAGES 130–131
Photo
This array of Spanish foods includes items that are eaten as *tapas,* the name for countless kinds of appetizers or bite-size snacks that are typical throughout Spain. Toothpicks serve as the primary eating utensil for olives and other *tapas* such as the large shrimp *(gambas),* sliced sausage *(chorizo),* croquettes *(croquetas),* and diced cheese seen on the cutting block. On the cake plate is the ubiquitous

tortilla española, also served for *tapas* when cut into small squares. No meal or snack is complete without bread, which is used to soak up sauces and juices. Peppers and strings of garlic are hung from the wall or ceiling not only to dry but also for storage and decoration.

PAGE 131
Additions to on-page notes
Notes: You may want to give students these questions before assigning the *Prólogo:* What is the name of the soup that is typical of Galicia? Where did *gazpacho* originate? How do you make *gazpacho?* Why is seafood so popular in Spain? Name some seafood dishes popular in northern Spain. What are some of *paella's* ingredients? What is Spain's favorite snack food? Name four foods that are staples in every Spanish home.

PAGE 134
Photo
Farm workers preparing a *parrillada* in Baradero, an agricultural center near Buenos Aires. A *parrillada* in Argentina is a combination of various cuts of beef and different types of sausage grilled over an open fire. Because Argentina is blessed with some of the most fertile land in Latin America, the country produces an abundance of beef as well as fruit, vegetables, and grain. Beef is so plentiful in Argentina that the government claims that there are one-and-a-half of cattle for each of Argentina's approximately 32 million inhabitants.

Additions to on-page notes
Reteach / Review: You may want to reinforce the use of the definite article in the last line of mini-dialogue 6 by asking students to suggest *Variaciones* for *el pavo asado.* Remind students that *sabroso* must agree in gender and number with the nouns that they substitute.

PAGE 135

Photo

Men tending cattle at Las Madres Ranch in Bolivia's eastern province of Beni. This semitropical region along the Rio Beni is sparsely populated because of heavy rainfall and the absence of railroads and highways. The majority of the inhabitants of the Beni area raise cattle and grow such crops as cocoa, sugar, coffee, and tropical fruits.

PAGE 138

Photo

Luquillo Beach, named for the friendly Indian spirit Yuquiyú, is located on Puerto Rico's northeastern coast. Tourists and residents alike come to enjoy this mile-long stretch of white sand and clear water. Coconut palms line the beach, providing shade for the *asados,* or barbecues, where the fare may vary from hamburgers and hot dogs to roast pig *(lechón asado),* an island favorite.

PAGE 139

Photo

Teenagers gathered around the fire in Mexico. The activities that teenagers enjoy are similar in many countries. Sitting around the campfire to sing and thell stories is fun in Mexico as it is in the United States or throughout the world.

PAGE 142

Photo

Camping in Costa Rica. Almost 60 percent of the country's territory is covered by woods and forest. Costa Ricans are environmentally conscious, and their parks and national reserves are well guarded. Costa Rica has a variety of ecosystems that house a great many forms of plant and animal life. There are 900 different species of birds in the Costa Rican forest (compared with 800 in the whole United States) and an enormous variety of butterflies.

PAGE 144

Photo

Hiking in the Gredos Mountains near Salamanca, Spain. The Gredos Mountains, at about 40 miles west of Madrid, have game and fishing preserves that are very attractive to tourists. Nearby River Tormes has excellent trout. Horse riding and mountain climbing are also favorite activities in the Gredos Mountains.

PAGE 145

Photo

A campground located near Buenaventura, Colombia's only port on the Pacific Ocean. Hikers can trek to swampy coastlands to the south or to jungle terrain to the north. Beaches in the area are accessible by launch.

Realia

A sing for the municipal campground site in Córdoba, Spain. Prices are based on the number of campers, the type and size of equipment used, and the type of vehicle driven to enter the site. For example, children under ten are charged 78 pesetas, while a one-person tent costs 84 pesetas. There are over 500 campsites in Spain, many of which are located on the eastern Mediterranean coast.

PAGE 146

Photos

(a) These adventurous soulds are hiking in Puerto Rico's Caribbean National Forest, which is located about 30 miles east of San Juan. The forest, generally referred to as El Yunque (named for a anvil-shaped peak), is the only tropical rain forest in U.S. territories, and is home to 240 varieties of trees and many kinds of exotic birds and flowers. The 29,000-acre forest is the perfect environment for millions of tiny tree frogs called *coquís.* The *coquí,* named for the loud, distinctive sound it makes, is found only in Puerto Rico.

(b) Visitor to a forest in Miranda del Castañar, Spain. Located near Portugal in Spain's central far western region, the town is the site of many castles and mansions. Miranda del Castañar is also close to the Sierra de Gredos, where visitors can enjoy mountain climbing, horseback riding, hunting, and fishing.

PAGE 153
Photo
A cattle market in Padrón, Spain. Because of the scarcity of good pastureland for cattle in Spain, most Spaniards cannot afford the high prices of beef. As a result, red meat is not as popular in Spain as it is in the U.S. Pork, poultry, goat, lamb, and rabbit are popular meats. Topping the list, however, is fish, which is plentiful and inexpensive in the coastal regions.

Realia
A U.S. government publication in Spanish on how to buy beef roasts. In 1987 about 7 percent of the population of the U.S. was Spanish-speaking. Because of the large number of Spanish speakers in the country, many U.S. government publications now appear in Spanish as well as in English.

PAGE 154
Additions to on-page notes
Enrichment: Additional questions for Ex. B: *¿Les prestas tus discos a tus amigos? ¿Les prestas tu ropa a tus hermanos? ¿Le escribes a tu actor (actriz) favorito(a)?*

PAGE 155
Photo
Young women preparing tortillas by hand in a café in Tonalá, located in Mexico's western state of Jalisco. Tortillas are made from *masa,* a doughy mixture of ground corn, water, and lime for corn tortillas, or of flour, hot water, and sugar or salt for flour tortillas. The *masa* is then shaped by hand or machine into thin disks and cooked quickly in a flat frying pan called a *comal.* Tortillas accompany most meals as a kind of bread. They are also used in such specialties as *tacos, tostadas,* and *enchiladas.*

Realia
This restaurant sign in Barcelona highlights the international flavor of both life and food in this Spanish city. Fish soup and octopus prepared Galician-style, spaghetti with meat sauce, and chicken Provence-style (from southern France) are among the featured items on the menu.

PAGE 156
Photos
(a) A buffet at a hotel on the island of Ibiza. Ibiza is the smallest of the three principal Balearic Islands, but its 45,000 inhabitants play host to nearly a million tourists every year. Ibiza's best-known dishes include *la burrida de ratjada,* which is boiled skate (a type of fish) in an almond sauce, and *el guisat de marisc,* a stew of assorted fish and shellfish. The language of the island is *ibicenco,* a dialect of *catalán.*

(b) The man of the house tends the grill at his home in Buenos Aires. The *parrillada* is a favorite treat throughout much of the Spanish-speaking world. *Morcilla,* or blood sausage, is a popular part of any Argentine parrillada. Beef is often marinated prior to cooking in *chimichurri,* a spiced sauce made of parsley, olive oil, and vinegar, which is also used to baste the meat while it is cooking. Latin Americans generally prefer their beef *bien cocido,* or well done.

Realia
A bill from a restaurant in Spain's northern region of Navarra. The date on the bill, *Fecha* 9-7, is July 9, reflecting the European style that states the day before the month. The cost of the meal includes a cover charge *(pan / vino)* and a 6 percent IVA, or *impuesto de valor añadido.* This value-added tax is based on the value that each stage of production adds to the total value of the item and is required of all businesses in Common Market countries.

PAGE 159
Photo
Students and their instructor in a classroom at the Universidad Javeriana in Cali, Colombia.

PAGE 160

Photos

(a) Teenagers hiking at Ordesa National Park, located in the Pyrenees Mountains of the Spanish region of Aragón. One of the numerous government-regulated campsites (called *campings*) located throughout Spain, Ordesa is open from April to September and has space for 624 campers.

(b) Campers in Colombia setting up their tent. There are 26 official campsites in Colombia, located primarily in the northern half of the country. These sites are found outside the capital city of Bogotá, in the hills and valleys northeast of Bogotá, along the Pacific Coast, and in the virgin Caribbean beach area of the National Park of Tayrona, east of the city of Santa Marta.

Answers to *Repaso*

1. Esta noche va de vacaciones al rancho. / Mañana Uds. van de pesca en el río. / Esta tarde van de compras en el pueblo.
2. ¿Dónde está la sandía? Ahora la traen. / ¿Dónde están las galletas? Ahora las traemos. / ¿Dónde está el aceite? Ahora lo traigo.
3. Mi mamá me dice: "Apágame las luces." / Me dicen: "Cómprale las aceitunas." / Te digo: "Muéstrame el sendero."
4. Le dicen a su invitado (invitada): "Enciende la lámpara en el comedor." / Le digo a mamá: "Haz un picnic en el valle." / Le dice a su sobrino: "Hierve el maíz en la olla."
5. "Contéstame," dice el policía. "A mí me gustaría saber ahora mismo." / "Muéstrame," dice la niña. "A mí me gustaría ver también." / "Dinos," dice el piloto. "A mí me gustaría aterrizar pronto."

PAGE 161

Answers to *Tema*

1. Hoy vamos de camping en el valle.
2. ¿Dónde está la parrilla? Ahora la traigo.
3. Mi papá (padre) me dice: "Tráeme el abrelatas."
4. Él le dice a mi hermano: "Pon las pilas en las linternas."
5. "Llévame," piensa el gato (la gata). "A mí me gustaría ir también."

PAGE 162

Answers to *Comprueba tu progreso*

A 1. b   3. a   5. b
     2. b   4. a

B
1. Ponemos (ponen) la (una) sandía en la mesa.
2. Pongo la (una) linterna y las (unas) pilas en la mochila.
3. Te traigo las (unas) galletas.
4. Oigo dos mosquitos.
5. Hago tortillas.
6. Hacemos las maletas.
7. Salgo a las dos.
8. Oímos las ranas.

C
1. Tráele la linterna. Tráela.
2. Ponnos la mesa. Ponla.
3. Búscales las aceitunas. Búscalas.
4. Hazme la cama. Hazla.
5. Recógenos las manzanas. Recógelas.
6. Muéstrame el hielo. Muéstralo.
7. Ábreles los sacos de dormir. Ábrelos.
8. Dales la sal. Dala.

D
1. Plánchale la falda a Elena.
2. Enchúfale la lámpara a papá.
3. Sécale las camisas a Diego.
4. Límpiales el dormitorio a los abuelos.
5. Bárrele el suelo a Elena.
6. Arréglales el proyector a los tíos.

E
1. Sé amable.
2. Ven temprano.
3. Di que salimos.
4. Pon sal y pimienta (en la mesa).
5. Sal a las cinco.
6. Ve al pueblo.

PAGE 163

Photo

A mural and decorations on the front of a bus in Panama. Scenes painted in brilliant colors on buses are a favorite form of pop art in this country. Although nobody knows when or how this practice started, the intent is to make the buses as entertaining, and as much like a moving party, as possible. The buses have continuous salsa music playing, and the drivers use the air horn liberally. The painted decorations may be anywhere on the bus, including the windows, bumpers, fenders, and steps. Names of women are often written on the windows in colorful lettering, and since the bus has over twenty windows, there is room for many names. The Themes of the murals vary greatly: some show religious scenes, others depict fantastic beings from outer space, and still others, like the one in the photograph, represent rural scenes. The name on the front window refers to the route that the bus follows-between the capital, Panama City, and La Chorrera, a small town to the west of it.

ORAL PROFICIENCY TEST
Directed Response
1. Your friend Pablo calls you from Madrid, and you have a terrible connection. Tell him you don't hear him well. *(No te oigo bien.)*
2. Your father asks what you are doing. Tell him you are washing the children's hands. *(Les lavo las manos a los niños.)*
3. Norma wants to know when she can reach you and Sandra. Tell her to call you at six o'clock. *(Llámanos a las seis.)*

Picture-Cued Response
4. Pointing to the photograph on p. 137, ask students to decide who is bringing what to the barbecue. Ask questions such as: ¿Quién trae el pan? *(Ana lo trae.)* ¿Quién puede traer los platos y las servilletas? *(Jorge los puede traer.* OR *Jorge puede traerlos.)* ¿Qué traes tú? *(Yo traigo una radio.)*

Using the visual on p. 140 or the overhead transparency for that page, ask:
5. ¿Para dónde sale este chico? *(Sale para el río (lago) para ir de pesca.)*
6. ¿Dice el otro niño que quiere ir con él o que prefiere comer algo? *(Dice que prefiere comer algo.)*

Situations
7. Your host is about to put the steaks on the grill, and he asks you how you would like yours done. What might you say?
   a. Asado.   b. *Poco cocido.*   c. Sabroso.

8. Your uncle is leaving. You offer to carry his suitcase to the car, but it weighs a ton! What might you say?
   a. ¡Está mojada!   b. ¡Está congelada!
   c. *¡Está pesada!*

Real-Life Questions
9. Cuando vas de camping, ¿prefieres ir a la playa o a las montañas?
10. Si vas de camping a la playa, ¿qué oyes? Y si vas a las montañas, ¿qué oyes?
11. ¿Qué les dices a tus amigos cuando llegas a la escuela por la mañana? ¿Y cuando sales para la casa?

ORAL PROFICIENCY TEST   CHAPTERS 1–4
Directed Response
1. Ask a classmate where she is from. *¿De dónde eres?)*
2. Your friend wants your to go to the library with him. Tell him you can't go now because you are eating lunch. *(No puedo ir ahora porque almuerzo.)*
3. Tell the salesclerk that you like these pants but that you prefer the ones over there. *(Me gustan estos pantalones pero prefiero aquéllos.)*

Picture-Cued Response
4. Using the visuals on pp. 64–65 or the overhead transparencies for those pages, ask questions such as: ¿Qué le dice mamá a papá? *(Pasa la aspiradora.)* ¿Qué le dice a su hijo? *(Barre la acera.)* ¿Qué le dice a su hija? *(Corta el césped.)*
5. Using the visuals on pp. 110–111, ask questions such as: ¿Qué le vas a dar a Juan para su cumpleaños? *(Le voy a dar una máquina de escribir.* OR *Voy a darle una máquina de escribir.)*

Situations
6. As you are leaving the restaurant, you spot Ana and her parents. They are just starting to eat. What would you say to them?
   a. *¡Buen provecho!*   b. ¡Feliz cumpleaños!
   c. ¡Por fin!

7. Your parents say you can't leave the house until all your chores are done. What might you think?

    a. ¡Qué alivio!   b. ¡Qué susto!   c. *¡Qué lata!*

8. ¿Cuánto hace que tienes esa camisa / blusa (ese vestido)?

9. ¿Te dan miedo los dentistas? ¿Te asusta ir al médico?

10. ¿Te gusta el pescado más que la carne?

11. ¿Siempre dices lo que piensas? ¿Por qué?

CAPÍTULO 5

OBJECTIVES

Communication
- to identify vocabulary related to sports

Grammar
- to use $e \rightarrow i$ stem-changing verbs
- to use ordinal numbers
- to use the definite article (el, la, los, las) with a nominalized adjective or a prepositional phrase
- to use the regular -ar preterite
- to use the preterite of the verb hacer

Culture
- to discuss tlachtli, a ball game that was played throughout the Aztec and Mayan regions of Mexico and Central America
- to describe the tlachtli court in Chichén Itzá
- to point out the significance of tlachtli in Mayan mythology

SUGGESTED MATERIALS

p. 165 (Prólogo cultural):   a wall map showing Mexico and Central America

pp. 166–167 (Palabras nuevas I):   magazine pictures showing people engaged in sports; magazine pictures and / or photographs of people smiling and laughing

p. 182 (Explicaciones I):   a wall calendar

PAGES 164–165

Photo
Ruins of the Mayan ceremonial city of Uxmal, located approximately 50 miles from Mérida on Mexico's Yucatán Peninsula. Although Uxmal means "thrice-built" in Maya, archaeologists believe that the ruins represent five different construction periods. The work started during the Mayans' Classic Period, between the sixth and seventh centuries. The city was completely abandoned by the middle of the fifteenth century, less than 100 years before Hernán Cortés landed in Mexico on April 21, 1519.

In the background of the photo is a structure referred to as the Cuadrángulo de las Monjas (Nunnery Quadrangle). The Spaniards gave the building this name because it resembles a convent with a central court surrounded by long galleries. On the right is the Pirámide del Adivino (Pyramid of the Magician, or Soothsayer) which, according to Mayan legend, was built by a magician in a single night.

PAGE 165

Additions to on-page notes
Notes: You may want to give students these questions before assigning the *Prólogo:* Who played tlachtli and where did these people live? What was the object of the game? Why was it difficult to score a goal? What did the players wear? Where is Chichén Itzá? Describe the *tlachtli* court there. How did two mythical heroes ensure humankind's destiny against evil? How do we know this?

PAGE 168

Photo
The Olympic-sized (50 × 12 meters) swimming pool at the Universidad Nacional Autónoma de México (UNAM) in southern Mexico City. Mexico's national university is the oldest in the Western Hemisphere, dating from the 1550s. Ciudad Universitaria, UNAM's campus, was built during the 1950s and extends over a threesquare-mile area.

Realia
A poster advertising the Twentieth National Youth Swimming Championship. Competing will be Bolivia's best swimmers selected from among the teams representing such cities as La Paz, the country's center of government and commerce; Sucre, the legal Bolivian capital; and Cochabamba and Santa Cruz, the nation's second and third most important cities.

PAGE 170

Photos

(a) Mexican long-jumper Carlos Casar at the *X Juegos Deportivos Panamericanos,* the Tenth Pan-American Games in Indianapolis (August 9-23, 1987). Held every four years, the Pan-American Games are patterned after the Olympics and follow most of the same rules and regulations. Participants in the Pan-Am Games, however, represent only the countries of the Western Hemisphere. The 4,350 athletes at the Indianapolis Games came from 38 countries to participate in more than 200 different competitive events. These Pan-Am Games were the second held in the U.S. since the 1951 inception of the event in Buenos Aires; Chicago hosted the 1959 Games.

(b) A scene from the opening ceremony of the 1983 Pan-American Games in Caracas, Venezuela. Depicted here by the crowd is the image of the famous *caraqueño* Simón Bolívar (1783-1830), who fought to free South American from Spanish rule. Known as *El Libertador,* Bolívar was instrumental in the liberation of Venezuela, Colombia, Ecuador, Peru, and Bolivia (which was named for him). In addition to various statues and monuments throughout the city, Caracas has three museums dedicated to Bolívar: the Casa Natal, Museo Bolivariano, and La Cuadra Bolívar, the family's country house.

Additions to on-page notes

Reteach / Review: After students complete Ex. C in class, you may want to base a written homework assignment on it. Ask students to choose five expressions from the list and to create a situation for each expression. Time allowing, ask volunteers to present their sentences to the class.

PAGE 171

Photo

Windsurfing in the Mexican resort area of Cancún, which is located in the southeastern state of Quintana Roo on a 12-mile elbow-shaped sandbar jutting into the Caribbean. On the interior side is a turquoise lagoon whose placid waters are perfect for windsurfing. Sailboards are available for rent by the hour at Playa Tortuga, or Turtle Beach. Novice windsurfers are encouraged to stay near the shore until they learn to maintain their balance and maneuver the board. Other popular beach activities at Cancún include snorkeling, scuba diving, water skiing, and parasailing.

PAGE 172

Photo

Soccer ball similar to the one used in the World Cup Championship held in Mexico in 1986. Soccer is the most popular sport not only in Spanish-speaking countries but in the world, and special care goes into manufacturing the balls for the World Cups, which are held every four years. The main international soccer organization, *Federación Internacional de Fútbol Asociado* (FIFA), with headquarters in Zurich, Switzerland, has chosen the Adidas company as its official supplier of balls for the World Cup.

Realia

Several official seals for the national soccer federations of Italy, Spain, and Mexico, all of which belong to the international organization, FIFA.

PAGE 173

Photos

(a) A crowd of 114,500 soccer fans watched at Aztec Stadium in Mexico City as Argentina's Diego Maradona led his team to victory over West Germany in the Thirteenth World Cup Tournament. World Cup '86 was held from May 31 through June 29 at 12 different sites throughout Mexico. This 52-game soccer tournament takes place every four years under the auspices of the international soccer organization, FIFA, and is the most popular and best-attended sporting event in the world.

(b) The Spanish professional soccer team Málaga C.F. (Club de Fútbol) is a second-division team that consistently draws high classification standings. The team is based at Málaga's 45,000-seat La Rosaleda (rose garden) Stadium.

Realia

One of the collector's item World Cup medals issued to raise advance funds for the 1986 event. This commemorative medal was produced under the authorization of the international soccer organization, FIFA. The medal displays the cup itself with the words "World Cup" written in Spanish, English, Italian, Portuguese, German, and French.

PAGE 174

Additions to on-page notes

Notes: You may want to present the *Contexto visual* on pp. 174-175 by asking students to keep their books closed as you point to transparency 16 and model each of the new vocabulary items.

Additions to on-page notes

Culture: Jai alai originated around the seventeenth century in *el País Vasco,* or the Basque country, in northern Spain. A fast-moving game involving either two, four, or six players, jai alai is played on a court that is approximately 176 feet long and 95 feet wide and closed in on the front, back, and one side by wals 44 feet high. The audience sits behind the fourth wall, which has a wire netting.

The object of jai alai is to hurl a hard-rubber ball in such a way that after hitting one of the side walls it cannot be returned to the front wall. The players each wear a curved wicker basket *(cesta)* that is attached to one arm.

PAGE 178

Photo

Women running in Barcelona. Women's sports have developed rapidly in Spain in the last few years, thanks in large part to changes in public attitudes. Spanish women athletes have yet to capture any world records, but they are getting close. Look for the names of these Spanish track-and-field stars in the next Olympic Games: Teresa Rione (100 meters), Gemma García Villamil (400 meters), Estrella roldán (broad jump), and Isabel Mozún (high jump).

PAGE 179

Additions to on-page notes

Reteach / Extra Help: You may want to reinforce the present tense of $e \rightarrow i$ verbs by asking these questions. Change subjects in order to practice all of the verb forms: *¿Qué pides para tu cumpleaños? ¿Qué sirves en las fiestas? ¿Repites palabras mucho en esta clase? ¿Ríes y sonríes mucho cuando estás con tus amigos?*

PAGE 180
Photo

A wendor exhibiting a wide selection of nuts outside Madrid's Santiago Bernabeu Soccer Stadium. Spectators can purchase the nuts by the gram. The 130,000-seat stadium is the residence for the Real Madrid, Spain's major first-division team. Madrid is also the home of one of the other principal contending first-division teams, Atleta de Madrid, which plays at the 75,000-seat Manzanares Stadium.

PAGE 181
Photo

A Mexican athlete at the Olympic Games. Held every four years in a different country, the games are regulated by the International Olympic Committee. At the 1984 Los Angeles Olympics, Mexico won two gold medals (Ernesto Cano winning the 20-kilometer and Raúl González the 50-kilometer walks), three silver, and one bronze.

PAGE 182
Photo

A young Filipino winning a race in Honolulu, Hawaii. Today's Filipinos come from one independent nation in which Filipino, Spanish, and American influences are blended. However, the Philippines only recently gained independence from the U.S., in 1946. Moreover, for over 300 years, from 1565 until the end of the Spanish-American War in 1898, the Philippine Islands were a Spanish colony. At one time, all educated Filipinos spoke Spanish, but this is no longer true. The official languages are Filipino (derived from Tagalog) and English.

Inspite of these changes, many signs of Spanish influence are still apparent today. Most Filipinos have Spanish surnames as a result of a decree passed in the 1800s by the Spanish government ordering the adoption of Spanish surnames in the islands. A great deal of contemporary Philippine folk music resembles that of Spain and Latin America. And many Spanish words are used in everyday language.

Additions to on-page notes
Reteach / Extra Help: After presenting the explanation of ordinal numbers, elicit additional examples for each of the three points. You may want to reinforce the forms by asking questions such as: *¿Cuál es el tercer mes del año? ¿Cuáles son tus dos primeras clases? ¿Es Isabel II (segunda) la reina de Inglaterra o de España?*

PAGE 185
Sample dialogues for *¿Qué pasa?*
Emilia and Benjamín are at the seashore talking about water sports that they enjoy.

B: ¿Participas en algún deporte?
E: Sí, soy nadadora en el equipo de mi colegio.
B: ¡Qué bueno! ¿Eres campeona?
E: Yo no, pero creo que nuestro equipo va a ganar el campeonato este año.

E: ¿Quién va a ganar la regata este año?
B: Pues, yo la puedo ganar, ¿no te parece?
E: ¿Tú? ¡Increíble!
B: No es tan increíble. Hace cinco años que navego y practico todos los días.

PAGE 187
Photo
Scuba diving and snorkeling are popular in the warm, clear waters of the Caribbean, where divers can swim alongside colorful tropical fish and explore sponge configurations, coral reefs, antique sunken boats, rock formations, and underwater caves. Average year-round undersea visibility in the Caribbean is 100 feet. Favored locations for divers include Mexico's Cancún, Isla Mujeres, Akumal, and the Palancar reef at

Cozumel; the Dominican Republic's undersea caves and coral reefs at La Caleta; and Puerto Rico's Humacao, La Parguera, and Icacos Island.

PAGE 188
Photos
(a) A Peruvian weight-lifter at the 1987 Pan-American Games in Indianapolis. The Games are a result of the 1940 Pan-American Congress held in Buenos Aires, attended by members of national Olympic committees from 16 countries. However, because of World War II, the first Pan-Am Games were not held until 1951.
(b) The Puerto Rican baseball team at the Tenth Pan-American Games. Baseball is one of the sports included at the Pan-American Games that does not figure into the Olympics. Men's and women's softball, roller skating, and table tennis are also not included. The Games are held under the auspices of the Pan-American Sports Organization (PASO), which was formed in 1967.
(c) Teens horseback riding in Venezuela. Ever since the Spanish *conquistadores* brought horses to the New World in the early sixteenth century, these animals have been an important part of everyday life, both in work and play.

Horses were integral to the rise of the "cowboy" cultures that developed in the cattle-raising areas of Latin America: the *gaucho* of Argentina, the *huaso* of Chile, the *llanero* of Venezuela, and the *charro* of Mexico, for example.

Additions to on-page notes
Notes: Before assigning Ex. C for oral or written work, you may want to point out that with the exception of *temprano,* the time expressions in the third column can go either at the beginning or at the end of the sentences.

PAGE 191
Photo
A los Angeles Times interview with Puerto Ricon golfer Juan A. Rodríguez Vila (right), better known as Chi Chi Rodríguez. Raised in a poor San Juan suburb, Rodríguez learned to play golf through his job

as a caddie. At the age of 17, he entered the Puerto Rican Open, where his powerful drive earned him second place. He turned pro in 1960, and over the years has ranked among the first five players in 35 official Professional Golf Association tournaments. By the end of the 1975 season, he had picked up seven titles and approximately $665,000 in prize money.

PAGE 192

Photo
Mexican tennis player Xochitl Escobedo at the 1987 Pan-American Games in Indianapolis. The host countries of the Pan-Am Games are chosen from among three zones: North (U.S., Canada, Mexico, Cuba, Puerto Rico), Central (Central America and Venezuela), and South (all South American countries). The Eleventh Pan-American Games will be hosted by Cuba in 1991.

Answers to *Repaso*
1. Somos unas esquiadoras muy enérgicas. Practicamos el esquí cuando podemos. / Roberto no es un nadador muy bueno. Lleva un salvavidas cuando navega. / La Sra. Gómez es una fotógrafa muy buena. Saca fotos cuando viaja.
2. El lunes pasado, buceé con Paco en el océano. / El jueves pasado, cambiaste de idea a las dos. / La semana pasada, tú y Luisa patinaron sobre ruedas en el club.
3. Anoche, hicimos planes con las entrenadoras. / El año pasado, hiciste un viaje a la isla. / Esta mañana, hice preguntas sobre el velero.
4. A la una pedimos una cancha de tenis libre. / Afortunadamente, sirven chuletas de cordero sabrosas. / Ahora pides zapatos de tenis nuevos.
5. Hoy terminamos la cuarta carrera. Mañana corremos en la quinta. / Ayer ganaron la novena regata. Hoy navegan en la décima. / Anteayer tiré las cajas vacías. Ahora busco en las llenas.

PAGE 193

Answers to *Tema*
1. Marta es una chica muy activa. Practica deportes cuando puede.
2. La semana pasada montó a caballo en el rancho.

3. Anteayer hizo gimnasia en el club.
4. Ahora pide una raqueta de tenis nueva.
5. La semana pasada ganó el primer partido. Mañana participa en el último.

PAGE 194

Answers to *Comprueba tu progreso*
A 1. Mamá siempre sirve comida sabrosa.
   2. Tomás y tú repiten las preguntas a menudo.
   3. Pedimos más cacahuates.
   4. Sirves paella por primera vez.
   5. Nunca repito lo que decimos.
   6. Ud. siempre pide más que los otros.

B 1. sonríes 4. sonríe
   2. reímos   5. sonríen
   3. ríen   6. sonrío

C 1. Tengo que leer el cuarto capítulo.
   2. Mónica Santos es la quinta nadadora.
   3. La fecha de hoy es el primero de febrero.
   4. Vivo en la tercera casa de la esquina.
   5. Las raquetas están en la segunda caja.
   6. Trabajo en el noveno piso.

D 1. No, prefiero los bajos.
   2. No, prefiero los pequeños.
   3. No, prefiero las cómicas (chistosas) (graciosas).
   4. No, prefiero los nuevos.
   5. No, prefiero el primero.
   6. No, prefiero el del oeste.

E 1. Corté el césped.
   2. Ud. planchó la ropa.
   3. Lavamos el coche.
   4. Tiraste la basura.
   5. Bucearon.
   6. Uds. pasaron la aspiradora.

F 1. Ya hicimos un viaje a San Juan.
   2. Esta mañana hice la cama antes de salir de casa.
   3. ¿Hiciste la maleta anoche?
   4. Anteayer la gente hizo cola para comprar las entradas.

5. ¿Ayer hicieron Uds. la tarea después de cenar?
6. El sábado pasado hicimos un asado.

PAGE 195
Photo
A Peruvian quilted and embroidered *tapiz* (wall hanging). This type of appliqué work is a popular folk-art form in many Latin American countries. Small, bright pieces of cloth, usually left over from making clothing, are sewn together to create a decorative tapestry that displays aspects of daily life. Artist Pedro Sulca, who comes from the south-central city of Cuzco, is one of Peru's most famous artisans working in this medium. He has received much international attention for his quilted *tapices.*

ORAL PROFICIENCY TEST
Directed Response
1. Pedro asks you about the results of last night's game. Tell him that the home team won for the first time. *(El equipo local ganó por primera vez.)*
2. Ask your teacher whether you have to answer all the questions in the third lesson. *(¿Tengo que contestar todas las preguntas en la tercera lección?)*
3. Conchita asks which bicycle you like better, the red one or the blue one. Tell her that you prefer the red one. *(Prefiero la roja.)*

Picture-Cued Response
4. Using the visuals on p. 174 or transparency 16, ask: "¿Qué hicieron los jóvenes ayer?" *(Hicieron gimnasia.)*
5. Pointing to the month of February on a wall calendar, ask: "¿Es éste el primer mes del año?" *(No, es el segundo (mes del año). OR No, no es el primer mes del año.) ¿Cuál es el primer mes del año? (Enero es el primer mes (del año). OR Enero es el primero.)*

Situations
6. You tell Ramón that you have three exams to study for tonight. How might he respond?
   a. ¡Qué milagro!   b. *¡Qué barbaridad!*
   c. ¡Ojalá!
7. The swimmers on the local team have asked their coach for new bathing suits and warm-up outfits. How might the coach tell his swimmers that their request is unreasonable?
   a. *Uds. piden mucho.*   b. Uds. hacen muchas preguntas.   c. Uds. preguntan mucho.

Real-Life Questions
8. ¿Hiciste la cama esta mañana?
9. ¿Te gustan los coches americanos o prefieres los japoneses y los alemanes?
10. ¿Descansaste el verano pasado o trabajaste?
11. ¿En qué clase sonríes y ríes más, en ésta o en la clase de matemáticas?

CAPÍTULO 6

OBJECTIVES

Communication
- to use vocabulary related to travel

Grammar
- to use the preterite of verbs that end in *-car, -gar,* and *-zar*
- to use the preterite of the verbs *ir* and *ser*
- to use the preterite of the verbs *dar* and *ver*
- to use negative words

Culture
- to point out some topographic characteristics of Central and South America
- to explain the uniqueness of the Pan American Highway
- to describe the roads of the Pan American Highway
- to tell about Panama's Darien Gap
- to discuss the *Pampa Colorada* in Peru

SUGGESTED MATERIALS

p. 197 (Prólogo cultural): wall map(s) showing the route of the Pan American Highway (from Arizona and Texas to Chile)

pp. 198–199 (Palabras nuevas I): a wall map of South America

p. 204 (Diálogo): a wall map showing the Andes Mountains

pp. 206–207 (Palabras nuevas II): items to reinforce travel-related vocabulary (city map, credit card, traveler's and bank checks)

p. 210 (Actividad): poster paper

p. 218 (Lectura): a wall map of Spain

PAGES 196–197
Photo
A section of the *Carretera Panamericana* in Chile, where the highway runs the length of the country from the city of Arica at the Peruvian border to Puerto Montt in the south. Chile, a narrow country that stretches along the Andes Mountains, is a land of surprising variety. The northern third of Chile is largely desert, important for its extensive mineral deposits. Most of the population lives in the central third of the country, a rich agricultural area with a mild climate. The southern third is an inhospitable mix of glaciated mountains, fjords, and thick forests.

PAGE 197
Additions to on-page notes
Notes: You may want to give students these questions before assigning the *Prólogo:* When did construction on the Pan American Highway begin? How many countries were involved in the project? In what year was the highway completed? What three conveniences are not available along the Pan American Highway? Where and why is the highway interrupted? If you were driving from Panama to Venezuela, how would you get there? What does *Pampa Colorada* mean? Describe the attraction that is located there and tell why it is unusual.

PAGE 200
Realia
A Spanish train ticket. Spain's state-owned railroad, *Red Nacional de Ferrocarriles Españoles* (RENFE), computerized its ticket-issuing operations in the 1960s. As a result, one can buy a ticket virtually anywhere in the country for a trip between any two points in Spain up to two months in advance. The ticket shown here was sold by an agency in Valencia on July 7 for seat number 67 in the non-smoking section of second-class car 21. This train left Valencia at 22:41 (10:41 P.M.) on July 10 and probably arrived in San Sebastián sometime before noon the following day.

PAGE 202

Photos

(a) *Ferrocarriles Argentinos* (Argentine Railways), with a network of 27,000 miles of tracks, have six different lines that service four stations in Buenos Aires: Retiro, Constitución, Once, and Lacroze. Built by the British at the end of the nineteenth century, the railroad provided easy transport of agricultural goods and livestock from the central pampas to the ports. Pulled by diesel engines, Argentine trains are cheaper than buses and offer air-conditioning, Pullman cars, new sleeping cars, and diners. Two of the most popular routes are the 30-hour Buenos Aires-San Carlos de Bariloche run and the 15-hour trip from Buenos Aires to Mendoza. The sign in the photo indicates the *tarifas,* or rates, for different destinations.

(b) A travel agency in Málaga, the capital of Spain's southern Costa del Sol. Although Spain has a reputation for attracting tourists, Spaniards themselves enjoy traveling as much as anyone else. In 1987 about 8 percent of vacationing Spaniards traveled to other countries. Of those who vacationed within Spain, nearly half went to the beaches and the rest to inland destinations.

PAGE 203

Additions to on-page notes

Reteach / Review: Before students begin Ex. C, you may want to reinforce the omission of the indefinite article with *ser* + nationality or profession by asking questions about popular sports and entertainment figures. For example: *Gabriela Sabatini es de la Argentina, ¿verdad? (Sí, es argentina) ¿Y cuál es su profesión? (Es tenista.)*

PAGE 204

Photo

Venezuelan teens waiting for a bus in Caracas. The round no-parking sign behind them displays the letter ''E,'' for *estacionamiento* (parking), with a prohibitive diagonal bar through it. Because of massive traffic problems, the city is currently installing a modern subway system, of which only the east-west line had been completed by 1988. Besides buses and taxis, residents also rely on collective cars and mini-buses called *por puestos,* which travel along set routes. They are faster and more expensive than buses and cheaper than taxis.

PAGE 205

Photo

The *Empresa Nacional de Ferrocarriles del Perú* (Peruvian National Railroad) boasts the world's highest standard-gauge railway. The Lima-La Oroya train climbs through the Andes to a height of more than 15,600 feet, offering a breathtaking panorama of the mountains. Much of Peru's state-owned rail system was built with the purpose of connecting the country's coastal cities and the inland mining communities. Today, Peruvian trains provide passenger transportation that is cheaper though generally slower than bus travel, as well as freight service.

PAGE 208

Photos

(a) A room at the Parador de Sigüenza in Sigüenza, a town about 77 miles from Madrid. *Paradores* (literally, stopping places) are government-run hotels located throughout Spain, many of which were deserted castles, monasteries, and palaces that the Spanish Department of Tourism has converted into tourist accommodations. The 75,000-square-foot *parador* in Sigüenza was originally a Moorish *alcázar,* or castle, and has been furnished with antiques and excellent reproductions.

(b) A front-desk clerk at a hotel in Torremolinos, a Mediterranean beach resort on Spain's Costa del Sol. Anyone who checks into a Spanish hotel must show either a foreign passport or an identification document called *documento nacional de identidad,* which Spaniards over 14 are required to carry with them at all times. This ID allows citizens of the European Economic Community, which Spain finally joined in 1986, to travel within member countries without a passport.

PAGE 210

Photo

Costa Rica's narrow-gauge Northern Railway runs approximately 100 miles, from the capital city of San José to Limón, the country's most important port. The express train makes only 7 stops, while the local (shown here) makes 52. There are numerous small settlements along the route that have no roads and therefore rely on the train for local transportation; children ride the morning train to the nearest school and take the evening train home. Because of the spectacular scenory, tourists often tak the San José-Limón trip; the Costa Rican government has remodeled four cars and a locomotive in 1930s' style and runs this tourist train three times a week.

PAGE 212

Additions to on-page notes

Enrichment: Point out that the $c \rightarrow qu$, $g \rightarrow gu$ and $z \rightarrow c$ spelling changes are needed to keep the pronunciation of the consonants the same as in the infinitive forms.

PAGE 216

Photo

The old diesel-engine train in Costa Rica travels from the capital city of San José to the Atlantic coast with a junction at the railyards in Siquirres, shown here. The railway was built by the British to provide transportation for coffee and banana crops. Approximately 6,000 laborers died, mostly of malaria, before the construction through the mountains to the coastal lowlands was completed in 1890. A modern electric train, *Ferrocarril Eléctrico al Pacífico,* runs from San José to the Pacific port city of Puntarenas. Costa Rica has almost 800 miles of tracks.

PAGE 217

Photo

A student field trip in Las Cañadas del Teide National Park on Tenerife, one of Spain's Canary Islands located about 60 miles from Africa. The Cañadas (ravines) del Teide are a reminder that the Canary Islands are volcanic in origin. A huge crater 46.5 miles in perimeter is one of the two main attractions of the park. The volcano is no longer active, but sulphurous smoke still issues from a fissure in the crater. The peak in the back of the photograph is the other attraction: the Pico del Teide, a mountain 12,162 feet high. A funicular rises to the summit, from which nearly all of the Canary archipelago can be viewed. The *pico* remains snow-covered all winter, even as a spring-like climate reigns along island's beaches. The pillarlike shape in the upper left of the photograph is a basalt massif, a volcanic rock formation.

PAGE 218

Photo

The Parador Carlos V in Jarandilla de la Vera, which is located in Spain's western province of Cáceres. This parador was a fortified palace where the Holy Roman Emperor Carlos V (1500-1558), also known as Carlos I of Spain, lived briefly before retiring to the nearby Monastery of Yuste. The suit of armor on the stairs is probably placed there in honor of the emperor, who collected such artifacts.

PAGE 219

Photos

(a) The Parador Marqués de Villena in Alarcón, a town located along Spain's Júcar River. One of the country's most beautiful castles was taken over to make this small *parador;* there are only 11 guest rooms. The castle, which stands on an outcropping in a loop of the Júcar River, was a Moorish fortress until it was captured by Hernán Martínez de Cevallos, who pulled himself up its walls by gripping a dagger in each hand. In this picture, it is framed by an entrance through one of several protective walls that surround the castle.

(b) The interior of the Parador Casa del Barón in Pontevedra, Spain. This building is a sixteenth-century country manor in the center of the city. Note the massive granite construction that is typical of the buildings here and in other older cities of Galicia. Pontevedra was originally settled by colonists from Crete, but its name comes from the Latin *Pontus Vetere* (Old Bridge). It is located in one of the more beautiful of the *rías bajas,* the estuaries of southern Galicia.

PAGE 223
Realia
A complimentary memo pad from a hotel chain in Spain's northern region of Asturias, which is located along the Cantabrian Mountains. Asturias was the site of the first Christian victory in 718, beginning the centuries-long struggle by the Spaniards to reclaim their peninsula from the Moors (711-1492). Today the region is important for its agriculture as well as its coal mines. Oviedo, the capital of Asturias, is remarkable for tis examples of pre-Romanesque architecture, some of which date back to the eighth and ninth centuries. Gijón is an attractive port city about 17 miles from Oviedo. Severely damaged at the outbreak of the Spanish Civil War (1936-1939), much of Gijón has been rebuilt.

PAGE 224
Realia
A deposit slip from a Spanish bank. This is a receipt *(recibo de pago)* for a payment to a checking account *(cuenta corriente)* using the bank's own credit card *(tarjeta de crédito carnet de oro).* The depositor must fill in the numbers of his or her account and write the deposit amount in both figures and words. The bank will make it official with a stamp *(sello)* and the signature of a teller *(cajero receptor).*

PAGE 226
Photo
The main hall of the Estación de Francia railroad station in Barcelona. Note that the signs are in both Spanish and *catalán,* the language of the autonomous region of Cataluña. The *taquilla,* or ticket window, on the right sells tickets for trips to nearby towns *(cercanías)* and the one on the left, for trips to more distant places *(largo recorrido).* Because so much of Cataluña is mountainous, *largo recorrido* travel is either northeast along the coast to France or southwest along the coast toward Valencia (or as far

as Tarragona and then through the Ebro River valley to Zaragoza and on to Madrid and other points).

Answers to *Repaso*
1. Cuando crucé en la esquina no vi nada ni a nadie. / Cuando busqué al inspector no vieron nada ni a nadie. / Cuando pagué a la dueña no vimos nada ni a nadie.
2. Saqué el bolígrafo i firmé un cheque de viajero. / Pagaste la cuenta y usaste una tarjeta de crédito. / Llegaron al campamento y buscaron su tienda.
3. Apagué la luz y fui a cobrar un cheque. / Sacamos el plano y fuimos a encontrar el correo. / Buscaron una escoba y fueron a limpiar la pensión.
4. Les dieron los horarios a los viajeros. Luego esperaron el tren local. / Les expliqué el problema a los pasajeros. Luego comenzamos el viaje largo. / Coloqué nuestras maletas en el suelo. Luego pagamos la habitación doble.
5. ¡Qué barbaridad! Nunca hay ningún periódico peruano en esta ciudad. / ¡Qué triste! Nunca hay ninguna comida brasileña en estos hoteles. / ¡Qué lástima! Nunca hay ningún autobús expreso en este pueblo.

PAGE 227
Answers to *Tema*
1. Cuando Eva llegó a la estación no vio nada ni a nadie.
2. Buscó la ventanilla y compró un boleto de ida.
3. Cruzó las vías y fue a esperar el tren.
4. Le dio su boleto al inspector. Luego buscó el coche comedor.
5. ¡Qué lata! Nunca hay ningún coche comedor en este tren.

PAGE 228
Answers to *Comprueba tu progreso*
A Llegué a la estación con un poco de retraso y busqué la ventanilla. Compré un boleto de ida y vuelta y crucé la vía para ir al andén. Después de subir al tren, coloqué el equipaje debajo del asiento. Le di el boleto al inspector. Luego fui al coche comedor y almorcé. Durante el viaje, practiqué el inglés con los otros pasajeros y

saqué unas fotos del campo. Llegué a Córdoba a
la una.

B 1. No, pero fuimos los primeros ayer.
   2. No, pero fue divertido el mes pasado.
   3. No, pero fueron fáciles el año pasado.
   4. No, pero fui de pesca anteayer.
   5. No, pero fue la última vez.
   6. No, pero fui la única (alumna ecuatoriana) en
      la otra clase.
   7. No, pero fueron a comprar las entradas para
      este concierto.

C 1. Ya la vieron. Ya le dieron los esquís.
   2. Ya lo vimos. Ya le dimos el cheque.
   3. Ya lo vieron. Ya le dieron los boletos.
   4. Ya los vio. Ya les dio una lección.
   5. Ya los vi. Ya les di los salvavidas.
   6. Ya lo vi. Ya le di la habitación individual.

D 1. No, no tengo ninguna idea buena.
   2. No, no vi ni a los paraguayos ni a los chilenos
      en el coche comedor.
   3. No, no compré nada en el mercado.
   4. Nunca fui a Salamanca (No fui nunca a
      Salamanca).
   5. No vi ni a mis primos ni a mis tíos.
   6. No, no hay ningún turista argentino allí.
   7. No, no vi ningún cuadro viejo (no vi nada) en el
      museo.
   8. No vi a nadie en la recepción.
   9. Tampoco fuimos (No fuimos tampoco) a la
      casa de cambio ayer.

PAGE 229

Photo

A Bolivian weaving whose *greca,* or ornamental
design, features native birds and animals such as
llamas and cows. Textiles woven or knitted from
llama, alpaca, and vicuña wools are coveted items in
the cold mountainous regions of South America. Cloth
goods include ponchos, sweaters, blankets, and bags.
Some of the best craft markets are found in and
around Cochabamba, Bolivia's second-largest city.
The valley town of Villa Rivero produces the only
tapestry weaving in the country.

ORAL PROFICIENCY TEST
Directed Response

1. How would you tell Esteban that the train is
arriving an hour late? *(El tren llega con una hora
de retraso.)*
2. Ask Elena what movie she saw the day before
yesterday. *(¿Qué película viste anteayer?)*
3. Your friend Paco was looking for you yesterday.
Tell him you crossed the bridge and had lunch in
the park. *(Crucé el puente y almorcé en el
parque.)*

Picture-Cued Response

4. Pointing to the photograph on p. 205, ask:
"¿Cómo fueron a Barcelona?" *(Fueron a
Barcelona en tren.)*
5. Pointing to the photograph on p. 208, ask: "¿Hay
alguien en la habitación?" *(No, no hay nadie en
la habitación.)*

Situations

6. Pedro says he has no energy. You find yourself in
the same situation. How would you express this?
   a. No me parece.   b. *Ni yo tampoco.*
   c. Ni él ni yo.
7. Mrs. Soler doesn't have enough cash to pay her
bill. What might she ask?
   a. ¿Puedo pagar al contado?   b. ¿Puedo
firmar el registro?   c. *¿Puedo pagar con
cheque?*

Real-Life Questions

8. ¿A qué hora llegaste a casa ayer después de las
clases? ¿Empezaste tu tarea inmediatamente?
9. ¿Cuánto tiempo tardas en vestirte cada mañana?
10. La última vez que viajaste, ¿adónde fuiste?
11. ¿Fuiste de pesca esta mañana o practicaste el
esquí acuático? ¿Hiciste estas cosas ayer?

CAPÍTULO 7

OBJECTIVES

Communication
- to identify vocabulary related to personal grooming
- to identify vocabulary related to shopping

Grammar
- to use the present tense of reflexive verbs
- to use afirmative *tú* commands with reflexive verbs
- to use cardinal numbers from 100 to 1,000,000
- to use the regular *-er* / *-ir* preterite
- to use the preterite of reflexive verbs

Culture
- to contrast past and present shopping places in San Juan, Puerto Rico
- to describe Plaza de las Américas, the largest shopping mall in the Caribbean
- to tell about Plaza del Mercado in the Río Piedras dristric of San Juan
- to discuss the Puerto Rican crafts found in El Viejo San Juan
- to point out the importance of local open-air markets in Puerto Rico's remote areas

SUGGESTED MATERIALS

p. 231 (Prólogo cultural): a wall map showing Puerto Rico and the rest of the Caribbean

pp. 232–233 (Palabras nuevas I): objects illustrating grooming-related vocabulary (perfume, scissors, nail polish, a nail file, lipstick, makeup, a razor, shoelaces, shaving cream)

pp. 242–243 (Palabras nuevas II): a piece of clothing with a label, objects illustrating the difference between *estrecho* and *ancho* (ties, books, pieces of paper, and so on)

p. 247 (Actividad): toy money (large bills)

PAGES 230–231

Photo
The central fountain area in Puerto Rico's ultramodern shopping center, Plaza de las Américas. Constructed in the Hato Rey section of San Juan, the three-level mall has approximately 200 businesses and retail establishments. Both underground and outdoor parking facilities are available.

PAGE 231

Additions to on-page notes
Notes: You may want to give students these questions before asigning the *Prólogo:* In the past, where did teenagers in San Juan go to shop and meet friends? Where do they go now? What is Plaza del Mercado? What else can you buy in Río Piedras? Name some crafts found in El Viejo San Juan. What is the name of Puerto Rico's native Indians? Where do Puerto Ricans who live in remote areas of the island go to shop and socialize?

PAGE 234

Realia
Fixonia offers a variety of hair-care products: mousse *(espuma),* shampoo *(champú),* two different types of hair spray *(laca),* one for dry hair and one for normal or oily hair, and a styling gel *(gomina)* in regular and extra strength.

Additions to on-page notes
Reteach / Extra Help: After presenting the *Contexto comunicativo,* you may want to reinforce the meaning of *quejarse* in mini-dialogue 1 by asking these questions about 3 and 4: *¿De qué se queja Mamá? (Del pelo de Juan.) ¿De qué se queja Carmen? (Del color de su pelo.)*

PAGE 236

Photos

(a) A young man is shown trimming his moustache in Chicago.
(b) Two sisters in Madrid, Spain, are shown applying makeup.
(c) Two teenagers are shown preparing to go to a party.

PAGE 239

Photo

The perfume counter at the Madrid branch of El Corte Inglés, Spain's most important department-store chain. Major international fragrances are featured here, as well as fine Spanish product lines such as Puig and Myrurgia. In addition to its three other stores in Madrid, El Corte Inglés has branches in ten other Spanish cities.

PAGE 240

Realia

(a) An ad from the Mexican yellow pages advertising the services of Julia's Beauty Parlor, which specializes in applying false eyelashes one by one and false nails. The ad indicates the *despacho,* or office number at the Bellavista building, located at 7 Jardín Juárez Street. Note that each of the two phone numbers contains only five digits, as is the case throughout most of Mexico except in the capital, where seven numbers are used.
(b) Gloria's Beauty Salon is featured in this display ad from the yellow pages for the city of Cuernavaca, which is located in the central Mexican state of Morelos. The salon boasts hairdressers and makeup artists who are highly trianed, with the most beautiful creations for brides-to-be.

PAGE 241

Photo

In Madrid a teenager is having her hair styled at one of the city's hundreds of beauty parlors, or *peluquerías.* A manicure *(manicura)* and facial *(limpieza de cutis)* are usually available as well. In Spain, men's barber shops are also called *peluquerías.* The unisex trend has become popular among *peluquerías* in large Spanish cities. Those that are not unisex are usually defined as *peluquerías de señoras* or *salones de belleza* (beauty salons) for women and *peluquerías de caballeros* for men.

PAGE 245

Realia

(a) This advertisement from a Mexican magazine for Express sportswear advises: "If you think differently, dress differently. Express yourself with Expres."
(b) The flyer *(volante)* announces a boutique called Duna. To celebrate the opening, the store is offering big savings on: all brands of jeans, skirts, blouses, bush jackets; all types of clothing at factory prices; today's styles. Customers are also told not to throw the flyer away, because upon presenting it, they will receive a 10 percent discount on any purchase.

PAGE 246

Photo

Spanish teenagers shopping for shoes. Running shoes have become popular for daily use throughout Spain. Another kind of footwear is *alpargatas,* a type of canvas espadrille with soles made of twined rope.

Realia

(a) A merchandise tag for a type of skirt indicating, among other things, the product's name, size, and number code. The initials *P.V.P.* stand for *precio de venta al público,* the standard retail price.
(b) A manufacturer's label for the Argentine textile company Tejidos Brigi, which is located in the coastal resort city of Mar del Plata. The word *tejidos* refers to woven or knitted goods; Mar del Plata is famous for distinctive and fashionable wool sweaters.

PAGE 247

Photo

Shopping for clothes at a department store in Puerto Rico. Because of the island's affiliation with the U.S., there are some familiar department-store chains such as Sears and J.C. Penney, both of which have large stores at Plaza de las Américas. González Padín, New York Department Store, Velasco, and Armstrong's are some of the domestic department stores located throughout the island.

PAGE 248

Photos

(a) Relatively new to Spain, modern shopping malls like this one in the city of Zaragoza, in the northeastern region of Aragón, are springing up in the country's major cities. The malls are filled with all kinds of stores, boutiques, and service establishments such as travel agencies, photocopy shops, and hairstyling salons. On the lower levels, called *bajos,* there are usually cafés, restaurants, and even discos, which are popular gathering places for teenagers.

(b) There are many delightful outdoor dining areas in Mexico City's famous Zona Rosa (Pink Zone), a chic section of the city that is filled with shoppers during the day and people seeking entertainment at night. The Zona Rosa offers a broad choice of tourist hotels, boutiques, movie theaters, record stores, discotheques, art galleries, and other attractions. In deference to its name, the 24-square-block area has been paved in pink bricks. The streets are named after European cities. This restaurant, formerly the Kineret Delicatessen and now Pan, Queso y Vino, is located at the corner of Génova (Genoa) and Hamburgo (Hamburg) streets.

PAGE 252

Additions to on-page notes

Notes: You may want to assign Ex. F as written homework. Tell students to use only present-tense forms in their answers.

Reteach / Extra Help: Before students begin the

Práctica on p. 253, you may want to give various commands with reflexive verbs and ask students to follow or pantomime them.

PAGE 254

Sample dialogues for *¿Qué pasa?*

Enrique tries to exchange a shirt that the bought a couple of days ago. He and the saleswoman discuss the matter.

E: Buenos días, señorita. Quiero devolver esta camisa. No me gusta quejarme de nada, pero no es mi talla y está sucia.

S: ¿Quisiera probarse una camisa distinta? Ésta es muy elegante.

E: A mí me parece anticuada. Prefiero las camisas estrechas.

S: Bueno. ¿Por qué no se prueba ésta? Está muy de moda.

E: Quisiera devolver esta camisa. Me queda muy ancha.

S: ¿Muy ancha? Pues, las camisas anchas están muy de moda.

E: Señorita, no me gusta esta camisa. Quiero devolverla y probarme algo distinto. Mi talla es 38.

S: ¡Pero esta camisa está sucia! Ud. no la puede devolver. Lo siento, señor.

E: De acuerdo. Adiós.

PAGE 256

Photo

The Banco Santa Cruz de la Sierra in Santa Cruz, which is located in the Bolivian plains approximately 340 miles southeast of La Paz. Bolivian banking hours are from 9:00 A.M. to noon, and from 2:00 to 4:30 P.M. Like most banks in the Spanish-speaking world, those in Bolivia close for lunch. Founded in 1561, Santa Cruz has boomed over the past three decades thanks to the area's agricultural resources and the development of its oil and gas reserves.

PAGE 258

Photo

An actor in Barcelona, Spain, is shown applying makeup.

PAGE 259

Additions to on-page notes

Reteach / Extra Help: You may want to ask volunteers to read the sentences in Ex. A, supplying the correct preterite forms. Students may them write the paragraph at home. Check students' work for correct spelling, capitalization and punctuation.

PAGE 260

Photo

Customers getting a shave and haircut at a barbershop *(peluquería de caballeros)* in Guatemala. At traditional barbershops like this one, it is still customary to get a haircut and a shave. In fact, many men in the Spanish-speaking world still follow the custom of going to a barbershop for their daily shave.

Answers to *Repaso*

1. Fueron al baño de la oficina para lavarse las manos. / Fuimos al gimnasio de la escuela para quitarnos los uniformes. / Fuiste al cuarto (dormitorio) de Ana para limarte las uñas.
2. Antes de irme (salir) de la tienda, devolvieron la crema de afeitar. / Después de probarse el vestido, compró un lápiz de labios. / Después de afeitarte el bigote, tiraste la maquinilla de afeitar.
3. Su mamá (madre) le preguntó: "¿Puedes también atarte los cordones?" / Les preguntó: "¿Quieren también quitarse los anteojos?" / María me preguntó: "¿Debes también cortarte las uñas?"
4. Me dice: "Es muy ancha. Quítate la falda y busca tu talla." / Le digo a Daniel: "Es bastante tarde. Lávate el pelo y usa el secador." / Le digo a ella: "Son demasiado estrechas. Pruébate estos zapatos y devuelve las sandalias."
5. ¡Qué lata! Devolvieron alrededor de mil cien tijeras. / ¡Qué suerte! Escribió más de mil quinientas etiquetas. / ¡Qué lástima! Vendimos menos de mil cajas.

PAGE 261

Answers to *Tema*

1. Consuelo fue a la peluquería del barrio para cortarse el pelo.
2. Antes de cortarse el pelo, miró las revistas de modas.
3. La peluquera le preguntó: "¿Quieres también probarte este maquillaje?"
4. La amiga de Consuelo le dice: "Es muy tarde. Date prisa y paga la cuenta."
5. ¡Qué barbaridad! ¡Gasté más de mil quinientos pesos!

PAGE 262

Answers to *Comprueba tu progreso*

A
1. ganga
2. la escalera mecánica
3. la etiqueta
4. el letrero
5. talla
6. dependiente
7. un ojo de la cara
8. el impuesto

B
1. Ana se cepilla el pelo.
2. Te limas mucho las uñas.
3. Mi hermano se prueba la corbata nueva.
4. Nos vestimos de prisa.
5. Me maquillo muy despacio.
6. Carmen se ata los cordones de los zapatos.
7. Mis hermanas se van temprano.
8. Luis y yo nos quejamos de todo.

C
1. Se cepilla el pelo.
2. Se lima las uñas.
3. Se seca el pelo.
4. Se maquilla la cara.
5. Se afeita.
6. Se cepilla los dientes.

D
1. Tengo que irme en dos minutos.
2. Mi tío tiene que cortarse el bigote.
3. Ud. tiene que darse prisa.
4. Tengo que ponerme el vestido rosado.
5. Tenemos que quejarnos de esa cajera.
6. Tienes que probarte los pantalones.
7. Mis hermanas tienen que limarse las uñas.
8. Tienen que acostarse después de la cena.

E
1. Vete ahora mismo.
2. Ponte el esmalte de uñas.
3. Lávate bien las manos.
4. Aféitate antes de salir.

5. Córtate el pelo.
6. Maquíllate en el baño.

F
1. saliste
2. Se escribieron
3. aprendí
4. devolvió
5. escogimos
6. rompió
7. Entendiste
8. prometió
9. nos vimos
10. me fui

PAGE 263

Photo

A carved wood Parachico dance mask from the southern Mexican border state of Chiapas. The pink, painted mask topped with a brush headdress represents a European. The slits under the eyes are holes through which the wearer can see. Throughout Mexican history, masks have played an important role in the lives of the different indigenous peoples. Depending on their place of origin, masks can be made from wood, baked ceramic clay, stone, leather, tin, cloth, paper, or woven fiber. Masks were used in many rituals and are still important in dances: priests wore masks of deities during special religious feasts; hunters donned masks representing beasts that they wished to capture; and storytellers related legends and stories through masks.

ORAL PROFICIENCY TEST

Directed Response

1. How would you tell Jaime to put on a dry bathing suit? *(Ponte un traje de baño seco.)*
2. Ask Paula if she returned the books to the library. *(¿Devolviste los libros a la biblioteca?)*
3. How would you ask Juana and Elena why they left so early last night? *(¿Por qué se fueron Uds. tan temprano anoche?)*

Picture-Cued Response

Pointing to the photograph on p. 241, ask:
4. ¿Dónde está la muchacha? *(Está en la peluquería.)*
5. ¿Con qué le seca el pelo la señora? *(Le seca el pelo con un secador.)*

Situations

6. Ángela hasn't been able to sleep because of a noisy neighbor. What advice would you give her?
   a. Hay que darte prisa.   b. Tienes que afeitarte.   c. *Debes quejarte.*
7. Luis asks Guillermo if he calls his girlfriend often. How might Guillermo respond?
   a. Se llama Inés.   b *Nos llamamos a veces.*
   c. La llamo Linda.

Real-Life Questions

8. ¿Te gusta ir de compras? Si ves algo que quieres comprar, ¿lo compras o esperas una liquidación?
9. ¿Cuál es tu departamento favorito en un almacén? ¿Por qué?
10. ¿Qué hiciste anoche? Si saliste, ¿volviste tarde o temprano?
11. ¿Cuántas veces al año te cortas el pelo?

CAPÍTULO 8

OBJECTIVES

Communication
- to identify vocabulary related to driving
- to identify vocabulary related to finding a location
- to identify automobile-related vocabulary

Grammar
- to use negative *tú* commands
- to use possessive adjectives before and after nouns
- to use possessive pronouns

Culture
- to identify Mexico City as the oldest city in the Americas and the second-largest and most rapidly growing metropolitan area in the world
- to discuss the founding and development of Mexico City by the Aztecs
- to point out how the arrival of the Spanish explorers in Mexico affected Mexico City
- to describe the *Plaza de las Tres Culturas*
- to tell about advancements made in Mexico City by 1620

SUGGESTED MATERIALS

p. 265 (Prólogo cultural): a wall map of Mexico

pp. 266–267 (Palabras nuevas I): magazine pictures of cars and street scenes

pp. 274–275 (Palabras nuevas II): a toy car

pp. 286–287 (Explicaciones II): classroom objects (pens, pencils, books, and so on) and other items to illustrate possessive adjectives and pronouns

PAGES 261–205

Photo
Mexico City's *Plaza de las Tres Culturas*, located in the Tlatelolco district. This square brings together three distinct periods of the nation's history. The Aztec pyramid represents the pre-Columbian age, marked by the presence of numerous Indian groups. The Iglesia de Santiago dates from the colonial years, and represents three centuries of Spanish rule that began when Hernán Cortés defeated the Aztecs in 1521. The Ministry of Foreign Affairs building is symbolic of today's Mexico.

PAGE 265

Additions to on-page notes
Notes: You may want to give students these questions before assigning the *Prólogo:* For how many years has Mexico City been inhabited? Who were the first inhabitants and how did they build their city? Describe the *Plaza de las Tres Culturas.* What special attractions are found in some Mexico City subway stations? Name three innovations that were created or developed in Mexico City before anywhere else in the Americas. What is the total population of Mexico City and its surrounding areas?

PAGE 268

Additions to on-page notes
Reteach / Review: In conjunction with mini-dialogue 4, point out that the *u* in *continuar* requires a written accent in the present-tense forms *continúo, continúas, continúa, continúan,* as well as in the affirmative *tú* command *continúa.*

PAGE 269

Photo
A police officer writing out a ticket to the owner of a car parked in a no-parking zone. Parking regulations vary from country to country in the Spanish-speaking world. In Spain, for example, parking is permitted on one-way streets only on the side with even numbers on even-numbered days of the month and on the side with odd numbers on odd-numbered days.

Realia

This parking ticket issued by the municipality of Madrid cites the owner for having parked illegally in a controlled parking area. Information written by the police officer on the ticket includes the vehicle registration (license plate) number, the date and time of the citation, and the street address in front of which the car was parked. The bottom of the ticket advises the owner of the vehicle to await further instructions, which will be mailed to his or her residence.

PAGE 270

Photo

This car with a student driver is registered in the province of Málaga, as indicated by the letters *MA* on the license plate. In Spain all license plates *(matrículas)* begin with one or two letters signifying the province of registration. (Spanish province names are the same as those of their capital cities.) Two letters are used to differentiate province names beginning with the same letter: *M* indicates Madrid, *MU* means Murcia. The *Z* at the end means that this is a late-model car.

Realia

A road sign in Spain advises that it is mandatory *(obligatorio)* for both drivers and front-seat passengers to use safety belts. This relatively new law is strictly enforced wherever these signs are posted, mainly on the country's highways.

PAGE 271

Realia

(a) In Spain, the U.P.A. Driving Schools advertise a program whereby a driver's license can be obtained *gratis,* or free. According to the program, which is offered at U.P.A.'s 200 affiliates, customers will recuperate the money they invested to obtain a car-registration document *(carnet),* as well as receive the financial benefits of supplementary insurance.

(b) A Mexican driver's license. The license lists the full name and birthdate of the driver, dates of issue and expiration of the license, the license

number, blood type of the operator, signature of the authorizing official, the type of license (operator's or chauffeur's), and the address and signature of the driver. An operator's license is valid for two years. In order to apply for a license, one must be 18 years old and produce an official birth certificate. While the law technically requires both a written and driving test, these formalities are often waived at the discretion of the examining officer. Very few high schools in Mexico offer driver's education courses.

PAGE 272

Photo

A student driving to school in Madrid. Although public transportation serves the suburbs and outskirts of the city, students with their own or family cars usually prefer to drive. For those whose schools and residences are located in the center of the city, it is more convenient to use subways or buses. In Madrid, the weekday traffic rush hour occurs four times a day—not only at the beginning (about 9:00 A.M.) and end (7:00 P.M.) of the business day, but also just before and after the midday lunch break that lasts from around 1:00 P.M. to 4:00 P.M.

Realia

International highway and street signs found in Spain. The one on the left posts a maximum speed limit of 100 kilometers per hour, equivalent to 62 miles per hour. The other signs indicate (from bottom to top) "stop," "no parking," "signal ahead," "two-way traffic," and "yield right-of-way."

PAGE 273

Photo

Approach to the city of Málaga, heading east on Spain's National Highway N-340. The sign on the right indicates the turnoff leading to the east side of the city, the seaport, and the continuation of the same highway east along the Mediterranean coastline to Almería. The sign on the left points the way to the city center, and beyond to National Highway N-321, which begins in Málaga and heads north, connecting with the highways to Granada, Sevilla, and Córdoba.

PAGE 276

Photo

A large PEMEX service station in Mexico City. PEMEX, or Petróleos Mexicanos, is Mexico's government-run petroleum industry. In 1938, after a nationwide strike by Mexican workers against foreign (mainly U.S. and British) oil companies, President Lázaro Cárdenas nationalized his nation's petroleum industry.

PAGE 277

Photo

A gas station in Bogotá, Colombia. Services include car washing, lubrication, and tire and battery services. The station sells gasoline that is filtered *(con filtro)* to eliminate impurities; however, unleaded gas is not required and is relatively scarce. Premium gas (called *extra* or *super*) is available only in urban areas and has an octane rating of 95. More commonly available is regular gas (termed *corriente*) with as 84 octane level. Automobiles are still a relative luxury in Colombia since they cost more than in the U.S. due to higher transport costs and import duties. Consequently, older cars are kept on the road as long as possible.

Realia

This flyer describes a special promotion for Spanish motorists featuring a tune-up for the price of 6,900 pesetas. An oil change, spark plugs, and air and oil filters, a maintenance check of the battery and headlights, and the balancing of the front tires are among the services offered.

PAGE 279

Additions to on-page notes

Enrichment: Additional questions you may want to ask for *Ex. D ¿Te asusta manejar de noche? ¿Por qué? ¿Te gusta estar en la carretera cuando llueve o nieva? ¿Por qué?*

PAGE 280

Photo

A pair of traffic signs in Panama City, the capital of Panama. The octagon *ALTO* (stop) sign is the same shape used in most countries of the world. In some Latin American countries, the sign bears te word *PARE* (the formal command form of the verb *parar,* "to stop"). The lower sign bears the international symbol for no left turn. The written message is a formal command ("Do not turn left").

Additions to on-page notes

Reteach / Extra Help: Reinforce the negative *tú* commands for regular and stem-changing verbs and those with spelling changes by making these statements about students and asking volunteers to give advice in the form of negative commands: ____ *va a llenar el tanque de su coche con agua. (____, no llenes . . .)* ____ *quiere hablar español en la clase de historia.* ____ *tiene tanta hambre que va a comer cinco sándwiches.* ____ *siempre abre la ventana del coche cuando llueve.* ____ *cuenta chistes en la clase de matemáticas.*

PAGE 281

Photo

Drivers experiencing the heavy traffic congestion typical of Paseo de la Reforma, one of the two major thoroughfares in Mexico City. (The other is Avenida Insurgentes, which intersects with the Paseo.) Government attempts to alleviate the city's transportation problems are constantly challenged by the rapid growth rate of the population, which totals overs 14 milion people. Despite the continual expansion of the subway sistem, overcrowding is a major problem on tho *Metro.* The building of two ring roads, one outside the city and the other within the city limits, both connected to a central area by a series of freeways laid out in a grid pattern, has only slightly alleviated urban traffic jams.

PAGE 284

Photo

In addition to experiencing frustration at being caught in a traffic jam on the Paseo de La Reforma in Mexico City, this driver is one of the millions affected by the pollution from the heavy traffic and industrial smog that plague this capital. Many instances of such physical discomforts as respiratory aliments, nosebleeds, and eye problems are attributed to the high levels of pollution there. The noise from the heavy traffic adds to drivers' distress, and is exacerbated by Mexican motorists' use of the horn to move traffic along as soon as a light has turned green.

Realia

This road sign indicating "no passing" is found in Guadalajara, the capital of the Mexican state of Jalisco. Guadalajara's population has risen to nearly three million, creating pollution problems and traffic congestion.

Additions to on-page notes

Notes: Before assigning Ex. D either as oral or written work, make sure students know that they should answer with negative *tú* commands.

PAGE 285

Photo

Teenagers checking mechanical problems with their car, which is stalled at the Plaza de la Cibeles in the heart of Madrid. This is one of the city's busiest intersections. In the background is the immense central post office called *Palacio de Comunicaciones* and affectionately nicknamed *Catedral de Comunicaciones.* Dominating the center of the beautiful plaza is Madrid's favorite fountain, the Fuente de la Cibeles, with a statue of Cybele, the Greek goddes of fertility, riding her chariot pulled by mythological lions.

PAGE 286

Realia

Seliauto is a used-car lot in Leganés, a town on the outskirts of Madrid. Advertised here are its specials of the week: used European cars that have been checked or overhauled in all thier "vital points" and are "ready for everything."

In the center, a variation of the "Baby on Board" window sticker announces that a nice *(simpático)* driver is on board. On the right is a parking stub.

PAGE 289

Photo

This *Bienvenido a la Argentina* sign greets those traveling by car via the Andes from Chile to Argentina at a town called *Las Cuevas* (The Caves). This small, modern mountain town houses the Argentine customs station where travelers are detained for approximately ten minutes to complete customs formalities.
A customs form declaring the contents and value of all personal belongings must be carried in foreign vehicles throughout visitors' stay in the country.
Las Cuevas lies at the end of a modern four-kilometer (2.5 mile) mountain tunnel. From June to October, the winter months in Argentina, snow chains are strongly recommended for vehicles traveling this route.
Las Cuevas has become a famous ski resort despite having suffered demage from landslides several years ago.

PAGE 292

Photo

Teens washing a car in Málaga, Spain. There are drive-in car washes in Spain, especially in the large cities, but they are not as plentiful as in the U.S.

Answers to *Repaso*

1. Paramos a las señales de tráfico. Tenemos suerte. / Cruzan en el paso de peatones. Tienen cuidado. / Acelero en el carril de la izquierda. Tengo prisa.
2. "¿Cuándo limpió Ud. ese coche suyo?," le pregunto al conductor (a la conductora). / "¿Dónde cambiaste esos cheques tuyos?," tu mamá te pregunta. / "¿Cuándo pagaron esa multa mía?," nos pregunta.
3. "No dobles tan lento," dice el instructor (la instructora). / "No seas tan impaciente," dice la bibliotecaria. / "No llegues demasiado tarde," dice mi padre.
4. Luego le decimos: "Sé inteligente. No repitas ese chiste." / Luego el profesor le dice: "Sé buena. No pierdas esos apuntes." / Ahora le digo: "Sé optimista. No digas esas cosas."
5. "No usé tu perfume," dice su sobrina. "Prefiero el suyo (el de ella)." / "¿Perdieron su secador?," preguntamos. "¿Quieren el nuestro?" / "¿Rompió

Ud. la raqueta?," pregunta el entrenador (la entrenadora). "¿Quiere la mía?"

PAGE 293

Answers to *Tema*

1. Carlota y su madre están en el estacionamiento del almacén. Tienen prisa.
2. "¿Dónde estacionaste ese cacharro tuyo?," su madre le pregunta.
3. "No manejes tan rápido," dice su madre.
4. Luego le dice: "Sé paciente. No toques la bocina."
5. "Olvidé el bolso," dice Carlota "¿Tienes el tuyo?"

PAGE 294

Answers to *Comprueba tu progreso*

A
1. Limpia el parabrisas.
2. Lee la placa.
3. Abre el capó.
4. Enciende los faros.
5. Cambia la llanta.
6. Toca la bocina.
7. Llena el tanque.
8. Ponte el cinturón de seguridad.

B
1. Pues, no compres el regalo.
2. Pues, no recojas los platos.
3. Pues, no juegues al ajedrez.
4. Pues, no toques el piano.
5. Pues, no hagas nada.
6. Pues, no tengas prisa.
7. Pues, no digas eso.
8. Pues, no des la vuelta.
9. Pues, no vayas al teatro.
10. Pues, no seas antipático.

C
1. ¡No comas dulces antes del almuerzo!
2. ¡Respeta las reglas de tráfico!
3. ¡Cruza en el paso de peatones!
4. ¡No corras por los pasillos de la escuela!
5. ¡No toques la bocina cerca del hospital!
6. ¡No abras el capó en la carretera!
7. ¡Llena el tanque con gasolina!
8. ¡No choques con ese coche!

D
1. María va a invitar a una compañera suya.
2. Eugenio y Luis van a invitar a unos amigos suyos.
3. Dolores y Silvia van a invitar a un profesor suyo.
4. Nosotros vamos a invitar a unas primas nuestras.
5. Tú vas a invitar a unos compañeros tuyos.
6. Ud. va a invitar a una sobrina suya.
7. Eugenio va a invitar a unas amigas suyas.
8. Teresa y yo vamos a invitar a una tía nuestra.

E
1. Las suyas están en el garaje.
2. Las mías están en el armario.
3. La suya está en el baúl.
4. Los nuestros están en el suelo.
5. Las mías están en la cartera.
6. La nuestra está cerca del establecimiento.
7. El suyo está detrás del coche comedor.
8. La mía está en el primer piso.

PAGE 295

Photo

A model truck made from painted batten wood. Colorful and charming toys such as this can be found in nearly all markets in Mexico. Personalized dolls made from cloth scraps or painted papier-mâché complete with earrings and beauty marks are also popular, as are miniature sets of dishes and other household items. Whistles and wind instruments are often shaped like winged angels or fantastic animals. A visit to a Mexican market proves that by using a bit of imagination and a playful dash of color, Mexicans can put together toys with almost any material at hand: wood, clay, tin, copper, glass, string, paper, cloth, or woven fiber.

ORAL PROFICIENCY TEST

Directed Response

1. Roberto tells you that he has his driver's license. How would you tell him that you don't have yours yet? (*Todavía no tengo el mío.* OR *No tengo el mío todavía.*)

2. Tell Jaime not to go out now because it's raining. *(No salgas ahora porque llueve.)*
3. How would you tell your family that you and Julio are going downtown with some friends of yours? *(Julio y yo vamos al centro con unos (algunos) amigos nuestros.)*

Picture-Cued Response
Pointing to the photograph on p. 269, ask questions such as:

4. ¿Qué le va a hacer al joven el policía? *(Le va a poner una multa.)*
5. ¿Qué crees que el policía le dice al joven? *(Ud. no puede (No puedes) estacionar aquí.* OR *¿Puedo ver su (tu) permiso de manejar, por favor?)*

Situations
6. A tourist stops you on the street to ask how far away the museum is. How might you respond?
   a. *Está a sólo dos cuadras.*
   b. Hay solamente dos cuadros.
   c. Es el único museo por aquí.
7. You're about to go on a long car trip. Which of the following might you do at a service station before you get going?
   a. Arrancar.   b. *Llenar el tanque.*
   c. Acelerar rápidamente.

Real-Life Questions
8. ¿Tienes tu permiso de manejar? Si no, ¿cuándo lo vas a obtener?
9. ¿Siempre usas el cinturón de seguridad? ¿Crees que la gente debe usarlo siempre?
10. ¿Cuál es la estación de servicio más cerca de tu casa? ¿Le puedes decir a un amigo cómo llegar allí?
11. ¿Crees que es más fácil manejar en el centro de la ciudad o en el campo? ¿Por qué?

ORAL PROFICIENCY TEST—CHAPTERS 5–8
Directed Response
1. Ask Alfredo if he took many pictures when he went to Argentina. *(¿Sacaste muchas fotos cuando fuiste a la Argentina?)*

2. Say that you want to buy your Mom a blouse but you don't know her size. *(Quiero comprarle una blusa a mi mamá pero no sé su talla.)*
3. How would you tell Pablo not to drive so fast because it's dangerous? *(No manejes tan rápido porque es peligroso.)*

Picture-Cued Response
Pointing to the visual on p. 203, ask questions such as:

4. ¿Qué tiene en la mano la segunda persona en la cola? *(Tiene una raqueta de tenis.)*
5. ¿En qué deporte va a participar la tercera persona? *(Va a esquiar.* OR *Va a participar en el esquí.)*
6. ¿Cuál es la profesión de la séptima persona? *(Es fotógrafa.)*

Situations
7. Pilar and Tomás are good friends, but she often gets tired of his constant complaining. What might she say to him?
   a. ¡Ay! ¿Por qué te das tanta prisa?   b. No te afeites tanto, chico.   c. *¡Uf! ¿Por qué te quejas tanto?*
8. You've just finished a fantastic book and are recommending it to your friend Conchita. When she asks how long it took you to read the book, how might you answer?
   a. *Tardé dos semanas en leerlo.*   b. Tardo muy poco en leerlo.   c. Hace un mes que lo leí.

Real-Life Questions
9. Cuando quieres comprar unos zapatos nuevos, ¿te pruebas varios antes de comprarlos?
10. ¿Cuál es la primera cosa que haces después de levantarte por la mañana? ¿Y la segunda?
11. Este libro es mío. ¿Dónde está el tuyo?

CAPÍTULO 9

OBJECTIVES
Communication
- to identify vocabulary related to food and diet
- to identify vocabulary related to illness, medical care, and the human body

Grammar
- to use commands with *Ud.* and *Uds.*
- to use the present subjunctive

Culture
- to point out Latin Americans' recent interest in keeping fit
- to discuss the popularity of jogging and working out in the larger Latin American cities
- to tell about the rise of team sports at schools and universities
- to describe how the growing interest in fitness and health has influenced eating habits in the Spanish-speaking world

SUGGESTED MATERIALS
pp. 298–299 (Palabras nuevas I):   magazine pictures of foods and activities associated with fitness and nutrition

p. 303 (Actividad):   menus from restaurants serving Spanish or Latin American cuisine

p. 323 (Actividad):   a paper bag

PAGES 296–297
Photo
Teens running in a Barcelona stadium. Jogging (known in Spain as *footing*) is an increasingly popular sport in Spain. This is due in part to foreign example and to a campaign by the *Consejo Superior de Deportes.* The *consejo* has published information about jogging in all four of Spain's languages —*español, catalán, gallego, vasco*—and provides expert advice. Many cities organize short-distance races (2.5 to 7.5 kilometers), and some have established jogging paths in parks. In the past, only boys got this kind of exercise—mainly as a result of playing *fútbol,* a sport that requires a great deal of running. Nowadays, people of both sexes and all ages can be seen running—an indication of a growing awareness of the value of exercise.

PAGE 297
Additions to on-page notes
Notes: We have provided pre-reading questions for the *Prólogo cultural* in Chaps. 1–8; however, because the Prólogo topics in the second half of the book are somewhat more general, these detailed questions will not appear in subsequent chapters.

PAGE 300
Photo
A lovely display of tropical fruits at a market stall in Colima, a small town near the Pacific coast of Mexico. Here one can purchase such delicacies as fresh figs, mangoes, melons, pomegranates, and pineapples.

Realia
An advertisement for the Vázquez fruit store in Cuernavaca, Mexico, which offers bananas, oranges, and watermelon all year long in addition to special seasonal fruits. This *frutería* also boasts the best wholesale prices around and offers home delivery. The store's address is given in typical Hispanic fashion—street name followed by the number.

Additions to on-page notes
Culture: In connection with mini-dialogue 4, remind students that *guacamole* is a sauce or dip that originated in Mexico. A popular ingredient not mentioned is green coriander *(cilantro),* known in many parts of the U.S. as Chinese parsley.

PAGE 302

Photo

On display at this market in Valencia is an array of freshly caught seafood including *pulpos* (octopus), a favorite delicacy enjoyed throughout Spain. *Pulpo* is usually boiled, cut into bite-size pieces, and served with olive oil and paprika as *tapas* (appetizers). It is also used in salads. Valencia is famous not only for its citrus fruit and rice growing, but also as an important Mediterranean fishing port, where the daily catch is auctioned to wholesalers, restauranteurs, and the general public.

Realia

An ad for a seafood restaurant called La Bombilla (here, meaning "ship's lamp") that boasts the best shellfish at the lowest prices.

Additions to on-page notes

Enrichment: You may want students to play a guessing game with some of the food-related nouns in Ex. C. Ask them to work in pairs to ask and answer questions. For example: *¿Qué pones en el pan?* *(Pongo mantequilla.)*

PAGE 303

Photo

The window of a café in Santiago, Chile. Snack seekers can enjoy the *oferta* (special of the day) with a choice of beverage including juice, Cristal (a local beer), or tea. Coffee is not on the list but is available at espresso bars that often feature a strong brew called *café-café.* The snack special offered is popular for teatime, around 5 P.M. Other favorites consumed with tea or *agüita* (hot water flavored with herbs such as mint, or lemon peel) include toast, *empanadas dulces* (sweet filled turnovers), or even a couple of fried eggs to tide one over until dinner, which is served sometime after 7 P.M.

Realia

A food bill from Mesón de la Ribera, an inn and restaurant in Zaragoza, the fifth-largest city in Spain, located halfway between Madrid and Barcelona. Among the food listings are *caza* (game) and *aves*

(fowl). In addition to food costs, the *descripción claves* (or *descripción de claves;* literally, "description of abbreviations") lists *habitaciones,* or room charges, and *mostrador,* referring to items purchased from a display case. The total of 1,500 pesetas includes I.V.A., or *impuesto al valor agregado,* a value-added tax on goods and services by Spain and other members of the European Economic Community, or Common Market.

PAGE 304

Realia

This advertisement for the "Natural Diner" offers patrons balanced lunches (referring to protein-balancing in vegetarian meals) for a fixed price. The special includes a main dish, salad, whole-grain bread, dessert, and fresh fruit juice. The lower price is for the main dish only. Open for lunch on weekdays from noon until 3:00 P.M. (12:00 until 15:00 on the 24-hour clock), the diner also offers the same foods for take-out.

PAGE 305

Photo

A couple working together to prepare a Mexican meal. Popular home-cooked Mexican meals include *mole* (chicken in a spicy chocolate, peanut, and chile sauce) or one of the many varieties of *enchiladas* (tortillas filled with meat, chicken, or cheese, smothered in a red or green sauce, laden with cheese, and baked).

Additions to on-page notes

Enrichment: You may want to bring some Spanish-language cookbooks to class. If students are interested, groups can prepare a dish and share it with the class.

PAGE 308

Additions to on-page notes

Reteach / Extra Help: In connection with mini-dialogue 4, you may want to reinforce the meaning and forms of *sentirse* by asking questions such as: *Cuando sales mal en un examen, ¿cómo te sientes?*

¿Cómo nos sentimos cuando nuestro equipo gana un partido?

PAGE 309
Photo
A Spanish *doctora* taking a patient's blood pressure. In Spain, more and more women are entering the field of medicine, often specializing in pediatrics or gynecology. Spain's most important medical schools are located in Madrid and Barcelona, and the entrance requirements are highly competitive. *Puericultura* (child care) is another very important profession for women, requiring a degree comparable to a master's.

PAGE 313
Photo
This young woman seems ready to have her cast removed by a female physician in her private office in Argentina. Access to medical care in this country is available to virtually everyone through a system of socialized *medicina.* Both employers and employees contribute a percentage of their wages into *Obra Social,* similar to a combined Medicaid and Social Security system in the U.S. For a small fee, patients can then purchase booklets of coupons with which to pay for visits to private physicians. This plan also covers most of the costs of hospitalization in private *sanatorios.* The unemployed have access to public clinics for minor ailments and to public *hospitales,* in which basic hospital care is provided at no charge. Special services, including the dispensing of medicine, require some payment.

Realia
This prescription was written—in the stereotypical "doctor's scribble"—at a *consultorio médico,* or physician's office, at the private Hospital Británico in Buenos Aires.

PAGE 315
Photo
A street market in the picturesque old section of Granada, in Spain's southern region of Andalucía.

A typical dish enjoyed by *granadinos,* or residents of Granada, is *patatas asadas,* potatoes baked on a small grill. Also popular are fruits transplanted from the Americas long ago and now grown here, such as the *chirimoya* (custard apple) and avocado. The most typical of all is the native *granada,* or pomegranate, which is also the symbol of Granada.

PAGE 316
Sample dialogues for *¿Qué pasa?*
Javier has hurt his leg, and he and the doctor are talking about his injury.

D: ¿Cómo te sientes, Javier? Estás pálido.

J: Me duele mucho la pierna. Creo que tengo un hueso roto.

D: No, el hueso no está roto. Pero vas a tener que caminar con muletas.

J: Pero no tengo que quedarme en cama, ¿verdad? ¡Qué bueno!

D: ¿Cómo te lastimaste la pierna, Javier?

J: Me lastimé durante un partido de básquetbol.

D: Pues voy a ponerte una venda y recetarte unas pastillas.

J: Bueno. Me duele muchísimo.

D: Vete a la casa ahora y descansa. Mañana te sientes mejor.

J: ¡Espero que sí! Gracias, doctor. Adiós.

PAGE 319
Photo
These teenagers came to weigh themselves at a *farmacia* in Caracas, Venezuela. The Hispanic *farmacia* is different from the self-service drugstore common in the U.S. A broader range of drugs and medicine, including herbal remedies, is available without a prescription. Self-service and non-medical items such as greeting cards are not usually offered by the *farmacia.*

Realia
In Spain and Latin America, many people typically visit their local *farmacia* to check their weight. Scales there dispense a written record of the weigh-in for a small fee. This receipt from Farmacia Lanza in Madrid

tells us that a rather hefty person checked in at 92.700 kilograms (204.5 pounds) on Monday, August 3, 1987, at 6:47 P.M.

PAGE 321
Additions to on-page notes
Enrichment: In conjunction with the presentation and practice of the subjunctive, you may want to create a class advice column. Ask each student to write one question that asks for advice. For example: *¿Qué debo hacer si quiero tocar bien la guitarra?*
¿Qué debo hacer si no quiero aumentar de peso?
Check their work for correct spelling, capitalization, and punctuation; then ask students to exchange papers. Tell them to write an answer, beginning their advice with *Te recomiendo.* Post the questions and answers on the bulletin board or ask pairs to present them orally.

PAGE 324
Photo
A physical-fitness test at a high school in Palma de Mallorca, capital of Spain's Balearic Islands in the Mediterranean. Gym classes and physical fitness activities in general, are essential as well as favorite elements of Spanish high school programs.

Answers to *Repaso*
1. El médico (La médica) está con un caso de urgencia. / Alguien estornuda durante la obra de teatro. / Ella duerme en la silla de ruedas.
2. El muchacho (chico) nos dice: ''Espero que mi gato baje del árbol.'' / Le digo: ''Espero que tú cambies de idea.'' / Les decimos: ''No queremos que Uds. contesten de prisa.''
3. Le pedimos a mamá que obtenga más duraznos y uvas. / Me pide que traiga más col y espinacas. / Nos dicen que traigamos más camarones y langostas.
4. Patinen, esquíen y coman ensaladas. Hagan gimnasia a menudo. / Escuche, aprenda y tome apuntes. No haga preguntas cada minuto. / Recojan, laven y sequen la ropa. No preparen la cena todavía.

5. Y no vuelva al baile, Julio. / Y no salgan (se vayan) de la pensión, muchachas (chicas). / Y no pese a los pacientes, señora.

PAGE 325
Answers to *Tema*
1. Mi hermano y yo estamos en la sala de espera.
2. El médico nos dice: ''Quiero que Uds. bajen de peso.''
3. Les pido que coman más frutas y verduras.
4. ¡Naden, corran y levanten pesas! ¡Hagan ejercicio todos los días!
5. Y no vayan a la heladería, muchachos (chicos).

PAGE 326
Answers to *Comprueba tu progreso*
A
1. Pues, no cuenten nada.
2. Pues, jueguen al ajedrez.
3. Pues, no vivan en la ciudad.
4. Pues, descanse.
5. Pues, no beba mucho.
6. Pues, vuelvan pronto.
7. Pues, empiece ahora.

B
1. Srta. Méndez, tenga cuidado con el horno.
2. Chicos, no vengan tarde.
3. Sra. Vidal, traiga más fresas y duraznos.
4. Sr. Giles, ponga estos camarones en el fregadero.
5. Isabel y Claudia, no hagan sopa todavía.
6. Srta. Porras, no diga que no.
7. Señoras, salgan de la cocina.

C
1. Dé estas pastillas al médico.
2. Vayan en la ambulancia con el paciente.
3. Sea paciente y espere media hora más.
4. Esté en la sala de espera temprano.
5. Den estas vendas al enfermero.
6. Vaya de prisa a la habitación número 34.
7. Sean generosos y ayuden en la clínica.

D
1.	examine	5.	estornuden
2.	abra	6.	tosa
3.	estacionemos	7.	asistamos
4.	anuncies	8.	corran (corramos)

E 1. La médica quiere que descansemos más.
   2. El Dr. Suárez les recomienda que Uds. caminen con muletas.
   3. Ojalá que ella no tome más pastillas.
   4. La profesora espera que Uds. no se lastimen.
   5. Ojalá que la ambulancia llegue pronto.
   6. Sus padres quieren que Elena se mejore en seguida.

F 1. c   3. c   5. c
   2. a   4. a   6. a

PAGE 327

Photo

Tissue paper cutouts used in prayers for rain and good crops by the Otomí Indians in San Pablito, which is located in the sierras in the south-central Mexican state of Puebla. The figures are meant to invoke the intercession of the gods for an abundant harvest. Colored paper silhouettes and decorations are commonly displayed during many Mexican holidays, notably the Day of the Dead (November 2) and the September 16th Independence Day celebrations.

ORAL PROFICIENCY TEST

Directed Response

1. How would you say that your father wants you to lose weight? *(Mi padre quiere que (yo) baje de peso.)*
2. Tell the children not to cross the street at this corner; tell them to go to the next one. *(No crucen la calle en esta esquina; vayan a la próxima.)*
3. Say that the nurse recommends that you stay in bed for two days. *(El (La) enfermero(a) recomienda que (yo) me quede en cama por dos días.)*

Picture-Cued Response

Pointing to the photograph on p. 313, ask questions such as:

4. ¿Con quién está la señorita? *(Está con la médica.)*
5. ¿Qué tiene la paciente? *(Tiene una pierna rota.)*

Using the photograph on p. 319 ask:

6. ¿Qué hacen estos jóvenes? *(Se pesan.)*

Situations

7. When you call your doctor, you find out that he isn't in today. How might the receptionist tell you so?
   a. No está allí hoy.   b. *Hoy no está.*   c. No es para hoy.
8. Felipe fell out of a tree and hurt his arm. How would he ask the nurse whether it's broken?
   a. *¿Está roto?*   b. ¿Tengo gripe?
   c. ¿Está descompuesto?

Real-Life Questions

9. ¿Siempre comes bien? Para ti, ¿qué es una dieta sana?
10. ¿Cuántas veces al año vas al (a la) médico(a)? ¿Te dice a veces el (la) médico(a) que debes bajar o aumentar de peso?
11. ¿Qué tipo de comida prefieres? Cuando comes, ¿piensas mucho en las calorías?

CAPÍTULO 10

OBJECTIVES

Communication
- to identify vocabulary related to telephone calls
- to identify vocabulary related to letter-writing

Grammar
- to use the verb *caer(se)*
- to use the verb *incluir*
- to use the infinitive after verbs and prepositions
- to use the present subjunctive of *-ir* stem-changing verbs
- to use the preterite of the verbs *creer, leer, oír, caer(se),* and *incluir*
- to use affirmative and negative words

Culture
- to describe Madrid's special phone booths
- to tell about the long-distance center at the telephone company in Madrid
- to describe the procedure for making long-distance calls in Latin America
- to mention phone tokens, or *fichas*
- to discuss the limited number of private phones in Spanish-speaking countries

SUGGESTED MATERIALS

p. 330 (Palabras nuevas I): a toy telephone

p. 335 (Actividad): a tape or cassette player and a blank tape

p. 336 (Diálogo): a wall map showing Bolivia

pp. 338–339 (Palabras nuevas II): a letter-size envelope, a form

p. 341 (Práctica B): blank envelopes

p. 350 (Lectura): a wall map showing northern Argentina

PAGES 328–329

Photo
A young man making a call from a public phone booth in Madrid's Plaza de España. In 1987 local phone calls cost ten pesetas (about eight cents). The cost of long-distance calls between Spanish cities varies with the distance; a short call from Madrid to Barcelona would have cost less than one hundred pesetas in 1987. On the walls of nearly every cabinet-style phone booth in Madrid, one sees signs in various languages urging tourists to call home and tell the folks that everything is fine. Note the metal push-button dial (a design that resists both the elements and vandalism) and the slanted slot at the top where the caller lines up coins of five, twenty-five, fifty, or one hundred pesetas to feed into the slot as each time period is up.

PAGE 332

Photo
A trouble-shooter at work on a switchboard in Santa Cruz, Bolivia. Throughout its history, the Bolivian telephone service has had to deal with a basic problem in developing countries: lack of funds for public services. Nevertheless, the telephone service has been improving steadily. Direct-dialing between most major Bolivian cities is possible. Direct international telephone dialing is also possible between the U.S. and most of the principal Bolivian cities.

Realia
A page from a card-sized pamphlet available in some hotels in Spain. The pamphlet explains in detail how to make calls within the city, to other towns within the same province, to cities in other provinces, and to other countries. It has only a few pages, each one giving the same instructions in a different language.

PAGE 334

Realia
These cards are available in hotels in U.S. cities such

as Miami where there are large numbers of Spanish-speaking travelers. They remind customers that they can make international calls from their own room.

PAGE 335
Photo
Using a public telephone in Puerto Rico. Long-distance calls to Puerto Rico can be direct-dialed from the continental U.S.; the island's area code is 809.

PAGE 337
Photo
Using a home telephone in Santander, Spain. The phone system in Spain is efficient in most respects. However, waiting lists for first-time applicants for phone service are usually very long. Moreover, in many cases there are restrictions on the number of phone receivers that a given area may have. And if an area already has all of the phones it is allowed, an applicant may have to wait until another person moves out of the area before receiving his or her own phone.

Realia
Logo for Spain's national phone company, known informally as *la Telefónica*. The logo seems to represent the front part of either the phone transmitter or the receiver, with the small holes arranged in the shape of a capital T for *Telefónica*.

PAGE 340
Additions to on-page notes
Reteach / Review: Reinforce the meaning of *o . . . o* in mini-dialogue 4 by contrasting it with *ni . . . ni.* Ask students to make the last line negative: *No estoy libre ni el lunes ni el miércoles.*

PAGE 343
Photo
The central post office, Correo Mayor, in Mexico City. This building is located directly across the street from the Palacio de Bellas Artes, the capital's principal art museum, and was designed by the same architect.

Italian Adamo Boari imitated the style that was typical of sixteenth-century Mexico even though the building was constructed between 1902 and 1908. The postal museum on the third floor contains an excellent collection of stamps and postmarks.

Realia
Stamps from three Latin American countries. Mexico salutes tourism and advertises one of its many attractions; Bolivia honors a distinguished figure in the revolution against Spain in the early nineteenth century; and Venezuela pays homage to German physician Robert Koch, whose investigation of tuberculosis merited one of the earliest Nobel Prizes (1905).

PAGE 348
Photo
Madrid's central post office. There are over 20 different entrances to this post office, each labeled with a letter and each housing some special form of service. In Spain, telegraph offices are usually found in or near post offices.

Realia
A telegram form. The sender fills in the name of the person it is being sent to *(destinatario),* that person's address *(señas)* and telephone or telex number, the message *(texto),* and his or her own name, address, and telephone number.

PAGE 350
Additions to on-page notes
Notes: Call attention to the *Antes de leer* questions before students begin the *Lectura.* You may want to use these pre-reading questions as the basis for a class discussion about the importance of telephones in daily life.

Photo
A letter carrier in Tonalá, Mexico, delivering the mail. Bicycles are often used for this purpose in small towns throughout the country. Tonalá, a village in the state of Jalisco, is one of the country's foremost centers for handicrafts, especially pottery.

PAGE 353

Photo

Making a call from a public booth in Mexico. Long-distance calls are difficult to make from most public phones in Mexico. Most towns have *larga distancia* offices where tourists and residents without private phone service go to place international calls.

PAGE 357

Photo

Madrid's central post office, officially known as Palacio de Comunicaciones, but commonly called *Correos.* Official hours for this post office are from 8:00 A.M. to 10:00 P.M., Monday through Friday, 8:00 A.M. to 8:00 P.M. on Saturday, and 9:00 A.M. to 1 P.M. on Sunday. In other branches, official hours are from 9:00 A.M. to 2 P.M., Monday through Friday, and 9:00 A.M. to 1:00 P.M. on Saturday.

Besides receiving and dispatching mail, Spanish post offices also offer telegraph and long-distance telephone service. Stamps can be purchased at post offices, at small tobacco shops *(estancos),* and at some hotels. Spanish stamps are valued highly by stamp collectors, and the government regularly issues elaborate series featuring local festivals, historical monuments, and regional costumes.

PAGE 358

Photo

A mail slot in Buenos Aires. An airmail letter mailed from the U.S. takes a week to ten days to reach Buenos Aires.

Answers to *Repaso*

1. Ayer oí una noticia interesante de mis primos. / Anteayer leyeron un telegrama importante de su padre. / La semana pasada oímos un cuento cómico (gracioso) de nuestros amigos.
2. Irene le vuelve a envolver un paquete. Ahora mismo corta un pedazo de papel. / Le tratamos de llenar un formulario. Pero olvido la fecha de hoy. / El mensajero (La mensajera) me acaba de entregar el telegrama. Probablemente anuncia la llegada del avión.

3. Antes de marcar el número, esperaste el tono. / Después de hacer la llamada, averigüé la respuesta. / Antes de escribir el cheque, ella incluyó el impuesto.
4. O incluimos el remitente correcto o no recibimos ninguna respuesta. / O alquila el apartado postal o no recibe ningún correo. / O escojo las espinacas frescas o no pido ninguna verdura.
5. No quieren que riamos porque olvidaron tantas cosas. / No quiere que nos durmamos porque oyó esos ruidos. / Ojalá que no rían porque perdimos nuestras linternas.

PAGE 359

Answers to *Tema*

1. Ayer Rafael leyó una carta larga de sus amigos.
2. Rafael les acaba de escribir una carta. También incluye una foto de Silvia.
3. Después de cerrar el sobre, escribió el remitente.
4. O Ud. manda una carta certificada o no obtiene (recibe) ningún recibo.
5. Ojalá que no rían porque gasté tanto dinero.

PAGE 360

Answers to *Comprueba tu progreso*

A
1. va a
2. empieza a
3. vienen a
4. vas a
5. enseñas a
6. vuelve a
7. comienza a
8. aprender a

B
1. para
2. sin
3. para
4. Antes de
5. Para
6. sin

C
1. oyó
2. Leyeron
3. incluyeron
4. creyeron
5. leíste
6. se cayó
7. oí
8. creyeron
9. Incluyó

D
1. Compré algo ayer.
2. Vi a algunos de los carteros.
3. Hay alguien en la tienda.
4. Siempre gano las carreras.
5. Sé algo de los premios de gimnasia.
6. Tengo algún cheque de viajero.
7. Alguien pagó el telegrama.
8. Vi algo en el buzón.

E 1. Esperan que no me sienta asustado.
   2. No quieren que nos sintamos nerviosos.
   3. Esperan que se duerma.
   4. No quieren que nos muramos de sed.
   5. Quieren que te vistas muy de moda.
   6. Quieren que vistamos a los niños.
   7. Esperan que sirvamos guacamole.
   8. Quieren que sirvas langostas, ¿no?
   9. Quieren que hierva los camarones.
   10. No quieren que hirvamos la col con las papas.

PAGE 361

Photo

A package mailed from Spain to the U.S. One of the stamps on it represents the Summer Olympic Games to be held in Barcelona in 1992; the others carry the image of King Juan Carlos. The king, who celebrated his 50th birthday on January 5, 1987, is a very popular monarch, and has the suport of Spain's political parties, including the conservative Popular Alliance, the ruling Socialists, and even the Communists.

   Although Juan Carlos, as other European monarchs, is not directly responsible for policy making, he has shown on several occasions that he is not merely a figurehead. He has been Head of State since General Francisco Franco's death in November, 1975. The period immediately, after Franco's death was a difficult one in Spain's history because Franco's supporters and many wealthy Spaniards feared a radical change from the status quo, while, many others wanted political liberalization. Complicating the situation were strident demands for autonomy in some regions of Spain, especially the Basque country. Juan Carlos had to achieve a delicate balance by supporting a pace of liberalization that was neither too fast nor too slow, because either extreme might have meant self-destruction. At first, skeptics predicted that he would not be able to remain in power for long, that he would be *Juan el Breve* (Juan the Short-lived). However, he has not only proven those skeptics wrong but also has helped continue a process of democratization that might have been far more difficult without his support.

ORAL PROFICIENCY TEST

Directed Response

   1. How would we say we hope that Antonio feels better and returns to the office soon? *(Esperamos que Antonio se sienta mejor y que vuelva pronto a la oficina.)*
   2. Say that you always fall down when you try to ski. *(Siempre me caigo cuando trato de esquiar.)*
   3. Ask Mrs. Sánchez why she didn't believe you. *(Sra. Sánchez, ¿por qué no me creyó Ud.?)*

Picture-Cued Response

Pointing to the visual on p. 359 or transparency, 35, ask questions such as:
   4. ¿Qué hizo Rafael inmediatamente después de recibir una carta ayer? *(La leyó.)*
   5. ¿Qué pone Rafael en el sobre de la carta que acaba de escribir? *(Pone el remitente.)*

Situations

   6. A strange-looking creature—possibly from another planet—approaches you on the street. It wants to know how to use the public phone. What is the first instruction you would give it?
      a. Primero cuelgue el teléfono.
      b. *Primero hay que descolgar el teléfono.*
      c. Haga primero una llamada por cobrar.
   7. Luisa has some incredible gossip to share with her friend Pedro. But Pedro doesn't like gossip. What might he say?
      a. *Prefiero no oír chismes.* b. No quiero que me cuentes chistes. c. No me gusta el cariño.

Real-Life Questions

   8. ¿Te mudas frecuentemente o hace mucho tiempo que vives en el mismo lugar?
   9. ¿Cómo averiguas las noticias? ¿Prefieres escuchar la radio o leer el periódico para averiguarlas?
   10. ¿Escribes muchas cartas? ¿Puedes recibir muchas cartas si no escribes ninguna?
   11. Si llamas a alguien y no está en casa, ¿dejas un recado o vuelves a llamar más tarde?

CAPÍTULO 11

OBJECTIVES

Communication
- to identify vocabulary related to television
- to identify vocabulary related to films

Grammar
- to use the preterite of verbs that end in *-ir*
- to use the preterite of the verb *venir*
- to use the conjunctions *pero, sino* and *sino que*
- to use the verbs *saber* and *conocer*
- to use verbs that end in *-cer* and *-cir*
- to use verbs that follow the pattern of *gustar*

Culture
- to discuss the popularity of movies in the Spanish-speaking world
- to describe moviegoing in Spanish-speaking countries
- to note the importance of the Spanish, Mexican, Venezuelan, Argentine, and Cuban film industries

SUGGESTED MATERIALS

p. 364 (Palabras nuevas I): television listings from magazines and / or newspapers

p. 368 (Diálogo): a Spanish-language tabloid or film magazine

p. 370 (Palabras nuevas II): magazine pictures of actors, actresses, and scenes from current films; movie ads and listings from local magazines and / or newspapers

PAGES 362–363
Photo
Teatro de los Insurgentes in Mexico City. In 1951 painter Diego Rivera (1886–1957) was commissioned to create this huge mural that mixes images from the country's cinematic and political history. The large mask at the bottom center of the photo establishes the theatrical theme. Above it, the actor Mario Moreno is seen taking money from the rich and giving it to the poor. (Rivera saw the comedian's character, Cantinflas, as representing Mexico's common man. Moreno has been to his people what Charlie Chaplin once was to the people of the U.S.) Elsewhere, portraits of virtually every figure from Mexico's past can be found, from Aztecs and Mayas to revolutionary heroes like Juárez, Zapata, and Hidalgo.

Although the building was originally a movie theater, it is also used for plays; *Tenorio 77,* a parody of José Zorrilla's *Don Juan Tenorio* (1844), has run there for many years. Most of the actors featured on the marquee are known for their comedy roles. Carmen Salinas is a film and theater actress known for *La Corcholata,* a satirical character that she created. The late Paco Malgesto, *Chabelo,* and Guillermo Rivas all achieved stardom on television. The abbreviation *act esp* stands for *actuación especial,* or "special appearance."

PAGE 367
Realia
This weather section from a Spanish periodical notes that it is cloudy in the northern part of the country. The paragraph below the headline gives a brief weather report for the rest of the country. The boxes at the bottom provide a key to the climatic conditions shown on the map. Spain and most of Latin America use the centigrade, or Celsius, scale to measure temperature.

PAGE 369
Photo
The Puerto Rican rock group, Menudo, skyrocketed to international stardom in the early 1980s. The members of this quintet, composed of young singers and dancers, change periodically: the boys leave the group on their fifteenth birthday and are replaced by new, younger talent. Menudo's success sparked the creation of similar groups in other Spanish-speaking countries, including Los Parchis from Spain, Timbiriche from Mexico, and Venezuela's Los Chomos.

PAGE 373

Photo

On the set of the Spanish film *Mitad del Cielo (Half of Heaven)* in Madrid. The movie, which won the Golden Shell Award for best film at the 1986 San Sebastián Film Festival, was directed by Manuel Gutiérrez Aragón. It stars popular actress Ángela Molina, who was featured in Gutiérrez Aragón's earlier work *Demonios en el Jardín (Demons in the Garden)*. Both of these films have been released in the U.S.

PAGE 375

Photos

(a) A scene from the 1956 movie version of Jules Verne's classic adventure novel *Around the World in 80 Days*. Produced by Michael Todd, the Oscar-winning film was Hollywood's first giant screen (70mm) extravaganza, featuring over 40 guest stars in cameo roles. Included in the photograph are David Niven (right) as Philers Fogg, accompanied by Mexican comedian Mario Moreno, better known as Cantinflas, who played Fogg's faithful Passe-Partout. Also in the photo are British actor Robert Newton (left) and Shirley MacLaine.

(b) Singer-actress Carmen Miranda (right) is joined by actors Alice Faye and John Payne in the 1941 musical *Weekend in Havana,* directed by Walter Lang. In the 1940s and 1950s, Havana was famous for its lavish nightclubs, gambling casinos, and tourist hotels. Carmen Miranda, whose real name was Maria do Carmo Miranda da Cunha, was born in Portugal in 1913, but lived in Brazil from the age of three. Considered one of the greatest Brazilian entertainers of all time, she was known for her colorful personality, makeup, and clothing. Her trademark was the "banana hat," head scarves topped with huge arrangements of tropical fruit.

(c) Cantinflas and David Niven riding a hot-air balloon over the Swiss Alps in *Around the World in 80 Days*. Born in 1911, Cantinflas has been called the Charlie Chaplin of Mexico, where he made many comedies including *Ahí Está el Detalle, El Bombero Atómico,* and *Águila o Sol (Heads or Tails)*. He starred in another English-language film, *Pepe,* which was made in 1960 by Columbia Pictures and featured 35 international guest stars.

PAGE 376

Photo

TV and radio coverage of a pop-music concert in Asunción, Paraguay. Television broadcasts began in Paraguay in 1965. There are two national channels, Canal 13 (Teledifusora Paraguaya) shown here and Canal 9 (Televisión Cerro Cora)

PAGE 379

Photo

A TV cameraman in Guadalajara, Mexico's second-largest city.

PAGE 380

Photo

A movie line in Antigua, which is located about 28 miles from the Guatemalan capital of Guatemala City. Movie-makers in Central American countries such as El Salvador, Nicaragua, Costa Rica, Panama and Guatemala produce fiction and documentary films. However, movies most frequently shown in those countries are usually from the U.S. or Mexico.

Realia

A ticket stub from the Atlas Cinema-Theater showing that the bearer sat in the orchestra *(platea)* for the first screening on Thursday night. It is noted that this half of the ticket is not valid for entrance into the cinema, but that it indicates the seat number.

PAGE 382

Photo

One of Madrid's largest and most popular cinemas, the movie palace Cine Callao is showing the 1983 U.S. film *The Big Chill,* translated as *Reencuentro (Reencounter),* Constructed in 1927, the Art Deco building also houses a discotheque downstairs with an entrance on te Gran Vía, the city's principal avenue.

Realia

A poster for the 1968 Mexican comedy western *Por Mis Pistolas (By My Pistols),* starring Cantinflas. The film, written by Cantinflas and directed by Miguel Delgado, is the story of a pharmacist who inherits a rich mine in Arizona, and his subsequent dealings with "bad guys" who try to take it away from him. The film co-stars Mexican actress Isela Vega.

PAGE 384

Sample dialogues for *¿Qué Pasa?*

Francisco and Susana walk by an appliance store exhibiting television sets in the window. They are discussing TV programs that they like and dislike.

F: ¡Mira Susana! Es mi telenovela favorita.

S: No sé por qué te gusta ese programa. Me hace bostezar.

F: A mí me encanta. Ocurre algo diferente todos los días.

S: Pues, yo prefiero las películas. Sobre todo las extranjeras.

S: ¿Miras a menudo ese programa de concursos?

F: Todos los programas de concursos me aburren. Prefiero los programas donde entrevistan a las estrellas de cine.

S: Mira a quién entrevistan hoy. Es la actriz que hace el papel de la policía en el nuevo programa policíaco.

F: Tienes razón. Y ese programa tiene lugar aquí en nuestra ciudad.

PAGE 387

Photos

(a) The large Cine Latino, located on Mexico City's major boulevard, Paseo de la Reforma, is screening the 1983 Academy Award-winning film *Terms of Endearment,* titled in Spanish *La fuerza del cariño.* Besides winning the Academy Award for best film, the movie also picked up Oscars for its director and main actors.

(b) A Madrid movie theater showing the 1987 Spanish film *Divinas Palabras (Divine Words),* directed by José Luis García Sánchez. The movie is a free adaptation of a work by twentieth-century writer Ramón de Valle-Inclán (1866–1936) and stars popular actress-singer Ana Belén, Francisco Rabal, and Imanol Arias.

PAGE 391

Photos

(a) Behind the scenes of a local news broadcast on Chicago's WSNS / TV-Channel 44. This station is an affiliate of the U.S. Spanish-language network Univisión, founded in 1961 as Spanish International Network (SIN). With over 400 affiliate stations located throughout the U.S., the network offers 24-hour satellite broadcasts of sports, comedies national news, musical variety programs, dramas, and the ever-popular soap operas (*telenovelas,* or more simply *novelas*).

(b) Anchorwoman Lolita Ayala on the Mexican evening newscast *24 Horas,* airing nightly on Mexico City's XEWTV-Channel 2. The program, carried nationwide, is produced by the privately run TV conglomerate Televisa. Televisa maintains three other broadcast channels in the capital, as well as a Mexico City cable TV company and various radio stations throughout the country. Televisa is the fourth-largest TV production company in the world, after NBC, CBS, and ABC. Many of its programs can be seen on the U.S. Spanish-language network Univisión.

Realia

Television listings from the *Diario de Navarra,* the major newspaper of Pamplona, in northern Spain. There are three channels listed: TVE (Televisión Española), a national network; Telenavarra, a local station that broadcasts in Castilian Spanish; and ETB (Euskal Telebista), a station that broadcasts in the Basque language of the neighboring *País Vasco.*

PAGE 392

Realia

(a) A theater ticket from the Instituto Nacional de Cinematografía in Lima, Peru.

(b) A theater ticket from Cine Capitol in Madrid, Spain.

Answers to *Repaso*

1. A mí me encanta toda clase de argumentos.
   A ellos les interesa toda clase de documentales. /
   A nosotros nos falta toda clase de cantantes.
2. Conozco a todos los jugadores del equipo. /
   Conocemos a todos los locutores de ese
   programa. / Ella conoce a todos los acomodadores
   del teatro.
3. Generalmente no va a la clínica con su madre
   (mamá), sino solo. / Afortunadamente no
   participas en los partidos (juegos) con nuestros
   tenistas, sino conmigo. / Probablemente no entran
   en la tienda con esos paquetes, sino que salen
   (se van).
4. La semana pasada viste a un director extranjero
   en el teatro y le pediste una entrevista. / Ayer
   vimos a nuestro equipo local en el club y les
   pedimos una foto. / Esta mañana vieron a la nueva
   gerente en la taquilla y le pidieron un horario.
5. Le dije: ''Nosotros sabemos usar la grabadora y
   mañana vamos a grabar un concierto para ti.'' /
   Me dijo: ''Ella sabe usar el cortacésped y esta
   tarde va a cortar el césped para mí.'' / Me dijiste:
   ''Ellos saben asar carne y esta noche van a hacer
   un asado con nosotros.''

PAGE 393

Answers to *Tema*

1. A Bernardo le encanta toda clase de películas.
2. Conoce a todos los taquilleros de la ciudad.
3. Generalmente no va al cine con amigos, sino solo.
4. Ayer vio a su actriz favorita (preferida) en la calle y
   le pidió el autógrafo.
5. Le dijo: ''Yo sé usar una cámara y algún día voy a
   filmar una película con Ud.''

PAGE 394

Answers to *Comprueba tu progreso*

A 1. Ya lo pedimos.
   2. Ya lo repitió.
   3. Ya la herví.
   4. Ya me reí (de tus chistes).
   5. Ya los serví.
   6. Ya se vistieron.
   7. Ya lo pedí.

B 1. ¿Cuándo vino?
      Vino el sábado pasado.
   2. ¿Por qué viniste?
      Vine por la función.
   3. ¿De dónde vinieron ellos?
      Vinieron de la estación.
   4. ¿Cómo vinieron Uds.?
      Vinimos en tren.
   5. ¿A qué hora vino?
      Vino a las 9 de la mañana.
   6. ¿Con quién vino?
      Vino con sus padres.
   7. ¿Por qué vinieron Uds.?
      Vinimos por tu cumpleaños.

C 1. pero   5. pero
   2. sino   6. sino
   3. sino   7. pero
   4. sino que

D 1. sabe   5. sé
   2. sabes   6. conocemos
   3. conocen   7. sabe
   4. conozco   8. Conoces

E 1. Le agradecemos (Uds. le agradecen) las
      entradas a la directora.
   2. Reconozco sólo a Pepe Culebra en este
      programa.
   3. Traduzco para mi médico que no entiende el
      idioma.
   4. Conozco muchas (reglas de tráfico).
   5. Les agradezco las flores a mis admiradores.
   6. Reconozco a mi padre en la foto.
   7. Te ofrezco un premio.

F 1. A nosotros no nos importa el público.
   2. A Uds. les falta un termómetro.
   3. A ti te interesan los argumentos complicados.
   4. A mí me encantan las versiones originales.
   5. A Ud. no le parece ser muy serio.
   6. A la directora le falta una actriz.

PAGE 395

Photo

A gold Incan ceremonial mask from Ecuador. The mask is currently on display at the Gold Museum located on the fifth floor of the Central Bank of Ecuador, which houses the best archaeological collection of gold in the country. Gold was greatly appreciated by the Incas because of its beatuy.

The highly developed Incan civilization, which at its peak extended from Ecuador in the north to what is today northern Chile, Bolivia, and western Argentina, was in the midst of a civil war when Spanish conquistador Francisco Pizarro landed in Peru in 1532. Some historical records indicate that when the Spaniards captured the Incan ruler Atahualpa, he tried to buy his freedom by offering to fill his prison cell once with gold and twice with silver. The Indian kept his end of the deal—giving Pizarro gold masks, jewelry, and artifacts which may have been worth about $30,000,000—but Atahualpa was not released, and the conquest of Peru was completed a few years later.

ORAL PROFICIENCY TEST

Directed Response

1. Say that Angela felt bad because the young people laughed at her. *(Ángela se sintió mal porque los jóvenes se rieron de ella.)*
2. How would you tell your aun that Julio Iglesias isn't an actor but rather a singer? *(Julio Iglesias no es actor sino cantante.)*
3. Say that you're very interested in documentaries. *(Me interesan mucho los documentales.)*

Picture-Cued Response

Pointing to the photograph on p. 369, ask:

4. ¿Reconoces a estos muchachos? *(Sí. (No, no) los reconozco.)*
5. ¿Sabes de dónde son? *(Sí. (No, no) sé de dónde son. Son de Puerto Rico.)*
6. ¿Son estrellas de cine o cantantes? *(Son cantantes.)*

Situations

7. Yolanda and Pedro have been watching TV all day. How might Yolanda respond when Pedro asks why she's yawning so much?
   a. Estoy despierta.　　b. Soy aburrida.
   c. *Me aburro.*
8. Many news programs employ people to give the news in sign language. Which of the following people benefit from this?
   a. Las personas ciegas.　　b. *La gente sorda.*
   c. Los extranjeros.

Real-Life Questions

9. ¿Qué libro lees ahora? ¿Es complicado el argumento? ¿Dónde tiene lugar? ¿Quién es el personaje principal?
10. ¿Quién es tu estrella de cine favorita? ¿Conoces todas sus películas? ¿Qué sabes de su vida?
11. ¿Qué pediste la última vez que fuiste a un restaurante?

CAPÍTULO 12

OBJECTIVES

Communication
- to identify vocabulary related to music
- to identify vocabulary related to art

Grammar
- to use the present progressive tense
- to use the verb *seguir*
- to place adjectives in their correct position in sentences

Culture
- to note the types of music heard in the U.S.
- to discuss the influence of Latin American music on that of the U.S.
- to point out musical instruments that originated in Mexico
- to name various Latin American dance rhythms popular in the U.S.
- to tell about the origin of "La Bamba" and to list several Spanish-language songs that have gained popularity in the U.S.

SUGGESTED MATERIALS

p. 397 (Prólogo cultural): recordings of Spanish-language songs

pp. 398–399 (Palabras nuevas I): a recording (of classical music, for example) demonstrating the sounds of as many instruments as possible

p. 402 (Diálogo): a recording of "La Adelita"

p. 404 (Palabras nuevas II): reproductions of different styles of paintings (portrait, landscape, modern, classical, abstract, mural)

p. 409 (Explicaciones I): magazine and / or newspaper pictures showing people in action

p. 419 (Explicaciones II): pictures to elicit descriptive adjectives

PAGES 396–397

Photo

Mariachis in Guadalajara, capital of the Mexican state of Jalisco. Mariachis are groups of men who sing *corridos,* or traditional ballads, and accompany themselves with such instruments as guitar, violin, an undersized guitar called a *guitarrillo,* and an oversized guitar known as a *guitarrón.* Originating in Jalisco, these musicians derived their name from the French word *mariage.* The mariachis entertained at weddings during the reign of Napoleon III's appointee Maximilian, who ruled as Emperor of Mexico from 1863 to 1867. Mariachis are most closely associated with two songs: *Despierta,* which is sung beneath a lady's window at the beginning of a midnight serenade, and *Las mañanitas,* the traditional birthday song of Mexico. Some other popular mariachi songs are *Guadalajara, ¡Ay Jalisco!, La llorona,* and *Cucurrucucú paloma.*

PAGE 402

Photo

Two Spanish guitar players. Spain has figured prominently in the development of the guitar as both a folk instrument and, in this century, as one suited to classical music. The folk guitar is particularly associated with Andalucía, the region where flamenco music originated. There the guitarist, dancers, singers, and rhythmic hand-clappers engage in an improvised musical form called *cante jondo* (deep song).

Additions to on-page notes

Culture: Remind students that much of the West and Southwest was once part of Mexico. Mexico won control of the western portion of Colorado from Spain in 1821; the U.S. took control during the Mexican War (1846–1848) and retained possession under the terms of the treaty that ended the war.

The Hispanic presence in Colorado is apparent not only in its population, but also in the state name (*colorado* means "red" or "ruddy" in Spanish), and the names of many of the cities and towns such as Huérfano, Pueblo, Conejos, and Costilla. Some of the state's rivers, Río Grande and Río Blanco, for example, also bear Spanish names.

PAGE 403
Photo
Pictured here are several members of a mariachi band playing at a *Cinco de mayo* celebration in Austin, Texas. This celebration is one of several that commemorate the stages in Mexico's independence from European domination. On May 5, 1862, a Mexican army defeated the French troops of Napoleon III, who had taken advantage of Mexico's internal political struggles for his own ends. Since Texas was part of Mexico until the beginning of the Mexican War (1846–1848), it is still quite common for present-day residents to celebrate their Mexican heritage and its holidays. Approximately one in five residents of the capital of Texas is Hispanic.

PAGE 405
Photo
This painting, titled *Shilshole Triptych,* was done by Alfredo Arreguín. Born in Morelia, Mexico, Arreguín has lived in Seattle, Washington, since 1959. The painting was commissioned by a Seattle woman who chose the color scheme for Arreguín's interpretation of the Olympic Mountains that surround Shilshole, a saltwater inlet near Seattle which still bears its original Indian name. The cool greens and blues of this painting are less intense than the warmer colors typical of Arreguín's "pattern-paintings," in which he repeats typical Mexican folkloric designs in vibrant, abstract Latin American jungle scenes. Arreguín has exhibited in local and national galleries, and his work has appeared in several well-known art magazines.

Additions to on-page notes
Culture: You may want to give students more information about Osvaldo Guayasamín (1919–   ), who is considered by many to be Ecuador's most famous modern painter. Guayasamín was influenced by the Mexican muralist school, which reached its height in the 1920s and 1930s and included such notable artists as Diego Rivera, José Clemente Orozco, and David Alfaro Biqueiros. This school of artists encouraged artists throughout Latin America to develop their own "indigenist" schools of modern painting, and Guayasamín responded with paintings (including murals) in which the theme of social protest is often incorporated. His paintings also reflect the influence of Picasso.

PAGE 407
Photo
A woman from San Miguel, a small town in El Salvador, in her studio. She wears a typical hand-embroidered dress made according to indigenous techniques handed down from generation to generation. Handicrafts such as hand-woven textiles, hammocks, ceramics, paintings, and leather goods are produced by artisans throughout the country.

PAGE 408
Photo
This young Hispanic girl is painting a mural on the side of the American Red Cross Building in Chicago. This Midwestern city has a relatively large Hispanic population (around 15–16 percent), the majority of Mexican descent.

PAGE 409
Realia
(a) This abstract layout heads the section of a Spanish newspaper dedicated to artistic and cultural events. The three figures to the left are symbols of art, and the guitarlike figure on the far right represents the world of music.

(b) This ticket stub from the Camino Real Hotel in Mexico City describes the December 31, 1986, New Year's Eve celebration held in the hotel ballroom. Continuous dance music provided by both the Venus Rey Orchestra and the smaller musical group *Los Cardenales* (The Cardinals) complemented the formal dinner *(cena de gala).* The owner of this ticket sat at table 21, seat 10.

PAGE 412

Realia

The cover of the pamphlet for the special program at Madrid's Teatro Real during the 1986 Festival of San Isidro. Located on the east side of the Plaza de Oriente, a large public square in central Madrid, the theater has been a music conservatory since 1966. The musical program supplements the main celebration held every May in honor of Madrid's patron saint. The actual feast day of San Isidro Labrador (Saint Isidore the Ploughman) is May 15. The saint's remains are buried in a shrine in the choir of the Catedral de San Isidro, a massive granite seventeenth-century cathedral with twin towers, located near the Plaza Mayor.

PAGE 414

Photo

This photograph of Blanche Hampton shows the serious side of the young Cuban-American ballerina. Blanche began to study ballet at age seven under the instruction Haydee Gutiérrez at the Busch Boulevard Classical Ballet Center in Tampa, Florida.

PAGE 415

Photo

Members of the Ballet Folklórico de México present one of the country's many regional dances, which form the company's repertoire. The Ballet also performs dances from Mexico's indigenous pre-Columbian cultures. The company's spectacular costumes are perhaps best spotlighted against the famous Tiffany-designed glass curtain in the troupe's home theater, which is located in the Palacio de Bellas Artes in Mexico City. The Palacio's theater also hosts performances of operas and concerts. The Art Deco Palacio houses a museum as well featuring ancient and modern paintings, murals by Rufino Tamayo, Diego Rivera, José Clemente Orozco, and David Siqueiros, and sculptures and handcrafted articles.

PAGE 417

Photo

Outdoor concerts such as the one shown here are common in Caracas, the cultural center and capital of Venezuela. For example, the city hosts free band concerts in Plaza Bolívar on Thursday and Sunday evenings. Even the Caracas subway system is involved in bringing culture to the people. The Metro's cultural department sponsors performances at major subway stops by such local groups as the Venezuelan Symphony Orchestra and the National University's Chorus.

PAGE 418

Photo

Andrés Segovia (1893–1987), the great Spanish virtuoso of the classical guitar. Even while in his 90's, Segovia rehearsed five hours a day and played some sixty concerts a year. Thanks in great part to Segovia's influence, classical guitar study is popular around the world. For example, classical guitar is taught at approximately 1,600 schools of music in the U.S.

PAGE 419

Realia

This ad for the Spanish Museum of Contemporary Art presents the dates (February 7–March 2) of a special exhibit of Spanish advertising art *(publicidad española)* of the 1980s. The museum is located on the extensive modern campus of the University of Madrid *(Ciudad Universitaria de Madrid).* The museum's regular collection features Spanish paintings and sculptures by such nineteenth- and twentieth-century artists as López, Esquivel, Miró, and Rosales.

PAGE 420

Photo

The Spanish painter Pablo Picasso (1881–1973). This famous artist lived in Paris much of his life and, together with the French painter Georges Braque, is credited with initiating the cubist movement in art.

Cubism makes use of geometric planes bounded by straight lines to form structures with a three-dimensional effect. Picasso's cubist portraits are particularly memorable. Art critics have noted that even his most ''distorted'' portraits approach a type of caricature, which he reserved primarily for male models.

Realia

This guidebook to the Picasso Museum in Barcelona, housed in a fourteenth-century palace, features Picasso's rendition of *Las Meninas (The Maidservants)*. In 1957 Picasso painted this version of the well-known painting of the same name by the famous Spanish baroque painter, Diego Velázquez (1599–1660). Picasso painted a series of variations on Velázquez's theme, focusing principally on Infanta (Princess) Margarita, one of several figures from the original work. Velázquez's *Las Meninas* hangs in a place of honor in Madrid's Museo del Prado.

PAGE 421

Photo

Visitors to the Joan Miró Foundation in Barcelona. This museum contains a collection of works by Miró and other contemporary artists. The Foundation, established by Miró in 1975, also includes archives and an art library and offers special workshops. Miró 1893–1983) was born in Barcelona. He spent some twenty years in Paris and was a leader in the various modernist movements, including cubism, surrealism, and futurism. He was prolific and versatile, creating paintings, ceramics, and sculptures.

PAGE 422

Photo

This mosaic mural adorns an exterior façade of the administration building of the Universidad Autónoma de México (UNAM) in Mexico City. Mexican muralist, David Alfaro Siqueiros created this work in the 1950s. It portrays scientists, humanists, and artists symbolically repaying the people of Mexico with talents developed within the public education system.

PAGE 422

Answers to *Repaso*

1. Los estudiantes (alumnos) de la Sra. González están leyendo una gran novela. / El director (La directora) de la banda está dirigiendo un concierto fantástico. / El hijo del pintor (de la pintora) está pintando un retrato elegante.
2. Los músicos están demostrando los sonidos de los instrumentos y la compositora está abriendo el piano. / Yo estoy firmando los cheques de viajero y mi hermano está contando los billetes. / Teresa está comprando ese esmalte de uñas y yo estoy mirando los perfumes.
3. Estamos incluyendo un aviso que explica cómo obtener información. / Están escogiendo una revista que demuestra cómo cortar pelo. / Estoy sacando un libro que describe cómo hacer cerámica.
4. Mis padres me dicen siempre que no les haga daño a los otros. / Nuestro entrenador (nos) recomienda generalmente que levantemos pesas con el equipo. / Yo les pido otra vez que presten atención por una hora.
5. Cuando ocurrió el accidente, siguió durmiendo. / Cuando se van (salen) los jugadores, sigo gritando. / Cuando empezó la lluvia, seguí ensayando.

PAGE 423

Answers to *Thema*

1. La clase del Sr. Pérez está pintando un mural grande.
2. Lucía está abriendo las latas de pintura y Jorge está mezclando colores.
3. María está leyendo un libro que explica cómo pintar murales.
4. El Sr. Pérez nos dice otra vez que tengamos cuidado con la pintura.
5. Cuando termina la clase, seguimos pintando.

PAGE 424

Answers to *Comprueba tu progreso*

A 1. La gente está aplaudiendo a los músicos.
  2. Ella está pidiendo otro saxofón.
  3. Los músicos están devolviendo los

instrumentos.

4. Yo estoy tocando el violoncelo.
5. El director está dirigiendo la orquesta.
6. Tú estás limpiando tu trompeta.
7. El coro está ensayando una canción diferente.
8. Nosotros estamos cantando en el coro.

B 1. Estamos recogiéndolos ahora mismo.
    2. Está escribiéndolo ahora mismo.
    3. Estoy ensayándola ahora mismo.
    4. Estamos terminándolo ahora mismo.
    5. Está arreglándola ahora mismo.
    6. Estoy oyéndolo ahora mismo.
    7. Están pidiéndolos ahora mismo.

C 1. g   3. c   5. f   7. e
    2. d   4. b   6. a

D 1. seguimos   4. siguió
    2. seguí   5. seguiste
    3. siguieron   6. siguió

E 1. vieja banda
    2. disco nuevo
    3. músico pobre
    4. gran éxito (éxito grande)
    5. canciones viejas
    6. instrumentos nuevos muy baratos
    7. pobre compositor
    8. armario grande

PAGE 425

Photo

This colorful painting depicts local Guatemalan Indians dancing a *son guatemalteco,* a native dance in which participants maneuver expertly around the male dancer's white straw hat, to the sound of a marimba and a guitar. This dance is popular around the mountainous region of Quezaltenango, the most important city in western Guatemala. Quezaltenango is famous for its native handicrafts and its artisans, who come from miles around to display their wares at the city's markets.

ORAL PROFICIENCY TEST

Directed response

1. Say that you and Andrea are dying of thirst. *(Andrea y yo estamos muriéndonos de sed.)* OR

(Andrea y yo nos estamos muriendo de sed.)

2. Mario needs help baking cupcakes. Since you don't know how to cook, tell him to follow the instructions on the box. *(Sigue las instrucciones en la caja.)*

3. Say that Juan's father was a great man. *(El padre de Juan fue un gran hombre.)*

Picture-Cued Response

Using the visual on p. 398 or transparency 40 ask questions such as.

4. ¿Qué están haciendo los admiradores? *(Están aplaudiendo.)*

5. ¿Te parece que el concierto tiene éxito o es un fracaso? *(Me parece que tiene éxito.)*

Situations

6. The director is upset because he can't hear the actors. What might he say to them?
    a. ¿Por qué gritan Uds. tanto?
    b. *¿Pueden Uds. hablar en voz más alta?*
    c. ¿Se fijan Uds. en el ruido en el fondo?

7. Mrs. Adalberto tells her children to turn the radio down. Which of the following probably describes what Mrs. Adalberto is thinking?
    a. ¡Qué sonido más suave!
    b. ¡Qué talento demuestran los músicos!
    c. *¡Me hace daño a los oídos!*

Real-Life Questions

8. ¿Tienes mucho talento? ¿En qué?

9. Si no haces algo muy bien la primera vez, ¿sigues practicando o no vuelves a hacerlo?

10. ¿Qué clase de arte prefieres? ¿Visitas mucho los museos? ¿Estás estudiando arte en la escuela?

11. ¿Tienes muchos amigos simpáticos? ¿Son muy parecidos a ti o son todos muy diferentes?

ORAL PROFICIENCY TEST   Chapters 9–12

Directed Response

1. Tell Mrs. Santos that you hope she feels better soon. *(Espero (Ojalá) que Ud. se sienta mejor pronto.)*

2. Ask the salesclerk if the price includes the tax. *(¿Incluye el precio el impuesto?)*

4. Tell Manuel to please be quiet because the musicians are still rehearsing. *(Cállate, por favor, porque los músicos todavía están ensayando.)*

Picture-Cued Response

Using the visual on p. 364 or transparency 36 ask questions such as:

4. ¿Qué están dando en el canal 5? *(Están dando un programa de noticias / el pronóstico del tiempo.)*
5. ¿De qué dos desastres hablan los locutores? *(Hablan de un terremoto y de un huracán.)*
6. ¿Qué clase de información indica el mapa? *(El mapa indica toda clase de información sobre el tiempo, que hay relámpagos en una parte del país y que la temperatura está a 20 grados.)*

Situations

7. Tomás calle his girlfriend with some interesting news. What might she say after greeting him?
   a. ¿Quién habla?   b. ¿De parte de quién?
   c. *¿Qué hay?*
8. Ana keeps dialing her friend's phone number. She won't give up because she says she knows someone is home. How does she know this?
   a. *La línea está ocupada.*   b. Hay tono.
   c. El teléfono está sonando.

Real-Life Questions

9. ¿Hablas mucho por teléfono? ¿Prefiere tu familia que hables por teléfono sólo los fines de semana o te permite hablar durante la semana también?
10. ¿Cómo es la comida en la cafetería de tu escuela? ¿Sirven la misma comida todas las semanas o cambian a menudo el menú?
11. ¿Te gustan los programas de concursos? ¿Cuál es tu (menos) favorito? ¿Dan a veces buenos premios en los programas de concursos? ¿Cuáles son algunos que dan?

CAPÍTULO 13

OBJECTIVES

Communication
- to identify vocabulary related to family relationships
- to identify vocabulary related to social behavior

Grammar
- to use the imperfect tense of -ar verbs
- to use the preposition por

Culture
- to point out the importance of gestures in conversations between Spanish speakers
- to describe and define some gestures commonly used by Spanish speakers
- to discuss and contrast the unconscious body language of English and Spanish speakers

SUGGESTED MATERIALS

p. 428 (Palabras nuevas I): magazine pictures or photos of ceremonies such as weddings, baptisms, or birthday parties

pp. 436–437 (Palabras nuevas II): magazine and/or newspaper pictures or photos illustrating different greeting styles (kissing, hugging, hand shaking)

PAGES 426–427

Photo
Students at the campus of the Universidad Autónoma of Barcelona. Spaniards typically gesture with their hands while speaking, as do other peoples of the Mediterranean and of Latin America. A fair amount of physical contact is also common among the Spanish, but it is an almost impersonal and unconscious contact. Even the ritual of kissing hello and good-by is a rather formal act, involving only a touching of cheeks while making the sound of a kiss.

PAGE 433

Photo
A church wedding in Mérida, which is located on Mexico's Yucatán Peninsula. Most Mexican weddings are followed by a formal reception either at the bride's home or at a rented hall or restaurant. Celebrants are treated to food, drink, music, and dancing before the newlyweds leave for their honeymoon (luna de miel).

Realia
An invitation to a wedding in Madrid, with a formal lunch reception to take place afterwards at the Jai-Alai Restaurant. The groom's parents are listed first on the invitation. The church ceremony will take place—God willing (Dios mediante)—May 26 at 1:30. In Spain, as in many other countries, the religious ceremony is not recognized legally. A couple must also go through a civil ceremony, usually a modest affair attended only by close family members.

PAGE 435

Photo
A wedding in Caracas. Venezuelans often celebrate the required civil ceremony in the morning before the formal church wedding in the evening. Placing a charm in the cake batter is a wedding tradition still followed in much of the Spanish-speaking world. The lucky guest who finds the charm will be the next to get married according to the tradition.

PAGE 438

Photo
Puerto Rican students interacting at school. Most public-school students in Puerto Rico wear uniforms. Private schools, however, have rather loose dress codes that allow students to dress for the weather—hot and humid most of the year—usually drawing the line at shorts and halter tops.

PAGE 441

Photo

Making a *piñata* por *las posadas* in Mexico City. *Las posadas* (literally "inns") are typical Mexican Christmas celebrations that commemorate Joseph and Mary's search for shelter during their trip to Bethlehem. They are held for nine consecutive evenings, beginning on December 16, and ending on Christmas Eve. The celebration begins with prayers and songs, and ends with dancing and merrymaking, including the breaking of the *piñata*. A *piñata* is a brightly decorated figure made of papier-mâché (usually in the shape of an animal ortoy) that covers a hollow container stuffed with candy, fruit, nuts, coina, and small gifts. Blindfolded children take turns trying to break the hanging *piñata* with long sticks or bats.

PAGE 442

Photo

A baptism in Madrid. In the Spanish-speaking world, the sacrament of baptism is extremely important because it marks a child's entrance as a member into the Catholic church. It usually takes place on a Sunday morning, within two weeks of the child's birth, and is followed by a reception for friends and relatives. A vital part of the ceremony is the selection of godparents, who will be responsible for the child's moral and religious education. *Padrinos* are part of the child's extended family and often are as close as any member of the immediate family.

PAGE 443

Photo

A Mexican-American family celebrating Christmas in the U.S. Many traditions—singing *villancicos* (Christmas carols), breaking *piñatas,* and observing *las posadas,* for example—are retained in areas such as Texas, New Mexico, and California, with large populations of Mexican origin.

PAGE 446

Photo

A 15-year-old cutting the birthday cake at her fifteenth-birthday party in Buenos Aires. In most Spanish-speaking countries, *los quince años* is a big occasion, often celebrated with a church service and a dinner dance given by her parents and / or godparents. The festivities, often written up in the society pages of the local newspaper, combine elements of the U.S. sweet-sixteen and debutante parties.

The ribbons leading from the top of the cake are an important part of the custom. A ring is tied to one of the ribbons. The guest of honor and her friends each pull a ribbon, and the girl who pulls that special ribbon will supposedly be the first to get married.

PAGE 447

Sample dialogues for *¿Qué pasa?*

At Julio and Raquel's wedding, Julio's parents are talking about two children who are misbehaving.

Padre: Creo que debes decirles a aquellos dos niños que se porten bien.

Madre: Tienes razón. Son bastante desagradables. ¿Qué te parece si hablo con sus padres?

Padre: Pues, espero que los padres no sean tan maleducados como los niños.

Madre: Y ojalá que yo no meta la pata.

Padre: Aquellos niños les están molestando a los otros invitados.

Madre: Es verdad. La muchacha sigue empujando a su hermano.

Padre: ¿Qué te parece si tú les dices que dejen de pelearse?

Madre: ¿Yo? A mí no me gustan los niños maleducados.

Padre: Es un problema muy desagradable. Mientras los mayores bailan, los niños deben portarse bien.

Madre: Tienes razón. Voy a hablarles ahora mismo.

PAGE 448

Photo

Easter lunch at a home a Popayán, a small city located in a mountain valley in southwestern Colombia. Because of the beauty of its colonial buildings, the entire town was declared a national monument. However, on Good Friday in 1983, a devastating earthquake destroyed 70 percent of the city. Much of the damage was quickly repaired, thanks to generous international donations. Popayán holds elaborate Holy Week celebrations starting on Palm Sunday, with solemn processions throughout the city and a festival of sacred music that attracts visitors from all over the world.

PAGE 449

Realia

A business card from Donls Restaurant, located in the medieval town of Arévalo in Spain's central province of Ávila. The restaurant advertises that it can be reserved for wedding parties, communion and baptismal receptions, meetings, and conventions. Its specialities include roast suckling pig, chops, seafood, fish, and special desserts.

PAGE 452

Photo

A first communion in Mexico City. In predominantly Catholic countries like Mexico, the first communion is not only of religious importance, but is also a social event attended by family and friends. It marks a child's entrance into active participation as a member of the church. Children between the ages of 7 and 9 receive instruction to prepare them for the event. Girls dress in elegant white lace, and boys wear dark suits.

Answers to *Repaso*

1. Juan y Pedro se reunieron anteayer. / Me aburrí anoche. / Nos despedimos esta tarde.
2. Trabajaron por diez minutos para desenvolver la caja. / Ensayó por ocho meses para ganar ese concurso. / Leí por tres días para terminar el libro.
3. Mientras los nietos se gritaban, los parientes se sentaban. / Mientras los padres se acostaban, el (la) bebé se despertaba. / Mientras tú te afeitabas, yo me pesaba.
4. Mientras empujaba el coche, mamá tocaba la bocina. / Mientras mirábamos la multa, el anciano estacionaba coches. / Mientras María llenaba el tanque, yo limpiaba el parabrisas.
5. Durante el concierto, mientras los músicos tocaban, el compositor repasaba la canción de él. /

En la cocina, mientras cocinábamos, recomendaban el guacamole de ellos. / Después del accidente, mientras esperábamos, la mecánica arreglaba el coche de ella.

PAGE 453

Answers to *Tema*

1. Patricia y Jorge se casaron ayer.
2. El tío Eduardo viajó por dos días para venir a la boda.
3. Mientras los novios se besaban, los suegros se abrazaban.
4. Mientras Patricia cortaba el pastel, el fotógrafo sacaba fotos.
5. Durante la fiesta, mientras los jóvenes bailaban, los mayores recordaban las bodas de ellos.

PAGE 454

Answers to *Comprueba tu progreso*

A
1. padrino
2. nieto
3. bisabuela
4. parientes
5. suegra
6. novio

B
1. beso
2. doy la mano
3. compartir
4. tengo celos
5. dejan de
6. molestan
7. nació
8. me despido
9. empujo
10. regalé

C
1. La madrina felicitaba al padrino.
2. Yo planchaba mientras tú pasabas la aspiradora.
3. Los ruidos fuertes asustaban a todos.
4. El padre estaba muy nervioso mientras esperaba el nacimiento de su hijo.
5. Uds. contaban el dinero en la caja.
6. Mandábamos las cartas por vía aérea.
7. El anciano compraba libros para su nieto.

D
1. Cada dos minutos los abuelos bostezaban.
2. El actor sordo siempre hablaba por señas.
3. Todos los días Jorge llamaba por teléfono a su novia.
4. Cada mañana Andrea saludaba al profesor.
5. Practicábamos para el concierto por la tarde.

6. Los martes ellos nadaban en el club.
7. Todos los días tomaba el autobús a las nueve.

E 1. Yolanda vendió el coche por doscientos dólares.
2. Javier va al sótano por la escoba.
3. No hay partido hoy por (la) lluvia.
4. Benjamín le dio las noticias a Elena por telegrama.
5. Susana va a dar un paseo por el parque.
6. Dolores sacó malas notas por estudiar poco.
7. Jorge va a la piscina dos veces por semana.

PAGE 455

Photo

Wood carvings from Monte Albán in the state of Oaxaca, Mexico. The figures represent the Virgin Mary with the Infant Jesus and Saint Joseph. Figures of this type are often made by unschooled part-time folk artists, who chop whitewood with a machete, carve it with a knife, and then paint it with dyes. Jesus is often depicted with Indian features in wood carvings from Oaxaca, where the Indian influence is strong.

ORAL PROFICIENCY TEST

Directed Response

1. Ask Pablo how much he paid for his new car. (*¿Cuánto pagaste por tu coche nuevo?*)
2. Say that Laura and Enrique always used to pull your leg, but now they don't speak to you anymore. (*Laura y Enrique siempre me tomaban el pelo, pero ya no me hablan.*)

3. Say that you used to talk on the telephone for two hours every night, but your mother no longer allows it. (*Hablaba por teléfono por dos horas cada noche, pero mi madre ya no lo permite.*)

Picture-Cued Response

Pointing to the photograph on p. 435, ask:
4. ¿Qué celebran los novios? (*Celebran la boda.*)
5. ¿Qué hace el señor a la derecha del recién casado? (*Lo felicita.*) OR (*Le da la mano.*)

Situations

6. There are about 40 people at Silvia's birthday party, and you want to know how she knows them all. What might her response be?
   a. Son mis padrinos.   b. Son mis padres.
   c. *Son mis parientes.*
7. Julia is in love with Raúl. How might she tell him so?
   a. Tengo celos de ti.
   b. *Estoy enamorada de ti.*
   c. Me tomas mucho el pelo.

Real-Life Questions

8. ¿Cuántos años vas a cumplir este año? ¿Cómo vas a celebrar tu cumpleaños?
9. ¿Dónde se reúnen tú y tus amigos después de las clases?
10. ¿A qué edad piensas casarte? ¿Con qué tipo de persona crees que vas a estar enamorado(a)?
11. Cuando eras niño(a), ¿cuánto costaba el chicle? ¿Mascabas chicle más que ahora o menos?

CAPÍTULO 14

OBJECTIVES

Communication
- to identify vocabulary related to ancient civilizations and ruins
- to identify vocabulary related to crime, accidents, and disasters

Grammar
- to use the imperfect tense of verbs that end in -er and -ir
- to use the future tense of verbs that end in -ar, -er, and -ir

Culture
- to identify Peru's Machu Picchu as a lost city discovered by Hiram Bingham in 1911
- to discuss the location of Machu Picchu
- to describe Machu Picchu's design and construction
- to tell who probably lived at Machu Picchu and why the city was abandoned

SUGGESTED MATERIALS

p. 457 (Prólogo cultural): a wall map shoving how extensive the Incan empire was at its peak (from Ecuador to Argentina, running some 2,000 miles along the Andes *cordillera*)

pp. 458–459 (Palabras nuevas I): magazine cutouts and / or objects illustrating materials (cotton, wool, gold, silver, paper, wood, leather, stone)

pp. 460–461 (Contexto comunicativo): wall map(s) showing the regions inhabited by the Aztecs (Mexico and parts of Central America), the Mayas the Yucatán Peninsula and southern Mexico, Guatemala, and Honduras), and the Incas (Peru, Bolivia, Ecuador, and Chile)

p. 466 (Palabras nuevas II): a Spanish-language newspaper

p. 476 (Actividad): a paper bag

PAGES 456–457

Photo
A view of Machu Picchu. The earliest Andean Indian group that is known to have existed in Peru, the Chavín culture, began around the year 1000 B.C. It was followed by the Paracas, Nazca, Mochica, and Tlahuanaco cultures. The Inca culture was a relatively late one, developing sometime after A.D. 1000. Its high period, however, did not begin until Pachacutec Inca Yupanqui became emperor (c. 1438). It was Pachacutec who consolidated the Incas and launched the campaign that expanded the reaches of the empire in every direction. When his son, Tupacluca Inca Yupanqui, succeeded to the throne in 1471, the pace of expansion increased. By the time Columbus arrived in the Americas, the Incas dominated much of Ecuador, Peru, Chile, and Bolivia. When Francisco Pizarro reached Peru in 1532, the decline of the Incas had already begun, due in large part to a civil war that had been instigated by the sons of the Emperor Huayna Capac.

PAGE 460

Photo
A view of El Castillo, also known as the Temple of Kukulkán, seen from the Platform of Tigers and Eagles at Chichén Itzá, which is about 75 miles east of Mérida on Mexico's Yucatán Peninsula. The five-square-mile site was founded by the Mayas in 432, and became the Toltec capital in the late tenth century. Each of the four sides of the 70-foot-high pyramid has 91 steps leading to a chamber dedicated to Kukulkán, the Mayan name for the god Quetzalcóatl, the plumed serpent. On the day of the summer solstice, the sun strikes the pyramid at such an angle that a shadow gives the illusion of a serpent descending the stairway.

PAGE 461

Photo
A Mayan exhibit at Mexico City's Museo Nacional de

Antropología, one of the world's foremost museums of anthropology. The Mayas inhabited the Yucatán Peninsula, southern Mexico, Guatemala, and Honduras; this highly evolved civilization flourished during its classic period, A.D. 250–1000, excelling in mathematics, astronomy, and architecture. Experts today are still puzzled by the collapse of the Mayan empire in the 1500s, when they simply abandoned their cities.

PAGE 463
Photo
A carved stone figure discovered in Mexico. Scientists are now in general agreement that the Americas were settled when nomad tribes crossed a landbridge from Asis as long as 35,000 years ago. Excavations at Tlapacoya, near Mexico City, show evidence of habitation dating back 21,000 years. From the ruined cities, ceremonial centers, and artifacts, we can see relics of the numerous civilizations that inhabited Mexico, including the Toltecs, Tarascans, Zapotecs, Olmecs, Mayas, Mixtecs, and the Mexica, better known as Aztecs.

PAGE 465
Photo
The ancient city of Tikal lies deep within the jungles of Guatemala's northern region of El Petén. Inhabited by the Mayas for approximately a millenium, the former ceremonial city consists of thousands of structures. Flanking the sweeping two-and-a-half-acre paved Great Plaza are the 145-foot Temple of the giant Jaguar, the 125-foot Temple of the Masks, and the North Acropolis complex. Within the area are pyramids and temples higher than 20-story buildings, ornate palaces, ball courts, shrines, and long causeways as wide as modern freeways. Scientists estimate that at its height, Tikal housed from 75,000 to 100,000 inhabitants and covered around 25 square miles.

PAGE 466
Additions to on-page notes
If students ask: Other related words you may want to present: *la bomba de incendios,* fire engine; *la manguera,* hose; *la boca de incendio,* five hydrant; *la estación de bomberos,* fire station; *el ejercicio contra incendios,* fire drill; *la escalera de emergencia,* fire escape.

PAGE 468
Photo
A fire station in Quito, Ecuador. The fire department *(cuerpo de bomberos)* in Quito is run by the municipal government, and Ecuadoran firefighters must go through extensive training in everything from first aid to building inspection for fire prevention.

PAGE 471
Photo
Frank Soler, former editor of the Spanish-language edition of the *Miami Herald,* with a circulation of approximately 85,000 copies daily. The large Hispanic community in Miami is predominantly of Cuban descent, but in recent years the population has become more diverse. In a 1987 study, Cubans were shown to make up just under two-thirds of Miami's Hispanic population, with South and Central Americans making up 32 percent.

PAGE 475
Photo
A feathered serpent adorns the side of the Temple of Quetzalcóatl at the ruins of Teotihuacán, about 30 miles from Mexico City. The stone carvings depict the god as a plumed serpent set within an eleven-petaled flower. Quetzalcóatl was the Toltec god who created man and invented corn, an important food to the early dwellers of the Americas. He sometimes assumed the shape of either a colorful quetzal bird or a serpent, hence his representation as a feathered snake. The Aztecs believed that he was a bearded white man who would one day return from the East. When Spanish conquistador Hernán Cortés and is

men arrived in 1519, Moctezuma, the Aztec king, thought that Quetzalcóatl had come back.

PAGE 476
Photo
In 1978 utility workers digging a trench to lay an electrical cable in downtown Mexico City discovered what turned out to be the archaeological find of the century: the ruins of the Templo Mayor (Great Temple) of the former Aztec capital city of Tenochtitlán. The site has since been excavated, and a large open air museum stands within a block of the National Palace, allowing visitors a glimpse into Mexico's pre-Hispanic past.

PAGE 477
Photo
A little after 7:00 A.M. on September 19, 1985, an earthquake struck Mexico City. Measuring 8.1 on the Richter Scale, the tremor wreaked havoc in the downtown area and caused buildings to collapse at a cost of thousands of lives.

PAGE 478
Photo
World-famous Spanish tenor, Plácido Domingo (left), joined the rescue efforts after Mexico City's 1985 earthquake. Born in Madrid in 1941, Domingo was raised in Mexico; several of his relatives perished when their apartments collapsed during the quake. Domingo canceled all professional engagements, and spent a year giving benefit concerts to aid Mexico's earthquake victims.

PAGE 479
Additions to on-page notes
Reteach / Extra Help: In preparation for the *Práctica* on pp. 480–481, you may want to lead a class discussion about life in the future. Initiate the discussion by asking questions such as *¿Trabajaremos más que ahora o menos? ¿Dónde estarás? ¿Todavía aprenderán español o francés los estudiantes en la escuela? ¿Serán amigos tú y ____?*

PAGE 480
Photo
An earthquake techinician. After the tremors hit Mexico City, many international seismologists arrived to study the seismic effects of the quake. Urban planners and architects use this information to design buildings that can withstand stress. Certain earthquake-prone areas, especially along the San Andreas fault, have established building codes that require reinforcements against seismic shocks.

PAGE 482
Photo
Archaeologists have uncovered more than 7,000 artifacts from the 10,000-square-meter Templo Mayor site in downtown Mexico City. Many of the pieces from the area where Tenochtitlán's main pyramid once stood still bear brightly painted designs and provide insights into the Aztecs' daily life.

Answers to *Repaso*
1. Cada mes asistía a una carrera. / Cada Navidad escribían al diario (periódico). / Cada domingo ella participaba en concursos.
2. Construían pirámides que tenían paredes de oro verdadero. / Él producía anuncios que ofrecían tesoros de religiones antiguas. / Leíamos un artículo que incluía titulares sobre desastres inolvidables.
3. A veces hallaba (encontraba) pirámides y templos impresionantes. / Frecuentemente destruían cuadros y estatuas importantes. / Él casi siempre reconocía actos y causas heroicos.
4. Esperamos que trabajes de ingeniera. / Quiero que ella trabaje de periodista. / Pide que nosotros trabajemos de bomberos.
5. Pero decimos que seremos periodistas. Escribiremos artículos. / Pero María dice que será ingeniera. Construirá puentes. / Pero piensan que serán astrónomos(as). Estudiarán estrellas.

PAGE 483

Answers to *Tema*

1. Cada verano la familia Morales huía de la ciudad.
2. Visitaban lugares donde había ruinas de civilizaciones antiguas.
3. A veces descubrían objetos y lugares asombrosos.
4. Los Morales esperan que Mateo trabaje de arqueólogo.
5. Pero Mateo dice que será artista. Pintará paisajes.

PAGE 484

Answers to *Comprueba tu progreso*

A
1. ladrón
2. bombero
3. astrónomo
4. periodista
5. humo
6. siglo
7. templo
8. titular

B
1. tenía
2. comíamos / teníamos
3. nos reuníamos
4. me sentía / leía / había
5. Vivías
6. pensaba / podíamos
7. ponía
8. descubrían

C
1. Daniel compartía sus cosas.
2. Daniel entendía sus lecciones.
3. Ramón empujaba a sus amigos.
4. Ramón comía con la boca abierta.
5. Ramón huía cuando alguien lo llamaba.
6. Ramón tenía celos de su hermano.

D
1. Hoy desayunaremos en el comedor.
2. Mañana llevaré un vestido a la escuela.
3. Esta noche regresaremos a casa más temprano.
4. Mañana llegaremos a la escuela a tiempo.
5. Hoy no compartiré nada.
6. Hoy comeremos en el jardín.
7. Esta tarde correré por la playa.
8. Ahora beberé agua.

E
1. Iré al bautizo de Juan Carlos.
2. Tu mamá se dará cuenta de que ese vaso está roto.
3. El ladrón se escapará.
4. La casa se quemará.
5. Tú salvarás a los niños.
6. Huiremos.
7. Clara y Miguel se quedarán.
8. Los periodistas extranjeros escribirán esos artículos.

PAGE 485

Photo

A pre-Columbian weaving from Peru, made in A.D. 13 by the Chancay Indians. The weaving represents the supreme god of the Incas, called Viracocha, or Wiracocha. The god is shown holding some symbols of power. The Chancay, who lived north of present-day Lima, incorporated many traditions of their conquerors, the Incas; and in turn, influenced Incan art. The Chancay produced textiles before and during the rise of the Incas, and left a wealth of weavings, ambroidery, and lacemaking.

ORAL PROFICIENCY TEST

Directed Response

1. Ask Rebeca when she realized that she wanted to study medicine. (*¿Cuándo te diste cuenta de que querías estudiar medicina?*)
2. Say that Carmen used to like her job because she learned something new every day. (*A Carmen le gustaba su trabajo porque aprendía algo nuevo todos los días (cada día).*)
3. Ask Elisa and Roberto what time they will get to the party. (*¿A qué hora llegarán Uds. a la fiesta?*)

Picture-Cued Response

Using the visuals on pp. 458–459 or transparency 47, ask questions such as:

4. ¿De qué hacían estatuas los incas? (*Las hacían de piedra / oro / madera.*)
5. ¿Crees que los mayas construían sus pirámides de madera? (*No, creo que las construían de piedra.*)
6. ¿Dónde vivían los aztecas? (*Vivían en México y en la América Central.*)

Situations

7. Luis wants to tell is friend Roberta about a scary

experience he had while babysitting last Saturday. How might he begin his story?

a. El bebé llorará pronto.

b. *De repente la niña empezó a llorar.*

c. Los muchachos están llorando por nada.

8. After digging for six years, an Argentine archaeologist has just uncovered some ancient ruins. How would she describe them?

a. *Son asombrosas.*

b. Están muertas.

c. Están enterradas.

Real-Life Questions

9. Si no sabes el significado de una palabra, ¿qué haces? ¿Dónde puedes averiguarlo?

10. ¿Prefieres los objetos de oro o de plata? ¿Por qué?

11. En tu opinión, ¿qué país tiene las ruinas más asombrosas? ¿Por qué?

CAPÍTULO 15

OBJECTIVES
Communication
- to identify vocabulary related to nature and expeditions / safaris
- to identify vocabulary related to professions and income

Grammar
- to use the irregular verbs *ir, ser,* and *ver* in the imperfect tense
- to understand the different uses of the imperfect tense
- to use the preposition *para*

Culture
- to point out the wide variety of exotic animals in South America
- to describe two interesting types of bats and fish
- to discuss two unusual South American mammals: the sloth and the giant anteater
- to explain why there are so many types of animals on the South American continent

SUGGESTED MATERIALS
p. 487 (Prólogo cultural):   photos of the vampire bat and the Mexican bulldog bat, the piranha and the electric eel, and the sloth and the giant anteater

p. 492 (Actividad):   magazine ads or travel brochures for interesting tours; a cassette or tape recorder

p. 495 (Palabras nuevas II):   magazine cutouts showing professions (scientist, orthodontist, pharmacist, lawyer, businessperson, secretary, computer programmer)

p. 508 (Actividad):   magazines and newspapers for students to cut from

PAGES 486–487
Photo
The jungles and rain forests of Colombia are home to a wide variety of exotic flora and fauna; the Amazon basin's beautiful wild orchids an seven-foot Queen Victoria lily pads; Andean condors, wil boars, jaguars, pumas, and tapirs; Putumayo's bright parrots, boa constrictors, and screeching monkeys. Colombia is the fourth-largest country in South America, with the third-largest population. The majority of Colombians live in the mountainous western region of the country, while the eastern and southeastern areas are inhabited almost exclusively by wildlife that lives in seclusion, protected from the modern world.

PAGE 488
Additions to on-page notes
If students ask: Other related words you may want to present: *el cocodrilo,* crocodile; *los bejucos,* reeds; *el alacrán* or *el escorpión,* scorpion; *el cacto,* cactus; *el lagarto,* lizard; *la erupción,* eruption; *el camello,* camel; *la roca,* rock.

PAGE 492
Photo
Macaws are the largest and most vividly colored members of the parrot family. They live in the Amazon rain forest, as seen here, an various species are found in Mexico, Central America, and as far south as Uruguay and central Argentina. They live high in tree tops, and eat fruits, seeds, and nuts that they crack open with their powerful beaks. Macaws are called *guacamayos* in some countries and *guacamayas* in others (regardless of their gender). These intelligent birds can be tamed and taught to talk, and they make affectionate pets. However, if mistreated they can become mean, biting and squawking in protest. Some Indian tribes use macaw feathers to adorn their costumes.

PAGE 494
Photo
Ruins of ancient Mayan cities, temples, and roads are found throughout Mexico's Yucatán Peninsula. Some

are well restored, such as Chichén Itzá, while others are still in the process of exploration and excavation. Seen here are remains of Bacán, in the south central section of the peninsula. Its structures, many still overgrown with tropical vegetation, include a pyramid crowned by a temple, several altars, and a ball court. The Mayan civilization, most of which mysteriously disappeared before the arrival of the Spaniards, also flourished in what is now the neighboring state of Chiapas, as well as in parts of Guatemala, Belize, and Honduras.

PAGE 498
Photo
A computer class at the Universidad Rafael Urdaneta in Maracaibo, the second-largest city in Venezuela. The city is located on the northeast banks of Lake Maracaibo, the largest lake in South America. Vast deposits of crude oil flow beneath the lake bed, and offshore drilling techniques used throughout the world today were pioneered in Lake Maracaibo. In addition to its computerized offshore and lakeside oil production installations at Lake Maracaibo, Petróleos de Venezuela, S.A., the national oil company, operates major research and development laboratories featuring state-of-the-art computer technology. The university was named for General Rafael Urdaneta, who was born in Maracaibo in 1789, became a hero in the revolutionary battles for independence against Spain, and later served as a Venezuelan diplomat.

PAGE 499
Photo
In Madrid, a pharmacist is shown helping a customer. Spanish pharmacies specialize in medicinal, surgical, and basic health-care products, and do not carry the range of nonrelated merchandise usually found in large U.S. drugstores. Customers are attended by professional college-graduate pharmacists (farmacéuticos) as well as knowledgeable, trained salespersons. There are may typical small pharmacies that are more than a century old. They proudly preserve their original traditional storefronts and decor, and antique apothecary jars and other collector's items remain on display.

PAGE 500
Realia
The course of study catalogue, including a section on the humanities, from the Universidad Rafael Landívar in Guatemala City. The university is named in honor of Rafael Landívar (1731–1793), a Guatemalan Jesuit intellectual and poet, whose words include a poem in Latin, *Rusticatio mexicana,* which describes regional country life and customs.

PAGE 501
Photo
An expert studying an Aztec artifact. Spanish *conquistador,* Hernán Cortés, ordered the construction of what is now the area of Mexico City's main square (El Zócalo) on top of the razed ceremonial center and Templo Mayor (Great Temple) of the defeated Aztec capital city of Tenochtitlán. In 1978, over four-and-a-half centuries later, Mexico City construction workers inadvertently discovered a section of the Great Temple within what turned out to be an Aztec ''time capsule.'' Buried intact at the time of the Conquest—rather than decaying amidst open ruins—thousands of artifacts of daily life, such as the incense vase seen here, have been uncovered.

PAGE 508
Additions to on-page notes
Enrichment: Additional questions for Ex. E: *Cuando eras niño(a), ¿cuáles eran tus comidas preferidas? ¿Qué clase de juegos o deportes preferías? ¿Soñabas con ser explorador(a) y con descubrir tesoros secretos?*

PAGE 509
Sample dialogues for *¿Qué pasa?*
Raúl has applied for a part-time job, and he and the interviewer are talking.

E: ¿Por qué le interesa a Ud. este trabajo?
R: Pues, quiero ganarme la vida mientras estudio.
E: ¿Cree Ud. que es capaz de trabajar y estudiar al mismo tiempo?

R: Claro que sí. Soy muy práctico y tengo mucha ambición.

E: ¿Sabe Ud. escribir a máquina?

R: Sí, señora. Lo aprendí en la escuela.

E: Muy bien. ¿Y cuánto espera Ud. ganar?

R: Quisiera ganar por lo menos cien dólares por semana.

E: Pues, ése es el sueldo que estamos ofreciendo. ¿Qué pienda Ud. hacer despúes de graduarse?

R: Si puedo ahorrar bastante dinero, voy a estudiar derecho. Me gustaría ser abogado.

PAGE 510

Photo

The shores of Lake Titicaca, the highest navigable lake in the world (12,500 feet above sea level), have been a center of Indian life since pre-Incan times. Here the Uru Indians continue using centuries-old methods of weaving boats from reeds growing along the marshy banks. They use the boats for fishing, and for traveling between different villages in Peru and Bolivia, the two countries surrounding the lake. From the reeds the Indians also build huts and rafts that are anchored by long taproots.

PAGE 513

Photo

Two *puertorriqueñas* chatting in the main plaza of Ponce, the second-largest city in Puerto Rico. This colonial-style plaza, lined with fountains and gardens, is dominated by the Cathedral of Our Lady of Guadalupe. Nearby is the famous Museo de Arte de Ponce, designed by Edward Durell Stone, who was also one of the architects of New York's Museum of Modern Art.

PAGE 514

Photo

The jaguar is the largest cat in the Western Hemisphere. It is found from northern Mexico all the way south to central Argentina, and is the most powerful and feared carnivorous animal of Latin America. Although it is often calle *tigre*, the jaguar's tawny fur is uniquely marked with black spots that form rosette patterns. The ancient Maya, who respected jaguars for their ferocity, depicted them in ceremonial centers. Examples can be seen in the stone carvings of the Temple of the Jaguar at Chichén Itzá on the Yucatán Peninsula, and also in the Temple of the Giant Jaguar at the Mayan ruins of Tikal in Guatemala.

Answers to *Repaso*

1. La semana pasada di un paseo por la ciudad. / El octubre pasado fue de pesca en el mar. / El invierno pasado hice un asado en las montañas.
2. Generalmente alquilábamos caballos jóvenes para subir al volcán. / A veces no había bastante algodón para hacer vendas. / Ella siempre llevaba sandalias cómodas para cruzar el desierto.
3. Esta mañana corría junto al lago cuando vi un jaguar. ¡Era peligrísimo! / La semana pasada viajaba por el desierto cuando vio a los antropólogos. ¡Estaban delgadísimos! / Anoche mirábamos por la ventana cuando vimos la ambulancia. ¡Estábamos preocupadísimos!
4. ''Conocía a muchos de los científicos en esa universidad, pero ya no,'' les dijo el ayudante. / ''Había demasiadas moscas en este restaurante, pero ya no,'' le dijo el gerente. / ''Veía a varios pacientes en esa clínica, pero ya no,'' le dijo el ortodoncista.
5. Ganó mucho dinero pero compró la mayoría de la ropa en venta. / Obtuvimos bastantes horarios y pedimos un boleto de ida en la ventanilla. / Cambié varios cheques y gasté la mitad de mi sueldo en comida.

PAGE 515

Answers to *Tema*

1. El año pasado hice una expedición por la selva.
2. Generalmente usábamos canoas pequeñas para explorar el río.
3. Un día íbamos por el río cuando vimos una tortuga. ¡Era grandísima!
4. ''Veíamos más tortugas en este sitio, pero ya no,'' nos dijo el explorador.
5. Sacamos unas fotos e hicimos el resto del viaje en helicóptero.

PAGE 516

Answers to *Comprueba tu progreso*

A
1. arqueólogos
2. expedición
3. explorar
4. helicóptero
5. capaz
6. canoas
7. loros
8. húmedo
9. práctico

B
1. era
2. iban
3. veíamos
4. Ibas
5. veían
6. Había, eran
7. veía

C
1. manejaba
2. hubo
3. iba, había
4. acompañaba, iba
5. exploraste
6. soñaban
7. se reunieron
8. era, tenía
9. Eran, oímos

D
1. Hay que estudiar arquitectura si quieres ser arquitecto (derecho si quieres ser abogado).
3. Ana quiere ser antropóloga porque le interesa estudiar las civilizaciones antiguas.
4. Los científicos tienen que pasar muchas horas en el laboratorio.
6. Mario quiere tener mucho dinero, y por eso sueña con ser millonario.

E
1. Para
2. para
3. por, para
4. para, para
5. para
6. por, para
7. por, para
8. Para, por
9. Para, para

PAGE 517

Photo

A papier-mâché lizard from Mexico City. This figure was made by the Linares family, whose name has become a trademark for this type of folk art throughout Mexico. Pedro Linares and his sons, who live in Mexico City, produce colorful, fantastic creatures called *alebrijes,* which include dragons, four-legged fish, winged lions, and lizard-like animals like the one shown in the photograph. The papier-mâché figures are whitewashed before being painted, decorated, and varnished.

ORAL PROFICIENCY TEST

Directed Response

1. Say that for a child so young, Sarita is very capable. *(Para una niña tan joven. Sarita es muy capaz.)*
2. Ask claudia and Rodolfo where they were going when they saw the fire. *(¿Adónde iban Uds. cuando vieron el incendio?)*
3. Ask Consuelo what time it was when Juana arrived. *(¿Qué hora era cuando llegó Juana?)*

Picture-Cued Response

4. Pointing to the visual on p. 488 or transparency 50, ask: "¿Por dónde remaban los exploradores cuando vieron el jaguar?" *(Remaban por la selva cuando vieron el jaguar.)*
5. Pointing to the photograph on p. 498, ask: "¿Son antropólogos?" *(No, son programadores de computadoras.)*

Situations

6. You want to buy a sweater that costs $29, but you have only $25. What might you say to the salesperson?
   a. Tengo demasiado dinero.
   b. Tengo por lo menos veintinueve dólares.
   c. *No tengo bastante dinero.*
7. Rita has always been interested in court cases. What do you think she might study at the university?
   a. *El derecho.* b. Las reglas.
   c. El tiempo

Real-Life Questions

8. ¿Con qué soñabas cuando eras joven?
9. ¿Qué consejos te dan los mayores? ¿Sigues todos los consejos o sólo algunos? ¿Cuáles sigues?
10. ¿Qué haces para ganar dinero? De lo que ganas, ¿cuánto gastas y cuánto ahorras?
11. ¿Crees que es bueno tener tu propio negocio? ¿Por qué? ¿Qué clase de negocio te gustaría tener?

CAPÍTULO 16

OBJECTIVES

Communication
- to identify vocabulary related to emotions, moods and temperament
- to identify vocabulary related to air travel

Grammar
- to use the subjunctive with verbs and expressions of emotion
- to use the subjunctive with verbs and expressions of doubt, denial, or uncertainty
- to use the subjunctive with impersonal expressions

Culture
- to discuss common U.S. superstitions
- to tell about the superstition associated with black cats in parts of Latin America
- to describe good-luck tokens and good omens in the Spanish-speaking world
- to point out the saying *la suerte es ciega*

SUGGESTED MATERIALS

p. 527 (Palabras nuevas II): ads and / or brochures for Hispanic airlines (Aeroméxico, Aerolíneas Argentinas, Avianca, Dominicana, Ecuatoriana, Iberia, Lan-Chile, Mexicana, Tan-Sahsa, Viasa-Venezuelan)

p. 529 (Práctica A): a wall map showing Barranquilla, Colombia

p. 538 (Lectura): a wall map showing Nazca, in southern Peru

p. 543 (Actividad): a paper bag

PAGES 518–519
Photo
Several good luck charms from Latin America. In the center we see Ekeko, an Indian mythical personage from Bolivia, laden with an assortment of miniature cooking utensils, coins, bills, balls of wool, tiny sacks of sugar, coffee, salt, rice and flour. These are

symbols that represent real things. Ekeko is given to friends and relatives around New Year's with the hope of bringing prosperity and granting wishes; he is a kind of Bolivian Santa Claus. You can buy plaster images of Ekeko at the *Feria de Alacitas,* a Bolivian festival dedicated to him. It is assumed that if you buy a toy house, cow, or sheep at the fair, you can expect a real one before the year is out.

PAGE 521
Photo
Milagros, good-luck charms from Mexico.

PAGE 522
Photo
Three teenage boys from Caracas, Venezuela. Evident in this photo is a teenage custom that transcends cultural boundaries—the wearing of tee shirts and jeans by both sexes. The short-sleeved button-down shirt worn by the young man in the center is typical of the more traditional male clothing worn in this tropical country.

PAGE 524
Photo
Two young women from Puerto Rico wearing lightweight summer clothing suited to the island's tropical climate. One rarely sees a *puertorriqueña* of any age without pierced earrings. Parents customarily have their infant daughters' ears pierced shortly after birth. Newborn baby girls come home from the hospital wearing tiny gold earrings.

PAGE 526
Realia
This mail-order flyer, produced by a New York-based company, invites Spanish speakers to "begin now to fill your pockets instantly with cash *(dinero en efectivo)*" by rubbing Aladdin's lamp to make money appear miraculously. Part of the sales pitch is a series

of questions asking readers if they need a lot of money right now; if they are drowning in debts and outstanding bills; if they could use an instant money miracle to resolve financial problems; and if they would like to have all money worries vanish in seconds, as if by magic.

Additions to on-page notes

Culture: In connection with the *Preguntas,* you may want to add these *refranes* and *dichos* to question 5: *"En el peligro se conoce al amigo."* (A friend in need is a friend indeed.) *"En menos que canta un gallo."* (In an instant.) *"Está en las nubes."* (He's / She's daydreaming.)

PAGE 529
Photo
Outside the Arturo Merino Benítez International Airport, which is located approximately fifteen miles from Santiago, Chile's capital. In addition to Ecuatoriana and Aeroperú, the national airlines of Ecuador and Peru, this airport also serves U.S. and European carriers. Chile's international airline is Lan-Chile (Lan: Línea Aérea Nacional); internal flights, especially those to the northern coppermine regions, are handled primarily by LADECO (Línea Aérea del Cobre). Since 90 percent of Chile's population lives in the central section of the country, small private airlines provide limited service to more remote areas, flying out of Los Cerrillos, an airport about twenty minutes from Santiago.

Realia
A bilingual boarding pass from AeroPerú. AeroPerú, the national airline of Peru, handles international flights, and, together with Compañía de Aviación Faucett, controls most internal flights between Andean towns that are inaccessible by land.

Additions to on-page notes
Reteach / Review: You may want to point out the use of *estar* in mini-dialogue 5. Clarify the sentence by asking *¿Es Carlos una persona extraña? (No, no es una persona extraña, pero está extraño estos días.)*

PAGE 530
Photo
This couple beckons a porter outside the San Juan International Airport in Puerto Rico. The man is wearing a lightweight, short-sleeved shirt known as a *guayabera*, which is commonly worn by men in tropical areas of the Spanish-speaking world. The San Juan airport serves the largest number of travelers in the Caribbean, with close to two million people a year. Bilingual signs, such as the one here that allows stopping only to drop off passengers, are common in this U.S. commonwealth. Puerto Ricans are U.S. citizens and, therefore, do not need visas or passports to travel between the island and the U.S.

PAGE 533
Photo
A young woman between classes at the University of Cartagena, a national university founded in 1827. The academic year in Colombia runs from February to December. This relatively small university offers degree programs to approximately 4,000 students in law, medicine, dentistry, pharmaceutical chemistry, and other fields. In Colombia, as in other Latin American countries, students enter directly into their field of study instead of spending two or more years fulfilling a liberal-arts requirement as is the case in most U.S. universities. The walled city of Cartagena, with close to a million inhabitants, is surrounded by water, and is protected by forts built by the Spaniards to safeguard their treasures and supplies during the seventeenth and eighteenth centuries.

PAGE 535
Realia
This flyer promotes the versatility of one of the leading tour operators in Spain, Ultramar Express. The ad's boast of "all the vacations in the world" seems accurate, since this well-known company sells travel packages in Spain to travel agencies in the U.S. and other countries; Ultramar also organizes trips to other countries for Spaniards.

PAGE 538
Photo
The huge desert markings pictured here are the famous Nazca lines. While they are usually associated with the Nazca Indian civilization in Peru which reached its peak around A.D., 800 other archaeologists attribute them to three different Indian cultures, the oldest dating back to 900 B.C.

PAGE 539
Photo
Pictured here is another of the famous Peruvian Nazca line drawings. In addition to the two theories mentioned in the reading, several others are offered to explain these mysterious land markings. One theory speculated that the ancient Nazca Indians flew in hot-air balloons. Many of the figures show evidence of burn pits that many have been launch pads, supporting this view. In addition, Nazca ceramics and tapestries feature images of balloonists. Another theory suggests that the symmetrical lines were the tracks for running contests along which contestants raced. The mystery of the lines continues to intrigue many, including the popular U.S. actress Shirley MacLaine, who described her visit to this magical place in her book and made-for-TV movie, *Out on a Limb.*

PAGE 541
Photo
Pre-Columbian ruins of an Incan fortress named Sacsahuamán, which is situated on a hill outside the Peruvian city of Cuzco. Mystery surrounds the transporting of these huge stones—weighing up to 300 tons—to this site, over 9,000 feet above sea level. The rocks are fitted together with absolute perfection, and are not held in place by any type of cement or mortar. The zigzag pattern of the wall apparently housed ''*chincha* grooves,'' channels through which a type of beer made from corn flowed during Incan festivals.

PAGE 543
Photo
These Spanish teenagers enjoy a group dance similar to the Caribbean *conga* line. Spanish teenagers tend to spend leisure time in groups, delaying dating until the age of 17 or 18. While chaperones no longer accompany dating couples, most teens do not bring partners home until the romance has become serious. Typical dating activities are similar to those in the U.S.: eating out, and going to the movies, to the beach, or dancing.

PAGE 544
Photo
The Simón Bolívar International Airport in Maiquetía, a nearby suburb of Caracas Venezuela. The airport serves the national carrier, VIASA, which is also actively involved in promoting Venezuelan tourism abroad. Airlines are allowed to issue 60-day tourist cards to those visiting the country, but extended stays for business or pleasure need consulate-issued visas. The airport also serves other local airlines such as AVENSA, which handles both national and international traffic and Aeropostal, which primarily serves other areas of the Caribbean.

Answers to *Repaso*
1. Es posible que viajes a Costa Rica. / Es importante que Uds. paguen a Francisco. / Es probable que naveguemos a Mallorca.
2. Pero dudo que lleguemos pronto a la frontera. / Pero la Sra. López no cree que vuelvas (regreses) temprano a casa. / Pero sienten que yo no vuelva otra vez al parador.
3. Creemos que él juega bien, pero dudamos que él gane el partido (juego). / No niega que Ud. enseña bien, pero no cree que Ud. sea paciente. / No niego que pinta bien, pero no creo que entienda (comprenda) el arte.
4. Estamos orgullosos (orgullosas) de que Ud. trabaje con nosotros (nosotras). / Está enojado de que yo empiece sin él. / Están felices de que nosotros (nosotras) corramos con ellos (ellas).
5. ¡Qué sorpresa! Me alegro de que mis padrinos me acompañen. / ¡Qué lástima! Se preocupan de que sus nietos no los hallen (encuentren). / ¡Qué alivio! Se alegra de que nadie la reconozca.

PAGE 545

Answers to *Tema*

1. Es necesario que Diego y Miguel vuelen a Caracas.
2. Pero Diego teme que ellos lleguen tarde al aeropuerto.
3. Diego cree que el avión sale a tiempo, pero Miguel duda que él tenga razón.
4. Diego está preocupado de que el avión despegue sin ellos.
5. ¡Qué susto! Diego se alegra de que su amigo lo despierte.

PAGE 546

Answers to *Comprueba tu progreso*

A
1. pista
2. demora
3. aduana, declarar
4. registra
5. puerta de embarque
6. escala
7. viaje

B
1. b   4. b   7. a
2. b   5. b   8. a
3. a   6. b   9. b

C
1. Me enoja que gastemos tanto dinero.
2. Es importante que tengas un sentido del humor.
3. ¿Te alegras de que recibamos un sueldo tan grande?
4. A Jorge no le molesta que pidan consejos.
5. Me sorprende que descubra eso.
6. Nos alegramos de que María pase la tarde aquí.
7. Temo que Uds. no comprendan nada.
8. Sentimos que no puedan conocer a tus suegros.

D
1. El profesor no está seguro de que entiendan el significado de eso.
2. Dudan que me enoje con Andrés.
3. Te alegras de que compartamos el trabajo.
4. El jefe siente que no empieces a las nueve.
5. Dudamos que nuestro equipo siempre gane.
6. Laura no cree que la aduanera registre el equipaje.

E
1. Es imposible que vuelva a intentar.
2. Es necesario que termines temprano.

3. Es una lástima que deba tanto dinero.
4. Es mejor que no mientan.
5. Es importante que asistamos al espectáculo.
6. Es posible que traiga las joyas.

PAGE 547

Photo

A contemporary paper cutout made by Otomi Indians from the San Pablito village in East Central Mexico. Paper-making has been an important craft among Mexican Indians since pre-Columbian times. Historical records indicate that paper was manufactured and used throughout the region by the time the Spaniards arrived in 1519. The Aztecs valued handmade bark paper as an almost sacred substance. However, most authorities believe that it was the Mayas of the Yucatán Peninsula who were the first to produce paper in the region.

Among the Otomi Indians, paper figures are cut by the shamans, or medicine men. The cutout shown in the photograph or is used for crop-curing ceremonies. It is made of two different types of bark paper: the dark background is fig bark, and the light foreground is mulberry bark, which was cut and pasted on the darker paper.

ORAL PROFICIENCY TEST

Directed Response

1. Tell Diana you're happy that she can accompany you. *(Me alegra de que puedas acompañarme (me puedas acompañar).)*
2. Say that you don't believe the customs official will inspect anyone's luggage. *(No creo que el(la) aduanero(a) registre el equipaje de nadie.)*
3. Say that you're sorry Ana and Olga believe in so many superstitions. *(Siento que Ana y Olga crean en tantas supersticiones.)*

Picture-Cued Response

4. Pointing to the photograph on p. 524, say: "Me parece que las chicas están enojadas." Then ask: "¿Qué crees tú?" *(Creo que están contentas (de buen humor) OR No creo que estén enojadas.)*

5. Pointing to the visual on p. 526, ask questions such as: ¿Es posible que la lámpara sea verdadera? *(Sí (No), (no) es posible que sea verdadera.)*

6. Pointing to the photograph on p. 543, ask: "¿Dudas que estos jóvenes se diviertan?" *(No, no dudo que se diviertan.)*

Situations

7. Anita wants to ask her teacher for an extension on her term paper, but she decides today isn't the best day to ask. What might be wrong?
   a. *La profesora está de mal humor.*
   b. La profesora tiene mucha paciencia.
   c. La profesora tiene un gran sentido del humor.

8. Domingo just received a college scholarship. What might you say to him?
   a. *¡Qué alegría!*   b. ¡Qué lástima!
   c. ¿Qué importa?

Real-Life Questions

9. ¿Qué haces si sabes que alguien te está diciendo mentiras? ¿Por qué es difícil ser amigo(a) de una persona que miente?

10. ¿Quién es tu mejor amigo(a)? ¿Cómo es? ¿De qué cosas se preocupa? ¿De qué cosas se alegra?

ORAL PROFICIENCY TEST   CHAPTERS 13–16
Directed Response

1. Say that you were cooking when the telephone rang. *(Cocinaba cuando sonó el teléfono.)*

2. Ask Ernesto if he went to the store for bread. *(¿Fuiste a la tienda por pan?)*

3. Say that you think the plane will land on time. *(Creo que el avión aterrizará a tiempo.)*

Picture-Cued Response

4. Pointing to the photograph on p. 442, ask: "¿Qué celebra la familia?" *(Celebra el bautizo del bebé.)*

5. Pointing to the photograph on p. 443, ask: "¿Qué hacía el señor durante la fiesta?" *(Tocaba la guitarra durante la fiesta.)*

Situations

6. Tito offers to help Marta study for an exam. How might she politely tell him it's not necessary?
   a. *No te molestes.*   b. No me molestes.
   c. No me importa.

7. The loudspeaker has just announced that Catalina's flight is ready for boarding. Where should she go?
   a. A la pista.   b. A la aduana.
   c. *A la puerta de embarque.*

Real-Life Questions

8. ¿Con quiénes haces citas durante el año? ¿Puedes hablar con tus profesores después de las clases o tienes que hacer una cita primero?

9. Cuando eras niño(a), ¿dónde vivías?

10. ¿Cuándo te graduarás de la escuela? ¿Qué piensas hacer después?

11. Si estudias mucho, ¿es cierto que siempre recibirás buenas notas? ¿Niegas que saques mejores notas cuando estudias?

INDEX OF CULTURAL REFERENCES

TEACHER NOTES

TEACHER NOTES

TEACHER NOTES

TEACHER NOTES

PASOS Y PUENTES

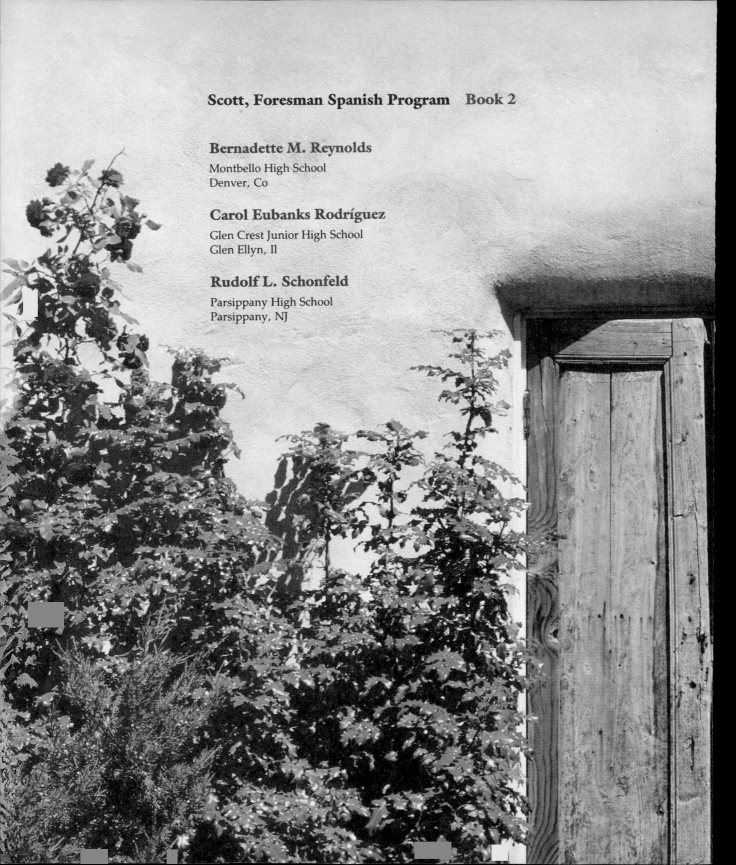

Scott, Foresman Spanish Program   Book 2

Bernadette M. Reynolds

Montbello High School
Denver, Co

Carol Eubanks Rodríguez

Glen Crest Junior High School
Glen Ellyn, Il

Rudolf L. Schonfeld

Parsippany High School
Parsippany, NJ

PASOS Y PUENTES

Scott, Foresman and Company

Editorial Offices: Glenview, Illinois

Regional Offices: Sunnyvale, California · Tucker, Georgia
Glenview, Illinois · Oakland, New Jersey · Dallas, Texas

ISBN: 0-673-20722-6

12345678910 RRC 9998979695949392919089 88

Acknowledgments of illustrations appear on page 611. The acknowledgments section should be considered an extension of the copyright page.

The authors and editors would like to express their heartfelt thanks to the following team of reader consultants. Each of them read the manuscript of all three levels of the Scott, Foresman Spanish Program. Chapter by chapter, each offered suggestions and provided encouragement. Their contribution has been invaluable.

Senior Reader Consultants

Estella M. Gahala, Ph.D.
National Foreign Language Consultant
Scott, Foresman and Company
Glenview, IL

Barbara Snyder, Ph.D.
Parma Public Schools
Parma, OH

Reader Consultants

Sheila Starr Ashley
Radnor High School
Radnor, PA

Elaine W. Baer
Foreign Language Dept. Chairperson
John Bartram High School
Philadelphia, PA

Barbara M. Berry, Ph.D.
Foreign Language Dept. Chairperson
Ypsilanti Public Schools
Ypsilanti, MI

Anna Budiwsky
Cardinal O'Hara High School
Springfield, PA

Susan R. Cole
San Francisco USD
San Francisco, CA

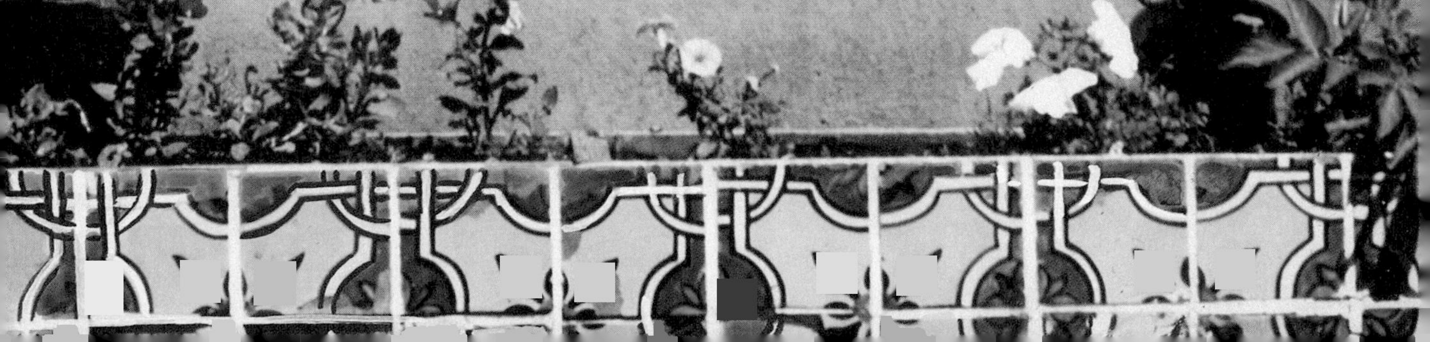

TABLA DE MATERIAS

CAPÍTULO 4

CAPÍTULO 5

CAPÍTULO 6

CAPÍTULO 7

CAPÍTULO 8

CAPÍTULO 9

CAPÍTULO 10

CAPÍTULO 11

CAPÍTULO 12

CAPÍTULO 13

CAPÍTULO 14

CAPÍTULO 15

CAPÍTULO 16

REPASO

REPASO

Práctica A
Review of greetings,
classroom vocabulary.
Answers will vary.

A **¡Hola!** Estás en la escuela otra vez, después de unas largas vacaciones. Mira los dibujos y las palabras siguientes para preparar un diálogo para cada situación.

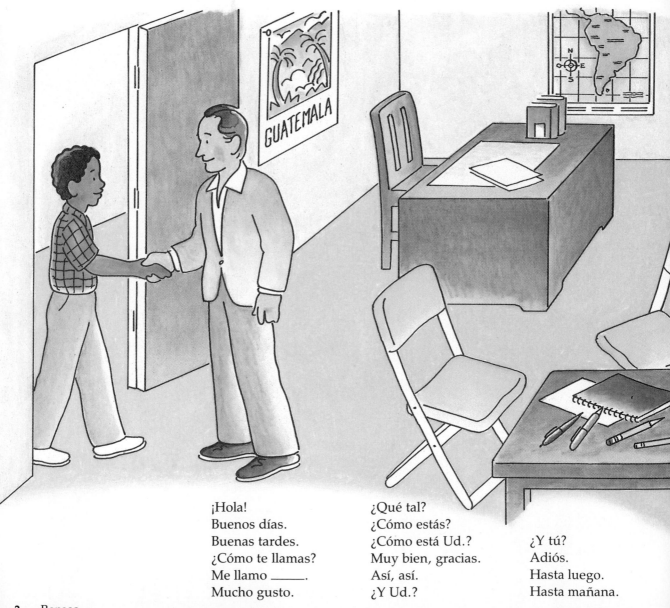

¡Hola!	¿Qué tal?	
Buenos días.	¿Cómo estás?	
Buenas tardes.	¿Cómo está Ud.?	¿Y tú?
¿Cómo te llamas?	Muy bien, gracias.	Adiós.
Me llamo ___.	Así, así.	Hasta luego.
Mucho gusto.	¿Y Ud.?	Hasta mañana.

B Las estaciones. Contesta según los dibujos.

Notes: You may want to do the first two sections of Ex. B as a whole-class activity. Then ask pairs to prepare answers for the third and fourth sections. Volunteers may present their answers to the class.

The questions in Ex. B may also be used for written work. Check students' work for correct spelling, capitalization, and punctuation.

Práctica B
Review of weather, calendar, days of the week, months, seasons, rooms of the house, -ar verbs.

1. a. Hoy es domingo.
   b. Es el veintiocho de junio.
   c. Es verano.
   d. Junio, julio, agosto (y septiembre).
   e. Hace calor.
   f. Están en la piscina.
   g. Nadan.
   h. Answers will vary.

1. a. ¿Qué día es hoy?
   b. ¿Cuál es la fecha?
   c. ¿Qué estación del año es?
   d. ¿Cuáles son los meses de esta estación?
   e. ¿Qué tiempo hace?
   f. ¿Dónde están los chicos?
   g. ¿Qué hacen los chicos?
   h. ¿Qué haces tú durante el verano?

2. a. Es otoño.
   b. Septiembre, octubre, noviembre (y diciembre).
   c. Hoy es viernes.
   d. Es el tres de octubre.
   e. (Practican) fútbol americano.
   f. Hace fresco y viento.
   g. Answers will vary.

2. a. ¿Qué estación del año es?
   b. ¿Cuáles son los meses de esta estación?
   c. ¿Qué día es hoy?
   d. ¿Cuál es la fecha?
   e. ¿Qué deporte practican?
   f. ¿Qué tiempo hace?
   g. ¿Qué haces tú durante esta estación?

3. a. ¿Cuál es la fecha?
   b. ¿Qué día es hoy?
   c. ¿Qué tiempo hace?
   d. ¿Qué hacen los chicos?
   e. ¿Qué estación del año es?
   f. ¿Cuáles son los meses de esta estación?
   g. ¿Qué te gusta hacer cuando hace frío?

3. a. Es el primero de febrero.
   b. Hoy es sábado.
   c. Hace frío. Nieva.
   d. Esquían.
   e. Es invierno.
   f. Diciembre, enero, febrero (y marzo).
   g. Answers will vary.

4. a. ¿Llueve o nieva?
   b. ¿Cuál es la fecha?
   c. ¿Qué estación del año es?
   d. ¿Cuáles son los meses de esta estación?
   e. ¿Dónde están los niños?
   f. ¿Qué hacen?
   g. ¿Dónde están sus padres? ¿Qué leen?
   h. ¿Te gusta la primavera? ¿Por qué?

4. a. Llueve.
   b. Es el catorce de abril.
   c. Es primavera.
   d. Marzo, abril, mayo (y junio).
   e. Están en la cocina.
   f. Lavan (los) platos.
   g. Están en la sala. Leen el periódico.
   h. Answers will vary.

Práctica C
Review of *gustar / prefiero*,
infinitives.
Answers will vary.

Notes: Ex. C may be used as
a chain drill or as pair work with
role switching.

C **Según el calendario.** ¿Qué te gusta hacer durante cada estación del
año? Pregunta y contesta según el modelo.

el invierno

ESTUDIANTE A ¿*Te gusta nadar en el invierno?*
ESTUDIANTE B *No, no me gusta. Prefiero esquiar.*
o: *Sí, me encanta.*

el invierno	nadar	ir a la escuela
la primavera	jugar al tenis	trabajar en el jardín
el verano	montar en bicicleta	jugar al golf
el otoño	jugar al béisbol	ir al campo
	ir de vacaciones	jugar al volibol
	viajar	jugar al básquetbol
	esquiar	tomar limonada
	jugar al fútbol americano	tomar chocolate
	ir de compras	ir al parque

Práctica D
Review of months, dates,
numbers, *más / menos / sin.*
Answers will vary.

Notes: If you have a large
class, you may want students to
work in small groups to ask and
answer the questions in Ex. D.
Volunteers from each group
may write the dates on the
board. When the results are in,
ask students to work
individually or in pairs to
prepare oral or written answers
to the questions. Circulate to
give help as needed.

D **¿Cuándo es tu cumpleaños?** Pregúntale a la persona que está a tu
lado *(side)* cuándo es su cumpleaños. Otro estudiante escribe las
fechas en la pizarra. Sigue el modelo.

ESTUDIANTE A ¿*Cuándo es tu cumpleaños?*
ESTUDIANTE B *Es el _____ de _____.*
ESTUDIANTE A *El cumpleaños de* (nombre) *es el _____ de _____.*

Ahora contesta las siguientes preguntas.

1. ¿Cuántos estudiantes tienen cumpleaños en enero? ¿En febrero?
   ¿En marzo, etc.?
2. ¿En qué mes hay más cumpleaños?
3. ¿En qué mes hay menos cumpleaños?
4. ¿Hay meses sin cumpleaños? ¿Cuáles son?
5. ¿En qué mes hay más cumpleaños de chicos? ¿De chicas?
6. ¿En qué mes es el cumpleaños de la persona a tu derecha?
   ¿de la persona a tu izquierda? ¿de tu mejor amigo(a)?

¡Feliz cumpleaños!

E De compras. Imagina que vas de compras. ¿Qué vas a comprar? Pregunta y contesta según el modelo.

ESTUDIANTE A *¿Qué desea Ud., señor(ita)?*

ESTUDIANTE B *Necesito lápices. ¿Cuánto cuestan?*

ESTUDIANTE A *Veinticinco pesos.*

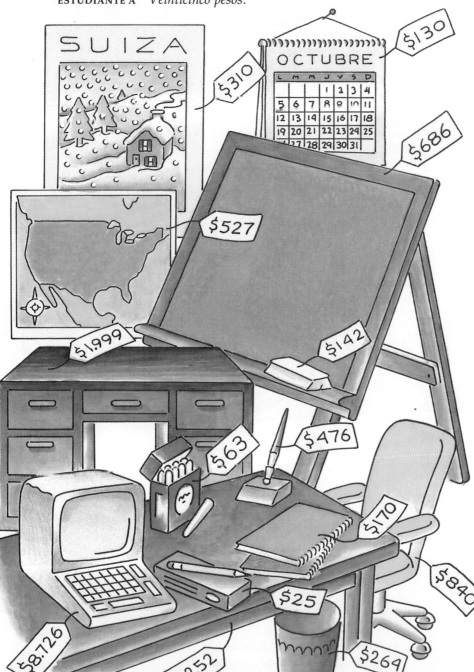

1. ¿A qué hora dan "Somos de la Luna"? A las dos.
2. ¿..."Pregunta y contesta"? A las cuatro menos diez.
3. ¿..."La hora mexicana"? A las cuatro y cuarto.
4. ¿...el "Fútbol americano"? A las cinco y cuarto.
5. ¿..."Estudiantes de Kung Fu"? A las siete y media.
6. ¿..."Qué pasa"? A las ocho.
7. ¿..."Cine de hoy"? A las ocho y media.
8. ¿..."Cocina con Carolina"? A las once menos veinte.
9. ¿..."¡No me digas!"? A las once.

F **¿A qué hora?** Imagina que tú y un(a) amigo(a) quieren saber a qué hora dan los siguientes programas de televisión. Pregunta y contesta según el modelo.

¡HOY!
EN EL CANAL 8

13:30
El pájaro loco—Dibujos animados con Paco el Pájaro

14:00
Somos de la luna—Película de ciencia ficción divertida para toda la familia

15:50
Pregunta y contesta—Juego de preguntas

16:15
La hora mexicana—Música y bailes folklóricos

17:15
Fútbol americano—Los Osos y los Leones

19:30
Estudiantes de Kung Fu—Programa de aventuras

20:00
¿Qué pasa?—Noticias de hoy

20:30
Cine de hoy: La montaña negra—Una película del oeste con Verónica Vaquera

22:40
Cocina con Carolina—Hoy enseña cómo cocinar una tortilla española

23:00
¡No me digas!—Las cosas más fantásticas de esta semana

El **8** ¡El canal para su vida!

Notes: Ask students to work in pairs to ask and answer the questions in Ex. F. Time allowing, ask students *¿A qué hora dan _____?* about TV programs they are familiar with.

ESTUDIANTE A *¿A qué hora dan "El Pájaro Loco"?*
ESTUDIANTE B *A la una y media.*

G ¿Cómo son? Escoge adjetivos de la lista para describir a las siguientes personas. Recuerda (*Remember*) que los adjetivos tienen que corresponder en género y número (*agree in gender and number*) con los nombres o pronombres.

Mi madre
Mi madre es alta, guapa y muy lista.

1. El (La) estudiante a mi derecha (izquierda)
2. (Yo)
3. Mi amigo (*nombre*) y yo
4. Mi mejor amigo(a)
5. Mi profesor(a) de español
6. Mi profesor(a) de (*materia*)

aburrido	feo	moreno
alto	gordo	pelirrojo
antipático	grande	pequeño
bajo	guapo	rubio
bilingüe	inteligente	simpático
bonito	joven	tonto
delgado	listo	viejo

Ahora, diles (*tell them*) a estas personas como tú crees que son.

7. Tu profesor(a) de español: "Señor(a), . . . "
8. Tu mejor amigo(a): "(*Nombre*), . . . "
9. Un miembro de tu familia: "(*Nombre*), . . . '
10. Dos personas que se parecen (*are alike*): "(*Nombres*), . . . "

Práctica G
Review of adjectives, *ser, tú* vs. *usted(es).*
Answers will vary.

Notes: The first part of this exercise is appropriate for written work. You may want to ask students to write the six sentences at home. After checking their work for correct spelling, capitalization, and punctuation, ask volunteers to present their answers for items 7 through 10 to the class.

Práctica H
Review of family members, possessive *de*.
1. la esposa / esposo
2. el hermano / hermana
3. los padres / hijos
4. la tía / sobrinos
5. el tío / sobrina
6. los padres / hija / hijo / los abuelos

Notes: Ask students to study the family tree and to read silently each of the six items in Ex. H. Then complete the exercise as a whole-class activity, asking volunteers to read the sentences aloud using the appropriate terms.

Before students begin Ex. I, you may want a volunteer to model the first item for the rest of the class. Then ask students to work in pairs to describe the clothing shown in the visuals. If time allows, students may enjoy talking about each other's clothing.

H La familia Torres. Completa las frases según el dibujo.

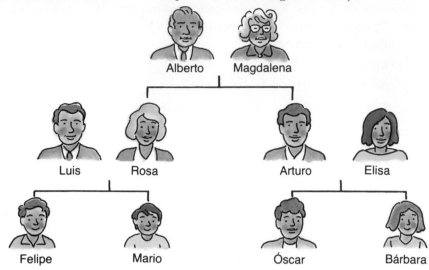

1. Magdalena es *(la madre / la tía / la esposa)* de Alberto. Alberto es su *(tío / esposo / padre)*.
2. Óscar es *(el primo / el hermano / el tío)* de Bárbara. Bárbara es su *(hermana / prima / tía)*.
3. Elisa y Arturo son *(los padres / los abuelos / los hermanos)* de Óscar y Bárbara. Óscar y Bárbara son sus *(primos / padres / hijos)*.
4. Elisa es *(la tía / la prima / la hermana)* de Felipe y Mario. Felipe y Mario son sus *(hijos / primos / sobrinos)*.
5. Luis es *(el padre / el tío / el hermano)* de Bárbara. Bárbara es su *(sobrina / hija / esposa)*.
6. Alberto y Magdalena son *(los padres / los tíos / los hijos)* de Rosa y Arturo. Rosa es su *(hermana / prima / hija)* y Arturo es su *(hermano / hijo / primo)*. Alberto y Magdalena son *(los abuelos / los padres / los tíos)* de los cuatro niños de la familia.

Práctica I
Review of clothing, colors.
1. Carmen lleva un vestido verde y zapatos negros.
2. Pedro lleva jeans, una camiseta amarilla, una chaqueta gris, calcetines amarillos y zapatos blancos.
3. Marta lleva una falda morada, una blusa blanca y botas negras.

I ¿Qué llevan hoy? Describe la ropa de cada persona.

1. Carmen   2. Pedro   3. Marta

4. Federico   5. Elena   6. Javier   7. Magdalena

4. Federico lleva un traje negro, una camisa blanca, calcetines grises y zapatos negros.
5. Elena lleva pantalones marrones, un suéter anaranjado y blanco y zapatos marrones.
6. Javier lleva un abrigo azul, una bufanda roja y verde, guantes negros y botas marrones.
7. Magdalena lleva un impermeable amarillo, botas azules y un paraguas azul y amarillo.

Práctica J
Review of *prefiero/prefieres*, foods.

1. ¿Cuál prefieres, sandwiches de jamón o hamburguesas? Prefiero…
2. ¿…jamón o queso?
3. ¿…jamón o chile con carne?
4. ¿…papas fritas o ensalada?
5. ¿…helado o yogur?
6. ¿…papas o pan?
7. ¿…burritos o tacos?
8. ¿…mantequilla o queso?

J **¿Cuál prefieres?** Imagina que tu y un(a) amigo(a) están en un restaurante. Pregunta y contesta según el modelo.

ESTUDIANTE A   *¿Cuál prefieres, leche o limonada?*
ESTUDIANTE B   *Prefiero leche.*
        o: *Prefiero limonada.*

Una familia mira la
televisión en Madrid,
España.

K **¿Sí o no?** Lee *(Read)* las siguientes frases. Si la frase es verdad, contesta *sí.* Si no es verdad, contesta *no,* y da *(give)* la información correcta. Sigue el modelo.

> Hablo francés y español.
> *Sí.*
> o: *No, no hablo francés y español.*

1. Vivo lejos de la escuela.
2. Voy a la escuela en autobús.
3. Asistimos a clase los sábados.
4. Me encanta la clase de español.
5. Mis padres y yo hablamos español en casa.
6. Voy a viajar a España mañana.
7. Tengo muchos primos.
8. Soy hijo(a) único(a).
9. Tengo muchos hermanos.
10. Mis amigos y yo nunca miramos la televisión.
11. Me encanta ayudar en casa.
12. Voy a una fiesta el sábado por la noche.

L Por la mañana. Contesta las preguntas según los dibujos.

¡Hasta luego!

Sra. Alba

Miguel

Sara

$3A^2 + 6AB - 7B^2 = ?$

David

1. ¿Dónde está la familia Alba?
2. ¿Qué hora es?
3. ¿Qué hace Miguel?
4. ¿Qué hace David?
5. ¿Qué come Sara?
6. ¿Qué bebe ella?
7. ¿Qué lleva Sara?
8. ¿Qué hace el gato?
9. ¿Llega o sale la Sra. Alba?
10. ¿Adónde crees que va?

Práctica L
Review of 3 sing. regular and irregular verb forms.
1. En la cocina.
2. Son las siete y diez (de la mañana).
3. Lava los platos.
4. Hace la tarea.
5. Come pan y mantequilla.
6. Bebe jugo de naranja.
7. Sara lleva jeans y un suéter marrón y anaranjado.
8. Bebe leche.
9. Sale.
10. Creo que va a trabajar (*or:* a la oficina).

Notes: You may want to lead Ex. L in a large group, encouraging rapid recitation. Then ask students to work in pairs to ask and answer questions about their own morning routines.

M El horario de Mónica. Lee el horario de Mónica y contesta las preguntas.

Colegio Superior Miguel Ángel

HORARIO

8:15 – 9:00	Álgebra	B-203	Sra. Ruiz
9:05 – 9:50	Historia	B-115	Sr. Ortega
9:55 –10:40	Español	A-200	Sr. Pardo
10:45 –11:30	Arte	A-209	Srta. Gasteazoro
11:35 –12:00	Almuerzo	Cafetería	
12:05 –12:50	Química	Laboratorio	Sra. Bolívar
12:55 – 1:40	Francés	A-201	Sr. Gómez
1:45 – 2:30	Educación física	Gimnasio	Sra. Borges

1. ¿Cuándo empieza la primera clase?
2. ¿Cuál es?
3. ¿Quién enseña historia?
4. ¿Qué materia enseña la Sra. Bolívar?
5. ¿Dónde enseña la Sra. Bolívar?
6. ¿Cuándo termina el almuerzo?
7. ¿Qué clase tiene Mónica a las dos menos cuarto? ¿Dónde es la clase?
8. ¿Dónde come?

N En la biblioteca. Contesta las preguntas.

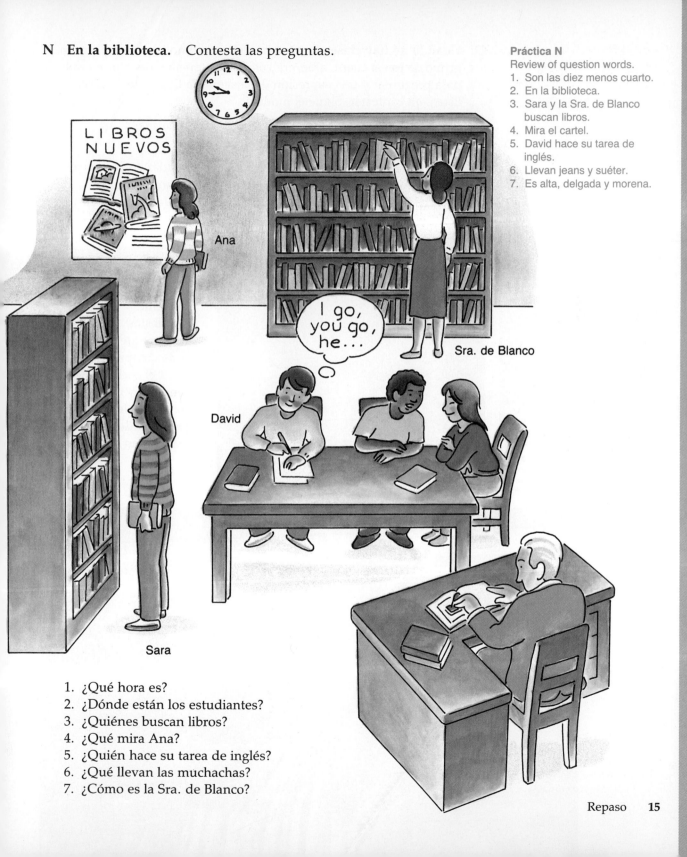

Práctica N
Review of question words.
1. Son las diez menos cuarto.
2. En la biblioteca.
3. Sara y la Sra. de Blanco buscan libros.
4. Mira el cartel.
5. David hace su tarea de inglés.
6. Llevan jeans y suéter.
7. Es alta, delgada y morena.

1. ¿Qué hora es?
2. ¿Dónde están los estudiantes?
3. ¿Quiénes buscan libros?
4. ¿Qué mira Ana?
5. ¿Quién hace su tarea de inglés?
6. ¿Qué llevan las muchachas?
7. ¿Cómo es la Sra. de Blanco?

Práctica O
Review of *-ar* verbs and *ir*.
Answers will vary.

O Cuando no hay clases. ¿Qué haces cuando no hay clases? En un grupo de tres o cuatro alumnos, usa una expresión de la primera lista para preguntar y una expresión de la segunda lista y de la tercera lista para contestar. Sigue el modelo.

ESTUDIANTE A *¿Qué haces los sábados por la mañana?*
ESTUDIANTE B *Bueno, a veces practico deportes.*

los sábados por la mañana	a menudo	ayudar en la cocina
los sábados por la tarde	a veces	cocinar
los sábados por la noche	nunca	cuidar a los niños
	siempre	escribir cartas

escuchar la radio
estudiar
hablar por teléfono
ir al campo
ir al cine
ir a fiestas
ir al parque
ir de compras
lavar el coche
limpiar mi dormitorio
mirar la televisión
practicar deportes
trabajar en el garaje

(izquierda) En España; (derecha) Cerca de la ciclovía en Bogotá, Colombia; (abajo) En Madrid, España

P **¿Qué hacen todos?** Describe qué hacen todas estas personas. Usa una palabra o expresión de cada columna para hacer frases completas. Sigue el modelo.

Práctica P
Review of *-ar / -er / -ir* verbs.
Answers will vary.

(nosotras)
Trabajamos en el jardín.

(nosotros)	aprender de memoria	a la profesora de matemáticas
Elena	asistir	a los niños
(yo)	ayudar	a una clase bilingüe
(tú)	cuidar	el autobús
Pedro y yo	esperar	el garaje
Rogelio y Enrique	estudiar	el horario
Ud.	hablar	el sol
tus amigos y tú	lavar	en bicicleta
el profesor	limpiar	en casa
	mirar	en el jardín
	montar	en el laboratorio
	repasar	fotos
	sacar	la guitarra
	terminar	la lección de química
	tocar	la tarea
	tomar	la televisión
	trabajar	los platos
		los poemas españoles
		para la prueba de álgebra
		por teléfono

En España

Práctica Q
Review of question words, question formation.
Choice of questions may vary.
1. a. ¿Quiénes van a una tienda de ropa?
   b. ¿Adónde van Inés y Jorge?
   c. ¿Qué buscan?
   d. ¿Por qué buscan una chaqueta?
   e. ¿Cuándo es el cumpleaños de Lolita?
2. a. ¿Quién está en casa?
   b. ¿Dónde está Norma?
   c. ¿Cómo está Norma?
   d. ¿Por qué está preocupada?
   e. ¿Cuándo tiene (or: hay) un examen de historia?
   f. ¿Qué tiene que hacer?
3. a. ¿De dónde son los estudiantes?
   b. ¿Quiénes son de España / México / Puerto Rico?
   c. ¿Cuántos estudiantes hay en la clase de inglés?
   d. ¿Con quién habla Esteban?

Práctica R
Review of *ir*, modes of transportation.
1. Voy a la piscina en bicicleta.
2. Vamos al aeropuerto en taxi.
3. Luis y Carolina van al cine en coche.

Q ¿Qué compramos? Lee los párrafos y usa las palabras que siguen para hacer preguntas.

1. Inés y Jorge van a una tienda de ropa. Buscan una chaqueta para su hermanita, Lolita, porque mañana es su cumpleaños. Quieren comprar una chaqueta bonita pero barata.

   a. ¿Quiénes?   b. ¿Adónde?   c. ¿Qué?   d. ¿Por qué?
   e. ¿Cuándo?

2. Norma está en casa hoy. Está bastante preocupada. Mañana hay un examen de historia y tiene que estudiar. Siempre saca buenas notas.

   a. ¿Quién?   b. ¿Dónde?   c. ¿Cómo?   d. ¿Por qué?
   e. ¿Cuándo?   f. ¿Qué?

3. Hay seis estudiantes en la clase de inglés. Esteban y María son de España. Rafael, Gregorio y Lourdes son de México y Gustavo es de Puerto Rico. Esteban habla con el profesor.

   a. ¿De dónde?   b. ¿Quiénes?   c. ¿Cuántos?   d. ¿Con quién?

R ¿Adónde van? Según los dibujos, indica adónde van estas personas y cómo van. Sigue el modelo.

(tú)
Vas al Perú en avión.

1. (yo)   2. (nosotros)   3. Luis y Carolina

4. mis padres

5. Teresa y yo

6. Sara

4. Mis padres van a la iglesia a pie.
5. Teresa y yo vamos al teatro en autobús.
6. Sara va al restaurante en moto.
7. Felipe va a la plaza en metro.
8. Los turistas van a España en barco.
9. El Sr. Ávila va a la estación en camión,

7. Felipe

8. los turistas

9. el Sr. Ávila

S **Mañana es sábado.** Imagina que hablas con unos amigos sobre lo que Uds. van a hacer el sábado. Forma frases completas con la forma correcta de *ir a*, un verbo de la segunda lista y una palabra o expresión de las otras dos listas. Sigue el modelo.

> *Cecilia va a cuidar a los niños españoles.*

(nosotros)	asistir a	a mis padres	aburrido
Elena	ayudar	bicicleta	barato
Jorge y María	comer en	el apartamento	blanco
Pablo y yo	comprar	el cine	cómodo
(tú)	cuidar a	el examen	de geometría
Uds.	escribir	el tren	en el patio
Ud.	escuchar	un restaurante	enorme
(yo)	estudiar para	la biblioteca	español
Cecilia	hacer	la ciudad	hoy
	ir a	la ropa	la próxima semana
	lavar	la tarea	mexicano
	leer	los niños	moderno
	limpiar	un partido de _____	por la mañana
	montar en	un suéter	rubio
	tomar	una carta	sucio
	trabajar en	unos discos	

Práctica T
Review of *estar* with prepositions.
Answers will vary.

Notes: You may want to help students prepare for Ex. T by asking questions about the location of classroom objects. For example: *¿Dónde está la pizarra? ¿Está a la izquierda de la puerta?*

T ¿Dónde está . . . ? Imagina que estás en la plaza y le preguntas a un policía dónde están los siguientes lugares (places). Usa las preposiciones de la lista. Pregunta y contesta. Por ejemplo:

ESTUDIANTE A	*¿Dónde está la farmacia? ¿Está lejos?*
ESTUDIANTE B	*No, no está lejos. Está entre el cine y el banco.*
ESTUDIANTE A	*Muchas gracias.*
ESTUDIANTE B	*De nada.*

a la izquierda de	enfrente de	entre
a la derecha de	delante de	lejos (de)
al lado de	detrás de	cerca (de)

U **¿Por qué no vienes?** Mucha gente no puede ir al teatro hoy. Para cada persona de la lista de la izquierda, escoge *(choose)* una excusa de la lista de la derecha. Pregunta y contesta según el modelo.

ESTUDIANTE A *¿Por qué no viene Roberto con nosotros?*
ESTUDIANTE B *Tiene que hacer la tarea.*

1. (tú)
2. ellos
3. Sara
4. Uds.
5. el Sr. Gómez
6. Ud.
7. las muchachas
8. tu amiga y tú

estudiar para un examen
cuidar a su hermanita
trabajar
hacer la tarea
hablar con su profesor
ir de compras
cocinar
ir a la oficina
practicar fútbol
esperar a su hermano
ir a los quince años de una sobrina

Notes: Review the present-tense forms of *venir* and *tener* before students begin Ex. U. Then ask pairs of students to practice asking and answering the questions. Circulate to give help as needed; encourage rapid recitation.

Práctica U
Review of *venir / tener que.*
Answers will vary.

(izquierda) La entrada del Palacio de Bellas Artes en México; (derecha) El Palacio de Bellas Artes en México

V ¿Qué haces? Con un(a) compañero(a) haz preguntas (*ask questions*) según los dibujos. Tu compañero(a) puede contestar con expresiones de la lista o dar otras respuestas apropiadas (*appropriate*). Sigue el modelo.

ESTUDIANTE A   *¿Qué haces cuando tienes sed?*
ESTUDIANTE B   *Bebo una limonada.*

1.

2.

3.

4.

5.

6.

7.

8.

beber (un(a)) _____	hablar con _____
buscar un restaurante / un café	ir a(l) _____
cantar	llamar a(l) _____
comer (un(a)) _____	llevar _____
correr	no hacer nada
estar contento(a) / triste	sacar una buena / mala nota

(izquierda) Unos jóvenes compran helados en Madrid, España;
(derecha) Dos amigos en un café en Bogotá, Colombia; (abajo)
Un día de lluvia en Madrid, España

W ¿Qué tienes ganas de hacer? Di *(tell)* qué tienen que hacer estas personas y qué quieren hacer. Sigue el modelo.

Cecilia

Cecilia tiene ganas de nadar, pero tiene que cuidar a los niños.

1. Carlos

2. (tú)

3. (nosotras)

4. tú y yo

5. Bernardo y Felipe

6. Uds.

7. (yo)

8. Ud.

X Una carta de Elizabeth.   Elizabeth le escribe a una amiga que vive en Puerto Rico. Usa la forma correcta de los verbos entre paréntesis *(parentheses)* para ayudarla a escribir la carta.

Querida Luisa:

¿Qué tal? ¿Cómo *(estar)*? Nosotros *(estar)* muy bien. Mi hermano Paul y yo *(asistir)* a un nuevo colegio donde *(estudiar)* español. Nuestra profesora de español *(ser)* muy simpática. (Nosotros) *(comprender)*
5 español muy bien y *(tener)* mucha tarea. (Yo) *(trabajar)* mucho en clase y siempre *(sacar)* buenas notas. Paul no *(trabajar)* mucho y nunca *(escuchar)* en clase. (Yo) *(leer)* todas las lecciones y *(escribir)* todos los ejercicios

(Tú) *(aprender)* inglés, ¿verdad? ¿Te gusta? ¿Por qué no *(escribir)*
10 una carta en inglés? ¿Y cuándo *(venir)* tú a los Estados Unidos? ¿El verano próximo? ¡Ojalá! (Yo) *(tener)* muchas ganas de hablar contigo.

Hasta luego,

Elizabeth

Práctica X
Review of verbs.
estás / estamos
asistimos / estudiamos
es / comprendemos
tenemos / trabajo
saco / trabaja
escucha / leo / escribo
aprendes / escribes
vienes
tengo

Dos estudiantes en la Universidad de Puerto Rico en San Juan

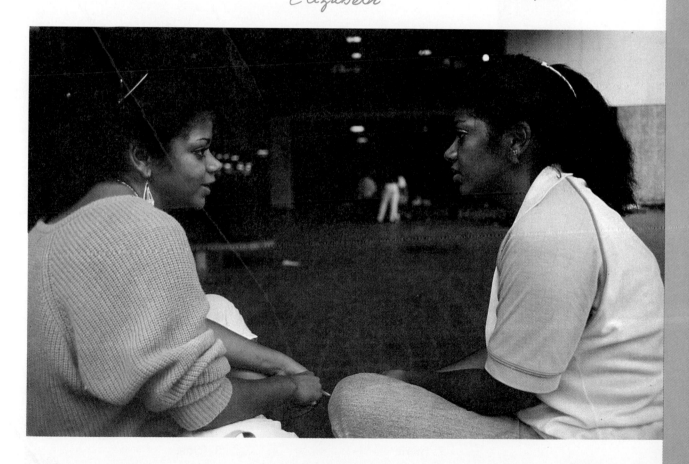

Y **¿Con quién vas?** Todo el mundo va a la fiesta el viernes. ¿Quién va con quién? Pregunta y contesta según el modelo.

ESTUDIANTE A	*¿Con quién va Elena?*
ESTUDIANTE B	*Va contigo.*

1. Pedro y Juan   2. (tú)

3. Uds.   4. Bernardo

5. Eduardo y Teresa   6. tu novio(a)

7. Silvia   8. Uds.

Dos amigas en Barcelona, España

Z Hablemos de ti.

1. ¿Cómo te llamas?
2. ¿Cuál es el nombre de la persona a tu izquierda? ¿a tu derecha? ¿Cuál es su apellido?
3. ¿Cuál es tu dirección? ¿Cuál es tu número de teléfono?
4. ¿Cuántos años tienes? ¿Cuándo es tu cumpleaños?
5. ¿Cómo eres?
6. ¿Cuál es la fecha de hoy? ¿Qué tiempo hace?
7. ¿Qué vas a hacer esta noche? ¿Qué vas a hacer durante el fin de semana?
8. ¿Cuál es tu materia favorita? ¿En qué materias estás flojo(a)? ¿En cuáles estás fuerte?
9. ¿Qué materias son fáciles para ti? ¿Cuáles son difíciles?

Práctica Z
Review of ability to answer questions about oneself (interviews, filling out forms, etc.)
Answers will vary.

Notes: Tell students that these questions are meant to give them a chance to talk about themselves. Through the **Hablemos de ti** questions, students will learn about their classmates' families, daily lives, opinions, interests, plans, and ambitions.

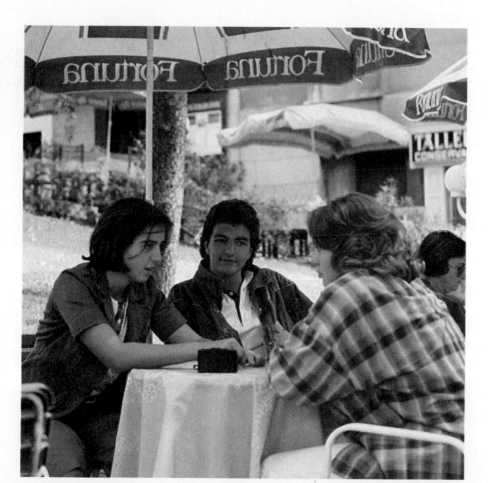

Tres jóvenes en un café en España

CAPÍTULO 1

PRÓLOGO CULTURAL

LA VIDA ESCOLAR

School is school no matter where you live. In Maine or Mexico, Arkansas or Argentina, students study, teachers teach, and there are textbooks, tests, and homework.

There are, however, a few major differences between our schools and those in most Spanish-speaking countries. For example, most Latin American high-school students must take 10 or 12 courses every year, and there are no electives. Instead of having classes in all subjects every day, students usually study each subject two or three times a week.

Another major difference is the lack of emphasis on sports at school. Though most high schools offer physical education, not too many have teams that compete with those of other schools. Instead, local clubs most often sponsor sports teams.

School holidays are also very different. In much of South America, summer vacation falls between November and February, which means that there is no separate Christmas vacation. And national holidays are different too, of course. Argentina's Independence Day, for example, is in the middle of winter—on July 9. It was on that date in 1816 that José de San Martín led the provinces of what is now Argentina to declare South America's independence from Spain.

There are many more private schools in Spanish-speaking countries than in the United States. Particularly popular are the international or foreign schools, where some of the subjects are taught in a language other than Spanish. English, French, and German schools are located in many major Spanish-speaking cities.

Some schools in Spanish-speaking countries host exchange students from the United States. In a year or two you might want to share in that exciting experience.

PALABRAS NUEVAS I

Essential

La América Central

Reteach / Review: Use a wall map to point out or to elicit the names of the countries in Central America and the Spanish-speaking Caribbean.

Transparency 1
CONTEXTO VISUAL

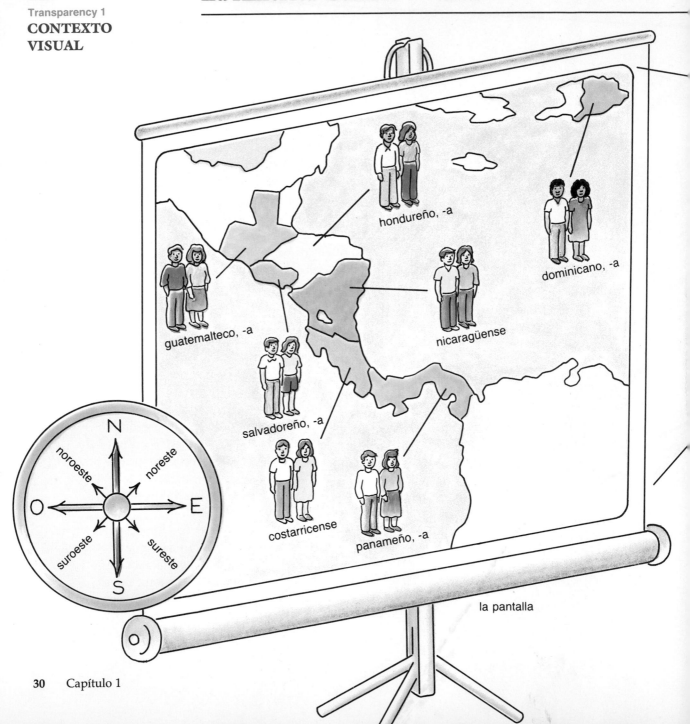

hondureño, -a

dominicano, -a

guatemalteco, -a

nicaragüense

salvadoreño, -a

costarricense

panameño, -a

la pantalla

N
noroeste   noreste
O   E
suroeste   sureste
S

el proyector

la diapositiva

CONTEXTO COMUNICATIVO  2

1 EVA   La diapositiva **siguiente** es de Guatemala.

   CÉSAR ¿En qué **parte** de la América Central está Guatemala?

   EVA   Está al sureste de México.

   CÉSAR ¿Cuántos **habitantes** hay en Guatemala?

   EVA   **Quizás** ocho **millones.***

   CÉSAR ¿Y qué lengua hablan?

   EVA   ¡El español, por supuesto!

Variaciones:

- diapositiva → foto
- Guatemala → Honduras *(3 veces)*
  sureste de México → noroeste de Nicaragua
  ocho millones → cuatro millones
- lengua →**idioma**

siguiente *nexl, following*
la parte *part*

el / la habitante *inhabitant*
quizás = tal vez
el millón, *pl.* **millones (de)**
  million

el idioma = la lengua

* When we use *millón (millones)* with a noun, we add *de*. For example: *cinco millones de habitantes*. Note that in English we use the singular form: "five million inhabitants."

Palabras Nuevas I   **31**

2 JUANA ¿Cuántos meses dura **el año escolar** en Costa Rica?
ÁNGEL Nueve. De septiembre a junio.
JUANA Dura el **mismo** tiempo que en Panamá, ¿verdad?
ÁNGEL Creo que sí.

■ Panamá → los Estados Unidos

el año escolar *school year*

mismo, -a *same*

3 DAVID ¿Qué piensas de la profesora Durán?
MARTA La **admiro** mucho. **Explica** muy bien las lecciones.
DAVID Pues yo no comprendo bien lo que ella enseña.
MARTA Entonces debes **prestar** más **atención** en clase.

■ explica → enseña

admirar *to admire*
explicar *to explain*
prestar atención *to pay attention*

Reteach / Review: You may want to ask students to vary mini-dialogue 3: *la profesora Durán → el profesor Gómez.* Elicit **Variaciones** for *la hija* in 4.

4 JORGE ¿Quién es esa chica?
PABLO Es la hija del **director.**
JORGE ¿Asiste a una escuela **pública**?
PABLO No, va a un **colegio particular.** Por eso lleva un **uniforme** azul.

■ del director → de la directora

el director, la directora *(school) principal*
público, -a *public*
el colegio particular *private school*
el uniforme *uniform*

EN OTRAS PARTES

Notes: The **En otras partes** is for enrichment, and the vocabulary is not considered active. You may want to assign this section for homework. Encourage students to add other regional variants that they know.

el colegio particular

También se dice *la transparencia.*

También se dice *el colegio privado.*

PRÁCTICA

A ¿De dónde son? David encontró a mucha gente cuando viajó por la América Central y el Caribe. Mira sus fotos y di *(tell)* cómo se llaman las personas y de dónde son. Sigue el modelo.

María es de Managua.
Es nicaragüense.

María
Managua, Nicaragua

Práctica A
1. … es de Copán. Es hondureño.
2. … son de Antigua. Son guatemaltecos.
3. … son de Santo Domingo. Son dominicanas.
4. … es de Colón. Es panameño.
5. … es de San Salvador. Es salvadoreña.
6. … son de San José. Son costarricenses.
7. … es de Cozumel. Es mexicana.
8. … es de Ponce. Es puertorriqueño.

1. Pedro
Copán, Honduras

2. José y Fernando
Antigua, Guatemala

3. Carmen y Marta
Santo Domingo,
la República Dominicana

4. Antonio
Colón, Panamá

5. Teresa
San Salvador,
El Salvador

6. Luisa y Jorge
San José, Costa Rica

7. Graciela
Cozumel, México

8. Esteban
Ponce, Puerto Rico

Palabras Nuevas I   **33**

B **¿Cómo son?** David escribió en el otro lado *(side)* de cada foto.
Escoge *(choose)* dos fotos de la Práctica A y escribe unas frases sobre
estas dos personas. Sigue el modelo.

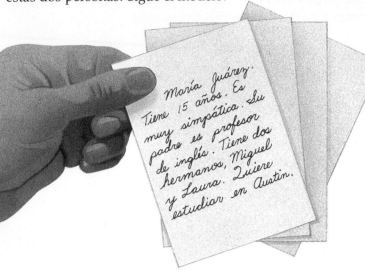

María Juárez.
Tiene 15 años. Es
muy simpática. Su
padre es profesor
de inglés. Tiene dos
hermanos, Miguel
y Laura. Quiere
estudiar en Austin.

C **Un poco de todo.** Completa cada frase con la palabra o expresión
apropiada *(appropriate)* de la lista.

admiro	explico	misma	proyector
año escolar	habitantes	pantalla	siguientes
director	idiomas	presto atención	uniforme

1. ¿Cuántos _____ habla el profesor Méndez?
2. Si tú no comprendes, debes escuchar. _____ qué quiere decir la
   palabra.
3. Jorge Luis Borges es un escritor difícil pero fantástico. Lo _____
   mucho.
4. El primer capítulo del libro es un poco aburrido. Pero los capítulos
   _____ son muy interesantes.
5. Si no _____ en clase voy a sacar malas notas.
6. Para mostrar diapositivas necesitas una _____ y un _____.
7. El _____ de mi equipo favorito es azul y blanco.
8. ¿Cuántos millones de _____ hay en Costa Rica?
9. Tú y yo vivimos en la _____ parte de la ciudad.

D **¡No, Jorge!** Jorge dice muchas cosas que no son correctas. Corrígelo
(correct him) según el modelo.

> ESTUDIANTE A   *El director lleva uniforme.*
> ESTUDIANTE B   *¡No! Los estudiantes llevan uniforme.*

1. Los habitantes de Honduras hablan portugués.
2. Costa Rica está al noroeste de Nicaragua.
3. En los Estados Unidos el año escolar dura seis meses.
4. En la Argentina celebran la Navidad durante el año escolar.
5. Arizona está en el sureste de los Estados Unidos.
6. Juan habla francés porque es guatemalteco.
7. Panamá está en la América del Sur.
8. Nicaragua es un país muy grande.

Práctica D
1. hablan español
2. está al sureste
3. dura nueve meses
4. durante las vacaciones de verano
5. está en el suroeste
6. habla español
7. está en la América Central
8. es (muy) pequeño

E Hablemos de ti.

1. ¿En qué parte de los Estados Unidos vives? ¿Vives cerca de México o del Canadá? ¿Vas allá a veces? ¿Quieres viajar por México? ¿Por qué?
2. ¿Vives en un barrio o cerca de un barrio donde hablan español? ¿Puedes hablar en español con los habitantes? ¿Puedes comprender lo que ellos dicen?
3. ¿Asistes a una escuela pública o a un colegio particular? ¿Hay que llevar uniforme en tu escuela? ¿Cómo es? ¿Crees que es una buena idea llevar uniforme? ¿Por qué sí? ¿Por qué no?
4. ¿A quiénes admiras mucho? ¿Por qué?
5. ¿Prefieres sacar diapositivas o fotos? ¿Sacas muchas? ¿De quién o de qué?

Práctica E
Answers will vary.

Practice Sheet 1–1   Workbook Exs. A–B

3 Tape Manual Exs. 1–2   Quiz 1–1

ACTIVIDAD

Nuestro uniforme nuevo.   With a partner, design a daily uniform for your school. You might consider the following questions:

¿De qué color o colores es el uniforme?
¿Tiene un dibujo de algo (un animal, por ejemplo)?
¿Llevan los chicos y las chicas la misma clase de uniforme?
¿Tiene el uniforme un sombrero? ¿Zapatos especiales?

When you have finished designing your school uniform, exchange your descriptions with another pair to see what they came up with.

APLICACIONES Discretionary

El primer día de clases 4 5 Pronunciación

Es el primer día del año escolar en una escuela de Texas. Roberto y Graciela hablan después de la primera clase.

ROBERTO	Graciela, tú eres panameña, ¿no?
GRACIELA	Sí, de la capital. ¿Y tú?
5 ROBERTO	Soy de aquí, pero mi familia es de origen mexicano.
GRACIELA	Ah, por eso hablas español.
ROBERTO	En el oeste y el suroeste de los Estados Unidos muchas personas hablan español. El profesor Díaz, por ejemplo. Él es de Nuevo México.
10 GRACIELA	¿El profesor de química? ¿Cómo es?
ROBERTO	Explica muy bien las lecciones, pero es muy exigente.[1] Nos da mucha tarea todos los días.
GRACIELA	¿Y qué?[2] En Panamá, todos los profesores dan tarea todos los días. Asistimos a la escuela para aprender, ¿no?
15 ROBERTO	Sí, pero yo tengo que trabajar en un restaurante por la tarde. No tengo mucho tiempo para ver a mis amigos.
GRACIELA	Sí, es bastante difícil, pero así es la vida,[3] ¿verdad?

---

[1]**exigente**   *tough, demanding*   [2]**¿y qué?**   *so what?*   [3]**así es la vida**   *that's life*

Culture: Do students remember that much of the West and Southwest was once part of Mexico? You may want to ask them to do research and give brief oral reports on the Mexican presence in the western and southwestern regions of the U.S.

Preguntas
Contesta según el diálogo.

1. ¿Qué día es?   2. ¿Dónde están Roberto y Graciela?   3. ¿Cuándo hablan?   4. ¿De qué ciudad es Graciela?   5. ¿De dónde es Roberto? 6. ¿Por qué habla español?   7. ¿Qué enseña el profesor Díaz?   8. Según Roberto, ¿cómo es él? ¿Por qué?   9. ¿Cómo crees que son los profesores en Panamá?   10. ¿Por qué no tiene tiempo Roberto para ver a sus amigos?   11. ¿Por qué asistes tú a la escuela?

Diálogo
1. Es el primer día del año escolar.
2. Están en una escuela de Texas.
3. Después de la primera clase.
4. Es de la capital de Panamá.
5. Es de Texas.
6. Su familia es de origen mexicano.
7. Enseña química.
8. Es muy exigente. Porque da mucha tarea.
9. Probable answer: Creo que son exigentes.
10. Porque trabaja por la tarde.
11. Answers will vary.

Participación

Working with a partner, create a dialogue in which you discuss aspects of school life. For example, what subjects do you study? Which is your favorite? Why? How long is the school day? When are vacations?

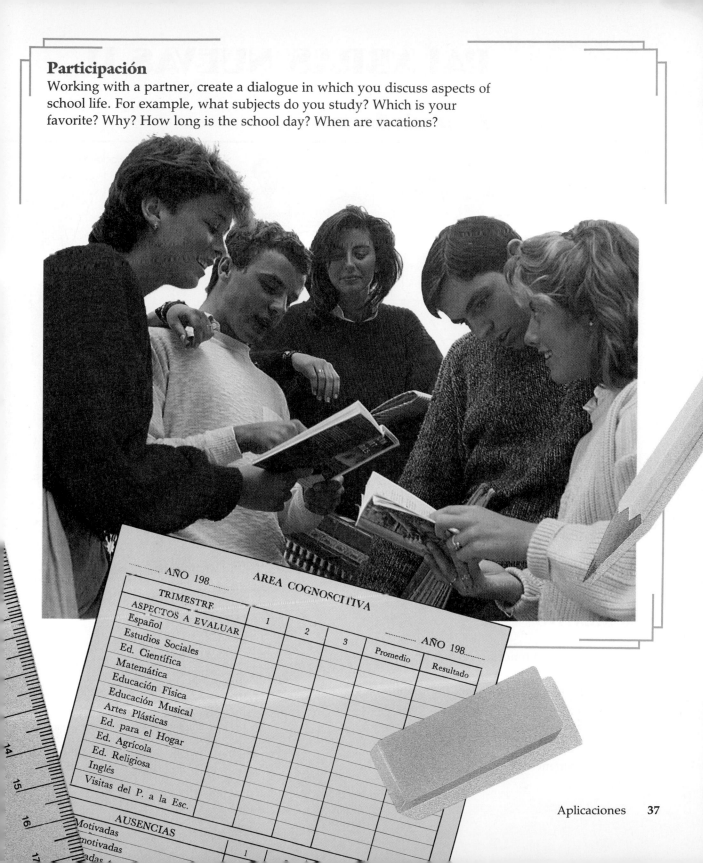

AREA COGNOSCITIVA					
AÑO 198......			AÑO 198......		
TRIMESTRE	1	2	3		
ASPECTOS A EVALUAR				Promedio	Resultado
Español					
Estudios Sociales					
Ed. Científica					
Matemática					
Educación Física					
Educación Musical					
Artes Plásticas					
Ed. para el Hogar					
Ed. Agrícola					
Ed. Religiosa					
Inglés					
Visitas del P. a la Esc.					

AUSENCIAS

Motivadas

...motivadas

...adas

PALABRAS NUEVAS II

Essential

En la sala de estudio

6
Transparency 2
**CONTEXTO
VISUAL**

el diccionario

el sujetapapeles
pl. los sujetapapeles

Notes: As you present the **Contexto visual** on pp. 38–39, you may want to point out that the compound nouns *sujetapapeles* and *sacapuntas* have the same form for both singular and plural. Explain that the article indicates number.

**CONTEXTO
COMUNICATIVO**

 7

1 INÉS   Vamos a tener un **repaso** hoy. ¿Me prestas tus **apuntes**?

   VÍCTOR   Lo siento, pero nunca tomo apuntes.

   INÉS   Y entonces, ¿cómo sales bien en los exámenes?

   VÍCTOR   Siempre presto atención en clase.

Variaciones:

■ en los exámenes → en las pruebas

el repaso *review*
el apunte *note*

If students ask: Other related words you may want to present: *el atril*, bookstand; *el letrero*, sign; *la enciclopedia*, encyclopedia; *investigar*, to research.

¡SILENCIO!

el bibliotecario

la bibliotecaria

la máquina de escribir

la grapadora

la grapa

el sacapuntas
pl. los sacapuntas

la calculadora

---

2 SUSANA ¿Qué lees, Miguel?
MIGUEL Una **biografía** de la reina Isabel de España.
SUSANA ¿Tienes que escribir **una composición**?
MIGUEL No, pero **la historia** de su **vida** es muy interesante.

■ una biografía de → un libro sobre
■ de la reina Isabel → del rey Fernando

la biografía *biography*
la composición, pl. **las composiciones** *composition*
la historia here: *story*
la vida *life*

3	JUAN	¿Cuál es **el tema** de tu composición?	**el tema** topic, subject
	LAURA	**No** sé **todavía.**	**no . . . todavía** (or: **todavía no**) not yet
	JUAN	Pero tienes que darle la composición al profesor esta tarde.	
	LAURA	La voy a escribir ahora, en **la sala de estudio.**	**la sala de estudio** study hall
	JUAN	Pero tenemos que **escribir**la **a máquina.**	**escribir a máquina** to type
	LAURA	¿A máquina? ¡No me digas!	

■ la sala de estudio → la biblioteca
■ ¡no me digas! → ay, ¡caramba!

4	LUIS	Perdón, ¿te puedo **hacer una pregunta**?	**hacer una pregunta** to ask a question
	SARA	Por supuesto.	
	LUIS	¿Qué tenemos que leer para la clase de inglés?	
	SARA	*The Cask of Amontillado.* Es **de** Edgar Allan Poe.	**de** here: by
	LUIS	¿Qué quiere decir la palabra *amontillado*?	
	SARA	Creo que es un vino español. ¿Por qué no la buscas en el diccionario?	

■ hacer una pregunta → preguntar algo
■ es de → **el autor** es

el autor, la autora   author

EN OTRAS PARTES

También se dice *el afilalápices* y *el cortalápices.*

También se dice *la presilla.*

También se dice *el engrapador, la engrapadora* y *el abrochador.*

También se dice *la máquina de calcular.*

UNIMAX CHILENA, S.A.

CALLE SAN MARTÍN 977
SANTIAGO 12
924-21-73

MÁQUINAS DE ESCRIBIR
NUEVAS, ELÉCTRICAS Y
MANUALES

CALCULADORAS
Y MÁQUINAS DE
ESCRIBIR
A PRECIOS
INCREÍBLES

TODAS LAS MARCAS
VENTA, RENTA Y SERVICIO GARANTIZADO
ENTREGA INMEDIATA

CASA GARCÍA ROLDÁN, S.A.
AVENIDA DE LOS REYES 373
MÉXICO 19, D.F.
729-52-00

PRÁCTICA

A **¿Qué necesitas?**   Siempre puedes encontrar cosas que necesitas en una venta de patio *(garage sale)*. Escoge *(Choose)* la palabra correcta para completar cada frase.

1. Voy a comprar *(este sacapuntas / esta cámara)* para mi hermano. Le gusta sacar fotos.
2. Necesito un *(mapa / sacapuntas)*. Siempre escribo con lápiz.
3. Esta *(máquina de escribir / grapadora)* va a ser perfecta para mis composiciones.
4. Aquí tienes *(un diccionario / una calculadora)* de cinco idiomas.
5. El Sr. Díaz todavía busca unos *(carteles / televisores)* para decorar la sala de estudio.
6. Voy a comprar este *(mapa / sujetapapeles)* de España para poner en la pared de mi dormitorio.
7. Necesitamos *(una cuchara / un cuchillo)* para abrir esa caja.
8. ¿Hay una *(grapadora / grabadora)*? Quiero poner juntas estas hojas de papel.
9. Todavía no tengo un buen *(sujetapapeles / bolígrafo)* para tomar apuntes en clase.

B **La composición.**   Laura y Enrique tienen que escribir juntos una composición. Están en la biblioteca y tratan de decidir el tema de su composición. Escoge *(Choose)* la palabra correcta para cada frase. Usa cada palabra sólo una vez.

apuntes	bibliotecario	diccionario	historias	repaso
autor	biografía	habitantes	idiomas	tema

ENRIQUE ¿Quién es el _____ de *The Cask of Amontillado?*

LAURA Creo que es Edgar Allan Poe, pero podemos preguntarle al _____.

ENRIQUE Las _____ de Poe son muy difíciles. Ya necesito un _____
5 porque no sé qué quiere decir "Cask." Quizás debemos escribir sobre otro _____.

LAURA ¿Por qué no escribimos sobre los mayas y los _____ de Guatemala de hoy? Va a ser muy interesante. Allí hablan varios _____, ¿no?

10 ENRIQUE Creo que sí. Podemos repasar nuestros _____ de historia.

LAURA Bueno. Vamos a buscar unos libros sobre Guatemala.

C   Hablemos de ti.

1. ¿Sabes escribir a máquina? ¿Qué escribes a máquina?
2. ¿Quién es tu autor favorito? ¿Cuáles de sus cuentos o novelas te gustan más? ¿Cuál prefieres leer, novelas o biografías? ¿Por qué?
3. ¿En qué clases tomas apuntes? ¿Te ayudan tus apuntes cuando estudias para los exámenes?
4. ¿Tienes un escritorio en tu dormitorio? ¿Qué hay en tu escritorio?

Practice Sheet 1–2   Workbook Exs. C–D   8 Tape Manual Ex. 3

 9 Refrán   Quiz 1–2

ESTUDIO DE PALABRAS

Did you know that Los Angeles means "City of the Angels"? When the Spaniards began to settle in the Americas, they gave some of their settlements religious names: San Francisco (St. Francis) and San Antonio (St. Anthony), for example.

Sometimes the explorers named places because of their first impressions. *Honduras* got its name from the deep waters off its northern coast (the Spanish word for "deep" is *hondo*). *Venezuela* means "Little Venice," because the people who lived on Lake Maracaibo had built their houses over the water, a scene that reminded the Spaniards of the Italian city of Venice. *Costa Rica* means "rich coast." What do you think *Puerto Rico* means?

Some Latin American countries kept their original names. *Chile* is an Indian name meaning "the place where the land ends," and *Uruguay* means "the river of the painted birds."

Sinónimos

Cambia las palabras en cursiva *(italics)* por un sinónimo.

1. El español es *la lengua* de los españoles.
2. Marta Morales es *la escritora* de esta novela.
3. Vamos hoy o *tal vez* mañana.
4. El capítulo *próximo* describe la vida de Cervantes.

Antónimos

Escoge un antónimo para cada palabra en cursiva *(italics)*. Luego usa ese antónimo en una frase.

1. *privado*	fuerte	público	listo
2. *las vacaciones*	el año escolar	el director	el habitante
3. *otro*	ese	algún	mismo
4. *noroeste*	sureste	noreste	suroeste

EXPLICACIONES I   Essential

Los usos de *ser* y *estar*

Review the present-tense forms of *ser* and *estar*.

SER		ESTAR	
soy	somos	estoy	estamos
eres	sois	estás	estáis
es	son	está	están

Notes: For examples of various uses of *ser* and *estar*, refer to the following mini-dialogues: 1 on p. 31, 4 on p. 32, 2 on p. 39, and 3 and 4 on p. 40.

◆ OBJECTIVES:

TO TELL THE TIME OF DAY AND THE DATE

TO TELL WHERE AND WHEN SOMETHING TAKES PLACE

TO DESCRIBE ORIGIN AND LOCATION

TO DESCRIBE PEOPLE AND THINGS

TO DESCRIBE HOW PEOPLE ARE FEELING

TO TELL WHAT SOMEONE DOES FOR A LIVING

1   Remember that we use *ser*
   a. to tell the time of day and the date:

   Son las dos.   *It's two o'clock.*
   Hoy **es** el tres de octubre.   *Today is October 3.*

   b. to indicate nationality or where someone or something comes from:

   Soy de Nicaragua.   *I'm from Nicaragua.*
   El Sr. Durán **es** hondureño.   *Mr. Durán is Honduran.*

   c. to describe characteristics that are usually associated with a person or a thing:

   ¿Cómo **es** Carlos?   *What's Carlos like?*
   Es alto.   *He's tall.*

   d. to connect a noun or a pronoun to another noun or pronoun:

   La Dra. Méndez **es** una dentista   *Dr. Méndez is an excellent*
   excelente.   *dentist.*

   Unless we use an adjective, we don't use the indefinite articles *un* and *una* with occupations or professions after *ser: La Dra. Méndez es dentista.*

2   We also use *ser*
   a. to tell what something is made of:

   El flan **es** de leche, huevos y   *Flan is made of milk, eggs, and*
   azúcar.   *sugar.*

   b. to tell the time and place of an event:

   La fiesta **es** a las ocho.   *The party is at eight.*
   La clase **es** en la biblioteca.   *The class is in the library.*

¡Te invitamos!

¿A qué? *fiesta de ...*
¿Cuándo? *3 de octu...*
¿A qué hora? *a los 7:3...*
¿Dónde? *en casa de ...*

¡Hasta entonces!

Explicaciones I   43

3 We use *estar*

    a. to tell where something or someone is located:

El diccionario **está** sobre la mesa.	*The dictionary **is** on the table.*
Estamos en la sala de estudio.	*We're in the study hall.*

    b. to describe conditions or characteristics that are not always associated with someone or something:

HEALTH:	**Estoy** enfermo.	*I'm sick.*
FEELINGS:	**Están** muy tristes.	*They're very sad.*
CONDITIONS:	**Estás** muy ocupado.	*You're very busy.*

4 Notice how the choice of *ser* or *estar* can give very different meanings.

USUALLY	{ ¿Cómo **son** los chiles?	*What **are** chili peppers like?*
	{ **Son** picantes.	*They're hot (spicy).*
TODAY	{ ¿Cómo **está** la sopa?	*How's the soup?*
	{ **Está** picante.	*It's hot (spicy).*

Some adjectives have a very different meaning depending on whether they are used with *ser* or *estar*.

Felipe **es aburrido**.	*Felipe is boring.*
Felipe **está aburrido**.	*Felipe is bored.*
La blusa **es verde**.	*The blouse is green.*
La naranja **está verde**.	*The orange is green (unripe).*

PRÁCTICA

A **¿Qué hacen?** Los miembros *(members)* de la familia de Pilar trabajan en muchas profesiones diferentes. Indica la profesión de cada persona. Sigue el modelo.

> Su madre es la persona más importante en la oficina del colegio.
> *Es directora.*

1. Su padre enseña inglés en un colegio particular panameño.
2. El hermano mayor de Pilar escribe una biografía de Goya.
3. Su prima Margarita vive y trabaja en una granja.
4. Pilar asiste a una escuela bilingüe.
5. Su tía trabaja en un restaurante.
6. Su primo Enrique saca fotos.
7. Su hermana mayor trabaja en un hospital para animales.
8. Su abuela trabaja en una tienda.
9. Su tío Raimundo trabaja en una biblioteca.

B **¿Dónde están?** Mira el dibujo y describe dónde está cada persona. Sigue el modelo.

> Mario
> *Mario está en el taxi.*

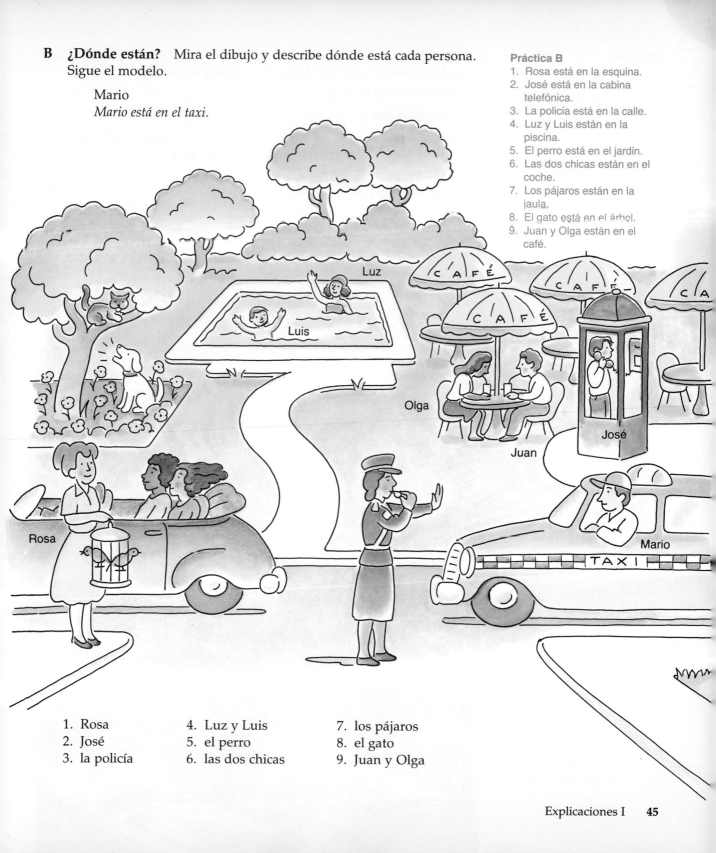

1. Rosa
2. José
3. la policía
4. Luz y Luis
5. el perro
6. las dos chicas
7. los pájaros
8. el gato
9. Juan y Olga

Práctica B
1. Rosa está en la esquina.
2. José está en la cabina telefónica.
3. La policía está en la calle.
4. Luz y Luis están en la piscina.
5. El perro está en el jardín.
6. Las dos chicas están en el coche.
7. Los pájaros están en la jaula.
8. El gato está en el árbol.
9. Juan y Olga están en el café.

C   Una carta.   Imagina que un compañero de clase escribió esta tarjeta postal sobre su viaje a España. Completa la tarjeta con las formas correctas de *ser* o *estar*.

Queridos amigos,

   Mis padres y yo _____ en San Sebastián. _____ una ciudad en el norte de España. _____ al lado del mar y las playas _____ muy bonitas.

5   Los mejores restaurantes _____ en un barrio viejo de la ciudad y las comidas que sirven _____ estupendas. Todos (nosotros) _____ más gordos que antes.

   (Yo) _____ muy contento. La vida aquí _____ fantástica. España _____ un país muy bello, y creo que San Sebastián _____ la ciudad

10   más bella de todas. No quiero volver nunca a la escuela. (¡_____ un chiste!)

                                        Su compañero,

                                        Felipe

D   ¿*Ser* o *estar*?   Completa las frases con la forma correcta de *ser* o *estar*.

1. ¡Qué aburridas _____ (nosotras) en este colegio particular!
2. Hoy _____ el primer día de octubre.
3. (Yo) _____ en la sala de estudio.
4. Ya _____ las tres y cuarto de la tarde.
5. El estudiante a mi izquierda _____ cansado.
6. Las niñas _____ guatemaltecas.
7. Las grapas _____ con los sujetapapeles.
8. (Nosotros) _____ pelirrojos.
9. La película _____ muy aburrida.
10. (Tú) _____ bibliotecaria, ¿no?

Una escuela secundaria en Buenos Aires, Argentina

La a personal

When the direct object of a verb is a definite person or a group of people, we use the personal *a* before it. Remember that *a + el → al*.

Admiro **a mis profesores.**	*I admire **my teachers.***
Llama **al director.**	*He's calling **the principal.***

When more than one person is mentioned, we usually repeat the *a*.

Espero **a Olga** y **a su amiga.**   *I'm waiting for **Olga** and **her friend.***

1   We also use the personal *a* before *¿quién?* and *¿quiénes?* when they are direct objects.

¿A quién invitas?	***Whom** are you inviting?*
¿A quiénes ayudan?	***Whom** are they helping?*

2   We generally do not use the personal *a* with *tener*.

Tengo tres hermanas.   *I have three sisters.*

3   We can also use the personal *a* with place names and with pets.

Voy a visitar **a España.**	*I'm going to visit **Spain.***
Ella busca **a su pájaro.**	*She's looking for **her bird.***

◆ OBJECTIVES:

TO DESCRIBE DOING THINGS THAT INVOLVE OTHER PEOPLE— LOOKING FOR, WAITING FOR, WATCHING THEM, ETC.

Notes: You may want to introduce the personal *a* orally before students open their books. As you write examples on the board, ask students for additional examples.
   Point out the use of the personal *a* in line 17 of the **Diálogo** on p. 36.

PRÁCTICA

¿A qué hora?   Horacio tiene mucho que hacer durante el día. Di *(tell)* lo que va a hacer. Usa la *a* personal cuando sea necesario *(when necessary)*. Sigue el modelo.

8:00 / despertar / su hermano
A las ocho va a despertar a su hermano.

1. 8:10 / escuchar / las noticias
2. 8:30 / llamar / el director
3. 9:00 / tomar / el autobús
4. 10:00 / visitar / el museo
5. 10:15 / mirar / el arte
6. 12:00 / visitar / el director
7. 1:00 / esperar / Carlos y Jorge
8. 1:30 / repasar / sus apuntes
9. 3:00 / bañar / el perro
10. 6:00 / comer / comida italiana
11. 7:30 / estudiar / química
12. 9:00 / llamar / su novia

Práctica
1. A las ocho y diez va a escuchar las noticias.
2. A las ocho y media va a llamar al director.
3. A las nueve ... tomar el autobús.
4. A las diez ... visitar el museo.
5. A las diez y cuarto ... mirar el arte.
6. A las doce (*or:* al mediodía) ... visitar al director.
7. A la una ... esperar a Carlos y a Jorge.
8. A la una y media ... repasar sus apuntes.
9. A las tres ... bañar al perro.
10. A las seis ... comer comida ...
11. A las siete y media ... estudiar química.
12. A las nueve ... llamar a su novia.

El complemento directo:
Los pronombres *lo, la, los, las*

◆ **OBJECTIVES:**

TO GO OVER A CHECKLIST

TO CONFIRM AN APPOINTMENT

TO AGREE (OR NOT TO AGREE) TO DO SOMETHING

TO RATE ACTIVITIES ON A FREQUENCY SCALE AND EXPLAIN WHY

Notes: Mini-dialogues 3 on p. 32 and 3–4 on p. 40 illustrate the use of direct object pronouns.

Here are the direct object pronouns meaning "him," "her," "it," "you" (formal), "them," and "you" (plural). Remember that a direct object tells who or what receives the action of the verb.

lo	*him, it, you* (masc. formal)	**los**	*them, you* (pl.)
la	*her, it, you* (fem. formal)	**las**	*them* (fem.), *you* (fem. pl.)

1 Direct object pronouns agree in gender and number with the nouns they replace. They come right before the verb.

¿Admiras **sus obras de teatro**?	*Do you admire **his plays**?*
Sí, **las** admiro.	*Yes, I admire **them**.*
¿Esperas **a tus tíos**?	*Are you waiting for **your aunt and uncle**?*
No, no **los** espero.	*No, I'm not waiting for **them**.*

2 When a pronoun replaces both a masculine and a feminine direct object noun, we use **los**.

¿Visitas **a Roberto y a María**?	*Do you visit **Roberto and María**?*
Sí, **los** visito.	*Yes, I visit **them**.*

3 We can attach a direct object pronoun to an infinitive or put it before the main verb.

¿Quieres ver **mis diapositivas**?	*Do you want to see **my slides**?*
Sí, quiero ver**las** ahora.	*Yes, I want to see **them** now.*
Si, **las** quiero ver ahora.	

Reteach / Extra Help Before students begin the **Práctica**, ask volunteers to identify each of the items in Ex. A. Make sure they include the correct definite article.

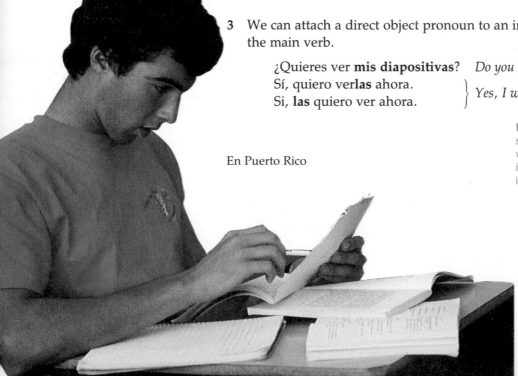

En Puerto Rico

PRÁCTICA

A De viaje. Imagina que vas de vacaciones y uno de tus padres te pregunta si tienes todo lo que necesitas. Pregunta y contesta según el modelo.

ESTUDIANTE A	*¿Tienes tu boleto?*
ESTUDIANTE B	*Sí, lo tengo.*
o:	*No, no lo tengo.*

1.   2.   3.   4.

5.   6.   7.   8.

Práctica A
1. ¿Tienes tu peine? Sí / No, no lo tengo.
2. ¿Tienes tu jabón? Sí / No, no lo tengo.
3. ¿Tienes tu cepillo de dientes? Sí / No, no lo tengo.
4. ¿Tienes tu pasta dentífrica? Sí / No, no la tengo.
5. ¿Tienes tu desodorante? Sí / No, no lo tengo.
6. ¿Tienes tu seda dental? Sí / No, no la tengo.
7. ¿Tienes tu champú? Sí / No, no lo tengo.
8. ¿Tienes tu despertador? Sí / No, no lo tengo.

B ¿A quién llamas? ¿Llamas por teléfono a estas personas? Usa la lista de la derecha para preguntar y contestar. Luego explica por qué las llamas o no las llamas.

Pedro

ESTUDIANTE A	*¿Llamas a Pedro?*
ESTUDIANTE B	*Sí, lo llamo a veces. Es muy simpático.*
o:	*No, no lo llamo nunca. No me gusta hablar con él.*

1. tu novio(a)	5. tus padres	todos los días
2. tu mejor amigo(a)	6. tus tíos	todas las noches
3. tu profesor(a) de español	7. tu médico(a)	a menudo
4. tus abuelos	8. tu dentista	a veces
		nunca

Práctica B
Answers will vary. All questions include personal *a*. Questions answered with *nunca* should include *No, no.*
1. ¿Llamas a tu novio(a)? Sí, lo (la) …
2. … Sí, lo (la) …
3. … Sí, lo (la) …
4. … Sí, los …
5. … Sí, los …
6. … Sí, los …
7. … Sí, lo (la) …
8. … Sí, lo (la) …

C ¿A qué hora? Gustavo es enfermero. Todas las tardes llama a los pacientes *(patients)* que tienen cita *(appointment)* el día siguiente. Sigue el modelo.

Sra. Ruiz / 5:00 P.M.
Sra. Ruiz, el médico la espera a las cinco de la tarde.

1. Sr. Sánchez / 10:00 A.M.	5. Sr. Morán / 11:45 A.M.
2. Sra. Casino / 3:00 P.M.	6. Sra. Alba / 1:30 P.M.
3. Srta. Hernández / 8:15 A.M.	7. Srta. Goytisolo / 9:30 A.M.
4. Sr. Jiménez / 7:00 P.M.	8. Sr. Martínez / 4:15 P.M.

Práctica C
1. … lo espera a las diez de la mañana.
2. … la espera a las tres de la tarde.
3. … la espera a las ocho y cuarto de la mañana.
4. … lo espera a las siete de la tarde.
5. … lo espera a las doce menos cuarto de la mañana.
6. … la espera a la una y media de la tarde.
7. … la espera a las nueve y media de la mañana.
8. … lo espera a las cuatro y cuarto de la tarde.

Práctica D
1. ¿Buscas a María?
   Sí, la necesito. ¿Puedes llamarla?
   Sí, la llamo ahora. / No, tú la puedes llamar.
2. ¿... a Jorge y a Raúl? ... los ...
3. ¿... al Sr. Ramírez? ... lo ...
4. ¿ ... a Paco y a Javier? ... los ...
5. ¿ ... a Ana y a Lucía? ... las ...
6. ¿... a Timoteo? ... lo ...
7. ¿... a la Sra. Ibáñez? ... la ...
8. ¿... a Sofía y a Pablo? ... los

Práctica E
Answers will vary.

Practice Sheet 1–5

Workbook Exs. E–F

 12 Tape Manual Ex. 6

Quiz 1–4

D ¿A quién buscas?   Imagina que tú y un(a) amigo(a) buscan a otras personas para ayudar a decorar el gimnasio para un baile. Pregunta y contesta según el modelo.

> Esteban
>
> ESTUDIANTE A *¿Buscas a Esteban?*
> ESTUDIANTE B *Sí, lo necesito. ¿Puedes llamarlo?*
> ESTUDIANTE A *Sí, lo llamo ahora.*
>   o: *No, tú lo puedes llamar.*

1. María   3. Sr. Ramírez   5. Ana y Lucía   7. Sra. Ibáñez
2. Jorge y Raúl   4. Paco y Javier 6. Timoteo   8. Sofía y Pablo

E Hablemos de ti.
1. ¿Cómo estás? ¿Cómo eres?
2. ¿Cómo es tu clase de español? ¿Cómo es tu profesor(a) de español?
3. ¿Cuándo estás triste? ¿Contento(a)? ¿Estás preocupado(a) a veces? ¿Aburrido(a)? ¿Cuándo?
4. ¿Qué haces cuando estás enfermo(a)?
5. ¿Qué haces cuando estás solo(a) en casa?
6. ¿Dónde está tu casa o apartamento?
7. ¿Ayudas a tus padres en casa? ¿Cuándo los ayudas?
8. ¿Hablas mucho por teléfono? ¿A quiénes llamas?

Enrichment: If the **Actividad** is particularly successful with your class and if time allows, you may want to refer students back to the visuals on p. 45. Ask them to work in pairs, taking turns choosing something or someone from the picture without saying who or what it is. The other partner should ask questions to find out who or what it is.

ACTIVIDAD

¿Quién es?   Send one student out of the room. Now choose another person whose identity the first student must try to discover. The student who is outside should then come back in and ask the class yes / no questions to find out whom they picked. For example:

> ¿Lleva una camisa roja?
> ¿Es alta?
> ¿Está a la izquierda del profesor?

Can the questioner discover whom the class picked in seven questions or less?

APLICACIONES

En la sala de estudio   Transparency 3

¿A quién ves en la sala de estudio? ¿Qué hace cada persona? ¿Qué ves sobre las mesas?

Arturo and Mónica have to write a composition about a Central American country for their history class. Make up a dialogue in which they discuss what country they are going to choose and why. Here are some words you might want to use:

buscar	escribir a máquina	mismo, -a
los carteles	explicar	tener
las diapositivas	los habitantes	tener que
dibujar / hacer un dibujo	el mapa	la vida

Notes: Sample dialogues for the **¿Qué pasa?** appear in the Teacher Notes. You may want to allow class time for pairs of students to prepare their dialogues. Circulate to give help as needed.

EXPLICACIONES II   Essential

Los verbos *dar* y *ver*

Here are the present-tense forms of *dar* ("to give") and *ver* ("to see"). Remember that they are irregular only in the *yo* form.

DAR			VER	
doy	damos		veo	vemos
das	dais		ves	véis
da	dan		ve	ven

PRÁCTICA

Reteach / Extra Help: Before students begin the Práctica, reinforce the present-tense forms of *dar* and *ver* by asking these questions. Change verb forms and point to a student, to yourself, to two or three students, and so on according to the form you are eliciting: *¿Das una fiesta el viernes? ¿A quién ves en la cafetería? ¿Qué vemos todos los días en la clase de español?*

Práctica A
1. Carmen les da unos diccionarios.
2. Les doy (unos) sujeta-papeles y grapas.
3. ... dan una pantalla.
4. ... da una calculadora.
5. ... da una máquina de escribir.
6. ... das un sacapuntas.
7. ... damos (unas) papeleras.
8. ... dan (unos) borradores.
9. ... dan (unas) diapositivas.

A   Unos regalos.   Imagina que los padres de una amiga abren una guardería (*day-care center*) y necesitan muchas cosas. ¿Quién va a darles qué? Sigue el modelo.

Gerardo
Gerardo les da una grapadora.

1. Carmen   2. (yo)   3. Tomás y Ángel

4. Esperanza   5. nuestra directora   6. (tú)

7. (nosotros)   8. Pablo y Ester   9. Tomás y tú

B **¿Qué película dan?** Los miembros de la familia Novás nunca van todos juntos al cine. Nunca hay más de dos personas que quieren ver la misma película. ¿Qué películas ven esta noche?

Verónica
Verónica ve una película cómica.

1. Nicolás y Norma

2. (yo)

3. la tía Rebeca

4. (tú)

5. (nosotros)

6. el tío Ricardo y tú

Práctica B
1. Nicolás y Norma ven una película de terror.
2. Veo una película policíaca.
3. La tía Rebeca ve una película del oeste.
4. Ves una película musical.
5. Vemos (unos) dibujos animados.
6. El tío Ricardo y tú ven una película de ciencia ficción.

Practice Sheet 1–6

Tape Manual Ex. 7 13

Quiz 1–5

(izquierda) En Buenos Aires, Argentina; (izquierda, abajo) En Costa Rica; (derecha) En Bogotá, Colombia

El complemento indirecto:
Los pronombres *le* y *les*

Remember that an indirect object tells *to whom* or *for whom* an action is performed. The indirect object pronouns *le* and *les* mean "to (or for) him, her, you" (formal and plural), and "them." Like direct object pronouns, they come right before the verb.

Le doy los uniformes.   *I'm giving the uniforms* $\begin{cases} \textbf{\textit{to him.}} \\ \textbf{\textit{to her.}} \\ \textbf{\textit{to you}} \text{ (Ud.)}. \end{cases}$

or: *I'm giving **him (her, you)** the uniforms.*

Les compro calculadoras.   *I'm buying calculators* $\begin{cases} \textbf{\textit{for them.}} \\ \textbf{\textit{for you}} \text{ (Uds.)}. \end{cases}$

or: *I'm buying **them (you)** calculators.*

Dinero mexicano

1   With *¿a quién(es)?* and when the indirect object is a noun, we generally also use an indirect object pronoun.

> **¿A quién le** das el dinero?   *To whom are you giving the money?*
> **Le** doy el dinero **a Juana.**   *I'm giving the money **to Juana.***

2   For emphasis or to clarify the meaning of *le* and *les*, we can add *a* + a prepositional pronoun.

> **Le** escribo una tarjeta postal **a él.**   *I'm writing a post card **to him.***
> **Les** presto los apuntes **a ellas.**   *I'm lending the notes **to them.***
> **Les** compro varias cosas **a Uds.,**   *I'm buying several things **for you,***
> no **a ella.**   *not **for her.***

3   We can attach *le* or *les* to an infinitive or put it before the main verb, just as we do with direct object pronouns.

> Tengo que dar**les** las grapas. $\Big\}$ *I have to give **them** the staples.*
> **Les** tengo que dar las grapas.

PRÁCTICA

A **¿A quiénes les escribes?**   Imagina que estudias en otro país. Pregunta y contesta según el modelo.

> tu sobrino favorito / a menudo
> **ESTUDIANTE A**   *¿A quién le escribes?*
> **ESTUDIANTE B**   *A mi sobrino favorito. Le escribo a menudo.*

1. mis padres / cuando necesito dinero
2. mi hermana(o) / cada mes
3. mi novio(a) / casi todos los días
4. mis amigos / a menudo
5. mis tíos / cuando tengo noticias
6. mi abuela / cada semana
7. mi profesor(a) de español / para practicar el español
8. mis primos / porque están enfermos

Práctica A
The question will be the same throughout.
1. ¿A quién le escribes? A mis padres. Les escribo cuando necesito dinero.
2. Le escribo …
3. Le escribo …
4. Les escribo …
5. Les escribo.
6. Le escribo …
7. Le escribo
8. Les escribo …

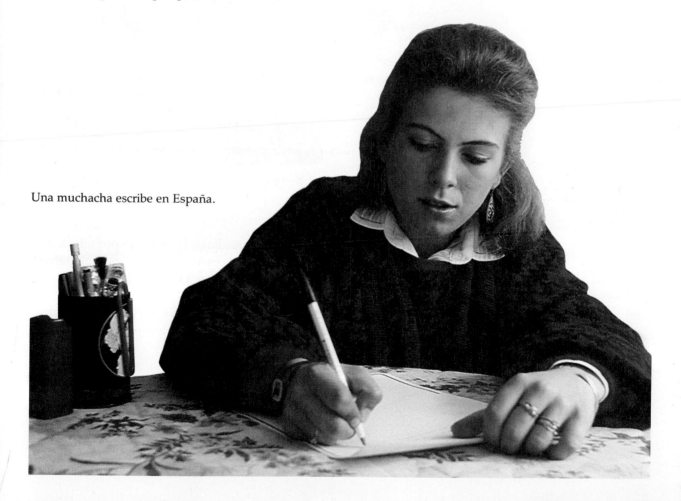

Una muchacha escribe en España.

B ¿Qué les das? Todas las personas en la familia de Yolanda van a cumplir años *(have a birthday)* pronto. Pregunta y contesta según el modelo.

Pablo

ESTUDIANTE A *¿Qué le vas a dar a Pablo?*
ESTUDIANTE B *Quizás voy a darle una corbata.*

1. tu prima Gloria   2. tu hermano Luis   3. tu abuela

4. tus sobrinas   5. tus tíos   6. tu hermanita

7. tu papá   8. tus primos   9. tu mamá

C Hablemos de ti.

1. ¿Te gusta escribir cartas o prefieres llamar a la gente por teléfono? ¿A quiénes les escribes cartas? ¿Las escribes con lápiz o bolígrafo o las escribes a máquina? ¿Cuando viajas, a quiénes les escribes tarjetas postales?
2. ¿A veces les prestas cosas a tus amigos? ¿Qué les prestas?
3. ¿Qué le vas a dar a tu novio(a) para su cumpleaños? ¿Qué les vas a dar a tus abuelos o a tus padres o hermanos?
4. ¿Qué clase de regalos te gusta recibir?

ACTIVIDAD

¡Regalos para todos!   With a partner, make a list of five or six items that you might give away. Discuss to whom you are going to give them and why. For example:

ESTUDIANTE A   *¿A quién le damos la máquina de escribir?*
ESTUDIANTE B   *Le damos la máquina de escribir a la profesora de inglés.*
ESTUDIANTE A   *¿Por qué?*
ESTUDIANTE B   *Porque no tiene ninguna.*
      o: *Porque no puedo leer lo que escribe.*
      o: *Porque su máquina de escribir es muy vieja.*

En la biblioteca en México

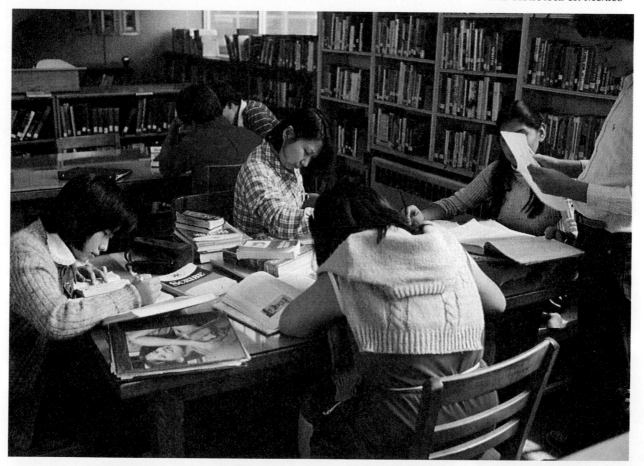

▼ APLICACIONES Discretionary

Notes: Answers to the **Repaso** and **Tema** appear in the Teacher Notes.

REPASO

Notes: Review of:
1. *ser*
   adjectives of nationality
   professions
   adjective agreement
2. *asistir a*
   position of adjectives
   adjective agreement
   time expressions
3. adjectives with *ser*
   adjective agreement
   indirect object pronouns
4. adjectives with *estar*
   tener
   mucho, -a
   adjective agreement
5. *ver*
   personal *a*
   direct object pronouns

Estudiantes en España

Mira las frases modelo. Luego cambia las frases que siguen *(follow)* al español según los modelos.

1. *Soy una médica dominicana.*
   (M. A. Asturias is a Guatemalan author.)
   (They (masc.) *are Panamanian pilots.)*
   (We (fem.) *are Nicaraguan librarians.)*

Enrichment: You may want to use the model sentences in the **Repaso** for dictation.

2. *Asisten a un partido importante mañana.*
   (Do you (fam.) *attend a private school now?)*
   (We're attending an interesting concert today.)
   (They're attending a bilingual class now.)

3. *Las muchachas son muy amables. Le explican palabras.*
   (I'm very generous. I give you (pl.) *paperclips.)*
   (She's very smart. Does she teach you (pl.) *languages?)*
   (The principal is very boring. She reads them biographies.)

4. *Están tristes porque tienen mucho trabajo.*
   (We're busy because we have a lot of homework.)
   (Luz is bored because she doesn't have many friends.)
   (I'm worried because I don't have many notes.)

5. *A veces ve a su primo y lo espera en la esquina.*
   (We often see the librarian and help him in the library.)
   (You (fam.) *always call your friends* (fem.) *or see them at the café.)*
   (I always admire that actress and see her on TV.)

TEMA

Escribe las frases en español.

1. Pablo is a Costa Rican student.

2. He attends a public school now.

3. The students are very nice. They're teaching him English.

4. Pablo is happy because he has a lot of friends.

5. He often calls his friends and invites them to his house.

REDACCIÓN

Ahora escoge *(choose)* uno de los siguientes temas para escribir tu propio *(own)* diálogo o párrafo *(paragraph)*.

1. Expand the *Tema* by writing about Pablo's experiences in his new school. Tell about his schedule, the subjects he's studying, his homework, and tests. Say how he feels about the students and the teachers.

2. Write a paragraph describing your school library. Describe the room and its furnishings. Tell what sorts of things occur there in a typical hour.

3. Imagine that Pablo is writing a letter to a friend in Costa Rica describing his school in the United States. Start the letter with *Querido(a)* and end it with *Hasta pronto*.

Aplicaciones **59**

COMPRUEBA TU PROGRESO   CAPÍTULO 1   Discretionary

Notes: Answers to the **Comprueba** appear in the Teacher Notes.

A   ¿Ser o estar?
Completa las frases con la forma correcta de *ser* o *estar*.

1. ¿_____ Ud. bibliotecario?
2. (Yo) _____ triste porque todavía no hace sol.
3. Manuel y su hermana _____ en Guatemala.
4. Su oficina _____ en la esquina sureste de la calle.
5. (Nosotros) _____ dominicanos.
6. Juana _____ muy atlética, pero _____ enferma hoy.
7. El estadio _____ al noroeste de la ciudad.

B   ¿Qué hacen?
Contesta cada pregunta con una frase completa. Sustituye *(substitute)* las palabras indicadas con un pronombre.

1. ¿Dónde pasa Pablo *el verano*?   (en Chile)
2. ¿Quién manda *esta tarjeta postal*?   (Daniel)
3. ¿Quién explica *la lección*?   (la profesora)
4. ¿Quiénes escuchan *las cintas*?   (los chicos)
5. ¿Adónde llevan *los libros*?   (al laboratorio)
6. ¿Quiénes hacen *los planes*?   (mis padres)

C   ¿Qué tiene que hacer?
Contesta cada pregunta dos veces. Usa el pronombre correcto. Sigue el modelo.

> ¿Tienes que lavar el coche? / Sí
> *Sí, tengo que lavarlo.*
> *Sí, lo tengo que lavar.*

1. ¿Vas a practicar el fútbol? / Sí
2. ¿Vas a mostrar las diapositivas? / Sí
3. ¿Tienes que llevar el uniforme todos los días? / No
4. ¿Quieres visitar a tu tía mañana? / No
5. ¿Prefieres comer la ensalada? / No

D   La *a* personal
Escribe frases completas. Usa la *a* personal cuando sea necesaria.

1. ¿llamar / (tú) / Juan?
2. ¿buscar / Javier / el médico?
3. (yo) / admirar / la profesora
4. ¿comprar / Mónica / la máquina de escribir?
5. los estudiantes / escuchar / el director
6. ¿usar / Uds. / el proyector?
7. Mario / invitar / todos los estudiantes
8. (yo) / ver / el policía

E   ¿Dar o ver?
Completa cada frase con la forma correcta de *dar* o *ver*.

1. Diego y Raúl le _____ flores a mamá.
2. ¿Qué _____ (tú) en la pantalla?
3. En la granja (nosotros) _____ muchos animales.
4. ¿Quién les _____ un millón de dólares a los García?
5. (Yo) siempre le _____ mis apuntes a Pilar.
6. (Yo) _____ a la directora.
7. ¿_____ (Uds.) esos carteles?
8. ¿Le _____ (nosotros) una corbata a papá?
9. Todos los días (ellos) le _____ de comer al gato.

F   ¿Qué pasa?
Pregunta y contesta según el modelo. Usa el pronombre correcto.

> dar / Ud. / la entrada / Elena
> *¿Le da Ud. la entrada a Elena?*
> *Voy a darle la entrada más tarde.*

1. prestar / Horacio / los diccionarios / su amigo
2. dar / (tú) / helados / los niños
3. escribir / ellos / cartas / sus hijos
4. explicar / Ana / la historia / su compañera
5. dar / Uds. / la grapadora / Patricia
6. prestar / Ud. / la grabadora / sus hijas
7. mandar / (ellos) / comida / los habitantes de esa parte del país

VOCABULARIO DEL CAPÍTULO 1

Sustantivos
el año escolar
el apunte
el autor, la autora
el bibliotecario, la bibliotecaria
la biografía
la calculadora
el colegio particular
la composición, *pl.* las
   composiciones
la diapositiva
el diccionario
el director, la directora
la grapa
la grapadora
el/la habitante
la historia
el idioma
la máquina de escribir
el millón (de), *pl.* millones (de)
el noreste
el noroeste
la pantalla
la parte
el proyector
el repaso
el sacapuntas, *pl.* los
   sacapuntas
la sala de estudio
el sujetapapeles, *pl.* los
   sujetapapeles
el sureste
el suroeste
el tema
el uniforme
la vida

Adjetivos
costarricense
dominicano, -a
guatemalteco, -a
hondureño, -a
mismo, -a
nicaragüense
panameño, -a
público, -a
salvadoreño, -a
siguiente

Verbos
admirar
explicar

Preposición
de *(by)*

Adverbios
quizás
todavía no (no . . . todavía)

Expresiones
escribir a máquina
hacer una pregunta
prestar atención
¡silencio!

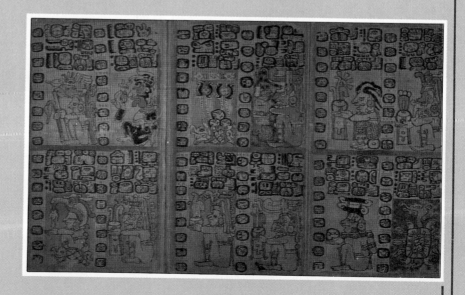

PRÓLOGO CULTURAL

LA CASA ESPAÑOLA

If you were visiting someone's home in southern Spain, you would probably notice many differences between it and your own home. Lawns and front yards are not traditional there, and the exterior of the houses is often quite plain. But you would see flowering plants on wrought-iron balconies or hung on decorative hooks attached to the outside wall. Many houses have front doors large enough for a car to enter. A smaller door may be built into the large one for people to pass through. Instead of bells, there are often door knockers, sometimes shaped like a lion's head or a woman's hand.

Behind the door there is usually a short passageway leading to a sunny patio at the center of the house. Here you might see an array of clay pots overflowing with geraniums and other plants. In warm weather this inner garden serves as an outdoor family room.

The inner garden is a tradition inherited from the Arabs, who invaded Spain in 711 and remained there for more than seven hundred years. The Spanish also learned from them how to build cool adobe houses made of blocks of baked mud painted white to reflect the sun. When the Spaniards settled in North America they continued building houses this way. Today you can see many examples of this in New Mexico and Arizona, where adobe is still used because of its excellent insulating properties.

Large homes in southern Spain may be two or three stories high, with galleries on each level overlooking the patio. Most of the rooms open onto the galleries. Their tiled floors and pastel walls are very inviting in the warm afternoons. They have high ceilings and tall windows with shutters that can be closed to block out the sun. In the Spanish-speaking world we are constantly reminded how climate influences the way we live.

If students ask: Other related words you may want to present: *el rastro / la rastra*, rake; *rastrillar*, to rake.

PALABRAS NUEVAS I

Essential

Transparency 5

1

CONTEXTO VISUAL

Hay que poner todo en orden

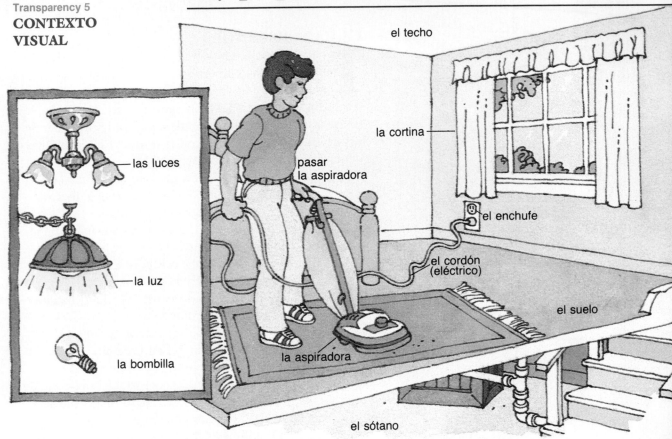

- el techo
- la cortina
- el enchufe
- pasar la aspiradora
- el cordón (eléctrico)
- el suelo
- la aspiradora
- el sótano

- las luces
- la luz
- la bombilla

CONTEXTO COMUNICATIVO

2

1   MAMÁ   Diego, ¿vas a limpiar el pasillo?

      DIEGO   Sí, pero la aspiradora no **funciona.**

      MAMÁ   Hay que **enchufar**la, hijo.

Variaciones:

- el pasillo → la alfombra
- no funciona → está **descompuesta**
- hay que enchufarla → acabas de **desenchufarla**

funcionar   *to work, to run (machines)*

enchufar   *to plug in*

descompuesto, -a   *broken, out of order (machines)*

desenchufar   *to unplug*

ordenado, -a   el pasillo   desordenado, -a

barrer

la escoba

cortar
el césped

el césped

el cortacésped

2 PAPÁ   ¡Ay, Sarita, qué **desorden**!

SARA   Lo siento, papá. Voy a **poner** todo **en orden ahora mismo**.

■ ¡qué desorden! → ¡qué dormitorio tan* desordenado!
■ ahora mismo → esta mañana

el desorden   *mess, disorder*
poner en orden   *to straighten out*
el orden   *order*
ahora mismo   *right away*

---

* You know that we use *Qué* to form exclamations with adjectives and nouns: *¡Qué hermoso!* ("How beautiful!"), *¡Qué día!* ("What a day!"). To form an exclamation using both an adjective and a noun we use *noun* + **tan** + *adjective*: *¡Qué día **tan** hermoso!* ("What a beautiful day!").

3 GUSTAVO ¿Adónde van Uds. a pasar las vacaciones?

  JUDIT Bueno, pensamos **alquilar** un coche para ir a Málaga.

  GUSTAVO Buena **idea.**

  ■ alquilar → pedir prestado

alquilar *to rent*

la idea *idea*

4 GERARDO ¡Uf! ¡Qué frío! ¿Qué **pasa** con **la calefacción**?

  SUSANA Está descompuesta.

  ■ frío → calor
  la calefacción → **el aire acondicionado**
  descompuesta → descompuesto

pasar *here: to happen*
la calefacción *heating (system)*

el aire acondicionado *air conditioning*

5 MAMÁ Tomás, ¿puedes **cortar** las zanahorias, por favor?

  TOMÁS Bueno. ¿Dónde está el cuchillo?

  ■ zanahorias → cebollas

cortar *to cut*

Enrichment: In connection with mini-dialogue 4, ask students to add two lines suggesting some action that Susana can take to solve the problem. In 5 elicit responses to Tomás's question.

EN OTRAS PARTES

También se dice *el bombillo* y *el foco.*

También se dice *la cortadora de césped* y *el cortacéspedes.*

También se dice *conectar.*

PRÁCTICA

Práctica A
Answers will vary but should follow the model.
The major substantive change will be in the direct object pronoun.

A **El sábado por la mañana.** Imagina que vas a ayudar en casa. Escoge *(choose)* elementos de cada columna para preguntar y contestar según el modelo.

  ESTUDIANTE A *¿Cuándo vas a cortar el césped?*
  ESTUDIANTE B *Voy a cortarlo por la mañana.*

arreglar	la aspiradora	ahora mismo
barrer	el baño	antes del almuerzo
cambiar	las bombillas	después del desayuno
comprar	la cama	por la mañana
cortar	el césped	esta noche
enchufar	el cortacésped	por la tarde
hacer	las cortinas	este fin de semana
lavar	el pasillo	la semana próxima
limpiar	las sábanas	mañana
pasar	el suelo	mañana por la mañana

Reteach / Extra Help: Before students begin Ex. A on p. 66, you may want to ask volunteers for appropriate verb-object combinations. Encourage students to use each element at least once.

In connection with Ex. B, make sure students can identify each of the drawings before they begin the exercise. You may want volunteers to write the names of the items on the board.

B ¿Dónde está? Mira los dibujos para preguntar y contestar dónde están estas cosas. Sigue el modelo.

ESTUDIANTE A	*¿Dónde están las revistas?*
ESTUDIANTE B	*En el estante.*

1.

2.

3.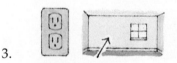

4.

5.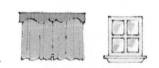

6.

7.

8.

Práctica B
1. ¿Dónde está la aspiradora? En el sótano.
2. ¿Dónde está la escoba? En el pasillo.
3. ¿Dónde está el enchufe? En la pared.
4. ¿Dónde están las luces? En el techo.
5. ¿Dónde están las cortinas? En la ventana.
6. ¿Dónde está la bombilla? En la lámpara.
7. ¿Dónde está el cordón (eléctrico)? En el suelo.
8. ¿Dónde está el corta-césped? En el garaje.

Práctica C
1. ¿Qué necesitas para limpiar …? Una aspiradora.
2. ¿Qué necesitas para barrer …? Una escoba.
3. ¿Qué necesitas para enchufar …? Un enchufe.
4. ¿Qué necesitas para abrir …? Una llave.
5. ¿Qué necesitas para poner …? Unos estantes.
6. ¿Qué necesitas para usar …? Una bombilla nueva.
7. ¿Qué necesitas para cortar …? Un cuchillo.
8. ¿Qué necesitas para hacer …? Sábanas y fundas.

C **¿Qué necesitas?** Pregunta y contesta. Escoge *(choose)* la palabra o expresión apropiada *(appropriate)* de la columna de la derecha para contestar. Sigue el modelo.

> escribir una carta
> ESTUDIANTE A   *¿Qué necesitas para escribir una carta?*
> ESTUDIANTE B   *Un bolígrafo.*

1. limpiar la alfombra	una bombilla nueva
2. barrer el suelo de la cocina	una aspiradora
3. enchufar el televisor	una llave
4. abrir la puerta del sótano	una escoba
5. poner los libros en orden	unos estantes
6. usar esa lámpara	sábanas y fundas
7. cortar algo	un cuchillo
8. hacer la cama	un enchufe
	un bolígrafo

En Marbella, España

D ¡Qué entusiasmo! Hay gente que exclama sobre todo. Usa cada sustantivo de la izquierda con un adjetivo apropiado de la derecha para hacer exclamaciones. No uses *(Don't use)* un adjetivo más de una vez. Sigue el modelo.

> diapositiva
> *¡Qué diapositivas tan bellas!*

1. día
2. gente
3. historia
4. hombre
5. muchacho(a)
6. mujer
7. novela
8. película
9. poema
10. programa

aburrido
amable
antipático
atlético
bueno
caliente
corto
chistoso
débil
emocionante

enérgico
fabuloso
fantástico
frío
fuerte
generoso
largo
perezoso
simpático
tacaño

E Hablemos de ti.
1. ¿Qué haces para ayudar en casa? ¿Cortas el césped? ¿Es un trabajo aburrido para ti o te gusta hacerlo?
2. ¿Prefieres pasar la aspiradora o barrer? ¿Por qué?
3. ¿Cómo es tu dormitorio? ¿Está ordenado o desordenado? ¿Quién lo limpia? ¿Cuándo? ¿Haces la cama todos los días?
4. ¿Hay un sótano en tu casa? ¿Qué tienes allí?
5. Donde tú vives, ¿necesitas aire acondicionado? ¿Durante qué meses? ¿Tienen casi todos los coches allí aire acondicionado?
6. ¿Hace mucho frío donde vives? ¿Necesitas calefacción todos los días en el invierno? ¿Prefieres el invierno o el verano? ¿Por qué?

Práctica D
Answers will vary.

Práctica E
Answers will vary.

(más arriba) En Caracas, Venezuela; (arriba) En Yucatán, México; (izquierda) En Buenos Aires, Argentina

Practice Sheet 2–1

Workbook Exs. A–B

Tape Manual Exs. 1–2 3

Quiz 2–1

Palabras Nuevas I   69

APLICACIONES

¡Qué desorden! 4 5 Pronunciación

Una discusión entre dos hermanos que comparten[1] un dormitorio.

JUAN PABLO ¡Qué desorden! Hay zapatos debajo de la cama, pantalones en la puerta, calcetines sucios en el suelo
5 y camisas en las sillas. ¿Por qué no pones las cosas donde deben estar?

JOSÉ LUIS Y tú, ¿por qué eres tan ordenado? Siempre tienes que poner toda tu ropa en la cómoda y en el armario.

10 JUAN PABLO Sí, cuando está limpia. Pero cuando está sucia la lavo y luego la guardo.[2]

JOSÉ LUIS ¿Ah sí? ¿Y quién limpia el cuarto?

JUAN PABLO ¡Yo! Tú nunca limpias nada. Nunca barres ni[3] pasas la aspiradora. Voy a poner el estante entre nuestras
15 camas. Así[4] no tengo que ver el desorden de *tu* dormitorio.

JOSÉ LUIS ¿De veras? Entonces no puedes usar el teléfono que está al lado de mi cama.

---

[1]**compartir** *to share*   [2]**guardar** *to put (something) away*   [3]**ni** *or (after a negative)*   [4]**así** *that way*

Culture: It is more common for boys to have compound names (Juan Antonio, Ángel Luis, and so on) in the Spanish-speaking world than in the U.S.

Preguntas
Contesta según el diálogo.

1. ¿De qué hablan los dos hermanos? ¿Están de acuerdo? ¿Por qué no?
2. ¿Cómo quiere tener el cuarto Juan Pablo? ¿Y José Luis?   3. ¿Qué hace con sus cosas Juan Pablo? ¿Y José Luis?   4. Según Juan Pablo, ¿qué no hace nunca José Luis?   5. ¿Qué dice Juan Pablo que va a hacer con el estante? ¿Por qué?   6. ¿Lo va a hacer de veras? ¿Qué crees tú? ¿Qué va a pasar? ¿Por qué?   7. ¿Estás de acuerdo con José Luis o con Juan Pablo? ¿Por qué?

Notes: Make sure students understand this cognate that has not been glossed: *la discusión*, discussion (often used in the sense of "argument").

Enrichment: As you model the **Diálogo** or play the tape, you may want to check comprehension with these questions: *Según Juan Pablo, ¿dónde pone José Luis los zapatos? (Debajo de la cama.) ¿Dónde pone los pantalones? (En la puerta.) ¿Y los calcetines y las camisas? (En el suelo y en las sillas.) ¿Está el teléfono en el centro del dormitorio? (No.) ¿Dónde está? (Está al lado de la cama de José Luis.)*

Diálogo
Answers may vary.
1. Del desorden del cuarto. No, no están de acuerdo porque …
2. A Juan Pablo le gusta tener el cuarto ordenado y a José Luis desordenado.
3. Juan Pablo las guarda y José Luis las deja en el suelo y en las sillas.
4. Nunca barre ni pasa la aspiradora.
5. Dice que va a ponerlo entre las camas porque no quiere ver el desorden.
6. No, porque quiere usar el teléfono.
7. Answers will vary.

Participación

Working with a partner, make up a dialogue about two brothers or sisters sharing a room. What might be some causes for disagreement? Messiness, borrowing things, using the other person's belongings?

PALABRAS NUEVAS II

If students ask: Other related words you may want to present: *el quehacer*, chore; *la licuadora*, blender; *la batidora*, mixer.

¿Quién lava los platos hoy?

🔊 6

Transparency 6
CONTEXTO VISUAL

quemado, -a

la tostadora

quemar

la olla

la sartén
pl. las sartenes

el horno

la cacerola

el fregadero

secar

la cucharita

CONTEXTO COMUNICATIVO

🔊 7

Enrichment: Point out that *fregadero* refers only to the kitchen sink; we use *el lavabo* to express "bathroom sink."

1 MAMÁ Los abuelos vienen a **almorzar** y no sé qué servir de postre.

HIJA ¿Por qué no preparas un flan? Yo te ayudo.

MAMÁ Bien, **trae aquella** cacerola y **aquellas** tazas. Voy a **batir** los huevos. Después puedes **mezclar**los con el azúcar y **añadir** la leche.

Variaciones:

■ a almorzar → a comer
■ servir → preparar
■ aquella cacerola → aquel tenedor
   aquellas tazas → aquellos platos

almorzar (o → ue) *to eat lunch, to have lunch*

trae (**tú** *command form of* **traer**) *bring*

aquel, aquella adj. *that (over there)*

aquellos, aquellas adj. *those (over there)*

batir *to beat*

mezclar *to mix*

añadir *to add*

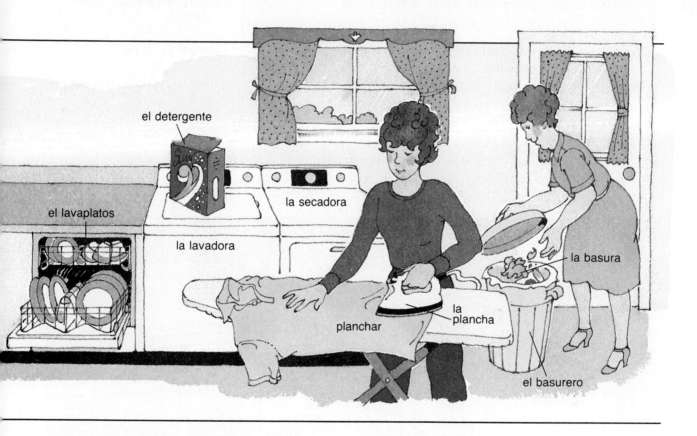

el detergente

el lavaplatos

la secadora

la lavadora

la basura

planchar

la plancha

el basurero

2   CÉSAR   ¿Qué servilletas pongo?

ANITA   No sé . . . es difícil **escoger.*** **Éstas** son demasiado grandes, ¿verdad?

CÉSAR   Sí, **ésas** no me gustan tampoco.

ANITA   Y **aquéllas** no son azules **como** el mantel.

■ servilletas → platos
   éstas → éstos
   ésas → ésos
   aquéllas → aquéllos

escoger (j)   *to choose*

éste, ésta; éstos, éstas
   pron.   *this one; these*

ése, ésa; ésos, ésas pron.   *that one; those*

**aquél, aquélla; aquéllos,
   aquéllas** pron.   *that one; those
   (over there)*

como   *like, as*

* In the present tense, verbs whose infinitives end in *-ger* change **g → j** in the *yo* form: **escojo.**
We will mark these verbs with a **(j).**

3 CECILIA ¿Qué es **eso**?

   ANDRÉS ¿**Esto**? Es un regalo para mi hermanito. Es su santo.

   CECILIA ¿Y **aquello**?

   ANDRÉS Es un regalo para ti. **¡Feliz cumpleaños!**

4 PAPÁ ¡Qué desordenada eres, hija! ¿Por qué no **recoges** los papeles del suelo?

   MARÍA Está bien, papá. Ahora mismo los recojo y los **tiro** a la basura.

   ■ los papeles → la ropa
   los → la
   los tiro a la basura → la pongo en la lavadora

eso *that*

esto *this*

aquello *that (over there)*

¡Feliz cumpleaños! *Happy birthday*

recoger (j) *to pick up*

tirar *to throw, to throw away*

Dos muchachas cocinan en España.

EN OTRAS PARTES

En la Argentina se dice *el tacho de basura*. En el Caribe se dice *el latón de basura*

En el Caribe se dice *la pila*.

En muchos países de la América Latina se dice *botar*.

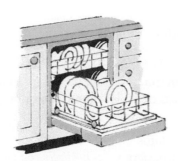

También se dice *el lavarropas*.

También se dice *el lavavajilla*.

PRÁCTICA

A ¿Dónde pongo esto? Es medianoche. El restaurante está cerrado y ahora hay que poner la cocina en orden. Escoge la palabra correcta. Sigue el modelo.

> platos sucios *(lavaplatos / basurero)*
> ESTUDIANTE A *¿Dónde pongo los platos sucios?*
> ESTUDIANTE B *En el lavaplatos.*

1. sartenes limpias *(armario / secadora)*
2. olla sucia *(fregadero / horno)*
3. pan quemado *(basurero / horno)*
4. cucharitas sucias *(secadora / lavaplatos)*
5. manteles sucios *(pasillo / lavadora)*
6. mantequilla *(fregadero / refrigerador)*
7. basura *(basurero / lavaplatos)*
8. detergente *(refrigerador / lavadora)*

En España

B **¿Qué hacen?**   Toda la familia ayuda en casa. Completa el párrafo (*paragraph*) con las palabras correctas.

Después de almorzar José (*quita / desenchufa*) los platos, los platillos, las cucharitas y los vasos sucios de la mesa. Yo lavo las ollas y las cacerolas en el (*refrigerador / fregadero*) y él las (*seca / lava*). Luego (yo) (*barro / quemo*) el suelo de la cocina con la escoba y él (*tira / escoge*) la
5 basura y lleva el basurero afuera. Mi hermana mayor (*enchufa / recoge*) la ropa sucia de nuestros cuartos y la pone primero en la (*lavadora / tostadora*) y después en la (*aspiradora / secadora*). Mi mamá (*plancha / corta*) las camisas y papá (*limpia / enchufa*) el sótano. Mi hermano mayor (*corta / seca*) el césped y (*barre / alquila*) el patio. A Josefina le
10 gusta pasar la (*aspiradora / plancha*) y poner en (*orden / desorden*) la sala y el comedor.

C **En la cocina.**   Raquel y Esteban ayudan en la cocina. Escoge elementos de cada columna para preguntar y contestar. Sigue el modelo.

> los platos
> ESTUDIANTE A   *¿Qué haces con los platos?*
> ESTUDIANTE B   *Los lavo y después los seco.*

1. la basura	contar	añadir a la sopa
2. las servilletas	cortar	batir
sucias	lavar	lavar
3. el pollo	mezclar con leche	limpiar
4. las cucharitas	planchar	poner en el armario
5. el mantel limpio	poner en el basurero	poner en el horno
6. las cacerolas sucias	poner en el fregadero	poner en la mesa
7. las papas y las	poner en la lavadora	poner en la secadora
zanahorias	preparar	secar
8. los huevos	recoger	tirar

D **Hablemos de ti.**
1. ¿Qué prefieres hacer en la cocina? ¿Te gusta cocinar? ¿Qué cocinas? ¿Cocinas a menudo? ¿Qué usas más cuando cocinas, el horno o la estufa? ¿Por qué?
2. ¿Tienes lavaplatos en tu casa? Si no tienes uno, ¿quién lava los platos? ¿Quién los seca? ¿Quién los pone en el armario?
3. De todos los aparatos (*machines*) eléctricos que tienes en tu casa, ¿cuál usas más a menudo? En tu opinión, ¿cuál es el más importante? ¿Por qué?

ACTIVIDAD

¿Haces la cama todos los días?   Find out what chores your classmates
do at home by participating in this class survey. Divide into small groups.
Each group then writes questions about what kinds of chores people have
to do at home. For example:

> ¿Quién tiene que lavar la ropa sucia?
> ¿Cuántos tienen que tirar la basura?
> Si tienes un perro o un gato, ¿quién tiene que darle de comer?

One person in each group should keep a tally of the questions and
responses. A sample tally sheet might look like the one below. Afterward
compare the results. Which are the most and the least common chores
among your classmates?

	Todos los días	A menudo	A veces	Nunca
lavar la ropa sucia				
tirar la basura				
dar de comer al perro/gato				

Sinónimos
1. añadir
2. barrerlo (or: lavarlo)
3. almorzar

Antónimos
1. desenchufar
2. desordenada
3. ahora (mismo)
4. calefacción
5. éste
6. techo

ESTUDIO DE PALABRAS

Written accents are often used to distinguish between words that are spelled the same but have different meanings. For example:

Él barre **el** suelo.	*He sweeps **the** floor.*
Tú y **tu** hermano pueden ir a la fiesta.	*You and **your** bröther can go to the party.*
Sí, si tú lo dices.	*Yes, **if** you say so.*

How do the following words change in meaning when we add an accent mark?

$$se \rightarrow sé \qquad solo \rightarrow sólo \qquad mi \rightarrow mí$$

We always use written accents on question words and exclamations.

¿Quién es tu profesor de inglés?	*Who's your English teacher?*
¿Dónde están las cucharitas?	*Where are the teaspoons?*
¡Qué desorden!	*What a mess!*

Familias de palabras

You have probably noticed that the adjective *quemado* is related to the verb *quemar*. What do you think these adjectives mean: *cortado, planchado, alquilado?*

Sinónimos

Completa las frases con una palabra parecida *(similar)* a la palabra en cursiva *(italics).*

1. Para preparar un flan necesitas *poner* azúcar *también.*
2. El suelo está muy sucio. ¿Te ayudo a *limpiarlo?*
3. Voy a *comer al mediodía* con mi primo.

Antónimos

Completa las frases con un antónimo de la palabra en cursiva.

1. Voy a *enchufar* la plancha.
2. Es una persona muy *ordenada.*
3. Quiero comer *más tarde.*
4. Mi coche no tiene *aire acondicionado.*
5. Voy a comprar *aquél.*
6. El *suelo* está limpio.

EXPLICACIONES I Essential

Notes: Point out the use of *almorzar* and of *poder* + infinitive in mini-dialogue 1 on p. 72.

Verbos con el cambio *o → ue*

Remember that in certain verbs, called stem-changing verbs, the stem vowel *o* changes to *ue* in all except the *nosotros* and *vosotros* forms of the present tense.

ENCONTRAR		PODER		DORMIR	
encuentro	encontramos	puedo	podemos	duermo	dormimos
encuentras	encontráis	puedes	podéis	duermes	dormís
encuentra	encuentran	puede	pueden	duerme	duermen

◆ **OBJECTIVES:**

TO RELATE ACTIVITIES AND EVENTS

TO DISCUSS SPORTS AND GAMES

1 Remember that *poder* is usually followed by an infinitive.

No **puedo encontrar** las bombillas.　*I **can't find** the lightbulbs.*
Podemos ir a la tienda mañana.　*We **can go** to the store tomorrow.*

2 Here are other *o → ue* stem-changing verbs that you have learned.

-*ar* verbs: almorzar, contar, costar, mostrar
-*er* verbs: doler, llover, volver

3 You also know one verb, *jugar*, whose stem changes from *u → ue* in all but the *nosotros* and *vosotros* forms of the present tense.

JUGAR	
juego	jugamos
juegas	jugáis
juega	juegan

4 Be careful, however, because not all verbs that have *o* as their stem vowel are stem-changing verbs. For example, *cortar: **Corto** el césped casi todos los fines de semana.*

Reteach / Extra Help: As you present the verb forms, call attention to the bold type used to highlight the stem vowels.
　Before students begin the **Práctica** on p. 80, provide practice with various *o → ue* verbs. You may want to write these phrases on the board: *dormir hasta el mediodía, mostrarles las fotos a los amigos, volver a casa, poder salir solo(a) por la noche, jugar al tenis.* Do a chain drill or ask students to work in pairs to ask and answer questions that use all the verb forms.

Práctica A
1. g (Cuenta …)
2. f (Juegan …)
3. d (Duerme …)
4. c (Almuerzan …)
5. h (Le muestra …)
6. b (Cuentan …)
7. e (Vuelve …)
8. a (Les muestra …)

PRÁCTICA

A ¿Qué hacen? Imagina que vas a una plaza. ¿Qué hace la gente que ves allí? Pregunta y contesta según el modelo. Escoge la frase más apropiada (*appropriate*).

> esas enfermeras
> ESTUDIANTE A *¿Qué hacen esas enfermeras?*
> ESTUDIANTE B *Vuelven del hospital.*

1. esa camarera
2. esas atletas
3. ese gato
4. esas mujeres
5. ese fotógrafo
6. esos turistas panameños
7. el piloto
8. la profesora de biología

a) mostrarles las hojas a los estudiantes
b) contar su dinero en español
c) almorzar juntas con sus hijos
d) dormir debajo del árbol
e) volver al aeropuerto
f) jugar al béisbol
g) contar su propina
h) mostrarle sus fotos a un cliente
i) volver del hospital

Práctica B
Llueve
puedo
juegan
duerme
cuentan
vuelvo / almuerzo / almorzamos
cuesta

B Mis vacaciones. Todos los días Emilia escribe lo que hace en su diario (*diary*). Escoge verbos de la lista para completar el párrafo (*paragraph*).

almorzar	costar	jugar	poder
contar	dormir	llover	volver

Lunes 15 de julio.
Estoy cansada de la lluvia. _____ casi todos los días. ¡Qué vacaciones tan aburridas! Nunca _____ salir del hotel.

Martes 16 de julio.
5 ¡Hoy hace buen tiempo! Ahora estoy en la playa. Hay mucha gente. Varios chicos _____ en la playa, otros en el agua. Mucha gente toma el sol, descansa sobre toallas de playa o _____ debajo de las sombrillas. Hay un vendedor de helados. Muchos niños hacen cola y casi todos _____ sus monedas. Son casi las dos, y tengo mucha hambre. En
10 seguida (yo) _____ al hotel. Hoy _____ con Josefina. (Nosotras) _____ en un restaurante mexicano muy bueno. La comida allá es excelente y no _____ mucho. Bueno, eso es todo por hoy.

Practice Sheet 2–3

 10 Tape Manual Ex. 5

Quiz 2–3

Mandatos afirmativos con *tú*

When you tell someone to do something, you are giving an affirmative command. For example, "Go away," "Eat your vegetables," "Be good" are commands. English has only one form for commands, but in Spanish there are several forms. Here is how you give an affirmative command to someone you address as *tú*.

1 The affirmative *tú* command form for regular and stem-changing verbs is the same as the *Ud. / él / ella* form of the present tense.

Elena contesta el teléfono.	*Elena is answering the phone.*
Elena, contesta el teléfono.	*Elena, answer the phone.*
Pepe abre la puerta.	*Pepe opens the door.*
Pepe, abre la puerta.	*Pepe, open the door.*
Graciela vuelve temprano.	*Graciela is coming back early.*
Graciela, vuelve temprano.	*Graciela, come back early.*
Jorge almuerza conmigo.	*Jorge is having lunch with me.*
Jorge, almuerza conmigo.	*Jorge, have lunch with me.*

2 Just as in English, we don't usually use the pronoun *tú* except for emphasis.

Marta, **desenchufa tú** la tostadora. Yo estoy ocupada.	*Marta, **you unplug** the toaster. I'm busy.*

◆ **OBJECTIVES:**

TO GIVE ORDERS TO SOMEONE

TO GIVE ADVICE OR MAKE SUGGESTIONS

TO GIVE INSTRUCTIONS

TO MAKE EXCUSES

Notes: Remind students that they have been hearing and responding to commands since they began their study of Spanish. Elicit some of the classroom instructions that you give as commands: *Escucha, Repite, Escribe, Contesta, Borra la pizarra,* for example.
  Point out the command forms in mini-dialogues 5 on p. 66 and 1 on p. 72.

Reteach / Extra Help: Reinforce *tú* commands by giving instructions and asking volunteers to follow them. Some of your commands may require that students mime the actions: *Cuenta tu dinero. Corta una manzana. Escribe mi nombre en la pizarra. Abre la ventana. Camina hasta la puerta. Juega al béisbol. Llama a ____ por teléfono.*

Un almuerzo en España

PRÁCTICA

A **¡Silencio!** ¿Qué dice la profesora al estudiante? Sigue el modelo.

Escribe tu nombre.

 1.

 3.

2.

 4.

 5.

 6.

Reteach / Review: Before students begin the **Práctica,** you may want them to work in pairs or small groups to take turns giving and following commands.

Práctica A
1. Cierra la ventana.
2. Mira la pizarra.
3. Mira la foto.
4. Escribe la fecha.
5. Levanta la mano.
6. Abre la puerta.

B **¿Qué hago primero?** Imagina que tienes que hacer muchas cosas. Le preguntas a alguien qué debes hacer primero. ¿Qué te dice? Sigue el modelo.

> limpiar la sala y lavar el suelo de la cocina
>
> ESTUDIANTE A *¿Qué hago primero? ¿Limpio la sala o lavo el suelo de la cocina?*
>
> ESTUDIANTE B *Limpia la sala primero.*
>
> o: *Lava el suelo de la cocina primero.*

1. planchar los pañuelos y lavar los platos
2. cortar el césped y arreglar la tostadora
3. contar aquellas monedas y secar aquellas ollas
4. buscar mis llaves y llevar aquellas cajas al garaje
5. pasar la aspiradora y limpiar todos los espejos
6. almorzar con mi abuela y repasar mis apuntes
7. limpiar el sótano y decorar la sala
8. lavar las cortinas y preparar la cena
9. alquilar una película y comprar comestibles

Práctica B
1. ¿Qué hago primero? ¿Plancho los pañuelos o lavo los platos? Plancha ... (*or:* Lava ...)
2. ... ¿Corto ... o arreglo? Corta ... (*or:* Arregla ...)
3. ... ¿Cuento ... o seco ...? Cuenta ... (*or:* Seca ...)
4. ... ¿Busco ... o llevo ...? Busca ... (*or:* Lleva ...)
5. ... ¿Paso ... o limpio ...? Pasa ... (*or:* Limpia ...)
6. ... ¿Almuerzo ... o repaso ...? Almuerza ... (*or:* Repasa ...)
7. ... ¿Limpio ... o decoro ...? Limpia ... (*or:* Decora ...)
8. ... ¿Lavo ... o preparo ...? Lava ... (*or:* Prepara ...)
9. ... ¿Alquilo ... o compro ...? Alquila ... (*or:* Compra ...)

C ¡Cómo habla! Hay gente que siempre nos dice qué debemos hacer. Sigue el modelo.

> Voy a pedir un postre. / escoger el pastel de queso
> ESTUDIANTE A *Voy a pedir un postre.*
> ESTUDIANTE B *Escoge el pastel de queso.*

1. Voy afuera. / volver pronto
2. Hay ropa sucia en el suelo. / recoger y lavar todo
3. El pasillo está sucio. / barrer el suelo ahora mismo
4. Llueve. / correr más rápidamente
5. No tengo mucha hambre. / comer más tarde
6. Voy a hacer un flan. / batir bien los huevos
7. Preparo una ensalada de frutas. / añadir más naranjas
8. Hace calor en casa. / abrir las ventanas

Práctica C
1. Vuelve pronto.
2. Recoge y lava todo.
3. Barre el suelo ahora mismo.
4. Corre más rápidamente.
5. Come más tarde.
6. Bate bien los huevos.
7. Añade más naranjas.
8. Abre las ventanas.

D Prepara la cena. En casa, tienes que hacer muchas cosas. Cambia las frases según el modelo.

> Para hacer la cama, tienes que cambiar las sábanas y las fundas.
> *Para hacer la cama, cambia las sábanas y las fundas.*

1. Antes de la cena, tienes que lavar y secar los vasos, llevar el mantel a la mesa, y después traer los platos, tenedores y cuchillos.
2. Para preparar pollo al horno, debes lavar y secar el pollo, cortar y añadir las cebollas y las papas y después cocinar todo junto por 45 minutos en un horno caliente.
3. Para preparar esta ensalada, tienes que lavar la lechuga, cortar los tomates y la cebolla, y añadir un poco de limón.
4. Después de la cena, tienes que quitar las cosas de la mesa, lavar los platos, platillos y vasos en el lavaplatos y las ollas en el fregadero, barrer el suelo y tirar la basura. Después puedes descansar.

Práctica D
1. Antes de la cena, lava y seca los vasos, lleva el mantel ... trae los platos, ...
2. Para preparar pollo al horno, lava y seca el pollo, corta y añade las cebollas ... cocina ....
3. Para preparar esta ensalada, lava la lechuga, corta los tomates ... y añade ...
4. Después de la cena, quita las cosas de la mesa, lava ... barre ... y tira ... Después, descansa.

Pollo asado

Ingredientes: 1 pollo Mantequilla 3 cebollas
2 zanahorias Papas pequeñas

Preparación: 1. Limpie el pollo. 2. Ponga el pollo en una cacerola. 3. Añada la mantequilla al pollo. 4. Corte las ... las cebollas y las

Práctica E
Answers will vary.

Practice Sheets 2–4, 2–5

Workbook Exs. E–F

11 Tape Manual Exs. 6–7

12 Refrán

Quiz 2–4

E Hablemos de ti.

1. ¿A qué deportes juegas en la escuela?
2. ¿A qué hora vuelves de la escuela por la tarde? ¿Dónde almuerzas? ¿Dónde almuerzas los sábados? ¿Con quién? ¿Qué comes generalmente para el almuerzo?
3. ¿Tienes algún animal en tu casa? ¿Un perro o un gato? ¿Cómo se llama? ¿Dónde pasa la noche, afuera o adentro?
4. ¿Qué tiempo hace ahora? ¿Llueve? ¿En qué estación llueve mucho? ¿Qué haces cuando llueve?

ACTIVIDAD

Hacer excusas Get together in groups of three or four. Write the verbs from the list below on separate slips of paper and place them upside down. Then take turns picking a verb and forming a command. The next person must reply with an excuse. Continue until each member of the group has given three commands and three excuses. Here are some examples:

Pasa la aspiradora.	Pero el suelo está limpio.
Come este pan tostado.	Pero está quemado.
Alquila un coche.	Pero ya tenemos uno.

abrir	batir	desenchufar	limpiar	quitar
almorzar	comer	enchufar	llevar	recoger
añadir	comprar	escribir	mandar	secar
aprender	contar	explicar	mezclar	subir
asistir a	contestar	jugar	mirar	tirar
bajar de	cortar	lavar	mostrar	tomar
barrer	dejar	leer	planchar	volver

APLICACIONES

¡Hogar, dulce hogar!¹ 13

Notes: Before presenting the **Lectura**, make sure students read the section marked **Antes de leer.**

Mi casa no es muy grande. Al contrario. Pero es cómoda y me gusta. No es moderna como la casa de Luis. Luis es un poco aburrido. ¡Siempre habla de su bello apartamento! Y sólo porque está en el edificio más grande y más alto del barrio. ¿Y qué importa? Yo nunca le digo a Luis que no me gusta su
5 casa. Claro que no. Pero yo encuentro más bonita la casa de mi amigo Raúl. Allí está, con su balcón, su jardín de muchos colores y el árbol viejo en la esquina.

   Mi casa no tiene jardín. No tiene balcón. Tampoco es moderna. Pero tiene dos enormes ventanas con rejas de hierro² y unas flores rojas muy
10 bonitas. No cambiaría³ por nada el patio interior. Si quiero, puedo acostarme allí para tomar el sol o puedo jugar con mi perro Ciclón. Nadie me ve desde la calle. Claro que me gustaría⁴ tener una casa más moderna con balcón y con vista al mar. Pero ¿saben algo? Me gusta vivir en esta casa vieja de paredes blancas y de grandes ventanas por donde entra mucha luz
15 y sol. Es que . . . ésta es mi casa y no quiero otra.

---

¹**hogar, dulce hogar**   *home, sweet home*   ²**rejas de hierro**   *iron grilles*
³**no cambiaría** (*from* **cambiar**)   *I wouldn't change*   ⁴**me gustaría**   *I'd like*

Preguntas

Contesta según la lectura.

1. ¿Dónde vive Luis? ¿Por qué habla siempre de su apartamento?
2. Según el autor, ¿por qué es más bonita la casa de Raúl que la casa de Luis?
3. ¿Por qué le gusta al autor tener un patio?
4. ¿Por qué le gusta al autor vivir en esa casa?
5. Cuando alguien dice "una casa moderna," ¿cómo la imaginas? Describe una casa moderna.
6. ¿Cómo es tu casa ideal?

ANTES DE LEER

As you read, think about choosing another title for this reading from the following:
1. No hay casa como mi casa
2. No hay casa perfecta
3. Mi casa preferida

Preguntas
1. En un apartamento moderno (y bello). Porque está en el edificio más grande y más alto del barrio.
2. Porque tiene un balcón y un jardín de muchos colores.
3. Porque puede tomar el sol y jugar con su perro y nadie puede verlo desde la calle.
4. Porque tiene paredes blancas y grandes ventanas (y porque es su casa).
5. Answers will vary.
6. Answers will vary.

EXPLICACIONES II Essential

Adjetivos y pronombres demostrativos

◆ OBJECTIVES:

TO POINT THINGS OUT

TO COMPARE AND CONTRAST

TO EXPRESS AGREEMENT AND DISAGREEMENT

TO STATE PREFERENCES

TO FIND OUT WHAT SOMETHING IS

You have already learned that we use demonstrative adjectives to point out people or things that are nearby.

este tenedor	*this fork*	**estos** tenedores	*these forks*
esta cuchara	*this spoon*	**estas** cucharas	*these spoons*
ese tenedor	*that fork*	**esos** tenedores	*those forks*
esa cuchara	*that spoon*	**esas** cucharas	*those spoons*

Remember that a demonstrative adjective always comes before the noun and agrees with it in gender and number.

1 To point out things that are farther away we use *aquel, aquella, aquellos, aquellas.*

aquel cuchillo	*that knife*	**aquellos** cuchillos	*those knives*
aquella servilleta	*that napkin*	**aquellas** servilletas	*those napkins*

aquella ensalada

esa ensalada

esta ensalada

2 We can also use all of these words as pronouns to replace a noun. In that case they have an accent mark.

Esta ensalada es de Sonia. Y **ésta,** ¿de quién es?	***This** salad is Sonia's. And whose is **this (one)**?*
Este chile relleno es de César, ¿verdad? No, **éste** es de César y **ése** es de Anita.	***This** stuffed pepper is César's, right? No, **this (one)** is César's and **that (one)** is Anita's.*
Aquella foto es bonita. **Aquéllas** son bastante feas.	***That** photo **(over there)** is pretty. **Those (over there)** are rather ugly.*

3 To refer to an idea, to an action, or to something that has not yet been identified, we use the demonstrative pronouns *esto, eso,* or *aquello.* None of them has an accent mark.

Esto es fácil.	*This is easy.*
Yo no hago **eso.**	*I don't do that.*
¿Qué es **aquello**?	*What is that (over there)?*

Notes: Make sure students understand that *esto, eso,* and *aquello* are neuter pronouns; they have no masculine, feminine, or plural forms.

	Cerca de ti		Cerca de la persona a quien hablas		Lejos de ti y de la otra persona	
ADJETIVOS	este	estos	ese	esos	aquel	aquellos
	esta	estas	esa	esas	aquella	aquellas
PRONOMBRES	éste	éstos	ése	ésos	aquél	aquéllos
	ésta	éstas	ésa	ésas	aquélla	aquéllas
	esto		eso		aquello	

PRÁCTICA

A ¿Qué te gusta más? Imagina que tú y un(a) amigo(a) están en una tienda donde venden muebles y otras cosas para la casa. Pregunta y contesta según el modelo.

> las almohadas
> ESTUDIANTE A *¿Te gustan estas almohadas?*
> ESTUDIANTE B *Sí, pero prefiero ésas.*

1. la cama
2. la lavadora
3. el horno
4. las sartenes
5. la tostadora
6. los sillones
7. la cacerola
8. la lámpara
9. las cortinas
10. la cómoda
11. las sábanas
12. el espejo
13. la alfombra
14. el sofá
15. las mantas
16. los muebles

Práctica A
1. ¿Te gusta esta cama?
   Sí, pero prefiero ésa.
2. ¿... esta lavadora?
   Sí, ... ésa.
3. ¿... este horno?
   Sí, ... ése.
4. ¿... estas sartenes?
   Sí, ... ésas.
5. ¿... esta tostadora?
   Sí, ... ésa.
6. ¿... estos sillones?
   Sí, ... ésos.
7. ¿... esta cacerola?
   Sí, ... ésa.
8. ¿... esta lámpara?
   Sí, ... ésa.
9. ¿... estas cortinas?
   Sí, ... ésas.
10. ¿.. esta cómoda?
    Sí, ... ésa.
11. ¿... estas sábanas?
    Sí, ... ésas.
12. ¿... este espejo?
    Sí, ... ése.
13. ¿... esta alfombra?
    Sí, ... ésa.
14. ¿... este sofá?
    Sí, ... ése.
15. ¿... estas mantas?
    Sí, ... ésas.
16. ¿... estos muebles?
    Sí, ... ésos.

Práctica B
este
ese
aquel
este
esa
aquella
aquella
esta

Enrichment: You may want to ask pairs of students to practice Ex. B; then lead the exercise in a large group.

B **De compras.** Clara y Lucía van de compras pero no saben qué comprar. Usa la forma correcta de los adjetivos demostrativos para completar el diálogo según el dibujo.

CLARA ¿Te gusta _____ sombrero rojo?

LUCÍA Prefiero _____ sombrero con las flores pequeñas.

CLARA ¿Y _____ sombrero mexicano?

LUCÍA Es hermoso pero muy caro.

5 CLARA Bueno, _____ sombrero verde es bonito y barato.

LUCÍA Pero a mí no me gusta.

CLARA Está bien, ¿quieres buscar otra cosa?

LUCÍA Sí, una falda.

CLARA ¿Te gusta _____ falda azul?

10 LUCÍA Es demasiado grande para mí.

CLARA ¿Y _____ falda con el cinturón negro?

LUCÍA Es interesante, pero no me gusta mucho.

CLARA Vámonos, entonces. No te gusta nada.

LUCÍA Un momento, ¿te gusta _____ bufanda marrón?

15 CLARA No es mi color favorito. Prefiero _____ bufanda verde.

LUCÍA No sé qué hacer. Es difícil escoger . . .

CLARA ¡También es difícil ir de compras contigo!

Práctica C
1. ¿Te gusta esa pelota?
   Prefiero aquélla.
2. ¿Te gusta ese barco?
   Prefiero aquél.
3. ¿Te gustan esos aviones?
   Prefiero aquéllos.
4. ¿Te gusta ese camión?
   Prefiero aquél.
5. ¿Te gusta ese tocadiscos?
   Prefiero aquél.
6. ¿Te gustan esos juegos?
   Prefiero aquéllos.
7. ¿Te gusta esa máscara?
   Prefiero aquélla.
8. ¿Te gustan esas calculadoras? Prefiero aquéllas.

C **Regalos.** Andrés va de compras con su hermanita. Pregunta y contesta según el modelo.

la piñata

ESTUDIANTE A   *¿Te gusta esa piñata?*

ESTUDIANTE B   *Prefiero aquélla.*

1. la pelota	3. los aviones	5. el tocadiscos	7. la máscara
2. el barco	4. el camión	6. los juegos	8. las calculadoras

La expresión *hace . . . que*

Remember that to tell how long something that began in the past has been going on we use this construction:

hace + period of time + **que** + present-tense verb

Hace mucho tiempo **que estudio** español.

I've been studying Spanish for a long time.

Hace cinco meses **que estamos** en esta ciudad.

We've been in this city for five months.

Hace una semana **que leo** esta novela.

I've been reading this novel for a week.

1 To form a question, we use this construction:

¿**Cuánto tiempo**
¿**Cuántos años (meses, etc.)**   } **hace que** + present-tense verb?
¿**Cuántas semanas (horas, etc.)**

¿**Cuánto tiempo hace que trabajas** en la farmacia?

How long have you been working at the drugstore?

¿**Cuántos meses hace que vives** en este apartamento?

How many months have you been living in this apartment?

◆ OBJECTIVES:

TO FIND OUT HOW LONG SOMETHING HAS BEEN GOING ON

TO TELL WHAT YOU HAVE BEEN DOING

Notes: Before students open their books to read the explanation of the *hace ... que* construction, you may want to write the following on the board: *hace* + period of time + *que* + present-tense verb. Elicit possible periods of time (*una semana, dos meses, tres años, cuatro minutos,* and so on) and present-tense verbs and write students' suggestions on the board. Then ask volunteers to combine the elements to form sentences.

Reteach / Extra Help: Ask students to work in pairs to practice asking and answering questions with the *hace ... que* construction. You may want to write those phrases on the board: *estudiar español, vivir en esta ciudad, asistir a esta escuela.*

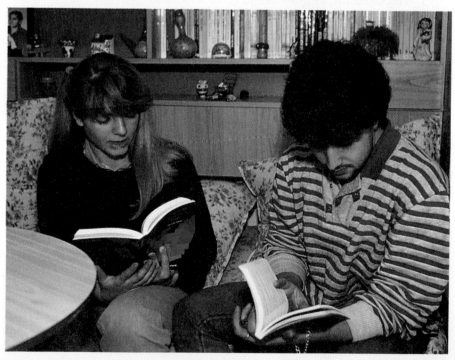

En Barcelona, España

PRÁCTICA

Práctica A

1. ¿Cuánto tiempo hace que busca (Ud.) ese número de teléfono? Hace sólo un minuto.
2. ¿Cuánto tiempo hace que hace (Ud.) cola? Hace más de quince minutos.
3. ¿Cuánto tiempo hace que va (Ud.) a esa agencia de viajes? Hace un mes.
4. ¿Cuánto tiempo hace que habla (Ud.) español? Hace sólo un año.
5. ¿Cuánto tiempo hace que viaja (Ud.)? Hace casi tres semanas.
6. ¿Cuánto tiempo hace que juega (Ud.) al tenis? Hace varios años.
7. ¿Cuánto tiempo hace que lee (Ud.) ese libro? Hace tres días.
8. ¿Cuánto tiempo hace que escribe (Ud.) esa tarjeta postal? Hace unos minutos.
9. ¿Cuánto tiempo hace que tiene (Ud.) esa cámara? Hace mucho tiempo.

Práctica B

1. ¿Cuántos meses hace que trabajas …?
2. ¿Cuántas semanas hace que asistes …?
3. ¿Cuántos días hace que estás …?
4. ¿Cuántas horas hace que escribes …?
5. ¿Cuántos minutos hace que hablas …?
6. ¿Cuántos días hace que almuerzas …?
7. ¿Cuántas semanas hace que sales …?

Práctica C
Answers will vary.

A Hacer cola.   Un grupo de turistas hacen cola en el aeropuerto. ¿Qué dicen? Pregunta y contesta según el modelo.

> estar en Caracas / una semana
> ESTUDIANTE A   *¿Cuánto tiempo hace que está Ud. en Caracas?*
> ESTUDIANTE B   *Hace una semana.*

1. buscar ese número de teléfono / sólo un minuto
2. hacer cola / más de quince minutos
3. ir a esa agencia de viajes / un mes
4. hablar español / sólo un año
5. viajar / casi tres semanas
6. jugar al tenis / varios años
7. leer ese libro / tres días
8. escribir esa tarjeta postal / unos minutos
9. tener esa cámara / mucho tiempo

B Una conversación en la oficina.   Lee cada una de las respuestas para hacer las preguntas. Sigue el modelo.

> *Hace tres años que vivo aquí.*
> *¿Cuántos años hace que vives aquí?*

1. Hace seis meses que trabajo en esta oficina.
2. Hace cuatro semanas que asisto a clases de computadoras.
3. Hace tres días que estoy aquí.
4. Hace varias horas que escribo a máquina.
5. Hace cinco minutos que hablo por teléfono.
6. Hace varios días que almuerzo solo(a).
7. Hace dos semanas que salgo tarde del trabajo.

C Hablemos de ti.

1. ¿Cuánto tiempo hace que estudias español?
2. ¿Cuánto tiempo hace que asistes a esta escuela?
3. ¿Cuántos minutos hace que estás en esta clase?
4. ¿Juegas a algunos deportes? ¿Qué deportes? ¿Cuánto tiempo que los juegas?
5. ¿Tocas la guitarra o el piano? ¿Cuánto tiempo hace que la/lo sabes tocar?
6. ¿Cuánto tiempo hace que vives en tu casa o apartamento?

ACTIVIDAD

¿Cuánto tiempo hace que . . . ?   Get together in groups of three or four. Each person should write on separate cards the names of five different household objects. Shuffle the cards and then distribute them in three piles marked *este(a)*, *ese(a)*, and *aquel(la)*. One person picks a card— for example, *la escoba* from the pile marked *este(a)*—and asks a question using the phrase *hace que*. For example:

> ¿Cuánto tiempo hace que tienes esta escoba?

The person to the questioner's left must give a reasonable answer. For example: *Hace un mes.*

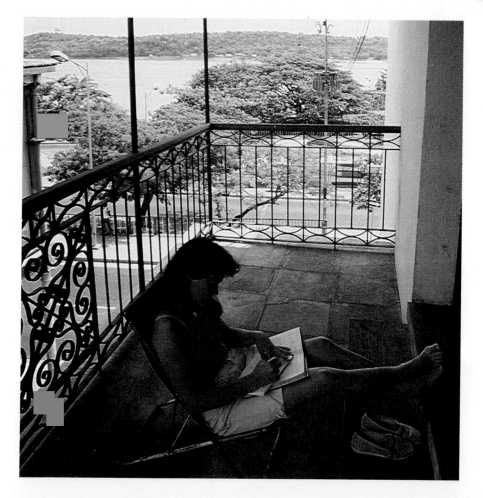

Una estudiante en Venezuela

APLICACIONES

Notes: Answers to the **Repaso** and **Tema** appear in the Teacher Notes.

REPASO

Notes: Review of:
1. days of the week
   hace … que
   noun phrases with *de*
   adjectives with *estar*
2. demonstrative adjectives /
   pronouns
   adjectives with *estar*
3. *poder*
   o → ue stem-changing verbs
   jugar
4. affirmative *tú* commands
   demonstrative adjectives
   ir a + infinitive

Enrichment: You may want to use the model sentences in the **Repaso** for dictation.

Mira las frases modelo. Luego cambia las frases que siguen al español según los modelos.

1. *Es lunes. Hace dos semanas que la ropa de Carolina está sucia.*
   (It's Thursday. The restaurant's dishwasher has been broken for two days.)
   (It's Sunday. The basement floor has been clean for a month.)
   (It's Friday. Pepe's sister has been sick for ten days.)

2. *Esta puerta está abierta y aquélla está cerrada.*
   (That pot (over there) is full, but this one is empty.)
   (These men are happy, but those (over there) are sad.)
   (This meat is burned, and that's cold.)

3. *No puedes cambiar la bombilla porque no encuentro una.*
   (I can't cut the grass because you (pl.) are playing there.)
   (They can't run the vacuum cleaner because their parents are sleeping now.)
   (We can't sweep the patio because you (fam.) are having lunch there.)

4. *Bate estos huevos, por favor. Voy a hacer un pastel.*
   (Please plug in that washing machine. I'm going to wash the clothes.)
   (Please pick up those cords. I'm going to sweep the floor.)
   (Please add that lemon (over there). He's going to mix the salad.)

En Zaragoza, España

Reteach / Review: In connection with the **Tema,** you may want students to write talk balloons for each of the first four pictures. Ask volunteers to present their conversations to the class.

Escribe las frases en español.

1. It's Saturday. Enrique's room has been messy for a week.

2. This closet is neat and that one is messy.

3. He can't make his bed because his dog is sleeping there.

4. Please clean this room, Chispa! I'm going to throw out the trash.

REDACCIÓN

Enrichment: Expand on the topics in the **Redacción** section: Write a ''Dear Abby'' letter asking for advice on how to deal with a sibling or roommate whose neatness or messiness is driving you crazy. Check students' work for correct spelling, punctuation, and capitalization.

Ahora escoge uno de los siguientes temas para escribir tu propio diálogo o párrafo.

1. Expand the *Tema* by contrasting the chores Enrique has to do on weekends with what he wants to do. Does he have to mow the lawn? Wash the dishes? What does he want to do?

2. Write a paragraph describing your ideal home. Do you want to live in an apartment or a house? How many rooms are there? Do you have air conditioning? What other appliances do you have? Do you do many chores around the house? Which ones? Is your room always neat? Who cleans it?

3. Create a dialogue between a parent and a child. The parent is telling the child what to do to help around the house. The child has a lot of excuses.

COMPRUEBA TU PROGRESO   CAPÍTULO 2   Discretionary

Notes: Answers to the **Comprueba** appear in the Teacher Notes.

A   Una casa desordenada
Completa cada frase con la forma correcta de la palabra apropiada.

ahora mismo	cortar	lavaplatos
barrer	enchufar	secadora
bombilla	hacer	suelo

1. El muchacho _____ la cama.
2. El perro duerme en el _____.
3. La madre _____ el balcón con su escoba.
4. Juan busca una _____ para la lámpara.
5. El muchacho pone las toallas en la _____.
6. Su hermanita _____ el césped.
7. El padre arregla el _____ descompuesto.
8. ¿Qué es eso en la pared? Hay que borrarlo _____.
9. (Yo) _____ la plancha.

B   Completa las frases
Completa cada frase con la forma correcta del verbo en el presente.

1. (Nosotros) no _____ salir porque _____.
   (poder, llover)
2. Teresa _____ al tenis con nosotros.   *(jugar)*
3. ¿A qué hora _____ Uds.?   *(volver)*
4. (Nosotros) no _____ en ese restaurante porque _____ demasiado.   *(almorzar, costar)*
5. (Yo) nunca _____ encontrar mis llaves, pero tú siempre las _____.   *(poder, encontrar)*
6. Ella _____ allá, en su dormitorio.   *(dormir)*
7. (Nosotros) siempre _____ nuestro dinero antes de salir del banco.   *(contar)*

C   Cambios
Escribe mandatos con *tú*. Sigue el modelo.

   tirar la basura
   Tira la basura.

1. volver temprano
2. escoger otro mantel
3. almorzar conmigo
4. batir los huevos con el azúcar
5. secar los cuchillos ahora mismo
6. añadir leche al café
7. enchufar la tostadora
8. alquilar esa película

D   La cocina
Completa las frases con el sustantivo y el demostrativo correctos.

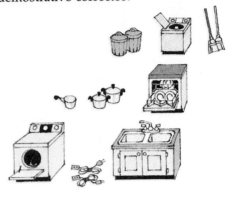

1. _____ no funciona.
2. Por favor, enchufa _____.
3. ¿Está limpio _____?
4. Pongo la sopa en _____.
5. No hay nada en _____.
6. Los platos están en _____.
7. _____ están vacíos.
8. ¿Tienes detergente para _____?
9. Uds. pueden barrer con _____.

E   Otra vez, por favor
Ahora vuelve a hacer (*redo*) la Práctica D.
Usa el pronombre demostrativo apropiado.

F   ¿Cuánto tiempo hace?
Contesta las preguntas.

1. ¿Cuánto tiempo hace que practicas el piano? (mucho tiempo)
2. ¿Cuánto tiempo hace que viven en esta ciudad? (tres meses)
3. ¿Cuánto tiempo hace que los Ramírez están de vacaciones?   (dos semanas)
4. ¿Cuánto tiempo hace que Pablo duerme? (media hora)
5. ¿Cuánto tiempo hace que ella barre el patio? (quince minutos)
6. ¿Cuánto tiempo hace que tu hermanito está enfermo?   (varios días)

Activity Masters   Chapter 2 Test   Listening Comprehension Test

VOCABULARIO DEL CAPÍTULO 2

Sustantivos
el aire acondicionado
la aspiradora
la basura
el basurero
la bombilla
la cacerola
la calefacción
el césped
el cordón, *pl.* los cordones
el cortacésped
la cortina
la cucharita
el desorden
el detergente
el enchufe
la escoba
el fregadero
el horno
la idea
la lavadora
el lavaplatos
la luz, *pl.* las luces
la olla
el orden
el pasillo
la plancha

la sartén, *pl.* las sartenes
la secadora
el sótano
el suelo
el techo
la tostadora

Pronombres demostrativos
aquél, aquélla, aquéllos, aquéllas
ése, -a, -os, -as
éste, -a, -os, -as
esto, eso, aquello

Adjetivos
descompuesto, -a
desordenado, -a
eléctrico, -a
ordenado, -a
quemado, -a

Adjetivo demostrativo
aquel, aquella

Verbos
almorzar (o → ue)
alquilar
añadir
barrer
batir
cortar
desenchufar
enchufar
escoger (j)
funcionar
mezclar
pasar *(to happen)*
planchar
quemar
recoger (j)
secar
tirar

Adverbio / Preposición
como

Expresiones
ahora mismo
¡Feliz cumpleaños!
pasar la aspiradora
poner en orden

PARQUES DEL MUNDO HISPANO

It's Sunday, and you're walking with your friends on a wide sidewalk through a park filled with tall trees. When one of you suggests a snack, you stop to buy slices of melon or mangos that have been carved and peeled to look like flowers. You probably couldn't do that in a park in the United States, but you could in Mexico City's Parque de Chapultepec.

Parks everywhere serve the same purpose: to provide open places with grass and trees where you can picnic, play games, or simply take a leisurely stroll.

Although it became a public park only in this century, Chapultepec has a long history. Its name, given to it by the Aztecs, means "Grasshopper Hill." There you will find a zoo, lakes, an amusement park, and the national history museum—El Castillo Chapultepec. This 200-year-old, 200-foot-high hilltop palace has served many purposes. From 1910 to 1944, for example, it was the home of Mexico's presidents. Today the presidential home is situated elsewhere in the park.

Madrid's El Retiro is a different type of park. It was once the garden of the king's summer palace. (Its name means "hideaway.") Unlike Chapultepec, El Retiro has a very formal design, with broad paths that cut through the trees in straight lines. The paths are bordered by hedges and numerous statues of Spanish royalty.

The most popular section of El Retiro is a large rectangular pool *(el estanque)*. You can rent a rowboat or sit at a nearby outdoor café and watch the people pass by. Another attraction is the Crystal Palace, a nineteenth-century exhibition building that presents contemporary art. But most of El Retiro's visitors are content simply to wander down the shaded lanes, enjoying a few hours' escape from the noise and traffic of the city.

Essential

If students ask: Other related words you may want to present: *la pista de patinaje*, skating rink; *la bolera;* bowling alley.

🔊 1

Transparency 8
CONTEXTO
VISUAL

¿Qué haces este sábado?

remar

la canasta

hacer un picnic

patinar (sobre ruedas)

el patín (de ruedas)
pl. los patines

la rueda

el hielo

patinar (sobre hielo)

el patín
pl. los patines

jugar a los bolos

la banda

la heladería

el cuadro

la exposición de arte
pl. las exposiciones de arte

CONTEXTO COMUNICATIVO   2

Enrichment: Reinforce the meaning of *me gustaría* in 3 by asking *¿Qué te gusta hacer los sábados? Y este sábado, ¿qué te gustaría hacer?*

1 PABLO Catalina, no puedo ir contigo a **la feria.**

CATALINA No te **entiendo.** Primero dices que sí, después que no. ¿Por qué **cambias de idea** tan rápidamente?

PABLO Mi padre me acaba de decir que tengo que ir con la familia.

Variaciones:

Enrichment: In connection with mini-dialogue 1, elicit other reasons for Pablo's *cambio de idea.*

■ la feria → la exposición de arte
■ rápidamente → **frecuentemente**

la feria *fair*
entender (e → ie) = comprender
cambiar de idea *to change one's mind*

frecuentemente *frequently*

2 DANIEL **Afortunadamente,** mañana es sábado y no hay clases. ¿Qué piensas hacer?

REBECA **Probablemente** voy al parque. Los sábados por la tarde dan **espectáculos gratis.** ¿Quieres ir conmigo?

DANIEL ¡Claro que sí!

■ afortunadamente → **¡qué maravilla!**
■ probablemente → quizás
■ gratis → muy **graciosos**

afortunadamente *fortunately*

probablemente *probably*
el espectáculo *show, performance*
gratis, pl. **gratis** *free*

¡qué maravilla! *how marvelous! great!*

gracioso, -a = cómico, -a

3 ROGELIO **Me gustaría ir de excursión** contigo, pero tengo que ir **antes** al dentista.

VERÓNICA **¡Qué lata!** Tenemos que salir en media hora. Tal vez otro día.

■ ir de excursión → **dar un paseo**
■ en media hora → ahora mismo

me gustaría *I'd like (to)*
ir de excursión *to go on a short trip or outing*
antes *before (that), first*
¡qué lata! *what a drag! what a bore!*
dar un paseo *to go for a walk or ride*

4 ELISA Para llegar al teatro temprano, es mejor salir a las seis. ¿Estás de acuerdo?

MARIO **Completamente.**

■ teatro → picnic
■ completamente → claro

completamente *completely*

5 CAROLINA   Esta camisa es **exactamente** lo que quiero. Pero ya
tengo **tantas** camisas . . . ¿Te gusta?

HORACIO   Sí. **Especialmente** el color.

CAROLINA   ¿La compro?

HORACIO   Sí, cómprala. Es muy bella.

■ esta camisa → este vestido
¿la compro? → ¿lo compro?
cómprala → cómpralo
bella → bello

exactamente   *exactly*

tanto, -a, -os, -as   *so much, so many*

especialmente   *especially*

Notes: Point out that
cómprala in mini-dialogue 5 is
the affirmative *tú* command of
comprar with the object
pronoun *la* attached to it. This
construction is explained and
practiced on pp. 113–114.

EN OTRAS PARTES

También se dice *la cesta*.

También se dice *jugar al boliche*.

También se dice *merendar en el campo* e *ir a un día de campo*.

Práctica A

exposición	gratis
cuadros	maravilla
espectáculo	canasta
Afortunadamente	especial-
banda	mente

En el Museo del Prado, Madrid, España

PRÁCTICA

A Una carta incompleta.   Mónica acaba de llegar a Madrid. Ella le escribe a su amigo Federico sobre sus planes para el día. Escoge palabras de la lista para completar la carta. Usa cada palabra sólo una vez.

afortunadamente	cuadros	exposición
banda	especialmente	gratis
canasta	espectáculo	maravilla

Querido Federico:

¿Cómo estás? Mi familia y yo acabamos de llegar a Madrid. Esta tarde vamos al Museo del Prado* para ver una _____ de arte nicaragüense. Les gustan mucho a mis padres los _____
5 centroamericanos de hoy.

Luego, mis padres van a ver un _____ en el teatro Juárez. _____, no tengo que ir con ellos. Yo voy a ir con mis primas a un concierto de una _____ fabulosa. ¡Las entradas son _____! Qué _____, ¿verdad?
Pensamos llevar una _____ con comida y bebidas para hacer un picnic

* The Museo del Prado, the national museum of Spain, is one of the world's great museums. It has a very extensive collection of art, but is best known for its works by such great Spanish artists as Diego Velázquez, Francisco Goya, and Pablo Picasso.

10 en el césped. Me gusta mucho la música de este grupo, _____ su canción "Siempre cambias de idea." Vamos a divertirnos mucho. Hay tantas cosas que quiero contarte, pero voy a tener que esperar. Hasta pronto.

Tu amiga,

Mónica

En el Parque del Retiro, Madrid, España

B **¿Qué hacen todos?** ¿Qué hacen estas personas? Usa una palabra o expresión de cada columna para hacer frases. Sigue el modelo.

Paco y Sara
Paco y Sara cambian de idea frecuentemente.

1. (yo)	cambiar	a los bolos	a la feria
2. Elena	correr	con unos amigos	a la playa
3. Jaime y Luisa	dar	de excursión	a menudo
4. (tú)	escuchar	de idea	al campo
5. Gloria y yo	hacer	juntos(as)	en el lago
6. Juan y tú	ir	los cuadros	en el museo
7. Uds.	jugar	planes	en el parque
8. mis padres	mirar	sobre ruedas	frecuentemente
	patinar	una banda	por la tarde
	remar	un grupo de rock	rápidamente
		un paseo	todos los días
		un picnic	

Práctica B
Answers will vary.

Reteach / Extra Help: You may want students to do Ex. B in pairs in order to come up with as many variations as possible. Ask volunteers to present their sentences to the class.

Práctica C
Answers will vary.

Practice Sheet 3–1

Workbook Exs. A–B

Tape Manual Exs, 1–? 0

Quiz 3–1

C **Hablemos de ti.**
1. ¿Qué prefieres hacer cuando tienes tiempo libre? ¿Te gusta jugar a los bolos? ¿Patinar sobre ruedas? ¿Con quiénes?
2. ¿Tienes un pasatiempo interesante? ¿Qué es? ¿Coleccionas algo? ¿Qué coleccionas?
3. ¿Te gusta hacer picnics o prefieres comer en casa o en un restaurante? ¿Por qué? ¿Por qué le gusta a la gente comer en el campo?
4. ¿Qué te gusta comer en un picnic? ¿Qué preparas tú cuando haces un picnic?
5. ¿A veces vas de excursión con tu familia? ¿Adónde van Uds.? ¿Qué hacen?
6. ¿Qué clase de espectáculo te gusta más? ¿Asistes a muchos espectáculos? ¿Son gratis o tienes que pagar? ¿Adónde vas para ver un espectáculo?
7. ¿Vas a exposiciones de arte? ¿Frecuentemente? ¿Tienes algunos cuadros favoritos? ¿De quiénes son? ¿Puedes describirlos?

APLICACIONES Discretionary

Doña* Clara Vidente 4 5 Pronunciación

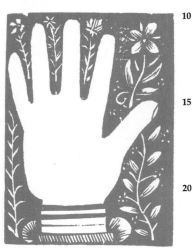

Es el cumpleaños de Rafael, y sus amigos Roberto y Pilar tienen una sorpresa[1] para él. Llegan a su casa con una mujer que lleva anteojos de sol, pulseras grandes en los brazos y muchos anillos en los dedos. Lleva también un pañuelo grande sobre la cabeza.
5 Dicen que es una adivina[2] que puede decirle cosas sobre su vida.

CLARA   Abre la mano por favor.

RAFAEL   ¡Qué tontería![3] Nadie puede leer nada en mi mano.

CLARA   ¡Silencio! ¡Sé lo que sé! ¡Veo lo que veo! *(Mira su palma con mucho cuidado.[4])* ¡Aquí veo algo!

10 RAFAEL   *(Un poco preocupado)* ¿Qué hay? ¿Qué ve Ud.?

CLARA   Escucha bien. Veo que a menudo no te lavas las manos.

RAFAEL   Para saber eso no hay que ser adivina.

CLARA   Hay más. Tu mano dice: "Estudia más" y "Come menos dulces."

15 RAFAEL   A todo el mundo le encantan los dulces.

CLARA   Yo lo sé. Soy adivina, ¿no? También veo que eres el mejor jugador de bolos de tu equipo.

RAFAEL   ¿Mi mano dice eso?

CLARA   No, tonto. ¡Tu amigo Roberto lo dice! *(Se quita los anteojos y el pañuelo.)* ¡Y yo soy su tía Clara! Feliz cumpleaños,
20   Rafael.

---

[1] **la sorpresa** *surprise*   [2] **la adivina** *fortune-teller*   [3] **la tontería** *nonsense*
[4] **con mucho cuidado** *very carefully*

*Doña is a title of respect generally used with a woman's first name. The masculine form is don.

Preguntas

Contesta según el diálogo.

1. ¿Quiénes le dan una sorpresa a Rafael? ¿Por qué?   2. ¿Cuál es la sorpresa?   3. Rafael dice que es una tontería, pero está preocupado. ¿Por qué?   4. ¿Qué ve doña Clara primero en la mano de Rafael?   5. Según la señora, ¿qué más dice la mano?   6. ¿Qué le gusta mucho a Rafael?
7. ¿Qué deporte practica Rafael?   8. Describe el disfraz de la adivina.
9. ¿Qué piensas tú de las adivinas?

Participación

Working with a partner, create a dialogue in which one of you tells the other's fortune.

PALABRAS NUEVAS II

Essential

La feria

If students ask: Related words you may want to present: *el algodón de azúcar*, cotton candy; *peligroso, -a*, dangerous.

El parque de diversiones

asustado, -a

la rueda de la feria

la montaña rusa

los cacahuates

la bolsa
(de papel)

la casa de los fantasmas

la casa de los espejos

las palomitas

el carrusel

el puesto

el globo

flaco, -a

tímido, -a

valiente

CONTEXTO COMUNICATIVO 7

1 En Bogotá, Colombia, hay un parque de diversiones que se llama El Salitre. Tiene **tantas atracciones como** el Parque de Chapultepec en México, que es el más **famoso** de la América Latina.

Variaciones:
■ famoso → conocido

tanto, -a, -os, -as + noun + **como** *as much . . . as / as many . . . as*
la atracción, pl. **las atracciones** *ride, attraction*
famoso, -a *famous*

2 RAÚL ¿**Damos una vuelta** en la montaña rusa?
SILVIA Sí, es muy emocionante.
RAÚL Y no es **tan** cara **como** la rueda de feria.

■ emocionante → divertida
■ rueda de feria → el carrusel

dar una vuelta *to take a ride*

tan + adj. / adv. + **como** *as . . . as*

3 MARÍA ¿Te da miedo la casa de los fantasmas?
ROSA No, lo que me **asusta** es la montaña rusa.
MARÍA ¡Ay, sí! **¡Qué susto** me da cuando baja!
ROSA ¡Y **qué alivio** cuando **para**!

■ montaña rusa → rueda de feria
baja → sube

asustar = dar miedo a
¡qué susto! *what a scare!*
¡qué alivio! *what a relief!*
parar *to stop*

4 EVA ¡**Por fin** llegamos! ¿Te gusta este **lugar**?
ÁNGEL Sí, está perfecto para hacer un picnic. ¿Tienes la canasta con la comida?
EVA ¡Ay, no! La **olvidé** en casa.
ÁNGEL ¡Qué lata!

■ olvidé → dejé

¡por fin! *at last! finally!*
el lugar *place*

olvidar *to forget (something)*

EN OTRAS PARTES

En Cuba se dice *la jaba*.
También se dice *el saco*.

En España se dice *la noria*.
También se dice *la estrella*.

En España se dice *el tiovivo*,
y en la Argentina y en el
Perú se dice *la calesita*.

También se dice *el parque de
atracciones*.

En Colombia se dice *las
crispetas*.

También se dice *el cacahuete*
y en muchos países se dice
el maní.

PRÁCTICA

Notes: Before students begin Ex. A, make sure that they understand the instructions and that they recognize *viste* as the preterite of *ver*. All of the preterite forms of *ver* are reintroduced and practiced in Chap. 6.

Práctica A
Exclamations will vary.
1. ¿Viste la montaña rusa?
2. ¿Viste el carrusel?
3. ¿Viste la casa de los espejos?
4. ¿Viste la rueda de feria?
5. ¿Viste el desfile?
6. ¿Viste los globos?
7. ¿Viste los puestos?
8. ¿Viste los fuegos artificiales?
9. ¿Viste la exposición de arte?

A **En la feria.** Imagina que tu amigo fue a la feria la semana pasada. Tú le preguntas lo que vio. Pregunta según el dibujo y escoge una palabra de la lista para contestar. Sigue el modelo.

aburrido	emocionante	gracioso	rápido
bonito	enorme	lata	susto
divertido	estupendo	maravilla	tonto

ESTUDIANTE A   *¿Viste la casa de los fantasmas?*
ESTUDIANTE B   *Sí, ¡qué susto!*

1.

2.

3.

4.

5.

6.

7.

8.

9.

B **¿Cómo describirlos?**   Usa la forma correcta del adjetivo apropiado
para describir a cada persona. Sigue el modelo.

asustado	flaco	listo	tacaño
desordenado	generoso	ordenado	tímido
famoso	gracioso	perezoso	valiente

Pedro nunca da nada a nadie.   *Es muy tacaño.*

1. Afortunadamente, Ana no tiene miedo de nada.
2. María siempre cuenta chistes a sus amigas.
3. Todo el mundo conoce al Dr. Martín.
4. Ester nunca olvida nada y por eso siempre saca buenas notas.
5. Ese perro probablemente come muy poco.
6. Luis les presta cosas a sus amigos muy frecuentemente.
7. Juan siempre pone su cuarto en orden.
8. Felipe nunca quiere contestar en la clase de inglés.
9. Alicia nunca hace nada.

Reteach / Extra Help: Before
beginning Ex. B, you may want
to ask volunteers to identify the
antonym pairs among the listed
adjectives *(asustado / valiente,
desordenado / ordenado,
generoso / tacaño).*
   Remind students that the
adjectives are given in the
masculine singular form;
students must change the
endings according to the nouns
that the adjectives modify.

Práctica B
1. valiente   6. generoso
2. graciosa   7. ordenado
3. famoso   8. tímido
4. lista   9. perezosa
5. flaco

C **¿Qué vas a comprar?**   Imagina que visitas los puestos en una feria y
preguntas cuánto cuesta cada cosa. Pregunta y contesta según el
modelo.

ESTUDIANTE A   *¿Cuánto cuestan las cajas de dulces?*
ESTUDIANTE B   *Veinticinco centavos.*

Práctica C
1. ¿Cuánto cuestan las bolsas
   de (*or:* los) cacahuates?
   Cuarenta centavos.
2. ¿… los globos? Veinte
   centavos.
3. ¿… las canastas? Setenta y
   cinco centavos.
4. ¿… las (bolsas de) palomitas? Treinta y cinco
   centavos.
5. ¿… los cuadros? Ochenta y
   cinco centavos.
6. ¿… las pelotas? Cuarenta y
   cinco centavos.

1.   2.

3.   4.

5.   6.

D Hablemos de ti.

1. ¿Vas a parques de diversiones? ¿Vas frecuentemente durante el verano? ¿Con quiénes vas? ¿Cuáles son tus atracciones preferidas? ¿Cuáles te gustan menos? ¿Por qué? ¿Hay atracciones que te asustan mucho? ¿Cuáles?

2. Cuando vas a un parque de diversiones, ¿cuánto tiempo pasas allí? ¿Todo el día? ¿Hay que hacer cola para subir a las atracciones? ¿Para comprar boletos o comida? ¿Generalmente son largas las colas?

3. ¿Cuesta mucho ir a un parque de diversiones? ¿Cuánto dinero necesitas para pasar un día allí? ¿Qué comes cuando estás en el parque de diversiones? ¿Generalmente es buena la comida? ¿Comes demasiado?

Notes: Ask students to limit verb tenses in their **Actividad** descriptions to the present and *ir a* + infinitive.

ACTIVIDAD

¿Quién tiene . . . ? With a partner, make a list of five famous superheroes, monsters, movie stars, rock stars, or other popular real or fictional figures. Working together, create descriptions of them. For example, King Kong: *Es un mono enorme y muy fuerte. Puede tener a una persona en la mano. Asusta a todo el mundo.* Join another pair of students and read them the descriptions you have prepared. Can they guess who or what is being described?

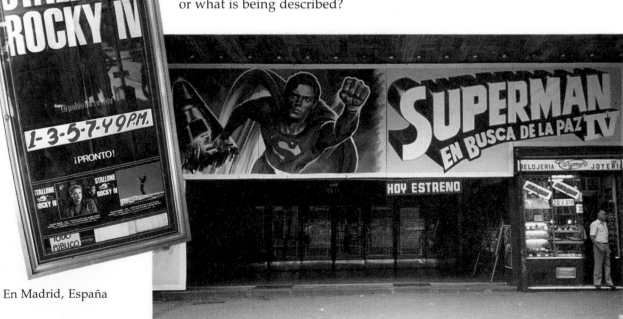

En Madrid, España

ESTUDIO DE PALABRAS

The Spanish suffix *-mente* corresponds to the English suffix *-ly*.

probablemente *probably*   exactamente *exactly*

We make these adverbs by adding *-mente* to the feminine form of an adjective. Remember that many adjectives have the same masculine and feminine form.

completa + mente = completamente *completely*
rápida + mente = rápidamente *rapidly*
especial + mente = especialmente *especially*
frecuente + mente = frecuentemente *frequently*

Note that if there is a written accent on the adjective it remains on the adverb. Can you form adverbs from these adjectives?

tímido   cómodo   perfecto   loco
agradable   valiente   triste   débil

Sinónimos

Cambia las palabras en cursiva por un sinónimo.

1. Esa señora es *muy conocida*.
2. Voy al cine *a menudo*.
3. Esta actriz es muy *cómica*.
4. Nadie me *comprende*.
5. ¿Jugar a los bolos? *¡Qué aburrido!*
6. *Quisiera* dar una vuelta en el carrusel.
7. Busco un lugar agradable para *caminar*.
8. Nada me *da miedo*.

Antónimos

Escoge el antónimo de cada palabra. Luego usa esa palabra en una frase.

1. flaco: fácil   gordo   delgado   listo
2. caro: generoso   gracioso   gratis   tacaño
3. valiente: tímido   caliente   famoso   cansado
4. gracioso: divertido serio   cómico   ordenado
5. empezar: asustar   olvidar   parar   remar

Notes: Refer students to mini-dialogues 1, 2, 4 on p. 99 and 5 on p. 100 for examples of adverbs that end in *-mente*.

Estudio de palabras
tímidamente
agradablemente
cómodamente
valientemente
perfectamente
tristemente
locamente
débilmente

Enrichment: You may want to write these unfamiliar adjectives on the board and ask students to form adverbs with *-mente: divino, verdadero, respetuoso, preciso (divinamente, verdaderamente, respetuosamente, precisamente)*.

Sinónimos
1. famosa
2. frecuentemente
3. graciosa
4. entiende
5. ¡Qué lata!
6. Me gustaría
7. dar un paseo
8. asusta

Antónimos
1. gordo
2. gratis
3. tímido
4. serio
5. parar

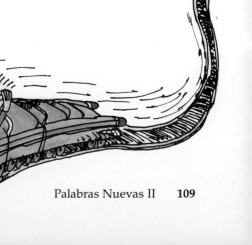

Notes: Refer to mini-dialogues
1 and 2 on p. 99 for examples
of *e → ie* stem-changing verbs
(*entender, pensar*).

EXPLICACIONES I

Verbos con el cambio *e → ie*

◆ **OBJECTIVES:**

**TO ASK SOMEONE
TO DO
SOMETHING WITH
YOU**

**TO DECLINE AN
INVITATION**

**TO STATE
PREFERENCES**

**TO MAKE A GIFT
LIST**

**TO EXPRESS
OPINIONS**

Here are all of the present-tense forms of *pensar** (''to think''), *querer* (''to want''), and *preferir* (''to prefer''). Remember that the endings are the same as those of regular *-ar*, *-er*, and *-ir* verbs, but that the stem vowel *e* changes to *ie* in all but the *nosotros* and *vosotros* forms. (Watch out! *Preferir* has two *e*'s in its stem. It is the second *e* that changes.) The other *e → ie* stem-changing verbs that you know are *cerrar, despertar(se), divertirse, empezar, entender,* and *perder.*

PENSAR		QUERER		PREFERIR	
pienso	pensamos	quiero	queremos	prefiero	preferimos
piensas	pensáis	quieres	queréis	prefieres	preferís
piensa	piensan	quiere	quieren	prefiere	prefieren

PRÁCTICA

Práctica A
1. ¿Qué quiere Olga? Quiere
un cortacésped.
2. ¿... quiere Juan? Quiere
una máquina de escribir.
3. ¿... quieren ...? Quieren un
proyector y una pantalla.

A Los cumpleaños.   Todos quieren algo diferente para su cumpleaños. ¿Qué quiere recibir cada persona?

¿Marcos?
ESTUDIANTE A   *¿Qué quiere Marcos?*
ESTUDIANTE B   *Quiere una cámara.*

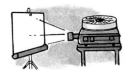

1. ¿Olga?   2. ¿Juan?   3. ¿Lola y Jaime?

* Remember that *pensar* + infinitive means ''to plan to, to intend to,'' *pensar en* means ''to think about,'' and *pensar de* means ''to think of, to have an opinion about.''

4. ¿su hermanito?　　5. ¿Uds.?　　6. ¿abuelita?

7. ¿Ud., Sr. Ortega?　　8. ¿Andrés?　　9. Y tú, ¿qué quieres recibir?

4. ¿… quiere …? Quiere unos globos.
5. ¿… quieren Uds.? Queremos unos patines (de ruedas).
6. ¿… quiere …? Quiere una lavadora y (una) secadora.
7. ¿… quiere Ud., Sr. Ortega? Quiero un lavaplatos.
8. ¿… quiere …? Quiere una calculadora
9. Answers will vary. Quiero …

B　¿En qué piensan?　Nadie presta atención. Cada uno piensa en algo diferente. Escoge una expresión de la columna de la derecha y pregunta y contesta según el modelo.

(tú) / vacaciones

ESTUDIANTE A　*¿En qué piensas?*
ESTUDIANTE B　*Pienso en las vacaciones.*
ESTUDIANTE A　*¡Vámonos!*

1. ellos / la heladería nueva
2. ella / el almuerzo
3. Uds. / la feria
4. Fernando / su grupo nuevo de rock
5. ella y tú / el partido de básquetbol
6. Ud., señor / los cuadros de la exposición
7. la directora / el fin de semana
8. ellas / el picnic del sábado
9. el profesor / los estudiantes que siempre olvidan la tarea
10. ¿Y en qué piensas tú?

¡ah, no!
¡caramba!
¡claro!
¡cómo no!
¿de veras?
¡imagínate!
¡por fin!
¡qué alivio!
¡qué chistoso!
¡qué lata!
¡qué maravilla!
¡vámonos!

Práctica B
Final remark will vary.
1. ¿En qué piensan ellos? Piensan en la heladería nueva.
2. ¿En qué piensa ella? Piensa en el almuerzo.
3. ¿En qué piensan Uds.? Pensamos en la feria.
4. ¿En qué piensa Fernando? Piensa en su grupo…
5. ¿En qué piensan ella y tú? Pensamos en el partido…
6. ¿En qué piensa Ud., señor? Pienso en los cuadros…
7. ¿En qué piensa la directora? Piensa en el fin de semana.
8. ¿En qué piensan ellas? Piensan en el picnic…
9. ¿En qué piensa el profesor? Piensa en los estudiantes…
10. ¿Y en qué piensas tú? (Answers will vary.)

Enrichment: You may want to expand on the practice in Ex. B by asking students to create explanations for each of the answers. For example: *Pienso en las vacaciones porque quiero ver a mis primos. Piensan en la heladería nueva porque tienen ganas de comer helado.*

Una exposición de arte en México

Unos jóvenes reman en Buenos Aires, Argentina.

Práctica C
1. ¿Qué piensa Ud. de esta biografía? Creo que es muy buena.
2. ¿Qué piensa ella de su aspiradora? Cree que es fabulosa.
3. ¿Qué piensas de mi abrigo? Creo que es demasiado grande.
4. ¿Qué piensan Uds. de mis sellos? Creemos que son muy bonitos.
5. ¿Qué piensan Jorge y Miguel de su juego de ajedrez? Creen que es excelente.
6. ¿Qué piensa Francisco de sus patines? Cree que son formidables.
7. ¿Qué piensa papá del cuadro? Cree que es demasiado caro.
8. ¿Qué piensa Irene de sus aretes? Cree que son bellísimos.

Práctica D
1. cierras / comer más palomitas
2. despertamos / Media hora antes de salir
3. entiendo / Afortunadamente
4. pierde / juega mucho a los bolos
5. prefieren / la heladería
6. piensa / especialmente
7. empezamos / Ahora mismo

Practice Sheets 3–3, 3–4

 10 Tape Manual Ex. 5

Quiz 3–3

C ¿Qué piensas de esto?   Hoy es el día después de Navidad, y todos los miembros de la familia Feliciano hablan de sus regalos. Pregunta y contesta según el modelo. Usa siempre la forma correcta del adjetivo.

> (tú) / mi nuevo radio / muy bonito
> ESTUDIANTE A   *¿Qué piensas de mi nuevo radio?*
> ESTUDIANTE B   *Creo que es muy bonito.*

1. Ud. / esta biografía / muy bueno
2. ella / su aspiradora / fabuloso
3. (tú) / mi abrigo / demasiado grande
4. Uds. / mis sellos / muy bonito
5. Jorge y Miguel / su juego de ajedrez / excelente
6. Francisco / sus patines / formidable
7. papá / el cuadro / demasiado caro
8. Irene / sus aretes / bellísimo

D Siempre tiene preguntas.   Mariana y Felipe siempre tienen que contestar las preguntas que les hace su hermano menor. Completa las frases. Escoge la forma correcta de los verbos para las preguntas y la mejor palabra o expresión para la respuesta.

1. ¿Por qué *(cerrar)* (tú) la bolsa? Porque no debo *(comer más palomitas / dar una vuelta más)*.
2. ¿Cuándo *(despertar)* (nosotros) a mamá y a papá? *(Media hora antes de salir. / Media hora después de salir.)*
3. ¡Qué maravilla! (Yo) *(entender)* completamente lo que dice esa gente. ¿Y tú? Sí. *(Afortunadamente / Frecuentemente)* aprendemos mucho este año.
4. ¿Por qué siempre *(perder)* (él) este juego? Probablemente porque no *(juega mucho a los bolos / cambia de idea)*.
5. ¿Dónde *(preferir)* Uds. comer? En *(la heladería / el puesto de globos)*.
6. ¿Qué *(pensar)* (ella) de este lugar? Le gustan todas las atracciones, *(especialmente / afortunadamente)* la montaña rusa.
7. ¿A qué hora *(empezar)* (nosotros)? *(Ahora mismo. / ¡Por fin!)*

Mandatos afirmativos
con *lo, la, los, las, le* y *les*

In Spanish we attach object pronouns to the end of affirmative commands. In writing we put an accent mark on the stressed syllable of the verb to show that the stress still remains there.

Abre la botella. **Ábrela.**   *Open* the bottle. ***Open it.***
Lee las revistas. **Léelas.**   *Read* the magazines. ***Read them.***
Para el coche. **Páralo.**   *Stop* the car. ***Stop it.***
Pregúntale al profesor. **Pregúntale.**   *Ask* the teacher. ***Ask him***

With *o* → *ue* and *i* → *ie* stem-changing verbs, the written accent goes over the *e* of the stem change.

Cierra la puerta. **Ciérrala.**   *Close* the door. ***Close it.***
Cuéntale el chiste a Diana. **Cuéntale** el chiste.   *Tell* Diana the joke. ***Tell her*** *the joke.*

◆ **OBJECTIVES:**
TO OFFER HELP
TO MAKE POLITE SUGGESTIONS
TO ASK FOR CLARIFICATION
TO TELL A FRIEND OR FAMILY MEMBER TO DO SOMETHING FOR SOMEONE

En el Parque de Chapultepec, México

Notes: Point out the affirmative *tú* command + object pronoun in mini-dialogue 5, p. 100.

Práctica A

1. barro / bárrela
2. cambio / cámbialas
3. limpio / límpialos
4. corto / córtalo
5. recojo / recógela
6. enchufo / enchúfala
7. acuesto / acuéstalo
8. preparo / prepáralo
9. abro / ábrelas
10. llamo / llámalos

Práctica B

1. ¿Por qué no le escribes una tarjeta postal a Pedro?
   ¿Qué debo escribirle?
   Escríbele una tarjeta postal.
2. ¿... les describes ... a los otros?
   ¿Qué debo describirles?
   Descríbeles el cuadro.
3. ¿... les mandas ... a tus tíos?
   ¿Qué debo mandarles?
   Mándales las diapositivas.
4. ¿... le cuentas ... a tu hermana?
   ¿Qué debo contarle?
   Cuéntale ese chiste divertido.
5. ¿... les lees ... a los niños?
   ¿Qué debo leerles?
   Léeles un cuento.
6. ¿... le prestas ... a Diana?
   ¿Qué debo prestarle?
   Préstale tus patines.
7. ¿... le explicas ... a tu profesor de química?
   ¿Qué debo explicarle?
   Explícale el problema.
8. ¿... le muestras ... a tu profesora de arte?
   ¿Qué debo mostrarle?
   Muéstrale los dibujos.
9. ¿... le llevas ... a la Sra. Gómez?
   ¿Qué debo llevarle?
   Llévale esta bolsa de dulces.

Práctica C

Answers will vary.

Practice Sheet 3–5

Workbook Exs. E–F

11 Tape Manual Ex. 6

Quiz 3–4

PRÁCTICA

A Ahora mismo.   La familia Martínez acaba de volver de sus vacaciones de seis semanas. Hay mucho que hacer. Afortunadamente hay muchas personas y todo el mundo quiere ayudar. Pregunta y contesta según el modelo.

> lavar esta ropa blanca
> ESTUDIANTE A *¿Lavo esta ropa blanca?*
> ESTUDIANTE B *Sí, lávala, por favor.*

1. barrer la cocina
2. cambiar las sábanas
3. limpiar los dormitorios
4. cortar el césped
5. recoger la basura
6. enchufar la aspiradora
7. acostar a Juanito
8. preparar el almuerzo
9. abrir las ventanas
10. llamar a los abuelos

B ¿Qué hago?   Esperanza no presta atención cuando su mamá le dice algo. Su mamá siempre tiene que repetir todo. Pregunta y contesta según el modelo.

> mostrar las fotos / Eva y Pedro
> ESTUDIANTE A *¿Por qué no les muestras las fotos a Eva y a Pedro?*
> ESTUDIANTE B *¿Qué debo mostrarles?*
> ESTUDIANTE A *Muéstrales las fotos.*

1. escribir una tarjeta postal / Pedro
2. describir el cuadro / los otros
3. mandar las diapositivas / los tíos
4. contar ese chiste divertido / tu hermana
5. leer un cuento / los niños
6. prestar tus patines / Diana
7. explicar el problema / tu profesor de química
8. mostrar los dibujos / tu profesora de arte
9. llevar esta bolsa de dulces / la Sra. Gómez

C Hablemos de ti.

1. ¿A qué hora empiezan las clases en tu escuela? ¿A qué hora terminan? ¿A qué hora empieza tu clase de español? ¿A qué hora termina?
2. ¿Qué piensas hacer esta noche? ¿Y este fin de semana? ¿Y durante las vacaciones de Navidad?
3. ¿Qué piensas de los programas que dan en la televisión este año? ¿Qué piensas de las películas que dan en tu ciudad esta semana? ¿Quieres ver algunas de ellas? ¿Cuáles? ¿Por qué?

APLICACIONES

Discretionary

Notes: Sample dialogues for the **¿Qué pasa?** appear in the Teacher Notes.

En el parque de diversiones   Transparency 10

¿Qué puestos y diversiones ves en el dibujo? ¿Cuánto cuesta cada cosa?

Victoria and Antonio can't decide which ride to go on next. Create a dialogue in which Victoria tries to persuade Antonio to ride the roller coaster. Here are some words you may want to use:

asustado, -a	¡por fin!	¡qué maravilla!
el carrusel	¡qué alivio!	¡qué susto!
me gustaría	¡qué lata!	valiente

Notes: You may want to set aside class time for pairs of students to prepare their dialogues. Circulate to give help as needed.

Aplicaciones   **115**

EXPLICACIONES II Essential

Los comparativos

◆ **OBJECTIVES:**

TO MAKE COMPARISONS

TO ASK FOR AND EXPRESS OPINIONS

TO DISAGREE EMPHATICALLY

TO DISAGREE POLITELY

TO HEDGE

Reteach / Extra Help: After presenting the material in **Explicaciones II** on pp. 116–117, provide practice with comparatives by asking questions about classroom items, places, popular TV, movie, and music personalities, and the students themselves. Encourage students to answer with full sentences: *¿Cuándo estás más ocupado(a), los domingos o los lunes? (Estoy más ocupado(a) los ___ que los ___.) ¿Cuándo tienes menos tarea, durante la semana o durante los fines de semana? (Tengo menos tarea ___ que ___.) ¿Quién es mayor, tu abuelo o tu papá? (Mi abuelo es mayor que mi papá.) ¿Y quién es menor? (Mi papá es menor.) ¿Qué banda toca mejor, ___ o ___?* and so on.

Estos patines son **más** caros **que** ésos.

Esta canasta es **menos** cara **que** ésa.

Remember that when we compare things that are not the same, we use *más* or *menos* + adjective + *que*. We compare adverbs in the same way.

Eva siempre llega **más tarde que** Luz.	*Eva always arrives **later than** Luz (does).*
Yo olvido cosas **menos frecuentemente que** tú.	*I forget things **less frequently than** you (do).*

Remember that adjectives agree in gender and number with the nouns they describe. Adverbs never change.

1 Remember that some adjectives have irregular comparative forms.

bueno → **mejor**   malo → **peor**   viejo → **mayor**   joven → **menor**

Este sombrero es **mejor que** aquél.	*This hat is **better than** that one.*
La nieve es **peor que** la lluvia.	*Snow is **worse than** rain.*
Bernardo es **mayor que** Graciela.	*Bernardo is **older than** Graciela.*
Mi tía es **menor que** mi papá.	*My aunt is **younger than** my dad.*

2 The adverbs *bien* and *mal* also have irregular comparative forms:
bien → **mejor**   *mal* → **peor**

Tú escribes **mejor que** yo.	*You write **better than** I (do).*
Antonio canta **peor que** José.	*Antonio sings **worse than** José (does).*

3 To compare things that are the same or equal, we use *tan* + adjective / adverb + *como*. In English we use "as . . . as."

> Él es **tan alto como** su hermano.   *He's **as tall as** his brother.*
> Corro **tan rápidamente como** él.   *I run **as fast as** he (does).*

4 To compare two verb actions, we use *más / menos que* or *tanto como*. In English, we use "more / less than" or "as much as."

> Trabajas $\begin{cases} \textbf{más que} \\ \textbf{menos que} \\ \textbf{tanto como} \end{cases}$ yo.   *You work* $\begin{cases} \textit{more than} \\ \textit{less than} \\ \textit{as much as} \end{cases}$ *I (do).*

Enrichment: You may want to further reinforce the comparative forms and structures by asking students to work in pairs and to take turns asking each other questions about the example sentences on pp. 116–117. For example: *¿Quién llega más tarde que Luz? ¿Quién olvida cosas menos frecuentemente, tú o yo? ¿Cuál es mejor, este sombrero o aquél?*

5 To use nouns in equal comparisons we use *tanto, -a* + noun + *como* ("as much . . . as / as many . . . as"). Because *tanto* is an adjective, it agrees with the noun that follows it in number and gender.

> Tengo **tanto** dinero **como** mi hermano.   *I have **as much** money **as** my brother.*
> Hay **tantos** chicos **como** chicas.   *There are **as many** boys **as** girls.*
> Voy a traer **tantas** bolsas de papel **como** cajas.   *I'm going to bring **as many** paper bags **as** boxes.*

We can also use *más* and *menos* with nouns.

> Hacemos **más picnics que** ellos.   *We have **more picnics than** they (do).*
> Tengo **menos palomitas que** él.   *I have **less popcorn than** he (does).*
> Olvido **menos cosas que** Uds.   *I forget **fewer things than** you (do).*

6 Remember that we use *más de* or *menos de* with numbers.

> Tengo $\begin{cases} \textbf{más de} \\ \textbf{menos de} \end{cases}$ cien pesos.   *I have* $\begin{cases} \textit{more than} \\ \textit{less than} \end{cases}$ *100 pesos.*

Un vendedor de bebidas en el Parque de Chapultepec, México

Reteach / Review: You may want to ask volunteers to identify each of the illustrations in Ex. A before students begin the exercise.

Práctica A
Adjectives may vary.
1. La jirafa es más alta que el oso / El oso es más bajo que la jirafa.
2. El mono es más pequeño (bajo) que la llama / La llama es más grande (alta) que…
3. El leopardo es más pequeño que el tigre / El tigre es más grande que…
4. La serpiente es más larga que el caimán / El caimán es más corto que…
5. La cebra es más tímida que el elefante / El elefante es más valiente que…
6. El hipopótamo es más gordo que la vaca / La vaca es más flaca que…
7. La iguana es más fea que el pato / El pez es más bonito que…
8. El perro es más flaco que el gato / El gato es más gordo que…

Enrichment: In connection with Exs. A on p. 118 and B on p. 119, you may want students to write five comparative sentences at home. Ask them to base their sentences on magazine pictures or on their own drawings. Check students' work for correct spelling, capitalization, and punctuation.

PRÁCTICA

A En el zoológico. Dos amigos comparan los animales que ven en el zoológico. Mira los dibujos y haz *(make)* comparaciones con *más . . . que* y un adjetivo apropiado. Usa cada adjetivo sólo una vez. Sigue el modelo.

La oveja es más pequeña que la vaca.
o: *La vaca es más grande que la oveja.*

alto	corto	gordo	pequeño
bajo	feo	grande	tímido
bonito	flaco	largo	valiente

1.

2.

3.

4.

5.

6.

7.

8.

B **¿Qué piensas?** Julio compara todo. Pregunta y contesta según el modelo. Usa siempre la forma correcta.

> película / divertido
>
> ESTUDIANTE A ¿Qué piensas de esta película?
> ESTUDIANTE B Es menos divertida que ésa.

1. cuento / interesante
2. vendedora / amable
3. flores / hermoso
4. lección / difícil
5. programas / serio
6. partido / aburrido
7. comida / picante
8. problemas / importante

Práctica B
1. este cuento / menos interesante que ése
2. esta vendedora / menos amable que ésa
3. estas flores / menos hermosas que ésas
4. esta lección / menos difícil que ésa
5. estos programas / menos serios que ésos
6. este partido / menos aburrido que ése
7. esta comida / menos picante que ésa
8. estos problemas / menos importantes que ésos

Entrada al Zoológico Chapultepec en México

C **¿Más o menos?** Graciela siempre compara lo que hace ella con lo que hacen sus amigos. Escoge un adverbio de la lista para hacer cada comparación. Sigue el modelo.

> Héctor / aprender lenguas
> *Héctor aprende lenguas más fácilmente que yo.*
> o: *Héctor aprende lenguas menos fácilmente que yo.*

1. Rosa / ir de excursión   completamente
2. Esteban / escribir a máquina   despacio
3. Julio y Samuel / trabajar en nuestro puesto exactamente
4. tú / llegar al colegio   fácilmente
5. Uds. / correr   frecuentemente
6. Patricia / cambiar de idea   rápidamente
7. Francisco / hablar   tarde
8. tú / explicar todo   temprano
                                                                            tímidamente

D **¿Mejor o peor?** ¿Qué hacen estas personas? ¿Quién lo hace mejor? ¿Quién lo hace peor? Contesta según el modelo.

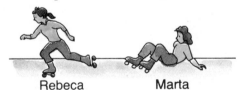

Rebeca   Marta

Rebeca patina mejor que Marta.
o: *Marta patina peor que Rebeca.*

1. nosotros   tú

2. Ud.   yo

3. ella   él

4. Ernesto · Víctor

5. Leonor · Judit

6. Uds. · nosotros

4. Ernesto juega a los bolos mejor que Víctor. / Víctor juega … peor que…
5. Judit rema mejor que Leonor. / Leonor rema peor…
6. Uds. cantan mejor que nosotros. / Cantamos peor…

E Al contrario.   Carmen y Antonio nunca están de acuerdo. Haz (*Make*) comparaciones según el modelo. Siempre usa la forma correcta del adjetivo.

> las novelas / divertido / las biografías
> ESTUDIANTE A   *Las novelas son más divertidas que las biografías.*
> ESTUDIANTE B   *Al contrario, son menos divertidas.*

1. el español / difícil / el francés
2. los chicos / débil / las chicas
3. la sopa de cebolla / picante / el chile con carne
4. la montaña rusa / emocionante / la rueda de feria
5. Superhombre / fuerte / King Kong
6. las mujeres / perezoso / los hombres
7. los ríos / frío / los lagos
8. los niños / tímido / las niñas
9. los gatos / valiente / los perros
10. los dibujos animados / bueno / las películas musicales

F ¿Qué crees tú?   Usa las frases de la Práctica E para hacer comparaciones iguales (*equal*). Sigue el modelo.

> las novelas / divertido / las biografías
> ESTUDIANTE A   *Creo que las novelas son tan divertidas como las biografías.*
> ESTUDIANTE B   *Estoy de acuerdo.*
> o: *No estoy de acuerdo. Yo creo que son más (o menos) divertidas.*

Práctica E
1. El español es más difícil que el francés / Al contrario, es menos difícil.
2. son más débiles que / menos débiles
3. es más picante que / menos picante
4. es más emocionante que / menos emocionante
5. es más fuerte que / menos fuerte
6. son más perezosas que / menos perezosas
7. son más fríos que / menos fríos
8. son más tímidos que / menos tímidos
9. son más valientes que / menos valientes
10. son mejores que / peores

Práctica F
If Student B responds negatively, comparative forms will be like those in Práctica E. In No. 10, negative reply would be *mejores* or *peores*.
1. tan difícil como
2. tan débiles como
3. tan picante como
4. tan emocionante como
5. tan fuerte como
6. tan perezosas como
7. tan fríos como
8. tan tímidos como
9. tan valientes como
10. tan buenos como

Explicaciones II   **121**

1. ¿Es Segura tan rico como
   yo?
   Pues tiene tanto dinero
   como tú.
2. ¿Es Segura tan fuerte
   como yo?
   Pues puede llevar tantas
   pelotas de golf como tú.
3. ¿… tan generoso…?
   … deja tantas propinas…
4. ¿… tan serio…?
   … ve tantos dibujos
   animados…
5. ¿Está Segura tan
   ocupado…?
   … tiene tanto trabajo…
6. ¿Es Segura tan famoso…?
   … recibe tantas cartas…
7. ¿… tan atlético…?
   … da tantos paseos…
8. ¿Está Segura tan
   preocupado…?
   … tiene tantos problemas…
9. ¿Es Segura tan inteligente…?
   … lee tantas revistas…
10. ¿… tan guapo…?
    … tiene tantos espejos…

Notes: In Ex. G, make sure
Estudiante A uses the
masculine form of the
adjectives. As pairs of students
work together, you may want to
circulate to give help as
needed. Encourage students to
dramatize and to concentrate
on correct pronunciation,
intonation, and rhythm.

Un parque de diversiones
en Aranjuez, España

Practice Sheets 3–6, 3–7

12 Tape Manual Exs. 7–8

Quiz 3–5

G ¿No soy mejor entonces?   A este actor famoso le gusta creer que
es mejor que su rival Juan Segura. Pero sus amigos le dicen (muy
amablemente) que no. Sigue el modelo.

> ser chistoso / contar chistes
> ESTUDIANTE A   *¿Es Segura tan chistoso como yo?*
> ESTUDIANTE B   *Pues cuenta tantos chistes como tú.*

1. ser rico / tener dinero
2. ser fuerte / poder llevar pelotas de golf
3. ser generoso / dejar propinas grandes
4. ser serio / ver dibujos animados
5. estar ocupado / tener trabajo
6. ser famoso / recibir cartas
7. ser atlético / dar paseos
8. estar preocupado / tener problemas importantes
9. ser inteligente / leer revistas sobre el cine
10. ser guapo / tener espejos

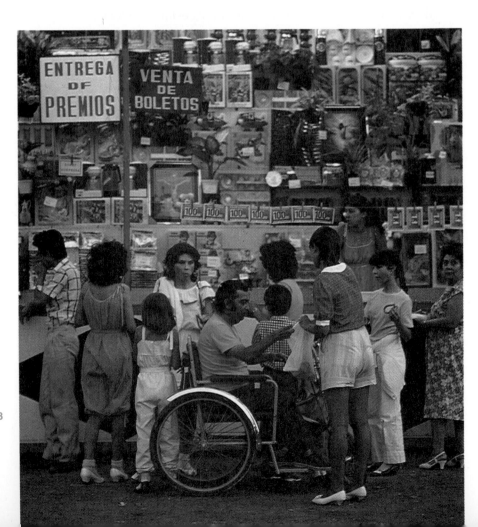

La forma superlativa

Notes: Refer to mini-dialogue 1 on p. 105 for an example of a superlative construction.

Remember that to say someone or something is the "most" or the "least" of a group, we use *de*.

$$\text{el / la / los / las} + \text{noun} + \left\{ \begin{array}{l} \textbf{más} \\ \textbf{menos} \end{array} \right\} + \text{adjective} + \textbf{de}$$

◆ **OBJECTIVES:**

TO SPEAK IN SUPERLATIVES

TO EXAGGERATE

TO EXPRESS STRONG OPINIONS

Reteach / Extra Help: Point out or elicit the spelling change that occurs before adding the -*ísimo, -a* suffix to adjectives that end in a vowel (the final vowel is dropped).

Ester es **la** alumna **más simpática de** la clase.	*Ester is **the nicest** student **in** the class.*
Juan y Manuel son **los** muchachos **menos enérgicos del** equipo.	*Juan and Manuel are **the least energetic** boys **on** the team.*
Sansón es **el** caballo **más grande de** la granja.	*Sansón is **the biggest** horse **on** the farm.*

Just as in English, we can omit the noun:

¿Quién es **la más simpática**?	*Who is **the nicest?***
Juan y Manuel son **los menos enérgicos**.	*Juan and Manuel are **the least energetic**.*

1 Remember that we also use the irregular forms *mayor, menor, mejor,* and *peor* in the superlative.

Graciela es **la mejor** escritora **de** nuestra familia.	*Graciela is **the best** writer **in** our family.*
¿Quién es **el mayor de** la banda?	*Who's **the oldest in** the band?*

2 We can also add the suffix -*ísimo, -a* to adjectives. It means "very" or "extremely" but has a lot of English equivalents.

La ropa es **carísima**.	*The clothes are **terribly expensive**.*
Los jardines son **grandísimos**.	*The gardens are **huge**.*
Este libro es **facilísimo**.	*This book is **awfully easy**.*

Una rueda de feria en San Juan, Puerto Rico

3 Adjectives ending in -*co, -ca* change to *qu* when the suffix -*ísimo, -a* is added. Adjectives ending in -*go, -ga* change to *gu*.

La médica es **simpatiquísima**.	*The doctor is **extremely nice**.*
Este programa es **larguísimo**.	*This program is **awfully long**.*

Explicaciones II   **123**

PRÁCTICA

A ¡Bienvenidos! Imagina que muestras tu ciudad a un(a) amigo(a) que es de otro país o de otro lugar. Usa palabras de las tres columnas para hacer frases según los modelos.

> *Éste es el hotel menos caro de la ciudad.*
> *Ésta es la ciudad más famosa del país.*

1. la calle	agradable	la América del Norte
2. la tienda	bonito	el barrio
3. el puente	caro	la calle
4. el parque	emocionante	el centro
5. la fuente	famoso	la ciudad
6. el zoológico	grande	los Estados Unidos
7. la casa	importante	el noroeste, etc.
8. el jardín	interesante	el país
9. el lugar	largo	
10. el barrio	viejo	

B ¡Mucho más! Algunas personas siempre exageran *(exaggerate).* Sigue el modelo.

> **ESTUDIANTE A** *Cervantes es un escritor muy famoso.*
> **ESTUDIANTE B** *Sí, es famosísimo.*

1. El caballo de Don Quijote es flaco.
2. Estos programas son bastante aburridos.
3. ¡Qué bellos son los cuadros de El Greco!
4. Creo que la cola es bastante larga.
5. Gálvez es un jugador muy rico.
6. La vendedora en esta heladería es graciosa.
7. Aquí el río Tajo es rápido.
8. Las cosas en este puesto son caras.

C Hablemos de ti.
1. ¿Cuál es el mejor programa de televisión de este año? ¿La mejor película?
2. ¿Quién es el actor más famoso de los Estados Unidos? ¿La actriz más famosa?
3. ¿Quién es el mejor atleta de tu escuela? ¿La mejor atleta? ¿Qué deportes practican?
4. ¿Cuál es el río más grande de la América del Norte? ¿De la América del Sur?

ACTIVIDAD

El más pequeño de todos   With a partner make up a *Libro de superlativos* arranged by subject. For example:

Las mejores y peores comidas de la cafetería de la escuela
Los estudiantes más listos (altos, atléticos, etc.) de la escuela
Los edificios más grandes (feos, bellos, etc.) de la ciudad
Los barrios más interesantes (viejos, hermosos, etc.) de la ciudad

En el Museo del Prado, Madrid, España

APLICACIONES Discretionary

Notes: Answers to the **Repaso** and **Tema** appear in the Teacher Notes.

REPASO

Notes: Review of:
1. days of the week
   e → ie verbs
   verb + infinitive
2. demonstrative adjectives
   noun phrases with *de*
   superlatives
   affirmative *tú* commands +
   direct object pronouns
3. *creer que*
   comparatives
   demonstrative adjectives
   adjectives
4. exclamations with *qué*
   tan … como
5. affirmative *tú* commands
   personal *a*
   affirmative *tú* commands +
   indirect object pronouns
   absolute superlatives

Enrichment: You may want
to use the model sentences in
the **Repaso** for dictation.

Mira las frases modelo. Luego cambia las frases que siguen al español según los modelos.

1. *Este sábado pienso jugar a los bolos.*
   (This afternoon I intend to take a walk.)
   (On Wednesday we want to have a picnic.)
   (This Thursday they prefer to go on an outing.)

2. *Esos actores de Venezuela son los más famosos del espectáculo. Míralos.*
   (These roller skates are the best in the store. Buy them.)
   (That amusement park is the largest in the southwest. Visit it.)
   (This art exhibit is the most interesting (one) of the year. Describe it.)

3. *Creen que el desfile es menos divertido que esa banda fabulosa.*
   (She thinks the rides are less exciting than those free balloons.)
   (I think the bag is smaller than this old basket.)
   (We think the peanuts are more expensive than that hot popcorn.)

4. *"¡Qué bueno! Las montañas son tan hermosas como las playas," dice mamá.*
   ("What a shame! He's as shy as his father," says grandfather.)
   ("How marvelous! He's as courageous as a lion," says Anita.)
   ("What a drag! She's (estar) as scared as I am," he says.)

5. *Después vamos a la exposición. "Mira a tu mamá," dice la tía Juana.*
   "Cómprale un cuadro. Son bellísimos."
   (Then we go to the show. "Look at those children," says Dad. "Buy them tickets. They're extremely cheap.")
   (Before, they go to the booths. "Look at your daughter," says Mom. "Buy her a mask. They're very funny.")
   (Now we're going to the zoo. "Look at those little girls," says Luz. "Buy them some peanuts. They're (estar) really delicious.")

En el Parque de
Chapultepec, México

TEMA

Escribe las frases en español.

1. This Sunday, María and Ángela plan to go to the fair.

2. This Ferris wheel is the tallest in the country. Look at it!

3. They think the merry-go-round is less exciting than this roller coaster.

4. "Gee! I'm as ugly as you (are)," says María.

5. Afterwards they go to the ice cream shop. "Look at that little boy," says Angela. "Buy him an ice cream. It's (estar) awfully good."

REDACCIÓN

Ahora escoge uno de los siguientes temas para escribir tu propio diálogo o párrafo.

1. Expand the *Tema* by writing a paragraph about María and Ángela at the fair. Tell how they go there, whether they meet friends, which rides they enjoy, and what their friends prefer to do. Are they going to go to the fair again? If so, when?

2. Write a paragraph about what you like to do best on weekends. Do you like to visit museums and art exhibits? Do you like to take walks, have picnics? Do you like to skate? Do you do these activities frequently? What do you plan to do next weekend?

3. Make up a telephone conversation between two friends who are planning a weekend outing. They are very enthusiastic and use a lot of superlatives.

COMPRUEBA TU PROGRESO   CAPÍTULO 3

A   La feria
Completa las siguientes frases con la palabra o expresión correcta.

1. ¿Quieres dar una vuelta en _____?   (el cuadro / la montaña rusa / la canasta)
2. En aquel _____ venden palomitas deliciosas. (carrusel / lago / puesto)
3. Ese caballo es muy _____. Todo le asusta. (tímido / valiente / famoso)
4. ¿Quiere Ud. comprar una _____ de dulces? (feria / bolsa / banda)
5. Los espectáculos en el parque no cuestan nada. Son _____.   (gratis / flacos / grises)
6. No podemos hacer un picnic porque va a llover. ¡_____!   (Qué lata / Qué maravilla / Qué susto)

B   Preguntas
Escribe preguntas. Luego contesta cada una afirmativamente.

1. ¿entender / Uds. / la obra de teatro?
2. ¿pensar / ella / dar un paseo?
3. ¿querer / tú / tomar algo?
4. ¿pensar / tú / hacer un picnic?
5. ¿querer / Uds. / ir de excursión?
6. ¿preferir / Ud. / el invierno?

C   Tienes mucho que hacer
Haz preguntas y luego contesta cada una con un mandato con *tú*. Sigue el modelo.

> limpiar la cocina / ahora mismo
> *¿Limpio la cocina?*
> *Sí, límpiala ahora mismo.*

1. leer los apuntes / en seguida
2. recoger mis cosas / por la mañana
3. cerrar la puerta / ahora mismo
4. visitar la exposición de arte / antes de salir
5. invitar a mis primos / esta noche
6. escribir la carta / mañana
7. empezar la canción / en unos minutos
8. comer las verduras / todas

D   Comparaciones
Completa las siguientes frases para hacer comparaciones.

> Elena es alta.

1. Pablo es _____ Elena.
2. Juana es _____ todos.

> El niño es joven.

3. La madre es _____ el niño.
4. La abuela es _____ todos.
5. La madre es _____ la abuela.
6. El niño es _____ todos.

E   ¡Es aburridísimo!
Answer each question according to the model.

> ¿Es muy aburrido José?
> *Sí, es aburridísimo.*

1. ¿Es muy famoso García Lorca?
2. ¿Es muy fácil patinar?
3. ¿Son muy ricas las niñas?
4. ¿Es muy grande la casa de los espejos?
5. ¿Son muy baratas las palomitas?
6. ¿Es muy rápido el metro?

F   ¿*Tan* o *tanto*?
Completa las siguientes frases con *tan . . . como* o con la forma apropiada de *tanto . . . como*.

1. La casa de los fantasmas no es _____ divertida _____ la montaña rusa.
2. La feria no tiene _____ puestos este año _____ el año pasado.
3. Las naranjas no tienen _____ azúcar _____ los dulces.
4. Diego Obregón es _____ famoso _____ Rosa Pinto.
5. El tren no está _____ lleno de gente _____ el autobús.
6. En mi casa no hay _____ espejos _____ en la casa de los espejos de la feria.
7. Hay _____ hielo en las calles _____ en el río.

VOCABULARIO DEL CAPÍTULO 3

Sustantivos

la atracción, *pl.* las atracciones
la banda
la bolsa
el cacahuate
la canasta
el carrusel
la casa de los espejos
la casa de los fantasmas
el cuadro
el espectáculo
la exposición de arte, *pl.* las
   exposiciones de arte
la feria
el globo
la heladería
el hielo
el lugar
la montaña rusa
las palomitas
el parque de diversiones
el patín, *pl.* los patines (de
   ruedas)
el picnic
el puesto
la rueda
la rueda de feria

Adjetivos

asustado, -a
famoso, -a
flaco, -a
gracioso, -a
gratis, *pl.* gratis
tanto, -a
tímido, -a
valiente

Verbos

asustar
entender (e → ie)
olvidar
parar
patinar (sobre ruedas / sobre
   hielo)
remar

Adverbios

afortunadamente
antes
completamente
especialmente
exactamente
frecuentemente
probablemente

Expresiones

cambiar de idea
dar un paseo
dar una vuelta
hacer un picnic
ir de excursión
jugar a los bolos
me gustaría
¡por fin!
¡qué alivio!
¡qué lata!
¡qué maravilla!
¡qué susto!
tan + *adj. / adv.* + como
tanto + *noun* + como

LA COMIDA ESPAÑOLA

I f you were in Spain at suppertime and wanted to try one of the local specialties, you would have a lot to choose from, because Spain offers a lot of variety. In Galicia, a cool, rainy region in the northwest, the favorite soup is a thick and hearty *caldo gallego*, made with meat and potatoes. In Andalucía, a region in the warm southern part of Spain, *gazpacho* is the classic soup. Served cold, it is a refreshing blend of tomatoes, cucumbers, olive oil, and garlic. Diced tomatoes, peppers, onions, and bread are added when the soup is served.

Fish is popular and plentiful. Look at the map, and you'll see why—Spain is nearly surrounded by water. Seafood dishes popular in the north are *merluza* (hake) *bacalao* (cod), *angulas* (baby eels fried in oil and garlic), and *pulpo* (octopus). Valencia, a port in the southeast, was the first to give us *paella*. Shrimp, crayfish, and clams are only part of *paella*'s special flavor. Chicken, rice (a major crop in that area), and the yellow-orange spice saffron are equally important ingredients.

Eggs are one of Spain's most popular foods. Spaniards often cook them by dropping them into a bowl of boiling garlic soup or by serving them fried with *patatas (papas) fritas*. The most popular egg dish is the *tortilla española*, an omelet made with potatoes and onions and cooked in olive oil. This is Spain's favorite snack food or side dish. It is usually served cold in wedges like pieces of pie.

It is no accident that the Spanish word for oil *(el aceite)* and olive *(la aceituna)* are closely related. Spain is the world's largest producer of olives and the oil derived from them. Like potatoes, eggs, and garlic, it is a staple in every Spanish home.

Essential

If students ask: Other related words you may want to present: *la cerca*, fence; *la salsa de tomate*, ketchup; *el panecillo / bollo*, roll; *el carbón*, charcoal.

Allá en el rancho

1

Transparency 12

CONTEXTO VISUAL

la colina — hill

el valle — valley

el pueblo — town

el ganado — cattle

el rancho — ranch

la salchicha — sausage

la parrilla — grill

la campesina — country woman

el campesino

la sandía — watermelon

la mostaza — mustard

el vinagre

el aceite

la sal

la pimienta

la tortilla

la aceituna

el perro caliente

el ajo

Notes: After presenting the **Contexto comunicativo** on pp. 133–134, you may want to ask volunteers to present the mini-dialogues to the rest of the class. Stress correct pronunciation, intonation, and rhythm.

CONTEXTO COMUNICATIVO 2

1 Hoy hay muchos invitados en el rancho. Queremos **hacer un asado.** Vamos a **asar** carne **a la parrilla** y servirla con papas y ensalada.

Variaciones:

- carne → pollos
  servirla → servirlos

hacer un asado *to have a barbecue*

el asado *barbecue*

asar a la parrilla *to barbecue, to grill*

(handwritten: Que necesita para un asado.)

2 NORMA ¿Puedo **probar** la carne?
PEDRO ¡Cómo no! ¿La quieres **bien cocida**?
NORMA No, la prefiero **medio cocida.**
PEDRO Entonces toma aquélla. ¡**Buen provecho!**

- bien cocida → **poco cocida**
- aquélla → ésa

(handwritten: te gusta su carne bien cocido o poco cocido)

probar (o → ue) *to taste*

bien cocido, -a *well done (referring to meat)*

medio cocido, -a *medium*

¡buen provecho! *enjoy your meal*

poco cocido, -a *rare*

3 RITA ¡Qué buen **sabor** tiene este pescado! ¿Es **fresco,** verdad?
LUIS *(handwritten: of course)* ¡Por supuesto! Nunca compro pescado **congelado.**

- sabor → **olor**
- nunca compro → no me gusta el

el sabor *taste*

fresco, -a *fresh*

congelado, -a *frozen*

el olor *odor, smell*

4 DAVID ¡Mira qué bello es este **paisaje**!
ÁNGEL Sí, sí. Muy bello. Pero estamos aquí para **recoger** frutas, no para mirar el paisaje.

- este paisaje → este valle
- frutas → manzanas

(handwritten: Estas su casa bella? es bello)

el paisaje *landscape*

recoger *here: to pick*

Enrichment: You may want to ask students to practice mini-dialogue 2 in pairs, substituting personalized information in the third line.

Reteach / Review: In connection with mini-dialogue 3, point out the shortened form of *bueno (buen)* before the noun *sabor*. Ask students to change the exclamation by using the opposite of *buen:* ¡Qué mal sabor tiene este pescado!

You may want to review *ser* vs. *estar* by asking these questions about mini-dialogue 3: ¿*Cómo está el pescado?* (Está delicioso / bueno / sabroso.) ¿Cómo es? (Es fresco.)

Palabras Nuevas I **133**

5 CARMEN ¿Viene Rogelio a nuestro asado?

JAVIER ¡Claro que sí! Las tres **actividades** que más le gustan son **desayunar**, almorzar y **cenar**.

- actividades → cosas
  desayunar → el desayuno
  almorzar → el almuerzo
  cenar → la cena

la actividad *activity*
desayunar *to eat breakfast*
cenar *to have dinner*

6 JOSEFINA ¿Qué vamos a cocinar hoy para la cena?

VIRGINIA Pienso **asar** un pavo.

JOSEFINA ¡Qué bueno! No hay nada tan **sabroso** como el pavo **asado**.

- cocinar → preparar
- sabroso → delicioso

asar *to roast*
sabroso, -a *tasty, flavorful*
asado, -a *roasted (meat)*

EN OTRAS PARTES

el asado

También se dice *la barbacoa*.

poco/bien cocido

También se dice *poco / bien hecho*.

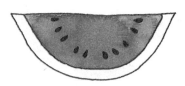

También se dice *el melón de agua*.

En España y en muchos países latinoamericanos se dice *la finca*. También se dice *la estancia* y *el fundo*.

Un asado cerca de Buenos Aires, Argentina

PRÁCTICA

A   ¿Qué hacen en el campo?   Imagina que estás en un rancho con un amigo. Escoge la palabra o expresión correcta.

1. ¿Cómo está el asado? Muy *(congelado / ganado / sabroso)*.
2. Cuando pongo la mesa frecuentemente olvido la sal y *(el paisaje / la pimienta / la salchicha)*.
3. ¿Qué vamos a hacer después del asado? Vamos a subir *(al valle / a la colina / a la parrilla)*.
4. ¿Qué más necesitamos para la ensalada? Un poco de aceite y *(olor / valle / vinagre)*.
5. ¿Qué hacen esas campesinas? *(Asan / Barren / Recogen)* frutas.
6. ¿Qué tiene que hacer el campesino? Tiene que dar de comer *(al ganado / al paisaje / al asado)*.
7. ¿Cómo puedo cocinar la carne? Puedes asarla a la *(colina / salchicha / parrilla)*.
8. ¿Qué añades a los perros calientes? *(Pueblos / Mostaza / Sandía)*.
9. ¿Qué hay en esos árboles? *(Ajo / Aceitunas / Aceite)*.

Práctica A
1. sabroso
2. la pimienta
3. a la colina
4. vinagre
5. Recogen
6. al ganado
7. parrilla
8. Mostaza
9. Aceitunas

B   Vamos a hacer un asado.   Escoge la mejor palabra o expresión para completar el párrafo.

asada	frescas	quemada
buen provecho	mostaza	sabor
congeladas	probar	sandía

¿A ti te gustan las salchichas o los perros calientes con _____ y cebolla? Pues yo prefiero la carne _____. Debe estar bien cocida, pero no _____. Tiene un _____ delicioso. ¡De veras! La tienes que _____. Y cómela con verduras _____. Nunca compro esas verduras _____ que
5   venden en el supermercado. Y de postre, claro que no hay nada mejor que _____ fría. Es deliciosa. Entonces, ¡_____!

Práctica B
mostaza
asada
quemada / sabor / probar
frescas / congeladas
sandía / buen provecho

En Bolivia

C En el restaurante. Imagina que tú y varios amigos están en un restaurante latinoamericano. Sólo tú sabes hablar español y tienes que pedir la comida para todos. Usa el menú, ¡y tu imaginación!

ESTUDIANTE A	*¿Y para el señor a su izquierda?*
ESTUDIANTE B	*Él quiere empezar con . . .*
ESTUDIANTE A	*Muy bien. ¿Y la carne?*
ESTUDIANTE B	*. . .*
ESTUDIANTE A	*¿Qué clase de verduras?*
ESTUDIANTE B	*. . .*
ESTUDIANTE A	*¿Y qué clase de ensalada?*
ESTUDIANTE B	*. . .*
ESTUDIANTE A	*¿Y para beber?*
ESTUDIANTE B	*. . .*
ESTUDIANTE A	*¿Y de postre?*
ESTUDIANTE B	*. . .*

Menú

Sopas
Sopa de pollo
Sopa de cebolla
Sopa de tomate
Sopa de ajo
Gazpacho

Carnes
Bistec a la parrilla
Chuleta de cerdo
Chuleta de cordero
Carne asada
Pollo frito
Pavo asado
Arroz con pollo

Verduras
Frijoles con arroz
Guisantes
Maíz
Zanahorias

Ensaladas
Ensalada de lechuga y tomate con aceite y vinagre
Ensalada de frutas

Postres
Helado
Pasteles
Flan
Fruta fresca

Bebidas
Vino
Refrescos
Naranjada
Limonada
Agua mineral
Jugos
Leche
Té, café o chocolate

D Hablemos de ti.

1. ¿Cómo te gusta la carne, poco cocida, bien cocida o medio cocida? ¿Con mucha o poca sal? ¿Con mucha o poca pimienta? ¿Te gusta el ajo?
2. ¿Cuál es tu comida favorita? ¿Qué comida no te gusta?
3. ¿Qué te gusta más comer cuando vas a un asado?
4. ¿Qué pones en los perros calientes? ¿En las hamburguesas?
5. ¿Qué clase de ensalada te gusta más? ¿Qué clase de sopa?
6. ¿A qué hora desayunas? ¿Quién prepara tu desayuno? ¿A qué hora cenas? ¿De qué habla tu familia durante la cena?
7. ¿Qué comes cuando cenas solo(a)?

Práctica D
Answers will vary.

Practice Sheet 4–1

Workbook Exs. A–B

Tape Manual Exs. 1–2 3

Quiz 4–1

ACTIVIDAD

Un asado en el campo   Imagine that you're planning a barbecue in the country with two or three of your classmates. First, each of you writes an answer to each of these questions:

¿Cuáles son tres cosas que quieres comer?
¿Cuáles son tres cosas que puedes traer?
¿Cuáles son tres cosas que prefieres hacer en el campo?

Then discuss what everyone wants to eat, and make a list of what each person can bring. Make any necessary changes to avoid repeating items. Finally, decide what activities would be the most fun for everyone.

Enrichment: In connection with the **Actividad,** you may want to ask students to create invitations for their barbecue.

APLICACIONES Discretionary

Un asado en la playa Luquillo*

🎞 4

🎞 5 Pronunciación

Playa Luquillo en Puerto Rico

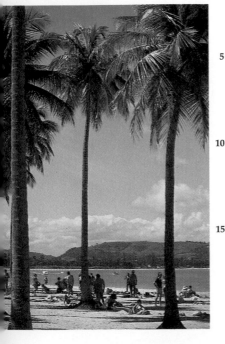

Ana y su hermano Jaime invitan a César, su primo de Nueva York, a un asado en la bella playa de Luquillo en Puerto Rico.

ANA   ¡Qué sabrosa está la carne!

JAIME   Siempre me parece que aquí en la playa el sabor de la
5   comida es mucho mejor que en la ciudad. Oye, César,
    ¿hace asados la gente en Nueva York?

CÉSAR   Sí, pero generalmente los hacemos en los parques.

ANA   ¿Por qué? ¿No van Uds. a la playa?

CÉSAR   Sí, pero no es tan fácil como aquí. Las playas están
10   bastante lejos y además[1] mucha gente no tiene coche.
    También, allá las playas no son tan bonitas como ésta.

JAIME   ¡Qué lata! Nunca quiero vivir lejos del mar.

ANA   Yo tampoco.

CÉSAR   Entonces, ¿por qué no hacemos otro asado mañana?

15 JAIME   ¡Sí, sí! Buena idea. Podemos hacerlo en el campo.

CÉSAR   Bien. Pero yo compro la carne esta vez. Y Uds. pueden
    traer el pan y los refrescos.

---

[1]**además**   *besides*

* Luquillo, una de las playas más bellas de Puerto Rico, está en el noreste de la isla *(island)*.

Reteach / Review: As you model the **Diálogo** or play the tape, you may want to remind students that *la gente* (lines 6 and 10) is a singular noun.

Preguntas

Contesta según el diálogo.

1. ¿De dónde es César?   2. ¿Qué es Luquillo? ¿Dónde está?   3. Según Ana, ¿cómo está la carne?   4. ¿Por qué le gusta a Jaime comer en la playa? Y tú, ¿estás de acuerdo con lo que él dice? ¿Por qué?   5. Según César, ¿dónde hacen los asados en Nueva York? ¿Por qué?   6. ¿Qué piensa César de las playas de Nueva York?   7. ¿Dónde no quiere vivir Jaime?   8. ¿En qué parte del país vives tú? ¿En qué parte te gustaría vivir? ¿Por qué?   9. ¿Por qué están tantos pueblos cerca de un lago o de un río? ¿Qué crees tú?

Diálogo
1. de Nueva York
2. una playa; cerca de San Juan, en el noreste de Puerto Rico
3. sabrosa
4. Porque la comida tiene mejor sabor que en la ciudad; Answers will vary.
5. En los parques; las playas están bastante lejos y mucha gente no tiene coche.
6. No son tan bonitas como Luquillo.
7. lejos del mar
8. Answers will vary.
9. Answers will vary.

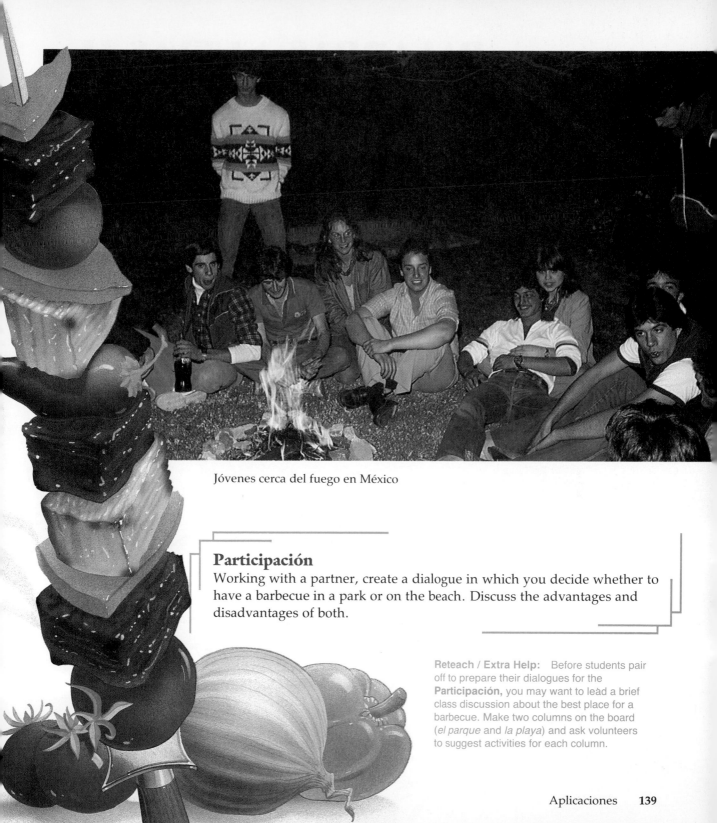

Jóvenes cerca del fuego en México

Participación

Working with a partner, create a dialogue in which you decide whether to have a barbecue in a park or on the beach. Discuss the advantages and disadvantages of both.

PALABRAS NUEVAS II

Essential

¿Vas de camping?

If students ask: Other related words you may want to present: *la fogata*, bonfire; *el malvavisco*, marshmallow; *la caña de pescar*, fishing rod.

6

Transparency 13
CONTEXTO VISUAL

el campamento

la tienda (de acampar)

la piedra

el saco de dormir

el sendero

ir de pesca

el fuego

la linterna

la pila

la lata

el abrelatas
pl. los abrelatas

la galleta

el ratón
pl. los ratones

la rana

la hormiga

la araña

el mosquito

la mosca

CONTEXTO COMUNICATIVO 7

1 Nos encanta **ir de camping** los fines de semana. Buscamos un lugar cerca de un lago porque nos gusta ir de pesca. No tenemos que **llevar** carne porque siempre tenemos mucha suerte y podemos comer pescado frito cada noche.

ir de camping	*to go camping*
llevar	here: *to take*

Variaciones:
- los fines de semana → durante el verano

2 ROSA Andrés, hay que **encender** el fuego si quieres **calentar** la sopa.

ANDRÉS Bien. También puedo **hervir** el agua para el café.

ROSA Buena idea, pero no debes olvidarte de **apagar** el fuego después.

- hay que encender → enciende

encender (e → ie) *to light, to turn on (a fire, light, appliance, etc.)*
calentar (e → ie) *to heat*
hervir (e → ie) *to boil*
apagar *to put out, to turn off (a fire, light, appliance, etc.)*

3 ANDREA Mira esto. Todo está **mojado.** ¿No va a parar nunca la lluvia?

ÁNGEL Afortunadamente, todavía hay algunas cosas **secas. Por ejemplo,** esta lata de café.

- algunas → varias

mojado, -a *wet*

seco, -a *dry*
por ejemplo *for example*

4 LUCÍA Esta mochila está muy **pesada.**

MANUEL ¿Sabes qué hay adentro?

LUCÍA No. ¿Piedras?

MANUEL Creo que tú llevas las latas y las linternas.

- muy pesada → pesadísima
- tú llevas → son

pesado, -a *heavy*

5 MAMÁ   ¿Haces la tarea, Judit?

JUDIT   Ahora no. Pero te **prometo** hacerla más tarde.

■ la tarea → las tortillas
  hacerla → hacerlas
■ más tarde → después

prometer   *to promise*

Enrichment: In connection with mini-dialogue 5, you may want to suggest these additional **Variaciones:** *¿Haces la tarea? → ¿Lavas los platos?, hacerla → lavarlos, más tarde → a las nueve.*

EN OTRAS PARTES

También se dice *la tienda de campaña* y *la carpa*.

En España se dice *el camping*.

En España también se dice *el bote*. También se dice *el pote*.

En México se dice *el abridor*.

También se dice *la bolsa de dormir*.

En Cuba, Puerto Rico y Costa Rica se dice *el trillo*.

encender

En muchos países latinoamericanos se dice *prender*.

En la Argentina se dice *la laucha*.

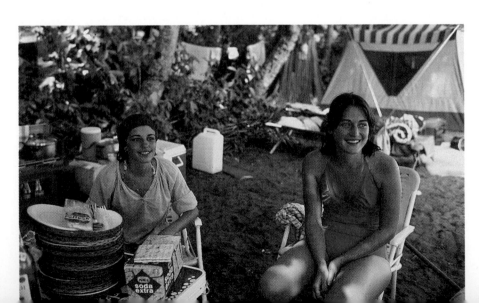

Un campamento en Costa Rica

PRÁCTICA

A **Vamos de camping.** Imagina que tú y un(a) amigo(a) hacen planes para ir de camping. ¿Tienen todo lo que necesitan? Sigue el modelo.

ESTUDIANTE A	*¿Tienes las tazas?*
ESTUDIANTE B	*Sí, las tengo.*
o:	*No, no las tengo.*

1.

2.

3.

4.

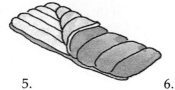
5.

6.

7.

8.

9.

Práctica A
1. ¿Tienes el abrelatas?
   Sí, (No, no) lo tengo.
2. ¿Tienes la linterna?
   Sí, (No, no) la tengo.
3. ¿Tienes la tienda
   (de acampar)?
   Sí, (No, no) la tengo.
4. ¿Tienes la mochila?
   Sí, (No, no) la tengo.
5. ¿Tienes el saco de dormir?
   Sí, (No, no) lo tengo.
6. ¿Tienes los tenedores?
   Sí, (No, no) los tengo.
7. ¿Tienes las cucharas?
   Sí, (No, no) las tengo.
8. ¿Tienes los cuchillos?
   Sí, (No, no) los tengo.
9. ¿Tienes las pilas?
   Sí, (No, no) las tengo.

B **¿Qué debo hacer?** Imagina que tú y otras personas van de camping. El director del campamento les dice a todos lo que deben hacer. Escoge el verbo correcto y úsalo para hacer un mandato. Sigue el modelo.

> María, _____ las latas. (parar / apagar / abrir)
> *María, abre las latas.*

1. Diego, _____ la sopa. (calentar / alquilar / almorzar)
2. Juan, _____ las tiendas de acampar. (planchar / traer / tirar)
3. Ester, _____ el fuego. (probar / hervir / encender)
4. Pedro, _____ las parrillas. (limpiar / asar / remar)
5. Luisa, _____ el aceite. (buscar / explicar / secar)
6. Juana, _____ las latas. (enchufar / recoger / asar)
7. Pepe, _____ las ollas. (alquilar / lavar / admirar)
8. Carmen, _____ la luz. (quemar / batir / apagar)
9. Julio, _____ el agua. (quemar / hervir / asar)

Práctica B
1. calienta
2. trae
3. enciende
4. limpia
5. busca
6. recoge
7. lava
8. apaga
9. hierve

Palabras Nuevas II **143**

Práctica C
Answers will vary.

C En el campamento. Escoge elementos de cada columna para describir lo que hacen estas personas. Sigue el modelo.

(tú)

ESTUDIANTE A *¿Qué haces?*
ESTUDIANTE B *Hiervo las papas.*

1. Luis y tú	apagar	el pollo
2. Cecilia y David	asar	el radio
3. nosotros	buscar	piedras
4. Isabel y Mario	calentar	en el río
5. Uds.	comer	la luz
6. Paco	dar un paseo	la parrilla
7. Leonor y Marta	encender	la sopa
8. Andrés	hervir	las galletas
9. Ud.	ir de pesca	las papas
10. (tú)	limpiar	pilas en la linterna
	poner	por ese sendero

Práctica D
Answers will vary.

Enrichment: After students answer items 1–5 of Ex. D orally, you may want to assign 6–7 as written homework Check students' work for correct spelling, punctuation, and capitalization.

Practice Sheet 4–2

Workbook Exs. C–D

8 Tape Manual Exs. 3–4

9 Refrán

Quiz 4–2

D Hablemos de ti.

1. ¿Te gusta ir de camping? ¿Con quién vas? ¿Adónde van Uds.?
2. Cuando vas de camping, ¿prefieres preparar la comida o encender el fuego? ¿Cuál es más fácil? ¿Qué comes para el desayuno cuando vas de camping? ¿A qué hora desayunas?
3. ¿Tienes un saco de dormir? ¿Cuándo lo usas? ¿Es cómodo?
4. ¿Puedes explicarle a la clase cómo abrir una lata o preparar una sopa?
5. ¿Tienes miedo de algunos animales? ¿De cuáles? ¿Te gustan las ranas? ¿Te asustan los ratones? ¿Hay ranas o ratones blancos en el laboratorio de biología de tu escuela?
6. Las hormigas están siempre muy ocupadas. ¿Puedes describirle a la clase lo que hacen estos insectos enérgicos?
7. Escoge uno o dos adjetivos para describir estos animales y explica por qué escogiste esa(s) palabra(s): las arañas, las moscas, los mosquitos, las ranas, el ganado.

En la Sierra de Gredos, España

ESTUDIO DE PALABRAS

Familias de palabras

What Spanish words or expressions do you know that are related to each of these words?

el campo	caliente	cocinar	el país
el pescado	el abrelatas	secar	cena

Antónimos

Escribe un antónimo para cada palabra en cursiva.

1. *Apaga* la tostadora, por favor.
2. El saco de dormir *está mojado*.
3. Prefiero la carne *bien cocida*.
4. *Esas colinas* son muy verdes.

Palabras con varios sentidos

¿Cuál es la palabra?

1.

2.

3. Sabes que la palabra *fresco* tiene dos sentidos. ¿Cuáles son?

Familias de palabras
campamento / campesino(a) / tienda de acampar / ir de camping
ir de pesca
calentar / hace calor / tener calor
abrir / lata
cocina / bien (poco, medio) cocido(a)
seco(a) / secadora
paisaje
cenar

Antónimos
1. Enciende
2. seco
3. poco cocida
4. Esos valles

Palabras con varios sentidos
1. la tienda
2. recoger
3. *cool, fresh*

Camping cerca de Buenaventura, Colombia

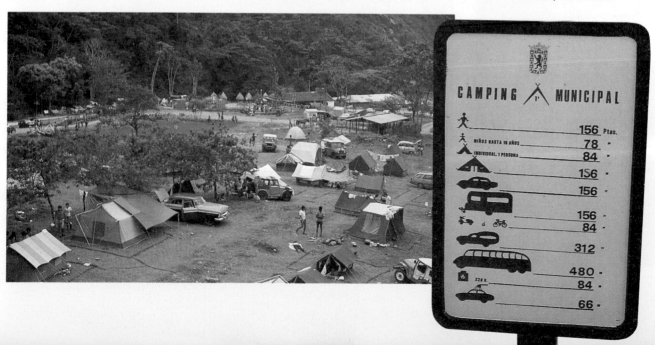

◆ **OBJECTIVES:**

TO ASK FOR CLARIFICATION

TO CLARIFY

TO ASSIGN TASKS

TO GIVE EXCUSES FOR ONESELF AND FOR OTHERS

EXPLICACIONES I Essential

Los verbos *decir*, *oír*, *hacer*, *poner*, *salir* y *traer*

1 Review the present-tense forms of *decir* ("to say, to tell").

DECIR	
digo	decimos
dices	decís
dice	dicen

Digo lo que pienso.	I **say** what I think.
¿Qué nos **dices**?	What **are you telling** us?
Dicen que va a llover.	**They say** (that) it's going to rain.

Remember that the *yo* form of *decir* ends in *-go* and that the *e* changes to *i* in all but the *nosotros* and *vosotros* forms.

(izquierda) En El Yunque, en Puerto Rico; (derecha) En Miranda del Castañar, España

2 Review the present-tense forms of *oír* ("to hear").

OÍR	
oigo	oímos
oyes	oís
oye	oyen

No te **oigo** bien.	*I can't **hear** you well.*
¿**Oyes** los pájaros?	*Do you **hear** the birds?*

Remember that the *yo* form of *oír* ends in *-go* and that the *i* changes to *y* except in the *yo*, *nosotros*, and *vosotros* forms. Note that the *nosotros* and *vosotros* forms have a written accent on the *i*.

3 Remember that there are many similarities among the verbs *hacer*, "to do," *poner*, "to put," *salir*, "to go out," and *traer*, "to bring."

HACER		PONER	
hago	hacemos	pongo	ponemos
haces	hacéis	pones	ponéis
hace	hacen	pone	ponen

SALIR		TRAER	
salgo	salimos	traigo	traemos
sales	salís	traes	traéis
sale	salen	trae	traen

All four verbs take regular *-er* / *-ir* endings, except in the *yo* forms. Note the *e* → *i* change in the *yo* form of *traer*.

4 Remember that we use *salir de* when we mean "to leave from (a place)."

Salimos de aquí esta tarde.	*We're leaving here this afternoon.*
El tren **sale de la estación** a las tres.	*The train **leaves the station** at three.*

We use *salir para* when we mean "to leave for (a place)."

Pronto **salen para** España.	*They'll leave for Spain soon.*

Enrichment: You may want to ask students to work in pairs to ask and answer questions that use the forms of *oír*. Students may choose a setting and focus on sounds associated with that place. For example: *Estamos en la playa. ¿Oyes el viento? ¿Oímos el mar?*

Notes: You may want to reread or highlight the **Diálogo** on p. 138, which contains several forms of *hacer*.

Reteach / Review: Elicit or point out the ending for the *yo* form in the verbs *hacer, poner, salir,* and *traer (-go)*.
  Review *salir de* and *salir para* by asking: *¿A qué hora sales para la escuela? ¿Y a qué hora salimos de aquí?*

PRÁCTICA

A ¿Qué dice? Imagina que estás en una fiesta y que la música está tan fuerte *(loud)* que no puedes oír lo que dice la gente. Escoge elementos de cada columna para contestar.

Juan

ESTUDIANTE A *¿Qué dice Juan?*
ESTUDIANTE B *Dice que pone la leche en el refrigerador.*

1. Laura y Amalia	aceite y vinagre	en la caja
2. (tú)	aceitunas	en la ensalada
3. Felipe	ajo	en el horno
4. Uds.	galletas	en la mesa
5. Norma	leche	en la parrilla
6. Ud.	mostaza	en los perros calientes
7. Benjamín	postre	en los platos
	sal y pimienta	en el pollo
	salchichas	en el refrigerador
	sandía	en la sartén
	tortillas	en los vasos

B ¿Oyen algo? Un grupo de niños pequeños visita un museo de ciencias. Con los ojos cerrados tienen que escuchar e identificar varios animales. Sigue el modelo.

¿Eduardo?
ESTUDIANTE A *¿Qué oye Eduardo?*
ESTUDIANTE B *Oye una vaca.*

1. ¿Juana? 2. ¿Diego y Sergio?

3. ¿yo? 4. ¿María?

5. ¿nosotras?

6. ¿tú, Luis?

7. ¿Ud., señora?

8. ¿Uds.?

C **¿Quién hace cada cosa?** Imagina que tú y tus amigos preparan un asado y nadie sabe lo que debe hacer. Sigue el modelo.

> ¿nosotros? / preparar la ensalada de frutas
> ESTUDIANTE A *¿Qué hacemos nosotros?*
> ESTUDIANTE B *Uds. preparan la ensalada de frutas.*

1. ¿tú? / hacer una ensalada
2. ¿Pedro? / encender el fuego
3. Carlos y Eugenio / abrir las latas de jugo de naranja
4. ¿Clara y Julia? / calentar el agua para el té
5. ¿yo? / poner la mesa
6. ¿Emilia? / hervir los huevos
7. ¿Uds.? / asar las chuletas de cerdo a la parrilla

D **Nadie está contento.** Imagina que llamas a tus amigos por teléfono, y que nadie está contento. Pregunta y contesta según el modelo.

> ¿Guillermo y Ángel / no decir la verdad? / estar asustado
> ESTUDIANTE A *¿Por qué no dicen la verdad Guillermo y Ángel?*
> ESTUDIANTE B *Porque están asustados.*

1. ¿Juanita / no poner en orden la casa? / tener fiebre
2. ¿(tú) / no oír las noticias? / no tener radio
3. ¿Héctor y Luis / no traer el tocadiscos? / estar demasiado pesado
4. ¿Uds. / no oír al profesor? / hay demasiado ruido
5. ¿(tú) / no hacer un asado afuera? / no salir cuando llueve
6. ¿Ud. / no traer la comida? / no querer preparar nada
7. ¿(nosotros) / no hacer el viaje? / no tener dinero
8. ¿Raúl / no decir nada? / ser tímido

5. ¿Qué oímos nosotras? Oyen un cordero.
6. ¿Qué oyes tú, Luis? Oigo una rana.
7. ¿Qué oye Ud., señora? Oigo un pato.
8. ¿Qué oyen Uds.? Oímos un gallo.

Práctica C
1. ¿Qué haces tú?
   Hago ...
2. ¿Qué hace Pedro?
   Enciende ...
3. ¿Qué hacen Carlos y Eugenio?
   Abren ...
4. ¿Qué hacen Clara y Julia?
   Calientan ...
5. ¿Qué hago yo?
   Pones ...
6. ¿Qué hace Emilia?
   Hierve ...
7. ¿Qué hacen Uds.?
   Asamos ...

Práctica D
1. ¿Por qué no pone en orden la casa Juanita?
   Porque tiene fiebre.
2. ¿... no oyes las noticias?
   ... no tengo radio.
3. ¿... no traen el tocadiscos Héctor y Luis?
   ... está demasiado pesado.
4. ¿... no oyen Uds. al profesor?
   ... hay demasiado ruido.
5. ¿... haces un asado afuera?
   ... no salgo cuando llueve.
6. ¿... no trae Ud. la comida?
   ... no quiero preparar nada.
7. ¿... no hacemos el viaje?
   ... no tenemos (*or:* Uds. no tienen) dinero.
8. ¿... no dice Raúl nada?
   ¿... es tímido.

Enrichment: After completing Ex. D, ask students to change the exercise to a *tú / yo* dialogue: *¿Por qué no dices ...? Porque estoy ...*

Los complementos directos e indirectos: *me, te, nos*

Remember that we use the pronouns *me, te,* and *nos* as either direct or indirect objects. In these examples, they are direct objects.

Las arañas **me** asustan.	*Spiders scare **me**.*
Los Ortega **nos** invitan.	*The Ortegas are inviting **us**.*
¿Dónde estás? No **te** veo.	*Where are you? I don't see **you**.*

In these examples, the pronouns are indirect objects. Note that they can mean *to* or *for me, you, us.*

¿**Me** muestras el sendero?
{ *Will you show the path **to me**?*
{ *Will you show **me** the path?*

Te doy el saco de dormir.
{ *I'm giving the sleeping bag **to you**.*
{ *I'm giving **you** the sleeping bag.*

Él **nos** presta su linterna.
{ *He's lending his flashlight **to us**.*
{ *He's lending **us** his flashlight.*

¿**Te** hiervo un huevo?
{ *Shall I boil an egg **for you**?*
{ *Shall I boil **you** an egg?*

OBJECTIVES:

TO CONTRADICT

TO ASK SOMEONE TO DO SOMETHING

TO AGREE TO DO SOMETHING

TO DESCRIBE DOING THINGS FOR OTHERS

1 Remember that the pronoun is placed just before the main verb or is attached to an infinitive or an affirmative command.

Lláma**me** más tarde. *Call **me** later.*
No **te** puedo llamar más tarde.
No puedo llamar**te** más tarde. } *I can't call **you** later.*

Enciénde**me** la luz, por favor. *Please turn on the light **for me**.*
Claro. **Te** puedo encender la luz. } *Of course. I can turn on the light*
Claro. Puedo encender**te** la luz. } ***for you**.*

2 Remember that when an indirect object is a personal possession or a part of the body, we use an indirect object pronoun and a definite article rather than a possessive form:

Él **me** barre **el** dormitorio. *He's sweeping **my** room.*
Nos secan **las** toallas mojadas. *They're drying **our** wet towels.*
Mamá va a cortar**te el** pelo. *Mom's going to cut **your** hair.*

In each of these English sentences, "for me, for us, for you" is implied. In Spanish we must use the pronoun, but then we use "the" instead of "my, our, your," etc.

PRÁCTICA

A Al contrario. Alfredo le cuenta historias absurdas al nuevo estudiante, pero Sonia le dice la verdad. Sigue el modelo.

>   el profesor Álvarez / dar mucha tarea
>   ESTUDIANTE A *El profesor Álvarez te va a dar mucha tarea.*
>   ESTUDIANTE B *Al contrario, no nos da mucha tarea.*

1. el profesor López / dar muchos exámenes
2. la profesora Gómez / hacer muchas preguntas
3. el profesor Ortiz / contar chistes
4. la profesora Fuentes / dar miedo
5. la profesora Molina / dar malas notas
6. el profesor Borau / prometer buenas notas
7. la profesora Núñez / traer churros
8. el profesor Suárez / vender pesos dominicanos

B Por favor. Guillermo siempre quiere algo. Sigue el modelo.

>   (yo) no encontrar un enchufe / ayudar
>   ESTUDIANTE A *No encuentro un enchufe. Ayúdame, por favor.*
>   ESTUDIANTE B *Bueno. Te ayudo.*

1. (yo) querer hablar contigo / llamar
2. (tú) nunca tener dinero / pagar
3. (yo) tener que salir temprano / despertar
4. (yo) poder hacer eso / mirar
5. (yo) ir a llegar tarde / esperar
6. (yo) tener algo importante que decirte / escuchar
7. (yo) nunca tener noticias de ti / escribir
8. (nosotros) no poder patinar porque el lago todavía no está congelado / creer

C Todos ayudan. ¿Qué hace cada persona? Sigue el modelo.

>   mi hermanita / lavar el coche / (a mí)
>   *Mi hermanita me lava el coche.*

1. el médico / examinar los ojos / (a ti)
2. mi madre / preparar el almuerzo / (a nosotros)
3. mi hermana / hacer la cama / (a mí)
4. papá y mamá / comprar la ropa / (a nosotros)
5. (yo) / hacer la maleta / (a ti)
6. mi abuela / poner en orden los armarios / (a nosotros)
7. la Dra. Sánchez / poner inyecciones / (a mí)
8. papá / pagar las lecciones de tenis / (a ti)

Práctica A
1. te va a dar …
   no nos da …
2. te va a hacer …
   no nos hace …
3. te va a contar …
   no nos cuenta …
4. te va a dar …
   no nos da …
5. te va a dar …
   no nos da …
6. te va a prometer
   no nos promete …
7. te va a traer …
   no nos trae …
8. te va a vender …
   no nos vende …

Práctica B
1. Quiero hablar contigo.
   Llámame, por favor.
   Bueno. Te llamo.
2. Nunca tienes dinero.
   Págame, por favor.
   Bueno. Te pago.
3. Tengo que … Despiértame …
   Bueno. Te despierto.
4. Puedo … Mírame …
   Bueno. Te miro.
5. Voy a llegar … Espérame …
   Bueno. Te espero.
6. Tengo … Escúchame …
   Bueno. Te escucho.
7. Nunca tengo … Escríbeme …
   Bueno. Te escribo.
8. No podemos … créeme …
   Bueno. Te creo.

Práctica C
1. El médico te examina los ojos.
2. … nos prepara …
3. … me hace …
4. … nos compran …
5. Te hago …
6. … nos pone en orden …
7. … me pone …
8. … te paga …

Practice Sheet 4–4

Tape Manual Ex. 6 11

Quiz 4–4

Los complementos directos e indirectos: Repaso

◆ OBJECTIVES:

**TO ASK SOMEONE
TO DO SOMETHING
FOR YOU OR FOR
SOMEONE ELSE**

**TO AGREE
ENTHUSIASTI-
CALLY**

Here are all of the direct and indirect object pronouns.

DIRECT OBJECT PRONOUNS

SINGULAR		PLURAL	
me	*me*	**nos**	*us*
te	*you*	**os**	*you*
lo	*him, you* (formal), *it*	**los**	*you, them* (masc. / masc. & fem.)
la	*her, you* (formal), *it*	**las**	*you, them* (fem.)

INDIRECT OBJECT PRONOUNS

SINGULAR		PLURAL	
me	*(to / for) me*	**nos**	*(to / for) us*
te	*(to / for) you*	**os**	*(to / for) you*
le	*(to / for) him, her, you* (formal), *it*	**les**	*(to / for) you, them*

1 All of these pronouns go before the main verb or are attached to an infinitive or an affirmative command.

Reteach / Extra Help: To reinforce point 2, ask students to work in groups of three. Make sure they have several objects that they can give each other. A gives an object to B, then C asks A: *¿Qué haces?* A answers *Le doy ... a ....*

To reinforce point 3, student B asks: *¿A quién le das ...?* A answers: *Le doy ... a ....*

2 When we use a noun as an indirect object, we usually also use the indirect object pronoun.

Le doy la mostaza **a Mario.**　　*I'm giving the mustard **to Mario.***
Les escribo **a mis abuelos.**　　*I'm writing **to my grandparents.***

3 We can emphasize the indirect object pronouns by using the preposition *a* + a prepositional pronoun.

¿A quién le escriben?　　***To whom** are they writing?*
Te escriben **a ti.**　　*They're writing **(to) you!***

Remember that we usually use *le* and *les* with *¿a quién(es)?*

4 When a direct object is a personal possession or a part of the body, we use an indirect object pronoun and a definite article rather than a possessive adjective.

> **Les** arreglo **la** aspiradora a Uds.
> Van a limpiar**nos la** estufa.
> Voy a lavar**les la** cara a los niños.

> *I'm fixing **your** vacuum cleaner.*
> *They're going to clean **our** stove.*
> *I'm going to wash the children's faces.*

Reteach / Extra Help: Before students begin the **Práctica** on p. 154, you may want to ask these questions: *¿Quién puede prestarme cinco dólares? ¿Viene el director / la directora a visitarnos a menudo? ¿Quién nos limpia la clase? ¿Te escriben tus primos?*

Una venta de vacas en Padrón, España

Cómo Comprar
LOS ASADOS
DE CARNE
DE VACA

U.S. DEPARTMENT OF AGRICULTURE

153

PRÁCTICA

Práctica A
Answers will vary.

Reteach / Extra Help: If your class finds Ex. A difficult, you may want to ask volunteers to suggest possible verb-object combinations: *apagar / linterna*, *abrir / latas, cerrar / cortinas*, and so on.

A Lo hago ahora mismo. Usa los dibujos y la lista de verbos para hacer ocho mandatos con *le, les, me* y *nos.* Luego usa el complemento directo apropiado (*lo, la, los* o *las*) para contestar. Sigue el modelo.

ESTUDIANTE A *Lávame la olla, por favor.*
o: *Lávanos la olla, por favor.*
o: *Lávale(s) la olla a papá (y a mamá), por favor.*
ESTUDIANTE B *Con mucho gusto. Voy a lavarla ahora mismo.*

abrir	cerrar	dibujar	limpiar	recoger
apagar	comprar	encender	mandar	secar
arreglar	decorar	enchufar	mostrar	tirar
calentar	desenchufar	lavar	prestar	traer

Práctica B
Answers will vary.

Practice Sheet 4–5

Workbook Exs. E–F

🔲 12 Tape Manual Ex. 7

Quiz 4–5

B Hablemos de ti.
1. ¿Les das regalos a tus amigos? ¿Cuándo? ¿Qué les das? ¿Qué clase de regalos te gusta recibir? ¿Qué clase de regalos te dan tus amigos?
2. ¿Qué cosas haces para tus mejores amigos o tu familia? ¿Qué hacen ellos para ti?
3. ¿Sales con tus amigos este fin de semana? ¿Adónde vas a ir? Cuéntales a los otros lo que quieres hacer.

APLICACIONES

Discretionary

¡Buen provecho! 13

Notes: You may want to assign the Antes de leer questions as written homework.

Antes de leer
1. cook
2. half kilo
3. Answers will vary.

LECTURA

Muchas personas quieren algo imposible. Ésta quiere ser astronauta. Aquélla quiere ser atleta. Otra quiere ser estrella de cine. Pero yo, Arturo Peret, estoy muy contento. ¡Soy un gran cocinero! Trabajo en un restaurante excelente. Preparo los platos más difíciles de comida española, mexicana
5 o americana. Sé preparar muchos platos diferentes de pollo, de carne o de pescado. ¡Todos son muy sabrosos! Mi paella, por ejemplo, es famosa. ¿Y mi gazpacho? ¡Pues, es el mejor de la ciudad!

Mi plato favorito es típico de la comida española: la fabada asturiana.[1] Es muy fácil prepararla. Los ingredientes que uso son: medio kilo de frijoles
10 blancos, un codito de jamón ahumado,[2] medio kilo de tocino,[3] una morcilla,[4] dos papas, una cebolla, dos cucharadas[5] de aceite.

Pongo los frijoles, el jamón y el tocino en una olla con agua. Pongo la olla al[6] fuego. Hiervo todo por una hora. Corto la cebolla y la pongo en una sartén con el aceite. La cocino por tres minutos. Corto la morcilla y las
15 papas en partes pequeñas. Añado la cebolla, la morcilla y las papas a la olla con los frijoles. Lo cocino todo por quince minutos y ¡ya está![7] ¡Qué olor! ¡Qué sabor! ¡Buen provecho!

---

[1]**la fabada asturiana**   *bean and bacon soup from Asturias, a region of northern Spain*
[2]**el codito de jamón ahumado**   *smoked ham hock*   [3]**el tocino**   *bacon*
[4]**la morcilla**   *a kind of Spanish sausage*   [5]**la cucharada**   *spoonful*   [6]**a**   here: *on*
[7]**ya está**   *that's it*

Haciendo tortillas en Tonalá, México

ANTES DE LEER

As you read, find the answers to the following questions.
1. Sabes lo que quieren decir *cocinar* y *cocina*. ¿Qué quiere decir *cocinero, -a*?
2. ¿Qué quiere decir *medio kilo*? (Piensa en la expresión *media hora*.)
3. En tu opinión, ¿es fácil o difícil ser cocinero(a)? ¿Es un trabajo aburrido o divertido? ¿Por qué?

En las Islas Baleares,
España

Preguntas

Contesta según la lectura.

1. ¿Cómo prepara Peret la fabada asturiana? Pon los pasos (*steps*) en el orden correcto.
   a. Añade la cebolla y la morcilla a los frijoles.
   b. Pone la olla en la estufa.
   c. Después de poner todos los ingredientes juntos en la olla, lo cocina todo por quince minutos más.
   d. Corta la cebolla.
   e. Pone los frijoles, el jamón y el tocino en la olla.
   f. Mezcla la cebolla con el aceite en una sartén.
   g. Hierve los frijoles, el jamón y el tocino.
2. ¿Por qué está Arturo Peret tan contento?
3. ¿Tienes ganas de probar la fabada asturiana? ¿Por qué? ¿Cuál de los ingredientes te gusta más? ¿Hay algunos que no te gustan?
4. ¿Te gustan las salchichas? ¿Las prefieres poco o muy picantes? ¿Te parecen más o menos sabrosas que los perros calientes?
5. Cuando desayunas en un restaurante, ¿qué pides? Cuando pides huevos, ¿pides también salchichas o tocino? ¿Cuestan mucho más los platos de huevos cuando los pides con carne? ¿Más o menos cuánto cuesta un vaso pequeño de jugo de naranja? ¿Y un vaso grande?

EXPLICACIONES II

Mandatos afirmativos con *tú:* Verbos irregulares

◆ **OBJECTIVES:**

TO NAG OR SHOW IMPATIENCE

TO MAKE POLITE REQUESTS TO SOMEONE YOU KNOW WELL

TO EXPLAIN WHY YOU WANT SOMEONE TO DO SOMETHING

You know how to form *tú* commands for regular and stem-changing verbs. The following verbs have irregular affirmative *tú* commands.

ser → **sé**	tener → **ten**	hacer → **haz**	poner → **pon**
ir → **ve**	venir → **ven**	decir → **di**	salir → **sal**

Sé amable	*Be nice.*
Ve a la tienda, Luis.	*Go to the store, Luis.*
Ten cuidado, Felipe.	*Be careful, Felipe.*
Ven a las cinco, Ana.	*Come at five, Ana.*
Haz un dibujo, Ignacio.	*Make a drawing, Ignacio.*
Di lo que piensas.	*Say what you think.*
Pon la mesa, Clara.	*Set the table, Clara.*
Sal de allí, Pedro.	*Get out of there, Pedro.*

1   Because these irregular command forms all have only one syllable, the stress remains on the verb when we use them with an object pronoun. Thus we do not have to add a written accent.

Dinos la verdad, por favor.	*Tell us the truth, please.*
Hazlo ahora mismo.	*Do it right now.*

This is also true of regular *tú* commands that have only one syllable.

Velos un poco más tarde.	*See them a little later.*
Dame la linterna.	*Give me the flashlight.*

PRÁCTICA

Práctica A

1. sal   5. pon
2. Di   6. Ve
3. Ven   7. ten
4. sé   8. haz

A ¡Ya son las diez! Francisco todavía está en la cama. Su mamá lo llama. Escoge el verbo correcto para completar cada frase. Usa mandatos con *tú*.

decir	ir	salir	tener
hacer	poner	ser	venir

1. Francisco, _____ de tu cuarto en seguida.
2. ¿A qué hora regresaste anoche? ¡_____ la verdad!
3. _____ aquí ahora mismo. Es la hora de desayunar.
4. ¡Francisco, por favor, _____ más ordenado!
5. Por favor, _____ la mesa.
6. Necesitamos pan fresco. _____ a la panadería, por favor.
7. Pero _____ cuidado en la calle.
8. Y después de regresar, por favor _____ tu cama.

Práctica B

1. ¿puedes poner ...? / pon
2. ¿puedes decir ...? / di
3. ¿puedes ser ...? / sé
4. ¿puedes venir ...? / ven
5. ¿puedes hacer ...? / haz
6. ¿puedes salir ...? / sal
7. ¿puedes ir ...? / ve
8. ¿puedes tener ...? / ten

B ¡Más rápido! Tú eres muy amable cuando quieres algo, ¿verdad? Pero imagina que tienes un(a) amigo(a) que no es tan amable y que siempre da mandatos. Cambia según el modelo.

Luisa / hacer la ensalada

ESTUDIANTE A *Luisa, ¿puedes hacer la ensalada?*
ESTUDIANTE B *Luisa, haz la ensalada.*

1. Héctor / poner el ratón en la jaula
2. Manuel / decir esto en francés
3. Mónica / ser más generosa
4. Carlota / venir a la puerta
5. Vicente / hacer el asado en tu casa
6. Sonia / salir de la tienda
7. Roberto / ir al campamento
8. Luz / tener cuidado con esas joyas

Práctica C

1. Préstanos
2. Llévanos
3. Diles
4. Ponle

Notes: You may want to assign Ex. C as written homework. Remind students to add an accent when they use object pronouns with command forms of more than one syllable.

C Un día en el rancho. Unos amigos visitan un rancho. Haz mandatos y añade el complemento directo o indirecto correcto. Sigue el modelo.

Aquí están las pilas. (Poner) _____ en el radio.
Aquí están las pilas. Ponlas en el radio.

1. Vamos a subir a la colina esta tarde. (Prestar) _____ las mochilas, por favor.
2. Nosotros queremos ir también. (Llevar) _____, por favor.
3. María y Luis quieren visitar el pueblo. (Decir) _____ dónde está.
4. Rosita tiene frío. (Poner) _____ ropa seca.

5. Me encanta el sabor del pollo asado. (Prometer) _____ que lo vas a preparar esta noche.
6. La sandía está estupenda. (Probar) _____, si quieres.
7. Estos perros calientes no tienen mucho sabor. (Poner) _____ más mostaza.
8. Tenemos mucha hambre. (Hacer) _____ unas salchichas con cebolla, por favor.

5. Prométeme
6. Pruébala
7. Ponles
8. Haznos

D Hablemos de ti.
1. ¿Qué mandatos te dan tus padres cuando sales por la noche con tus amigos?
2. ¿Qué mandatos le das a un(a) niño(a) pequeño(a) a quien cuidas?

Práctica D
Answers will vary.

Practice Sheet 4–6

Workbook Exs. G–J

Tape Manual Ex. 8 14

Refrán 15

Canción 16

Quiz 4–6

ACTIVIDAD

Haz lo que te digo. Think of five commands you might give a classmate. They should be things that can be done easily in the classroom. Then get together in a small group and take turns telling each other what to do and then doing what you have been told.

Notes: In connection with the **Actividad,** you may want to ask students to give commands that classmates can pantomime in addition to those that can be followed in the classroom.

APLICACIONES Discretionary

Notes: Answers to the **Repaso** and **Tema** appear in the Teacher Notes.

REPASO

Notes: Review of:
1. time expressions
   expressions with *ir + de*
2. *¿Dónde está(n)?*
   traer
   direct object pronouns
3. *decir*
   indirect object pronouns
   affirmative *tú* commands
      + object pronouns
4. *decir*
   redundant *le(s)* with indirect
      object pronouns
   affirmative *tú* commands
5. affirmative *tú* commands
      + object pronouns
   a mí me gustaría + infinitive

Mira las frases modelo. Luego cambia las frases que siguen al español según los modelos.

1. *Esta tarde voy de excursión al lago.*
   (Tonight she's going on vacation to the ranch.)
   (Tomorrow you (pl.) are going fishing in the river.)
   (This afternoon they're going shopping in the town.)

   Enrichment: You may want to use the model sentences in the **Repaso** for dictation.

2. *¿Dónde está la tienda? Ahora la traen.*
   (Where's the watermelon? They're bringing it now.)
   (Where are the crackers? We're bringing them now.)
   (Where's the oil? I'm bringing it now.)

3. *Sus padres le dicen: "Descríbenos el olor."*
   (My mom says to me: "Turn off the lights for me.")
   (They tell me: "Buy her the olives.")
   (I say to you: (fam.) "Show me the path.")

4. *El campesino le dice a su compañero: "Tira las latas en el basurero."*
   (They tell their guest: "Light the lamp in the dining room.")
   (I tell Mom: "Have a picnic in the valley.")
   (She says to her rephew: "Boil the corn in the pot.")

5. *"Escúchame," dice el niño. "A mí me gustaría salir también."*
   ("Answer me," says the police officer (m.). "I'd like to know right now.")
   ("Show me," says the little girl. "I'd like to see too.")
   ("Tell us," says the pilot. "I'd like to land soon.")

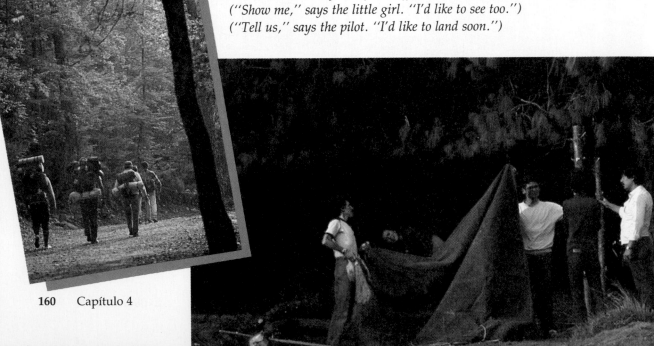

Escribe las frases en español.

1. Today we're going camping in the valley.

2. "Where's the grill?" "I'm bringing it now."

3. My father says to me, "Bring me the can opener."

4. He says to my brother, "Put the batteries in the flashlights."

5. "Take me," thinks the cat. "I'd like to go too."

REDACCIÓN

Ahora escoge uno de los siguientes temas para escribir tu propio diálogo o párrafo.

1. Expand the *Tema* by writing a paragraph about the family's camping trip. Where are they going? What things are they taking to eat? What equipment do they have? Why do they like to go camping?

2. Write a dialogue between Luis and his little brother as they walk along a path near a lake. What kinds of animals do they see? Do they want to go swimming, or is the water too cold?

3. Write a simple recipe using *tú* commands.

COMPRUEBA TU PROGRESO CAPÍTULO 4 Discretionary

Notes: Answers to the **Comprueba** appear in the Teacher Notes.

A En el rancho
Escoge la respuesta correcta.

1. ¿Cómo te gusta la carne?
   a. Congelada.
   b. Poco cocida.
   c. Buen provecho.
2. ¿Dónde pongo la carne?
   a. En la mostaza.
   b. En la parrilla.
   c. En la piedra.
3. ¿Te gusta el paisaje?
   a. Sí, es muy hermoso.
   b. Sí, es muy sabroso.
   c. Sí, medio cocido.
4. ¿Está fresco el pescado?
   a. No, está congelado.
   b. No, está mojado.
   c. No, está pesado.
5. ¿Dónde trabajan los campesinos?
   a. Allá, en la rana.
   b. Allá, en el rancho.
   c. Allá, en la parrilla.

B Preguntas
Mira los dibujos y contesta las preguntas. Usa
frases completas.

1. ¿Qué ponemos en la
   mesa?

2. ¿Qué pones en la
   mochila?

3. ¿Qué me traes?

4. ¿Qué oyes?

5. ¿Qué haces?

6. ¿Qué hacen Uds.?

7. ¿Cuándo sales?   8. ¿Qué oyen Uds.?

C Los mandatos
Haz mandatos según el modelo.

   decirme / la respuesta
   Dime la respuesta. Dila.

1. traerle / la linterna
2. ponernos / la mesa
3. buscarles / las aceitunas
4. hacerme / la cama
5. recogernos / las manzanas
6. mostrarme / el hielo
7. abrirles / los sacos de dormir
8. darles / la sal

D En casa
Haz mandatos según el modelo.

   lavar el pelo de Juanito
   Lávale el pelo a Juanito.

1. planchar la falda de Elena
2. enchufar la lámpara de papá
3. secar las camisas de Diego
4. limpiar el dormitorio de los abuelos
5. barrer el suelo de Elena
6. arreglar el proyector de los tíos

E ¿Qué debo hacer?
Contesta con un mandato según el modelo.

   ¿Qué debo hacer? (un asado)
   Haz un asado.

1. ¿Cómo debo ser?   (amable)
2. ¿Cuándo debo venir?   (temprano)
3. ¿Qué debo decir?   (que salimos)
4. ¿Qué debo poner en la mesa?   (sal y pimienta)
5. ¿Cuándo debo salir?   (a las cinco)
6. ¿Adónde debo ir?   (pueblo)

Activity Masters   Chapter 4 Test   Listening Comprehension Test
Workbook Review: Chapters 1–4   Cumulative Test: Chapters 1–4

VOCABULARIO DEL CAPÍTULO 4

Sustantivos

el abrelatas, *pl.* los abrelatas
el aceite
la aceituna
la actividad
el ajo
la araña
el asado
el campamento
el campesino, la campesina
la colina
el fuego
la galleta
el ganado
la hormiga
la lata
la linterna
la mosca
el mosquito
la mostaza
el olor
el paisaje
la parrilla
el perro caliente
la piedra
la pila
la pimienta
el pueblo
la rana
el rancho
el ratón, *pl.* los ratones
el sabor
el saco de dormir
la sal
la salchicha

la sandía
el sendero
la tienda (de acampar)
la tortilla
el valle
el vinagre

Adjetivos

asado, -a
congelado, -a
fresco, -a
mojado, -a
pesado, -a
sabroso, -a
seco, -a

Verbos

apagar
asar
calentar (e → ie)
cenar
desayunar
encender (e → ie)
hervir (e → ie)
llevar *(to take)*
probar (o → ue)
prometer
recoger (j) *(to pick)*

Expresiones

asar a la parrilla
bien / medio / poco cocido, -a
¡buen provecho!
hacer un asado
ir de camping
ir de pesca
por ejemplo

UN DEPORTE AMERICANO

He's taking a shot, it's in the air, and . . . it's a goal! It's absolutely incredible, ladies and gentlemen! The Aztec Arrows have won again." There were no sportscasters in Mexico a thousand years ago, but if there had been, they might have sounded something like that as they breathlessly reported a game called *tlachtli*, the most popular sport of that time.

Tlachtli was something of a cross between basketball and soccer. The object of the game was very simple: to get a rubber ball through a stone ring that stuck out of the wall at each end of the court. But there was a catch: Players could use only their knees, thighs, and elbows. Little wonder that it took only one goal to win, or that games sometimes went on for days.

Tlachtli was played throughout the Aztec and Mayan regions of Mexico and Central America. The best-preserved court is located in Chichén Itzá, on Mexico's Yucatán Peninsula. The court is 168 meters long, and its stone rings are almost three meters above the ground (not as high as a basketball net, but high enough if you're trying to slam-dunk with your elbow).

Another thing that made the game difficult was the ball itself, which was made of solid rubber. It was so hard and heavy that players were often injured and sometimes even killed by it. To protect themselves from bruises, players wore gloves, armpads, helmets, and heavy leather aprons.

Some scholars believe that the game might have been part of a religious ceremony. According to the *Popol Vuh*, the sacred book of the Mayas, two mythical heroes once played a game of *tlachtli* against the gods of evil for control over the destiny of humankind. Fortunately, they won!

PALABRAS NUEVAS I

Essential

En el club de deportes

If students ask: Other related words you may want to present: *el jinete*, jockey; *la vela*, sail; *la pista*, racetrack.

Transparency 15
CONTEXTO
VISUAL

la carrera

el velero

la carrera

la regata

primero, -a
segundo, -a
tercero, -a
cuarto, -a
quinto, -a
sexto, -a
séptimo, -a
octavo, -a
noveno, -a
décimo, -a
último, -a

reír (e → i)

sonreír (e —

CONTEXTO
COMUNICATIVO   2

1   **El club deportivo** de nuestro barrio tiene un buen programa. Para **participar** en los deportes sólo hay que tener **el carné** del club.

Variaciones:
■ los deportes → las actividades

el club, pl. **los clubes**   *club*
deportivo, -a adj.   *sports*
participar   *to participate, to take part*
el carné   *membership or ID card*

Enrichment: In connection with mini-dialogue 1, you may want to point out that *carné* is also spelled *carnet*.

el tanteo

el equipo perdedor

el equipo ganador

la campeona

el campeón
pl. los campeones

la ganadora

el ganador

la natación

el entrenador

la entrenadora

el empate

la nadadora

el nadador

2 MARIO ¿Es ésta la primera regata?

  SONIA No, es la tercera pero es la mejor de todas.
    Participan veleros de otros países.

  MARIO ¡Cómo me gustaría **navegar**!

  navegar *to sail*

- primera → cuarta
- la tercera → la quinta
- la mejor → la más interesante

Palabras Nuevas I   **167**

3	CLAUDIA	¿Vienes al partido con nosotros?	el / la visitante *visitor; visiting team*

3   CLAUDIA   ¿Vienes al partido con nosotros?

      ERNESTO   Sí. Dicen que **los visitantes** son formidables.

      CLAUDIA   Es verdad, pero **el equipo local** es excelente también.

   ■ es verdad → **de acuerdo**

el / la visitante   *visitor; visiting team*

el equipo local   *home team*

de acuerdo   *right, okay, all right*

4   LEONOR   ¡Uf! Estoy cansadísima. Hace una hora que practicamos para la carrera.

      IGNACIO   ¿Es muy **estricta** la Sra. Núñez?

      LEONOR   Sí. A veces nos asusta con su **voz fuerte** pero es una gran entrenadora. Aprendemos mucho de ella.

   ■ practicamos para la carrera → corremos

estricto, -a   *strict*

la voz, pl. **las voces**   *voice*

fuerte   here: *loud*

5   RAQUEL   El domingo juega Veracruz **contra** Los Leones **por** primera **vez**.

      RODOLFO   Va a ser un partido fantástico.

      RAQUEL   De acuerdo. Pero creo que Los Leones van a ganar **el campeonato,** porque son los mejores jugadores.

   ■ Veracruz → el equipo local

contra   *against, versus*

por (primera / segunda / última, etc.) vez   *for the (first / second / last, etc.) time*

el campeonato   *championship*

6   LOLA   Estás muy **activo** hoy. ¡Qué **milagro**!

      LUIS   Sí. Hace dos horas que limpio mi cuarto.

      LOLA   **¡Qué barbaridad!** Y todavía está desordenado.

   ■ está desordenado → no está en orden

activo, -a = enérgico, -a

el milagro   *miracle*

¡qué barbaridad!   *how awful! good grief!*

Natación en México

XX CAMPEONATO NACIONAL DE NATACION JUVENIL Y PRIMERA FUERZA

vea en competencia a los mejores nadadores del país

participan las selecciones de:

Cochabamba
Catavi Santa Cruz Sucre
Beni Corocoro La Paz

viernes 28 sabado 29 domingo 30
Hrs. 9.00 y 18.00

PRÁCTICA

A **El campamento de veraneo** *(summer camp).*   Antes de salir para el campamento, todos los chicos reciben una lista de "Actividades especiales." Imagina que recibes esta lista. Escoge dos actividades para cada una de las ocho semanas en que está abierto el campamento. Puedes escoger una actividad sólo una vez. Sigue el modelo.

> *La primera semana quisiera preparar un jardín*
> *y participar en carreras de bicicleta.*

preparar un jardín *(sólo en las dos primeras semanas)*
aprender a escribir a máquina *(dura cuatro semanas: desde la primera semana hasta la cuarta, y desde la quinta hasta la octava)*

aprender a tomar buenos apuntes	hacer canastas
estudiar piedras	leer cuentos de ciencia ficción
estudiar árboles y flores	leer revistas deportivas
estudiar pájaros	aprender a navegar
estudiar hormigas	aprender a patinar sobre hielo
estudiar peces, ranas y serpientes acuáticas	participar en regatas
aprender canciones folklóricas de varios idiomas	participar en carreras de bicicleta
dibujar paisajes	participar en carreras de natación
hacer lámparas con botellas	ir de pesca
	jugar a los bolos
	aprender juegos de naipes

Práctica A
Answers will vary.

Enrichment: After students complete Ex. A, ask them to say why they made the choices they did. For example: *Quisiera preparar un jardín porque me gustan las flores.*

B **¿Qué dicen?**   Completa cada frase con la palabra correcta.

1. El equipo local gana cada *(partido / club / carné).*
2. Nuestro equipo de natación tiene dos *(entrenadoras / regatas / voces)* muy buenas.
3. Necesitas mostrar tu *(carné / velero / carrera)* para entrar en el club.
4. Esperamos ganar *(la campeona / la jugadora / el campeonato)* de bolos.
5. El entrenador de los visitantes tiene *(una voz / un balón / un velero)* tan fuerte como un tren.
6. Esta noche es el *(estricto / activo / último)* partido del campeonato.
7. Creo que este equipo va a *(participar / navegar / patinar)* en el campeonato de fútbol.
8. Me gustaría aprender a *(navegar / reír / sonreír)* para poder participar en *(una regata / un empate / un tanteo).*
9. Mi hermano nunca practica deportes. Él es muy *(activo / estricto / perezoso).*

Reteach / Extra Help: Before students begin Ex. B, you may want to remind them to read the entire sentence before choosing the correct word to complete it.

Práctica B
1. partido
2. entrenadoras
3. carné
4. el campeonato
5. una voz
6. último
7. participar
8. navegar / una regata
9. perezoso

C ¡Qué barbaridad! ¿Qué dices tú en estas situaciones? Escoge una expresión apropiada de la lista. Usa cada expresión sólo una vez.

1. Tu equipo favorito pierde el partido.
2. Tu amiga gana el campeonato de natación.
3. Pierdes tu carné del club.
4. Ganas el partido de golf.
5. Tu entrenador dice que no puedes participar en la carrera.
6. Llueve y no hay partido.
7. El partido termina en un empate.
8. Tu velero llega en último lugar.
9. Tu escuela está en primer lugar del campeonato de ajedrez.

¡Felicitaciones!
¡Imagínate!
¡No me digas!
¡Por fin!
¡Por supuesto!
¡Qué barbaridad!
¡Qué lástima!
¡Qué lata!
¡Qué mala suerte!
¡Qué milagro!

D Hablemos de ti.

1. ¿A qué deportes eres aficionado(a)? ¿Cuál es tu deporte preferido? ¿Por qué?
2. ¿Prefieres participar en algunos deportes y en otros no? ¿Por qué? ¿Te gusta ir al estadio o prefieres mirar los partidos en la televisión? ¿Por qué?
3. ¿Tiene tu escuela un buen equipo de béisbol? ¿Y de básquetbol? ¿De qué color son los uniformes? ¿Ganan a menudo o generalmente pierden?
4. ¿Hay un club deportivo cerca de tu casa? ¿Vas allí a veces? ¿Puedes practicar natación allí?
5. En tu opinión, ¿cuál es el mejor equipo de fútbol americano? ¿Por qué es el mejor?
6. ¿Qué equipo va a ganar el campeonato de béisbol el próximo verano? ¿Por qué crees eso?

Juegos Panamericanos en Indianápolis y en Caracas

ACTIVIDAD

¿Por qué me llamas?   Write down half of a phone conversation. Write only your responses to what the caller might be saying. Use two positive and two negative exclamations from the list below.

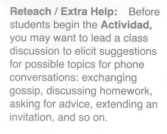

Reteach / Extra Help: Before students begin the **Actividad,** you may want to lead a class discussion to elicit suggestions for possible topics for phone conversations: exchanging gossip, discussing homework, asking for advice, extending an invitation, and so on.

¡Caramba!	¡Por fin!	¡Qué lata!
¿De veras?	¡Qué alivio!	¡Qué maravilla!
¡Espero que sí / no!	¡Qué barbaridad!	¡Qué milagro!
¡Imagínate!	¡Qué bueno!	¡Qué (mala) suerte!
¡Ojalá!	¿Qué importa?	¡Uf!

Leave a line or two blank before each exclamation. For example:

ESTUDIANTE A   . . .
ESTUDIANTE B   ¡Uf!
ESTUDIANTE A   . . .
ESTUDIANTE B   ¡Qué bueno!

Now exchange sheets with another student. Complete each other's dialogues so that the responses are appropriate. A complete dialogue might look like this:

ESTUDIANTE A   ¿Aló?
ESTUDIANTE B   Aló. Habla *(nombre)*. ¿Quieres ir a patinar esta tarde?
ESTUDIANTE A   ¡Uf!
ESTUDIANTE B   ¿Prefieres ver la regata entonces?
ESTUDIANTE A   ¡Qué bueno!
ESTUDIANTE B   Pero primero tengo que limpiar el sótano.
ESTUDIANTE A   ¡Qué lata!
ESTUDIANTE B   No importa. Voy a hacerlo en seguida.
ESTUDIANTE A   ¡Qué alivio!

When both conversations are complete, read them aloud together.

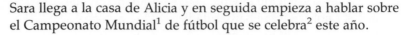

APLICACIONES Discretionary

El deporte número uno 4 5 Pronunciación

DIÁLOGO

Notes: Make sure students understand this cognate that has not been glossed: *la comunicación*, communication.

Culture: You may want to ask students to do research on the World Cup and present brief oral reports.

Sara llega a la casa de Alicia y en seguida empieza a hablar sobre el Campeonato Mundial[1] de fútbol que se celebra[2] este año.

SARA   Hola, Alicia. ¿Qué te parece el Campeonato Mundial?

ALICIA   ¡Fútbol! ¡Fútbol! ¿No quieres saber cómo estoy?

5   SARA   ¡Qué emocionante! ¿verdad? ¿Quién crees que va a ganar el Campeonato? ¿México?

ALICIA   Yo estoy muy bien, gracias. ¿Y tú?

SARA   Si México sale[3] campeón, ¡vamos a celebrar todo el año!

ALICIA   Y eso va a resolver[4] todos los problemas del país, ¿no?

10   SARA   Pero, ¿no comprendes que el fútbol es muy importante? Contribuye[5] a la comunicación entre la gente de todos los países.

ALICIA   ¡No contribuye nada a la comunicación entre nosotras! Bueno, ¿vamos al cine?

15   SARA   Pero, ¿no sabes que hoy México juega contra Alemania?

ALICIA   No. Tampoco quiero saberlo. Yo voy al cine.

---

[1]**mundial** adj. *world*   [2]**celebrarse** *to take place*   [3]**salir** here: *to end up as*   [4]**resolver** *to solve*   [5]**contribuir** *to contribute*

Diálogo
1. El Campeonato Mundial de fútbol.
2. A Sara.
3. Van a celebrar todo el año.
4. Answers will vary. Example: No le gusta.
5. Alemania / No / Answers will vary.
6. Porque contribuye a la comunicación entre la gente. / Answers will vary.
7. Answers will vary.

Preguntas
Contesta según el diálogo.

1. ¿Qué campeonato se celebra este año?   2. ¿A quién le gusta mucho el fútbol?   3. Según Sara, ¿qué va a pasar si México sale campeón? 4. ¿Qué piensa Alicia del fútbol?   5. ¿Qué país juega contra México? ¿Van Sara y Alicia juntas al partido? ¿Qué pasa entre las dos amigas? 6. ¿Por qué cree Sara que el fútbol es muy importante? ¿Estás de acuerdo? ¿Por qué? ¿Qué piensas de Alicia?   7. ¿Te gusta ver los juegos Olímpicos? ¿Prefieres los juegos de invierno o de verano? ¿Por qué? ¿Participas en algunos de estos deportes? ¿En cuáles?

Participación

Working with a partner, make up a phone conversation about a sports event such as the Super Bowl *(Campeonato de fútbol americano)* or the World Series *(Serie Mundial de béisbol)*. Arrange with your partner to go to the game. Set the time, date, and place, and mention the teams that are playing. Which team do you think is going to win? Why?

Diego Maradona

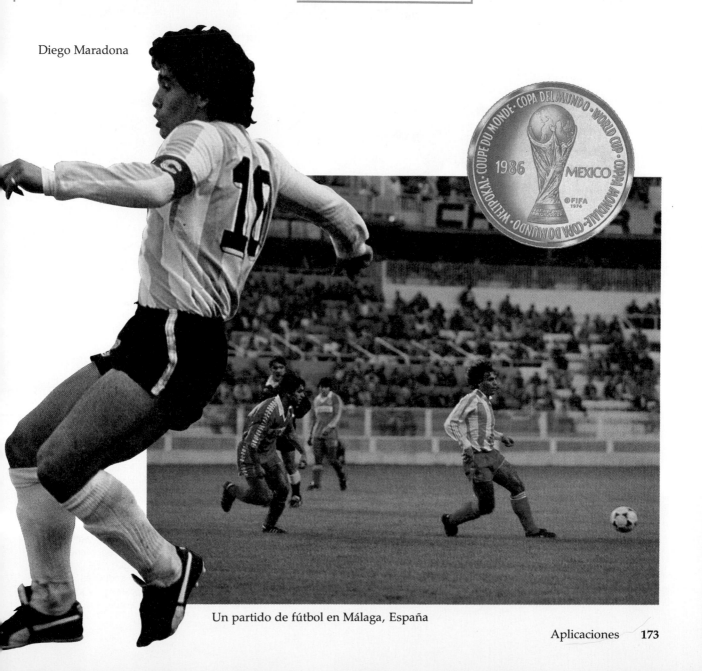

Un partido de fútbol en Málaga, España

PALABRAS NUEVAS II

Essential

 6

Transparency 16

CONTEXTO VISUAL

If students ask: Other related words you may want to present: *el frontón,* jai alai court; *el / la gimnasta,* gymnast; *la red,* net; *las aletas,* flippers.

Otros deportes

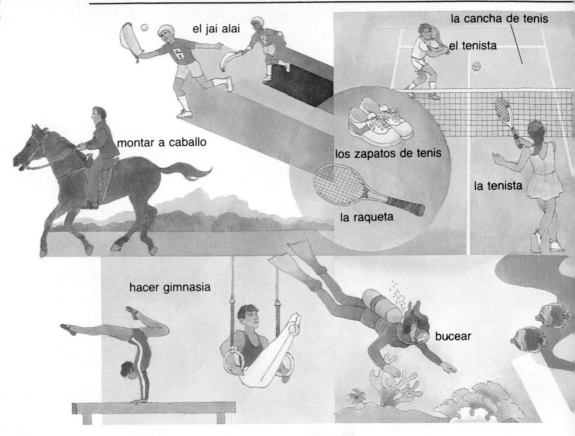

- el jai alai
- la cancha de tenis
- el tenista
- montar a caballo
- los zapatos de tenis
- la raqueta
- la tenista
- hacer gimnasia
- bucear

CONTEXTO COMUNICATIVO   7

1 PILAR **Anteayer** nadé tres horas sin parar.

TOMÁS **¡Increíble!**

PILAR Bueno, no es tan increíble. Hace muchos años que practico la natación.

Variaciones:

■ nadé → esquié

■ la natación → el esquí

anteayer *the day before yesterday*

increíble *incredible*

Enrichment: You may want to reinforce the concept of the past in mini-dialogue 1 by suggesting these additional **Variaciones:** *anteayer → ayer, anoche, el viernes pasado.*

If students ask: Other related words you may want to present: *el bastón de esquiar*, ski pole; *la pista de patinaje*, skating rink.

Reteach / Extra Help: You may want to point out the compound noun *salvavidas*. Elicit other familiar compound nouns (*abrelatas, lavaplatos, sacapuntas, sujetapapeles*) and ask what distinguishes the singular and plural forms (the article).

practicar el esquí

la esquiadora

el esquiador

el esquí

el patinador   la patinadora

levantar pesas

las pesas

el levantador de pesas

la levantadora
de pesas

practicar
el esquí acuático

la isla

el salvavidas

salvavidas

el salvavidas

2 SUSANA ¿Vamos en velero **hasta** la isla?

HORACIO Sí. Pero debes llevar el salvavidas. Es muy importante usarlo, **¿no te parece?**

SUSANA Sí. Tienes razón.

- vamos → damos un paseo
- en velero → a navegar
- tienes razón → estoy de acuerdo

hasta here: *to, out to, as far as*

¿no te parece? *don't you think so?*

EN OTRAS PARTES

También se dice *los tenis* y *las zapatillas de tenis*.

También se dice *el campo de tenis* y *la pista de tenis*.

Notes: Before students begin Ex. A, make sure they understand that they will be practicing plural nouns and the corresponding direct object pronouns.

Práctica A
1. ¿Tenemos todos los zapatos de tenis? Sí, los tenemos.
2. ¿Tenemos todas las raquetas? Sí, las tenemos.
3. ¿Tenemos todos los patines (de ruedas)? Sí, los tenemos.
4. ¿Tenemos todas las pelotas de tenis? Sí, las tenemos.
5. ¿Tenemos todas las pesas? Sí, las tenemos.
6. ¿Tenemos todos los trajes de baño? Sí, los tenemos.
7. ¿Tenemos todos los salvavidas? Sí, los tenemos.
8. ¿Tenemos todos los esquís? Sí, los tenemos.

PRÁCTICA

A **¿Tenemos todo?** La familia Ayala es muy atlética. Van de vacaciones y quieren saber si llevan todo lo que necesitan. Pregunta y contesta según el modelo.

ESTUDIANTE A *¿Tenemos todas las bicicletas?*
ESTUDIANTE B *Sí, las tenemos.*

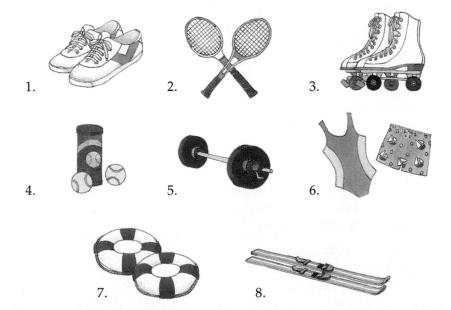

1. 2. 3.

4. 5. 6.

7. 8.

B **¿Qué le gusta hacer?**   Mira los dibujos y describe lo que le gusta hacer a Juan José. Sigue el modelo.

En el otoño
En el otoño monta en bicicleta.

1. En el club

2. En el verano

3. En el invierno

4. En el lago

5. En el campo

6. Cuando hace fresco

7. En la primavera

8. Cuando hace calor

9. Y tú, ¿qué deportes practicas en cada estación del año?

Práctica B
1. En el club juega al jai alai.
2. En el verano bucea y nada.
3. En el invierno patina sobre hielo.
4. En el lago practica el esquí acuático.
5. En el campo monta a caballo.
6. Cuando hace fresco patina sobre ruedas.
7. En la primavera hace gimnasia.
8. Cuando hace calor navega.
9. Answers will vary.

Reteach / Review: After students complete Ex. B either orally or in writing, you may want to expand on the practice by asking them to talk about Juan José and his friend Elena María. Remind students to change the verb forms from singular to plural.

C **Hablemos de ti.**
1. ¿Participas en carreras de bicicleta? ¿Generalmente, ganas o pierdes?
2. ¿Sabes patinar? ¿Dónde patinas? ¿Cuál te gusta más, patinar sobre hielo o patinar sobre ruedas? ¿Por qué?
3. ¿Puedes levantar pesas en algún club deportivo cerca de tu casa? ¿Te gusta hacerlo? ¿Lo haces a menudo?
4. ¿Hay un equipo de gimnasia en tu escuela? ¿Cómo es? En tu opinión, ¿cuál es más difícil, hacer gimnasia o levantar pesas? ¿Hay que ser más fuerte para hacer gimnasia o para levantar pesas?
5. ¿A veces montas a caballo? ¿Dónde? ¿Montas generalmente el mismo caballo? ¿Cómo se llama? ¿De qué color es?
6. ¿Eres buen(a) nadador(a)? ¿Te gustaría trabajar como salvavidas? ¿Dónde? ¿Por qué?
7. ¿Quién es tu tenista favorito(a)? ¿Por qué? ¿Juegas tú al tenis? ¿Eres un(a) buen(a) tenista? ¿Dónde juegas? ¿Tienes que reservar la cancha de tenis para hacerlo?

Práctica C
Answers will vary.

Practice Sheet 5–2

Workbook Exs. C–D

Tape Manual Exs. 3–4   8

Refrán   9

Quiz 5–2

Familias de palabras
trabajar / pensar / correr
tostadora / calculadora /
borrador / computadora /
lavadora / despertador

En Barcelona, España

Antónimos
1. activa / enérgica
2. perdedor
3. primera

Palabras con varios sentidos
1. el cuarto
2. el salvavidas

Notes: You may want to
assign the **Estudio de
palabras** as written homework.
Then go over the answers in
class by calling volunteers to
the board. Ask students to
correct their own work.

ESTUDIO DE PALABRAS

Familias de palabras

Did you notice that the nouns *el patinador / la patinadora* are related to the verb *patinar*? Or that *el nadador / la nadadora* are related to the verb *nadar*? In Spanish the suffixes *-dor* and *-dora* added to a verb stem often indicate the person who performs an action. Sometimes suffixes name certain utensils or appliances: *el refrigerador* (from *refrigerar*), *la aspiradora* (from *aspirar*). Many English words that end in *-er* or *-or* end in *-dor* or *-dora* in Spanish.

What verbs do you think the following nouns are related to? What do you think these nouns mean?

el trabajador   la pensadora   el corredor

What nouns have you learned that are related to each of these verbs?

tostar	borrar	lavar
calcular	computar	despertar

Antónimos

Escribe un antónimo para cada palabra en cursiva.

1. Es una persona muy *perezosa*.
2. El equipo *ganador* lleva el uniforme azul.
3. La *última* carrera empieza a las tres.

Palabras con varios sentidos

¿Cuál es la palabra?

1.

2.

EXPLICACIONES I

Essential

Verbos con el cambio *e → i*

Notes: As you present the forms of the *e → i* stem-changing verbs, make sure students remember that the endings are those of regular *-ir* verbs.

Remember that in some stem-changing verbs, the stem vowel changes from *e → i* in all of the present-tense forms except *nosotros* and *vosotros*.

PEDIR*	
pido	pedimos
pides	pedís
pide	piden

◆ **OBJECTIVES:**

TO FIND OUT WHAT PEOPLE WANT TO ORDER OR WHAT THEY SERVE IN A RESTAURANT

TO DESCRIBE AMUSING SITUATIONS

All verbs of this type have infinitives that end in *-ir*. For example: *servir*, *vestir(se)*, and *repetir*. Which *e* in *repetir* changes to *i*?

1 *Reír* ("to laugh") and *sonreír* ("to smile") show the same *e → i* stem change, but they have an accent mark on the *i* in all of their present-tense forms.

REÍR		SONREÍR	
río	reímos	sonrío	sonreímos
ríes	reís	sonríes	sonreís
ríe	ríen	sonríe	sonríen

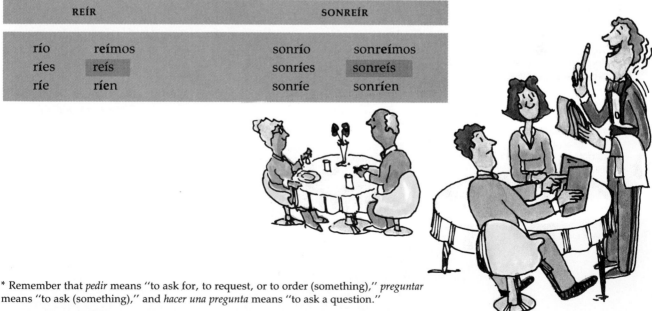

---

* Remember that *pedir* means "to ask for, to request, or to order (something)," *preguntar* means "to ask (something)," and *hacer una pregunta* means "to ask a question."

Siempre les **piden** el coche los sábados.	*They always **ask** them **for** the car on Saturdays.*
Voy a **preguntar** dónde vive.	*I'm going to **ask** where she lives.*
Hacen tantas **preguntas**.	*They **ask** so many **questions**.*

A **En el restaurante y en un asado.** Pregunta y contesta según los modelos.

en un restaurante		en un asado	
ESTUDIANTE A	*¿Qué pides cuando vas a un restaurante?*	ESTUDIANTE A	*¿Qué sirves cuando haces un asado?*
ESTUDIANTE B	*Generalmente pido . . .*	ESTUDIANTE B	*A menudo sirvo . . .*
ESTUDIANTE A	*¿Y qué pides de postre?*	ESTUDIANTE A	*¿Y qué sirves de postre?*
ESTUDIANTE B	*Pido . . .*	ESTUDIANTE B	*Sirvo . . .*

bistec	frutas y queso	pavo asado
carne asada	galletas y queso	perros calientes
chiles rellenos	hamburguesas	pescado frito
chuletas de cerdo	helado	pollo asado
chuletas de cordero	paella	pollo frito
empanadas de pollo	pan con ajo	salchichas
ensalada de . . .	papas fritas	sandía
flan	pastel de . . .	sopa de . . .

Un vendedor de cacahuates en Madrid

B **Todavía en el restaurante y en el asado.** Varios amigos hablan sobre lo que piden en un restaurante y lo que sirven en un asado. Usa la lista de la Práctica A para preguntar y contestar. Sigue el modelo.

en un restaurante		en un asado	
ESTUDIANTE A	*¿Qué piden cuando van a un restaurante?*	ESTUDIANTE A	*¿Qué sirven cuando hacen un asado?*
ESTUDIANTE B	*Generalmente pedimos . . .*	ESTUDIANTE B	*A menudo servimos . . .*
ESTUDIANTE A	*¿Y qué piden de postre?*	ESTUDIANTE A	*¿Y qué sirven de postre?*
ESTUDIANTE B	*Pedimos . . .*	ESTUDIANTE B	*Servimos . . .*

C ¿Ríen o sonríen? ¿Qué hacen las siguientes personas en estas situaciones? Escoge el verbo apropiado. Sigue el modelo.

> sus padres
> *Sus padres ríen cuando Jorge cuenta un chiste.*
> o: *Sus padres sonríen cuando los niños tratan de asustarlos.*

1. mis padres
2. (yo)
3. nuestro(a) entrenador(a)
4. (tú)
5. mi novio(a) y yo
6. Uds.
7. el profesor
8. (nosotros)
9. todo el mundo

cuando / tratar de asustar (a alguien)
cuando / contar un chiste
cuando / dar una vuelta en la
   montaña rusa
cuando / salir bien en una prueba
cuando / sacar buenas notas
cuando / ganar el campeonato
cuando / tratar de levantar pesas
cuando / estar contento
cuando / hablar con el (la) salvavidas
cuando / ganar regatas
cuando / empezar a tocar el piano
cuando / ver una película cómica
cuando / oír el tanteo

Notes: Make sure students understand that there are numerous possible answers for Ex. C.

Reteach / Review: Before students begin Ex. C, you may want to elicit the present-tense forms of the irregular and stem-changing verbs in the right-hand column *(contar, dar, salir, estar, empezar, ver, oír).*

Práctica C
Answers will vary.

Practice Sheet 5–3

Tape Manual Ex. 5 10

Quiz 5–3

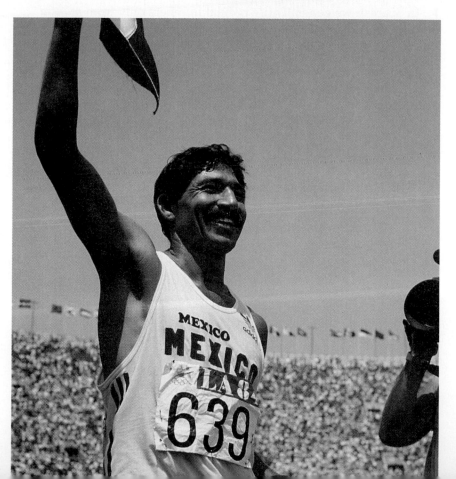

Un atleta mexicano

Los números ordinales

◆ **OBJECTIVES:**

TO IDENTIFY OR POINT THINGS OUT IN SEQUENCE

TO IDENTIFY PRIORITIES

TO DESCRIBE OR ORGANIZE EVENTS OR ACTIVITIES

We use ordinal numbers to describe people or things in a series. When we use them as adjectives, they agree in gender and number with the nouns they describe, and they usually go before the noun. Remember that *primero* and *tercero* drop the final *o* before a masculine singular noun.

Ésta es la **cuarta** regata del verano.	*This is the **fourth** boat race of the summer.*
Repite la **novena** palabra, por favor.	*Repeat the **ninth** word, please.*
Gané el **primer** partido.	*I won the **first** game.*
El **tercer** levantador de pesas es muy fuerte.	*The **third** weight lifter is very strong.*

When we abbreviate an ordinal number, we write the Arabic numeral with a small letter *o* or *a* after the number and above it.

María es la **5ª** nadadora.	*María is the **5th** swimmer.*
Estoy en **3º** lugar.	*I'm in **3rd** place.*

Una carrera en Honolulú

Notes: Refer to mini-dialogue 2 on p. 167 for examples of ordinal numbers. You may want to use a calendar to identify the months with ordinal numbers: *Enero es el primer mes del año, febrero es el segundo mes,* and so on.

1 In Spanish we generally use ordinal numbers only from *primero* through *décimo*. After *décimo* we use the cardinal numbers (*once, doce,* etc.) after the noun.

Tenemos que leer desde la **primera** lección hasta la lección **quince**.	*We have to read from the **first** lesson to the **fifteenth** lesson.*
Su oficina está en el piso **veintitrés**.	*His office is on the **23rd** floor.*

2 With the names of kings and queens we write Roman numerals and say them as ordinal numbers. But we do not say the definite article as we do in English.

Isabel **II** *(segunda)* es la reina de Inglaterra.	*Elizabeth **II** (the second) is the queen of England.*
La hija de Fernando **V** *(quinto)* se llama Juana la Loca.	*The daughter of Ferdinand **V** (the fifth) is called Juana la Loca.*

3 A cardinal number comes before an ordinal number when both are used together.

Necesitas leer **los dos primeros** capítulos para el examen.	*You need to read the **first two** chapters for the exam.*

PRÁCTICA

A **¿En qué lugar está . . . ?** Imagina que eres un locutor de deportes *(sports announcer)*. Indica las posiciones de los diferentes coches que participan en la carrera. Sigue este modelo.

El coche (color) *está en* (número) *lugar.*

Práctica A

El coche amarillo está en primer lugar.
... negro está en segundo ...
... verde está en tercer ...
... azul está en cuarto ...
... blanco está en quinto ...
... rojo está en sexto ...
... morado está en séptimo ...
... marrón está en octavo ...
... anaranjado está en noveno ...
... gris está en décimo ...

Práctica B

1. Es el nueve de junio. Es el noveno día del sexto mes.
2. Es el veintiséis de noviembre. Es el día veintiséis del mes once.
3. Es el trece de julio. Es el día trece del séptimo mes.
4. Es el ocho de enero. Es el octavo día del primer mes.
5. Es el doce de marzo. Es el día doce del tercer mes.
6. Es el quince de septiembre. Es el día quince del noveno mes.
7. Es el primero de diciembre. Es el primer día del mes doce.
8. Es el cuatro de febrero. Es el cuarto día del segundo mes.
9. Es el veintiuno de octubre. Es el día veintiuno del décimo mes.
10. Es el treinta y uno de mayo. Es el día treinta y uno del quinto mes.
11. Es el tres de agosto. Es el tercer día del octavo mes.
12. Es el diecisiete de abril. Es el día diecisiete del cuarto mes.

Practice Sheet 5–4

Tape Manual Ex. 6   11

B **¿Cuál es la fecha?** Primero, di estas fechas. Después, explícalas en español. Usa números cardinales y ordinales. Sigue el modelo.

5/12 *Es el cinco de diciembre.*
Es el quinto día del mes doce.

1. 9/6
2. 26/11
3. 13/7
4. 8/1
5. 12/3
6. 15/9
7. 1/12
8. 4/2
9. 21/10
10. 31/5
11. 3/8
12. 17/4

Práctica A

1. ¿Cuál prefieres, los anteojos de sol grandes o los pequeños?
Prefiero los grandes (*or:* los pequeños).
2. ¿… la chaqueta larga o la corta?
… la larga (*or:* la corta)
3. ¿… la foto de la regata o la de la carrera de caballos?
… la de la …
4. ¿… la manta nicaragüense o la hondureña? … la …
5. ¿… el abrigo gris o el marrón? … el …
6. ¿… los calcetines largos o los cortos? … los …
7. ¿… el suéter guatemalteco o el mexicano? … el …
8. ¿… el primer dibujo o el último? … el …
9. ¿… los coches alemanes o los ingleses? … los …
10. ¿… las aceitunas verdes o las negras? … las …
11. ¿… los zapatos de tenis americanos o los franceses? … los …
12. ¿… la voz de Plácido Domingo o la de José Carreras? … la de …

Práctica B
Answers will vary.

Practice Sheet 5–5

Workbook Exs. E–F

🔲 **12 Tape Manual Ex. 7**

Quiz 5–4

Nominalización de adjetivos

In Spanish we often avoid repeating a noun by using the definite article *el, la, los,* or *las* with an adjective or a prepositional phrase (*de inglés, de tenis,* etc.). The adjective agrees in gender and number with the noun that it replaces.

¿Quieres las bombillas amarillas? No, prefiero **las blancas**.	*Do you want the yellow light bulbs? No, I prefer **the white ones**.*
Terminamos el tercer capítulo. Ya empiezo **el cuarto**.	*We're finishing the third chapter. I'm already starting the **fourth one**.*
¿Te gustan las películas de terror? Sí, pero prefiero **las del oeste**.	*Do you like horror films? Yes, but I prefer **westerns**.*

PRÁCTICA

A **De compras.** El Sr. Barrios nunca va de compras solo porque nunca puede decidir qué comprar. Pregunta y contesta según el modelo.

> camisa roja / azul
> ESTUDIANTE A *¿Cuál prefieres, la camisa roja o la azul?*
> ESTUDIANTE B *Prefiero la azul.* (o: *la roja*)

1. anteojos de sol grandes / pequeños
2. chaqueta larga / corta
3. foto de la regata / de la carrera de caballos
4. manta nicaragüense / hondureña
5. abrigo gris / marrón
6. calcetines largos / cortos
7. suéter guatemalteco / mexicano
8. primer dibujo / último
9. coches alemanes / ingleses
10. aceitunas verdes / negras
11. zapatos de tenis americanos / franceses
12. voz de Plácido Domingo / de José Carreras

B **Hablemos de ti.**
1. ¿Cuáles son las tres primeras cosas que haces cuando llegas a casa?
2. ¿Cuál es tu primera clase del día? ¿Cuál es la última?
3. ¿A quién le pides dinero cuando lo necesitas? ¿Por qué escoges a esta persona?
4. ¿Cuáles son dos situaciones en que ríes? ¿Dos en que sonríes? Por ejemplo, ¿sonríes cuando un(a) amigo(a) te presenta a alguien?

APLICACIONES

Discretionary

Deportes de verano   Transparency 17

En el verano, ¿participas en deportes como éstos? ¿Qué deportes puede la gente practicar en el mar? ¿Cuáles practicas tú? ¿Qué más hace la gente en la playa?

Enrichment: You may want to show transparency 17 before students open their books. Ask students to talk about the drawing in pairs or small groups.

Emilia and Benjamín are at the seashore. Make up a dialogue in which they talk about water sports they enjoy. Are they on a team? Do their teams win often? You might want to use these words or phrases:

el campeón / la campeona	el empate	increíble
el campeonato (de . . .)	el tanteo	¿No te parece?

Notes: Sample dialogues for the **¿Qué pasa?** appear in the Teacher Notes.

EXPLICACIONES II

Notes: Refer to mini-
dialogue 1 on p. 174 for
examples of preterite forms of
-ar verbs.

El pretérito de los verbos que terminan en -ar

◆ **OBJECTIVES:**

TO DESCRIBE OR REPORT EVENTS THAT HAPPENED IN THE PAST

Remember that we use the preterite tense to talk about actions or events that occurred at a particular time in the past and have now ended. Here are all of the preterite forms for regular -ar verbs.

CANTAR	
canté	cantamos
cantaste	cantasteis
cantó	cantaron

Remember that the *yo* and *Ud. / él / ella* forms have an accent mark on the final vowel. Remember, too, that the *nosotros* form of regular -ar verbs is the same in the preterite and present tenses.

El pájaro rojo **cantó** anteayer por primera vez.
Ayer **cantaron** los dos amarillos.

*The red bird **sang** for the first time the day before yesterday.*
*Yesterday the two yellow ones **sang**.*

PRÁCTICA

Reteach / Extra Help: In
preparation for the **Práctica**,
you may want to ask these
questions: ¿Cuándo celebraste
tu cumpleaños? ¿Quién borró
la pizarra ayer? ¿Trabajamos
mucho en la clase la semana
pasada?

Práctica A
1. Ayer planché (la) ropa.
   Anteayer lavé (la) ropa).
2. Ayer patiné sobre hielo.
   Anteayer esquié.

A ¿Y ayer? Dos amigos hablan sobre lo que cada uno hizo ayer y anteayer. Sigue el modelo.

ESTUDIANTE A	*¿Qué hiciste ayer?*	ESTUDIANTE A	*¿Y anteayer?*
ESTUDIANTE B	*Ayer nadé.*	ESTUDIANTE B	*Anteayer buceé.*

1.   2.

3.

4.

5.

6.

3. Ayer monté a caballo.
   Anteayer monté en bicicleta.
4. Ayer corté el césped.
   Anteayer tomé el sol.
5. Ayer remé. Anteayer patiné
   sobre ruedas.
6. Ayer cociné. Anteayer miré
   la tele(visión).

B **Las vacaciones de verano.** La Sra. Anaya quiere saber lo que hizo todo el mundo durante las vacaciones. Pregunta y contesta según el modelo.

> Uds. / descansar en la playa / nadar mucho
>
> ESTUDIANTE A *¿Descansaron Uds. en la playa?*
> ESTUDIANTE B *Sí. Y también nadamos mucho.*

1. Ud. / cantar con la banda otra vez / bailar en el espectáculo del parque de diversiones
2. (tú) / montar a caballo / ganar varias carreras de bicicletas
3. Rosa / patinar mucho sobre ruedas / caminar en el parque cada mañana
4. tú y tu familia / viajar a Puerto Rico / bucear en el Mar Caribe
5. tus tíos / alquilar un velero / participar en la regata por primera vez
6. Víctor / visitar a sus abuelos / dibujar el paisaje allí
7. tu hermanito / trabajar en el rancho / ayudar con el ganado
8. Armando y Enrique / montar mucho en bicicleta / levantar pesas todos los días
9. Uds. / participar en varias carreras / ganar muchas

Práctica B

1. ¿Cantó Ud. con la banda otra vez?
   Sí. Y también bailé en el espectáculo del parque de diversiones.
2. ¿Montaste a caballo?
   … gané …
3. ¿Patinó Rosa mucho sobre ruedas?
   … caminó …
4. ¿Viajaron a Puerto Rico tú y tu familia?
   … buceamos …
5. ¿Alquilaron un velero tus tíos?
   … participaron en …
6. ¿Visitó Víctor a sus abuelos?
   … dibujó …
7. ¿Trabajó tu hermanito en el rancho?
   … ayudó con …
8. Montaron mucho en bicicleta Armando y Enrique?
   … levantaron …
9. ¿Participaron Uds. en varias carreras?
   … ganamos …

Una mujer bucea en
el Mar Caribe.

C ¿El año pasado? Usa un elemento de cada lista para describir lo que hizo todo el mundo. Usa el pretérito. Sigue el modelo.

> Mario y yo
> *Mario y yo buceamos en el lago anoche.*
> o: *Anoche Mario y yo buceamos en el lago.*

1. mi hermana	admirar el paisaje	anoche
2. Carlos	bucear en el lago	anteayer
3. mis primos	cambiar de idea	ayer
4. (yo)	cenar	el año pasado
5. Jorge y Eva	desayunar	el mes pasado
6. (nosotros)	esquiar en el Perú	el verano pasado
7. (tú)	ganar el campeonato de	la semana pasada
8. Luz	natación	por la mañana
9. el equipo local	lavar las sábanas y fundas	por la tarde
	levantar pesas	por primera vez
	olvidar los salvavidas	temprano
	prestar atención	
	quemar la comida	
	tomar muchos apuntes	
	visitar una exposición	
	de arte panameño	

Juegos Panamericanos,
Indianápolis, 1987

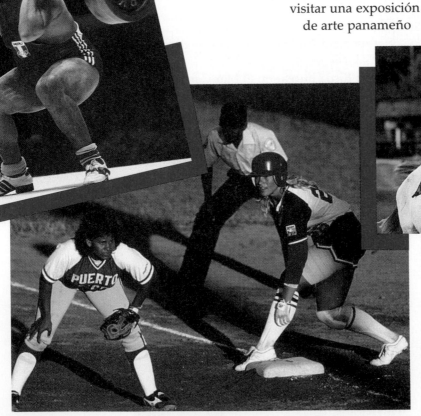

(arriba) Jóvenes montan
a caballo en Venezuela;
(izquierda) Béisbol en los
Juegos Panamericanos,
Indianápolis, 1987

El pretérito del verbo *hacer*

The verb *hacer* is irregular in the preterite tense.

HACER	
hice	hicimos
hiciste	hicisteis
hizo	hicieron

¿Qué **hiciste** ayer?   *What **did you do** yesterday?*
Asé pollo a la parrilla.   *I barbecued chicken.*

Note that in the *Ud. / él / ella* form, the *c* changes to *z* to maintain the soft *c* sound.

¿Quién **hizo** el pastel de chocolate?   *Who **made** the chocolate cake?*
Él lo **hizo**.   *He **made** it.*

PRÁCTICA

A   **¿Qué hizo cada uno?**   Imagina que asistes a una clase de trabajos manuales *(crafts)*. ¿Qué cosas hicieron los alumnos? Sigue el modelo.

(yo)
Hice una piñata.

1. (tú)   2. Juan   3. (nosotros)

4. Olga y Julia   5. Pedro y yo   6. Luisa

7. Cristina y tú   8. Daniel y Eugenio   9. (yo)

◆ **OBJECTIVES:**

TO TELL WHAT PEOPLE DID OR MADE

TO INTERVIEW SOMEONE

Reteach / Extra Help: You may want to present the preterite of *hacer* using choral repetition. Then reinforce the forms with a substitution drill: *Ayer hicimos un picnic. Esta mañana no hice mi cama. ¿Hiciste la tarea anoche?*

Práctica A
1. Hiciste un cinturón.
2. Juan hizo una canasta.
3. Hicimos un estante.
4. Olga y Julia hicieron (unos) aretes.
5. Pedro y yo hicimos una lámpara.
6. Luisa hizo un bolso.
7. Cristina y tú hicieron (unas) máscaras.
8. Daniel y Eugenio hicieron una alfombra.
9. Hice un reloj.

B Las vacaciones de invierno. La clase habla sobre lo que hizo todo el mundo durante las vacaciones de invierno. Haz preguntas. Luego escoge frases de la derecha para contestar.

(tú)

ESTUDIANTE A *¿Qué hiciste?*
ESTUDIANTE B *Esquié en las montañas.*

1. Uds.   alquilar una casa en la isla San Padre
2. tus primos   comprar ropa deportiva
3. Federico   esquiar en las montañas
4. (tú)   hacer gimnasia
5. tú y tu familia   hacer un viaje al Caribe
6. Laura   montar a caballo
7. los López   participar en el campeonato de esquí
8. Ud., señor(a)   pasar mucho tiempo en el club deportivo
                          patinar sobre hielo
                          practicar el esquí acuático en Puerto Rico
                          trabajar y estudiar cada día
                          tratar de practicar español
                          visitar varios lugares interesantes

C Un viaje. Un estudiante de Guyana, donde hablan inglés, tiene que escribir una composición sobre su viaje a la Argentina. Completa el párrafo con la forma correcta del pretérito de cada verbo.

El verano pasado mi familia y yo *(hacer)* un viaje a la Argentina. (Nosotros) *(pasar)* sólo una semana en Buenos Aires pero *(disfrutar)* mucho de nuestra visita. Es una ciudad moderna y muy interesante. El primer día (nosotros) *(caminar)* por la calle Florida y mamá *(comprar)*
5 regalos para toda la familia. Luego (nosotros) *(tomar)* un autobús y *(visitar)* el famoso Teatro Colón. Es un edificio bellísimo donde hay conciertos, ópera y baile. El segundo día (yo) *(visitar)* la Casa Rosada y *(caminar)* por la Plaza de Mayo. Esa tarde (yo) *(entrar)* en varias librerías de la avenida Santa Fe y *(tratar de)* hablar en español con la
10 gente. Papá y mamá *(caminar)* por el centro, donde *(cenar)* y *(escuchar)* tangos en un restaurante. El tercer día (nosotros) *(pasar)* la mañana en el Museo de Bellas Artes. Mis padres *(admirar)* mucho la exposición de arte argentino. Los últimos cuatro días en Buenos Aires (yo) no *(hacer)* mucho. (Yo) *(regresar)* a casa cansado pero muy contento.

D Hablemos de ti.

1. ¿Qué hiciste anoche?
2. ¿Qué hiciste el fin de semana pasado?
3. ¿Qué hiciste durante las vacaciones de invierno? ¿Y las de verano? ¿Hiciste algún viaje? ¿Lo hiciste en avión, en autobús, en tren o en coche? ¿Visitaste a alguien? ¿A quién?

Práctica D
Answers will vary.

Practice Sheet 5–7

Workbook Exs. G–J

Tape Manual Ex. 9 🔲 14

Refrán 🔲 15

Canción 🔲 16

Quiz 5 6

ACTIVIDAD

Y ahora . . . los deportes.   You and a partner take the roles of a sportscaster and an athlete. The sportscaster should interview the athlete, basing the interview on these seven basic questions: Who, what, when, where, which, how, and why.

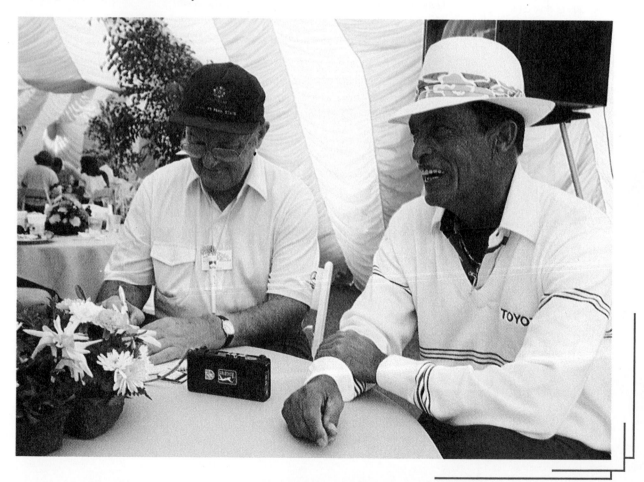

Notes: If some of your students are not interested in sports, you may want to offer this variation on the **Actividad.** You and a partner take the roles of a writer of an entertainment column and an actor / actress. The journalist should interview the actor / actress.

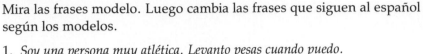 APLICACIONES Discretionary

Notes: Answers to the **Repaso** and **Tema** appear in the Teacher Notes.

REPASO

Notes: Review of:
1. *ser* + noun + adjective
   present tense of *-ar* verbs
2. expressions of past time
   preterite of *-ar* verbs
3. expressions of past time
   preterite of *hacer*
   expressions with *hacer*
4. *e → i* verbs
   noun phrases with *de*
   adjectives
5. expressions of past time
   preterite of *-ar* verbs
   ordinal numbers
   nominalization of adjectives

Una tenista de México

Mira las frases modelo. Luego cambia las frases que siguen al español según los modelos.

1. *Soy una persona muy atlética. Levanto pesas cuando puedo.*
   (We're (fem.) very energetic skiers. We practice skiing when(ever) we can.)
   (Roberto is not a very good swimmer. He wears a life preserver when(ever) he sails.)
   (Mrs. Gómez is a very good photographer. She takes pictures when(ever) she travels.)

2. *El mes pasado, patinamos sobre hielo en el lago.*
   (Last Monday I scuba dived with Paco in the ocean.)
   (Last Thursday you (fam.) changed your mind at 2:00.)
   (Last week you (fam.) and Luisa roller-skated at the club.)

3. *Anteayer, hicieron un picnic con los visitantes.*
   (Last night we made plans with the coaches (fem.).)
   (Last year you (fam.) took a trip to the island.)
   (This morning I asked questions about the sailboat.)

4. *Quizás pido una tienda de acampar grande.*
   (At 1:00 we request a free tennis court.)
   (Fortunately they serve tasty lamb chops.)
   (Now you (fam.) are asking for new tennis shoes.)

5. *Ayer hiciste la cama grande. Ahora descansas en la pequeña.*
   (Today we finished the fourth race. Tomorrow we run in the fifth.)
   (Yesterday afternoon they won the ninth boat race. Today they sail in the tenth.)
   (The day before yesterday I threw away the empty boxes. Now I'm looking (buscar) in the full ones.)

Enrichment: You may want to use the model sentences in the **Repaso** for dictation.

Escribe las frases en español.

1. Marta is a very active girl. She practices sports whenever she can.

2. Last week she went horseback riding at the ranch.

3. The day before yesterday she did gymnastics at the club.

4. Now she's asking for a new tennis racquet.

5. Last week she won the first match. Tomorrow she takes part in the last one.

REDACCIÓN

Ahora escoge uno de los siguientes temas para escribir tu propio diálogo o párrafo.

1. Expand the *Tema* by telling what other sports Marta participated in recently. What other pieces of sports equipment does she own? Are they expensive? Does she have to ask her parents for money? What type of person do you think Marta is?

2. Write a paragraph about the sports you like or don't like. Tell why. Did your school win any championship last year? If so, which one? If not, how does your team rank compared to the teams of other schools?

3. Make up a dialogue in which you interview your favorite sports figure.

Notes: Answers to the **Comprueba** appear in the Teacher Notes.

A   ¿Qué hacen?
Haz frases con las siguientes palabras.

1. mamá / siempre servir comida sabrosa
2. Tomás y tú / repetir a menudo las respuestas
3. (nosotros) / pedir más cacahuates
4. (tú) / servir paella por primera vez
5. (yo) / nunca repetir lo que decimos
6. Ud. / siempre pedir más que los otros

B   ¿Qué haces?
Completa cada frase con la forma correcta del verbo entre paréntesis.

1. ¿Por qué no (*sonreír*) cuando te saco una foto?
2. Cuando Daniel viene a casa, (nosotros) (*reír*) mucho.
3. Ellas (*reír*) cuando les cuento chistes.
4. María (*sonreír*) porque es la nueva campeona de natación.
5. Juan y Carlos son muy tímidos. Nunca (*sonreír*).
6. Siempre (*sonreír*) cuando recibo cartas de mi hermano.

C   ¿Primero o segundo?
Contesta las preguntas.

1. ¿Qué tienes qué leer? / 4º capítulo
2. ¿Quién es Mónica Santos? / 5ª nadadora
3. ¿Cuál es la fecha de hoy? / 1º de febrero
4. ¿Dónde vives? / 3ª casa de la esquina
5. ¿Dónde están las raquetas? / 2ª caja
6. ¿Dónde trabajas? / 9º piso

D   ¿Cuál prefieres?
Contesta cada pregunta con el antónimo correcto. Sigue el modelo.

> *¿Te gustan los cuentos largos?*
> *No, prefiero los cortos.*

1. ¿Te gustan los edificios altos?
2. ¿Te gustan los anillos grandes?

3. ¿Te gustan las películas serias?
4. ¿Te gustan los cuadros viejos?
5. ¿Te gusta el último velero?
6. ¿Te gusta el paisaje del este?

E   ¿Qué hicieron?
Di lo que hizo cada una de las siguientes personas. Usa la forma correcta del pretérito.

1. (yo)   2. Ud.

3. (nosotros)   4. (tú)

5. (ellos)   6. Uds.

F   Ayer por la mañana
Escribe las frases siguientes otra vez. Usa el pretérito y reemplaza (*substitute*) las palabras en cursiva por (*with*) las palabras entre paréntesis.

1. *Cada año* hacemos un viaje a San Juan.   (ya)
2. *Todos los días* hago la cama antes de salir de casa.   (esta mañana)
3. ¿Haces la maleta *hoy*?   (anoche)
4. *Ahora* la gente hace cola para comprar las entradas.   (anteayer)
5. *¿Siempre* hacen Uds. la tarea después de cenar?   (ayer)
6. *Hoy* hacemos un asado.   (el sábado pasado)

VOCABULARIO DEL CAPÍTULO 5

Sustantivos
el campeón (*pl.* los
   campeones), la campeona
el campeonato
la cancha de tenis
el carné
la carrera
el club, *pl.* los clubes
el empate
el entrenador, la entrenadora
el equipo local
el esquí
el esquí acuático
el esquiador, la esquiadora
el ganador, la ganadora
la isla
el jai alai
el levantador / la levantadora
   de pesas
el milagro
el nadador, la nadadora
la natación
el patinador, la patinadora
las pesas
la raqueta
la regata
el salvavidas, *pl.* los salvavidas
   (*life preserver*)
el salvavidas, la salvavidas
el tanteo
el/la tenista
el velero
el/la visitante
la voz, *pl.* las voces
los zapatos de tenis

Adjetivos
activo, -a
deportivo, -a
estricto, -a
fuerte (*loud*)
ganador, -a
increíble
perdedor, -a
último, -a

Números ordinales
cuarto, -a
quinto, -a
sexto, -a
séptimo, -a
octavo, -a
noveno, -a
décimo, -a

Verbos
bucear
navegar
participar
reír (e → i)
sonreír (e →i)

Adverbio
anteayer

Preposiciones
contra
hasta (*to, as far as*)

Expresiones
de acuerdo
hacer gimnasia
levantar pesas
montar a caballo
¿no te parece?
por + *número ordinal* + vez
¡qué barbaridad!

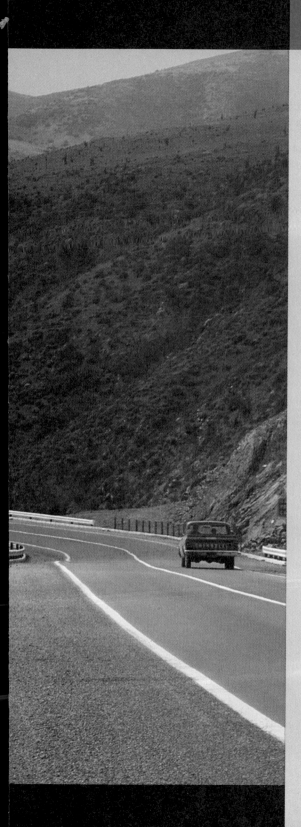

PRÓLOGO CULTURAL

UNA CARRETERA PARA LAS AMÉRICAS

How would you like to try a highway that passes through deserts, mountains, jungles, and plains? You can if you take the Pan American Highway from the United States to Chile.

La carretera panamericana is unique. A joint project of nineteen countries, it was begun in the 1920s and was largely completed by 1950. It is actually made up of numerous roads that crisscross Latin America, connecting the capitals of seventeen countries. All together, this famous highway is 47,516 kilometers long! (Though Canada and the United States are co-sponsors, they have never actually named any of their roads as part of the highway. But you can begin your trip at Nogales, Arizona, or El Paso, Eagle Pass, or Laredo, Texas.)

The roads of the Pan American Highway are often rather narrow, and they are not lined with gas stations, motels, and restaurants. Travelers often have to carry gas and food with them, because towns may be many hours apart. In some areas, this is the only route through dense jungles or high mountain ranges.

The highway is interrupted at only one point: the Darien Gap in Panama. The land there is so swampy, the rain forest so dense, and the mosquitoes so numerous that construction has never been completed. Cars can reach Colombia or Venezuela only by ferry.

Perhaps the most unusual attraction along the route is the *Pampa Colorada* (Red Plain) in Peru, where a series of canals were carved into the earth some 5,000 years ago. Viewed from the ground, these canals make no apparent sense; seen from a plane, they create an enormous picture of a man and several animals. Unlike the modern highway that passes by them, no one knows who built these, why, or how they created a master plan for something they were never able to see in its entirety.

📼 1

PALABRAS NUEVAS I

Essential

En la estación de tren

el coche cama
pl. los coches cama

el coche comedor
pl. los coches comedor

ANDÉN 5

ANDÉN 6

BOLETOS

la ventanilla

el bolsillo

la pasajera

el inspector

el pasajero

la inspectora

el andén
pl. los andenes

Notes: Present the **Contexto comunicativo** on pp. 199–201 by modeling each of the seven mini-dialogues or by playing the tape.

Reteach / Review: In connection with mini-dialogue 1, you may want to remind students that the numbers 200 through 999 agree in gender and number with the nouns they modify. Suggest these additional **Variaciones:** *Santiago → Salamanca, mil novecientos pesos → mil cuatrocientas pesetas.*

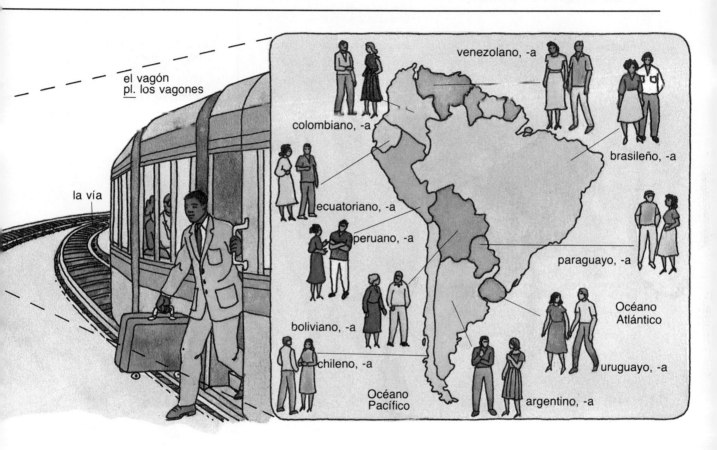

CONTEXTO COMUNICATIVO 2

1 INÉS   Buenas tardes. Dos boletos **de primera clase** para Santiago, por favor.

VENDEDOR   **¿De ida** o **de ida y vuelta?**

INÉS   De ida. ¿Cuánto es?

VENDEDOR   Mil novecientos pesos.

Variaciones:
- de primera clase → de segunda clase
  novecientos → quinientos

de primera (segunda) clase   *first (second) class*

de ida   *one way*

de ida y vuelta   *round trip*

2 MÓNICA ¡Vámonos! Ya **anunciaron la salida** del tren.

JULIO ¡Qué lata! No tengo tiempo para comprar una revista.

- salida → **llegada**
- una revista → un periódico

3 MARIANA Aquí estamos. ¡Por fin! **Tardamos** veinte minutos **en** llegar a la estación. ¿A qué hora llega el tren?

FEDERICO Acaban de anunciar que el tren de Guadalajara llega **con retraso.**

- ¡por fin! → ¡qué alivio!
- con retraso → **con media hora de retraso**

4 SR. CASAS ¿De qué andén sale el tren **local,*** Rosita?

ROSA Del 5, papá. Tenemos que **cruzar** el puente **sobre** las vías.

- local → **expreso**

5 RAFAEL ¿Dónde **coloco** las maletas?

ELISA Debajo del asiento.

- coloco → pongo

6 MARIO ¿Fuiste a Lima?

CLARA Sí, fui el verano pasado.

MARIO ¿Fuiste sola?

CLARA No, mi hermana Silvia fue conmigo.

- Lima → Cuzco
- verano → año

---

anunciar *to announce*
la salida here: *departure*

la llegada *arrival*

tardar (en + inf.) *to take* + time (+ verb)

con retraso *late*

con (media hora de) retraso *(a half hour) late*

local *local*
cruzar *to cross*
sobre here: *over*

expreso *express*

colocar = poner

---

* A local train is one that stops at all stations along a particular route. An express train stops only at the major, well-traveled stations.

7 **EDUARDO** Acabo de leer una novela del profesor Ortiz. Él nos dice que muchos escritores son profesores **de profesión.**

TERESA ¿De veras? ¿Te gustó el libro?

EDUARDO Sí, **fue** muy emocionante. Ahora **comienzo a** leer una biografía de Felipe IV.

- muy emocionante → fabuloso
- comienzo → empiezo

la profesión, pl. **las profesiones** *profession*

de profesión *by profession*

fue here: preterite of **ser** *was*

comenzar (a + inf.) (e → ie) = empezar (a)

EN OTRAS PARTES

En México, la América Central y el Perú se dice *la bolsa.*

En España se dice *el revisor.*

En España se dice *la taquilla.*

el tren expreso

En España también se dice *el tren rápido.*

Reteach / Extra Help: In preparation for Ex. A, you may want to ask volunteers to use each of the words in the three columns in an original sentence.

PRÁCTICA

A **Un viaje en tren.** Imagina que un(a) amigo(a) acaba de llegar en tren y te habla de su viaje. Completa cada frase con la palabra o expresión correcta.

andén	expreso	pasajeros
boleto de ida y vuelta	inspector	retraso
coche comedor	llegada	ventanilla

Cuando llegamos a la estación fui a la _____ para comprar un _____ a Madrid. Esperé el tren con varios otros _____ en el _____ número 5. El tren _____ llegó a la estación con casi una hora de _____. Ya en el tren fui al _____ para almorzar. Una hora más tarde el _____ anunció

5 nuestra _____ a la estación Atocha en Madrid. Fue un viaje agradable.

Práctica A
ventanilla
boleto de ida y vuelta
pasajeros
andén
expreso
retraso
coche comedor
inspector
llegada

Palabras Nuevas I **201**

1. (boletos) de ida
2. en el primer vagón (*or:* en el primero)
3. en primera (clase)
4. el (tren) local
5. (está) a la izquierda
6. (llega) con retraso
7. las llegadas
8. bajan (del tren)

B ¿Están Uds. juntos? Dos amigos hacen un viaje juntos, pero tienen ideas diferentes. Contesta con lo contrario (*opposite*) según el modelo.

> ESTUDIANTE A *¿Está lleno el coche comedor?*
>
> ESTUDIANTE B *No, está vacío.*

1. ¿Compramos boletos de ida y vuelta?
2. ¿Nuestros asientos están en el último vagón?
3. ¿Viajamos en segunda clase?
4. ¿Tomamos el tren expreso?
5. ¿Está a la derecha el andén número 14?
6. ¿Llega a tiempo el tren?
7. ¿Anuncian las salidas?
8. ¿Suben al tren esos pasajeros?

(izquierda) En Buenos Aires

(derecha) En Málaga

C En la oficina de inmigración. Imagina que trabajas en la oficina de inmigración y que entrevistas *(interview)* a la gente que viene de varios países. Pregunta y contesta según el modelo.

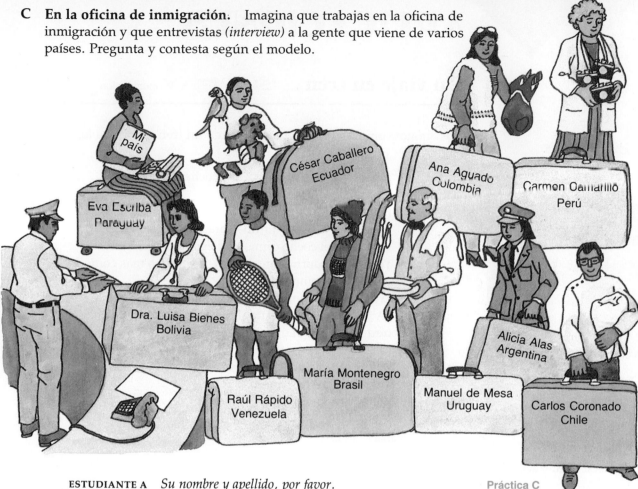

ESTUDIANTE A	*Su nombre y apellido, por favor.*
ESTUDIANTE B	*Luisa Bienes.*
ESTUDIANTE A	*¿Ud. es de Bolivia?*
ESTUDIANTE B	*Sí, soy boliviana.*
ESTUDIANTE A	*¿Y cuál es su profesión?*
ESTUDIANTE B	*Soy médica.*

D Hablemos de ti.
1. ¿Prefieres viajar en tren o en avión? ¿Por qué? ¿Hay una estación de tren en tu ciudad? ¿Dónde está? Descríbela.
2. ¿Generalmente llegas a la escuela a tiempo o con retraso? ¿Qué pasa cuando llegas con retraso? ¿Por qué no llegas siempre a tiempo?
3. ¿Cuánto tiempo tardas en llegar a la escuela? ¿Cómo vas allí?
4. ¿A qué hora comienzas a hacer tu tarea por la noche? Generalmente, ¿cuánto tiempo tardas en hacerlo?

Práctica C
1. venezolano / tenista
2. brasileña / esquiadora
3. uruguayo / camarero
4. argentina / piloto
5. chileno / dentista
6. peruana / fotógrafa
7. colombiana / nadadora
8. ecuatoriano / veterinario
9. paraguaya / escritora
   (*or:* autora)

Práctica D
Answers will vary.

Practice Sheet 6–1

Workbook Exs. A–B

Tape Manual Exs. 1–2 3

Quiz 6–1

APLICACIONES

Un viaje en tren   4   5 Pronunciación

En Caracas, Venezuela

Dos amigos compran boletos para viajar en un tren que cruza los Andes.

IGNACIO	¿Compramos boletos para el coche cama?
GREGORIO	No, hombre, eso es carísimo.
5 IGNACIO	Pero siempre hay mucha gente en este tren. Nunca tienes dos asientos juntos para acostarte bien. Si vamos en el coche cama, no llegamos cansados.
GREGORIO	Yo prefiero dormir en el hotel. Es mucho más cómodo y tenemos tiempo.
10 IGNACIO	Eres muy tacaño, Gregorio.
GREGORIO	¿A mí me llamas tacaño, Ignacio? Fue tu idea tomar el tren local y no el expreso. El viaje va a durar tres horas más.
IGNACIO	Bueno, chico, de alguna manera[1] tenemos que
15	ahorrar[2] nuestro dinero.
GREGORIO	¡Qué barbaridad!

---

[1] **de alguna manera** *somehow*   [2] **ahorrar** *to save*

Preguntas

Contesta según el diálogo.

1. ¿Por qué no quiere Gregorio comprar boletos para el coche cama?
2. ¿Por qué quiere Ignacio comprarlos?   3. ¿Dónde prefiere descansar Gregorio? ¿Por qué?   4. ¿Por qué dice Ignacio que Gregorio es tacaño?   5. Según lo que dicen Gregorio e Ignacio en las líneas 11–16, ¿cuál cuesta más, tomar el tren local o el tren expreso? ¿Por qué cuesta uno más que el otro?   6. En tu opinión, ¿cuál es más importante, la comodidad *(comfort)* o el tiempo que dura un viaje? ¿Por qué?

Diálogo

1. es carísimo (*or:* son carísimos)
2. hay mucha gente; si van en coche cama no llegan cansados
3. en el hotel; es más cómodo
4. porque Gregorio no quiere ir en coche cama
5. tomar el tren expreso; porque va más rápidamente (*or:* llega más pronto)
6. Answers will vary.

Participación

Work with a partner to prepare a dialogue about taking a trip. Imagine
that you are going by train. Where do you want to go? Do you prefer to
take the local or the express train? Why? Do you want to be in the
sleeping car? Why? Do you prefer to travel at night or during the day?

🔲 6

Transparency 20

CONTEXTO VISUAL

¿Tiene Ud. reservación?

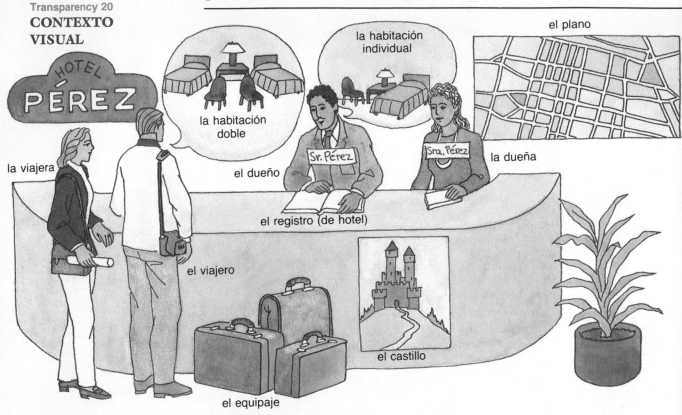

la habitación doble

la habitación individual

el plano

HOTEL PÉREZ

la viajera

el dueño   Sr. Pérez

Sra. Pérez   la dueña

el registro (de hotel)

el viajero

el castillo

el equipaje

CONTEXTO COMUNICATIVO   🔲 7

1   En España hay muchas **pensiones*** buenas y baratas. También hay **paradores** que generalmente son edificios **históricos** muy viejos y muy bellos. Algunos de ellos son castillos.

Variaciones:
■ buenas → cómodas
■ muy bellos → **maravillosos**

la pensión, pl. **las pensiones**   *boardinghouse*
el parador   *government-run inn*
histórico, -a   *historic*

maravilloso, -a   *marvelous, wonderful*

* A *pensión* is a boardinghouse where one can rent rooms for long or short periods of time and have three meals a day. The meals are included in the price of the room.

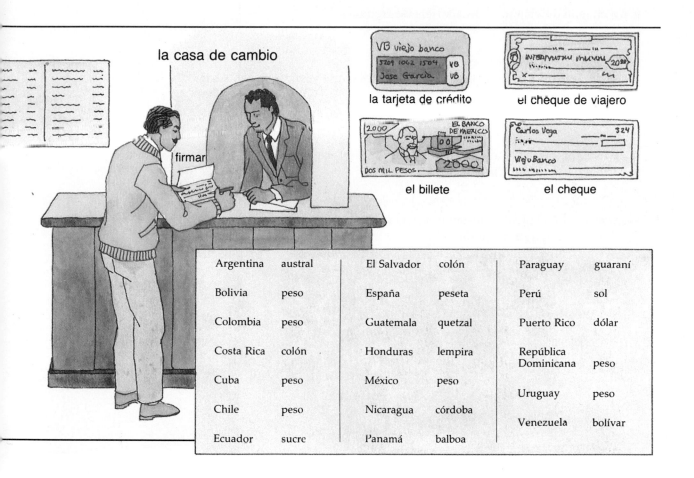

la casa de cambio

firmar

la tarjeta de crédito

el cheque de viajero

el billete

el cheque

Argentina	austral	El Salvador	colón	Paraguay	guaraní
Bolivia	peso	España	peseta	Perú	sol
Colombia	peso	Guatemala	quetzal	Puerto Rico	dólar
Costa Rica	colón	Honduras	lempira	República Dominicana	peso
Cuba	peso	México	peso		
Chile	peso	Nicaragua	córdoba	Uruguay	peso
Ecuador	sucre	Panamá	balboa	Venezuela	bolívar

2 DUEÑA   ¿Tiene Ud. una reservación?

SR. QUIROZ   Sí. Soy Rafael Quiroz.

DUEÑA   Aquí está, Sr. Quiroz. ¿**Quiere** firmar el registro, por favor?

SR. QUIROZ   Muy bien. ¿Y dónde puedo **cobrar un cheque**?

DUEÑA   Hay un banco en la esquina.

■ cobrar un cheque → cambiar unos billetes
un banco → una casa de cambio

¿**quiere(n)** + inf.?   here: *will you . . . ?*

cobrar un cheque   *to cash a check*

* Like banks, currency exchanges, found in all major cities, change foreign money into local money for travelers. They accept cash and traveler's checks but not personal checks.

3 DUEÑO	¿Prefiere Ud. una habitación individual o doble?	
JOSEFINA	Individual, por favor.	
DUEÑO	¿Va a **pagar al contado**?	**pagar al contado** *to pay cash*
JOSEFINA	No, prefiero usar un cheque de viajero.	

■ un cheque de viajero → una tarjeta de crédito

4 JULIA	¿Va a hacer buen tiempo hoy?	
NICOLÁS	No, el cielo no está muy **claro.** Creo que va a llover.	**claro, -a** *bright, clear*
JULIA	¡Caramba! Entonces hoy **no** podemos **ni** nadar **ni** remar.	**no . . . ni . . . ni** *neither . . . nor, not . . . or*

■ no está muy claro → está bastante **oscuro**

oscuro, -a *dark*

■ el cielo no está muy claro → está nublado

5 SR. AYALA	Los boletos cuestan casi seiscientas pesetas y **no** tengo **ni** un centavo.	**no . . . ni** *not even*
SRA. AYALA	**Ni yo tampoco.** Pero puedo usar la tarjeta de crédito.	**ni (yo) tampoco** *not either (I don't either), neither (neither do I)*
SR. AYALA	¡Qué alivio!	

■ ¡qué alivio! → ¡qué susto!

(izquierda) En un parador en Sigüenza, España; (derecha) En Torremolinos, España

EN OTRAS PARTES

la pensión

También se dice *la casa de huéspedes*.

También se dice *el cuarto sencillo*.

PRÁCTICA

A En la recepción. Imagina que estás cerca de la recepción de un hotel. Oyes partes de varias conversaciones. Usa los dibujos para completar las frases.

1. Cuando viajo, siempre llevo mucha ropa. Por eso necesito tanto ____.
2. Si queremos saber adónde vamos, necesitamos un ____ de la ciudad.
3. Necesito cambiar unos dólares. ¿Dónde está la ____?
4. Cuando algo cuesta mucho mis padres generalmente pagan con una ____.
5. ¿Puede Ud. cambiar un ____ de cincuenta dólares?
6. Las ____ cuestan menos que las ____ porque son más pequeñas y tienen sólo una cama.
7. Cuando viajo siempre compro ____ porque no me gusta llevar mucho dinero.
8. Perdón, señor, ¿dónde está la ____? Necesito firmar el ____.

B En la pensión. Imagina que hablas con la dueña de una pensión. De la lista a la derecha escoge la mejor respuesta para cada pregunta.

1. ¿Tiene Ud. una habitación libre con vista al mar?
2. ¿Tiene Ud. habitaciones individuales?
3. ¿Vienen muchos viajeros de Europa?
4. ¿Es Ud. la dueña?
5. ¿Puedo darle un cheque?
6. ¿Hay algún parador cerca de aquí?
7. ¿Hay una casa de cambio en este barrio?
8. ¿Tiene planos de la ciudad?

a. Sí, los tenemos y una guía excelente también.
b. Sí, hay uno en un castillo muy viejo.
c. No, señorita. Soy la gerente.
d. No, sólo dobles.
e. Lo siento. Hay que pagar al contado o con una tarjeta de crédito.
f. Sí, y hay muchos sudamericanos también.
g. No, pero hay un banco en la esquina.
h. Sí, tenemos dos. Pero no tienen balcón.

Práctica C
1. Firma / ¿Quiere Ud. firmar …?
2. Lee / ¿Quiere Ud. leer …?
3. Habla / Quiere Ud. hablar …?
4. Anuncia / ¿Quiere Ud. anunciar …?
5. Deja / ¿Quiere Ud. dejar …?
6. Coloca / ¿Quiere Ud. colocar …?
7. Saca / ¿Quiere Ud. sacar …?
8. Espérame / ¿Quiere Ud. esperarme …?

Práctica D
Answers will vary.

Practice Sheet 6–2

Workbook Exs. C–D

 8 Tape Manual Exs. 3–4

9 Refrán

Quiz 6–2

En Costa Rica

C En el club. Es una buena idea ser cortés *(polite)* con los clientes. Ayer dos amigos trabajaron en el club. Hoy sólo uno está todavía allí. Sigue el modelo.

> darme el carné
> ESTUDIANTE A   *Dame el carné.*
> ESTUDIANTE B   *¿Quiere Ud. darme el carné, por favor?*

1. firmar el registro en la recepción
2. leer el horario de actividades
3. hablar con el entrenador
4. anunciar el tanteo
5. dejar las toallas sucias aquí
6. colocar su ropa en este armario
7. sacar la bicicleta del pasillo
8. esperarme en la oficina.

Culture: In connection with Ex. C, the first employee addressed the customer as *tú* rather than *Ud.*, something that is considered impolite in most of the Spanish-speaking world.

D Hablemos de ti.
1. ¿Adónde te gustaría ir de vacaciones? ¿Al campo? ¿Al mar? ¿A las montañas? ¿Por qué?
2. ¿Cómo viajas cuando vas de vacaciones? ¿En coche? ¿En tren? ¿En avión? ¿Cuál prefieres? ¿Por qué?
3. ¿Viajas siempre con tu familia, o viajas a veces solo(a)? Si viajas con tu familia, ¿quién hace los planes de viaje? ¿Quién hace las reservaciones?
4. Imagina que haces un viaje. ¿Qué cosas llevas en el bolsillo? ¿En la cartera? ¿En el bolso? ¿En el equipaje?
5. ¿Te gusta quedarte en un hotel o motel? ¿Por qué? ¿Cuáles prefieres, moteles u hoteles? ¿Por qué?
6. Describe tu dormitorio. ¿Es grande o pequeño? ¿Es claro u oscuro? ¿Cuántas ventanas hay? ¿Tiene vista a la calle? ¿Al jardín? ¿Al patio?

Enrichment: In connection with the **Actividad,** students may want to prepare a TV commercial for their *pensión.*

ACTIVIDAD

¿Necesitas una habitación?   Imagine that you and two partners have opened a *pensión.* Working together, write an advertisement or create a poster designed to encourage travelers to stay there. For example:

> **La Estrella**—la mejor pensión de (la ciudad). Tenemos veinte cuartos con baño privado. Todos los cuartos tienen vista al mar. Gratis para niños menores de 12 años. Puede pagar con tarjeta de crédito.

ESTUDIO DE PALABRAS

Sometimes in English we use only one word for more than one idea or object, where Spanish uses two different words. For example, both of these pictures mean "country" to an English speaker. To a Spanish speaker the pictures represent two very different ideas and words:

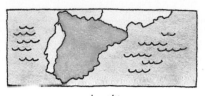
el país

el campo

What are these words?

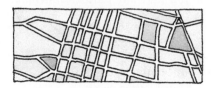

Estudio de palabras
el plano / el mapa

Sometimes it works the other way. English uses different words where in Spanish only one is used:

la entrada

la salida

Notes: You may want to ask students to write the *Sinónimos* and *Antónimos* sentences at home. Then go over the answers in class by asking volunteers to write their sentences on the board as students correct their own work. Or you may prefer that students exchange papers.

Sinónimos:
Cambia las palabras en cursiva por sinónimos.

1. ¿Me puede decir cuándo va a *comenzar* la película?
2. Queremos reservar *un cuarto* para este fin de semana.
3. ¿Por qué *pones* las monedas en tu bolsillo?

Sinónimos
1. empezar
2. una habitación
3. colocas

Antónimos:
Escribe un antónimo para cada palabra en cursiva.

1. El cielo está muy *claro* hoy.
2. *Terminamos* el libro hoy por la mañana.
3. ¿Cuándo van a anunciar *la salida* del tren?
4. Los pasajeros llegaron *temprano*.

Antónimos
1. oscuro
2. empezamos / comenzamos
3. la llegada
4. con retraso / tarde

Palabras Nuevas II   **211**

EXPLICACIONES I Essential

El pretérito: Verbos que terminan en *-car*, *-gar* y *-zar*

◆ OBJECTIVES:

TO DESCRIBE OR REPORT EVENTS THAT HAPPENED IN THE PAST

TO CORRECT WRONG ASSUMPTIONS

TO DESCRIBE A PLANE TRIP

In the preterite, verbs whose infinitive form ends in *-car*, *-gar*, and *-zar* have a spelling change in the *yo* form. All of their other preterite forms are regular.

-car (c → qu)
SACAR
¿Sacaste fotos ayer?   *Did you take any pictures yesterday?*
Sí, saqué muchas.   *Yes, I took a lot.*

-gar (g → gu)
PAGAR
¿Pagaste al contado?   *Did you pay in cash?*
No, pagué con un cheque.   *No, I paid with a check.*

-zar (z → c)
CRUZAR
¿Cruzaste la Calle 8?   *Did you cross 8th Street?*
Sí, la crucé.   *Yes, I crossed it.*

Here are the other verbs that you know that follow these patterns.

-car: *buscar, colocar, explicar, practicar, secar,* and *tocar*

-gar: *apagar, despegar, jugar, llegar,* and *navegar*

-zar: *almorzar, aterrizar, comenzar,* and *empezar*

Remember that stem-changing *-ar* verbs do not have a stem change in the preterite.

Almuerzan en el coche comedor.   *They're eating in the dining car.*
Almorzaron en el coche comedor.   *They ate in the dining car.*

Los invitados **comienzan** a llegar a las ocho.   *The guests begin to arrive at 8:00.*

Los invitados **comenzaron** a llegar a las ocho.   *The guests began to arrive at 8:00.*

212   Capítulo 6

PRÁCTICA

A ¿Qué hizo la familia de Elena?
Escoge palabras de cada columna para describir lo que hicieron Elena y su familia. Sigue el modelo.

Ayer por la tarde mi hermano colocó los muebles viejos en el sótano.

anoche	(yo)	almorzar en el centro
anteayer	mi hermano	buscar un plano de Quito
ayer por la mañana	mis padres	colocar los muebles
ayer por la tarde	mi hermanita	viejos en el sótano
esta mañana	Ricardo y yo	comenzar un libro
el lunes pasado	mi hermana y	nuevo
	su esposo	jugar a los bolos
	Ricardo y tú	sacar unas novelas
		históricas de la
		biblioteca
		secar la ropa
		practicar canciones
		folklóricas peruanas

B El viaje.
Pedro acaba de regresar a casa después de pasar unos días con sus primos en otra ciudad. Sus padres le preguntan qué hizo. Pregunta y contesta según el modelo.

llegar con retraso a la estación / a tiempo
ESTUDIANTE A   *¿Llegaste con retraso a la estación?*
ESTUDIANTE B   *No. Llegué a tiempo.*

1. pagar el boleto con cheques de viajero / al contado
2. colocar las maletas en el pasillo / sobre el asiento
3. almorzar en el coche comedor / en mi vagón
4. practicar el español con los otros pasajeros / con el inspector
5. buscar a tus primos en el andén / afuera
6. comenzar la biografía de ese poeta colombiano / una novela chilena
7. tocar la guitarra frecuentemente / nunca
8. jugar al jai alai con tu primo / al tenis con él
9. cruzar muchos ríos grandes / sólo el río Paraná
10. navegar mucho / sólo una vez

Reteach / Extra Help: Before students begin Ex. A, you may want to do a transformation drill in order to practice some of the verbs with a spelling change in the *yo* form. Ask students to change these sentences from present to preterite and to use past time expressions such as *ayer, anteayer, anoche, el mes pasado: Busco a mis amigos y almorzamos juntos. Toco la guitarra. Apago la luz del baño. Empiezo a entender los verbos.*

Práctica A
Answers will vary.

Práctica B
Better students may use direct object pronouns on 1, 2, 4, 5, and 7.
1. pagaste / (lo) pagué
2. colocaste / (las) coloqué
3. almorzaste / almorcé
4. practicaste / (lo) practiqué
5. buscaste / (los) busqué
6. comenzaste / comencé
7. tocaste / (la) toqué
8. jugaste / jugué
9. cruzaste / crucé
10. navegaste / navegué

Enrichment: Students may expand on their answers to Ex. B by adding explanations. For example: *Llegué a tiempo porque sólo tardé media hora en llegar.*

Práctica C
cruce
despegó / tardó
empecé
comencé / terminé
hablaron
invitaron
almorcé / saqué
aterrizó
busqué / encontré
tomé / llegué

Reteach / Extra Help: You
may want to ask volunteers to
read each sentence in Ex. C
using the correct preterite form.
Then ask them to write the
verbs on the board.

C El viaje de Esteban. Esteban escribe sobre su primer viaje a Caracas. Completa el párrafo con las formas correctas del pretérito.

Ayer por la mañana (yo) *(cruzar)* el Mar Caribe en avión. El avión *(despegar)* con unos minutos de retraso y el viaje *(tardar)* más de dos horas y media. Durante el viaje *(empezar)* a leer una novela venezolana y *(comenzar)* a escribirle una carta a mi abuela, pero no la *(terminar)*.

5 Unos muchachos que asisten a la universidad de Miami *(hablar)* conmigo y me *(invitar)* a su casa este fin de semana. Al mediodía (yo) *(almorzar)*. Antes de aterrizar (yo) *(sacar)* varias fotos maravillosas de la ciudad de Caracas desde el avión. El avión *(aterrizar)* a la una. En el aeropuerto (yo) *(buscar)* mi equipaje y lo *(encontrar)* todo sin problema.

10 ¡Qué milagro! Luego yo *(tomar)* un taxi y *(llegar)* al hotel antes de las dos.

Practice Sheet 6–3   10 Tape Manual Ex. 5   Quiz 6–3

El pretérito de *ir* y *ser*

◆ **OBJECTIVES:**

TO COMPARE TRIPS AND ACTIVITIES

TO MAKE EXCUSES FOR OTHERS

TO REMINISCE

Notes: Mini-dialogues 6 and 7
on pp. 200–201 contain
examples of the preterite of *ir*
and *ser*.

The verbs *ir* and *ser* have identical forms in the preterite tense. The context makes the meaning clear.

INFINITIVOS   **ser / ir**

	SINGULAR			PLURAL	
1 (yo)	**fui**	I was / I went	(nosotros) (nosotras)	**fuimos**	we were / we went
2 (tú)	**fuiste**	you were / you went	(vosotros) (vosotras)	**fuisteis**	you were / you went
3 Ud.	**fue**	you were / you went	Uds.	**fueron**	you were / you went
(él)		he was / he went	(ellos)		they were / they went
(ella)		she was / she went	(ellas)		they were / they went

Compare the following sentences.

Su esposo **fue** profesor en San Antonio. *Her husband **was** a teacher in San Antonio.*

Su esposo **fue** a San Antonio. *Her husband **went** to San Antonio.*

| Mi tío **fue** médico. | My uncle **was** a doctor. |
| Mi tío **fue** al médico. | My uncle **went** to the doctor. |

1   We can also use the preterite of *ir a* + infinitive to describe what someone went to do.

¿Adónde **fue** papá?	Where **did Dad go**?
Fue a firmar el registro.	**He went to sign** the register.
¿Adónde **fuiste**?	Where **did you go**?
Fui a navegar.	**I went sailing.**

PRÁCTICA

A ¿Adónde fueron?   Es lunes y un grupo de amigos habla sobre adónde fueron durante la semana de vacaciones. Sigue el modelo.

el 24 (yo)   Uds.

ESTUDIANTE A   *El 24 fui al teatro. Y Uds., ¿adónde fueron?*
ESTUDIANTE B   *Fuimos al museo.*

1. el lunes (yo)   él   2. el martes (yo)   tú

3. el miércoles (yo)   Marta   4. el jueves (yo)   ellos

5. el viernes (yo)   tú   6. el sábado (yo)   Daniel y tú

7. ayer (yo)   Uds.   8. anoche (yo)   José

Reteach / Extra Help: In preparation for the **Práctica** on pp. 215–217, you may want to ask students to create additional examples with the preterite forms of *ir* and *ser*.

Práctica A
1. El lunes fui al parque de diversiones. Y él, ¿adónde fue?
    Fue al castillo.
2. El martes fui al desfile. Y tú, ¿adónde fuiste?
    Fui a la isla.
3. El miércoles fui a la playa. Y Marta, ¿adónde fue?
    Fue al rancho.
4. El jueves fui a las montañas. Y ellos, ¿adónde fueron?
    Fueron al zoológico.
5. El viernes fui a la corrida. Y tú, ¿adónde fuiste?
    Fui al cine.
6. El sábado fui al campamento. Y Daniel y tú, ¿adónde fueron?
    Fuimos a la piscina.
7. Ayer fui al parque. Y Uds., ¿adónde fueron?
    Fuimos al valle.
8. Anoche fui a la heladería. Y José, ¿adónde fue?
    Fue al concierto de rock.

Enrichment: After students have completed Ex. A in class, you may want to ask them to bring in photographs of places they have visited. Ask students to write a sentence or two about their trip using the preterite of *ir* and / or *ser*.

B Actividades deportivas. ¿Qué fueron a hacer las siguientes personas? Sigue el modelo.

> los hermanos Ábalo / jugar al jai alai
> ESTUDIANTE A *¿Qué fueron a hacer los hermanos Ábalo?*
> ESTUDIANTE B *Fueron a jugar al jai alai.*

1. Leonor / montar a caballo
2. el Dr. Peralta y su hija / remar
3. Virginia y Sofía / bucear
4. el Sr. Fernández / patinar sobre ruedas
5. Uds. / levantar pesas
6. la familia Donoso / hacer gimnasia
7. la Dra. Vélez / jugar al golf
8. Ester y tú / montar en bicicleta
9. ¿y tú / ?

C Fotos de familia. Agustín y Carlota miran el álbum de fotos de su familia. Usa el pretérito de *ser* y sigue los modelos.

> una pensión muy cómoda
> *Fue una pensión muy cómoda.*
> nosotros / compañeros de clase
> *Nosotros fuimos compañeros de clase.*

1. un día muy oscuro
2. (tú) / un alumno excelente
3. la tía Marta / la dueña de esa tienda
4. mis mejores vacaciones
5. mi disfraz favorito
6. el Sr. Escobar / campeón de natación
7. (yo) / la ganadora de esa carrera
8. Emilia y tú / no . . . allá
9. (nosotros) / los últimos en la regata

En Siquirres, Costa Rica

D Hablemos de ti.

1. ¿Dónde almorzaste ayer? ¿Con quién?
2. ¿Practicaste un deporte ayer? ¿Cuál?
3. ¿Adónde fuiste anoche? ¿Adónde fuiste el fin de semana pasado?
4. ¿Fuiste de compras la semana pasada? ¿Qué compraste? ¿Fuiste de excursión? ¿Adónde? ¿Con quién? ¿Cuánto tiempo duró la excursión?
5. ¿Fuiste de pesca o de camping el año pasado? ¿Adónde? ¿Con quién?

Práctica D
Answers will vary.

Practice Sheet 6–4

Workbook Exs. E–F

Tape Manual Ex. 6 11

Quiz 6–4

ACTIVIDAD

El último viaje   Get together with two or three students to talk about a trip each of you took. You might ask each other questions such as these:

¿Cuál fue el viaje más largo que hiciste?
¿Adónde fuiste?
¿Cuándo fuiste?
¿Quiénes fueron contigo?
¿Cómo fue el viaje?

Notes: You may want students to prepare for the **Actividad** at home. Ask them to jot down notes that will help them remember details when classmates ask questions about their trip.

APLICACIONES Discretionary

¡Una noche en un castillo! 12

Notes: You may want to use the **Antes de leer** questions for small-group or class discussion.

ANTES DE LEER

Contesta las preguntas.
1. ¿Te gustan las casas y los edificios viejos o prefieres los modernos? ¿Por qué?
2. ¿Te gustaría ser rey o reina? ¿Por qué?
3. ¿Te gustaría vivir en un castillo? ¿Te parece una buena idea convertir un castillo histórico en un hotel más o menos moderno?

Antes de leer
1–3. Answers will vary.

El Parador Carlos V
en España

Querida[1] Sofía:

   ¡Hola! Aquí en España vemos muchas cosas fabulosas. ¡Imagínate! ¡Acabamos de pasar unos días en un castillo! Aterrizamos en España el viernes y papá anunció, "Vamos a quedarnos en un parador." Papá alquiló un
5 coche y viajamos dos horas por los campos[2] de Castilla.* Por fin, encontramos el castillo en un hermoso valle entre dos colinas.

   Sofía, estos castillos históricos de España son fantásticos. No pierden nada de su aspecto[3] viejo, pero las habitaciones son cómodas, modernas y elegantes. La cama en la habitación individual es tan grande que mi herma-
10 na y yo podemos dormir juntas en ella. En las paredes todavía hay armas[4] viejas, pero afortunadamente nadie las usa. Son sólo una decoración. Nuestra habitación tiene vista a los jardines llenos de flores de muchos colores. Las rosas son increíbles. ¡Qué hermoso está todo! ¡Y qué buena idea es convertir un castillo en un hotel!

15   Recorrí[5] todo el parador. Desde una de las torres[6] miré el paisaje verde de Castilla. ¡Qué bonito! Pensé en las aventuras románticas del pasado, de la gente tan rica que antes vivieron aquí y de los reyes y reinas que la visitaron.

   En unas horas voy a decirle adiós a mi castillo. Mamá no quiere volver a
20 casa. ¡Ni yo tampoco! Ahora te digo adiós a ti porque tengo que hacer las maletas. ¡Y tengo tanto equipaje! ¡Hay una maleta pequeña sólo para los recuerdos que compramos! Hasta luego.

Tu amiga,

Lupe

---

[1]**querido, -a** *dear*   [2]**el campo** here: *field*   [3]**el aspecto** *appearance*
[4]**las armas** *weapons*   [5]**recorrí** (preterite of **recorrer**) *I went through*
[6]**la torre** *tower*

* La región central de España se llama Castilla. El nombre quiere decir "tierra de castillos."

Preguntas

Contesta según la lectura.

1. ¿Cómo viajan Lupe y su familia?
2. ¿En qué parte de España están?
3. ¿En qué clase de parador se quedan?
4. Describe el paisaje donde está el castillo.
5. Según Lupe, ¿cómo son las habitaciones?
6. Describe la habitación de Lupe. Compara esto a los muebles y decoraciones de una habitación en un hotel o motel que tú conoces.
7. ¿Qué vista tiene el cuarto?
8. ¿Por qué piensa Lupe en aventuras cuando está en el castillo?

Preguntas
1. En avión y en coche
2. En Castilla
3. En un castillo
4. Es un hermoso valle entre dos colinas.
5. Cómodas, modernas y elegantes
6. Es una habitación individual con cama grande y armas viejas en las paredes. / Answers will vary.
7. Tiene vista a los jardines.
8. Answers will vary.

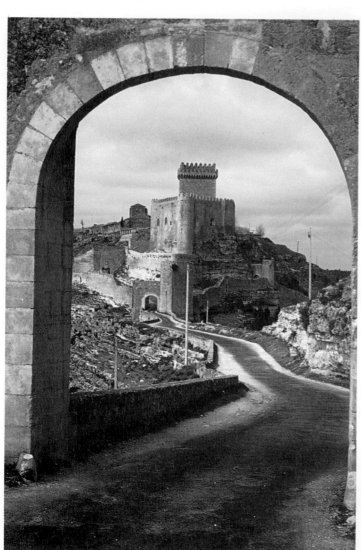

(izquierda) Un parador en Alarcón, España; (abajo) El Parador Casa del Barón en Pontevedra, España

EXPLICACIONES II

El pretérito de *dar* y *ver*

Here are all of the preterite forms of *dar* and *ver*.

DAR		VER	
di	dimos	vi	vimos
diste	disteis	viste	visteis
dio	dieron	vio	vieron

PRÁCTICA

A **¡Tantos regalos!** Los amigos de Marta hablan de los regalos que le dieron para sus quince años. Sigue el modelo.

Juan
Juan le dio un reloj.

1. (yo)

2. Teresa

3. Uds.

4. su hermano menor 5. (tú)

6. sus tíos

7. Ángel

8. (nosotros)

9. Diego y Lucía

B De viaje. El avión de Alfredo despega en seis horas y él no puede encontrar nada. Le hace muchas preguntas a su hermano. Sigue el modelo.

> mi pasaporte
> ESTUDIANTE A   *¿Viste mi pasaporte?*
> ESTUDIANTE B   *No, no lo vi.*

1. mi cinturón argentino
2. mis cheques de viajero
3. mi cámara
4. mi paraguas
5. mi boleto
6. mi reloj
7. mis tarjetas de crédito
8. mis planos
9. la dirección de la pensión

C Todavía busca sus cosas. Cuando su hermano no puede ayudarlo, Alfredo les hace las mismas preguntas a sus padres. Sigue el modelo.

> mi pasaporte
> ESTUDIANTE A   *¿Vieron Uds. mi pasaporte?*
> ESTUDIANTE B   *No, no lo vimos.*

D Una visita al zoológico. Rosa les habla a sus amigos de su visita al zoológico. Completa las frases con la forma correcta del pretérito de cada verbo.

Ayer mi familia y yo *(ir)* al zoológico donde *(ver)* unos animales muy interesantes. Por ejemplo, mi hermana *(ir)* al jardín de los pájaros donde *(ver)* un pájaro maravilloso en una jaula grande. Ella le *(sacar)* muchas fotos.

5   Yo *(ir)* a ver los elefantes. Mis padres me *(dar)* dinero para comprar cacahuates para ellos. (Yo) *(ver)* un elefante pequeño con orejas enormes. Les *(dar)* a él y a los otros elefantes casi toda la bolsa de cacahuates.

Mis padres y mi hermanito Pablo *(ir)* a la casa de los monos donde
10   *(ver)* unos monos muy graciosos. La guardiana les *(dar)* plátanos, lechuga y zanahorias. Después nosotros *(ir)* a una heladería. *(ser)* un día perfecto.   Practice Sheet 6–5   🔲 13 Tape Manual Ex. 7

Quiz 6–5

Práctica B
1. viste / lo vi
2. viste / los vi
3. viste / la vi
4. viste / lo vi
5. viste / lo vi
6. viste / lo vi
7. viste / las vi
8. viste / los vi
9. viste / la vi

Práctica C
vieron / vimos
Throughout, direct object pronouns as in Práctica B.

Práctica D
fuimos / vimos
fue
vio / sacó
fui / dieron
vi
di
fueron
vieron / dio
fuimos / Fue

Palabras negativas

◆ OBJECTIVES:

**TO HEDGE OR
AVOID
ANSWERING**

TO DENY

**TO CORRECT
WRONG
ASSUMPTIONS**

**TO AVOID GIVING
INFORMATION**

Notes: Point out the negative
words in mini-dialogues 4 and 5
on p. 208.

Remember that when we use a negative word we can either put it in front of the verb or put *no* before the verb and the negative word after.

Nunca fuimos a Alemania. }
No fuimos **nunca** a Alemania. }   We **never** went to Germany.

Nadie lo vio. }
No lo vio **nadie**. }   **Nobody** saw him.

Tampoco lo vi. }
No lo vi **tampoco**. }   I did**n't** see him **either**.

No me gusta **nada** aquí. }
Nada me gusta aquí. }   I don**'t** like **anything** here.

We can also use another negative word before the verb instead of *no*.

Nunca veo a **nadie**.   I **never** see **anyone**.

1   Remember that *ningún* and *ninguna* are adjectives and agree with the noun they describe.

     No hay **ningún pasajero** en ese vagón.   *There aren**'t any passengers** in that (train) car.*

     No tengo **ninguna tarjeta de crédito.**   *I don**'t** have **any credit cards.***

Remember that we use a singular noun in Spanish where English uses a plural noun.

2   *Ninguno, -a* is a pronoun that agrees in gender with the noun it refers to. We usually use it, too, in the singular.

     ¿Fuiste a muchos lugares interesantes?   *Did you go to many interesting places?*

     No, **no** fui a **ninguno.**   *No, I did**n't** go to **any.***

     ¿Hiciste reservaciones?   *Did you make reservations?*

     No, **no** hice **ninguna.**   *No, I did**n't** make **any.***

3   Remember that we use the personal *a* with *nadie* when it is a direct object. We also use the personal *a* before *ninguno, -a* when it is a direct object referring to people.

     No veo **a nadie** en la recepción.   *I don**'t** see **anyone** at the reception desk.*

     No vi **a ninguno** de los dueños.   *I did**n't** see **any** of the owners.*

4 *Ni* means "neither," "nor," or "not even." We often use it with *tampoco* for emphasis.

No tengo **ni** un peso.	*I don't have **even** one peso.*
No quiero ir al museo.	*I don't want to go to the museum.*
¡**Ni** él **tampoco**!	***Neither** does he (He doesn't either)!*

5 *Ni . . . ni* means "neither . . . nor" or "not . . . or."

No como **ni** arroz **ni** papas.	*I eat **neither** rice **nor** potatoes.*
No me gusta **ni** esquiar **ni** patinar.	*I don't like skiing **or** skating.*

Here are all of the negative words you have learned.

nada	*nothing, not anything*
nadie	*no one, nobody, not anyone*
ni . . . ni	*neither . . . nor, not . . . or*
ningún, ninguna	*no, not any (adj.)*
ninguno, -a	*none, not any (pron.)*
nunca	*never*
tampoco	*neither, not either*

PRÁCTICA

A No hice nada. Javier nunca le dice nada a nadie. Esta vez hizo un viaje y sus amigos quieren saber qué pasó. Contesta cada pregunta con una palabra negativa. Sigue el modelo.

ESTUDIANTE A   *¿Llevaste mucho equipaje?*
ESTUDIANTE B   *No, no llevé nada.*

1. ¿Quién fue contigo?
2. ¿Cuántas tarjetas postales mandaste?
3. ¿Practicaste el esquí acuático muchas veces?
4. ¿Sacaste muchas fotos?
5. ¿Qué compraste?
6. ¿A quién viste en la playa?
7. ¿Fuiste de pesca muchas veces?
8. ¿Nadaste todos los días?
9. ¿Qué hiciste entonces?

Reteach / Extra Help: You may want to reinforce the forms and meanings of negative words by asking questions designed to elicit negative responses: *¿Cuántas tarjetas de crédito tienes? ¿Cuándo viajaste a la Argentina? ¿Quién fue a Madrid la semana pasada? ¿A quién ves en aquella esquina?*

Práctica A
1. No fue nadie (*or:* Nadie fue) conmigo.
2. No mandé ninguna (tarjeta postal).
3. No practiqué nunca el esquí acuático.
4. No saqué ninguna (foto).
5. No compré nada.
6. No vi a nadie.
7. No fui nunca de pesca.
8. No nadé nunca.
9. No hice nada.

Práctica B

1. ¿Comes carne o pescado? No como ni carne ni pescado. Como verduras.
2. ¿Lees …? No leo ni novelas ni biografías. Leo periódicos y revistas.
3. ¿Juegas …? No juego ni al golf ni al tenis. Juego a los bolos.
4. ¿Quieres …? No quiero pagar ni al contado ni con cheque. Quiero pagar con tarjeta de crédito.
5. ¿Estudias …? No estudio ni química ni física. Estudio biología.
6. ¿Tomas …? No tomo ni café ni chocolate. Tomo leche.
7. ¿Vas …? No voy (al colegio) ni a pie ni en autobús. Voy en coche.
8. ¿Tienes …? No tengo ni perro ni gato. Tengo peces.
9. ¿Pides …? No pido ni la comida argentina ni la colombiana. Pido la brasileña.

Reteach / Review: In preparation for Exs. C and D, write several nouns on the board: *trenes, conductoras, perros, pensiones, paradores, hoteles.* Then ask volunteers to give negative answers to *¿Cuántos / Cuántas ___ hay?*, using both *ningún / ninguna +* noun and the pronoun *ninguno, -a.*

Práctica C

1. ¿Qué fuente? No vi ninguna. Ni yo tampoco.
2. No vi ninguno.
3. No fui a ninguno.
4. No vi ninguna.
5. No fui a ninguna.
6. No fui a ninguno.
7. No vi ninguna.
8. No compré ninguno.
9. Answers will vary.

B   Ni . . . ni.   Un amigo de Mauricio lo quiere conocer mejor. Le pregunta si hace varias cosas, pero él no hace ninguna de ellas. Pregunta y contesta según el modelo.

> hablar francés o italiano / inglés y español
> **ESTUDIANTE A**   *¿Hablas francés o italiano?*
> **ESTUDIANTE B**   *No hablo ni francés ni italiano. Hablo inglés y español.*

1. comer carne o pescado / verduras
2. leer novelas o biografías / revistas y periódicos
3. jugar al golf o al tenis / a los bolos
4. querer pagar al contado o con cheque / con tarjeta de crédito
5. estudiar química o física / biología
6. tomar café o chocolate / leche
7. ir al colegio a pie o en autobús / en coche
8. tener un perro o un gato / peces
9. pedir la comida argentina o la colombiana / la brasileña

C   De paseo.   Sonia y su hermana fueron a pasar el día en el centro. Cuando vuelven a casa, su madre les pregunta qué hicieron. Contesta según el modelo. Usa *ninguno* o *ninguna.*

> ¿Disfrutaron de la exposición de arte? (visitar)
> **ESTUDIANTE A**   *¿Disfrutaron de la exposición de arte?*
> **ESTUDIANTE B**   *¿Qué exposición de arte? No visité ninguna.*
> **ESTUDIANTE C**   *Ni yo tampoco.*

1. ¿Vieron la nueva fuente?   (ver)
2. ¿Les gustó el restaurante peruano?   (ver)
3. ¿Disfrutaron del espectáculo?   (ir)
4. ¿Fueron a la casa de cambio?   (ver)
5. ¿Disfrutaron de esa nueva película uruguaya?   (ir)
6. ¿Les gustó el museo?   (ir)
7. ¿Qué pensaron de las nuevas canchas de tenis en el parque?   (ver)
8. ¿Cuánto pagaron los boletos de ida y vuelta?   (comprar)
9. En tu opinión, ¿qué hicieron las chicas? ¿Cómo pasaron el día? ¿Fueron de excursión al centro?

D El viaje horrible.   Lourdes acaba de llegar a la estación de tren en un pueblo muy pequeño. Ella no tiene ningún plano y no puede encontrar nada. Contesta sus preguntas según el modelo.

> ¿Dónde está la ventanilla?
> *No hay ninguna ventanilla.*

1. ¿Dónde está la iglesia histórica?
2. ¿Puedo usar el teléfono?
3. ¿Cuándo sale el tren expreso?
4. ¿Dónde está la casa de cambio?
5. ¿Cómo puedo reservar un coche cama?
6. ¿Dónde están los horarios?
7. ¿Cuándo salen los trenes por la tarde?
8. ¿Dónde están las pensiones en este pueblo?

E Hablemos de ti.
1. ¿Qué regalos te dieron tus padres para tu último cumpleaños? ¿Y para la Navidad? ¿Qué les diste tú a ellos?
2. ¿Fuiste al cine el fin de semana pasado? ¿Con quién fuiste? ¿Qué película viste? ¿Cómo fue?
3. ¿Fuiste al centro el fin de semana pasado? ¿Con quién fuiste? ¿Qué hiciste? ¿Viste algo interesante?
4. En tu escuela, ¿cuántos alumnos llevan traje? ¿Cuántos llevan uniforme? ¿Corbata? ¿Sombrero?
5. ¿Te gusta limpiar el sótano o el garaje? ¿Lavar la ropa o planchar? ¿Limpiar las sartenes o cortar el césped?
6. ¿Eres desordenado(a)? ¿Cuándo pones tu dormitorio en orden? ¿Cómo lo haces?

ACTIVIDAD

Ni el uno ni el otro.   Working with a partner, make up a list of a dozen things that you think no one likes to do. Afterwards, join another pair of students and give them some of your most undesirable choices. They should answer truthfully, but if you have made a good enough list, they probably won't like any of the possibilities. For example:

ESTUDIANTE A ¿Qué prefieren Uds., tirar la basura o lavar los platos?
ESTUDIANTE B No nos gusta ni tirar la basura ni lavar los platos.
ESTUDIANTE A ¿Qué quieren hacer, llevar cajas pesadas o correr hasta el aeropuerto?
ESTUDIANTE B No queremos ni llevar cajas pesadas ni correr hasta el aeropuerto.

Práctica D
1. No hay ninguna iglesia histórica.
2. No hay ningún teléfono.
3. No hay ningún tren expreso.
4. No hay ninguna casa de cambio.
5. No hay ningún coche cama.
6. No hay ningún horario.
7. No hay ningún tren por la tarde.
9. No hay ninguna pensión en este pueblo.

Práctica E
Answers will vary.

Practice Sheet 6–6

Workbook Exs. G–J

Tape Manual Exs. 8–9 14

Refrán 15

Canción 16

Quiz 6–6

Explicaciones II   **225**

APLICACIONES Discretionary

Notes: Answers to the **Repaso** and **Tema** appear in the Teacher Notes.

REPASO

Notes: Review of:
1. preterite of *-car* / *-gar* / *-zar* verbs
   preterite of *ver*
   negative words
   personal *a*
2. preterite of *-car* / *-gar* verbs
   noun phrases with *de*
3. preterite of *-car* / *-gar* verbs
   preterite of *ir a* + infinitive
4. preterite of *dar*
   preterite of *-car* / *-gar* / *-zar* verbs
5. exclamations with *qué*
   negative words
   demonstrative adjectives

Enrichment: You may want to use the model sentences in the **Repaso** for dictation.

Mira las frases modelo. Luego cambia las frases que siguen al español según los modelos.

1. *Cuando jugaste al golf no viste nada ni a nadie.*
   (When I crossed at the corner I didn't see anything or anyone.)
   (When I looked for the conductor (m.) they didn't see anything or anyone.)
   (When I paid the owner (f.) we didn't see anything or anyone.)

2. *Sacaste los billetes y buscaste una casa de cambio.*
   (I took out the pen and signed a traveler's check.)
   (You (fam.) paid the (restaurant) check and used a credit card.)
   (They arrived at the campground and looked for their tent.)

3. *Sacó la guitarra y fue a tocar unas canciones.*
   (I turned off the light and went to cash a check.)
   (We took out the (street) map and went to find the post office.)
   (They looked for a broom and went to clean the boardinghouse.)

4. *Le dio el equipaje a su esposo. Luego encontró un sillón cómodo.*
   (They gave the travelers the schedules. Then they waited for the local train.)
   (I explained the problem to the passengers. Then we began the long trip.)
   (I put (colocar) our suitcases on the floor. Then we paid for the double room.)

5. *¡Qué barbaridad! Nunca hay ningún asiento libre en este vagón.*
   (How awful! There are never any Peruvian newspapers in this city.)
   (How sad! There's never any Brazilian food in these hotels.)
   (What a shame! There's never any express bus in this town.)

La Estación de Francia en Barcelona, España

TEMA

Transparency 21

Notes: You may want students to work in pairs to prepare the **Tema** sentences.

Reteach / Review: When students have completed the Tema sentences, you may want to ask volunteers to change the subject in the first four captions from *ella* to *yo*. For example: *Cuando llegué a la estación no vi nada ni a nadie.*

Escribe las frases en español.

1. When Eva arrived at the station she didn't see anything or anyone.

2. She looked for the ticket window and bought a one-way ticket.

3. She crossed the tracks and went to wait for the train.

4. She gave the conductor her ticket. Then she looked for the dining car.

5. "What a drag! There's never any dining car on this train."

REDACCIÓN

Ahora escoge uno de los siguientes temas para escribir tu propio diálogo o párrafo.

1. Expand the *Tema* by writing several additional sentences. Give some background information on picture 1. Where is Eva coming from? Where do you think she's going? What is she going to do there?

2. Write a short paragraph about a real or imaginary train trip you took. Where did you go? What did you see from the window? Did the train arrive on time? Would you like to take another trip by train?

3. Make up a dialogue between the owner of a boardinghouse and a guest arriving at the reception desk.

COMPRUEBA TU PROGRESO   CAPÍTULO 6   Discretionary

Notes: Answers to the **Comprueba** appear in the Teacher Notes.

A   Un viaje en tren
Escribe el siguiente párrafo. Usa el pretérito.

Llego a la estación con un poco de retraso y busco la ventanilla. Compro un boleto de ida y vuelta y cruzo la vía para ir al andén. Después de subir al tren, coloco el equipaje debajo del asiento. Le doy el boleto al inspector. Luego voy al coche comedor y almuerzo. Durante el viaje, practico el inglés con los otros pasajeros y saco unas fotos del campo. Llego a Córdoba a la una.

B   *Ser* e *ir*
Contesta cada pregunta con una frase completa en el pretérito. Sigue el modelo.

> ¿Siempre vas sola al club?   (anoche)
> *No, pero fui sola anoche.*

1. ¿Son Uds. siempre los primeros?   (ayer)
2. ¿Siempre es tan divertido el viaje?   (el mes pasado)
3. ¿Siempre son fáciles las pruebas?   (el año pasado)
4. ¿Vas de pesca cada semana?   (anteayer)
5. ¿Siempre va ella en el tren local?   (la última vez)
6. ¿Soy la única alumna ecuatoriana?   (en la otra clase)
7. ¿Siempre van Carlos y Ana a comprar las entradas?   (para este concierto)

C   *Dar* y *ver*
Contesta las preguntas en el pretérito. Usa complementos directos o indirectos. Sigue el modelo.

> ¿Vas a ver a José?
> *Ya lo vi.*
> ¿Vas a darle la cuenta?
> *Ya le di la cuenta.*

1. ¿Tus padres van a ver a Teresa? ¿Van a darle los esquís?
2. ¿Van Uds. a ver al dueño? ¿Van a darle el cheque?
3. ¿Los chicos van a ver al inspector? ¿Van a darle los boletos?
4. ¿Va a ver María a los tenistas? ¿Va a darles una lección?
5. ¿Va Ud. a ver a los niños? ¿Va a darles los salvavidas?
6. ¿Vas a ver al Sr. Núñez? ¿Vas a darle la habitación individual?

D   Los negativos
Contesta las preguntas. Usa *nada, nadie, nunca, ningún, ninguno, -a, ni . . . ni* o *tampoco.*

1. ¿Tienes muchas ideas buenas?
2. ¿Viste a los paraguayos o a los chilenos en el coche comedor?
3. ¿Compraste fruta en el mercado?
4. ¿Cuándo fuiste a Salamanca?
5. ¿Viste a tus primos o a tus tíos?
6. ¿Hay muchos turistas argentinos allí?
7. ¿Viste los cuadros viejos en el museo?
8. ¿A quién viste en la recepción?
9. No fui a la casa de cambio ayer. ¿Y Uds.?

VOCABULARIO DEL CAPÍTULO 6

Sustantivos
el andén, *pl.* los andenes
el billete
el bolsillo
la casa de cambio
el castillo
el coche cama, *pl.* los coches
    cama
el coche comedor, *pl.* los coches
    comedor
el cheque
el cheque de viajero
el dueño, la dueña
el equipaje
la habitación (individual / doble),
    pl. las habitaciones
    (individuales / dobles)
el inspector, la inspectora
la llegada
el parador
el pasajero, la pasajera
la pensión, *pl.* las pensiones
el plano
la profesión, *pl.* las profesiones
la recepción, *pl.* las recepciones
el registro (de hotel)
la salida *(departure)*
la tarjeta de crédito
el vagón, *pl.* los vagones
la ventanilla *(ticket window)*
la vía
el viajero, la viajera

Adjetivos
argentino, -a
boliviano, -a
brasileño, -a
claro, -a
colombiano, -a
chileno, -a
ecuatoriano, -a
expreso
histórico, -a
local
maravilloso, -a
oscuro, -a
paraguayo, -a
peruano, -a
uruguayo, -a
venezolano, -a

Verbos
anunciar
colocar
comenzar (a + *inf.*) (e → ie)
cruzar
firmar
tardar (en + *inf.*)

Preposición
sobre *(over)*

Conjunciones
ni . . . tampoco
(no . . .) ni
(no . . .) ni . . . ni

Expresiones
cobrar un cheque
con (+ *time* + de) retraso
de ida (y vuelta)
de primera / segunda clase
de profesión
pagar al contado
quiere + *inf.*

PRÓLOGO CULTURAL

VAMOS DE COMPRAS

In the past, if you had lived in San Juan, Puerto Rico, you would have gone to the central plaza in the heart of the city to shop and meet your friends in the open air. Today you would more likely go to the Plaza de las Américas. This ultramodern shopping center is the largest in the Caribbean. Whether you are shopping or just out for a walk, you can escape the heat and wander in air-conditioned comfort through this busy mall. There are locally owned specialty shops and major chain stores on the ground floor. On the third level, you'll find several restaurants, cafés, food shops, and a movie theater.

When shopping for food, there is no better place than the markets in la Plaza del Mercado in the Río Piedras district of the city. There, you'll find farmers from other parts of the island selling their produce just as they have done for centuries. While in the area, you can also buy handmade guitars, flutes, and drums in all shapes and sizes.

In El Viejo San Juan, you can explore the many craft shops and perhaps buy a beautifully carved wood sculpture, some lace or ornate needlework, or a colorfully painted mask made of coconut shells. In other shops in this old section of the city, you can find ceramics decorated with the traditional patterns of the native Taíno Indians: images of lizards and insects, stick figures, and geometric patterns.

For people who live in Puerto Rico's more remote areas, getting to the commercial center of San Juan can be a difficult trip. For them, the local open-air market remains the most important center of business and social activity.

1

Transparency 22
**CONTEXTO
VISUAL**

Essential

Pelo largo, pelo corto

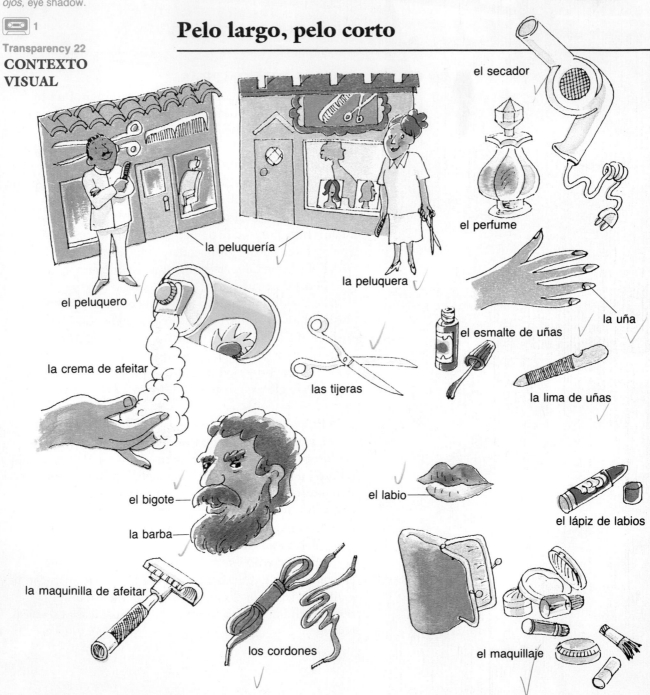

el secador

el perfume

la peluquería

la peluquera

el peluquero

la crema de afeitar

las tijeras

el esmalte de uñas

la uña

la lima de uñas

el bigote

la barba

el labio

el lápiz de labios

la maquinilla de afeitar

los cordones

el maquillaje

el cepillo
el peine

cortar el pelo

El peluquero le corta el pelo al niño.

cortarse el pelo

El niño se corta el pelo.

maquillar

Él maquilla a la actriz.

maquillarse

La actriz se maquilla.

afeitar

Él afeita al señor.

afeitarse

Él se afeita.

cortar las uñas

Su madre le corta las uñas a Paco.

cortarse las uñas

Paco se corta las uñas.

limar las uñas

Le lima las uñas también.

limarse las uñas

Se lima las uñas también.

limpiar

Le limpia los zapatos al señor.

limpiarse

Se limpia los zapatos.

atar

Luego le ata los cordones de los zapatos.

atarse

Se ata los cordones de los zapatos.

* *Cortar el pelo* means "to cut (someone's) hair." *Cortarse el pelo* can mean "to cut your own hair," but we usually use it to mean "to get a haircut."

1 MARTA   No me gusta el color de este lápiz de labios. Es demasiado **rosado.**

    TERESA   ¿Y ése?

    MARTA   ¡Uf! Ése no está **de moda.** Es demasiado rojo.

    TERESA   ¡Ay! Siempre **te quejas de** todo.

Variaciones:

- lápiz de labios → esmalte de uñas
- rosado → anaranjado
- siempre te quejas de todo →, nunca te gusta nada

rosado, -a *pink*

la moda *fashion*
de moda *fashionable, in fashion*
quejarse (de) (yo me quejo, tú te quejas) *to complain (about)*

2 MAMÁ   Hugo, son las siete. Tienes que **darte prisa.**

    HUGO   ¿Qué dices, mamá?

    MAMÁ   Hay que salir.

    HUGO   Sólo tengo que limpiarme los zapatos.

- limpiarme los zapatos → cortarme las uñas
- limpiarme los zapatos → atarme los cordones de los zapatos
- limpiarme → ponerme

darse prisa (yo me doy prisa, tú te das prisa) *to hurry*

3 JUAN   **Me voy,** mamá.

    MAMÁ   ¿Vas a la peluquería? Tienes el pelo demasiado largo.

- me voy → voy a salir
- tienes el pelo demasiado largo → tienes que cortarte el pelo

irse (yo me voy, tú te vas) *to leave, to go away*

4 CARMEN   La peluquera dice que mi pelo **castaño** es hermoso.

    PATRICIA   Estoy de acuerdo.

    CARMEN   Pero a mí me gusta el pelo negro.

- a mí me gusta → yo prefiero

castaño, -a *chestnut-colored*

EN OTRAS PARTES

En México y en otros países se dice también *rasurarse*.

En México se dice *las agujetas*.

También se dice *el lápiz labial* o *la barra de labios*.

En el Caribe y en otros países se dice *la pintura de uñas*.

En México y en el Caribe se dice *pintarse*.

También se dice *el salón de belleza*.

También se dice *el barbero*.

También se dice *amarrarse los cordones de los zapatos*.

PRÁCTICA

A ¿Qué necesitas? Di lo que necesitas para hacer las siguientes cosas. Pregunta y contesta según el modelo.

cortarse el pelo
ESTUDIANTE A *¿Qué necesitas para cortarte el pelo?*
ESTUDIANTE B *Unas tijeras y un espejo.*

1. secarse el pelo
2. lavarse el pelo
3. afeitarse
4. cepillarse los dientes
5. bañarse
6. limarse las uñas
7. peinarse
8. maquillarse

new vocab

Notes: Before students begin Ex. A, you may want to call attention to the transformation from reflexive pronoun *se* in the cues to *te* in the answers.

Práctica A
1. ¿Qué necesitas para secarte el pelo?
Un secador y una toalla.
2. ¿ ... para lavarte el pelo?
Champú y agua (caliente).
3. ¿ ... para afeitarte?
Una maquinilla de afeitar, crema de afeitar y agua caliente.
4. ¿ ... para cepillarte los dientes?
Un cepillo de dientes y pasta dentífrica.
5. ¿ ... para bañarte?
Jabón y agua (caliente)
6. ¿ ... para limarte las uñas?
Una lima de uñas.
7. ¿... para peinarte?
Un peine.
8. ¿ ... para maquillarte?
Maquillaje (y un lápiz de labios).

B Antes de la fiesta.

B Antes de la fiesta. ¿Qué hacen estas personas antes de la fiesta? Pregunta y contesta según el modelo.

Rita

ESTUDIANTE A *Rita, ¿qué haces?*
ESTUDIANTE B *Me corto el pelo.*

Práctica B
1. Anita, ¿qué haces?
   Me limo las uñas.
2. Me peino.
3. Me lavo las manos.
4. Me maquillo.
5. Me corto las uñas.
6. Me cepillo los dientes.
7. Me ato los cordones de los zapatos.
8. Me afeito.
9. Me baño.

1. Anita

2. Alfonso

3. Benjamín

4. Julia

5. Gerardo

6. Yolanda

7. Isabel

8. Papá

9. Luz

Práctica C

1. ¿A quién le limas las uñas?
   Le limo las uñas a
   Esperanza.
2. ¿A quién afeitas?
   Afeito al Sr. Márquez.
3. ¿A quién maquillas?
   Maquillo a la Sra. Muñoz.
4. ¿A quién le cepillas el pelo?
   Le cepillo el pelo a la Sra.
   Meléndez.
5. ¿A quién le limpias los
   zapatos?
   Le limpio los zapatos al
   Sr. Arenas.
6. ¿A quién le cortas el pelo?
   Le corto el pelo a Ernesto.
7. ¿A quién le lavas el pelo?
   Le lavo el pelo a Sonia.
8. ¿A quién le cortas las uñas?
   Le corto las uñas a Felipe.

C En la peluquería. En la peluquería todo el mundo está ocupado.
Pregunta y contesta según el modelo. ¡Cuidado! Algunas preguntas y
respuestas necesitan el complemento indirecto *le*.

ESTUDIANTE A	*¿A quién le cortas el pelo?*
ESTUDIANTE B	*Le corto el pelo a Fernando.*

Fernando

1. Esperanza   2. el Sr. Márquez   3. la Sra. Muñoz

4. la Sra. Meléndez   5. el Sr. Arenas

6. Ernesto   7. Sonia   8. Felipe

D Hablemos de ti.

1. ¿Tienes el pelo largo o corto? ¿De qué color es? ¿Qué piensan tus padres? ¿Se quejan ellos de la moda de hoy?

2. ¿Te cortas el pelo a menudo? ¿Adónde vas para cortarte el pelo? ¿Te gusta el color de pelo que tienes? ¿Por qué?

3. Si eres una chica, ¿te gusta el maquillaje y el lápiz de labios? ¿Por qué? ¿Usas esmalte de uñas? ¿De qué color? ¿Qué perfume te gusta más? Si eres un chico, ¿te gusta la barba o el bigote? ¿Qué clase de barba o de bigote te gusta más? ¿El bigote pequeño o grande, largo o corto? ¿La barba corta o larga?

4. ¿Te quejas mucho? ¿De qué te quejas? ¿De qué se quejan tus padres? ¿Y tus amigos?

5. ¿Tienes que darte prisa a menudo? ¿Cuándo? ¿Por qué?

6. ¿Te gusta vestirte de moda? ¿Por qué? ¿Qué clase de ropa está de moda ahora? ¿Qué colores están de moda este año?

Práctica D
Answers will vary.

Notes: You may want to assign some of the questions in Ex. D as written homework. Check students' work for correct spelling, capitalization, and punctuation.

Practice Sheet 7–1

Workbook Exs. A–B

Tape Manual Exs. 1–2 3

Quiz 7–1

Un mostrador de perfumes en Madrid, España

APLICACIONES Discretionary

En la peluquería 4  5 Pronunciación

Diálogo

Preguntas are on facing page.

1. Están en la peluquería porque la hija quiere cortarse el pelo.
2. No quiere un corte de pelo corto y rizado para su hija. Le gusta el pelo largo que ella tiene.
3. Porque su mamá tiene el pelo rizado. / Answers will vary.
4. Cree que son demasiado jóvenes para usar maquillaje. Answers will vary.
5. Answers will vary, but may include *Porque él es calvo* or *Porque él no tiene pelo.*
6. Answers will vary.

Un señor calvo[1] y su hija de diez años entran en una peluquería.

PELUQUERA   Buenos días.

PADRE   Buenos días, señora. Mi hija quiere cortarse el pelo.

PELUQUERA   ¿Qué corte de pelo[2] te gusta?

HIJA   El corte que está de moda, corto y muy rizado.[3]

PADRE   Pero hija, tu pelo es hermoso.

HIJA   Papá, a mí me gusta el pelo rizado. Mamá lo tiene rizado.

PADRE   Sí, lo sé. Pero tú no eres mamá.

HIJA   No te entiendo. Siempre te quejas de las cosas que me gustan a mí. Todas mis amigas tienen el pelo corto. También usan maquillaje para los ojos, esmalte de uñas, lápiz de labios . . .

PADRE   ¡Cómo! ¿Las chicas de diez años usan lápiz de labios? Tú no necesitas maquillaje porque ya eres bonita. También tienes un hermoso pelo largo. Vámonos. *(a la peluquera)* Lo siento, señorita.

PELUQUERA   No importa, señor.

HIJA   ¡Qué lata! ¿Por qué siempre cree la gente sin pelo que es mejor tener mucho pelo?

---

[1]**calvo, -a**   *bald*   [2]**el corte de pelo**   *haircut*   [3]**rizado, -a**   *curly*

Preguntas

Contesta según el diálogo.

1. ¿Dónde están el padre y la hija y qué hacen allí?   2. ¿Qué no quiere el padre? ¿Por qué?   3. ¿Por qué quiere la hija tener el pelo corto y rizado? ¿Cómo lo tienes tú? ¿Y tus amigas?   4. ¿Qué piensa el padre de las niñas de diez años que usan maquillaje? ¿Estás de acuerdo con lo que él dice? ¿Por qué sí o por qué no?   5. ¿Por qué crees tú que el padre admira tanto *(so much)* el pelo largo? En tu opinión, ¿tiene razón la hija cuando dice que su padre admira el pelo largo porque él no tiene pelo?   6. ¿Puedes describir al padre y a la hija? Usa tu imaginación.

Participación

Work with a partner to create a dialogue between a hairdresser or barber and a client. What kinds of questions does the barber or hairdresser ask? What does the client need or want? How does the client want his or her hair done?

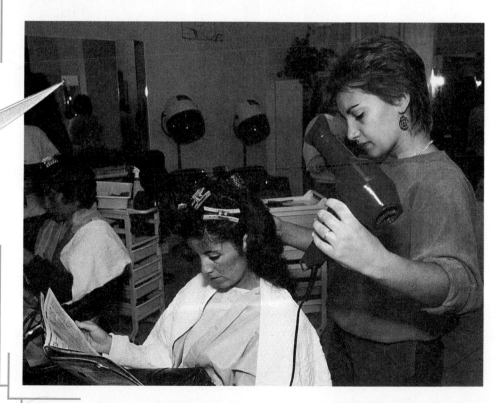

PALABRAS NUEVAS II

Transparency 23
CONTEXTO VISUAL

En el almacén

If students ask: Other related words you may want to present: *el maniquí*, mannequin; *la puerta giratoria*, revolving door; *la mercancía*, merchandise.

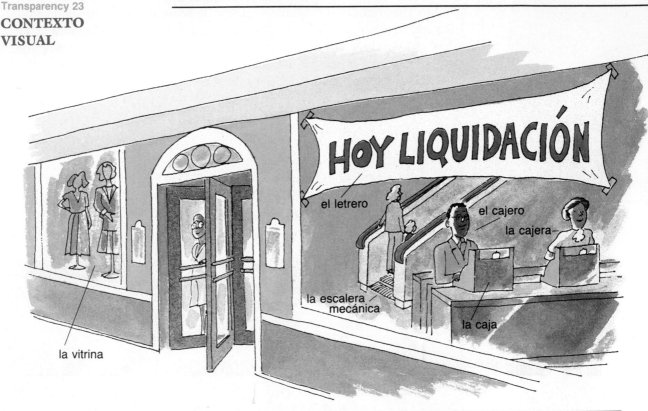

HOY LIQUIDACIÓN

el letrero

el cajero

la cajera

la escalera mecánica

la caja

la vitrina

CONTEXTO COMUNICATIVO

 7

1 MARÍA   Ayer fui a **una liquidación** en el almacén Blanco y Negro.

    LUZ   Me gusta mucho el **departamento** de ropa deportiva. ¿Compraste algo allí?

    MARÍA   Sí, fui a la planta baja y encontré unas ollas muy baratas.

Variaciones:

■ una liquidación → una venta

■ unas ollas → una lavadora y una secadora

■ unas ollas muy baratas → un secador muy barato

la liquidación, las liquidaciones
(clearance) sale

el departamento *department*

Reteach / Review: You may want to point out that *ropa deportiva* in mini-dialogue 1 has the same broad meaning as its English equivalent, '''sportswear.''

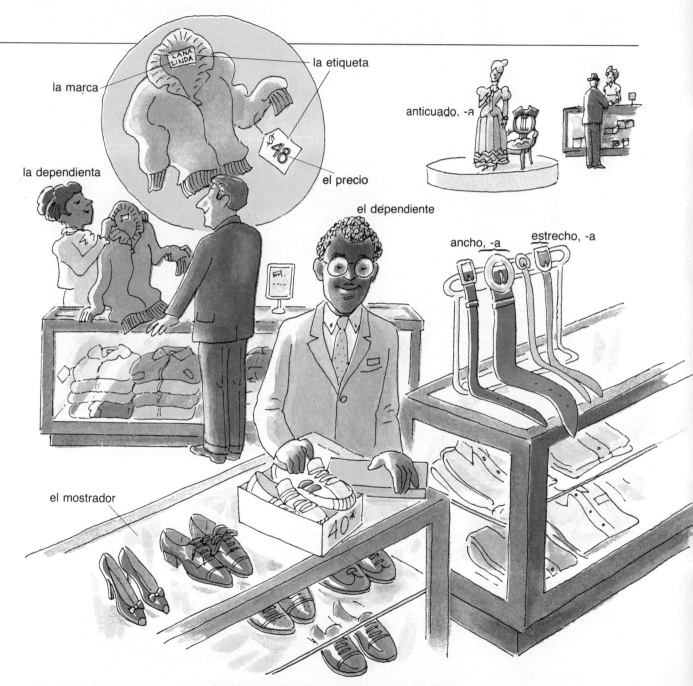

la marca

la etiqueta

el precio

la dependienta

el dependiente

anticuado, -a

ancho, -a

estrecho, -a

el mostrador

* Clothing sizes differ from country to country. For a chart of sizes in Spain see page 247.

2 MARÍA   No quiero este vestido.

DEPENDIENTE   Pero es muy **elegante** y le **queda** muy bien.

MARÍA   Sí, y también **cuesta un ojo de la cara.**

- vestido → traje
- cuesta un ojo de la cara → es carísimo

elegante   *elegant*

quedar   *to fit, to look (good) on*

costar un ojo de la cara   *to cost an arm and a leg*

3 PEPE   Carlos, el almacén Blanco y Negro anuncia **miles de gangas. La mayoría de** su ropa está en venta.

CARLOS   Entonces debo darme prisa. Necesito zapatos.

PEPE   ¿Qué **número**?

CARLOS   El 41.

- miles de → millones de
- miles de → docenas de

miles (de)   pl. of **mil**

la ganga   *bargain*

la mayoría de   *most (of), the majority of*

el número   *(shoe) size*

> **Enrichment:** Refer students to the size chart on p. 247. Then ask them to practice mini-dialogue 3 using personalized information.

4 ALICIA   Quisiera comprar una camisa **talla** 40.

DEPENDIENTA   ¿Quiere Ud. **probarse** esta rosada que está muy de moda?

ALICIA   No gracias. Es para un regalo. ¿Cuánto cuesta? Pienso **gastar alrededor de** $ 20,00.*

DEPENDIENTA   Ésta cuesta sólo $ 18,00. Con **el impuesto**† $ 19,80 *(diecinueve dólares con ochenta centavos).* Si a ella no le queda bien puede **devolverla.**

- pienso → no quiero
  alrededor de → más de
- que está muy de moda → **hecha** en México
- está muy de moda → es muy **distinta de** las otras
- si no le queda bien → si no le gusta

la talla   *(clothing) size*

probarse (o → ue)   *to try on*

gastar   *to spend*

alrededor de   *around, about*

el impuesto   *tax*

devolver (o → ue)   *to return (something), to give back, to take back*

hecho, -a   *made*

distinto, -a (de)   *different (from)*

5 DOLORES   ¿Conoces a Raúl Silva?

LEONARDO   ¡Por supuesto! **Nos** vemos casi todos los días.

- conoces → conocen ellos
  nos vemos → **se** ven

nos   here: *each other*

se   here: *each other*

---

* In Spanish-speaking countries they usually use a period in numbers where we use a comma. Where we use a period, they use a comma: $ 10.000.000,00 = *diez millones de dólares con cero centavos.*

† In Spanish-speaking countries the tax is often not a separate sales tax, but a value-added tax. The tax is already included in the sales price.

EN OTRAS PARTES

devolver

En España se dice *el escaparate*. También se dice *la vidriera*.

En México se dice *regresar*

PRÁCTICA

A Me encanta ir de compras. Escoge las palabras correctas para completar el párrafo.

Hoy tengo que darme *(prisa / moda / maquillaje)* porque hay una gran *(etiqueta / marca / liquidación)* en la tienda La Mundial. A menudo esta tienda tiene *(gangas / vitrinas / tijeras)* fantásticas y todo está baratísimo. Cuando llego, busco la escalera *(distinta / mecánica /*
5 *anticuada)* y voy al *(letrero / departamento / impuesto)* de ropa deportiva. Veo unas blusas baratas y bonitas. Me *(ata / maquilla / pruebo)* una azul y una amarilla. La blusa azul me *(queda / quema / devuelve)* muy bien. Quiero comprarla pero el cajero me dice que el precio en la *(etiqueta / talla / marca)* no es correcto. ¡Yo no quiero *(costar / gastar / cortar)*
10 3.000 pesetas! Pongo la blusa en *(la moda / el mostrador / el secador)* y voy a buscar una falda. Le pido a la *(dependienta / peluquera / camarera)* una falda roja, pero me dice que no tienen ninguna en mi *(número / talla / marca)*. ¡Caramba! ¡Qué mala suerte tengo hoy!

Práctica A
prisa
liquidación
gangas
mecánica
departamento
pruebo
queda
etiqueta
gastar
el mostrador
dependienta
talla

Si piensas
diferente,
vístete
diferente.

Exprésate con EXPRESS

En España

B **¿Qué dices?** Imagina que estás en un almacén con un(a) amigo(a). Escoge la respuesta correcta para cada pregunta.

1. ¿Hay ascensor?
2. ¿Cuánto es el impuesto?
3. ¿Pago en este piso?
4. ¿Qué hago si a ella no le gusta esta pulsera?
5. ¿Qué dice esta etiqueta? No puedo leerla.
6. ¿En qué piso está el departamento de perfumes?
7. Mira esos precios. ¿Qué pasa entonces?
8. ¿Cómo te quedan esos zapatos? Me parecen un poco anchos.
9. ¿Está de moda este traje?
10. ¿Es dependiente ese hombre?

a. No, son muy cómodos.
b. Sí, en la caja número 4.
c. No sé. A mí me parece un poco anticuado.
d. Alrededor de $ 1,60.
e. Hay una liquidación hoy.
f. No, es cajero.
g. No, pero hay una escalera mecánica.
h. Puede devolverla.
i. Hecho en Guatemala.
j. En la planta baja, cerca del mostrador de maquillaje.

C **Hablemos de ti.**

1. ¿Te gusta ir a las liquidaciones? ¿Por qué? ¿Te gusta ir de compras? ¿Te gusta mirar las vitrinas sin comprar nada?
2. ¿Tienes una marca favorita de ropa? ¿Cuál és? ¿Es ropa elegante o deportiva?
3. ¿Llevas ropa o zapatos hechos en otros países? ¿Sabes dónde fue hecha la ropa que llevas hoy?
4. ¿A veces devuelves regalos que recibes? ¿Por qué los devuelves? ¿Qué clases de regalos te gustan recibir?
5. ¿Siempre te pruebas la ropa antes de comprarla? ¿Por qué?
6. Cuando vas al cine, ¿gastas mucho dinero? ¿Pagas mucho por una entrada? ¿Cuánto? ¿Compras palomitas o dulces? ¿Cuánto cuestan? ¿Compras refrescos? ¿Grandes o pequeños? ¿Cuánto pagas por ellos? En total, ¿más o menos cuánto gastas cuando vas al cine?

ACTIVIDAD

En el almacén   Get together in groups of two or three students to set up a shopping trip. One or two people are the *clientes* and the other is the *dependiente(a) / cajero(a)*. The *clientes* should first write down how many thousand pesetas they have. After deciding on an item to buy, they ask for it, specifying such things as the desired style, size, and color. Price should also be discussed. The *dependiente(a)* should ask questions to get more information. Use the chart of sizes, and you may want to use some of the following phrases:

Reteach / Extra Help: Before students begin to prepare their conversation for the **Actividad**, you may want to remind them that they should address each other as *Ud(s)*.

DEPENDIENTE(A)
¿Qué desea(n) Ud(s).?
¿Cuál es su talla / número?
¿Qué color prefiere(n) Ud(s).?
¿Le(s) queda(n)?
¿Quiere(n) Ud(s). probarse el / la . . . ?

CLIENTE(S)
¿Cuánto cuesta(n)?
¿Puedo probarme el / la . . . ?
¿Dónde pago?
¿Puedo pagar con cheques de viajero? ¿Tarjeta de crédito?
¿Hay que pagar al contado?
¿Cuánto es el impuesto?

En Puerto Rico

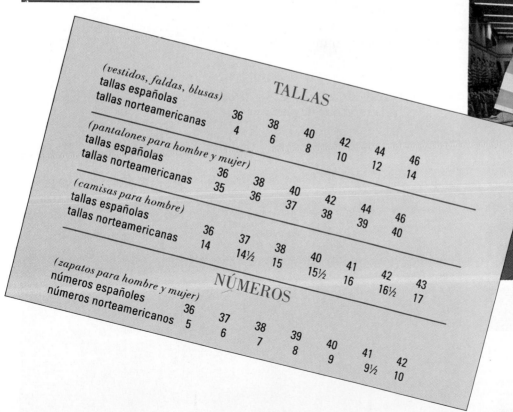

TALLAS						
(vestidos, faldas, blusas)						
tallas españolas	36	38	40	42	44	46
tallas norteamericanas	4	6	8	10	12	14
(pantalones para hombre y mujer)						
tallas españolas	36	38	40	42	44	46
tallas norteamericanas	35	36	37	38	39	40
(camisas para hombre)						
tallas españolas	36	37	38	40	41	42	43
tallas norteamericanas	14	14½	15	15½	16	16½	17

NÚMEROS						
(zapatos para hombre y mujer)						
números españoles	36	37	38	39	40	41	42
números norteamericanos	5	6	7	8	9	9½	10

Estudio de palabras
lima / maquillaje
secar / mostrar / peinar(se) /
cepillar(se) / duchar(se)

Sinónimos
1. liquidación
2. dependientes
3. irse

Antónimos
1. anticuada
2. anchos

ESTUDIO DE PALABRAS

You have already seen several verb and noun pairs that have a common root. For example, *el vendedor* is related to the verb *vender*, and *el anuncio* is related to *anunciar*. In this chapter you learned several more noun and verb pairs:

What nouns are related to these verbs?

limarse   maquillarse

To what verbs are these nouns related?

el secador   el mostrador   el peine   el cepillo   la ducha

Sinónimos:
Cambia las palabras en cursiva por sinónimos.
1. La tienda de la esquina tiene una gran *venta*.
2. Quiero comprar perfume. ¿Dónde están *los vendedores*?
3. La peluquera espera *salir* a las tres.

Antónimos:
Cambia las palabras en cursiva por antónimos.
1. Esa escalera mecánica es muy *moderna*.
2. Estos pasillos son muy *estrechos*.

(arriba) En Zaragoza,
España; (derecha) En
México

EXPLICACIONES I

Los verbos reflexivos

You know that a reflexive verb has two parts—a reflexive pronoun and a verb form. The reflexive pronoun refers to the subject of the sentence. Look at the difference between these reflexive and nonreflexive verbs.

Baño al perro.	*I'm bathing the dog.*
Me baño.	*I'm taking a bath* (= *bathing myself*).
Acuesto a los niños.	*I'm putting the children to bed.*
Me acuesto.	*I'm going to bed* (= *putting myself to bed*).

Here are all of the present-tense forms of the verb *levantarse*, "to get up."

LEVANTARSE	
me levanto	**nos** levantamos
te levantas	**os** levantáis
se levanta	**se** levantan

1 Remember that except for *se*, all of the reflexive pronouns have the same forms as the direct and indirect object pronouns. They generally come before the verb, or they may be attached to an infinitive.

Me voy a **poner** la blusa gris. ⎫
Voy a **ponerme** la blusa gris. ⎭ *I'm going **to put on** the gray blouse.*

2 Remember that with reflexive verbs we usually use the definite article with parts of the body or articles of clothing. Even when we are talking about more than one person we use the singular form unless the objects come in pairs (*calcetines, manos*) or are logically plural (*pantalones, dientes*).

Nos afeitamos **la barba**.	*We're shaving **our beards**.*
Se ponen **la chaqueta**.	*They're putting on **their jackets**.*
Se liman **las uñas**.	*They're filing **their nails**.*

3 Sometimes we use the reflexive pronouns *se* and *nos* to express the idea of "each other."

Nos escribimos a menudo.	*We **write to each other** often.*
Se entienden bien.	*They **understand each other** well.*

◆ **OBJECTIVES:**

TO DESCRIBE DAILY ROUTINE

TO POINT OUT THINGS PEOPLE DO FOR EACH OTHER

TO INTERVIEW SOMEONE

Notes: For additional examples of reflexive verbs, you may want to refer students to the **Contexto visual** on pp. 232–233 and to mini-dialogues 1–3 on p. 234 and 3–5 on p. 244.

Reteach / Extra Help: Reinforce the forms and meanings of various reflexive verbs by asking these questions: *¿A qué hora te levantas? ¿Nos levantamos todos a la misma hora? ¿A tu mejor amigo le gusta irse temprano de las fiestas? ¿Te despiertas temprano o tarde durante los fines de semana? ¿Quiénes se liman más las uñas, los muchachos o las muchachas?*

4 Some verbs have a change in meaning when we use them reflexively.

Nicolás **va a** la peluquería.　　Nicolás **goes** to the barber shop.
Se va a las tres.　　He **leaves** at 3:00.

Duermo bien en esa cama.　　I **sleep** well in that bed.
Me duermo fácilmente.　　I **fall asleep** easily.

Él **llama a** Clara todos los días.　　He **calls** Clara every day.
Se llama Clara Bermúdez.　　**Her name is** Clara Bermúdez.

¿Puedo **probar** la sopa?　　May I **taste** the soup?
¿Puedo **probarme** ese vestido?　　May I **try on** that dress?

PRÁCTICA

A **¿Qué hacen?** Describe lo que hacen estas personas. Usa verbos reflexivos o no reflexivos según los dibujos. Sigue los modelos.

Despierta a su hijo.　　　　*Se despierta.*

1.　　　　2.　　　　3.　　　　4.

5.　　　　6.　　　　7.　　　　8.

B **¿Cuándo?** Imagina que un niño muy joven viene a visitarte y quiere saber tu rutina diaria (*daily routine*). Por ejemplo:

despertarse
ESTUDIANTE A *¿Cuándo te despiertas?*
ESTUDIANTE B *Me despierto alrededor de las siete.*
　　o: *Me despierto cuando oigo el despertador.*

1. levantarse
2. bañarse o ducharse
3. cepillarse los dientes
4. vestirse
5. lavarse las manos
6. peinarse
7. irse para la escuela
8. acostarse

C Visitantes de Guanajuato.   Imagina que tu clase de español entrevista (*interviews*) a unas visitantes de Guanajuato, México. Pregunta y contesta según el modelo.

> ¿cuándo? / levantarse / muy temprano
> ESTUDIANTE A   *¿Cuándo se levantan Uds.?*
> ESTUDIANTE B   *Nos levantamos muy temprano.*

1. ¿cuánto tiempo / quedarse en los Estados Unidos? / una semana
2. ¿dónde / quedarse? / en una pensión en el centro
3. ¿a qué hora / despertarse? / alrededor de las 7:30
4. ¿hay algo de qué / quejarse? / sí, . . . del horario
5. ¿darse prisa todo el tiempo? / sí, siempre
6. ¿divertirse? / sí, . . . mucho
7. ¿cuándo / acostarse? / alrededor de la medianoche
8. ¿dormirse fácilmente? / en seguida
9. ¿cuándo / irse para Guanajuato? / el domingo por la tarde

3. ¿A qué hora se despiertan Uds.? Nos despertamos alrededor de las siete y media.
4. ¿Hay algo de qué se quejan Uds.? Sí, nos quejamos del horario.
5. ¿Se dan Uds. prisa todo el tiempo? Sí, siempre nos damos prisa.
6. ¿Se divierten Uds.? Sí, nos divertimos mucho.
7. ¿Cuándo se acuestan Uds.? Nos acostamos alrededor de la medianoche.
8. ¿Se duermen Uds. fácilmente? Nos dormimos en seguida.
9. ¿Cuándo se van Uds. para Guanajuato? Nos vamos el domingo por la tarde.

Práctica D
1. Se cepillan el pelo. Les cepillan el pelo a sus hijas.
2. Se atan los cordones de los zapatos. Les atan los cordones de los zapatos a sus hijos.
3. Se pone el abrigo. Les ponen el abrigo a sus hijos.
4. Se quita las botas. Les quitan las botas a sus hijos.

D Hay que ayudar a los niños.   Describe lo que hacen estas personas. Usa verbos reflexivos o no reflexivos según los dibujos. Sigue el modelo.

Se lavan la cara.   *Les lavan la cara a sus hijas.*

1.

2.

3.

4.

Práctica E

1. ¿Se escriben José y tú? Sí, nos escribimos a menudo.
2. ¿Se prestan Uds. ropa? Sí, siempre nos prestamos ropa.
3. ¿Se visitan …? Sí, nos visitamos …
4. ¿Se entienden …? Sí, nos entendemos …
5. ¿Se ayudan …? Sí, nos ayudamos …
6. ¿Se llaman …? Sí, nos llamamos …
7. ¿Se ven …? Sí, nos vemos …
8. ¿Se mandan …? Sí, nos mandamos …

Práctica F

1. se duerme
2. probarse
3. pruebas
4. nos vamos
5. va
6. se llama
7. Llamas
8. Pongo
9. ponerse

Practice Sheets 7–3, 7–4

 **10 Tape Manual Exs. 5–6**

Quiz 7–3

E Nos conocemos muy bien.   Varios amigos se hacen preguntas para conocerse mejor. Sigue el modelo.

> Uds. / conocer bien / muy bien
>> ESTUDIANTE A   *¿Se conocen bien Uds.?*
>> ESTUDIANTE B   *Sí, nos conocemos muy bien.*

1. José y tú / escribir / a menudo
2. Uds. / prestar ropa / siempre
3. María, Inés y tú / visitar / todos los meses
4. las hermanas Ochoa y tú / entender bien / muy bien
5. Uds. / ayudar en la escuela / muchas veces
6. tú y tu novia / llamar por teléfono / todos los días
7. Uds. / ver / durante el verano / a menudo
8. Marta y tú / mandar tarjetas postales / frecuentemente

F ¿Reflexivo o no?   Completa las frases con la forma correcta del verbo reflexivo o no reflexivo.

1. Mi hermanito siempre *(dormir / dormirse)* en seguida después de acostarse.
2. Luisa quiere *(probar / probarse)* una nueva marca de maquillaje.
3. ¿Por qué no *(probar / probarse)* (tú) los guisantes?
4. ¿A qué hora (nosotros) *(ir / irse)* del campamento?
5. La mayoría de las veces él *(ir / irse)* a la peluquería conmigo.
6. Este lápiz de labios *(llamar / llamarse)* ''Fuego rosado.''
7. ¿(Tú) *(llamar / llamarse)* al dependiente?
8. (Yo) *(poner / ponerse)* el secador en la maleta.
9. Guillermo quiere *(poner / ponerse)* un traje elegante para la fiesta.

Mandatos con pronombres reflexivos

◆ **OBJECTIVES:**

TO REFUSE TO DO SOMETHING

TO TELL A CHILD WHAT TO DO

Just as with other object pronouns, we attach reflexive pronouns to affirmative *tú* commands. When we attach a reflexive pronoun to a command form of more than one syllable, we place a written accent mark over the stressed syllable.

Ponte el traje de baño nuevo.	*Put on your new bathing suit.*
Vete ahora.	*Leave now.*
Quítate la chaqueta si tienes calor.	*Take off your jacket if you're warm.*
Córtate el pelo pronto.	*Get your hair cut soon.*
Levántate por favor.	*Get up please.*

PRÁCTICA

A ¡Qué niño tan antipático! Imagina que eres el padre o la madre de un niño obstinado *(stubborn)*. Haz mandatos y contesta según el modelo.

> cortarse el pelo
> ESTUDIANTE A   *Córtate el pelo.*
> ESTUDIANTE B   *No quiero cortarme el pelo.*

1. limpiarse las uñas
2. lavarse el pelo
3. ponerse la bufanda
4. cepillarse los dientes
5. darse prisa
6. irse ahora mismo
7. quitarse las botas mojadas
8. probarse los zapatos nuevos
9. atarse los cordones de los zapatos
10. acostarse temprano
11. quedarse en el comedor
12. despertarse ahora mismo

B Hablemos de ti.

1. Describe lo que haces por la mañana. ¿Cuándo te despiertas? ¿Prefieres bañarte o ducharte? ¿Cuánto tiempo tardas en vestirte? Si tienes que darte prisa, ¿puedes vestirte en cinco minutos?
2. ¿Qué haces los sábados o los domingos que no haces durante los otros días de la semana? ¿Cómo te diviertes? ¿Te pones ropa distinta los fines de semana? ¿Cómo es?
3. ¿Te gusta levantarte temprano o tarde? ¿Por qué? ¿Cuántas horas duermes generalmente? ¿Prefieres la mañana o la noche? ¿Por qué?
4. ¿Te acostaste tarde o temprano anoche? ¿Por qué?
5. ¿Cuántos años hace que sabes atarte la corbata? ¿Y atarte los cordones de los zapatos?
6. ¿Te quejaste de algo esta mañana? ¿De qué?
7. ¿Cuáles son algunos de los mandatos que te da tu papá? ¿Tu mamá? ¿Tus profesores? ¿Tus entrenadores o entrenadoras?

ACTIVIDAD

¡Despiértate! Get together with two or three students for this variation of charades. One person starts by pointing at someone in the group and giving a command that includes a reflexive verb. That person pantomimes the action, and then everyone mentions something the mimer needs. For example, if the person pantomimes combing his or her hair, people might say things like *necesita un peine, necesita un espejo,* and so on. Continue until everyone has given two commands and pantomimed two actions.

APLICACIONES

Discretionary

La liquidación   Transparency 24

Después de las cinco el almacén está lleno de gente. ¿Qué precio ves en la caja? ¿Cuántas personas suben por la escalera mecánica? ¿Qué está en liquidación?

Enrique bought a shirt from this department store two days ago. Create a dialogue in which he asks the saleswoman if he can exchange it. Give the reason why. You may want to use these words or phrases:

devolver	la talla	distinto, -a
probarse	ancho, -a	estrecho, -a
quejarse de	anticuado, -a	sucio, -a

EXPLICACIONES II

Essential

Los números de 100 a 1.000.000

1 You know how to count by hundreds.

100 cien(to)	400 cuatrocientos, -as	700 setecientos, -as
200 doscientos, -as	500 quinientos, -as	800 ochocientos, -as
300 trescientos, -as	600 seiscientos, -as	900 novecientos, -as

You also know how to say all numbers up to 999. Look at the following examples:

211 doscientos once	567 quinientos sesenta y siete
817 ochocientos diecisiete	999 novecientos noventa y nueve

◆ **OBJECTIVES:**

TO GIVE EXACT DATES

TO TELL HOW MUCH EXPENSIVE ITEMS COST

2 Notice the use of *mil* in the following sentences.

Mis abuelas llegaron a los Estados Unidos en **mil ochocientos noventa y tres.**

*My grandparents arrived in the United States in **1893.***

En esta biblioteca hay más de **diez mil quinientos** libros.

*There are more than **10,500** books in this library.*

We use the plural form *miles* in the same way that we use "thousands" in English.

Hay **miles** de personas en el parque.

*There are **thousands** of people in the park.*

3 Remember that after *millón* and *millones* we use *de* before a noun.

Esta ciudad tiene casi **un millón de** habitantes.

*This city has almost **a million** inhabitants.*

La Argentina tiene cerca de **treinta millones de** habitantes.

*Argentina has close to **thirty million** inhabitants.*

While we usually use the singular in English, in Spanish we use the plural form *millones* for everything over one million.

Práctica A

1. ... mil ochocientos dieciocho
2. ... mil ochocientos veintiuno
3. ... mil ochocientos veinticinco
4. ... mil ochocientos treinta
5. ... mil ochocientos noventa y ocho
6. ... mil novecientos tres
7. ... mil setecientos setenta y seis
8. ... mil ochocientos treinta y ocho y treinta y nueve

Práctica B

1. El segundo cajero tiene más de setenta mil dólares.
2. ... casi cuarenta mil dólares.
3. ... casi un millón de dólares.
4. ... más de doscientos cincuenta mil dólares.
5. ... alrededor de cuatrocientos mil dólares.
6. ... cerca de tres millones de dólares.
7. ... más de setecientos mil dólares.
8. ... alrededor de veinticinco mil dólares.
9. ... menos de diez mil dólares.

Practice Sheet 7–6

📼 12 Tape Manual Ex. 8

Quiz 7–5

Un banco en Santa Cruz, Bolivia

PRÁCTICA

A **¿Cuál es la fecha de la independencia?**   Los estudiantes de la clase de historia aprenden de memoria el año de la independencia de varios países. Sigue el modelo.

> la Argentina / 1810
> *la Argentina, mil ochocientos diez*

1. Chile / 1818
2. México / 1821
3. el Uruguay / 1825
4. el Ecuador / 1830
5. Cuba / 1898
6. Panamá / 1903
7. los Estados Unidos / 1776
8. la mayoría de los países centroamericanos / 1838 y '39

B **¿Cuánto tiene cada uno?**   Antes de irse a casa, cada cajero del banco tiene que contar el dinero que hay en su caja: los billetes, las monedas, los cheques y los cheques de viajero. ¿Más o menos cuánto tiene cada uno? Sigue el modelo.

> el primer cajero / casi $ 30.000
> *El primer cajero tiene casi treinta mil dólares.*

1. el segundo cajero / más de $ 70.000
2. el tercer cajero / casi $ 40.000
3. el cuarto cajero / casi $ 1.000.000
4. el quinto cajero / más de $ 250.000
5. el sexto cajero / alrededor de $ 400.000
6. el séptimo cajero / cerca de $ 3.000.000
7. el octavo cajero / más de $ 700.000
8. el noveno cajero / alrededor de $ 25.000
9. el décimo cajero / menos de $ 10.000

El pretérito de los verbos que terminan en -er e -ir

Review the preterite forms of regular -er and -ir verbs. Remember that the endings are the same for both types of verbs.

COMER			VIVIR	
comí	comimos		viví	vivimos
comiste	comisteis		viviste	vivisteis
comió	comieron		vivió	vivieron

Ayer **comimos** en la pensión.	*Yesterday we **ate** at the boardinghouse.*
Jaime **vivió** en Bolivia el año pasado.	*Jaime **lived** in Bolivia last year.*

Note that stem-changing -er verbs do not have the stem change in the preterite.

¿Enciendo ahora la estufa?	***Shall I light** the stove now?*
No, ya la **encendí**.	*No, I already **lit** it.*

PRÁCTICA

A Ya es lunes. Di lo que hicieron estos chicos durante el fin de semana. Sigue el modelo.

> Pedro / asistir a un concierto de música clásica
> *Pedro asistió a un concierto de música clásica.*

1. Carlos / devolver un secador descompuesto
2. Ellos / salir para la peluquería antes del mediodía / y no volver hasta las seis
3. Uds. / escoger una botella de perfume para el santo de Alicia
4. Mis amigos / ver una película de ciencia ficción
5. Susana / correr en una carrera / y perder
6. Juan / escribir letreros y etiquetas para la liquidación en la tienda de su mamá
7. Pablo y Ramón / comer en un restaurante dominicano
8. Cristina / recoger revistas viejas / y venderlas
9. Y tú, ¿qué hiciste?

◆ OBJECTIVES:

TO TELL WHAT PEOPLE DID AND DID NOT DO AT A CERTAIN TIME

Reteach / Extra Help: You may want to reinforce the preterite forms of -er and -ir verbs by doing an oral question / answer drill before beginning the **Práctica:** *¿Me vieron Uds. ayer? ¿A qué hora saliste de casa hoy? ¿Salió alguien contigo? ¿Te escribió _____ una carta la semana pasada? ¿Escribiste una carta ayer? ¿Quiénes comieron ayer en la cafetería? ¿Qué comieron?*

Práctica A
1. devolvió
2. salieron … no volvieron
3. escogieron
4. vieron
5. corrió … y perdió
6. escribió
7. comieron
8. recogió … y las vendió
9. Answers will vary.

1. respondiste ... respondí
2. entendiste ... entendí
3. escribiste ... escribí (no escribí nada)
4. devolviste ... devolví (no devolví ningún libro ...)
5. aprendiste ... aprendí (no aprendí nada nuevo ...)
6. recibiste ... recibí (no recibí ninguna ...)
7. perdiste ... perdí (no perdí nada importante)
8. saliste ... salí
9. volviste ... volví

Práctica C

1. respondieron ... respondimos
2. entendieron ... entendimos
3. escribieron ... escribimos (no escribimos nada)
4. devolvieron ... devolvimos (no devolvimos ningún libro ...)
5. aprendieron ... aprendimos (no aprendimos nada nuevo ...)
6. recibieron ... recibimos (no recibimos ninguna ...)
7. perdieron ... perdimos (no perdimos nada importante)
8. salieron ... salimos
9. volvieron ... volvimos

Practice Sheet 7–7

 13 Tape Manual Ex. 9

Quiz 7–6

B **¿Lo hiciste o no?** Pregúntale a un(a) compañero(a) si hizo las siguientes cosas ayer. Sigue el modelo.

> asistir a clase
> ESTUDIANTE A *¿Asististe a clase?*
> ESTUDIANTE B *Sí, asistí a clase.*
> o: *No, no asistí a clase.*

1. responder a todas las preguntas de la tarea de español
2. entender todos los problemas de matemáticas
3. escribir algo a máquina
4. devolver algunos libros a la bibliotecaria
5. aprender algo nuevo en esta clase
6. recibir una carta o tarjeta postal
7. perder algo importante
8. salir temprano de la escuela
9. volver tarde a casa

C **¿Lo hicieron o no?** Ahora usa los elementos de la Práctica B para preguntar y contestar según el modelo.

> asistir a clase
> ESTUDIANTE A *¿Asistieron Uds. a clase?*
> ESTUDIANTE B *Sí, asistimos a clase.*
> o: *No, no asistimos a clase.*

El pretérito de los verbos reflexivos

We form the preterite of reflexive verbs in the same way that we form the preterite of nonreflexive verbs. The reflexive pronoun comes before the verb just as in the present tense.

No **me duché, me bañé.**	*I didn't take a shower; I took a bath.*
¿A qué hora **se acostaron** Uds.?	*What time **did you go** to bed?*
Nos fuimos temprano.	*We left early.*

◆ **OBJECTIVES:**

TO TELL WHAT HAPPENED IN THE PAST

TO DESCRIBE PREPARATIONS FOR AN EVENT

PRÁCTICA

A **En el teatro.** ¿Qué hicieron los actores y las actrices antes y después de la obra de teatro? Completa el párrafo con la forma correcta de los verbos en el pretérito.

A las siete y cuarto, los cuatro actores *(llegar)* al teatro. Las dos actrices *(probarse)* los vestidos y *(escoger)* sus joyas elegantes. Luego *(cortarse)* y *(limarse)* las uñas y después *(maquillarse)*. El maquillaje les *(quedar)* muy bien.

5   Los dos actores *(afeitarse)* y *(peinarse.)* También ellos *(ayudarse)* a ponerse la barba y el bigote y a maquillarse. Todos *(darse prisa)*. La obra *(comenzar)* exactamente a las ocho.

Después de la obra, los actores y las actrices *(quitarse)* el maquillaje y *(lavarse)* la cara con mucho jabón. Alrededor de las once, todos *(irse)*
10 del teatro.

B **Hablemos de ti.**

1. ¿Saliste este fin de semana? ¿Con quién? ¿Qué hicieron Uds.?
2. Hoy por la mañana, ¿te levantaste temprano o tarde? ¿A qué hora? ¿Te bañaste o te duchaste? ¿Te cepillaste los dientes? ¿Qué marca de pasta dentífrica usaste?
3. ¿A qué hora desayunaste esta mañana? ¿Qué comiste? ¿Qué bebiste? ¿Quién preparó la comida? ¿A qué hora cenaste anoche? ¿Qué hiciste después? ¿Miraste la televisión? ¿Qué programas viste?

Práctica A
llegaron
se probaron
escogieron
se cortaron
se limaron
se maquillaron
quedó
se afeitaron
se peinaron
se ayudaron
se dieron
comenzó
se quitaron
se lavaron
se fueron

Práctica B
Answers will vary.

Practice Sheet 7–8

Workbook Exs. G–J

Tape Manual Ex. 10   14

Refrán   15

Canción   16

Quiz 7–7

APLICACIONES Discretionary

Notes: Answers to the **Repaso** and **Tema** appear in the Teacher Notes.

REPASO

Notes: Review of:
1. preterite of *ir*
   noun phrases with *de*
   para + infinitive
   reflexive verbs +
      clothing / parts of
      the body
2. preposition +
      infinitive
   reflexive verbs
   preterite of *-ar*
      verbs
   noun phrases with *de*
3. indirect object pronouns
   reflexive verbs +
      clothing / parts of
      the body
4. *decir*
   indirect object pronouns
   affirmative *tú* commands
      with reflexive verbs
5. exclamations with *qué*
   preterite of *-er* / *-ir*
      verbs
   más / *menos de*
   numbers over 1,000

Enrichment: You may want
to use the model sentences in
the **Repaso** for dictation.

Mira las frases modelo. Luego cambia las frases que siguen al español según los modelos.

1. *Armando fue a la peluquería del hotel para cortarse la barba.*
   (They went to the office bathroom to wash their hands.)
   (We went to the school gym to take off our uniforms.)
   (You (fam.) went to Ana's room to file your nails.)

2. *Después de maquillarse los ojos, usó el esmalte de uñas.*
   (Before leaving the store, they returned the shaving cream.)
   (After trying on the dress, she bought a lipstick.)
   (After shaving your mustache, you (fam.) threw away the razor.)

3. *La dependienta le preguntó: "¿Quiere también ponerse estos zapatos?"*
   (His mother asked him: "Can you (fam.) also tie your laces?")
   (He asked them: "Do you also want to take off your glasses?")
   (María asked me: "Should you (fam.) also cut your nails?")

4. *Su mamá le dice: "Es muy tarde. Cepíllate los dientes y apaga la luz."*
   (She says to me: "It's very wide (fem.) Take off the skirt and look for your size.")
   (I say to Daniel: "It's rather late. Wash your hair and use the hair dryer.")
   (I say to her: "They're too narrow (fem.) Try on these shoes and return the sandals.)

5. *¡Qué milagro! Vendiste más de un millón de secadores.*
   (What a drag! They returned about 1,100 scissors.)
   (How lucky! She wrote more than 1,500 labels.)
   (What a shame! We sold fewer than a thousand cash registers.)

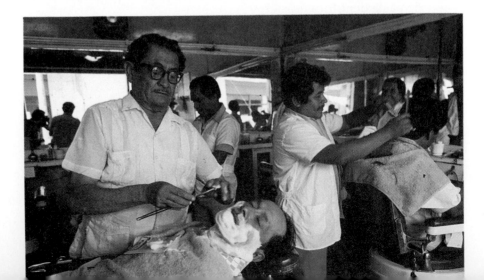

TEMA

Escribe las frases en español.

1. Consuelo went to the neighborhood beauty shop to have her hair cut.

2. Before having her hair cut, she looked at the fashion (pl.) magazines.

3. The hairdresser asked her: "Do you also want to try (on) this makeup?"

4. Consuelo's friend says to her: "It's very late. Hurry up and pay the bill."

5. "Good grief! I spent more than 1,500 pesos!"

REDACCIÓN

Ahora escoge uno de los siguientes temas para escribir tu propio diálogo o párrafo.

1. Write a paragraph describing what you or a member of your family does to get ready in the morning.

2. Create a dialogue between two friends in a department store that is having a sale. To which departments do they go? What do they try on? Do they buy anything?

3. Imagine that someone you know is working as a salesclerk at a neighborhood clothing store. Write a paragraph describing what he or she does during a typical day. What are the customers like? Does your friend like the work? Does he or she complain about anything?

Aplicaciones   **261**

COMPRUEBA TU PROGRESO   CAPÍTULO 7   Discretionary

Notes: Answers to the **Comprueba** appear in the Teacher Notes.

A   En la tienda

Escoge la palabra correcta para completar cada frase.

dependiente	el impuesto
la escalera mecánica	el letrero
la etiqueta	un ojo de la cara
ganga	talla

1. Estos jeans son muy baratos. ¡Qué _____!
2. El ascensor está descompuesto. Hay que buscar _____.
3. El precio de la ropa está en _____.
4. No puedo leer _____. Es muy pequeño.
5. Tengo que devolver esta camisa. No es mi _____.
6. Él es _____ en una tienda de música.
7. ¡Qué caro es! Cuesta _____.
8. Luis dice que _____ va a ser más de 1.100 pesos.

B   Por la mañana

Forma frases. Usa la forma reflexiva correcta.

1. Ana / cepillarse el pelo
2. (tú) / limarse mucho las uñas
3. mi hermano / probarse la corbata nueva
4. (nosotros) / vestirse de prisa
5. (yo) / maquillarse muy despacio
6. Carmen / atarse los cordones de los zapatos
7. mis hermanas / irse temprano
8. Luis y yo / quejarse de todo

C   ¿Qué hace?

Di lo que hace Laura con las siguientes cosas. Sigue el modelo.

Se lava la cara y las manos.

 1.   2.   3.

 4.   5.   6.

D   Lo que van a hacer

Haz frases según el modelo.

(él) / afeitarse por la mañana
Tiene que afeitarse por la mañana.

1. (yo) / irse en dos minutos
2. mi tío / cortarse el bigote
3. Ud. / darse prisa
4. (yo) / ponerse el vestido rosado
5. (nosotros) / quejarse de esa cajera
6. (tú) / probarse los pantalones
7. mis hermanas / limarse las uñas
8. (ellos) / acostarse después de la cena

E   Los mandatos

Haz mandatos afirmativos con *tú*.

1. irse ahora mismo
2. ponerse el esmalte de uñas
3. lavarse bien las manos
4. afeitarse antes de salir
5. cortarse el pelo
6. maquillarse en el baño

F   El pretérito

Completa cada frase con la forma correcta del verbo en el pretérito.

1. ¿A qué hora _____ (tú) anoche?   *(salir)*
2. ¿_____ Uds. a menudo?   *(escribirse)*
3. (Yo) _____ eso el año pasado.   *(aprender)*
4. ¿Lo _____ Ud. al dependiente?   *(devolver)*
5. (Nosotros) _____ muchas gangas.   *(escoger)*
6. ¿Quién _____ el plato?   *(romper)*
7. ¿_____ (tú) el letrero?   *(entender)*
8. Elena me _____ un lápiz de labios nuevo.   *(prometer)*
9. (Nosotros) _____ en la farmacia.   *(verse)*
10. (Yo) _____ del departamento a las tres.   *(irse)*

Sustantivos
la barba
el bigote
la caja *(cash register)*
el cajero, la cajera
los cordones (de los zapatos)
la crema de afeitar
el departamento
el dependiente, la dependienta
la escalera mecánica
el esmalte de uñas
la etiqueta
la ganga
el impuesto
el labio
el lápiz de labios
el letrero
la lima de uñas
la liquidación, *pl.* las
   liquidaciones
el maquillaje
la maquinilla de afeitar
la marca
la moda
el mostrador
el número *(shoe size)*
la peluquería
el peluquero, la peluquera
el perfume
el precio
el secador
la talla
las tijeras
la uña
la vitrina

Adjetivos
ancho, -a
anticuado, -a
castaño, -a
distinto, -a (de)
elegante
estrecho, -a
hecho, a
rosado, -a

Verbos
afeitar(se)
atar
devolver (o → ue)
gastar
irse
maquillar(se)
probarse (o → ue)
quedar
quejarse (de)

Pronombres reflexivos
nos *(each other)*
se *(each other)*

Preposición
alrededor de

Expresiones
atar(se) la corbata / los cordones
   de los zapatos
cortar(se) el pelo / las uñas
costar un ojo de la cara
darse prisa
de moda
limar(se) las uñas
limpiar(se) los zapatos / los
   anteojos
la mayoría de
miles (de)

PRÓLOGO CULTURAL

MÉXICO, D.F.

What do you think it's like to live in the oldest city in the Americas? Mexico City has been inhabited since 1325. In that year the Aztecs founded the city they called Tenochtitlán on an island in the middle of *el lago de Texcoco*. As the population grew, they created more land by layering mud and aquatic plants on woven frames, and by the time the Spanish explorers arrived in 1519, they found a magnificent city of houses, pyramids, and temples. In conquering the Aztecs, they destroyed much of the Indian civilization and then built their own colonial city on top of the ruins. In the 1600s the Spaniards drained Texcoco, and now the *Distrito Federal*, or D.F., has almost completely covered the dry lake bed.

The people of Mexico City live with the past on a daily basis. Nowhere is the contrast between old and new more evident than in *la Plaza de las Tres Culturas*, not far from the heart of downtown Mexico City. There you can see the ruins of a fourteenth-century Aztec pyramid next to a sixteenth-century Spanish church and, towering over both, a twentieth-century office building. Below ground, if you ride certain routes on the very efficient and quiet Mexico City subway system, you will pass pyramids and glass cases displaying Aztec artifacts that were discovered when workers excavated the subway tunnel.

By the time the Pilgrims landed at Plymouth Rock in 1620, Mexico City was a thriving center of more than 100,000 inhabitants. It was the home of the first university, printing press, and mint in the Americas. Today, with a population of 9 million, and with 5 million more in the suburbs and outlying areas, Mexico City is the second-largest and most rapidly growing metropolitan area in the world.

PALABRAS NUEVAS I

Essential

1

CONTEXTO VISUAL

Las reglas de tráfico

la carretera

el parquímetro

el semáforo

el cruce (de calles)

el paso de peatones

la conductora

el conductor

el peatón
pl. los peatones

ALTO

las señales de tráfico

* In Spain and many other countries, the word STOP appears on stop signs. In some countries of Latin America (Colombia, for example) they use PARE. In others, such as Mexico, they use ALTO.

el cinturón de seguridad
pl. los cinturones de seguridad

el instructor

la instructora

tocar la bocina

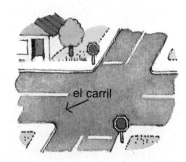

el carril

CONTEXTO COMUNICATIVO

 2

1 NORMA Estoy **nerviosa.** Hoy voy a tomar el examen para **obtener un permiso de manejar.**

MATEO Pero manejas bien y aprendiste **las reglas** de **tráfico.**

NORMA Pero, ¿qué va a pasar si salgo mal en el examen?

MATEO **No seas** tan pesimista, Norma. Si manejas **con cuidado** vas a salir muy bien en el examen.

Variaciones:

- nerviosa → preocupada
- no seas tan pesimista → sé más optimista

2 IGNACIO No seas tan **impaciente.**

BEATRIZ Lo siento, Ignacio, pero **tengo prisa.**

IGNACIO Nunca **respetas la velocidad máxima.** Si tú no tienes cuidado, ese policía te va a **poner una multa.**

- no seas tan impaciente → sé más **paciente**
- no seas tan impaciente → no puedes **estacionar** aquí
  la velocidad máxima → las señales de tráfico

nervioso, -a *nervous*

obtener (yo obtengo, tú obtienes) *to get, to obtain*

el permiso de manejar *driver's license*

manejar *to drive*

la regla *rule, law*

el tráfico *traffic*

no seas (negative **tú** command form of **ser**) *don't be*

con cuidado *carefully*

impaciente *impatient*

tener prisa *to be in a hurry*

respetar *to respect, to obey*

la velocidad máxima *speed limit*

poner una multa *to give a ticket*

la multa *fine; (traffic) ticket*

paciente *patient*

estacionar *to park*

3 RAQUEL   Por favor, ¿**queda por aquí** la estación de tren?

    MANUEL   No, **por allí.** Ud. tiene que **dar la vuelta.**

■ queda → está
■ la estación del tren → la casa de cambio

4 ARMANDO   ¿**Doblo** a la izquierda para llegar al parador?

    BÁRBARA   No. Continúa **todo derecho.** Pero ten cuidado. La calle es muy estrecha y es bastante **peligrosa.**

■ a la izquierda → en la esquina
■ es muy estrecha → no es muy ancha

5 FELIPE   Mamá, tengo que ir a la biblioteca. ¿Me puedes llevar en coche?

    MAMÁ   Pero hijo, ¿no ves que estoy ocupada? Tienes que caminar sólo quince **cuadras.**

    FELIPE   ¡Quince cuadras! ¡Qué lata!

    MAMÁ   ¡Qué niño tan perezoso!

■ la biblioteca → el club
■ ¡qué lata! → ¿no quieres cambiar de idea?

---

quedar   *here: to be (located)*

por aquí   *around here, over here, this way*

por allí   *around there, over there, that way*

dar la vuelta   *here: to turn around, to go around*

doblar   *to turn*

(todo) derecho   *straight ahead*

peligroso, -a   *dangerous*

la cuadra   *(city) block*

Reteach / Extra Help: In connection with mini-dialogue 4, reinforce the difference between *derecho* and *(a la) derecha* by asking questions about familiar locations: *¿Doblo a la derecha para llegar a la (al) _____ o continúo derecho?*

EN OTRAS PARTES

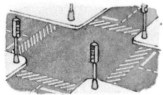

También se dice *el crucero, la bocacalle* y *la encrucijada.*

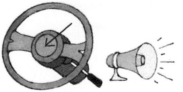

También se dice *el claxón.*

En España se dice *aparcar.*

También se dice *el chofer.*

manejar

También se dice *conducir.*

el permiso de manejar

En España se dice *el carné, la licencia* y *el permiso de conducir.*

doblar

También se dice *torcer.*

PRÁCTICA

A   ¿Por qué?   Cuando Javier maneja el coche sus hermanitos le hacen muchas preguntas. Completa cada una de sus respuestas con la palabra correcta.

1. ¿Dónde cruzan las personas? En *(el carril / la carretera / el paso)* de peatones.
2. ¿Por qué toca ese hombre la bocina? Él es muy *(impaciente / perezoso / peligroso)*.
3. ¿Por qué doblas? Porque quiero ir a aquella tienda y acabo de ver *(un carril / un parquímetro / una regla)*.
4. ¿Cómo se llaman esas luces rojas y verdes? Es *(un semáforo / una cuadra / una multa)*.
5. ¿Dónde vas a doblar? En *(la multa / el tráfico / el cruce de calles)*.
6. ¿Por qué estás tan nervioso? Porque la bocina no *(funciona / dobla / maneja)*.
7. ¿Cómo son los instructores que dan clases de manejar? La mayoría de ellos son muy *(nerviosos / pacientes / peligrosos)*.
8. ¿Cuál es la primera cosa que te dice el instructor? Ponte *(el parquímetro / el cinturón de seguridad / el permiso de manejar)*.
9. ¿Por qué manejas siempre tan despacio? Porque yo *(obtengo / llevo / respeto)* todas las reglas de tráfico.
10. ¿Puedes llevarnos a la casa de Anita esta tarde? No, su casa *(dobla / queda / estaciona)* demasiado lejos de aquí.

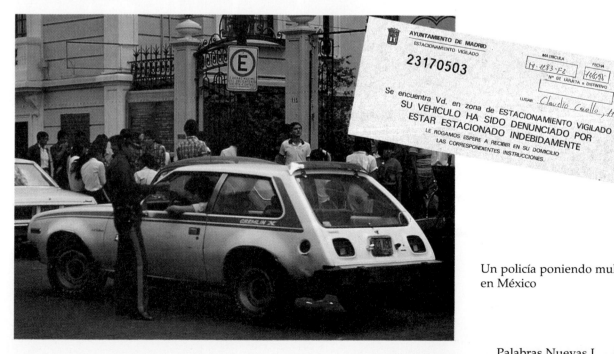

Un policía poniendo multa en México

Práctica B
1. con cuidado
2. poner una multa
3. respetar
4. gente
5. continuar todo derecho
6. velocidad máxima
7. carril
8. vuelta de la esquina
9. semáforo
10. llevar

B La lección de manejar. El Sr. Alvarado le dio a su hijo una lección de manejar. Completa las frases con las palabras de la columna a la derecha.

1. Es peligroso por aquí. ¡Maneja ____!
2. ¡Más despacio! El policía te va a ____.
3. Hay que ____ las señales de tráfico.
4. Siempre hay que parar cuando hay ____ en el paso de peatones.
5. ¿Por qué doblas? Para llegar a la carretera hay que ____.
6. Es peligroso ir más rápido que la ____.
7. Para doblar a la derecha, debes estar en el otro ____.
8. Dobla aquí. Hay parquímetros a la ____.
9. Hay mucho tráfico allí porque el ____ no funciona.
10. ¿Me puedes ____ a casa ahora? Necesito descansar.

carril
con cuidado
continuar todo derecho
gente
llevar
poner una multa
respetar
semáforo
velocidad máxima
vuelta de la esquina

Una lección de manejar en España

C Hablemos de ti.

1. ¿Cuántas personas manejan en tu familia? ¿Quién es el mejor conductor de tu familia? ¿Por qué? ¿Qué debes hacer para ser un(a) buen(a) conductor(a)?

2. ¿Sabes manejar? Si no manejas, ¿quién te lleva a lugares lejos de tu casa?

3. ¿Crees que es fácil o difícil el examen que hay que tomar para obtener el permiso de manejar? ¿Por qué? En el estado donde vives, ¿cuántos años debes tener para obtener el permiso de manejar? En tu escuela, ¿hay clases para aprender a manejar? ¿Cómo son?

4. ¿Siempre respetas las señales de tráfico cuando montas en bicicleta? ¿Qué pasa si no las respetas?

5. Cuando cruzas la calle, ¿siempre usas el paso de peatones? ¿Siempre respetas las señales de tráfico para peatones? ¿Cuáles no respetas? ¿Por qué?

Práctica C
Answers will vary.

Practice Sheet 8–1

Workbook Exs. A–B

Tape Manual Exs. 1–2  3

Quiz 8–1

APLICACIONES

Una lección de manejar 4 5 Pronunciación

En Madrid, España

El instructor le da a Ramón su primera lección de manejar.
Acaban de subir al coche.

INSTRUCTOR Primera lección, Ramón: Hay que ponerse el
cinturón de seguridad. No vayas[1] rápido. Mira
5   siempre adelante,[2] pero presta atención a los otros
coches, a los semáforos, a los peatones, a las . . .

RAMÓN Pero, Sr. López, eso es mucho, yo . . .

INSTRUCTOR No, Ramón. Eso es muy poco. Pero podemos
empezar ahora. Aquí tienes la llave.
10   *(Varios minutos después . . .)*

INSTRUCTOR No vayas tan rápido. Continúa todo derecho hasta
la próxima señal de . . . ¡Cuidado, Ramón, la
bicicleta!

RAMÓN ¿Qué pasó, Sr. López? Yo no vi nada.

15 **INSTRUCTOR** ¡Claro que no! Te dije[3] que tienes que mirar siempre
adelante. Pero hay que saber lo que pasa a tu
derecha, a tu izquierda . . .

RAMÓN Sí, señor, pero no sea[4] impaciente.

INSTRUCTOR Está bien, Ramón. Ahora continúa hasta la esquina.
20   Para. Bueno. Puedes doblar si no viene otro coche.

RAMÓN Señor López, ¿cuándo voy a saber manejar?

INSTRUCTOR Muy pronto, Ramón. Sólo tienes que manejar con
cuidado, conocer las reglas de tráfico, aprender a
doblar y a estacionar bien . . .

---

[1]**no vayas** *don't go*   [2]**adelante** *forward*   [3]**dije** (preterite of **decir**) *told*
[4]**no sea** (negative *Ud.* command form of **ser**) *don't be*

Enrichment: Before
presenting the **Diálogo,** you
may want to ask students to
cover the glosses and to try to
guess the meaning of each of
the words and phrases from the
context.

Culture: Point out to students
that *100 máxima* on the road
sign refers to the speed limit,
which is 100 kilometers per
hour or approximately 60 miles
per hour. Explain that in most
Spanish-speaking countries, as
in most of the world, the metric
system is used.

Preguntas
Contesta según el diálogo.

1. Cuando la gente sube a un coche, ¿qué debe hacer primero? ¿Haces eso tú?   2. ¿Cómo puedes mirar siempre adelante y también prestar atención a otras cosas? ¿Por qué crees que Ramón dice que es mucho? 3. ¿Por qué no vio Ramón la bicicleta?   4. ¿Por qué está impaciente el Sr. López?   5. ¿Cómo crees que está Ramón después de su primera lección?   6. En tu opinión, ¿qué debe hacer Ramón para aprender a manejar?   7. ¿Cuándo piensas aprender a manejar? ¿O ya sabes? ¿Quién te enseñó o cómo piensas aprender?   8. ¿Por qué quiere casi todo el mundo en los Estados Unidos aprender a manejar? En tu opinión, ¿cómo es la vida diaria (*daily*) para la gente que no sabe manejar?

Diálogo
1. Debe ponerse el cinturón de seguridad. / Answers will vary.   2. Usas los espejos. / Answers will vary.   3. No miró adelante.   4. Answers will vary, but may include *porque tiene que repetir todo muchas veces*.   5. Answers will vary, but may include *cansado, nervioso, preocupado, asustado*.   6–8. Answers will vary.

Participación
Work with a partner to make up a dialogue in which you give directions about how to get to each other's house.

PALABRAS NUEVAS II

Essential

Transparency 27

**CONTEXTO
VISUAL**

En la estación de servicio

el accidente

el mecánico

la mecánica

el coche deportivo

la gasolina

**CONTEXTO
COMUNICATIVO**

1	CARMEN	¿Puedo usar el coche hoy?
	PAPÁ	Sí, pero tienes que **llenar** el tanque.
	CARMEN	¿No compraste gasolina ayer?
	PAPÁ	No, me olvidé de hacerlo.

llenar   *to fill (up)*

Variaciones:

■ el coche → la moto

If students ask: Other related words you may want to present: *la grúa,* tow truck; *el limpiaparabrisas,* windshield wiper; *el asiento delantero,* front seat; *el asiento trasero,* back seat; *la palanca de cambio,* gearshift.

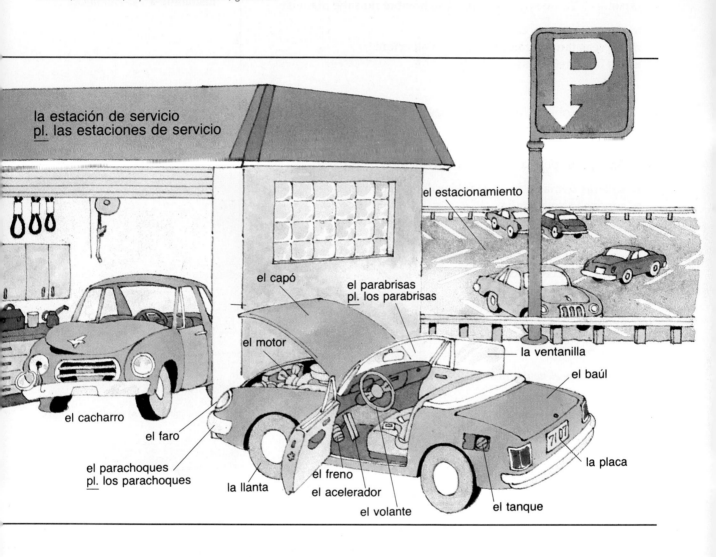

la estación de servicio
pl. las estaciones de servicio

el estacionamiento

el capó

el parabrisas
pl. los parabrisas

el motor

la ventanilla

el baúl

el cacharro

el faro

la placa

el parachoques
pl. los parachoques

la llanta

el freno

el acelerador

el volante

el tanque

---

2 ALFONSO ¿De quién es ese coche deportivo? **El tuyo** es mucho más viejo, ¿verdad?

CECILIA Sí, **el mío** es un cacharro. A veces no **arranca.**

ALFONSO ¿Y qué dice tu mecánico?

CECILIA Que necesito un coche nuevo.

■ el tuyo → tu coche
■ el mío → mi coche
    un coche nuevo → uno nuevo

el tuyo, la tuya *yours*

el mío, la mía *mine*
arrancar *to start (a car)*

3 CLARA   ¡Cuidado, Jaime! Casi **chocaste con** esa moto. ¡No seas tan **distraído**!

JAIME   Yo no soy distraído. Ese hombre no sabe manejar.

- esa moto → ese camión
- ¡no seas tan distraído! → ¡presta atención!
- ese hombre → ese conductor

chocar (con)   *to hit (something), to bump (into), to crash (into)*
distraído, -a   *absent-minded*

4 LUISA   Roberto, **aceleras** demasiado.

ROBERTO   ¿Por qué estás tan nerviosa? Este coche tiene buenos frenos.

LUISA   Sí, pero a veces no tienes tiempo para parar.

- aceleras demasiado → manejas demasiado rápido
- nerviosa → asustada

acelerar   *to speed up, to accelerate*

EN OTRAS PARTES

También se dice *el neumático* y *la goma*.

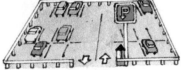

En España se dice *el aparcamiento* o *el parqueo*.

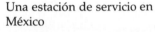
Una estación de servicio en México

En muchos países se dice *la gasolinera*.

También se dice *la cajuela, la maletera, el maletero* y *el portaequipaje(s)*.

En España se dice *la (placa de) matrícula*. En Cuba se dice *la chapa*.

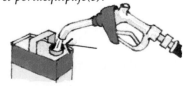

En la Argentina se dice *la nafta*.

PRÁCTICA

A Mecánicos. En la clase para aprender a manejar el instructor le dice a cada estudiante lo que tiene que hacer. ¿Qué mandato le da a cada estudiante? Sigue el modelo.

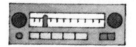

Mario / apagar
Mario, apaga el radio.

1. Rosa / encender

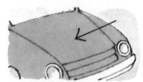

2. Diego / examinar

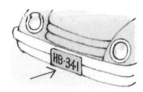

3. Esteban / limpiar

4. Sara / levantar

5. Ana / tomar

6. Jorge / llenar

7. Tomás / abrir

8. Ester / lavar

9. Vicente / encender

En Bogotá, Colombia

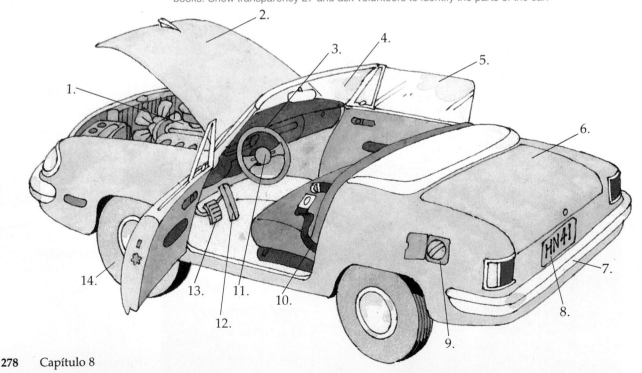

Práctica B
1. Segundo, Raúl olvidó el …
2. Tercero, él no llenó …
3. Cuarto, Raúl y Pilar no encontraron una …
4. Quinto, Raúl no respetó la …
5. Sexto, los frenos no funcionaron …
6. Séptimo, Raúl y Pilar no doblaron …
7. Octavo, Raúl chocó …
8. Noveno, Raúl y Pilar llegaron al …

Práctica C
1. el motor
2. el capó
3. el volante
4. el parabrisas
5. la ventanilla
6. el baúl
7. el parachoques
8. la placa
9. el tanque
10. el cinturón de seguridad
11. la bocina
12. el acelerador
13. el freno
14. la llanta

B **Un viaje difícil.** Raúl y Pilar fueron al aeropuerto a buscar a sus padres, pero fue un viaje lleno de problemas. Completa las frases con el pretérito del verbo correcto. Sigue el modelo.

> Primero, el coche no (*arrancar / estacionar / chocar*).
> *Primero, el coche no arrancó.*

1. Segundo, Raúl (*respetar / olvidar / doblar*) el permiso de manejar.
2. Tercero, él no (*manejar / llenar / gastar*) el tanque.
3. Cuarto, Raúl y Pilar no (*encontrar / tocar / llevar*) una estación de servicio.
4. Quinto, Raúl no (*cruzar / respetar / acelerar*) la velocidad máxima.
5. Sexto, los frenos no (*llenar / manejar / funcionar*) bien.
6. Séptimo, Raúl y Pilar no (*doblar / quedar / tardar*) a tiempo.
7. Octavo, Raúl (*chocar / encontrar / cruzar*) con otro coche.
8. Noveno, Raúl y Pilar (*devolver / estacionar / llegar*) al aeropuerto con mucho retraso.

C **¿Qué es?** Los estudiantes que toman el examen para obtener el permiso de manejar tienen que identificar las partes del coche. Identifica cada parte en español.

Notes: In connection with Ex. C, you may want to ask students to work with closed books. Show transparency 27 and ask volunteers to identify the parts of the car.

D Hablemos de ti.

1. ¿Tiene coche tu familia? ¿Cómo es? ¿De qué color es? ¿Puedes describir tu coche favorito?
2. ¿Prefieres los coches pequeños o los grandes? ¿Por qué? ¿Prefieres los coches con baúles grandes o pequeños? ¿Por qué? Para ti, ¿cuál es la cosa más importante que un coche debe tener?
3. ¿Prefieres los coches deportivos o los cacharros? ¿Por qué?

Práctica D
Answers will vary.

Practice Sheet 8–2

Workbook Exs. C–D

Tape Manual Exs. 3–4  8

Refrán [▭] 9

Quiz 8–2

ACTIVIDAD

Un coche nuevo. With a partner, create and draw a picture of a new, advanced car and label all the parts. Then get together with other pairs of students and describe your car, explaining any unusual features you came up with.

ESTUDIO DE PALABRAS

Palabras compuestas:

A word that is made by combining two or more other words is called a compound word: For example, thumbnail, snowman, brother-in-law.

Spanish, too, has *palabras compuestas.* Can you tell what two words are combined to make each of these compound words?

el parabrisas	el tocadiscos	el salvavidas
el parachoques	el lavaplatos	el paraguas
el abrelatas	el sujetapapeles	el sacapuntas

You know what most of those individual words mean. What do you think *brisa, choque, sujetar, salvar,* and *sacar + punta* mean?

Palabras compuestas
parar + brisa *(breeze)*
parar + choque *(bump, crash)*
abrir + lata
tocar + disco
lavar + plato
sujetar *(to fasten)* + papel
salvar *(to save)* + vida
parar + agua
sacar *(to bring out)* + punta *(point)*

Antónimos

Cambia las palabras en cursiva por un antónimo.

1. Nuestro instructor es una persona muy *paciente.*
2. La estación de servicio queda por *aquí.*
3. *Los conductores* deben respetar las reglas de tráfico.
4. Pon el pie en *el freno* para *parar.*

Antónimos
1. impaciente
2. allí
3. los peatones
4. el acelerador / acelerar

Palabras Nuevas II   **279**

EXPLICACIONES I

Los mandatos negativos con *tú*

◆ **OBJECTIVES:**

TO TELL PEOPLE NOT TO DO THINGS

TO REQUEST AND GIVE ADVICE

TO CONTRADICT

TO SHOW IMPATIENCE

You know that to form regular affirmative *tú* commands we simply use the *Ud.* / *él* / *ella* form of the present tense. To tell someone *not* to do something we use a negative command, which has a very different form.

Habla con el mecánico, Luis.	*Talk to the mechanic, Luis.*
No hables ahora, Luis.	*Don't talk now, Luis.*

To form negative *tú* commands with regular verbs, we drop the *o* of the present-tense *yo* form and add the following endings. For -*ar* verbs we add -*es*; for -*er* and -*ir* verbs we add -*as*.

CANTAR	cantø → cant + **es**	**No cantes** ahora.	*Don't sing now.*
COMER	comø → com + **as**	**No comas** eso.	*Don't eat that.*
ABRIR	abrø → abr + **as**	**No abras** esto.	*Don't open this.*

1   Stem-changing verbs follow the same rule.

En Panamá

o → ue
CONTAR
cuentø → cuent + **es**   **No cuentes** todavía.   *Don't count yet.*

e → ie
ENCENDER
enciendø → enciend + **as**   **No enciendas** eso.   *Don't light that.*

e → i
REPETIR
repitø → repit + **as**   **No repitas** eso.   *Don't repeat that.*

2   Verbs ending in -*car*, -*gar*, and -*zar* have the following spelling changes in order to maintain the original sound.

-car (c → qu)
TOCAR
tocø → toqu + **es**   **No toques** el piano.   *Don't play the piano.*

-gar (g → gu)
LLEGAR
llegø → llegu + **es**   **No llegues** tarde.   *Don't arrive late.*

-zar (z → c)
CRUZAR
cruzø → cruc + **es**   **No cruces** aquí.   *Don't cross here.*

3 Remember that verbs ending in *-ger* already have a spelling change in the *yo* form.

ESCOGER

escoj∅ → escoj + **as**   **No escojas** todavía.   *Don't choose yet.*

RECOGER

recoj∅ → recoj + **as**   **No recojas** eso.   *Don't pick that up.*

PRÁCTICA

A ¡No, no, no! Imagina que cuidas a un(a) niño(a) que siempre quiere hacer cosas que no debe hacer. Tú le dices que no. Sigue el modelo.

atar eso
No ates eso.

1. patinar en el pasillo	6. enchufar el proyector
2. bajar al sótano	7. bañar al gato
3. desenchufar la tostadora	8. tirar esas salchichas
4. llenar ese vaso	9. asustar a los peces
5. cortar el cordón eléctrico	10. afeitar al perro

B De camping. Imagina que vas de camping con dos amigos. Cuando les preguntas qué debes hacer, ellos nunca están de acuerdo. Sigue el modelo.

abrir las latas
ESTUDIANTE A   *¿Abro las latas?*
ESTUDIANTE B   *Sí, ábrelas ahora.*
ESTUDIANTE C   *No, no abras las latas todavía.*

1. barrer la tienda de acampar	5. servir el pescado
2. encender el fuego	6. comer el postre
3. hervir el agua	7. devolver las linternas
4. añadir el ajo	8. recoger los platos

Tráfico en el Paseo de la Reforma, México

Práctica A
1. No patines en …
2. No bajes al …
3. No desenchufes la …
4. No llenes ese …
5. No cortes el …
6. No enchufes el …
7. No bañes al …
8. No tires esas …
9. No asustes a los …
10. No afeites …

Notes: Before students break into pairs to do Ex. B, tell them not to use object pronouns in *Estudiante C*'s negative responses. Object pronouns with negative *tú* commands will be practiced in Level III.

Práctica B
1. ¿Barro la tienda de acampar? Sí, bárrela ahora. No, no barras …
2. ¿Enciendo el fuego? Sí, enciéndelo. No, no enciendas …
3. ¿Hiervo el agua? Sí, hiérvela. No, no hiervas …
4. ¿Añado el ajo? Sí, añádelo. No, no añadas …
5. ¿Sirvo el pescado? Sí, sírvelo. No, no sirvas …
6. ¿Como el postre? Sí, cómelo. No, no comas …
7. ¿Devuelvo las linternas? Sí, devuélvelas. No, no devuelvas …
8. ¿Recojo los platos? Sí, recógelos. No, no recojas …

Práctica C

Exclamations will vary.
1. ... No apagues ...
2. ... No comiences ...
3. ... No choques ...
4. ... No toques ...
5. ... No cruces ...
6. ... No coloques ...
7. ... No empieces ...
8. ... No expliques ...
9. ... No juegues ...

C El pasajero nervioso. Paco acaba de obtener el permiso de manejar. ¿Qué consejos *(advice)* le da su hermano mayor? Escoge una expresión de la lista de la derecha. Sigue el modelo.

> pagar demasiado por la gasolina
> *¡Oye! No pagues demasiado por la gasolina.*

1. apagar el motor antes de parar
2. comenzar a llenar el tanque
3. chocar con el parquímetro
4. tocar la bocina tan frecuentemente
5. cruzar cuando hay gente en el paso de peatones
6. colocar las llaves en el baúl
7. empezar a doblar todavía
8. explicar todas las reglas
9. jugar con el cinturón de seguridad

¡ay, chico!
¡caramba!
¡cuidado!
¡oye!
por favor
¡qué barbaridad!
¡qué susto!
¡uf!

Práctica D

1. No esquíes.
2. No juegues al fútbol.
3. No bucees.
4. No remes.
5. No corras.
6. No rías.
7. No toques la guitarra.
8. No saques fotos.
9. No duermas.

Enrichment: You may want to expand on the practice in Ex. D by asking students to work in pairs to create four or five signs illustrating additional negative *tú* commands. Pairs should then exchange drawings and guess what command is depicted on each sign.

Practice Sheet 8–3

📼 10 Tape Manual Ex. 5

Quiz 8–3

D No puedes hacerlo. ¿Qué quieren decir estas señales nuevas?

No bailes.

1.

2.

3.

4.

5.

6.

7.

8.

9.

Otros mandatos negativos con *tú*

1 All verbs whose present-tense *yo* form ends in *-go* form their negative *tú* commands according to the regular rule. We drop the *o* and add *-es* for *-ar* verbs and *-as* for *-er* / *-ir* verbs.

TENER
tengø → **teng + as**   **No tengas miedo.**   *Don't be afraid.*

VENIR
vengø → **veng + as**   **No vengas** solo.   *Don't come alone.*

DECIR
digø → **dig + as**   **No digas** eso.   *Don't say that.*

HACER
hagø → **hag + as**   **No hagas** nada más.   *Don't do anything more.*

TRAER
traigø → **traig + as**   **No traigas** eso.   *Don't bring that.*

PONER
pongø → **pong + as**   **No pongas** eso allí.   *Don't put that there.*

SALIR
salgø → **salg + as**   **No salgas** ahora.   *Don't leave now.*

2 The following verbs have irregular negative *tú* command forms.

DAR   → **No des la vuelta** aquí.   *Don't turn around here.*
ESTAR → **No estés** tan nervioso.   *Don't be so nervous.*
IR   → **No vayas** al cine.   *Don't go to the movies.*
SER   → **No seas** tímido.   *Don't be shy.*

PRÁCTICA

A   En la feria.   Imagina que estás en la feria y visitas a una adivinadora *(fortune teller)*. ¿Qué consejos *(advice)* te da? Sigue el modelo.

> hacer un viaje mañana
> *No hagas un viaje mañana.*

1. poner dinero en el banco esta semana
2. salir sin visitar todos los puestos
3. tener miedo de decir la verdad
4. hacer planes para el jueves
5. salir el sábado por la noche
6. decir a tus amigos lo que te cuento
7. traer cheques de viajero la próxima vez
8. venir aquí sin dinero

◆ OBJECTIVES:

TO GIVE ADVICE

TO SUGGEST ALTERNATIVE ACTIONS

TO TELL PEOPLE WHAT TO DO AND WHAT NOT TO DO

Notes: Refer to mini-dialogues 1 and 2 on p. 267 and 3 on p. 276 as well as the **Diálogo** on p. 272 for examples of irregular negative *tú* commands.

Reteach / Extra Help: You may want to reinforce the irregular negative *tú* commands by asking volunteers to suggest additional examples with each of the four verbs.

Práctica A
1. No pongas dinero en el banco …
2. No salgas …
3. No tengas miedo …
4. No hagas planes …
5. No salgas …
6. No digas …
7. No traigas …
8. No vengas …

Práctica B
1. No seas tan distraído. Mira el semáforo.
2. No vayas al parque todavía. Corta el césped.
3. No des de comer al perro. Cena tú primero.
4. No seas tan impaciente. Termina tu cena.
5. No estés tan triste. Sonríe un poco.
6. No pongas los pies en la mesa. Sé bueno.
7. No vayas a la calle. Ven conmigo.
8. No des excusas tontas. Sal a tiempo.
9. No estés tan asustado. Sé más valiente.

Práctica C
1. No hagas eso. Haz cola.
2. No estés preocupado. Está contento.
3. No vayas solo. Ve con los otros.
4. No vengas hoy. Ven mañana.
5. No digas eso. Di la verdad.
6. No seas tonto. Sé listo.
7. No salgas ahora. Sal más tarde.
8. No traigas regalos. Trae comida.

Práctica D
Answers will vary.

Practice Sheet 8–4

Workbook Exs. E–F

 11 Tape Manual Ex. 6

Quiz 8–4

B **En casa.** ¿Qué le dice Bernardo a su hermanito? Sigue el modelo.

> dar un paseo ahora / hacer la tarea
> *No des un paseo ahora. Haz la tarea.*

1. ser tan distraído / mirar el semáforo
2. ir al parque todavía / cortar el césped
3. dar de comer al perro / cenar tú primero
4. ser tan impaciente / terminar tu cena
5. estar tan triste / sonreír un poco
6. poner los pies en la mesa / ser bueno
7. ir a la calle / venir conmigo
8. dar excusas tontas / salir a tiempo
9. estar tan asustado / ser más valiente

C **¡Escúchame!** La abuela de Diego siempre le dice qué hacer. ¿Qué le dice? Sigue el modelo.

> tener miedo / cuidado
> *No tengas miedo. Ten cuidado.*

1. hacer eso / cola
2. estar preocupado / contento
3. ir solo / con los otros
4. venir hoy / mañana
5. decir eso / la verdad
6. ser tonto / listo
7. salir ahora / más tarde
8. traer regalos / comida

D **Hablemos de ti.**
1. Cuando comes con tus padres, ¿qué clase de mandatos te dan?
2. Si tienes que estudiar para un examen, ¿qué no debes hacer, según tus padres?
3. En la escuela, ¿qué no debes hacer? ¿Qué te dicen tus profesores? ¿Qué te dicen tus compañeros?
4. Si un(a) amigo(a) aprende a manejar, ¿qué no debe hacer? ¿Qué le dices tú?

En el Paseo de la Reforma, México

APLICACIONES

Discretionary

Marta, la mecánica 12

A Marta no le interesan ni la ropa nueva ni la música popular. A ella sólo le encantan los coches. Cuando Marta era[1] muy pequeña, le gustaba[2] jugar con los cochecitos.[3] Más tarde, cuando aprendió a leer, comenzó a buscar libros y revistas sobre los coches. Entonces empezó a ayudar a su padre a
5 arreglar el cacharro viejo de la familia.

Cuando el padre de Marta compró un coche nuevo, le dio el cacharro a ella, y desde ese momento Marta pasó todo su tiempo libre con ese coche viejo. Era su pasatiempo favorito. Trabajó días y semanas con el motor. ¡Quién sabe cuántas partes le[4] cambió!

10 Después de arreglar el motor, compró de segunda mano[5] los parachoques y las llantas de coches de otros modelos. Luego fue necesario comprar frenos nuevos. Su padre le prestó el dinero y su hermano la ayudó a poner todo en su lugar. Por fin el cacharro funcionó maravillosamente. Pero, era tan feo que la madre de Marta la ayudó a pintarlo.[6] Y ahora la gente no
15 puede creer lo que ve. No es un cacharro. ¡Es casi como un coche deportivo!

---

[1]**era** (from **ser**)   *was*   [2]**le gustaba** (from **gustar**)   *she used to like*
[3]**los cochecitos**   *toy cars*   [4]**le**   here: *on it*   [5]**de segunda mano**   *second-hand*
[6]**pintar**   *to paint*

Preguntas

Usa las frases de la columna de la derecha para completar las de la izquierda. Luego pon las frases completas en el orden correcto.

1. A Marta le encantan . . .
2. Nadie . . .
3. Marta trabaja con su cacharro . . .
4. El papá de Marta . . .
5. Su hermano y ella . . .
6. Le gusta leer . . .
7. Marta y su mamá . . .
8. Tiene que comprar . . .

a. lo pintan.
b. ponen todo en orden.
c. frenos nuevos.
d. sobre los coches.
e. puede creer que esto era un cacharro viejo.
f. por mucho tiempo.
g. todos los coches.
h. obtiene un coche nuevo.

En Madrid, España

EXPLICACIONES II Essential

Los adjetivos posesivos

TO REFER TO PEOPLE WHOM THE LISTENER DOES NOT KNOW

TO REFER TO PEOPLE WHOM YOU DON'T WANT TO IDENTIFY

Remember that possessive adjectives agree in number with the nouns they describe.

mi / tu / su $\begin{cases} \text{instructor} \\ \text{instructora} \end{cases}$ **mis / tus / sus** $\begin{cases} \text{instructores} \\ \text{instructoras} \end{cases}$

Nuestro and *vuestro* agree in gender as well as number.

nuestro entrenador   nuestros entrenadores
nuestra entrenadora   nuestras entrenadoras

1 Since *su* and *sus* have many meanings, for clarity or emphasis we can use a prepositional phrase instead.

de $\begin{cases} \text{Ud.} \\ \text{él} \\ \text{ella} \end{cases}$ **de** $\begin{cases} \text{Uds.} \\ \text{ellos} \\ \text{ellas} \end{cases}$

¡**Sus** cuadros son maravillosos!	*(His / Her / Your / Their)* paintings *are marvelous.*
¿Los cuadros **de ellos**?	***Their*** *paintings?*
No, los cuadros **de Ud.**	*No,* ***your*** *paintings.*

2 Like English, Spanish has another set of possessive adjectives that come *after* the noun. Compare these pairs of sentences.

Es **mi** prima.	*She's* ***my*** *cousin.*
Es una prima **mía**.	*She's a cousin* ***of mine.***
Invito a **nuestros** amigos.	*I'm inviting* ***our*** *friends.*
Invito a unos amigos **nuestros**.	*I'm inviting some friends* ***of ours.***

We also use these forms for emphasis. Note that they agree in number and gender with the nouns they refer to.

Estas son nuestras ofertas de la semana.

MODELO	AÑO	PRECIO
PEUGEOT 205 SR	1985	865.000
PEUGEOT 505 GL	1985	1.155.000
RENAULT 11 GTL	1986	1.085.000
CORSA TR 4P	1986	875.000
CAPRI 2.0 EXTRAS	1981	1.155.000
BX 16 TRS (A.A.)	1985	1.155.000
ESCORT 1.3 GL	1986	985.000
VISA CHALLENGER	1986	725.000
ESCORT 1.1	1983	695.000

Vehículos revisados en todos sus puntos vitales. Con 3 meses de garantía. Con 6 meses de asistencia gratuita. Y con planes de financiación a su medida.
     Venga a probarlos y lo comprobará. Nuestros vehículos están preparados para todo.

VAYA SOBRE SEGURO. VENGA A NUESTRO CONCESIONARIO.

SELIAUTO

Ctra. de Madrid a Leganés, Km. 3,700
Tel. 686 18 88 - LEGANES (Madrid)

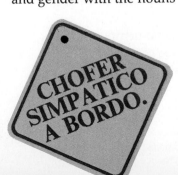

Here are the possessive adjectives that follow a noun.

mío(s), mía(s)	*my, (of) mine*	**nuestro(s), nuestra(s)**	*our, (of) ours*
tuyo(s), tuya(s)	*your, (of) yours*	vuestro(s), vuestra(s)	*your, (of) yours*
suyo(s), suya(s)	*your, (of) yours* *his, (of) his* *her, (of) hers*	**suyo(s), suya(s)**	*your, (of) yours* *their, (of) theirs*

3   To clarify or emphasize, we can use *de* + a prepositional pronoun instead of a form of *suyo*.

¿Es el boleto **suyo**?   *Is it (**his / her / your / their**) ticket?*
Sí, es el boleto **de ella**.   *Yes, it's **her** ticket.*

4   We can also use these forms of the possessive adjectives after *ser*.

¿De quién es este velero?   *Whose sailboat is this?*
Es nuestro.   ***It's ours.***

Esas placas son **tuyas**, ¿verdad?   *Those license plates are **yours**, right?*
Sí, **son mías**.   *Yes, **they're mine**.*

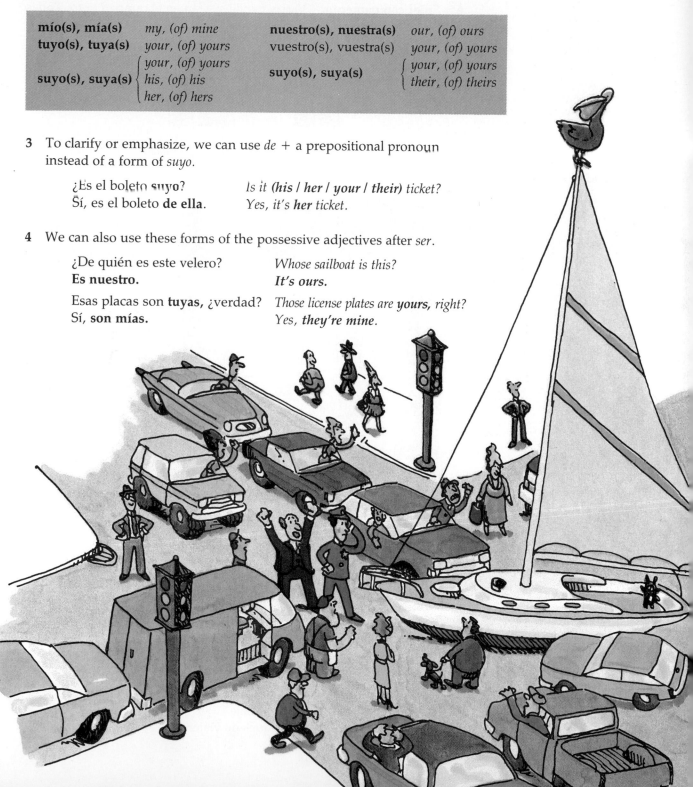

Práctica A

1. Estos cepillos son tuyos, ¿verdad? No, no son míos. Son de ellos.
2. Este esmalte de uñas es tuyo, ¿verdad? No, no es mío. Es de ella.
3. Esta maquinilla de afeitar es tuya, ¿verdad? No, no es mía. Es de él.
4. Esta crema de afeitar es tuya, ¿verdad? No, no es mía. Es de Uds.
5. Este desodorante es tuyo, ¿verdad? No, no es mío. Es de ella.
6. Esta lima de uñas es tuya, ¿verdad? No, no es mía. Es de Ud.
7. Estas tijeras son tuyas, ¿verdad? No, no son mías. Son de él.
8. Estos lápices de labios son tuyos, ¿verdad? No, no son míos. Son de ellas.

Práctica B

1. ¿Son suyas estas diapositivas? Sí, son nuestras.
2. ¿Es suya esta plancha? Sí, es nuestra.
3. ¿Son suyos estos boletos? Sí, son nuestros.
4. ¿Son suyas estas raquetas de tenis? Sí, son nuestras.
5. ¿Es suyo este maquillaje? Sí, es nuestro.
6. ¿Son suyos estos cheques de viajero? Sí, son nuestros.
7. ¿Son suyos estos perfumes? Sí, son nuestros.
8. ¿Es suya esta canasta? Sí, es nuestra.
9. ¿Es suyo este secador? Sí, es nuestro.

PRÁCTICA

A En el campamento. Varias familias están en el campamento. Todas sus cosas están mezcladas (*mixed up*). ¿De quiénes son estas cosas?

ESTUDIANTE A   *Estos peines son tuyos, ¿verdad?*
ESTUDIANTE B   *No, no son míos. Son de ellas.*

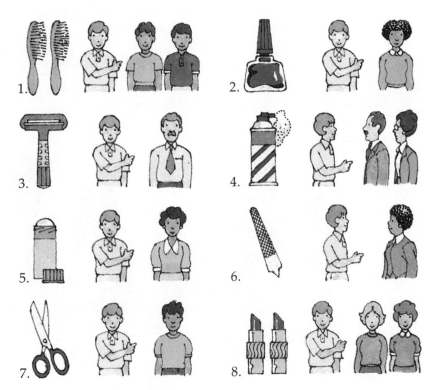

1.
2.
3.
4.
5.
6.
7.
8.

B En la aduana (*customs*). Imagina que tú y tu familia regresan de México y pasan por la aduana. ¿Qué les pregunta el inspector? ¿Qué le contestan Uds.? Sigue el modelo.

ESTUDIANTE A   *¿Es suyo este equipaje?*
ESTUDIANTE B   *Sí, es nuestro.*

1. diapositivas
2. plancha
3. boletos
4. raquetas de tenis
5. maquillaje
6. cheques de viajero
7. perfumes
8. canasta
9. secador

C ¿Con quién van? Hay una gran fiesta este fin de semana. ¿Con quién va cada persona? Sigue los modelos.

Carolina / un primo
ESTUDIANTE A *¿Con quién va Carolina?*
ESTUDIANTE B *Va con un primo suyo.*

Uds. / una prima
ESTUDIANTE A *¿Con quién van Uds.?*
ESTUDIANTE B *Vamos con una prima nuestra.*

1. (tú) / una amiga
2. Raquel / unos amigos
3. Uds. / un sobrino
4. Enrique / unas primas
5. Ud. / unos alumnos
6. tú y Javier / unas compañeras
7. Nicolás y Ángel / unas invitadas
8. Leonor y David / una tía

Practice Sheet 8–5 **13 Tape Manual Ex. 7 Quiz 8–5**

Práctica C
1. ¿Con quién vas?
   Voy con una amiga mía.
2. ¿… va Raquel?
   Va con unos amigos suyos.
3. ¿… van Uds.?
   Vamos con un sobrino nuestro.
4. ¿… va Enrique?
   Va con unas primas suyas.
5. ¿… va Ud.?
   Voy con unos alumnos míos.
6. ¿… van tú y Javier?
   Vamos con unas compañeras nuestras.
7. ¿… van Nicolás y Ángel?
   Van con unas invitadas suyas.
8. ¿… van Leonor y David?
   Van con una tía suya.

Entre la Argentina y Chile

Explicaciones II **289**

Los pronombres posesivos

◆ OBJECTIVES:

TO DIVIDE THINGS UP AMONG PEOPLE

TO CATEGORIZE ACCORDING TO OWNERSHIP

TO COMPARE AND CONTRAST

Notes: Mini-dialogue 2 on p. 275 contains examples of possessive pronouns.

A possessive pronoun takes the place of a noun and a possessive adjective.

Me quedo en mi carril y tú te quedas en **el tuyo**.	*I'll stay in my lane and you stay in **yours**.*
Nuestras maletas están en el baúl. ¿Tiene Eva **la suya**?	*Our suitcases are in the trunk. Does Eva have **hers**?*

To form a possessive pronoun, we simply put the appropriate definite article before the long form of the possessive adjective. For example: *el mío, la mía, los míos, las mías*. Remember that after the verb *ser* we say *es mío, es tuya*, etc., without the definite article.

PRÁCTICA

A ¿Me prestas . . . ? Imagina que estás en el club deportivo y le pides a tu compañero(a) varias cosas suyas. Sigue el modelo.

> toalla
> ESTUDIANTE A *No encuentro mi toalla. ¿Me prestas la tuya?*
> ESTUDIANTE B *¿La mía? Está bien.*
> o: *¿La mía? No, no puedo.*

1. anteojos de sol	5. raqueta
2. sombrilla	6. revistas de deportes
3. secador	7. cinturón
4. calcetines limpios	8. pelotas de tenis

B ¡El nuestro también! Varios alumnos hablan de sus escuelas. Sigue el modelo.

> equipo de béisbol / formidable
> ESTUDIANTE A *Nuestro equipo de béisbol es formidable.*
> *¿Y el suyo?*
> ESTUDIANTE B *El nuestro también.*

1. profesores / excelente
2. biblioteca / enorme
3. entrenador de natación / muy estricto
4. clases de historia / interesante
5. bailes / fabuloso
6. gimnasio / magnífico
7. laboratorios / muy moderno
8. directora / muy simpático
9. club de español / popular

Práctica A
1. No encuentro mis anteojos de sol. ¿Me prestas los tuyos? ¿Los míos? …
2. … mi sombrilla. ¿… la tuya? ¿La mía? …
3. … mi secador. ¿… el tuyo? ¿El mío? …
4. … mis calcetines limpios. ¿… los tuyos? ¿Los míos?…
5. … mi raqueta. ¿… la tuya? ¿La mía? …
6. … mis revistas de deportes. ¿… las tuyas? ¿Las mías? …
7. … mi cinturón. ¿… el tuyo? ¿El mío? …
8. … mis pelotas de tenis. ¿… las tuyas? ¿Las mías? …

Práctica B
1. Nuestros profesores son excelentes. ¿Y los suyos? Los nuestros también.
2. Nuestra biblioteca es enorme. ¿Y la suya? La nuestra también.
3. Nuestro entrenador de natación es muy estricto. ¿Y el suyo? El nuestro también.
4. Nuestras clases de historia son interesantes. ¿Y las suyas? Las nuestras también.

C **¡Qué hotel!** El dueño de este hotel nunca sabe dónde están las cosas. Pregunta y contesta según el modelo.

> el equipaje del Sr. Palacios / en su cuarto
> ESTUDIANTE A *¿Dónde está el equipaje del Sr. Palacios?*
> ESTUDIANTE B *El suyo está en su cuarto.*

1. el pasaporte de la Dra. Ramos / con los otros pasaportes
2. las mantas de estas señoras / en el armario del cuarto de ellas
3. la máquina de escribir del gerente / descompuesta y no funciona
4. la cuenta del Sr. Vidal / aquí en la recepción
5. el horario de la gerente / allá en la pared
6. los cheques de viajero del profesor Vidal / en su mano
7. el equipaje de la familia Vidal / en el estacionamiento
8. las llantas nuevas del coche del guía / en el sótano con las otras nuevas

D **Hablemos de ti.**

1. ¿Les prestas tu ropa a tus hermanos o amigos? ¿Qué les prestas? Y ellos, ¿te prestan la suya? ¿Qué te prestan?
2. Si tienes amigos en otra escuela, ¿cómo es la escuela de ellos? ¿Puedes compararla con la tuya?
3. ¿Son estrictos los padres de tus amigos? Y los tuyos, ¿cómo son? ¿Quiénes son más estrictos, los tuyos o los suyos?
4. ¿Viven algunos de tus amigos en otra ciudad? ¿Cuál? ¿Dónde crees que es más divertido vivir, en la ciudad tuya o en la suya? ¿Por qué? Si conoces la ciudad de ellos, ¿cómo es? ¿Cómo es la tuya?

Practice Sheet 8–6   Workbook Exs. G–J

📼 **14 Tape Manual Ex. 8**   📼 **15 Refrán**

📼 **16 Canción**   **Quiz 8–6**

ACTIVIDAD

Los míos también   Get together in groups of three or four. Thinking of an article of clothing (pants, for example), one person begins by saying *Los míos son azules.* A second person, who thinks he or she knows what is being referred to, might say *Los míos también* or *Los míos son negros* or, pointing to another group member, *Los suyos también.* If the second person answers correctly, the first student says, for example, *Sí, los tuyos también.* If the answer is incorrect, the first student might say *No, los tuyos no son azules. Son marrones.* The first person to guess what the article of clothing is begins the next round.

5. Nuestros bailes son fabulosos. ¿Y los suyos? Los nuestros también.
6. Nuestro gimnasio es magnífico. ¿Y el suyo? El nuestro también.
7. Nuestros laboratorios son muy modernos. ¿Y los suyos? Los nuestros también.
8. Nuestra directora es muy simpática. ¿Y la suya? La nuestra también.
0. Nuestro club de español es popular. ¿Y el suyo? El nuestro también.

Práctica C
1. ¿Dónde está el pasaporte de la Dra. Ramos? El suyo está con los otros pasaportes.
2. Las suyas …
3. La suya …
4. La suya …
5. El suyo …
6. Los suyos …
7. El suyo …
8. Las suyas …

Práctica D
Answers will vary.

APLICACIONES

REPASO

Notes: Review of:
1. present tense of -*ar* verbs
   noun phrases with *de*
   expressions with *tener*
2. preterite of -*ar* verbs
   demonstrative adjectives
   long form of possessive
      adjectives
   indirect object pronouns
3. negative *tú* commands
   tan + adjective / adverb
4. indirect object pronouns
   present tense of *decir*
   affirmative *tú* command of
      ser
   adjective agreement
   negative *tú* commands
   demonstrative adjectives
5. preterite of -*ar* and -*er*
      verbs
   possessive adjectives
   e → ie stem-changing verbs
   possessive pronouns

Enrichment: You may want to use the model sentences in the **Repaso** for dictation.

Mira las frases modelo. Luego cambia las frases que siguen al español según los modelos.

1. *Cristina para en la estación de servicio. Tiene cuidado.*
   (We stop at traffic signs. We're lucky.)
   (They cross at the crosswalk. They're careful.)
   (I speed up in the left-hand lane. I'm in a hurry.)

2. *"¿Dónde compró Ud. esas llantas suyas?" le pregunta el mecánico.*
   ("When did you (formal) clean that car of yours?" I ask the driver.)
   ("Where did you cash those checks of yours?" your mom asks you (fam.).)
   ("When did you pay that fine of mine?" she asks us.)

3. *"No salgas tan temprano," digo yo.*
   ("Don't turn so slowly," says the instructor.)
   ("Don't be so impatient," says the librarian (fem.).)
   ("Don't arrive too late," says my father.)

4. *Luego le dice: "Sé amable. No hagas esas preguntas."*
   (Then we say to him: "Be smart. Don't repeat that joke.")
   (Later the teacher (masc.) says to her: "Be good. Don't lose those notes.")
   (Now I say to him: "Be optimistic. Don't say those things.")

5. *"Olvidé las llaves," dice mi hermano. "¿Tienes las tuyas?"*
   ("I didn't use your perfume," says her niece. "I prefer hers.")
   ("Did you lose your hair dryer?" we ask. "Do you want ours?")
   ("Did you (formal) break your racket?" the coach asks. "Do you want mine?")

Lavando el coche en Málaga, España

Escribe las frases en español.

1. Carlota and her mother are in the department store parking lot. They're in a hurry.

2. "Where did you park that jalopy of yours?" her mother asks her.

3. "Don't drive so fast," says her mother.

4. Then she says to her: "Be patient. Don't honk that horn."

5. "I forgot my purse," Carlota says. "Do you have yours?"

REDACCIÓN

Ahora escoge uno de los siguientes temas para escribir tu propio diálogo o párrafo.

1. Expand the *Tema* by writing a paragraph about Carlota. How does she drive? Does she wear a seatbelt? Does she obey all the traffic laws? In your opinion, is she a good driver?

2. Write a paragraph in which you describe your ideal car. Is it a sports car? A jalopy? Describe the way it looks outside and inside. Who fixes it when it doesn't run well?

3. Imagine that you are teaching someone to drive. List at least three things you would tell your student to do and three things not to do.

COMPRUEBA TU PROGRESO CAPÍTULO 8 Discretionary

Notes: Answers to the **Comprueba** appear in the Teacher Notes.

A El coche

Haz mandatos con *tú* según el dibujo. Sigue el modelo.

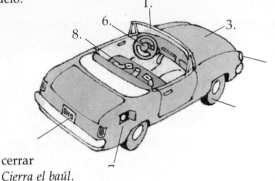

cerrar
Cierra el baúl.

1. limpiar
2. leer
3. abrir
4. encender
5. cambiar
6. tocar
7. llenar
8. ponerse

B No hagas lo que no quieres hacer

Haz mandatos con *tú* según el modelo.

No quiero estar tan nervioso.
Pues, no estés tan nervioso.

1. No quiero comprar el regalo.
2. No quiero recoger los platos.
3. No quiero jugar al ajedrez.
4. No quiero tocar el piano.
5. No quiero hacer nada.
6. No quiero tener prisa.
7. No quiero decir eso.
8. No quiero dar la vuelta.
9. No quiero ir al teatro.
10. No quiero ser antipático.

C ¿Debo hacerlo o no?

Haz mandatos afirmativos o negativos con *tú* según la situación. Sigue el modelo.

manejar rápido cerca de la escuela
¡No manejes rápido cerca de la escuela!

1. comer dulces antes del almuerzo
2. respetar las reglas de tráfico
3. cruzar en el paso de peatones
4. correr por los pasillos de la escuela
5. tocar la bocina cerca del hospital
6. abrir el capó en la carretera
7. llenar el tanque con gasolina
8. chocar con ese coche

D ¿A quiénes van a invitar?

Di a quién(es) van a invitar estas personas. Usa el adjetivo posesivo correcto. Sigue el modelo.

yo / amigo
Yo voy a invitar a un amigo mío.

1. María/compañera
2. Eugenio y Luis / amigos
3. Dolores y Silvia / profesor
4. nosotros / primas
5. tú / compañeros
6. Ud. / sobrina
7. Eugenio / amigas
8. Teresa y yo / tía

E ¿Dónde están?

Usa el pronombre posesivo correcto y las palabras entre paréntesis para contestar las preguntas. Sigue el modelo.

¿Dónde está el permiso de manejar de Carlos? (en la mesa)
El suyo está en la mesa.

1. ¿Dónde están las llantas del mecánico? (en el garaje)
2. ¿Dónde están mis tijeras? (en el armario)
3. ¿Dónde está la pantalla de Laura? (en el baúl)
4. ¿Dónde están los patines de Uds.? (en el suelo)
5. ¿Dónde están tus tarjetas de crédito? (en la cartera)
6. ¿Dónde está la pensión de Uds.? (cerca del estacionamiento)
7. ¿Dónde está el coche cama de Enrique? (detrás del coche comedor)
8. ¿Dónde está la habitación de Ud.? (en el primer piso)

Activity Masters Chapter 8 Test Listening Comprehension Test
Workbook Review: Chapters 5–8 Cumulative Test: Chapters 5–8

VOCABULARIO DEL CAPÍTULO 8

Sustantivos
el accidente
el acelerador
el baúl
la bocina
el cacharro
el capó
la carretera
el carril
el cinturón de seguridad, *pl.* los cinturones de seguridad
el coche deportivo
el conductor, la conductora
el cruce (de calles)
la cuadra
el estacionamiento
la estación de servicio, *pl.* las estaciones de servicio
el faro
el freno
la gasolina
el instructor, la instructora
la llanta
el mecánico, la mecánica
el motor
la multa
el parabrisas, *pl.* los parabrisas
el parachoques, *pl.* los parachoques
el parquímetro
el paso de peatones
el peatón, *pl.* los peatones
el permiso de manejar
la placa
la regla
el semáforo
la señal de tráfico
el tanque
el tráfico
la velocidad máxima
la ventanilla *(car window)*
el volante

Adjetivos
distraído, -a
impaciente
nervioso, -a
paciente
peligroso, -a

Adjetivos posesivos
mío, -a
nuestro, -a
suyo, -a
tuyo, -a

Pronombres posesivos
el mío, la mía; los míos, las mías
el nuestro, la nuestra; los nuestros, las nuestras
el suyo, la suya; los suyos, las suyas
el tuyo, la tuya; los tuyos, las tuyas

Verbos
acelerar
arrancar
chocar (con)
doblar
estacionar
llenar
manejar
obtener
quedar *(to be located)*
respetar

Expresiones
con cuidado
dar la vuelta *(to turn around)*
poner una multa
por aquí/allí
tener prisa
tocar la bocina
(todo) derecho

PRÓLOGO CULTURAL

LA BUENA SALUD

Like their neighbors to the north, Latin Americans have in recent years discovered the benefits of keeping fit. Office workers who spend their days behind desks have every reason to be concerned about their health. So in the early morning, when the air is cool and not yet filled with exhaust fumes, a large number of people can be seen jogging in city streets and parks.

Many gyms and health clubs have opened in the larger Latin American cities, where few if any existed before. Men and women whose only exercise used to consist of going for a stroll or dancing on weekends now show up at the clubs several times a week for an hour or so of aerobics or other kinds of workouts.

At the same time, team sports are on the rise, along with athletics in general. Quite a few schools and universities have developed track and field programs. Of course team sports have long been popular, especially soccer, baseball, and volleyball. But they have not often been as popular a school activity as in the United States. Instead, like boxing, tennis, cycling, and so on, they have been sponsored by *clubes deportivos*.

The growing interest in fitness and good health has also helped to change eating habits in Spanish-speaking countries. Traditionally, meals there have been composed of four or five separate dishes—a soup, rice or potatoes, meat or fish, a vegetable or salad, and dessert. But for many people today, such meals seem too large and heavy, especially at midday. Though this tradition continues in smaller towns, health-conscious city dwellers are turning to lighter, simpler meals that take full advantage of the rich variety of fruits, grains, and vegetables that Latin America produces.

PALABRAS NUEVAS I

Essential

If students ask: Other related words you may want to present: *el apio*, celery; *el pepino*, cucumber.

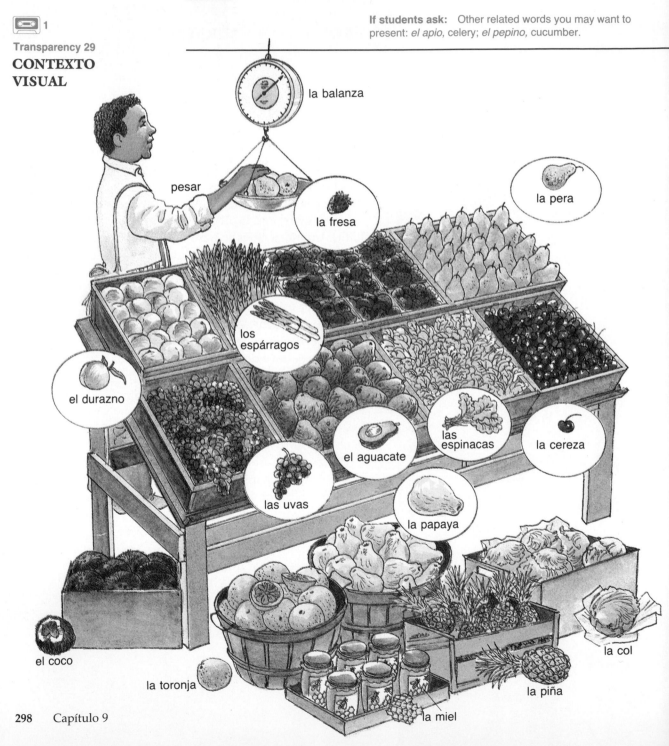

la balanza

pesar

la fresa

la pera

los espárragos

el durazno

el aguacate

las espinacas

la cereza

las uvas

la papaya

el coco

la toronja

la miel

la col

la piña

la langosta

el camarón
pl. los camarones

el cereal

hacer ejercicio

pesarse

CONTEXTO COMUNICATIVO   2

1 CARLOS **¡Me muero** de hambre! ¿Cuál es **el plato del día**?

CAMARERO **Mariscos** o ensalada de espinacas.

CARLOS Quisiera la ensalada de espinacas, por favor. No tiene muchas **calorías.**

Variaciones:
- mariscos → camarones
- quisiera → me gustaría

morirse (o → ue) *to die*
el plato del día *special of the day*
los mariscos *seafood, shellfish*
las calorías *calories*

2 JORGE Para tener buena **salud** necesitas una **dieta sana.**

INÉS También debes hacer ejercicio.

- una dieta sana → comer bien
- ejercicio → gimnasia

la salud *health*
la dieta *diet*
sano, -a *healthy*

3 ANDRÉS Voy a **estar a dieta** hasta el sábado. Tengo que **aumentar de peso** para el partido.

TERESA ¡Ay, qué lata! ¿Cuánto pesas?

ANDRÉS Cincuenta kilos. Soy el jugador más pequeño del equipo.

- aumentar de peso → **bajar de peso**
  cincuenta kilos → ochenta kilos
  pequeño → grande

estar a dieta *to be on a diet*
aumentar de peso *to gain weight*
el peso here: *weight*

bajar de peso *to lose weight*

4 SR. MILLER ¿Cómo preparo **el guacamole**?
  SRA. LÓPEZ **Mezcle** dos aguacates, un tomate, una cebolla y un chile verde. Luego **añada** un poco de limón.
  SR. MILLER ¿Y **mayonesa**?
  SRA. LÓPEZ No, nunca.

  ■ preparo → hago

el guacamole *guacamole, a Mexican avocado spread or salad*

mezcle (**Ud.** command form of **mezclar**) *mix*

añada (**Ud.** command form of **añadir**) *add*

la mayonesa *mayonnaise*

EN OTRAS PARTES

En España y el Caribe se dice *el melocotón*.

También se dice *el ananá* o *el ananás*.

También se dice *el pomelo*.

Un mercado en Colima, México

En la América del Sur se dice también *la palta*.

En la América del Sur se dice también *la frutilla*.

PRÁCTICA

A ¡Buen provecho! Contesta las preguntas. Usa frases completas.

1. ¿Qué pesas?

2. ¿Qué lavas?

3. ¿De qué sabor es el helado?

4. ¿Qué hierves?

5. ¿Qué pones en la ensalada?

6. ¿Qué frutas te gustan?

7. ¿Qué quieres de postre?

8. ¿Qué cortas?

9. ¿Qué clase de jugo pides?

10. Para empezar, ¿qué quieres?

Práctica A
1. Peso la (or: una) langosta.
2. Lavo las (or: unas) espinacas.
3. Es de fresa.
4. Hiervo camarones.
5. Pongo col (en la ensalada).
6. Me gustan los duraznos y las uvas.
7. Quiero peras.
8. Corto el (or: un) aguacate.
9. Pido jugo de piña
10. (Para empezar,) quiero una toronja.

Notes: You may want students to do Ex. A in pairs.

Reteach / Review: After students have completed Ex. A, you may want to expand the practice by asking volunteers to change the questions and answers for items 1, 2, 4, 6, 8, and 9 to the preterite.

B ¿Qué van a comer? Varias personas están en un restaurante. ¿Qué dicen? Completa cada frase con la palabra correcta.

1. No añado azúcar al té. Prefiero usar la *(col / miel / pera)*. Es más sana.
2. Generalmente desayuno con *(cereal / coco / cereza)* y café.
3. No quiero dulces, gracias. Estoy a *(pie / dieta / tiempo)*.
4. ¿Quieres el sandwich de jamón con mostaza o con *(mariscos / mayonesa / espinacas)*?
5. La ensalada de *(espárragos / mariscos / toronjas)* tiene langosta y camarones.
6. Si quieres saber cuánto pesas, usa *(la dieta / las calorías / la balanza)*.
7. Hijo, me pareces un poco delgado. Debes *(bajar / aumentar / subir)* de peso.
8. Si no almuerzo pronto, me voy a *(morir / pesar / aumentar)* de hambre.

Práctica B
1. miel
2. cereal
3. dieta
4. mayonesa
5. mariscos
6. la balanza
7. aumentar
8. morir

Palabras Nuevas I   **301**

C ¿Qué clase de palabra es?

En cada grupo de palabras hay una que no debe estar. ¿Cuál es? Búscala y luego úsala en una frase completa.

1. a. calorías   b. balanza   c. coles   d. peso
2. a. coco   b. langosta   c. camarones   d. mariscos
3. a. plato del día   b. durazno   c. plátano   d. manzana
4. a. cuchillo   b. cuchara   c. cereza   d. tenedor
5. a. mantequilla   b. espárragos   c. miel   d. mermelada
6. a. piña   b. mantel   c. taza   d. servilleta
7. a. burrito   b. empanada   c. taco   d. mayonesa
8. a. cereza   b. toronja   c. flan   d. fresa
9. a. jugo   b. guacamole   c. leche   d. agua mineral
10. a. espinacas   b. uvas   c. verduras   d. espárragos

D Hablemos de ti.

1. ¿Qué hay que hacer para tener buena salud?
2. Para aumentar de peso, ¿qué hay que comer? ¿Y para bajar de peso? ¿Es bueno para la salud bajar rápidamente de peso? ¿Por qué?
3. Cuando vas a la tienda de comestibles, ¿qué compras? ¿Generalmente haces una lista? ¿Por qué?
4. ¿Qué frutas y verduras te gustan más? ¿Cuáles te gustan menos? ¿Las prefieres frescas, congeladas o enlatadas (= en lata)?
5. ¿Haces ejercicio? ¿Cuándo? ¿Dónde? ¿Cuántas veces lo haces cada semana?

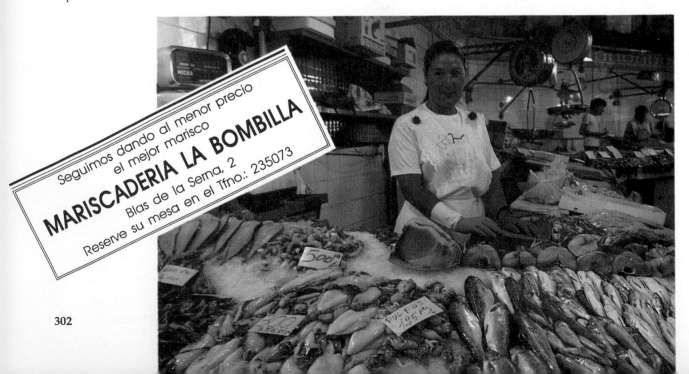

ACTIVIDAD

¡Qué comida tan sabrosa!   Imagine that you are opening a new restaurant. What dishes will you serve? Work in pairs to create a menu. Include the food headings below and fill in several choices under each. Then switch menus with another pair and play the parts of a waiter or waitress and a customer.

Sopas

Ensaladas

Plato(s) dcl día

Carnes

Pescado y mariscos

Verduras

Frutas y postres

Bebidas frías

Bebidas calientes

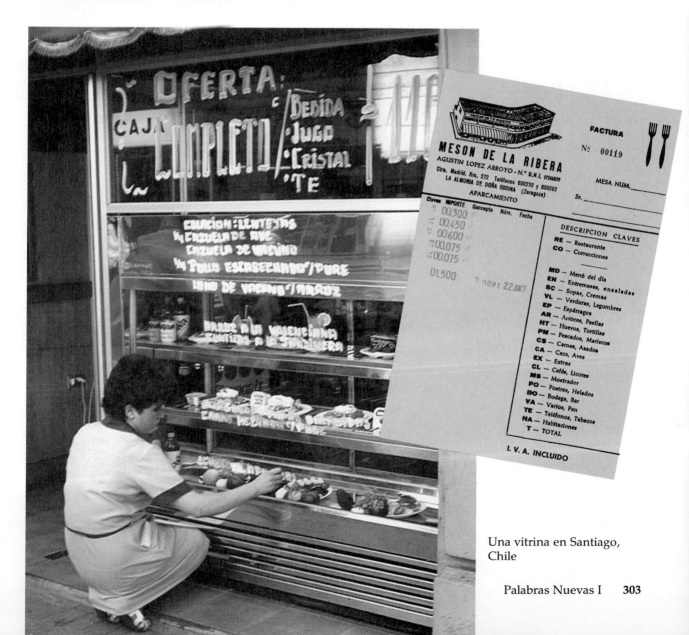

Una vitrina en Santiago, Chile

APLICACIONES Discretionary

La dieta ideal 4 5 Pronunciación

En la cafetería de una escuela en Los Ángeles.

RICARDO   ¿Sabes cuál es el plato del día? Me muero de hambre.

CONSUELO   Salchichas fritas con salsa de tomate y con espaguetis.

RICARDO   ¡Mmm, qué sabroso!

5 CONSUELO   Pues hace mucho tiempo que traigo mi propia[1] comida.

RICARDO   ¿Ah sí? ¿Por qué?

CONSUELO   Porque así[2] como lo que me gusta y también como mejor.

RICARDO   No me digas que quieres bajar de peso.

10 CONSUELO   Claro que no. Mi peso está bien así. Pero prefiero comer frutas y verduras, y sólo un poco de carne.

RICARDO   Yo no tengo tiempo para preparar comidas. Por la mañana siempre me muero de sueño.

CONSUELO   Y ahora te mueres de hambre.

15 RICARDO   Sí, pero no pienso comer una ensalada de frutas. Siempre tengo ganas de comer el plato del día, como hamburguesas, papas fritas, pollo frito, carne misteriosa,[3] ¡pizza!

CONSUELO   ¡Uf! Somos muy distintos, tú y yo.

---

[1]**propio, -a** *own*   [2]**así** *this way*   [3]**la carne misteriosa** *mystery meat*

Diálogo
1. Hablan de comida (*or:* del plato del día). / Answers will vary.
2. No, ella trae su propia comida. / Porque así come lo que le gusta y también come mejor. / Come frutas y verduras y un poco de carne. / Porque las prefiere (*or:* es comida sana). / Ella prepara su propia comida.
3. Porque siempre se muere de (*or:* tiene) sueño. / Él prefiere comer el plato del día.
4. Answers will vary.

Preguntas

Contesta según el diálogo.

1. ¿De qué hablan Ricardo y Consuelo?   ¿Qué piensas tú del plato de ese día?   2. ¿Come Consuelo la comida de la cafetería? ¿Por qué? ¿Qué come ella? ¿Por qué? ¿Quién le prepara la comida a Consuelo?   3. ¿Por qué no tiene tiempo Ricardo por las mañanas? ¿Qué prefiere comer él?   4. ¿Con quién estás de acuerdo, con Ricardo o con Consuelo? ¿Por qué? Describe la dieta ideal para ti.

Cocinando comida mexicana en Texas

Participación

Work with a partner to prepare a dialogue in which you discuss a menu for a party or picnic. Afterwards, make a shopping list. For example, if you are going to make a fruit salad, what fruits do you need?

If students ask: Other related words you may want to present: *la cadera*, hip; *la mejilla*, cheek; *la camilla*, stretcher; *el yeso*, cast.

Una visita al médico

▭ 6

Transparency 30

CONTEXTO VISUAL

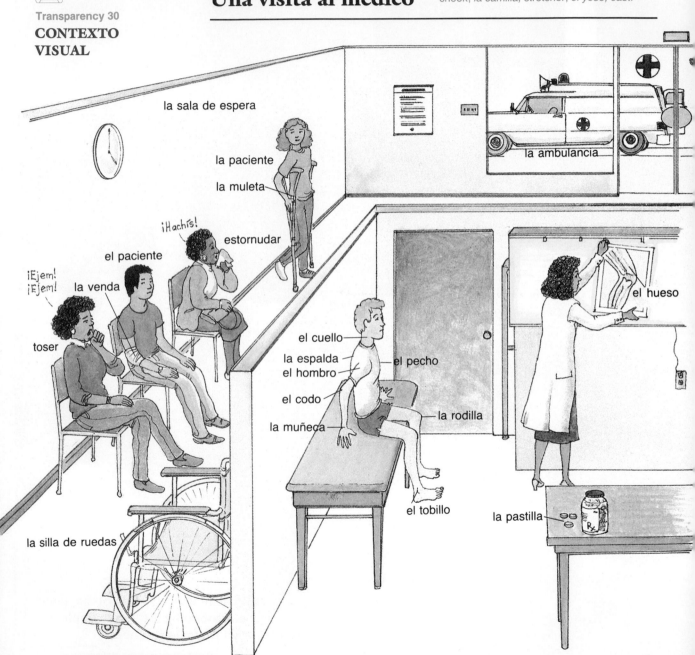

la sala de espera

la paciente

la muleta

la ambulancia

¡Hachís!

estornudar

el paciente

¡Ejem! ¡Ejem!

la venda

toser

el cuello

la espalda
el hombro

el pecho

el codo

la muñeca

la rodilla

el hueso

el tobillo

la pastilla

la silla de ruedas

CONTEXTO COMUNICATIVO 7

1 BENJAMÍN **¿Qué tienes,** Lucía? Estás muy **pálida.**

LUCÍA Tengo un resfriado. Estornudo mucho y estoy tan cansada que no puedo hacer nada.

BENJAMÍN ¡Qué lástima!

Variaciones:

■ un resfriado → gripe

■ estornudo → toso

¿qué tienes / tiene Ud.? *what's wrong with you?*

pálido, -a *pale*

2 PABLO Mamá, me muero de sed.

MAMÁ ¡Pobrecito! Tienes fiebre. Te voy a traer un vaso de agua.

PABLO Voy a **mejorarme** pronto, ¿verdad?

MAMÁ ¡Claro que sí, hijito! Pero tienes que quedarte en cama **por** varios días.

■ me muero de → tengo mucha

■ un vaso de agua → un jugo de naranja

■ pronto → antes del partido

mejorarse *to get better, to improve*

por *for* (+ time)

3 SRA. LÓPEZ Habla la Sra. López. ¿Está* la doctora Vargas?

SECRETARIA Está en **la clínica.** ¿Es **un caso de urgencia**?

SRA. LÓPEZ Sí. Es mi hijo mayor. Creo que **se rompió** el brazo.

■ la clínica → el hospital

■ se rompió → **se lastimó**

■ el brazo → el tobillo

■ se rompió el brazo → tiene un hueso **roto**†

la clínica *clinic*

un caso de urgencia *an emergency (case)*

romperse *to break (a bone)*

lastimarse *to hurt (a part of one's body)*

roto, -a *broken*

---

* We can use *estar* by itself to mean "to be there" or "to be in."

† We use *roto, -a* with bones or with things that break or shatter. We use *descompuesto, -a* to mean "broken" in the sense of not working: *La lavadora no funciona. Está descompuesta.*

4 MÉDICA   ¿Cómo **te sientes,** Julio?

    JULIO   Todavía me duele la rodilla.

    MÉDICA   Entonces te voy a **recetar** unas pastillas.

- la rodilla → la pierna
- unas pastillas → esta **medicina**
- recetar unas pastillas → cambiar las vendas

sentirse (e → ie) *to feel*

recetar *to prescribe*

la medicina *medicine*

5 MÉDICO   Felicitaciones, Sr. Gómez. Ud. **ya** está sano.

  SR. GÓMEZ   ¡Qué maravilla! ¿Ya no tengo que estar a dieta?
No, pero **recomiendo** que coma* más verduras
y menos carne.

  SR. GÓMEZ   Sí, doctor. Espero que mi familia comprenda.*
A ellos les gusta mucho la carne.

- sano → bien
- recomiendo → quiero
- espero que → ojalá que

ya here: = ahora

recomendar (e → ie) *to recommend, to advise*

PRÁCTICA

Práctica A

1. ... Me duele el cuello.
2. ... la espalda.
3. ... el tobillo.
4. ... el brazo.
5. ... el codo.
6. ... el pecho.
7. ... el hombro.
8. ... el dedo.
9. ... la muñeca.
10. ... la rodilla.

A ¿Cómo te sientes? Después del partido de fútbol, a todos los jugadores les duele algo. Pregunta y contesta según el modelo.

ESTUDIANTE A   *¿Cómo te sientes?*
ESTUDIANTE B   *Me siento mal. Me duele el pie.*

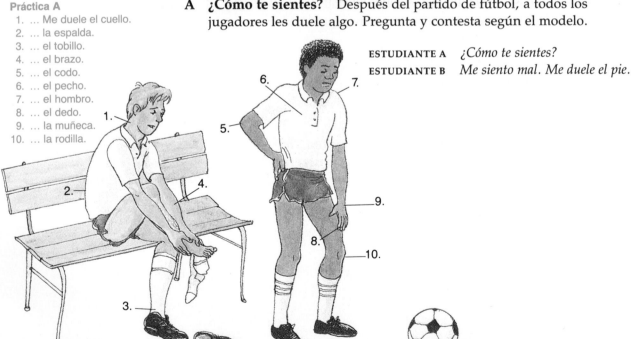

* These forms of *comer* and *comprender* are called ''subjunctive.'' Their English equivalents are the same as *Ud. come* and *mi familia comprende.*

B Un caso de urgencia. Escoge una palabra o expresión de cada uno de los tres grupos para hacer frases.

1. el médico	estar	a la gente enferma	la muñeca
2. el paciente	estornudar		pálido(a)
3. el enfermero	examinar(le)	a la gente al hospital	peor
4. la ambulancia	llevar		sano(a)
5. la sala de espera	ponerle	la espalda	el tobillo
	recetarle	fiebre	un hueso roto
6. la paciente	romperse	gripe	una inyección
7. el muchacho	sentirse	llena de gente	una silla de ruedas
8. la médica	tener	mejor	
9. la clínica	toser	menos	una venda
	usar	mucho	unas pastillas
		muletas	

Práctica B
Answers will vary.

Notes: Make sure students see that the last two columns in Ex. B make up a single group.

Enrichment: After students do oral work with Ex. B, you may want to ask them to write five additional sentences at home.

C Hablemos de ti.

1. ¿Qué haces cuando no te sientes bien? Y después de hacerlo, ¿te sientes mejor?
2. ¿Qué te duele si comes demasiado? ¿Qué partes del cuerpo te duelen después de practicar deportes o hacer ejercicio?
3. ¿Cuándo estornudas y toses? ¿Qué tomas para mejorarte? ¿Qué te receta el médico o la médica cuando tienes gripe o un resfriado? ¿Cuándo vas al médico o a la médica?
4. Cuando vas al médico, ¿generalmente está llena de gente la sala de espera? ¿Más o menos cuánto tiempo tienes que esperar?
5. ¿Te rompiste un hueso alguna vez *(once)*? ¿Qué hiciste? ¿Te llevaron a un hospital?
6. ¿Qué haces cuando te lastimas un brazo o una pierna? ¿Qué haces cuando te cortas un dedo?

Práctica C
Answers will vary.

Practice Sheet 9–2

Workbook Exs. C–D

Tape Manual Exs. 3–4 🔲 8

Refrán 🔲 9

Quiz 9–2

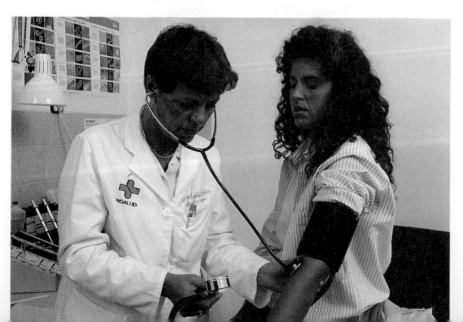

Con la médica en España

ESTUDIO DE PALABRAS

Many languages that the native Indians spoke when Europeans first arrived in the Americas are still spoken today. In Mexico about one million people speak Náhuatl, the language of the Aztecs. More than two million Mexicans and Guatemalans speak one or another of the Mayan languages, the most important of which are Quiché, Cakchiquel, Mam, Kekchí, Yucatec, Tzeltal, and Tzotzil. In South America about six million people in the region of Peru and Bolivia speak either Quechua, the language of the Incas, or Aymará. In Paraguay most of the population is bilingual, speaking both Spanish and Guaraní.

The Spaniards borrowed many words from these native languages, often because the words named things that the Europeans had never seen before, such as *papaya* (from a Caribbean language), *aguacate*, and *guacamole* (both from Náhuatl). Other borrowed words include the Quechua words *cancha*, *llama*, and *papa*; the Náhuatl words *cacahuete*, *coyote*, *chile*, *chocolate*, *tiza*, and *tomate*; the Caribbean words *maíz* and *caimán*; and *poncho*, from Araucana, a language of southern Chile. Still later, of course, English speakers borrowed many of these words from Spanish.

These Spanish words came from Indian languages. What do you think they mean?

canoa   caníbal   hamaca   huracán   chicle

Notes: Before students begin the *Familias de palabras* section of the **Estudio de palabras,** point out that infinitives of verbs are given but that some sentences require a conjugated form—either present tense or preterite.

Familias de palabras
1. pesas / peso / pesarte
2. calientes / caliente / calor / calorías
3. médica / medicina
4. recetó / receta
5. se mejoró / mejor
6. esperar / espera
7. mariscos / mar

Familias de palabras
Completa las frases con la forma correcta de la palabra apropiada.

1. peso, pesas, pesarse
   Después de comenzar a levantar _____, probablemente vas a aumentar de _____. Debes _____ cada dos o tres días.
2. calor, calorías, calentar, caliente
   No _____ (tú) la sopa porque no me gusta tomar sopa _____ cuando hace _____, y esa sopa tiene muchas _____.
3. médica, medicina
   La _____ les da _____ a los pacientes.
4. receta, recetar
   Ayer el médico me _____ unas pastillas pero perdí la _____.
5. mejorarse, mejor
   Lucía _____ la semana pasada y ya está _____.
6. espera, esperar
   Tenemos que _____ en la sala de _____.
7. mar, mariscos
   Los _____ viven en el _____.

EXPLICACIONES I Essential

Mandatos con *Ud.* y *Uds.*

You know how to give a command to someone you address as *tú*. Here is how we give commands to more than one person and to people we address as *Ud.*

1 To form *Ud.* commands with regular verbs, we drop the *-o* of the present-tense *yo* form and add the following endings. For *-ar* verbs we add *-e;* for *-er* / *-ir* verbs we add *-a.*

CANTAR
cantø → cant + **e**   **Cante** una canción.   *Sing a song.*

COMER
comø → com + **a**   **Coma** las uvas.   *Eat the grapes.*

ABRIR
abrø → abr + **a**   **Abra** la boca.   *Open your mouth.*

2 To form *Uds.* commands with regular verbs, we add *-en* to the stem for *-ar* verbs and *-an* for *-er* / *-ir* verbs.

CANTAR
cantø → cant + **en**   **Canten** más fuerte.   *Sing louder.*

COMER
comø → com + **an**   **Coman** la col.   *Eat the cabbage.*

ABRIR
abrø → abr + **an**   **Abran** los ojos.   *Open your eyes.*

We just add *no* before these commands to make them negative.

No cante(n) ninguna canción.   *Don't sing any songs.*
No coma(n) las uvas.   *Don't eat the grapes.*
No abra(n) los ojos.   *Don't open your eyes.*

Notes: Mini-dialogue 4 on p. 300 contains examples of *Ud.* commands.

◆ **OBJECTIVES:**

TO TELL PEOPLE WHAT TO DO AND WHAT NOT TO DO

TO SUPERVISE OTHERS

TO WARN PEOPLE OR GIVE THEM ADVICE

Reteach / Review: Ask students to name types of people whom they address as *Ud.*: teachers, waiters and waitresses, friends' parents, salesclerks, employers, members of the clergy, doctors, dentists, and so on.

3 Stem-changing verbs follow the same rule.

o → ue

CONTAR
cuentø + **e(n)**

Cuente
Cuenten } el dinero.   *Count the money.*

e → ie

ENCENDER
enciendø + **a(n)**

Encienda
Enciendan } la luz.   *Turn on the light.*

e → i

REPETIR
repitø + **a(n)**

No repita
No repitan } eso.   *Don't repeat that.*

4 Verbs ending in *-car*, *-gar*, and *-zar* have spelling changes to keep the original sound.

-car (c → qu)

BUSCAR
buscø → busqu + **e(n)**

Busque
Busquen } al gato.   *Look for the cat.*

-gar (g → gu)

PAGAR
pagø → pagu + **e(n)**

No pague
No paguen } la cuenta.   *Don't pay the check.*

-zar (z → c)

CRUZAR
cruzø → cruc + **e(n)**

Cruce
Crucen } conmigo.   *Cross with me.*

Remember that verbs ending in *-ger* already have a spelling change in the *yo* form.

ESCOGER
escojø → escoj + **a(n)**

Escoja
Escojan } las peras.   *Choose the pears.*

5 For verbs whose present-tense *yo* form ends in *-go* or *-zco*, we drop the *-o* and add *-a(n)*.

DECIR
digø → dig**a(n)**

Diga
Digan } la verdad.   *Tell the truth.*

TRAER
traigø → traig**a(n)**

Traiga
Traigan } el coco.   *Bring the coconut.*

CONOCER
conozcø → conozc**a(n)**

Conozca
Conozcan } su país.   *Know your country.*

6 The following verbs have irregular *Ud(s).* command forms.

DAR **Dé**
     Den } la respuesta.   *Give* the answer.

ESTAR **Esté**
      Estén } aquí mañana.   *Be* here tomorrow.

IR   **Vaya**
     Vayan } a la clínica.   *Go* to the clinic.

SABER **Sepa**
      Sepan } esto para la prueba. *Know* this for the exam.

SER **Sea** } amable.
     Sean } amables.   *Be* nice.

Enrichment: You may want to point out the written accent mark on *dé* and ask why it is necessary (to distinguish the verb from the preposition *de*).

Reteach / Extra Help: In preparation for the **Práctica** on pp. 314–315, you may want to write these phrases on the board and ask volunteers to give the *Ud.* and *Uds.* commands: *contar calorías, escoger / pedir el plato del día, hacer ejercicio, no comer mucho, escribir una composición.*

7 We sometimes use *Ud.* or *Uds.* with commands for politeness or emphasis.

No puedo ir. **Vaya Ud.**   *I can't go.* **You go.**
Vuelvan Uds. mañana.   *Come back* tomorrow.

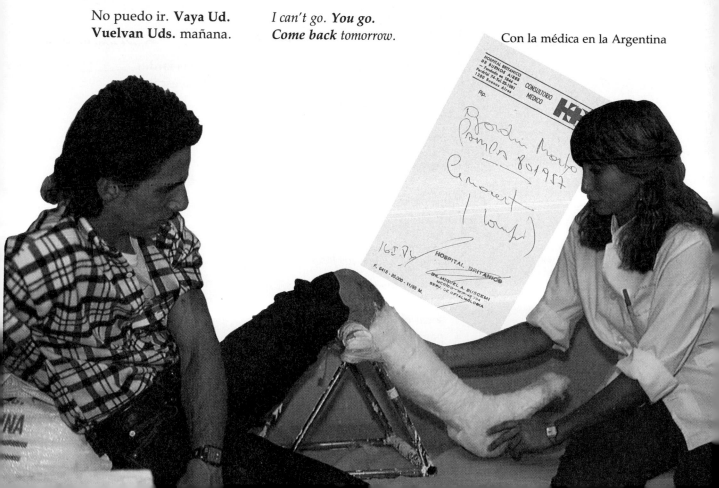

Con la médica en la Argentina

PRÁCTICA

A En el restaurante. La Sra. Gómez trabaja en un restaurante. La dueña le dice qué hacer. Da mandatos según el modelo.

> usar los platos azules
> *Use los platos azules, por favor.*

1. planchar las servilletas
2. cambiar los manteles
3. cortar el pan
4. preparar la mayonesa
5. lavar las cacerolas
6. desenchufar la tostadora

7. llamar a la cajera
8. descansar un poco
9. contestar el teléfono
10. limpiar los camarones
11. probar este aguacate
12. calentar las espinacas

B En la oficina. El Sr. Mandamás siempre les dice a todos los dependientes lo que tienen que hacer. Da mandatos con *Ud.* según el modelo.

> ¡Qué sucio está todo! (barrer la oficina)
> *Barra la oficina.*

1. ¡Hace calor aquí! (abrir las ventanas)
2. Esta carta es demasiado larga. (escribir otra)
3. No le oigo. (leer los precios otra vez)
4. Ya no hay tiempo para almorzar. (comer más tarde)
5. El ascensor está descompuesto. (subir por la escalera)
6. Ya no hay sellos. (correr al correo)
7. Esto no es lo que pedí. (devolver este paquete)
8. No hay mucha luz aquí. (encender esa lámpara)
9. Le conté un chiste. (sonreír)

C ¡Qué perezoso! Fernando es el mayor y siempre les dice a sus hermanos qué hacer. Da mandatos según el modelo.

> apagar los faros
> *Apaguen Uds. los faros.*

1. recoger los papeles
2. buscar en el baúl
3. secar el parabrisas
4. pagar la gasolina y el aceite
5. no tocar la bocina
6. cruzar en la esquina

7. no jugar con el freno
8. no almorzar en el coche
9. no decirle nada a papá
10. traer las placas
11. no poner nada sobre el capó
12. conocer las reglas de tráfico

D **¿Qué más les digo?** Los Jiménez se van de vacaciones por una semana. Antes de irse, dejan una lista de las cosas que sus hijas tienen que hacer y lo que no deben hacer. ¡Cuidado! Algunos mandatos deben ser afirmativos y otros negativos. Sigue el modelo.

> hacer mucho desorden
> *No hagan mucho desorden.*

1. tocar el piano muy fuerte
2. empezar su tarea a las diez de la noche
3. apagar el radio antes de salir
4. perder las llaves
5. volver a casa después de las clases
6. dar de comer al pájaro
7. ser amables con la tía Ana
8. hacer su tarea antes de mirar la tele
9. estar demasiado tiempo en la piscina
10. ir al cine más de una vez
11. recoger la ropa sucia
12. saber lo que tienen que saber para los exámenes

Práctica D
1. No toquen…
2. No empiecen…
3. Apaguen…
4. No pierdan…
5. Vuelvan…
6. Den…
7. Sean…
8. Hagan…
9. No estén…
10. No vayan…
11. Recojan…
12. Sepan…

E **Hablemos de ti.**
1. ¿Qué les dice su profesor(a) a Uds. cuando empieza la clase de español? ¿Y cuando termina? ¿Qué les dice cuando Uds. hablan demasiado en clase? ¿Y cuando Uds. no saben la respuesta correcta?
2. ¿Te gustaría algún día decirles a los adultos lo que deben hacer? ¿Qué te gustaría decirles? ¿Por qué?
3. En los parques hay letreros que dicen lo que no debemos hacer allí. ¿Qué dicen?
4. En las carreteras hay letreros que nos dicen lo que debemos y no debemos hacer. ¿Qué nos dicen?

Práctica E
Answers will vary.

Practice Sheets 9–3, 9–4

Workbook Exs. E–F

Tape Manual Exs. 5–6  10

Quiz 9–3

Un mercado en Granada, España

APLICACIONES
Discretionary

En la clínica   Transparency 31

Notes: You may want to show transparency 31 and ask students to work in pairs or small groups to talk about the picture.

Sample dialogues for the **¿Qué pasa?** appear in the Teacher Notes.

Muchos pacientes vienen a la clínica. Están en la sala de espera. ¿Cuántas personas esperan? ¿Por qué viene cada uno a ver a la médica?

Javier hurt his leg while playing basketball. Create a dialogue in which he and the doctor discuss his condition. You may want to use some of these words:

descansar	quedarse en cama	el hueso	la venda
doler	recetar	las muletas	pálido
lastimarse	sentirse bien / mal	las pastillas	roto

EXPLICACIONES II Essential

El subjuntivo

Up to now you have been using verbs in the present and preterite tenses of the *indicative mood*. We use the indicative mood to talk about facts or actual events.

Limpian su cuarto.   *They're cleaning their room.*
Rita gana todas las carreras. *Rita wins all the races.*
No se despiertan temprano.   *They don't wake up early.*

The following sentences use the *subjunctive mood*. What differences do you see between the indicative and the subjunctive?

Su mamá **quiere que limpien** el cuarto.
*Their mother **wants them to clean** their room.*

Raúl **espera que Rita gane** la carrera.
*Raúl **hopes Rita wins** the race.*

¡**Ojalá que no se despierten** temprano!
I hope they don't wake up early!

We use the subjunctive to tell what someone *wants*, *wishes*, or *hopes* that someone else will do. We also use the subjunctive to tell what someone *asks*, *tells*, or *recommends* that someone else do.

El cliente **le pide al camarero que llene** su vaso.
*The customer **is asking the waiter to fill** his glass.*

Notes: Point out the examples of the subjunctive in mini-dialogue 5 on p. 308.

◆ **OBJECTIVES:**

TO EXPRESS HOPES AND WISHES ABOUT OTHER PEOPLE

TO MAKE RECOMMENDATIONS AND SUGGESTIONS

TO MAKE EXCUSES

TO EXPLAIN WHAT OTHERS WANT

La profesora **le dice a Pablo que lea.**

*The teacher **is telling Pablo to read.***

El médico **le recomienda a Susana que descanse** más.

*The doctor **advises Susana to rest** more.*

Notice that these are like commands: "Fill the glass, please," "Read, Pablo," "Rest more, Susana." In fact, sometimes we speak of them as "implied" or "indirect" commands.

1 We form the present subjunctive of most -*ar*, -*er*, and -*ir* verbs the same way we form *Ud(s.)* and negative *tú* commands. We drop the -*o* of the present-tense indicative *yo* form and add the subjunctive endings.

INFINITIVO **-ar**

	SINGULAR		PLURAL
1	que (yo) cant**e**	que (nosotros) que (nosotras)	cant**emos**
2	que (tú) cant**es**	que (vosotros) que (vosotras)	cant**éis**
3	que Ud. que él } cant**e** que ella	que Uds. que ellos } cant**en** que ellas	

INFINITIVO **-er / -ir**

	SINGULAR		PLURAL
1	que (yo) com**a** / viv**a**	que (nosotros) que (nosotras)	com**amos** / viv**amos**
2	que (tú) com**as** / viv**as**	que (vosotros) que (vosotras)	com**áis** / viv**áis**
3	que Ud. que él } com**a** / viv**a** que ella	que Uds. que ellos } com**an** / viv**an** que ellas	

Reteach / Extra Help: Before introducing the subjunctive forms of regular verbs, you may want to ask these questions: *¿Quieren Uds. que yo cante o prefieren que baile? ¿Le recomiendas a ___ que coma en la cafetería? ¿Esperamos que el equipo de básquetbol gane este año?*

Reinforce the present-subjunctive endings by doing a substitution drill: *El dentista recomienda que nosotros no comamos muchos dulces (tú), (Uds.). Quiero que tú me llames por teléfono esta noche (ella, ellos). Los profesores piden que Uds. no escriban con lápiz, ¿verdad? (nosotros, tú).*

2 Compare these sentences.

Elena **quiere manejar.**	*Elena wants to drive.*
Elena **quiere que Ud. maneje.**	*Elena wants you to drive.*

In the first sentence, Elena wants to drive herself, so we use the infinitive after *quiere*. In the second sentence, she wants someone else to drive, so we use the subjunctive.

Sentences that use the subjunctive usually have two parts connected by *que*. Each part has a different subject (*Elena / Ud.*) The part that begins with *que* contains the subjunctive. What do you think the following sentences mean?

Raúl **espera ganar.**	Raúl **espera que ganemos.**
¿No **quieres manejar** hoy?	¿**Me pides que yo maneje** hoy?
Quiero abrir la puerta.	**Te digo que abras** la puerta.

We always use the subjunctive after **ojalá que,** never the infinitive.

Ojalá que yo gane el campeonato.	*I hope I win the championship.*
Ojalá que regresen pronto.	*I hope they come back soon.*

PRÁCTICA

A Con tantas ideas, no hay tiempo para estudiar.   Gloria debe estudiar para un examen, pero piensa siempre en otras cosas. ¿En qué piensa? Usa *ojalá que* y sigue el modelo.

> Julio / mejorarse pronto
> *Ojalá que Julio se mejore pronto.*

1. (él) / no lastimarse otra vez
2. el médico / recetarle algo bueno
3. (nosotros) / visitar al abuelo este fin de semana
4. (ellos) / arreglar mi pulsera
5. los profesores / no preguntar nada difícil
6. Julio / estudiar
7. la profesora de geometría / anunciar que no vamos a tener un examen
8. (nosotros) / terminar este libro pronto

En una farmacia en Caracas, Venezuela

1. ¿Quieres patinar (sobre hielo)? No, mis padres no quieren que yo patine.
2. ¿Quieres mirar la tele? No, mis padres no quieren que yo mire la tele.
3. ¿... manejar? ... no quieren que yo maneje.
4. ¿... remar? ... no quieren que yo reme.
5. ¿... nadar? ... no quieren que yo nade.
6. ¿... cocinar? ... no quieren que yo cocine.
7. ¿... montar a caballo? ... no quieren que yo monte a caballo.
8. ¿... levantar pesas? ... no quieren que yo levante pesas.
9. ¿... esquiar? ... no quieren que yo esquíe.

Práctica C

1. ¿Qué más recomienda papá? Recomienda que Raquel coma ...
2. ¿Qué más dice mamá? Le dice a Fernando que aprenda ...
3. ¿Qué más piden mamá y papá? Piden que yo les escriba una carta.
4. ¿Qué más pide mamá? Pide que barramos ...
5. ¿Qué más dice papá? Le dice a Raquel que no corra ...
6. ¿Qué más recomiendan mamá y papá? Recomiendan que leamos
7. ¿Qué más dice mamá? Le dice a Fernando que no rompa ...
8. ¿Qué más pide papá? Pide que yo beba ...

Practice Sheet 9–5

11 **Tape Manual Ex. 7**

Quiz 9–4

B **¡A mis padres no les gusta nada!**   Hay muchas cosas que nuestros padres no quieren que hagamos. Pregunta y contesta según el modelo.

ESTUDIANTE A   *¿Quieres bucear?*
ESTUDIANTE B   *No, mis padres no quieren que yo bucee.*

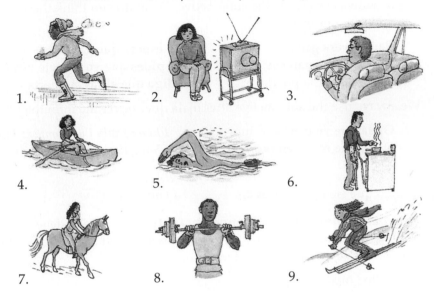

1.   2.   3.

4.   5.   6.

7.   8.   9.

C **Cartas de mamá y papá.**   Los padres de Rogelio, Fernando y Raquel viajan por el Canadá. Los hermanos reciben muchas tarjetas postales con muchos consejos (*advice*). Pregunta y contesta según el modelo.

mamá / decirnos / asistir a la escuela todos los días
ESTUDIANTE A   *¿Qué más dice mamá?*
ESTUDIANTE B   *Nos dice que asistamos a la escuela todos los días.*

1. papá / recomendar / Raquel / comer más espinacas y lechuga
2. mamá / decirle a Fernando / aprender a atarse la corbata
3. mamá y papá / pedir / yo / escribirles una carta
4. mamá / pedir / (nosotros) / barrer el garaje
5. papá / decirle a Raquel / no correr demasiado
6. mamá y papá / recomendar / (nosotros) / leer más libros
7. mamá / decirle a Fernando / no romper el proyector que le mandaron
8. papá / pedir / yo / beber más leche y menos refrescos

El subjuntivo: Continuación

Most verbs form the present subjunctive in the same way we form *Ud(s).* and negative *tú* commands.

◆ OBJECTIVES:

TO EXPRESS WISHES

TO ASK FOR REASSURANCE

TO REASSURE SOMEONE

TO ASK FOR AND GIVE REASONS

TO STALL SOMEONE

TO EXPRESS EXPECTATIONS

1 Verbs whose infinitives end in *-car*, *-gar*, and *-zar* have the spelling change in all of their present subjunctive forms.

-car (c → qu)
TOCAR
No tocamos la guitarra. | *We aren't playing the guitar.*
No quieren que toquemos. | *They don't want us to play.*

-gar (g → gu)
PAGAR
Pago al cajero. | *I pay the cashier.*
Mamá **pide que yo pague** al cajero. | *Mom asks me to pay the cashier.*

-zar (z → c)
CRUZAR
¿Siempre cruzas en el paso de peatones? | *Do you always cross at the crosswalk?*
Espero que siempre **cruces** en el paso de peatones. | *I hope you always cross at the crosswalk.*

And verbs that end in *-ger* have the *j* of the present-tense *yo* form: *¡Ojalá que me escojan!*

Reteach / Extra Help:
Reinforce the present-subjunctive forms of spelling-changing, irregular *yo* form, and stem-changing verbs by asking volunteers to create additional example sentences for each of the verbs given on p. 321.

2 Verbs whose present indicative *yo* form is irregular keep the change in all of their present subjunctive forms.

Esperamos que el guía **conozca** este barrio. | *We hope the guide knows this neighborhood.*
Quiero que me **digas** la verdad. | *I want you to tell me the truth.*
Ojalá que obtengan algo agradable. | *Let's hope they get something nice.*

3 Stem-changing *-ar* and *-er* verbs have the stem change in all except the *nosotros* and *vosotros* forms.*

Espero que la entrada **no cueste** mucho. | *I hope the ticket doesn't cost much.*
Nos **pide que contemos** lo que pasó. | *He asks us to tell what happened.*

* Stem-changing *-ir* verbs are different. We will discuss them in Chapter 10.

Práctica A

1. Espero que naveguemos
 … Siempre navegamos …
2. Espero que empecemos …
 Siempre empezamos …
3. … lleguemos … llegamos …
4. … comencemos … comen-
 zamos …
5. … toquemos … tocamos …
6. … paguemos … pagamos …
7. … aterricemos … aterrizamos …
8. … escojamos … escoge-
 mos …
9. … saquemos … sacamos …
10. … recojamos … recoge-
 mos …

Práctica B

1. ¡Ojalá que yo navegue …!
 Siempre navegas …
2. ¡Ojalá que yo empiece …!
 Siempre empiezas …
3. … llegue … llegas …
4. … comience … comienzas
 …
5. … toque … tocas …
6. … pague … pagas …
7. … aterrice … aterrizas …
8. … escoja … escoges …
9. … saque … sacas …
10. … recoja … recoges …

Práctica C

1. ¿Por qué quieres que yo
 ponga el dinero en mi
 bolsillo? Porque no quiero
 que lo pierdas.
2. ¿Por qué quieres que yo
 cuelgue el teléfono? Porque
 no quiero que digas nada
 más.
3. ¿… que yo salga …? … que
 encuentres …
4. ¿… que yo encienda …? …
 que tengas …
5. ¿… que yo cuente …? …
 que traigas …
6. ¿… que yo vuelva …? …
 que vengas …
7. ¿… que me pruebe …? …
 que la devuelvas …
8. ¿… que me acueste …? …
 que juegues …

PRÁCTICA

A **¿Eres optimista?** Algunas personas esperan cosas. Otras están seguras. Sigue el modelo.

> sacar fotos claras
> ESTUDIANTE A *Espero que saquemos fotos claras.*
> ESTUDIANTE B *Siempre sacamos fotos claras.*

1. navegar en la regata
2. empezar bien
3. llegar temprano
4. comenzar antes de las tres
5. tocar bien la noche del concierto
6. pagar al contado
7. aterrizar a tiempo
8. escoger buenos asientos
9. sacar unas biografías de la biblioteca
10. recoger cerezas

B **Otra vez.** Vuelve a hacer la Práctica A según el nuevo modelo.

> sacar fotos claras
> ESTUDIANTE A *¡Ojalá que yo saque fotos claras!*
> ESTUDIANTE B *Siempre sacas fotos claras.*

C **¿Por qué entonces?** Luis siempre quiere comprender por qué tiene que hacer algunas cosas. Pregunta y contesta según el modelo.

> ¿cerrar la puerta? / oír lo que dicen los otros
> ESTUDIANTE A *¿Por qué quieres que yo cierre la puerta?*
> ESTUDIANTE B *Porque no quiero que oigas lo que dicen los otros.*

1. ¿poner el dinero en mi bolsillo? / perderlo
2. ¿colgar el teléfono? / decir nada más
3. ¿salir tan pronto? / encontrar tus regalos
4. ¿encender la calefacción? / tener frío
5. ¿contar mi dinero? / traer más de $20,00
6. ¿volver ahora? / venir conmigo
7. ¿probarme la camisa? / devolverla más tarde
8. ¿acostarme? / jugar más a los naipes

D **Y los otros también.** Los hermanitos de Luis también quieren comprender por qué deben hacer cosas. Pregunta y contesta.

> ¿cerrar la puerta? / oír lo que digo
> ESTUDIANTE A *¿Por qué quieres que cerremos la puerta?*
> ESTUDIANTE B *Porque no quiero que oigan lo que digo.*

1. ¿poner los sellos en el escritorio? / perderlos
2. ¿colgar el teléfono? / jugar con él

3. ¿salir contigo? / buscar tus regalos de Navidad
4. ¿encender el aire acondicionado? / tener calor
5. ¿acostarnos? / hacer ruido
6. ¿traer nuestros carnés? / venir sin ellos
7. ¿probar la sopa? / decir más tarde que no les gusta
8. ¿tener cuidado? / chocar con los muebles

E   ¡Qué lata!   El padre de Raúl y Esperanza dejó una carta en la cocina. Complétala con la forma correcta de cada verbo. Usa el infinitivo, el indicativo o el subjuntivo.

Raúl,

    Sabes que (yo) *(tener que)* salir por unos días. Durante este tiempo quiero que (tú) *(cuidar)* a tu hermanita y que la *(llevar)* a jugar a la casa de Susana. Te pido que no *(regresar)* tarde por la noche. No quiero que
5 tú y tus amigos *(tocar)* música hasta las dos o las tres de la mañana, para no *(despertar)* a la niña. Tampoco quiero que Uds. *(montar)* en bicicleta en el jardín. Les recomiendo que no le *(prestar)* nada al Sr. Aguilera, porque él nunca *(devolver)* las cosas. Espero que tú y Esperanza *(asistir)* todos los días a la escuela y que *(preparar)* las tareas.
10 Ojalá que yo no *(encontrar)* la casa en un gran desorden.

                                       Hasta pronto,
                                       Papá

F   Hablemos de ti.
1. ¿Qué quieren tus padres que hagas después de regresar de la escuela? ¿Por qué? Y tú, ¿qué prefieres hacer? ¿Por qué?
2. ¿Tus padres te dicen a menudo que pongas en orden tu cuarto? ¿Te piden que hagas otras cosas en casa? ¿Qué te piden que hagas?
3. ¿Qué cosas no quieren tus padres que tú y tus hermanos o tú y tus amigos hagan? ¿Por qué? ¿Qué les dicen?

ACTIVIDAD

¡Ojalá!   On separate slips of paper, write four things that you hope will or will not happen. In small groups, take turns picking them and reading them aloud. Try to guess who wrote each one and explain why you think so. For example:

Ojalá que no llueva el sábado.
(*Nombre* lo escribió porque le gusta jugar al tenis los fines de semana.)

Espero que alguien me invite a una fiesta.
(*Nombre* lo escribió porque siempre quiere ir a fiestas.)

Práctica D
1. ¿Por qué quieres que pongamos los sellos en el escritorio? Porque no quiero que los pierdan.
2. ¿… colguemos …? … jueguen …
3. ¿… salgamos …? … busquen …
4. ¿… encendamos …? … tengan …
5. ¿… nos acostemos …? … hagan …
6. ¿… traigamos …? … vengan …
7. ¿… probemos …? … digan …
8. ¿… tengamos …? … choquen …

Práctica E
tengo que
cuides / lleves
regreses
toquen
despertar / monten
presten
devuelve
asistan / preparen
encuentre

Práctica F
Answers will vary.

Practice Sheet 9–6

Workbook Exs. G–J

Tape Manual Ex. 8   12

Refrán   13

Canción   14

Quiz 9–5

Notes: You may want students to put their **Actividad** slips in a paper bag.

APLICACIONES Discretionary

Notes: Answers to the **Repaso** and **Tema** appear in the Teacher Notes.

REPASO

Notes: Review of:
1. noun phrases with *de*
2. indirect object pronouns
   present subjunctive
   of *-ar* verbs
   expressions with *de*
3. indirect object pronouns
   decir / pedir + present
   subjunctive of *traer /
   obtener*
4. affirmative / negative
   Ud(s.) commands
5. negative *Ud(s.)* commands

Mira con cuidado las frases modelo. Luego cambia las siguientes frases al español según los modelos.

Enrichment: You may want to use the **Repaso** model sentences for dictation.

1. *Los pacientes esperan en la clínica del barrio.*
   (The doctor is with an emergency case.)
   (Someone sneezes during the play.)
   (She's sleeping in the wheelchair.)

2. *La enfermera le dice: "Quiero que Ud. aumente de peso."*
   (The boy says to us: "I hope my cat comes down from the tree.")
   (I say to her: "I hope you (fam.) change your mind.")
   (We tell them: "We don't want you (pl.) to answer in a hurry.")

3. *La médica le dice a Ud. que traiga más agua y jugos.*
   (We ask Mom to get more peaches and grapes.)
   (He asks me to bring more cabbage and spinach.)
   (They tell us to bring more shrimp(s) and lobster(s).)

4. *Limpie, barra y pase la aspiradora. Haga las camas ahora mismo.*
   (Skate (pl.), ski, and eat salads. Do (pl.) gymnastics often.)
   (Listen (formal), learn, and take notes. Don't ask questions every minute.)
   (Pick up (pl.), wash, and dry the clothes. Don't prepare dinner yet.)

5. *Y no vaya a la recepción, Sr. Gálvez.*
   (And don't come back (formal) to the dance, Julio.)
   (And don't leave (pl.) the boardinghouse, girls.)
   (And don't weigh (formal) the patients, ma'am.)

Haciendo ejercicio en
Palma de Mallorca, España

TEMA

Transparency 32

Reteach / Extra Help: Before students begin work on the **Tema** sentences, you may want to show transparency 32 as the class discusses the cartoon strip

Escribe las frases en español.

1. My brother and I are in the waiting room.

2. The doctor says to us: "I want you to lose weight."

3. "I'm asking you to eat more fruit and vegetables."

4. "Swim, run, and lift weights! Exercise every day!"

5. "And don't go to the ice-cream parlor, boys."

REDACCIÓN

Ahora escoge uno de los siguientes temas para escribir tu propio diálogo o párrafo.

1. Expand the *Tema* by writing about the boys' visit to the doctor. The doctor wants them to eat some foods (list three) and not others (list three). The doctor also wants them to do certain activities (list three). He wants them to visit him again after six months.

2. Have you ever broken any bones? If so, write a paragraph about your experience. What did you break, and how did it happen? Did you go to the emergency room *(la sala de emergencia)*? Did the doctor prescribe any medicine? Did you stay in bed or use crutches or a wheelchair? How do you feel now?

3. Imagine that you are a doctor telling a patient how to stay healthy. Using the *Ud.* command form, tell the person to do six health-maintaining activities.

Aplicaciones   **325**

COMPRUEBA TU PROGRESO   CAPÍTULO 9   Discretionary

Notes: Answers to the **Comprueba** appear in the Teacher Notes.

A   ¿Qué hacemos?

Usa mandatos afirmativos o negativos con *Ud.* o *Uds.* para contestar. Sigue los modelos.

> No queremos bajar de peso.
> *Pues no bajen de peso.*
> Quiero cantar un poco.
> *Pues cante un poco.*

1. No queremos contar nada.
2. Queremos jugar al ajedrez.
3. No queremos vivir en la ciudad.
4. Quiero descansar.
5. No quiero beber mucho.
6. Queremos volver pronto.
7. Quiero empezar ahora.

B   En la cocina

Da mandatos con *Ud.* o *Uds.* Sigue el modelo.

> Sra. González / hacer el guacamole
> *Sra. González, haga el guacamole.*

1. Srta. Méndez / tener cuidado con el horno
2. chicos / no venir tarde
3. Sra. Vidal / traer más fresas y duraznos
4. Sr. Giles / poner estos camarones en el fregadero
5. Isabel y Claudia / no hacer sopa todavía
6. Srta. Porras / no decir que no
7. señoras / salir de la cocina

C   En la clínica

Haz mandatos con *Ud.* o *Uds.* Sigue el modelo.

> estar a dieta sólo por una semana (Uds.)
> *Estén a dieta sólo por una semana.*

1. dar estas pastillas al médico   (Ud.)
2. ir en la ambulancia con el paciente   (Uds.)
3. ser paciente y esperar media hora más   (Ud.)
4. estar en la sala de espera temprano   (Ud.)
5. dar estas vendas al enfermero   (Uds.)
6. ir de prisa a la habitación número 34   (Ud.)
7. ser generosos y ayudar en la clínica   (Uds.)

D   ¿Qué quieres?

Completa cada frase con la forma correcta del verbo.

1. Diego quiere que el médico le *(examinar)* la rodilla.
2. La enfermera quiere que (yo) *(abrir)* la boca.
3. Papá nos recomienda que *(estacionar)* aquí.
4. Quieren que (tú) *(anunciar)* el tanteo.
5. Ojalá que Uds. no *(estornudar)* mucho durante el espectáculo.
6. Todos esperan que (yo) no *(toser)* mucho.
7. Mis padres nos piden que *(asistir)* al concierto.
8. La profesora de gimnasia quiere que todos *(correr)* un poco cada día.

E   ¿Qué quiere el médico?

Escribe cada frase otra vez. Empieza con la expresión entre paréntesis.

1. Descansamos más.   (la médica quiere que)
2. Uds. caminan con muletas.   (el Dr. Suárez les recomienda que)
3. Ella no toma más pastillas.   (ojalá que)
4. Uds. no se lastiman.   (la profesora espera que)
5. La ambulancia llega pronto.   (ojalá que)
6. Elena se mejora en seguida.   (sus padres quieren que)

F   ¿Cuál es correcto?

Escoge la forma correcta del verbo.

1. Quiero que (tú) _____ el periódico.
   a. leer   b. lees   c. leas
2. No quiero _____ tan temprano.
   a. comer   b. comes   c. comas
3. La médica recomienda que (yo) _____ más.
   a. pesarme   b. me peso   c. me pese
4. Ellos quieren _____ a su hijo.
   a. visitar   b. visitan   c. visiten
5. Paco espera que Uds. no _____ el dinero.
   a. perder   b. pierden   c. pierdan
6. Queremos _____ en autobús.
   a. viajar   b. viajamos   c. viajemos

VOCABULARIO DEL CAPÍTULO 9

Sustantivos
el aguacate
la ambulancia
la balanza
las calorías
el camarón, *pl.* los camarones
un caso de urgencia
el cereal
la cereza
la clínica
el coco
el codo
la col
el cuello
la dieta
el durazno
la espalda
los espárragos
las espinacas
la fresa
el guacamole
el hombro
el hueso
la langosta
los mariscos
la mayonesa
la medicina
la miel
la muleta
la muñeca
el/la paciente
la papaya
la pastilla
el pecho
la pera
el peso *(weight)*
la piña
el plato del día
la rodilla
la sala de espera
la salud

la silla de ruedas
el tobillo
la toronja
las uvas
la venda

Adjetivos
pálido, -a
roto, -a
sano, -a

Adverbio
ya *(now)*

Preposición
por *(for)*

Verbos
estornudar
lastimarse
mejorarse
morirse (o → ue)
pesar(se)
recetar
recomendar (e → ie)
romperse
sentirse (e → ie)
toser

Expresiones
aumentar / bajar de peso
estar a dieta
hacer ejercicio
¿qué tienes / tiene Ud.?

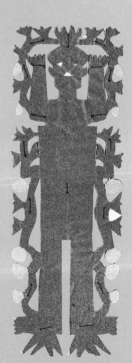

PRÓLOGO CULTURAL

HOLA, ¿QUIÉN HABLA?

Suppose you're in Madrid on vacation and want to call home. Just look around the center of the city and you will find special phone booths that can be used for transatlantic calls as well as for local ones. The booths have lists of international area codes, instructions in several languages, and digital meters that register when to put in more coins. It's almost as easy as calling next door.

If you don't happen to have a pocketful of coins, you can go to the phone company office just off the Gran Vía and call from the public long-distance center. An operator will place your call and send you to a booth. Afterward you pay a cashier.

In most cities of the Spanish-speaking world, however, public phones are still limited to local calls. And international calls, even from a long-distance center, may turn out to be very complicated. If you phone the United States from Paraguay, for example, your call will head south first because it must be routed through Buenos Aires.

Public telephones in some countries require the use of a special token, or *ficha*. You can usually buy *fichas* at the post office, newsstands, or at any store or business that has a public phone.

Private telephones are not as common in Spanish-speaking countries as they are in the United States. The larger cities are growing so quickly that the phone companies cannot keep up with the demand. In small towns, people have no real need for telephones because they see each other every day. And since in very small towns of the Hispanic world people still often spend their lives where they were born, phones are not needed for families to stay in touch.

PALABRAS NUEVAS I

Essential

¿De parte de quién?

If students ask: Other related words you may want to present: *el auricular,* receiver; *la llamada de persona a persona,* person-to-person call.

Transparency 33

**CONTEXTO
VISUAL**

descolgar (o → ue)

el operador

Olga:
El Sr. Gómez llamó a
las 10:15.

el recado

la operadora

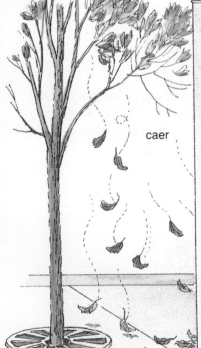

caer

colgar (o → ue)

caerse

CONTEXTO COMUNICATIVO 2

1

VÍCTOR	¿Aló? ¿Quién habla?	
ELISA	Elisa.	
VÍCTOR	Ah, Elisa, **¿qué hay?**	**¿qué hay?** *what's new?*
ELISA	Tengo **un chisme** increíble.	**el chisme** *piece of gossip;* pl. *gossip*
VÍCTOR	No hables **en voz** tan **baja.**	
ELISA	No quiero que los otros me oigan.	**en voz baja** *softly, in a low voice*

Variaciones:

- un chisme → **una noticia**
- no hables en voz tan baja →habla **en voz** más **alta**
- en voz tan baja → tan **lentamente**
  no quiero que los otros me oigan → quiero que oigas cada palabra

la noticia *piece of news, news item*

en voz alta *in a loud voice; out loud*

lentamente = despacio

2

CLARA	Quiero hacer **una llamada de larga distancia** a Buenos Aires. Es una **llamada por cobrar.**	**la llamada** *call* **de larga distancia** *long-distance* **la llamada por cobrar** *collect call*
OPERADORA	El número y su nombre, por favor.	
CLARA	54–1–89–45–16.* Clara Morales.	
OPERADORA	Lo siento, pero las líneas están ocupadas. Por favor, cuelgue y **vuelva a**[†] llamar más tarde.	**volver (o → ue) a** + inf. *to (do something) again, to re- (+ verb)*

- vuelva a llamar más tarde → llame otra vez

3

SRA. IBARRA	¿Puedo hablar con la Sra. López?	
SECRETARIO	**¿De parte de quién?**	**¿de parte de quién?** *who's calling?*
SRA. IBARRA	De la Sra. Ibarra.	
SECRETARIO	Un momento, por favor . . . La Sra. López no está. ¿Quiere Ud. dejar un recado?	
SRA. IBARRA	**Tenga la bondad de** decirle que me gustaría verla esta tarde.	**tenga la bondad de** + inf. = ¿quiere Ud. + inf.?

- no está → no está en la oficina

* The number 54 is the telephone code for Argentina; 1 is the code for Buenos Aires.
[†] In English we often use the prefix "re-" where Spanish uses *volver a: Volver a llenar* ("to refill"), *volver a calentar* ("to reheat"), *volver a cortar* ("to recut"), and so on.

4 LILIANA	¿Qué pasa con el teléfono de María? **Suena** y suena pero no contesta nadie.	**sonar (o → ue)** *to ring*
CARLOS	Quizás **marcaste** un número **equivocado**. Marca el número otra vez.	**marcar** *to dial* **equivocado, -a** *wrong*
LILIANA	¡Qué mala suerte! Ahora no hay **tono**.	**el tono** *dial tone*

- un número equivocado → otro número
- no hay tono → el teléfono no funciona

EN OTRAS PARTES

También se dice *el / la telefonista*.

También se dice *discar*.

la llamada por cobrar

También se dice *la llamada con cargo*. En España se dice *la llamada de cobro revertido*.

el tono

También se dice *el tono de marcar* o *la señal para marcar*.

Un operador en Santa Cruz, Bolivia

INSTRUCCIONES PARA EL USO DEL TELEFONO DURANTE SU ESTANCIA EN ESPAÑA

SERVICIO AUTOMATICO

1. Descuelgue el microteléfono y espere la señal para marcar.
2. LLAMADAS URBANAS E INTERURBANAS DENTRO DE LA MISMA PROVINCIA. Marque el número deseado.
3. LLAMADAS INTERURBANAS. Marque el código interurbano de la ciudad a la cual va destinada la llamada, y a continuación el número del abonado deseado.
4. LLAMADAS INTERNACIONALES. Marque el 07. Espere un segundo tono más agudo que el normal. A continuación el indicativo del país (*) hacia el cual va encaminada la llamada, seguido del de la ciudad (**), y del número del abonado deseado.

(*) Consulte los indicativos de países en la última página.

(**) Recuerde que no debe marcar el prefijo de acceso al servicio automático interurbano del país de destino, que generalmente es un 0 (cero).

NOTA: Para conferencias no automáticas llame a la operadora. Marque el 003 para información general

PRÁCTICA

A Pequeños problemas. Escoge la palabra correcta para completar las frases.

1. Hablen en (*voz alta* / *voz baja*) por favor. Me duele mucho la cabeza.
2. Éste no es el 22–75–84. Ud. tiene (*el número equivocado* / *la línea ocupada*).
3. El teléfono no funciona. Ojalá que lo (*descuelguen* / *arreglen*) hoy.
4. La doctora no está todavía. (*Tenga la bondad de* / *Tenga miedo de*) esperar en la sala.
5. El Sr. Torres no está. ¿Quiere dejar (*un chisme* / *un recado*)?
6. Antes de marcar el número debes (*descolgar* / *colgar*) el teléfono y escuchar si hay (*recado* / *tono*).
7. ¡Qué aburrido! Alejandro siempre quiere saber los (*chismes* / *operadores*) de la oficina.
8. Tengo que hacer una llamada (*de larga distancia* / *por cobrar*) porque no tengo dinero.
9. Tengo las manos mojadas. ¿Me puede (*marcar* / *sonar*) el número?
10. ¡Tengan cuidado! Uds. van a (*descolgar* / *caerse*) si corren al teléfono.

B ¿Qué dicen? Varias personas hablan por teléfono. A la izquierda está una parte de la conversación. ¿Cuál fue la otra parte? Escoge la respuesta correcta.

ESTUDIANTE A *¿Está Georgina?*
ESTUDIANTE B *Lo siento. Tiene el número equivocado.*

1. ¿Me oye Ud. bien?
2. ¿Qué clase de llamada quiere hacer?
3. ¿De parte de quién?
4. Necesito hablar con la profesora Silva, por favor.
5. No sé cómo funcionan los teléfonos aquí. ¿Me puede ayudar?
6. ¿Es una llamada de larga distancia?
7. Estoy ocupada. ¿Me puedes volver a llamar?
8. ¿Puedo hablar con el Sr. o la Sra. López?

a. Acaban de salir. ¿Quiere dejar un recado?
b. No, es una llamada local.
c. Primero, marque el número.
d. Sí, te llamo alrededor de la una.
e. ¿Puede hablar en voz más alta?
f. No está. Tenga la bondad de llamarla más tarde.
g. De Leonardo.
h. Lo siento. Tiene el número equivocado.
i. Una llamada por cobrar.

C Una llamada. Imagina que una persona acaba de llegar a los Estados Unidos y no sabe hacer una llamada en el teléfono público. Escoge palabras de cada columna para explicarle cómo hacerlo. Explícale también lo que debe hacer si marca un número equivocado. Usa mandatos con *Ud*.

colgar	las monedas
descolgar	el número
esperar	el teléfono
marcar	el tono
poner	
volver a	

D Hablemos de ti.

1. ¿Quién usa más el teléfono en tu casa?
2. ¿Tienes un teléfono en tu cuarto? ¿A quiénes llamas más frecuentemente? ¿Quiénes te llaman? ¿Cuántas llamadas haces y recibes cada día?
3. ¿Haces muchas llamadas de larga distancia? ¿Adónde? ¿Con quién hablas? ¿A veces haces llamadas por cobrar? ¿Cuesta mucho?
4. Si quieres llamar a otro país, ¿qué tienes que hacer?
5. Si llamas a alguien y no está, ¿generalmente vuelves a llamar o prefieres dejar un recado? ¿Por qué?
6. ¿Qué dices cuando marcas un número equivocado? ¿Qué haces entonces? ¿Qué haces cuando quieres llamar a alguien y no sabes el número de teléfono?
7. Imagínate la vida en un pueblo donde no hay teléfonos. Por ejemplo, ¿qué hace la gente en caso de urgencia?

ACTIVIDAD

El recado   Work with a partner to invent both a telephone answering machine recording and a message that you might leave on the machine if you were calling. For example:

ESTUDIANTE A   Buenos días. Habla con el 555–1753. Después del tono, deje su nombre, su número de teléfono y su recado.

ESTUDIANTE B   Hola, Javier. Habla Josefina. ¿Qué hay? Yo tengo un chisme increíble. Llámame a casa, 555–8052.

APLICACIONES Discretionary

 4 5 Pronunciación

Una llamada de larga distancia

Notes: Make sure students understand these cognates that have not been glossed: *la llamada de persona a persona,* person-to-person call; *un momento,* one moment.

Culture: In connection with line 4 of the **Diálogo,** you may want to ask students to find out the time differences between your town and five locations in the Spanish-speaking world.

Hace un mes que Daniel está en Bolivia. Hoy trata de llamar a sus padres en los Estados Unidos porque extraña a la familia.[1]

DANIEL	Quisiera hacer una llamada a Iowa, Estados Unidos. Hay una hora de diferencia,[2] ¿verdad?
5 **OPERADORA**	Sí. El número y la ciudad, por favor.
DANIEL	El código del área[3] es 518, y el número es el 111–5714, Des Moines.
OPERADORA	Des . . . ¿qué? Por favor, hable más lentamente.
DANIEL	D-e-s M-o-i-n-e-s. El número es . . .
10 **OPERADORA**	Ya tengo el número, gracias.
DANIEL	Es una llamada de persona a persona.
OPERADORA	¿Con quién quiere hablar y de parte de quién?
DANIEL	Con la Sra. Charlotte Zeller, de parte de Daniel Zeller.
15 **OPERADORA**	Repita el nombre por favor.
DANIEL	Ch-a-r-l-o-t-t-e Z-e-ll-e-r.
OPERADORA	Un momento. No cuelgue, por favor . . . Lo siento, Sr. Zeller. La línea está ocupada. Tenga la bondad de llamar más tarde.

---

[1]**extrañar a la familia** *to be homesick*   [2]**una hora de diferencia** *an hour's difference*   [3]**el código del área** *area code*

Preguntas

Contesta según el diálogo.

1. ¿Por qué extraña Daniel a la familia?   2. ¿Adónde y a quiénes quiere llamar? ¿Qué clase de llamada es?   3. ¿Sabes cuántas horas de diferencia hay entre la ciudad donde tú vives y Bolivia? ¿Sabes cuántas horas de diferencia hay entre tu ciudad y España? ¿Es más temprano o más tarde en España?   4. ¿Por qué crees que la operadora no entiende bien lo que Daniel dice?   5. ¿Por qué no puede Daniel hablar con sus padres? ¿Qué tiene que hacer para hablar con ellos?   6. En tu opinión, ¿cómo se siente Daniel cuando la operadora le dice que la línea está ocupada?

Diálogo
1. Porque hace un mes que está en Bolivia.
2. A Iowa, Estados Unidos / a sus padres / una llamada de persona a persona (*or:* de larga distancia)
3. Answers will vary.
4. Answers will vary, but may include: Porque no conoce los nombres ingleses (*or:* norteamericanos).
5. Porque la línea está ocupada. / Tiene que llamar más tarde (*or:* Volver a llamar).
6. Answers will vary.

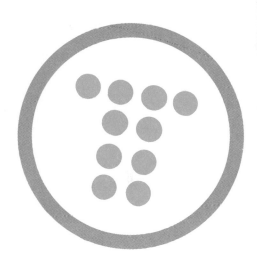

Llamando por teléfono
en Santander, España

Participación

Work with a partner to make up a dialogue between a caller and a telephone operator. What kind of a call is it? What kinds of questions does the operator ask?

PALABRAS NUEVAS II

Essential

Por correo

If students ask: Other related words you may want to present: *asegurar*, to insure; *la entrega inmediata*, special delivery.

VÍA AÉREA

vía aérea

el cartero

el remitente

Ana Cano
276 Ridge Road
Lyndhurst, T.J. 07143

Hotel Bamer
Avenida Juárez 52
México 1, D.F.

el código postal

el sobre

envolver (o → ue)

el apartado postal

el paquete

338   Capítulo 10

el telegrama

el formulario

la firma

el buzón
pl. los buzones

la cartera

entregar

la mensajera

el mensajero

CONTEXTO COMUNICATIVO 7

1 Querida Josefina:

Hoy alquilé un apartamento. **Incluyo** una foto de él. Estoy contentísima porque ahora puedo **mudarme** pronto. Todavía no tengo tu respuesta a mi última carta. Espero que me escribas pronto. Llámame si no tienes ganas de contestar **por correo. Saluda** a Pablo y a los chicos **de mi parte.**

Con cariño,
Beatriz

Variaciones:
- me escribas pronto → **respondas** pronto **a** ésta
- con cariño → muchos **besos**

querido, -a *dear*

incluir (yo incluyo, tú incluyes) *to include; to enclose*

mudarse *to move (to a new residence)*

el correo here: *mail*

por correo *by mail*

saludar *to greet, to say hello / good-by*

de mi parte *from me, for me*

el cariño *affection*

con cariño *affectionately*

responder a = contestar

el beso *kiss*

2 ALFREDO   Luisa, ¿viste este **aviso**? Hay una carta **certificada** para ti.

      LUISA   ¿Dónde está?

      ALFREDO   Tienes que recogerla en el correo. Necesitan tu firma en **el recibo.**

■ recogerla en el → **ir a buscar**la al
■ necesitan tu firma en → quieren que firmes

3 ARMANDO   ¿Sales ahora, Teresa?

      TERESA   Sí, voy al correo para **averiguar*** cómo mandar este paquete.

      ARMANDO   Probablemente tienes que **llenar** varios formularios.

      TERESA   ¡Uf! ¡Qué lata!

■ averiguar → preguntar
■ este paquete → un telegrama

4 SR. MUÑOZ   Srta. Millán, quiero que visite nuestra **compañía** la semana próxima. ¿Qué día puede venir?

      SRTA. MILLÁN   Estoy libre **o** el lunes **o** el miércoles.

■ quiero → espero
■ compañía → oficina

---

el aviso   *notice; warning*
cèrtificado, -a   *registered*

el recibo   *receipt*

ir (venir) a buscar   *to go (come) get, to pick up*

averiguar   *to find out*

llenar   here: *to fill out (a form), to fill in (a blank)*

la compañía   *company*

o . . . o   *either . . . or*

EN OTRAS PARTES

También se dice *el apartado de correos* y *la casilla postal.*

mudarse

También se dice *cambiarse.*

También se dice *por avión.*

También se dice *la planilla.*

En España también se dice *el distrito postal.*

* In *averiguar* the *gu* changes to *gü* when it is followed by the letter *e:*
     in the *yo* form of the preterite: *averigüé*
     in all of the present subjunctive forms: *averigüe, averigües, averigüe, averigüemos, averigüéis, averigüen*
     in the commands: *no averigües* and *averigüe(n).*

PRÁCTICA

A Una carta a España.   Lolita acaba de escribirle una carta a su amigo español. Contesta las preguntas según la carta.

Nueva York

3 de julio de 1989

Querido Carlos:

¿Cómo estás? Recibí tu carta la semana pasada. Me gustaron mucho los chismes de tu escuela. Me gustaría conocer a algunos de esos chicos. Me parecen muy cómicos. Y ahora tengo una noticia increíble. ¡Acabo de comprar un boleto para ir a España! Me costó un ojo de la cara, pero ya lo tengo y es mío. Salgo el 18 de julio por la tarde y llego a Madrid el 19 por la mañana. Espero que vengas a buscarme al aeropuerto. Te llamo el 16 por la tarde. Saluda a tus padres de mi parte.

Con cariño,

Lolita

1. ¿En qué ciudad vive Lolita?
2. ¿Cuál es la fecha de la carta?
3. ¿A quién le escribe Lolita?
4. ¿Qué anuncia Lolita en su carta?
5. ¿A quién quiere que Carlos salude de su parte?
6. ¿Qué va a hacer el 16 de julio?
7. ¿Cómo comienza la carta?
8. ¿Cómo termina?

B Ahora el sobre.   Carlos acaba de recibir la carta de Lolita. Contesta las preguntas según el sobre.

1. ¿Cuál es el remitente?
2. ¿Cuál es el código postal de Lolita? ¿Y el código postal de Carlos?
3. ¿Cuál es la dirección de Carlos?
4. ¿En qué país vive?
5. ¿Cómo mandó Lolita la carta?
6. ¿Cuánto costaron los sellos?

Práctica A
1. en Nueva York
2. tres de julio de mil novecientos ochenta y nueve
3. a Carlos
4. que llega a Madrid el 19 (*or:* que va a Madrid / que tiene un boleto para ir a España)
5. a sus padres
6. va a llamar a Carlos
7. Querido Carlos
8. Con cariño

Práctica B
1. Lolita Camacho
   718 Broadway
   New York, NY 10012
   U.S.A.
2. 10012 / 28050
3. Paseo de la Castellana 50
4. en España
5. por vía aérea
6. 44 centavos

Enrichment: After students complete Ex. B in class, you may want to ask them to address their own envelopes with real or imaginary addresses in Spanish-speaking countries. Ask them to label the parts of the addresses: *remitente, código postal, dirección, ciudad, país.*

Práctica C
1. entregue
2. llenar / formulario
3. saluda / besos
4. mudarse
5. el sobre / el buzón
6. el código postal / mandar
7. el recibo / entrega
8. Envolví
9. la dirección / el remitente / correo / por vía aérea

C No olvides el remitente.   A todo el mundo le gusta recibir cartas. Escoge las palabras correctas para completar cada frase.

1. Espero que la cartera (*averigüe / entregue*) las cartas temprano.
2. Si quieres mandar un telegrama debes (*envolver / llenar*) este (*buzón / formulario*).
3. Mi abuelo siempre me (*envuelve / saluda*) con cariño cuando nos vemos. Me da (*besos / firmas*) y me hace muchas preguntas.
4. Nuestros amigos acaban de (*envolver / mudarse*) del barrio.
5. Elena cierra (*el formulario / el sobre*) y lo pone en (*el buzón / el recibo*).
6. Tengo que averiguar (*el código postal / el aviso*) de la compañía antes de (*mandar / marcar*) el paquete.
7. Necesitas firmar (*el recibo / la noticia*) cuando el mensajero te (*entrega / envuelve*) la carta.
8. (*Entregué / Envolví*) el paquete y espero mandarlo esta tarde.
9. Después de escribir la carta, pon (*la firma / la dirección*) y (*el remitente / el formulario*) en el sobre, ve al (*correo / código postal*) y mándala (*por vía aérea / por cobrar*).

Práctica D
Answers will vary.

Practice Sheet 10–2

Workbook Exs. C–D

8 Tape Manual Exs. 3–4

9 Refrán

Quiz 10–2

D Hablemos de ti.

1. ¿A quiénes mandas cartas? ¿A veces mandas paquetes? ¿A quién?
2. ¿Te gusta comprar cosas por correo? ¿Por qué? ¿Qué clase de cosas compras por correo? ¿Cuánto tiempo tardan en llegar? ¿Te entregan el paquete o tienes que recogerlo en el correo?
3. ¿Te gustaría mudarte a otra ciudad o a otro barrio? ¿Por qué? Imagina que trabajas para una compañía que va a mandarte o a México o a España. ¿Cuál de los dos escoges? ¿Por qué?
4. ¿Esperas viajar a otro país algún día? ¿A cuál? ¿Por qué escoges ése?

ESTUDIO DE PALABRAS

Familias de palabras

Familias de palabras
viajar / bailar / caminar / enchufar

Sometimes we can guess the meaning of a word because it resembles a word that we already know. For example, look at the following related words:

VERB		NOUN	
firmar	*to sign*	la firma	*signature*
entrar	*to enter*	la entrada	*entrance*
llamar	*to call*	la llamada	*call*
recibir	*to receive*	el recibo	*receipt*

To what verbs are the following nouns related?

viaje   baile   camino   enchufe

Sinónimos

Cambia cada palabra en cursiva por un sinónimo.

1. No sé *contestar* este recado.
2. *¿Aló? ¿Qué tal?*
3. *¿Quiere Ud.* firmar el registro?
4. Voy a mandar el paquete *por avión.*
5. Por favor, habla *despacio.*

Sinónimos

1. responder a
2. ¿Qué hay?
3. Tenga la bondad de
4. por vía aérea
5. lentamente

Antónimos

Cambia cada palabra en cursiva por un antónimo.

1. Háblame *en voz baja.*
2. ¿Por qué manejas tan *lentamente?*
3. Por favor, *cuelga* el teléfono.

Antónimos

1. en voz alta
2. rápidamente
3. descuelga

Correo Central, México

EXPLICACIONES I Essential

El verbo *caer(se)*

Caer(se) ''to fall (down)'' follows the same pattern as *traer*.

◆ **OBJECTIVE:**

TO DESCRIBE HOW WELL OR BADLY SOMEONE DOES SOMETHING

Reteach / Extra Help:
Reinforce the forms of *caer(se)* by asking these questions: *¿Te caes a veces cuando corres? ¿Me caigo en la nieve? ¿Cuándo cae más lluvia, en la primavera o en el verano? ¿Se caen Uds. a veces cuando juegan al volibol? Y los futbolistas, ¿se caen frecuentemente?*

INFINITIVO   caer(se)

	SINGULAR		PLURAL	
1	(yo)	(me) **caigo**	(nosotros) (nosotras)	(nos) **caemos**
2	(tú)	(te) **caes**	(vosotros) (vosotras)	(os) **caéis**
3	Ud. (él) (ella)	(se) **cae**	Uds. (ellos) (ellas)	(se) **caen**

Una fuerte lluvia **cae** sobre la ciudad.   *A heavy rain **falls** on the city.*
Siempre **me caigo** en la nieve.   *I always **fall down** in the snow.*

Notice that, like many other verbs, only the *yo* form of *caer* is irregular.

Práctica
1. ¿Cómo patinan …?
   Nunca se caen (or: No se caen nunca).
2. ¿Cómo patina Ana?
   Se cae a menudo.
3. ¿Cómo patinan …?
   Nos caemos frecuentemente.
4. ¿Cómo patinan …?
   Se caen a veces.
5. ¿Cómo patino?
   Te caes siempre.
6. ¿Cómo patina …?
   Casi nunca se cae.
7. ¿Cómo patinamos …?
   Se caen siempre.
8. Y tú, ¿cómo patinas?
   Answers will vary: … me caigo …

PRÁCTICA

Sobre el hielo.   Un grupo de amigos piensan ir a patinar. Algunos son buenos patinadores y otros no. Pregunta y contesta según el modelo.

Eduardo / a veces
ESTUDIANTE A   *¿Cómo patina Eduardo?*
ESTUDIANTE B   *Se cae a veces.*

1. Felipe y Raquel / nunca
2. Ana / a menudo
3. Cecilia y tú / frecuentemente
4. Luz y Mariana / a veces
5. (yo) / siempre
6. Marcos / casi nunca
7. Gustavo y yo / siempre
8. ¿Y tú?

El verbo *incluir*

In the present tense of *incluir* ("to include"), the *i* changes to *y* in all except the *nosotros* and *vosotros* forms. Note that there is no accent in the *nosotros* form.

Notes: Refer to mini-dialogue 1 on p. 339 for an example of the *yo* form of *incluir*.

◆ **OBJECTIVE:**

TO EXPRESS UNCERTAINTY

	SINGULAR		PLURAL	
1	(yo)	incluyo	(nosotros) (nosotras) }	incluimos
2	(tú)	incluyes	(vosotros) (vosotras) }	incluís
3	Ud. (él) (ella) }	incluye	Uds. (ellos) (ellas) }	incluyen

Reteach / Extra Help: You may want to reinforce the forms of *incluir* by telling students to imagine that they are preparing a time capsule, *una cápsula de tiempo*. Ask students to work in pairs or small groups to ask and answer *¿Qué?* + all the present-tense forms of *incluir*. For example: *¿Qué incluyes? Incluyo el periódico de hoy.*

PRÁCTICA

¿Qué incluimos?   Los García comienzan a hacer un paquete grande que van a mandar a una tía que vive en México. ¿Qué pone cada persona en el paquete? Sigue el modelo.

> mamá / fotos de los quince años de Ana
> **ESTUDIANTE A**   *¿Qué incluye mamá?*
> **ESTUDIANTE B**   *Incluye fotos de los quince años de Ana.*

1. Ricardo / una botella de perfume
2. papá y tú / dibujos de los chicos
3. Ud., señora / una nueva marca de secador
4. la abuela Antonia / un suéter azul que ella hizo
5. Jorge y Ana / una cinta con canciones folklóricas
6. el tío Juan / una caja de chocolate canadiense
7. Uds. / un libro de cuentos fantásticos
8. ¿y tú? / ?

Práctica
1. ¿Qué incluye …? Incluye …
2. ¿Qué incluyen …? Incluimos …
3. ¿Qué incluye Ud., señora? Incluyo …
4. ¿Qué incluye …? Incluye …
5. ¿Qué incluyen …? Incluyen …
6. ¿Qué incluye …? Incluye …
7. ¿Qué incluyen …? Incluimos …
8. ¿Qué incluyes tú? Incluyo …

Practice Sheet 10–3

Tape Manual Ex. 5   10

Quiz 10–3

Usos del infinitivo

Notes: Mini-dialogues 2–3 on p. 331, 1 on p. 339, and 2–4 on p. 340 illustrate various uses of the infinitive.

◆ OBJECTIVES:

TO MAKE SUGGESTIONS

TO EXPRESS DESIRES, PREFERENCES, AND PLANS

TO REPORT RECENT EVENTS AND ACTIVITIES

TO EXPLAIN HOW TO DO SOMETHING

TO TELL WHAT SOMEONE FORGOT OR FAILED TO DO

TO DESCRIBE OR EXPLAIN SEQUENCE OF EVENTS

TO SET PRIORITIES

You know that we use the infinitive after many verbs.

¿Puedo dejar un recado?	*Can I leave a message?*
Preferimos hablar en voz baja.	*We prefer to speak softly.*
Necesito hacer una llamada de larga distancia.	*I need to make a long-distance call.*

With some verbs we must use *a, de,* or *en* before the infinitive.

1   The following verbs take *a* + infinitive: *aprender a, ayudar a, comenzar a, empezar a, enseñar a, invitar a, ir a, venir a, volver a.*

No vuelvan a usar la tarjeta de crédito.	*Don't use the credit card again.*
Vengo a entregar los paquetes.	*I'm coming to deliver the packages.*
Los teléfonos **empiezan a sonar.**	*The phones are starting to ring.*

2   The following verbs take *de* + infinitive: *acabar de, disfrutar de, olvidarse de, tratar de.*

Acaban de anunciar el tanteo.	*They just announced the score.*
Trata de salir temprano.	*Try to leave early.*
Disfrutan de gastar dinero.	*They enjoy spending money.*
Me olvidé de leer el aviso.	*I forgot to read the warning.*

3   *Tardar* and *pensar* take *en* + infinitive. (But remember that *pensar en* + infinitive means "to think about," while *pensar* + infinitive means "to plan.")

¿Cuánto tiempo **tardaste en cobrar** el cheque?	*How long did it take you to cash the check?*
Pienso en mudarme a un apartamento.	*I'm thinking about moving to an apartment.*
Espero que **pienses volver a atar** ese paquete.	*I hope you plan to retie that package.*

PARA _Dorotea_

FECHA _23/7/89_ HORA _2_ A.M./P.M.

MIENTRAS UD. NO ESTUVO

SR./SRA./SRTA. _Rafael Jiménez_

DE _Escuela San Vicente_

NÚMERO DE TELÉFONO _555-59-76_

○ LLAMÓ POR TELÉFONO   ○ FAVOR DE LLAMARLO
⊶ LLAMÓ PARA UNA CITA   ○ VOLVERÁ A LLAMARLO
○ DESEA VERLO   ○ VENGA A VERME

RECADO _Le gustaría verla el lunes por la mañana._

RECADO TOMADO POR _Cristina_

4 In Spanish, the infinitive is the only verb form that we can use after a preposition.

Llámenos **antes de venir.**
Después de almorzar fuimos
al cine.
No puedo marcar el número
sin saberlo.
Necesita muletas **para caminar.**

*Call us **before you come.***
***After we ate lunch** we went to
the movies.*
*I can't dial the number **without
knowing (unless I know)** it.*
*He needs crutches **to walk.***

Reteach / Extra Help: You
may want to reinforce the
structures by suggesting or
eliciting additional examples.
For example: *¿Pueden Uds.
oírme si hablo en voz baja?
¿Quieres ir al cine esta noche o
prefieres estudiar?,* and
so on.

Notoo1 Before students begin
Ex. A, make sure they
understand that there are many
possible answers.

PRÁCTICA

A El fin de semana. La familia López está de vacaciones y no sabe qué hacer esta tarde. Escoge una palabra o expresión de cada columna para formar frases. Por ejemplo:

Práctica A
Answers will vary.

(yo)
ESTUDIANTE A *¿Qué debo* (or: *puedo*) *hacer?*
ESTUDIANTE B *Debes* (or: *Puedes*) *montar a caballo.*

1. papá y abuelito	querer	ir a nadar o de pesca
2. mamá	preferir	hacer un asado
3. Manuel y tú	deber	escribir tarjetas postales
4. Diego	necesitar	dar un paseo
5. Juanita y yo	poder	montar a caballo o en bicicleta
6. Beatriz y Elenita	pensar	hacer un picnic
7. (tú)	esperar	ver una película

B ¿Aprendiste a bailar? Varios amigos hablan de lo que hicieron durante el fin de semana pasado. Sigue el modelo.

tú / empezar a estudiar música
ESTUDIANTE A *¿Qué hiciste tú?*
ESTUDIANTE B *Empecé a estudiar música.*

1. Pablo / invitar a cenar a su novia
2. Juan y Jorge / comenzar a cortar el césped
3. María / volver a caerse en el hielo
4. Lupe / ayudar a asar un cordero a la parrilla
5. Uds. / enseñarle a jugar a los bolos a Jorge
6. tú / empezar a leer una novela de ciencia ficción
7. ellas / aprender a manejar un camión

Práctica B
1. ¿Qué hizo …? Invitó a cenar
…
2. ¿Qué hicieron …?
Comenzaron a cortar …
3. ¿Qué hizo …? Volvió a
caerse …
4. ¿Qué hizo …? Ayudó a asar
…
5. ¿Qué hicieron …? Le
enseñamos a jugar …
6. ¿Qué hiciste …? Empecé a
leer …
7. ¿Qué hicieron …?
Aprendieron a manejar …

C   **¿Qué necesitas?**   ¿Qué necesitas para hacer las siguientes cosas? Sigue el modelo.

> salir bien en los exámenes
> *Para salir bien en los exámenes necesitas estudiar más.*

1. hacer una llamada por cobrar
2. manejar bien
3. envolver un paquete
4. escribir el remitente
5. pedir algo por correo
6. viajar a Costa Rica
7. bajar de peso
8. recoger una carta certificada del correo

a. buscar papel y tijeras
b. incluir tu código postal
c. hablar primero con el operador
d. firmar un recibo
e. aprender las reglas de tráfico
f. estar a dieta
g. obtener un pasaporte
h. estudiar más
i. averiguar la dirección de la compañía

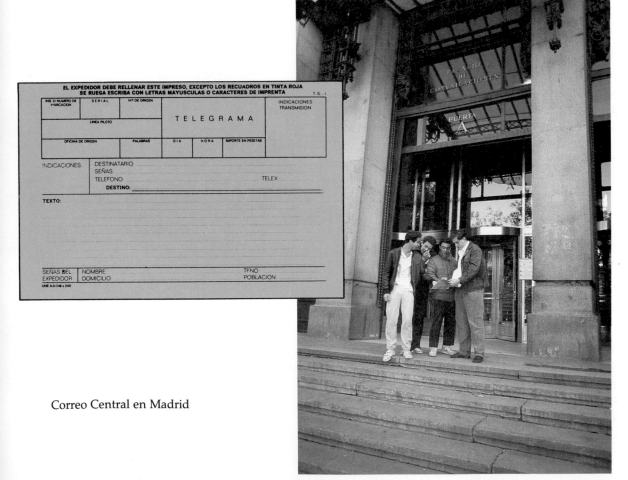

Correo Central en Madrid

D Los distraídos.   Las siguientes personas son bastante distraídas y se olvidan de hacer cosas. Vuelve a formar estas frases según el modelo.

> Juan Carlos sube al tren pero no compra el boleto.
> *Juan Carlos sube al tren sin comprar el boleto.*

1. Jorge se va del restaurante pero no deja una propina.
2. Mi hermana se acuesta pero no apaga la luz.
3. Josefina entra en la casa pero no saluda a nadie.
4. La mensajera entrega el telegrama pero no dice nada.
5. El Sr. Montalvo llena el formulario pero no incluye su firma.
6. Cristina pide prestadas cosas pero no las devuelve.
7. Tomás escribe cheques pero no los firma.
8. Eugenio cuelga el teléfono pero no dice adiós.

Práctica D
1. sin dejar
2. sin apagar
3. sin saludar
4. sin decir
5. sin incluir
6. sin devolverlas
7. sin firmarlos
8. sin decir

E ¿Antes o después?   Di lo que haces antes y lo que haces después. Por ejemplo:

> comer
> *Antes de comer me lavo las manos.*
> *Después de comer quito los platos.*

1. entrar en el paso de peatones
2. pasar la aspiradora
3. descolgar el teléfono
4. comprar algo
5. irse de casa
6. envolver un paquete
7. llenar un formulario
8. poner una carta en el sobre
9. comenzar un viaje largo
10. patinar sobre hielo

Práctica E
Answers will vary but should follow the model.

F Hablemos de ti.
1. ¿Qué prefieres hacer después de la clase? ¿A qué hora comienzas a hacer la tarea? ¿Cuánto tardas en hacerla? ¿Qué haces antes de acostarte?
2. ¿A veces te olvidas de hacer cosas? ¿Te olvidaste de hacer algo ayer? ¿Qué te olvidaste de hacer?
3. ¿Aprendiste a hacer algo nuevo el año pasado? ¿Qué aprendiste a hacer? ¿Le enseñaste algo a alguien? ¿Qué? ¿A quién?
4. ¿Qué disfrutas de hacer los fines de semana?
5. ¿Sabes patinar sobre hielo o sobre ruedas? ¿Hay un lugar para ir a patinar donde tú vives? ¿Quién te enseñó a patinar? ¿Patinas bien o te caes mucho?

Práctica F
Answers will vary.

Practice Sheet 10–4

Workbook Exs. E–F

Tape Manual Ex. 6 11

Quiz 10–4

APLICACIONES Discretionary

El mensajero telefónico 12

ANTES DE LEER

Piensa en estas preguntas mientras *(while)* lees.

1. ¿Cómo es la vida donde no hay teléfonos?
2. ¿Cómo es la vida donde hay muchos turistas pero muy pocos habitantes durante varias semanas?
3. ¿Puedes darle otro título a esta lectura?

Un cartero en México

Hace poco tiempo que Ignacio Martínez vive en Las Cruces, pero todo el mundo lo conoce. Tiene un trabajo muy importante: es el mensajero telefónico del pueblo.

Las Cruces es un pequeño pueblo en el norte de la Argentina. Durante
5 las vacaciones de verano, los turistas llenan los cuatro hoteles del pueblo. El resto del año, sólo doscientas personas viven aquí y los hoteles están cerrados. No hay ningún teléfono particular[1] y hay sólo una cabina telefónica en todo el pueblo. Todos lo usan para hacer y recibir llamadas de larga distancia. Cuando hay una llamada, Ignacio contesta y luego va a buscar a
10 esa persona en bicicleta. Él casi siempre sabe dónde está cada persona en cada momento. Si no la encuentra, deja un recado.

Todos dicen que Ignacio parece ser el mensajero perfecto porque, aunque[2] sabe todo lo que pasa en Las Cruces, no le gustan los chismes y nunca repite nada de lo que oye. Pero también hay personas que creen que Igna-
15 cio no se mudó al pueblo para ser mensajero; están seguras de que es realmente un escritor y que piensa usar todo lo que aprende sobre la vida en Las Cruces para escribir su nueva novela. Otras dicen que Raúl empezó este rumor, porque él siempre soñó con[3] ser el mensajero del pueblo. ¿Quién sabe? Quizás Ignacio o Raúl, pero ellos no dicen nada. ¡Qué com-
20 plicada es la vida, aun[4] en los pueblos más pequeños.

---

[1]**particular** *private*   [2]**aunque** *although*   [3]**soñar con** *to dream of*   [4]**aun** *even*

Preguntas
1. En el norte de la Argentina / doscientos.
2. Answers will vary.
3. Porque es el mensajero telefónico del pueblo.
4. Deja un recado.
5.–7. Answers will vary.

Preguntas

1. ¿Dónde está Las Cruces? ¿Cuántos habitantes tiene?
2. En tu opinión, ¿cómo es el paisaje cerca de Las Cruces y qué tiempo hace allí en el verano?
3. ¿Por qué es importante el trabajo de Ignacio?
4. ¿Qué hace Ignacio cuando no encuentra a la persona que busca?
5. ¿Cuál crees tú que es la verdadera *(true)* profesión de Ignacio? ¿Por qué?
6. ¿Cómo piensas que es el pueblo de Las Cruces? Descríbelo.
7. ¿Cómo cambia la vida en Las Cruces en el verano?

EXPLICACIONES II Essential

El subjuntivo de ciertos verbos que terminan en *-ir*

Remember that in the present subjunctive, stem-changing *-ar* and *-er* verbs have the stem change in all except the *nosotros* and *vosotros* forms.

Quieren que { yo **cuente** chistes.
{ **contemos** chistes.

They want { *me to tell jokes.*
{ *us to tell jokes.*

Ojalá que { **entiendan.**
{ **entendamos.**

I hope { *they understand.*
{ *we understand.*

◆ OBJECTIVES:

TO ASK FOR ADVICE OR SUGGESTIONS

TO EXPRESS HOPES AND WISHES

Stem-changing *-ir* verbs, however, have a stem change in all of their present subjunctive forms.

1 Stem-changing *e* → i verbs have the same stem change throughout.

PEDIR	
pida	**pidamos**
pidas	pidáis
pida	pidan

2 Stem-changing *e* → *ie* and *o* → *ue* verbs whose infinitives end in *-ir* also keep the stem change in the subjunctive. But in the *nosotros* and *vosotros* forms, we drop the *e*.

SENTIRSE		DORMIR	
me **sienta**	nos **sintamos**	**duerma**	**durmamos**
te **sientas**	os sintáis	**duermas**	durmáis
se **sienta**	se **sientan**	**duerma**	**duerman**

Other verbs you know that follow these patterns are:

e → i: *reír, repetir, servir, sonreír, vestir(se)*
e → *ie*: *divertirse, hervir, preferir*
o → *ue*: *morirse*

PRÁCTICA

A No quiero cambiar.   Unas personas siempre sirven la misma comida. Pregunta y contesta según el modelo.

papayas

ESTUDIANTE A   *Siempre servimos papayas. ¿Qué quieres que sirvamos esta noche?*

ESTUDIANTE B   *Sirvan papayas.*

1. cerezas	5. coco
2. duraznos	6. fresas
3. uvas	7. peras
4. piña	8. toronja

Práctica B
Questions will follow the model exactly. Answers as follows:
1. Pídelas *(or:* No las pidas).
2. Pídelas *(or:* No las pidas).
3. Pídelo *(or:* No lo pidas).
4. Pídelos *(or:* No los pidas).
5. Pídelos *(or:* No los pidas).
6. Pídelos *(or:* No los pidas).
7. Pídela *(or:* No la pidas).
8. Pídelos *(or:* No los pidas).

B En el restaurante.   La madre de Eugenio averigua lo que él quiere que ella pida para él. Sigue el modelo.

frijoles

ESTUDIANTE A   *¿Quieres que yo pida frijoles?*
ESTUDIANTE B   *Sí. Pídelos.*
o: *No. No los pidas.*

1. espinacas	5. guisantes
2. zanahorias	6. espárragos
3. maíz	7. col
4. aguacates	8. plátanos fritos

Práctica C
1. Espero que no hiervas el agua para el té.
2. Ojalá que no nos durmamos.
3. Espero que ella no se muera de sed.
4. Ellos quieren que durmamos lejos del fuego.
5. Ojalá que nos divirtamos en la feria.
6. Él recomienda que me duerma tan temprano como él.
7. Ojalá que te sientas mejor.
8. Ella espera que no nos durmamos sin cepillarnos los dientes.
9. Ojalá que el café no hierva.
10. Ellos esperan que nos sintamos mejor.
11. Ojalá que él no repita ese chisme.
12. Esperan que prefiramos salir con ellos.

C Yo no quiero.   Forma frases según el modelo.

(yo) / no querer / (tú) / morirse de hambre
No quiero que te mueras de hambre.

1. (yo) / esperar / (tú) / no hervir el agua para el té
2. ojalá / (nosotros) / no dormirse
3. (yo) / esperar / ella / no morirse de sed
4. ellos / querer / (nosotros) / dormir lejos del fuego
5. ojalá / (nosotros) / divertirse en la feria
6. él / recomendar / (yo) / dormirse tan temprano como él
7. ojalá / (tú) / sentirse mejor
8. ella / esperar / (nosotros) / no dormirse sin cepillarse los dientes
9. ojalá / el café / no hervir
10. ellos / esperar / (nosotros) / sentirse mejor
11. ojalá / él / no repetir ese chisme
12. (ellos) / esperar / (nosotros) / preferir salir con ellos

El pretérito de *creer, leer, oír, caer(se)* e *incluir*

Here are the preterite forms of *leer* ("to read").

	SINGULAR		PLURAL	
1	(yo)	**leí**	(nosotros) (nosotras) }	**leímos**
?	(tú)	**leíste**	(vosotros) (vosotras) }	leísteis
3	Ud. (él) (ella) }	**leyó**	Uds. (ellos) (ellas) }	**leyeron**

Anoche **leyó** el último capítulo.   *Last night **he read** the last chapter.*
Nosotros lo **leímos** anteayer.   *We read it the day before yesterday.*

Note that the *i* becomes *y* in the *Ud. / él / ella* and *Uds. / ellos / ellas* forms. There is an accent on the *i* in all of the other forms. The verbs *creer, oír,* and *caer(se)* form the preterite in the same way.

¿Creíste esa noticia que **oíste?**   ***Did you believe** that piece of news **you heard?***

No oí ningún chisme.   ***I didn't hear** any gossip.*
Oyó el ruido cuando los niños **se cayeron.**   ***He heard** the noise when the children **fell down.***

1   *Incluir* follows the same pattern except that it has an accent mark only on the *i* of the *yo* form *(incluí)* and the *o* of the *Ud. / él / ella* form *(incluyó).*

No incluí mi cuenta.   ***I didn't include** my bill.*
¿Incluiste el recibo?   ***Did you enclose** the receipt?*
Los precios **incluyeron** el impuesto.   *The prices **included** the tax.*

Llamando por teléfono en México

Práctica A

1. leímos
2. leyó
3. leyeron
4. leíste
5. leí
6. leyeron
7. leyeron
8. leyó

Práctica B

1. Un avión 707 con 150 pasajeros cayó en el océano.
2. Miles de personas oyeron una banda en el estadio.
3. Una exposición incluyó (unos) dibujos de un muchacho de 15 años.
4. (Unos) niños leyeron poemas en la Casa Blanca.
5. Nadie creyó los chismes sobre la vida de Juan Galán.
6. Un puente se cayó después de la lluvia.
7. El inspector no creyó la historia del accidente.
8. El desfile incluyó una compañía de baile brasileña.

Reteach / Extra Help: If your class finds Ex. B difficult, you may want to ask volunteers to model the first few items.

Práctica C

Leíste
oí
Incluyeron
se cayó
creíste
creí / leí / oíste
leyó / oyó

Practice Sheet 10–6

 14 Tape Manual Ex. 8

Quiz 10–6

PRÁCTICA

A Una tarea que no es como las otras. La directora del club de periodismo (*journalism*) les dio a los miembros la tarea de leer varios periódicos latinoamericanos para aprender más sobre esos países. Di qué leyeron. Sigue el modelo.

> Óscar / un periódico argentino, *El Clarín* de Buenos Aires
> *Óscar leyó* El Clarín *de Buenos Aires.*

1. (nosotros) / un periódico peruano, *El Comercio* de Lima
2. Josefina / un periódico colombiano, *El Tiempo* de Bogotá
3. Jorge y Martín / un periódico mexicano, *El Excelsior* de México
4. (tú) / un periódico costarricense, *La Nación* de San José
5. (yo) / un periódico dominicano, *El Caribe* de Santo Domingo
6. Pilar y Celia / un periódico puertorriqueño, *El Día* de Ponce
7. Esteban y tú / un periódico uruguayo, *El País* de Montevideo
8. Ana / un periódico venezolano, *El Mundo* de Caracas

B ¿Que pasó ayer? Imagina que lees los titulares (*headlines*) del periódico de hoy. Usa el pretérito para contar lo que pasó ayer. Sigue el modelo.

> "Niño se cae del tercer piso"
> *Un niño se cayó del tercer piso.*

1. "Avión 707 con 150 pasajeros cae en el océano"
2. "Miles de personas oyen banda en estadio"
3. "Exposición incluye dibujos de muchacho de 15 años"
4. "Niños leen poemas en la Casa Blanca"
5. "Nadie cree chismes sobre vida de Juan Galán"
6. "Puente se cae después de la lluvia"
7. "Inspector no cree la historia del accidente"
8. "Desfile incluye compañía de baile brasileña"

C Una llamada importante. Completa el diálogo con las formas correctas del pretérito.

ROSA ¿(*Leer*) el periódico ayer?

MARÍA No, pero (*oír*) las noticias por la radio. ¿Por qué preguntas?

ROSA (*Ellos*) (*Incluir*) una noticia de nuestra escuela. Dicen que (*caerse*) el techo y no vamos a tener clases hasta lunes.

5 MARÍA ¿Y tú lo (*creer*)?

ROSA Claro que lo (*creer*). Lo (*leer*) en el periódico. Tú no (*oír*) nada por la radio, ¿verdad?

MARÍA No, nada. Voy a llamar a Jorge. Tal vez él (*leer*) u (*oír*) algo.

Palabras afirmativas y negativas

Review the affirmative and negative words that you know. Remember that they are antonyms.

AFFIRMATIVE	NEGATIVE
alguien	nadie
algo	nada
alguno, -a *(pron.)*	ninguno, -a *(pron.)*
algún, alguna *(adj.)*	ningún, ninguna *(adj.)*
siempre	nunca
también	tampoco
o . . . o	ni . . . ni

Notes: Refer to mini-dialogue 4 on pp. 332 and 340 for examples of affirmative and negative words.

Don't forget that if a negative word comes *after* a verb we must use *no* or another negative word *before* the verb: *Nunca escribo / No escribo nunca.*

1 When we use *alguien* or *nadie* as a direct object, we use the personal *a*.

¿Saludas **a alguien?**   *Are you greeting **someone?***
No espero **a nadie.**   *I'm **not** waiting for **anyone.***

When we use the pronouns *alguno* and *ninguno* to refer to people and we are using them as direct objects, we also use the personal *a*.

No encontré **a ninguno** de mis amigos.   *I did**n't** find **any** of my friends.*

2 The pronouns *alguno* and *ninguno* agree in gender with the nouns they replace.

¿Tienes planes para hoy?   *Do you have plans for today?*
No tengo **ninguno.**   *I don't have **any.***
Respondí a **algunas** de las llamadas.   *I answered **some** of the calls.*

Remember that we usually use *ninguno(a)* in the singular.

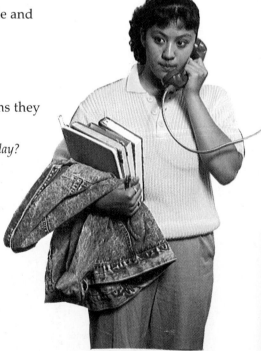

3 In questions, we often use the affirmative adjectives in the singular. We almost always use the negative adjectives in the singular. In English we usually use the plural.

¿Tienes **algún plan** para hoy?	*Do you have **any plans** for today?*
No respondí a **ninguna llamada**.	*I did**n't** answer **any calls**.*

4 Remember that *ni . . . ni* means "not . . . or" or "neither . . . nor" and that *o . . . o* means "either . . . or."

No vi **ni** al cartero **ni** a ningún mensajero.	*I did**n't** see the mail carrier **or** any messengers.*
Ni los costarricenses **ni** los hondureños son sudamericanos. Son centroamericanos.	***Neither** Costa Ricans **nor** Honduras are South Americans. They're Central Americans.*
O le mandas un telegrama **o** la llamas por teléfono.	***Either** you send her a telegram **or** you call her.*
Puedes **o** dejar un recado **o** volver a llamar.	*You can **either** leave a message **or** call back.*

PRÁCTICA

A Ninguno. Pregunta y contesta según el modelo.

> tener un libro de física
> ESTUDIANTE A *¿Tienes algún libro de física?*
> ESTUDIANTE B *No, no tengo ninguno.*

1. dejar un recado
2. llenar un formulario
3. envolver un regalo
4. incluir un chisme
5. poner una carta en el buzón
6. hacer una llamada por cobrar
7. recibir una caja por vía aérea
8. averiguar una dirección

B Ojalá que . . . ¿Qué dices en las siguientes situaciones? Haz frases con *ojalá que* y una palabra afirmativa. Sigue el modelo.

> El cartero no te entrega nada.
> *Ojalá que el cartero me entregue algo.*

1. Nadie te invita a la fiesta.
2. No encuentras ningún lugar para estacionar el coche.
3. Tu equipo no gana ninguna carrera.
4. Nadie dice nada interesante.
5. Nadie te deja ningún recado.
6. La médica no te receta nada para el resfriado.
7. No tienes ningún tema bueno para la composición de inglés.
8. Ninguno de tus amigos contesta el teléfono.

Práctica A
1. ¿Dejas algún recado?
   No, no dejo ninguno.
2. ¿Llenas algún formulario?
   No, no lleno ninguno.
3. ¿Envuelves algún regalo?
   No, no envuelvo ninguno.
4. ¿Incluyes algún chisme?
   No, no incluyo ninguno.
5. ¿Pones alguna carta en el buzón?
   No, no pongo ninguna.
6. ¿Haces alguna llamada por cobrar?
   No, no hago ninguna.
7. ¿Recibes alguna caja por vía aérea?
   No, no recibo ninguna.
8. ¿Averiguas alguna dirección?
   No, no averiguo ninguna.

Práctica B
1. Ojalá que alguien me invite a la fiesta.
2. Ojalá que encuentre algún lugar para estacionar el coche.
3. Ojalá que mi equipo gane alguna carrera.
4. Ojalá que alguien diga algo interesante.
5. Ojalá que alguien me deje algún recado.
6. Ojalá que la médica me recete algo para el resfriado.
7. Ojalá que tenga algún tema bueno para la composición de inglés.
8. Ojalá que alguno de mis amigos conteste el teléfono.

C ¿Siempre o nunca? Dos niños pequeños hablan de lo que sus padres quieren que ellos hagan siempre o que no hagan nunca. Sigue el modelo.

limpiar el dormitorio
Mamá quiere que siempre limpiemos el dormitorio.

1. lavarse las manos antes de comer
2. hablar con personas que no conocemos
3. hacer la cama
4. pedir comida sana
5. hablar en voz alta en la iglesia
6. comer tan lentamente como ella
7. dejar la ropa en el suelo
8. abrir la puerta sin preguntar quién es
9. cruzar la calle solos
10. dormir en el sofá nuevo
11. vestirse de prisa
12. sentirse bien

D Hablemos de ti.

1. ¿Leíste algún libro interesante el mes pasado? ¿Cuál fue tu favorito? ¿Por qué? ¿Leíste algo importante en el periódico hoy? ¿Qué leíste?
2. ¿Crees todo lo que oyes? ¿Por qué? ¿Crees todo lo que lees? ¿Por qué? ¿Qué noticias importantes oíste ayer por la tele o la radio?
3. ¿Algunas veces das excusas cuando no haces la tarea? ¿Diste alguna excusa recientemente *(recently)*? ¿Te creyó tu profesor(a)?
4. ¿Este año cayó mucha nieve donde tú vives? ¿Fuiste a esquiar? ¿Adónde? ¿Te caíste muchas veces?
5. ¿Vas a ir a algún lugar especial este fin de semana? ¿Piensas ir con alguien o solo(a)? ¿Vas a comprar algo? ¿Qué?

Práctica C
1. Mamá quiere que siempre nos lavemos las manos antes de comer.
2. Mamá quiere que nunca hablemos con personas que no conozcamos.
3. Mamá quiere que siempre hagamos la cama.
4. Mamá quiere que siempre pidamos comida sana.
5. Mamá quiere que nunca hablemos en voz alta en la iglesia.
6. Mamá quiere que siempre comamos tan lentamente como ella.
7. Mamá quiere que nunca dejemos la ropa en el suelo.
8. Mamá quiere que nunca abramos la puerta sin preguntar quién es.
9. Mamá quiere que nunca crucemos la calle solos.
10. Mamá quiere que nunca durmamos en el sofá nuevo.
11. Mamá quiere que siempre nos vistamos de prisa.
12. Mamá quiere que siempre nos sintamos bien.

Práctica D
Answers will vary.

Practice Sheet 10–7

Workbook Exs. G–J

Tape Manual Ex. 9　15

Refrán　16

Canción　17

Quiz 10–7

Correo Central en Madrid

APLICACIONES Discretionary

Notes: Answers to the **Repaso** and **Tema** appear in the Teacher Notes.

REPASO

Notes: Review of:
1. preterite of *leer* and *oír*
   possessive adjectives
2. indirect object pronouns
   verb + infinitive
   uses of *de*
3. preposition + infinitive
   preterite of regular and
   spelling-changing verbs
4. *o . . . o*
   ningún / ninguna
5. present subjunctive of *-ir*
   stem changing verbs
   preterite

Enrichment: You may want
to use the **Repaso** model
sentences for dictation.

Mira con cuidado las frases modelo. Luego cambia las frases que siguen al español según el modelo.

1. *Anoche leí un cuento corto de mi hermano.*
   (Yesterday I heard an interesting piece of news from my cousins.)
   (The day before yesterday they read an important telegram from their father.)
   (Last week we heard a funny story from our friends.)

2. *Les acabo de escoger el regalo. Ahora busco mis cheques de viajero.*
   (Irene is rewrapping a package for him. Right now she's cutting a piece of paper.)
   (We're trying to fill out a form for her. But I forget today's date.)
   (The messenger just delivered the telegram to me. It probably announces the arrival of the plane.)

3. *Antes de mandar el paquete, Ud. escribió la dirección.*
   (Before dialing the number, you (fam.) waited for the dial tone.)
   (After making the call, I found out the answer.)
   (Before writing the check, she included the tax.)

4. *O dan la respuesta correcta o no reciben ningún premio.*
   (We either enclose the correct return address or we won't receive any answer.)
   (She either rents the post office box or she doesn't get any mail.)
   (I('ll) either choose the fresh spinach or I won't order any vegetable.)

5. *Ojalá que no se duerma porque comió tanta comida.*
   (They don't want us to laugh because they forgot so many things.)
   (He doesn't want us to go to sleep because he heard those noises.)
   (I hope they don't laugh because we lost our flashlights.)

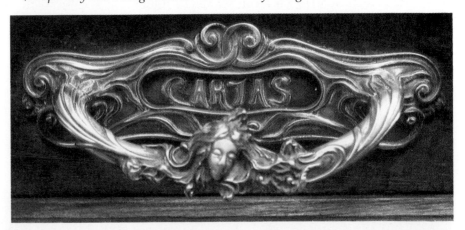

Un buzón en Buenos Aires,
Argentina

TEMA

Transparency 35

Notes: Time allowing, ask volunteers to present their **Tema** sentences to the class.

Escribe las frases en español.

1. Yesterday Rafael read a long letter from his friends.

2. Rafael just wrote to them. He's also enclosing a photograph of Silvia.

3. After closing the envelope, he wrote the return address.

4. You (formal) either send a registered letter or you don't get any receipt.

5. I hope they don't laugh because I spent so much money.

REDACCIÓN

Notes: Students may want to develop topic 3 of the **Redacción** as a dialogue rather than a paragraph.

Ahora escoge uno de los siguientes temas para escribir tu propio diálogo o párrafo.

1. Imagine that you are writing the letter Rafael wrote to his friend. Begin with a salutation and end with *Con cariño.* Mention the photograph of Silvia, who took it, and where it was taken.

2. Make up a phone conversation in which one person dials a wrong number.

3. Write a short paragraph about a long-distance call to another country. Whom are you trying to call and in what country? Do you have to ask the operator to get the number for you? What type of call are you making? Is it easy or difficult to talk on the phone with someone in another country?

COMPRUEBA TU PROGRESO   CAPÍTULO 10   Discretionary

Notes: Answers to the **Comprueba** appear in the Teacher Notes.

A   Completa las frases

Usa la forma correcta del verbo apropiado para completar cada frase.

1. Marta te _____ contar un chisme increíble.
   (ir a / aprender a)
2. Mi madre _____ trabajar a las nueve.
   (empezar a / aprender a)
3. Ellos _____ comer esta noche a mi casa.
   (venir a / empezar a)
4. ¿(Tú) _____ viajar a España este verano?
   (comenzar a / ir a)
5. ¿Por qué (tú) no me _____ llenar los formularios? (aprender a / enseñar a)
6. Si el teléfono _____ sonar, no contestes.
   (venir a / volver a)
7. El teatro _____ vender entradas para el concierto a las tres. (comenzar a / venir a)
8. Si quieres _____ dibujar, ésa es la mejor escuela. (venir a / aprender a)

B   ¿Qué hacemos?

Escoge la(s) palabra(s) correcta(s).

1. Por la mañana salgo de prisa (*para / antes de*) encontrar un buen estacionamiento.
2. Tengo que ir al correo pero no puedo mandar la carta (*sin / después de*) averiguar la dirección.
3. Necesitamos dinero (*para / sin*) pagar la cuenta.
4. (*Antes de / Después de*) hacer una llamada por cobrar tienes que decir tu nombre a la operadora.
5. (*Para / Sin*) obtener el permiso de manejar debes pasar un examen.
6. No puedes ganar el campeonato (*sin / después de*) practicar mucho.

C   El pretérito

Completa cada frase con la forma correcta del pretérito del verbo entre paréntesis.

1. Alicia _____ al mensajero cuando llegó.   (*oír*)
2. ¿ _____ David y Ana su correo anoche?   (*leer*)

3. ¿Qué _____ Uds. en la composición que escribieron?   (*incluir*)
4. Uds. no _____ que su equipo ganó.   (*creer*)
5. ¿Cuándo _____ (tú) el aviso?   (*leer*)
6. Él _____ enfrente del museo.   (*caerse*)
7. Descolgué el teléfono pero no _____ ningún tono.   (*oír*)
8. (Ellas) _____ todo lo que les contó.   (*creer*)
9. ¿ _____ (Ud.) el recibo?   (*incluir*)

D   Las palabras afirmativas

Contesta cada pregunta con una frase afirmativa.

1. ¿No compraste nada ayer?
2. ¿No viste a ninguno de los carteros?
3. ¿No hay nadie en la tienda?
4. ¿Nunca ganas las carreras?
5. ¿No sabes nada de los premios de gimnasia?
6. ¿No tienes ningún cheque de viajero?
7. ¿Nadie pagó el telegrama?
8. ¿No viste nada en el buzón?

E   ¿Qué quieren?

Vuelve a escribir las frases. Di lo que quieren o esperan los otros. Sigue los modelos.

> Pido mariscos.   (querer)
> *Quieren que pida mariscos.*
> Pedimos bistec.   (querer)
> *Quieren que pidamos bistec.*

1. No me siento asustado.   (esperar)
2. Nos sentimos nerviosos.   (no querer)
3. Se duerme.   (esperar)
4. Nos morimos de sed.   (no querer)
5. Te vistes muy de moda.   (querer)
6. Vestimos a los niños.   (querer)
7. Servimos guacamole.   (esperar)
8. Sirves langostas, ¿no?   (querer)
9. Hiervo los camarones.   (querer)
10. Hervimos la col con las papas.   (no querer)

Activity Masters   Chapter 10 Test   🖭 Listening Comprehension Test

VOCABULARIO DEL CAPÍTULO 10

Sustantivos
el apartado postal
el aviso
el beso
el buzón, *pl.* los buzones
el cariño
el cartero, la cartera
el código postal
la compañía
el correo *(mail)*
el chisme
la firma
el formulario
la llamada
el mensajero, la mensajera
la noticia
el operador, la operadora
el paquete
el recado
el recibo
el remitente
el sobre
el telegrama
el tono

Adjetivos
certificado, -a
equivocado, -a
querido, -a

Verbos
averiguar
caer(se)
colgar (o → ue)
descolgar (o → ue)
entregar
envolver (o → ue)
incluir
llenar *(to fill out / in)*
marcar
mudarse
responder (a)
saludar
sonar (o → ue)
volver (o → ue) a + *inf.*

Adverbios
en voz alta / baja
lentamente
por correo
por vía aérea

Expresiones
con cariño
de larga distancia
de mi parte
¿de parte de quién?
ir / venir a buscar
por cobrar
¿qué hay?
tenga la bondad de + *inf.*

Conjunción
o . . . o

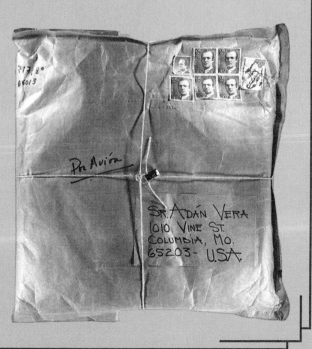

EL CINE DE HABLA ESPAÑOLA

The first Spanish movie was made nearly a hundred years ago in Spain, in 1896. Only a minute long, it was entitled *Salida de las alumnas del Colegio de San Luis de los Franceses,* and it showed just what the title promised: students leaving school. Because the new technology fascinated the public, this very short movie was a smash hit. Now, almost a century later, the movies are still a popular form of entertainment throughout the Spanish-speaking world. In spite of the spread of television, most large movie theaters are filled every weekend.

In some ways, moviegoing in a Spanish-speaking country is different from what you are used to. Theaters are usually richly decorated and very large, with orchestra seats, a mezzanine, and one or more balconies. Since tickets are sold according to the section, the higher you sit and the farther you are from the screen, the less your ticket will cost.

The show usually begins with one or more of the following: a short, a cartoon, or previews of coming attractions. This may be followed by an intermission, which is partly to allow latecomers to be seated and partly to give the audience a chance to buy refreshments. Candy vendors sometimes come down the aisle calling *"Bombones, chocolates, caramelos."* During the intermission, theaters may show commercials for local stores or restaurants.

American and other non-Spanish-language films are very popular, but they are sometimes dubbed into Spanish. Spain, Mexico, Venezuela, Argentina, and Cuba have major film industries. Many of their films have won international awards. Argentina's *La historia oficial,* for example, won the Oscar for best foreign-language film of 1985.

PALABRAS NUEVAS I

If students ask: Other related words you may want to present: *el camarógrafo,* cameraman; *la camarógrafa,* camerawoman.

¿Telenovela o documental?

Transparency 36
CONTEXTO VISUAL

el terremoto

el huracán
pl. los huracanes

el pronóstico del tiempo

el relámpago

el grado

30°

la temperatura

la locutora   el locutor

CANAL 5

el termómetro

To ask and give the temperature we say: *¿Cuál es la temperatura? Es **de** diez grados.*

el programa de concursos

los premios

el cantante

despierto, -a

dormido, -a

el público

bostezar

la cantante

hablar por señas

CONTEXTO COMUNICATIVO 2

1	PILAR	Esta **telenovela** me **aburre**. ¿Podemos ver **otra cosa**?
	GLORIA	Ya te **dije** que no. Quiero saber qué le **ocurre** a Pedro.
	PILAR	Pero es **el personaje** más aburrido de todos.
	GLORIA	¡Ay, Pilar, **cállate**!

Variaciones:

■ esta telenovela → este programa
■ me aburre → es aburrida

2	CARLOS	Ayer **conocí** a tu hermana mayor.
	EUGENIO	Si hablas de Luz, no es la mayor, **sino** la menor.
	CARLOS	¡No me digas! Pues **parece** mayor que tú.

■ conocí → vi
■ ¡no me digas! → ¡caramba!

3	MIGUEL	¿Te divertiste en **el concurso** de disfraces?
	ROBERTO	No fui al concurso, **sino que** jugué al jai alai con mi hermano.
	MIGUEL	¿Y quién ganó?
	ROBERTO	Él. Fue **un desastre**. Por fin **se aburrió** y se fue a jugar con **otra persona**.

■ el concurso → la fiesta
  al concurso → a la fiesta

4	JULIO	Esta mañana a las nueve **entrevistan** al profesor Sánchez **por** la televisión. Va a mostrar **toda clase de** recuerdos de su viaje.
	ESTER	¡Qué lástima! Todos tenemos clase a las nueve.
	JULIO	Eso no es un problema. Mi mamá va a **grabar** el programa. Podemos verlo más tarde.

■ ¡qué lástima! → ¡qué lata!

la telenovela *soap opera*

aburrir *to bore*

otra cosa *something else, anything else*

(yo) dije, (tú) dijiste, (Ud. / él / ella) dijo *(from* **decir***) told, said*

ocurrir *to happen, to occur*

el personaje *character (in a play, novel, etc.)*

cállate *be quiet!*

conocer *here: to meet, to get to know*

sino *(after negative) but, but rather*

parecer (yo parezco, tú pareces) *to seem (to be), to look like*

el concurso *contest, competition*

sino que + verb *(after a negative) but, but rather*

el desastre *disaster*

aburrirse *to be bored, to get bored*

otra persona *someone else, no one else*

entrevistar *to interview*

por *here: on*

toda clase de *all kinds of*

grabar *to record*

Palabras Nuevas I   **365**

5 CARLITOS	Te **traje** unas flores, mamá.	**(yo) traje, (tú) trajiste, (Ud. / él / ella) trajo** *(from* **traer***)* *brought*
SRA. GUZMÁN	¿Me **trajiste** flores? ¡Qué amable eres, hijito! Ponlas en esa canasta, por favor.	

6 RAFAEL   ¿Oyes esos **truenos**? Creo que pronto va a llover.

el trueno   *thunder, thunderclap*

GUADALUPE   Sí, está muy oscuro. Parece que llega **una tormenta.**

la tormenta   *storm*

- ¿oyes esos truenos? → ¿oíste ese trueno?
- ¿oyes esos truenos? → ¿viste esos relámpagos?
- creo → **indican**

indicar   *to indicate, to show*

- parece que → estoy segura de que*

7 SONIA   A las ocho y media hay un **documental** sobre una escuela para niños **sordos.**

el documental   *documentary*
sordo, -a   *deaf*

LUIS   ¿Ah sí? A mí me gustaría aprender a hablar por señas.

SONIA   Estoy segura de que van a dar **información** sobre eso.

la información   *information*

- documental → programa especial
- sordos → **ciegos**

ciego, -a   *blind*

  a hablar por señas → sobre el Braille

PRÁCTICA

Práctica A
1. toda clase de
2. bosteza
3. se aburre
4. hablar por señas
5. indica
6. se queja de / sorda
7. tormenta / grados
8. dormida

Reteach / Review: After students do Ex. A either orally or in writing, you may want to ask volunteers to make up sentences with the words not used to complete the sentences in the exercise.

A   Tele y más tele.   Hace mal tiempo y Eva pasa todo el fin de semana delante del televisor. Escoge la palabra o expresión correcta para completar cada frase.

1. Con nueve canales, Eva piensa que puede escoger entre *(sólo algunos / toda clase de / muy pocos)* programas.
2. Durante un documental sobre unas cantantes francesas, Eva *(graba / bosteza / ocurre)* cada cinco minutos.
3. Después de tres horas de programas deportivos, Eva *(se aburre / habla por señas / indica)* mucho.
4. Ve un programa sobre unos niños sordos que aprenden a *(parecer oscuros / hablar por señas / estornudar).*
5. El periódico no *(indica / graba / entrevista)* cuáles de las películas son buenas y cuáles son malas.

* When we use *seguro, -a (de)* before a verb, we use *de que.*

6. La madre de Eva (receta / recomienda / se queja de) un programa de música rock y dice que toda la familia va a estar (pálida / sorda / sana).

7. El pronóstico del tiempo dice que una (locutora / tormenta / telenovela) viene del mar y que la temperatura va a bajar a diez (truenos / huracanes / grados).

8. Después de ocho horas de televisión, Eva está (congelada / fea / dormida) en el sofá.

B El pronóstico del tiempo. Es la hora del pronóstico del tiempo en el Canal 4. Completa las frases con las palabras correctas de la lista.

| fecha | información | relámpago | termómetro | tormenta |
| grados | lluvia | temperatura | tiempo | truenos |

''Buenas noches, señores y señoras. El huracán de ayer trajo temperaturas muy bajas a la ciudad. Cayeron más de 30 centímetros de _____. Y yo espero no volver a oír nunca _____ tan fuertes. Esta mañana a las cinco, el _____ indicó una temperatura de 14 _____,
5 la más baja en los últimos años para esta _____. Afortunadamente, pronto la _____ va a subir otra vez. En este momento es de 17 grados. Mañana esperamos tener buen _____, con una temperatura entre 22 y 27 grados. Pero parece que en pocos días vamos a tener mal tiempo otra vez. En este momento empieza otra fuerte _____ en el Golfo de
10 México. Más _____ sobre esto después de este anuncio comercial.''

C Hablemos de ti.

1. ¿Cuáles son tus programas preferidos de televisión? ¿Qué clase de programas son? ¿Te gustan las telenovelas? ¿Cuáles ves? ¿Puedes contar lo que ocurrió la semana pasada en tu telenovela preferida?

2. ¿A veces no estás de acuerdo con tus padres o hermanos sobre qué programa quieren mirar? ¿Quién gana? ¿Qué clase de programas les gustan más? ¿Y a ti?

3. ¿Miras programas de concursos? ¿Qué tienen que hacer las personas que participan? ¿Qué te parecen estos programas?

4. ¿Miras a menudo el pronóstico del tiempo? ¿Lo miras más frecuentemente en el verano o en el invierno? ¿Por qué? ¿Qué temperatura indica el termómetro estos días?

5. ¿Ocurren desastres de la naturaleza (nature) donde vives? ¿Qué clase?

6. ¿Te gustan las tormentas? ¿Por qué? ¿Te asustan los relámpagos? ¿Por qué? ¿Qué debes hacer y no hacer cuando hay relámpagos?

Práctica B
lluvia / truenos
termómetro / grados
fecha
temperatura
tiempo
tormenta
información

Enrichment: In connection with Ex. B, you may want to ask students to read the weather forecast in a local newspaper or to watch a weather report on TV and prepare a brief forecast of their own. Ask volunteers to present their reports to the class.

Práctica C
Answers will vary.

APLICACIONES

🔲 4 🔲 5 Pronunciación

Una entrevista con Ángel Galán

Enrichment: Before presenting the **Diálogo,** you may want to ask students to cover the glosses and to try to guess the meaning of each of the words and phrases from the context.

You may want to point out that Gloria Alba and Ángel Galán are fictional characters. Their names literally mean "Glory Dawn" and "Angel Elegant Fellow."

Gloria Alba, locutora del Canal 8, entrevista a Ángel Galán, actor de cine muy conocido de la América del Sur.

GLORIA   Dime, Ángel, ¿qué es lo que haces hoy día?[1]

ÁNGEL   Ahora trabajo en una película que se llama *Entre tú y yo.*
5   En mayo pienso hacer un documental sobre los
terremotos. Y después vuelvo a trabajar en el teatro en
Buenos Aires.

GLORIA   Es una vida muy activa. ¿Nunca vas de vacaciones?

ÁNGEL   No las necesito, Gloria. Cuando uno hace lo que le
10   gusta, no se cansa.[2]

GLORIA   El periódico *Hoy* dijo que te casaste[3] el mes pasado con
una escritora peruana.

ÁNGEL   Los periódicos cuentan toda clase de chismes sobre mí.
No es verdad. La verdad es que sólo vivo para mi
15   profesión y no tengo tiempo para otra cosa.

GLORIA   Pero, ¿no te aburre vivir solo?

ÁNGEL   No, nunca me aburro. Mi trabajo es muy interesante.

GLORIA   Pues, gracias por la entrevista, Ángel.

ÁNGEL   De nada, Gloria. Fue un gran placer.[4]

---

[1]**hoy día** *nowadays*   [2]**cansarse** *to get tired*   [3]**casarse con** *to get married to*   [4]**el placer** *pleasure*

Diálogo
1. Es locutora.
2. Es un actor de cine muy conocido (de la América del Sur).
3. *Entre tú y yo.* Answers will vary, but most will probably say *una película romántica.*
4. Piensa hacer un documental sobre los terremotos. Y después vuelve a trabajar en el teatro en Buenos Aires.
5. Porque le gusta su trabajo.

Preguntas
Contesta según el diálogo.

1. ¿Cuál es la profesión de Gloria Alba?   2. ¿Quién es Ángel Galán?
3. ¿Cómo se llama la película que él hace ahora? ¿Qué clase de película crees que es?   4. ¿Qué piensa hacer Ángel después de terminar la película?   5. ¿Por qué nunca va de vacaciones Ángel?   6. ¿Qué dice Ángel de los periódicos? ¿Qué piensas tú de lo que dicen los periódicos

sobre las personas muy conocidas? ¿Crees todo lo que lees en los periódicos y en las revistas?   7. Según Ángel, ¿por qué no se aburre?   8. En tu opinión, ¿por qué le importa a la gente lo que hacen y dicen las personas famosas? ¿Te importa a ti? ¿Por qué?   9. ¿Ves programas o lees revistas en que entrevistan a actores o a cantantes famosos? ¿Por qué disfrutas de ellos?   10. En tu opinión, ¿cómo es la vida de un actor o una actriz famoso(a)? ¿Es divertida? ¿Difícil? ¿Por qué?

6. Dice que los periódicos cuentan toda clase de chismes sobre él y que no dicen la verdad. / Answers will vary.
7. Porque su trabajo es muy interesante.
8–10. Answers will vary.

Notes: In connection with the **Participación,** you may want to ask students to agree on which partner will play which role. Once they decide on the basic questions for their interview, students may prepare their parts of the dialogue at home.

Participación
Work with a partner to make up a dialogue between an interviewer and a TV, movie, or rock star.

El grupo Menudo de Puerto Rico

PALABRAS NUEVAS II

Essential

¿A qué hora es la función?

If students ask: Other related words you may want to present: *el vaquero*, cowboy; *la marquesina*, marquee; *la limosina*, limousine.

CONTEXTO VISUAL

"Se fueron por allá."

They went that-a-way.

el director

la directora

la taquillera

el taquillero

la taquilla

la estrella de cine

el subtítulo

el autógrafo

María Morena

el admirador *

la admiradora

sentarse (e→ie)

el acomodador

la acomodadora

la fila

* Although *aficionado(a)* and *admirador(a)* both mean "fan," we use them differently. We use *aficionado(a) a* with activities and *admirador(a) de* with people: *Somos aficionados al béisbol / Somos admiradores de Fernando Valenzuela.*

CONTEXTO COMUNICATIVO 7

1 DIANA ¿Vamos al Cine Rex esta noche? Dan una película italiana **en versión original.**

PABLO No me gustan los subtítulos. Es difícil leerlos. Prefiero las **películas dobladas.**

DIANA Yo no. Nunca las **traducen** bien y no puedo **reírme de** chistes que no entiendo.

Variaciones:
- italiana → **extranjera**
- traducen → **hacen**

en versión original *in the original (foreign) language*

la película doblada *dubbed film*

traducir (yo traduzco, tú traduces) *to translate*

reírse (de) *to laugh (at)*

extranjero, -a *foreign*

2 DIANA Quiero ver esta película. **Tiene** mucho **éxito.**

PABLO No **reconozco** ni el título ni los nombres de los actores.

DIANA No importa. Alicia me dijo que nos va a gustar porque los personajes son muy divertidos.

- reconozco → conozco
- personajes → actores **principales**

tener éxito *to be successful*

reconocer (yo reconozco, tú reconoces) *to recognize*

principal *main, leading*

3 JUDIT ¿Qué sabes de la película que dan en el Cine Rex?

MARIO Es norteamericana. Cliff Muggins **hace el papel de** un policía en Nueva York. ¿Te **interesa** verla? ¿Quieres ir conmigo esta tarde?

JUDIT Te **agradezco** la invitación, pero hoy no puedo ir.

- te agradezco → gracias por

hacer el papel de *to play the role of*

interesar *to interest*

agradecer (yo agradezco, tú agradeces) *to thank (for), to appreciate*

4 JAIME Paco me **ofreció** unas entradas para **la función** de las ocho. ¿Quieres ir?

MARTA Tengo que estar en casa temprano. ¿Cuánto dura?

JAIME Dos horas y media con **el intervalo.**

MARTA Bueno, entonces puedo ir.

- la función → el espectáculo
- temprano → antes de medianoche

ofrecer (yo ofrezco, tú ofreces) *to offer*

la función, pl. las funciones *show*

el intervalo *intermission*

5 ENRIQUE   ¿No te pareció **complicado el argumento** de esa película?

BEATRIZ   Sólo **al principio.** Después fue muy **sencillo.**

ENRIQUE   ¿Sencillo? ¿Una historia que **tiene lugar** en un hotel en la luna? ¿Con jirafas?

BEATRIZ   Mira, no quiero **discutir** contigo y especialmente no quiero **discutir** más **de** cine.

- complicado → difícil
- hotel → castillo
- jirafas → ratones y arañas

complicado, -a   *complicated*
el argumento   *plot*
al principio   *at first*
sencillo, -a   *simple*
tener lugar   *to take place*
discutir   *to argue*
discutir de   *to discuss, to talk about*

6 DIEGO   ¿Quién es esa mujer que está **rodeada de** tantas personas?

LEONOR   Se llama Guadalupe Limón. Es una cantante ciega. Van a **filmar una entrevista** con ella para el Canal 5.

- filmar → grabar

rodeado, -a de   *surrounded by*

filmar   *to film*
la entrevista   *interview*

7 SRA. DÍAZ   ¿Qué piensan **los jóvenes** de la película de Iowa Smith?

JORGE   Algunos dicen que es un **éxito,** otros que es un **fracaso.**

- piensan → dicen
  dicen → creen

el/la joven, pl. **los/las jóvenes**   *young person*
el éxito   *success*
el fracaso   *failure*

EN OTRAS PARTES

el intervalo

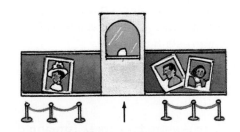

Se dice también *el descanso, el receso* y *el intermedio.*

También se dice *la boletería.*

PRÁCTICA

A Vamos a discutir de cine.   Unos turistas visitan un estudio (*studio*) de cine y hacen muchas preguntas. Escoge la respuesta correcta.

1. ¿Qué papel hace, señor?
2. ¿Qué filman esas personas?
3. ¿Es complicado el argumento?
4. ¿Qué hace ese hombre rodeado de chicas?
5. ¿Están de acuerdo el director y el actor principal?
6. ¿Qué hace esa mujer?
7. ¿A quién entrevista la locutora?
8. ¿Quién es esa mujer tan guapa?

a. ¡Nunca! ¡Ellos siempre discuten!
b. Traduce para los sordos en el grupo.
c. A la estrella de cine española.
d. Les da su autógrafo.
e. Al contrario, es muy sencillo.
f. Una cantante cubana.
g. Soy el hijo de una señora rica.
h. Una película romántica.

B ¡Qué película!   Imagina que estás delante de un cine cuando termina la película. La gente que sale habla sobre la película, pero hay tanto ruido que no oyes algunas palabras. Escoge las palabras de la lista para completar las frases.

argumento	hizo el papel	me parecieron	sencillo
ciegos	intervalo	principal	sentarnos
extranjero	me aburro	reconocí	trajiste
fila			

1. —¿Te gustó?
   —No. No entendí muy bien el _____.
   —Pues no sé por qué. Es muy _____, como todas las historias románticas.
2. —¿Quién es la actriz que _____ de profesora?
   —¿No conoces a Cristina Conde?
   —¿Cristina Conde? Pues, con ese pelo castaño, no la _____.
3. —No me gustó. Todos los personajes _____ antipáticos.
   —A mí me gustó el actor _____, Pedro Martín.
   —No es de aquí, ¿verdad?
   —No, él es _____. Creo que es del Uruguay.
4. —¡Ay, me duelen los ojos! ¿Por qué siempre tenemos que _____ en la primera _____? En unos años vamos a estar _____.
5. —¿Por qué _____ un libro al cine?
   —Siempre llevo algo para leer en el _____. Si no, no tengo nada que hacer y _____.

Filmando una película en Madrid, España

C ¿Qué palabra es distinta? En cada grupo hay una palabra o expresión que no debe estar. ¿Cuál es? Haz una frase completa con ella.

1. a. premio   b. cuento   c. historia   d. argumento
2. a. ser popular   b. tener éxito   c. ser conocido   d. tener lugar
3. a. taquillera   b. vendedora   c. dependienta   d. admiradora
4. a. relámpago   b. trueno   c. fracaso   d. tormenta
5. a. telenovela   b. taquilla   c. documental   d. noticias
6. a. función   b. película   c. programa   d. relámpago
7. a. terremoto   b. desastre   c. éxito   d. huracán
8. a. concurso   b. temperatura   c. grado   d. termómetro

D ¿Qué dan en el Canal 4? Unos muchachos miran la guía de espectáculos para buscar un buen programa de televisión. Lee la guía y contesta las preguntas.

NOCHE

8:00 ❷ Noticias

8:00 ❺ El tiempo

8:00 ❸ El amor (*love*) ciego. Telenovela. En este capítulo Clara deja a Gustavo y vuelve a vivir con sus padres. Cristina enseña a bailar a Ernesto porque quiere que él baile en la fiesta de cumpleaños de Gloria. Continúan los problemas de Margarita en el trabajo. Estrella invitada (*guest star*): Dolores Milonga.

8:30 ❷ Los leones del África. Documental. El conocido director ecuatoriano Rafael Molina presenta otro de sus estupendos documentales sobre los animales. Filmó éste en distintos países del África en 1988.

8:30 ❹ CINE: ¡Paren ese elefante! Comedia. Pepe Culebra hace el papel de un torero sin trabajo que tiene que aprender a trabajar con un elefante. Con Ana Medina y el elefante Sultán.

8:30 ❺ CINE: De los relámpagos viene el fuego. (Estados Unidos, 1939) Las complicadas aventuras del conocido personaje de las novelas de Freddy Schmitz. Zambango va con su amigo Trak a la ciudad de los hombres-rana. Allí conocen a la bella Susana y a su padre, el profesor Goldstein, quien estudia la vida de los monos. Pero Trak quiere las joyas de Susana y empiezan los problemas . . . Versión original con subtítulos en español.

9:30 ❸ La hora de los millones. Concurso. El popular y simpático José Carrasco presenta, como siempre, este programa. Premios fabulosos para los ganadores.

9:30 ❹ FÚTBOL. Repetimos el partido del domingo. Partido del Campeonato de Europa: Atlético de Bilbao contra Dínamo de Moscú.

1. En la telenovela, ¿qué hace Clara? ¿Quién crees tú que es Gustavo? ¿Qué le pasa a Margarita?
2. Imagina que tú eres Rafael Molina y que haces *Los leones de África*. Describe el documental y cómo lo hiciste.
3. ¿En qué canal dan el programa deportivo y a qué hora? ¿Crees que es un partido importante? ¿Por qué? ¿Es la primera vez que lo dan?
4. ¿Quién es Zambango? ¿Adónde va Zambango y con quién? ¿A quién encuentran allí? ¿Qué busca Trak? ¿En qué idioma es esta película? ¿Cómo lo sabes?
5. En *¡Paren ese elefante!*, ¿qué papel hace Pepe Culebra? ¿Crees que es un personaje cómico o serio? ¿Por qué?
6. ¿Qué clase de programa dan a las 9:30 en el Canal 3? ¿Qué clase de premios crees que dan? ¿Cómo lo sabes?

E Hablemos de ti.
1. ¿Te gustaría ser estrella de cine o director(a)? ¿Por qué?
2. ¿A veces vas a ver películas con subtítulos? ¿Ves películas dobladas de otros idiomas? ¿Cuál prefieres? ¿Por qué?
3. ¿Qué crees que es más importante para un actor? ¿Ser famoso, ser rico o hacer papeles interesantes? ¿Por qué?
4. ¿Te gustaría trabajar como taquillero(a) o como acomodador(a)? ¿Por qué?
5. Cuando vas al cine, ¿en qué fila prefieres sentarte? ¿Por qué?

Práctica E
Answers will vary.

Practice Sheet 11–2

Workbook Exs. C–D

Tape Manual Exs. 3–4 8

Refrán 9

Quiz 11–2

Enrichment: If the **Actividad** is particularly successful with your class, you may want to expand on it by asking students to prepare a very brief summary of the movie's plot, a few remarks from critics, and a poster advertising the film.

ACTIVIDAD

¿Qué dice?   Bring to class six pictures from magazines or newspapers. Imagine that these are scenes from a movie that need Spanish subtitles. Work with a partner to make up appropriate subtitles for each of the pictures.

ESTUDIO DE PALABRAS

By now you have discovered that there are many Spanish words that are very similar to English words, but some of them have very different meanings. For example, you may have noticed the similarity between the Spanish word *éxito*, which means "success," and the English word "exit" (*la salida*). These kinds of words are called *amigos falsos*. Here are some others that you have learned:

el argumento	*plot*
la etiqueta	*tag, label*
asistir a	*to attend*

Which of the words in the following sentences are *amigos falsos*? What do they really mean?

> Ésta es una pensión muy cara.
> No reconozco tu firma.
> Ese globo es muy largo.
> Aquella librería vende libros extranjeros.
> Pon la ropa en el armario.
> Nuestro dormitorio está en el segundo piso.

Sinónimos

Cambia las palabras en cursiva por un sinónimo.
1. *El espectáculo* comienza a las nueve.
2. Aquí tienes *la firma* de Picasso.
3. Me encanta *hablar de* cine.

Antónimos

Cambia las palabras en cursiva por un antónimo.
1. Su última película fue *un éxito*.
2. Me parece demasiado *sencillo* para tener éxito.
3. *Me divertí* cuando vi el programa de concursos.
4. Son las diez y todo el mundo está *dormido*.

Notes: You may want to cover the first part of the **Estudio de palabras** in class. Then students may write the *Sinónimos* and *Antónimos* sentences at home. Ask volunteers to write the answers on the board so that students may correct their own work.

Estudio de palabras

pensión	*boardinghouse*
firma	*signature*
globo	*balloon*
largo	*long*
librería	*bookstore*
ropa	*clothing*
dormitorio	*bedroom*

Sinónimos
1. La función
2. el autógrafo
3. discutir de

Antónimos
1. un fracaso
2. complicado
3. me aburrió
4. despierto

Un concierto de música popular en Asunción, Paraguay

EXPLICACIONES I   Essential

El pretérito de ciertos verbos que terminan en *-ir*

You know that stem-changing *-ar* and *-er* verbs are regular in the preterite and do not have the stem change: *contar* → *conté*, *contaste*, etc., *volver* → *volví*, *volviste*, etc. Stem-changing *-ir* verbs, however, do have a stem change in the *Ud. / él / ella* and *Uds. / ellos / ellas* forms in the preterite.

PEDIR		PREFERIR		DORMIR	
pedí	pedimos	preferí	preferimos	dormí	dormimos
pediste	pedisteis	preferiste	preferisteis	dormiste	dormisteis
pidió	pidieron	prefirió	prefirieron	durmió	durmieron

Luz **se vistió** en cinco minutos.   *Luz **got dressed** in five minutes.*
La cantante **se sintió** mal durante   *The singer **felt** sick during*
el concurso.   *the contest.*
Mi tío **se murió** el año pasado.   *My uncle **died** last year.*

1 *Reír(se)* and *sonreír* have the same *e* → *i* change as *pedir*. However, they have an accent mark in all of their forms, except the *Uds. / ellos / ellas* forms.

REÍR	
reí	reímos
reíste	reísteis
rió	rieron

Me reí del actor principal.   *I **laughed** at the leading actor.*
¿Te **sonrió** Fernando?   ***Did** Fernando **smile** at you?*
Los jóvenes **se rieron** del   *The young people **laughed** at the*
argumento.   *plot.*

PRÁCTICA

Práctica A

1. ¿Cómo te sentiste en el avión?
   Me sentí …
2. ¿… se sintió …?
   Se sintió …
3. ¿… se sintieron …?
   Se sintieron …
4. ¿… se sintió …?
   Me sentí …
5. ¿… te sentiste …?
   Me sentí …
6. ¿… se sintieron …?
   Nos sentimos …
7. ¿… se sintieron …?
   Nos sentimos …
8. ¿… se sintió …?
   … se sintió …
9. ¿… te sentiste …?
   Me sentí …
10. ¿… se sintieron …?
    Se sintieron …

A Vamos a comparar apuntes.   Un grupo de turistas discuten su viaje. Pregunta y contesta según el modelo. Usa los adjetivos de la lista.

aburrido	cansado	contento	estupendo	impaciente
bienvenido	cómodo	enfermo	fuerte	nervioso

(tú) / cuando llegamos
ESTUDIANTE A   *¿Cómo te sentiste cuando llegamos?*
ESTUDIANTE B   *Me sentí cansado(a).*

1. (tú) / en el avión
2. Elena / cuando bajó del avión
3. Felipe y María / en el museo
4. Ud. / al principio del viaje
5. (tú) / por la noche
6. María y tú / en el autobús del aeropuerto
7. Uds. / cuando subieron a la montaña
8. el profesor / después de comer esas langostas
9. (tú) / cuando regresaste al hotel
10. Cristina y Clara / después de dar el paseo en barco

Práctica B

1. ¿Se durmió Carlota? Sí, se durmió cuando la función empezó.
2. ¿Te dormiste? … me dormí …
3. ¿Se durmieron …? … se durmieron …
4. ¿Se durmieron …? … se durmieron …
5. ¿Se durmió …? … se durmió …
6. ¿Se durmieron …? … se durmieron …
7. ¿Se durmieron …? … nos dormimos …
8. ¿Te dormiste …? … me dormí …

B Una película aburrida.   *Iowa Smith y la montaña de fuego* fue un fracaso. El público se durmió durante la función. Indica cuándo se durmió cada uno. Sigue el modelo.

Diego / durante el intervalo
ESTUDIANTE A   *¿Se durmió Diego?*
ESTUDIANTE B   *Sí, se durmió durante el intervalo.*

1. Carlota / cuando la función empezó
2. (tú) / cuando Iowa comenzó a hablar por señas
3. los acomodadores / cuando apagaron las luces
4. María y su hermana / después de esa canción tan tonta
5. Gerardo / al principio
6. Ana y Eva / cuando Iowa le dio el premio a la cantante
7. Alfredo y tú / antes del terremoto
8. (tú) / cuando ocurrió la tormenta

C ¡Qué camarero!   Imagina que estás en un restaurante con tu familia y unos invitados. El restaurante no tiene buenos camareros. Pregunta y contesta según el modelo. ¡Ten cuidado con los complementos indirectos!

(tú) / pescado / el camarero / mariscos
ESTUDIANTE A   *¿Qué pediste?*
ESTUDIANTE B   *Pedí pescado, pero el camarero me sirvió mariscos.*

1. (tú) / agua / (él) / vino
2. el Sr. Ortega / sopa / (ellos) / ensalada
3. Alicia / arroz / (él) / papas fritas
4. Uds. / chuletas de cordero / (ellos) / chuletas de cerdo
5. mamá / guisantes / (ellos) / frijoles
6. ellos / paella / (él) / gazpacho
7. (nosotros) / flan / (ellos) / pasteles
8. papá / café / (él) / té
9. mamá / fruta / (él) / un helado

D **El baile de carnaval.** Completa el siguiente párrafo con las formas correctas del pretérito de los verbos de la lista. Puedes usar algunos verbos más de una vez.

divertirse	pedir	reír	repetir	servir
dormirse	preferir	reírse	sentirse	vestirse

Anoche fuimos a una fiesta de carnaval. Yo _____ de fantasma y Alberto _____ de torero. Para mi disfraz, (yo) le _____ prestada a mamá una sábana, y Alberto le _____ prestado el mantel rojo del comedor. Ella _____ mucho de nosotros. Clarita no _____ de nada; es
5 un poco tímida y _____ ir sin disfraz.

Cuando llegamos a la fiesta empezamos a bailar. Encontramos a varios amigos y _____ mucho con ellos. Yo _____ muy contenta con mi disfraz. Alberto contó chistes y todos (nosotros) _____ mucho de ellos, pero después (él) _____ casi todos los mismos chistes y yo ya no
10 _____ más. (Ellos) _____ sandwiches y ensalada de frutas.

Nos quedamos hasta la una de la mañana, pero la fiesta continuó por dos horas más. Clarita _____ en el coche. Yo la llevé dormida a su cama. Luego me acosté y _____ en seguida.

Práctica C
1. ¿Qué pediste? Pedí agua, pero me sirvió vino.
2. ¿... pidió el Sr. Ortega? Pidió ... le sirvieron ...
3. ¿... pidió ...? Pidió ... le sirvió ...
4. ¿... pidieron ...? Pedimos ... nos sirvieron ...
5. ¿... pidió ...? Pidió ... le sirvieron ...
6. ¿... pidieron ...? Pidieron ... les sirvió ...
7. ¿... pedimos ...? Uds. pidieron (or: pedimos) ... les (or: nos) sirvieron ...
8. ¿... pidió ...? Pidió ... le sirvió ...
9. ¿... pidió ...? Pidió ... le sirvió ...

Práctica D
me vestí
se vistió / pedí
pidió
se rió / se vistió
prefirió
nos divertimos (or: nos reímos) / me sentí
nos reímos
repitió
reí / sirvieron
se durmió
me dormí

Practice Sheet 11–3

Tape Manual Ex. 5 🔲 10

Televisión en Guadalajara, México

El pretérito de *venir*

◆ **OBJECTIVE:**

**TO TELL WHY
PEOPLE CAME TO A
PLACE OR AN
EVENT**

Reteach / Review: You may
want to contrast the present-
tense and preterite forms of
venir by doing an oral
transformation drill: *Siempre
vengo temprano a clase. ¿Y
ayer? (Ud. vino temprano a
clase.)*

Here are the preterite forms of *venir*.

VENIR	
vine	vinimos
viniste	vinisteis
vino	vinieron

Note that the *e* of the stem changes to *i* in all of the preterite forms. The endings are regular except for the *yo* and *Ud.* / *él* / *ella* forms. None of the endings has a written accent.

PRÁCTICA

¿Por qué viniste al rancho?   ¿Por qué vino toda esta gente al Rancho Relámpago? Sigue el modelo.

>   todos (nosotros) / descansar
>   *Todos vinimos para descansar.*

1. mi mamá / disfrutar del campo
2. (yo) / montar a caballo
3. ese director de cine / filmar una película del oeste
4. mis hermanas mayores / ver a las estrellas de cine
5. mi hermanito / ver el ganado
6. ese locutor / entrevistar al director y a las estrellas
7. Uds. / maquillar a los actores, ¿no?
8. (tú) / ayudar a los dueños, ¿no?
9. casi todos (nosotros) / admirar el paisaje

Práctica
1. Mi mamá vino para disfrutar
   del campo.
2. Vine …
3. … vino …
4. … vinieron …
5. … vino …
6. … vino …
7. … vinieron …
8. … Viniste …
9. … vinimos …

Practice Sheet 11–4

 11   Tape Manual Ex. 6

Quiz 11–3

En el cine en Antigua,
Guatemala

Pero, sino y sino que

Notes: There are examples of *sino* and *sino que* in mini-dialogues 2 and 3 on p. 365.

You know that *pero* means "but." After a negative, to contradict what came before, we use *sino* instead of *pero*. It means "but" or "but rather."

No es el cartero **sino** un mensajero.	*He isn't the mailman **but** a messenger.*
El formulario no es sencillo **sino** muy complicado.	*The form isn't simple **but** very complicated.*
No me gusta discutir de películas **sino** verlas.	*I don't like to talk about films **but** to see them*
No me interesa escribir cartas **sino** recibirlas.	*I'm not interested in writing letters **but rather** (in) receiving them.*

Notice that in each sentence what follows *sino* contradicts the first part of the statement.

1 In the last two examples you saw that we can use an infinitive after *sino*. But if the verb is not an infinitive, we must use *sino que*.

No le receté nada **sino que** le recomendé bajar de peso.	*I didn't prescribe anything for him **but** recommended that he lose weight.*
No quiero que hagas la llamada **sino que** busques el número en la guía telefónica.	*I don't want you to make the call **but rather** to look for the number in the phone book.*

PRÁCTICA

A No fui allí, sino allá. Escoge la palabra o expresión apropiada de la derecha para completar las frases. Sigue el modelo.

No es un argumento sencillo . . .
No es un argumento sencillo sino complicado.

1. Mi mamá no tiene el pelo corto . . .
2. Jorge no está dormido . . .
3. Éste no es un tren local . . .
4. No fue sólo un pequeño fracaso . . .
5. No recibí ningún regalo . . .
6. No dije gordo . . .
7. No traje una pila . . .
8. El cantante no está rodeado de admiradores . . .

una bombilla
de fotógrafos
complicado
largo
un desastre
un premio
despierto
expreso
sordo

Práctica A
1. ... sino largo
2. ... sino despierto
3. ... sino expreso
4. ... sino un desastre
5. ... sino un premio
6. ... sino sordo
7. ... sino una bombilla
8. ... sino de fotógrafos

Reteach / Extra Help: After students complete Ex. A, you may want to reinforce the difference between *sino* and *sino que*. Ask students to redo Ex. A adding a verb and using *sino que*. For example: *No es un argumento sencillo sino que es muy complicado.*

Práctica B
pero
sino
Pero
sino
sino
pero
sino
sino
sino
Pero
sino

B **En el cine.** Raúl encuentra a Julia delante del cine. Completa el diálogo con *pero* o *sino*.

JULIA Fui a la taquilla, _____ no te vi.

RAÚL No te dije en la taquilla, _____ en la esquina.

JULIA Pues no te oí. _____ no importa, porque nos encontramos.

5 RAÚL Bueno, no vinimos para discutir en la calle, _____ para ver una película. Vamos. . . . Veo unos asientos allá en la segunda fila.

JULIA No me gusta sentarme en la segunda fila, _____ en la séptima o la octava.

(Por fin encuentran dos asientos que les gustan y pronto empieza la película.)

10 RAÚL Dijiste que es una película doblada, _____ es una con subtítulos. ¡Y mira! La historia no tiene lugar en Caracas, _____ en Río. La mayoría de las películas venezolanas no tienen lugar en un país extranjero, _____ en Venezuela, ¿no?

JULIA Ésta no es una película venezolana, _____ una brasileña. ¿No

15 oyes que hablan en portugués?

RAÚL _____ reconozco a esa actriz, y no conozco a ninguna actriz brasileña.

JULIA ¡Cállate, Raúl! No vine al cine para discutir contigo, _____ para ver la película.

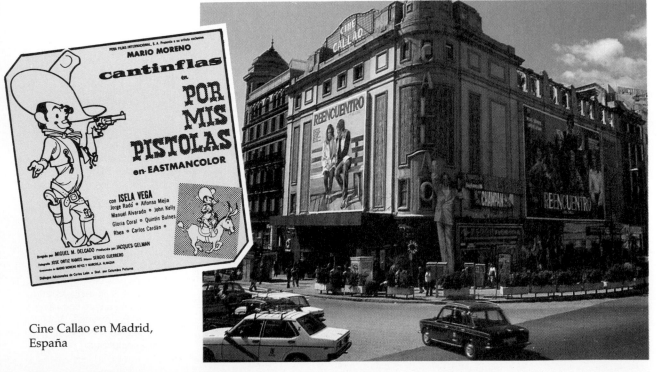

Cine Callao en Madrid, España

C   No seas tan pesimista.   Unos amigos hacen un picnic y tratan de
ser optimistas. Completa las frases con la palabra correcta: *sino* o *sino
que*.

1. No tenemos que caminar una hora _____ 55 minutos.
2. Ésos no son mosquitos _____ moscas pequeñas.
3. No viene un huracán _____ un viento fuerte.
4. Las salchichas no están quemadas _____ bien cocidas.
5. No hace frío _____ hace poco sol.
6. Las nubes grises no indican una tormenta _____ puede llover.
7. No me dan miedo los relámpagos _____ no me gustan.
8. Cuando llueve aquí, nunca dura mucho _____ termina en pocos
   minutos.

D   Hablemos de ti.

1. ¿Cuándo fue la última vez que fuiste a una fiesta de disfraces?
   ¿De qué te vestiste? ¿Ganaste algún premio? ¿De qué se vistieron
   las personas que ganaron premios?
2. ¿Te divertiste mucho en tu último cumpleaños? ¿Cuántos invitados
   vinieron a tu última fiesta? ¿Se divirtieron? ¿Qué hicieron Uds.?
   ¿Qué les dijiste a tus invitados cuando te dieron regalos?
3. ¿Cuántas horas dormiste anoche? ¿Cuántas horas duermes
   generalmente?
4. ¿Cuándo fue la última vez que fuiste a un restaurante?
   ¿Qué pediste?
5. ¿Qué pediste para el almuerzo ayer? ¿Trajiste tu almuerzo a la
   escuela hoy? ¿Qué trajiste?

Práctica C
1. sino
2. sino
3. sino
4. sino
5. sino que
6. sino que
7. sino que
8. sino que

Práctica D
Answers will vary.

Practice Sheet 11–5

Workbook Exs. E–F

Tape Manual Ex. 7   12

Quiz 11–4

ACTIVIDAD

Notes: Before students begin the **Actividad,** you
may want to ask volunteers to suggest various themes.

No como col, sino coco.   Work in groups of four or five. One person
begins by choosing a theme and making up a sentence that includes *sino*.
For example, if the theme is television, the person might say:

No miro los documentales sino los programas de concursos.

The next person then says a sentence that begins with the last phrase of
the preceding one. For example:

No miro los programas de concursos sino las telenovelas.

The round ends when the person who began it has completed a second
sentence. The next person then chooses a new theme with a new verb
and starts a new round.

APLICACIONES Discretionary

La tele Transparency 38

Es difícil aburrirse con cinco programas distintos. ¿Cuál es el pronóstico del tiempo para mañana? ¿En qué programa dan premios? ¿Qué van a discutir en el documental?

Make up a dialogue in which Francisco and Susana discuss the programs. What do they think of them? Which do they prefer and why? Here are some words and phrases you might want to use:

aburrirse	entrevistar	ocurrir
al principio	extranjero, -a	tener lugar
bostezar	hacer el papel de	toda clase de

EXPLICACIONES II

Essential

Los verbos *saber* y *conocer*

Remember that *saber* and *conocer* both mean "to know." We use *saber* to talk about knowing *facts* or *information*. *Conocer* means "to know" in the sense of being *acquainted* or *familiar with* a person, place, or thing.

SABER		CONOCER	
sé	sabemos	conozco	conocemos
sabes	sabéis	conoces	conocéis
sabe	saben	conoce	conocen

Except for the *yo* forms, both *saber* and *conocer* follow the pattern of regular *-er* verbs.

1 Remember that when we use *saber* with an infinitive it means "to know how (to)."

   Ester **sabe usar** la cámara.   *Ester **knows how to use** the camera.*

2 When *saber* is followed by a question word, such as *qué* or *cuándo* or *quién*, the question word must have an accent.

   No **sé qué** ocurre.   *I don't **know what**'s happening.*
   Ella no **sabe dónde** se   *She doesn't **know where** they're*
   sientan.   *sitting.*

3 Remember that though we can omit "that" in English, we must always use *que* in a similar sentence in Spanish.

   Sabemos que no debemos   *We **know (that)** we shouldn't*
   bostezar.   *yawn.*

4 *Conocer* also means "to get to know someone or something" or "to meet someone (for the first time)."

   ¿Quieres **conocer** a una   *Do you want **to meet** a movie*
   estrella de cine?   *star?*
   Conocimos a la locutora.   *We **met** the announcer.*
   Ayer **conocí** el mercado.   *Yesterday **I got to know** the market.*

Notes: Point out the uses of *saber* and *conocer* in mini-dialogues 1 and 2 on p. 365 and 2 and 3 on p. 371.

◆ **OBJECTIVES:**

   TO ASK FOR INFORMATION OR DIRECTIONS

   TO TELL WHAT AND WHOM YOU KNOW

   TO BRAG

Reteach / Extra Help: Reinforce the forms and uses of *saber* and *conocer* by asking questions such as *¿Cuánto tiempo hace que Uds. me conocen? ¿Sabes dónde vivo? ¿Sabes usar una computadora?*

5 After *conocer*, we often use the personal *a* before a direct object that names a specific place.

¿**Conoces** bien **a Albuquerque**?   *Do you know Albuquerque well?*

PRÁCTICA

A Un viaje en tren.   Felipe va con unos amigos extranjeros de Madrid a El Escorial. Haz preguntas con la forma correcta de *saber* y de *conocer*. Sigue los modelos.

¿Conoces un buen restaurante cerca de aquí?
¿Sabes dónde encontrar un taxi?

¿(tú) { saber
         conocer }
  El Escorial?
  cuánto tiempo dura el viaje?
  qué tren vamos a tomar?
  dónde está la estación?
  cuánto cuestan los boletos?
  el camino de la estación a El Escorial?
  que allí vivieron los reyes de España?
  a qué hora cierran El Escorial?
  algún otro lugar interesante cerca de allí?

B Una fiesta.   Elena y Alfredo no saben qué hacer. Completa las frases con la forma correcta de *saber* o de *conocer*.

ELENA   ¿_____ (tú) qué día es hoy?

ALFREDO   Sí, es viernes.

ELENA   ¡Ay, caramba! Hoy es la fiesta de Gregorio y no tengo ningún regalo para él.

5 ALFREDO   ¿Quién es Gregorio? No lo _____.

ELENA   Es un amigo mío. Es muy alto y tiene pelo castaño. Tu hermana lo _____.

ALFREDO   ¡Ah! ¡Ya _____ quién es! ¿A qué hora es la fiesta?

ELENA   A las siete. Va a tener lugar en su casa. Yo _____ la
10   dirección, pero Anita y yo no _____ cómo llegar. Es en el Barrio de la Estrella. ¿Lo _____ tú?

ALFREDO   No _____ su casa sino el barrio. ¿_____ Uds. manejar?

ELENA   ¡Claro que sí! Tú _____ mi cacharro, Alfredo, el viejo SEAT rojo.

15 ALFREDO   ¡Ah sí! Ya _____ cuál es. Bueno, dime la dirección de Gregorio, y yo te explico cómo llegar.

ELENA   Muchas gracias.

Los verbos que terminan en -cer y -cir

Notes: See mini-dialogues 2 on p. 365 and 1–4 on p. 371 for examples of verbs ending in -cer and -cir.

Many verbs that end in a vowel + -cer or -cir follow the pattern of *conocer*. Their *yo* form ends in -*zco*. The verbs you know that follow this pattern are *agradecer, ofrecer, parecer, reconocer,* and *traducir*.

Le **agradezco** su visita.	*I **appreciate** your visit.*
María **parece** estar dormida.	*María **looks like** she's asleep.*
Ofrecemos trabajo a acomodadores.	*We're **offering** work to ushers.*
Reconozco ese argumento.	*I **recognize** that plot.*

◆ **OBJECTIVES:**

TO THANK SOMEONE

TO TELL WHAT THINGS LOOK LIKE OR HOW THEY APPEAR TO YOU

PRÁCTICA

A **Un aficionado al cine.** Pepe Rodríguez, de España, es aficionado al cine de su país. Usa la forma correcta del verbo apropiado para completar cada frase.

agradecer ofrecer parecer reconocer traducir

1. Cada año, España _____ un premio para la mejor película.
2. A veces (yo) _____ para actores extranjeros que no hablan español.
3. Mucha gente dice que (yo) _____ un cantante de rock famoso.
4. (Yo) Te _____ mucho el libro de obras de teatro que me prestaste.
5. (Yo) Le _____ mi apartamento a un director de cine que va a usarlo durante todo el verano.
6. _____ fácil filmar entrevistas, pero la verdad es que es muy difícil.
7. Mucha gente que trabaja en el cine me _____ cuando me ve en la calle.
8. Hay muchas actrices aquí en España que _____ norteamericanas.
9. Creo que esa taquillera es argentina. (Yo) _____ el acento.
10. Claro que nosotros _____ estar cansados. La película duró más de cuatro horas.

Práctica A
1. ofrece
2. traduzco
3. parezco
4. agradezco
5. ofrezco (*or:* ofrecí)
6. Parece
7. reconoce
8. parecen
9. Reconozco (*or:* Reconocí)
10. parecemos

En México y en España

B **El éxito de José.** El director José Montalbán habla con su viejo amigo Manuel. Completa las frases con la forma apropiada de los verbos entre paréntesis. ¡Cuidado! No todos van a estar en el presente.

> JOSÉ Ayer le escribí a Carlos Lenguado.
>
> MANUEL ¿Ah sí? ¿Y qué le dijiste?
>
> JOSÉ Le (*agradecer*) todo el trabajo que hizo para mí cuando filmé *El trueno en el valle*. Sabes que Carlos siempre (*traducir*) para
> 5 mí cuando estoy en Alemania.
>
> MANUEL (*Parecer*) que te van a dar un premio por ésa, ¿no?
>
> JOSÉ Sí, es el premio más importante que (*ofrecer*) los periodistas de cine de Alemania a la mejor película extranjera.
>
> MANUEL ¡Qué suerte, José!
>
> 10 JOSÉ No, Manuel. No es suerte sino trabajo. Y eso no es todo. También le dije que todo el mundo (*reconocer*) mi éxito y que (ellos) me (*ofrecer*) trabajo en varios países. ¿Qué te (*parecer*)?
>
> MANUEL Me (*parecer*) fantástico que (tú) le (*agradecer*) a Carlos su trabajo. ¡Es un milagro! Después de tantos fracasos, un
> 15 director tan poco conocido ya es una estrella. Y yo, su viejo amigo, ya no lo (*reconocer*).

Practice Sheet 11–7 14 Tape Manual Ex. 9 Quiz 11–5

Los verbos como *gustar*

You know that the verb *gustar* actually means "to be pleasing," and that whatever is pleasing is the subject of the sentence.

Me gustan los concursos.	*I like contests. (Contests are pleasing to me.)*
Nos gusta el arte moderno.	*We like modern art. (Modern art is pleasing to us.)*
A Marta le gustó la función.	*Marta liked the show. (The show was pleasing to Marta.)*

Gustar agrees with the subject (*los concursos, el arte, la función*). The person who likes them is the indirect object (*me, nos, Marta*).

1 Remember that, to make the meaning clear, or for emphasis, we can add *a* + a noun or prepositional pronoun.

A ella le gusta grabar telenovelas. **A mí me gustan** las películas dobladas, pero **a Jorge no le gustan.**	*She likes to record soap operas. I like dubbed movies, but **Jorge** doesn't like them.*

2 Other verbs that follow this pattern are *doler*, "to hurt," *encantar*, "to love," *faltar*, "to need or lack (something), to be missing (something)," *importar*, "to matter, to be important," *interesar*, "to interest," and *parecer*, "to seem."

¿Te duelen los pies?	*Do **your** feet **hurt**?*
Nos encanta obtener autógrafos.	*We **love** to get autographs.*
Me faltan tres dólares.	*I **need** three dollars.*
¿Te importa el dinero?	*Is money **important to you**?*
A él le interesan los idiomas.	*He's **interested in** languages.*
¿A Uds. les parece interesante la entrevista?	*Does the interview **seem interesting to you**?*

PRÁCTICA

A **¡Ay!** Después de esquiar, a todo el mundo le dolió algo. Sigue el modelo.

> a Inés
> *A Inés le dolió la cabeza.*

1. a ti	4. a María	7. a nosotros	10. a Paco y a Luz
2. a Raúl	5. a Julio	8. a ti y a mí	11. a ti
3. a mí	6. a Ud.	9. a Uds.	12. a Juan y a mí

Reteach / Extra Help: If students have difficulty making correct subject-verb agreement with *gustar* and similar verbs, make two columns on the board: *plural* and *singular*. Elicit subjects for each of the columns. Then ask volunteers to make up sentences using elements from each column and the verbs discussed on pp. 000–389.

Reteach / Review: Before students begin Ex. A, you may want to remind them to use definite articles with parts of the body.

Práctica A
1. A ti te dolieron los ojos.
2. A Raúl le dolió la nariz.
3. A mí me dolieron las orejas.
4. A María le dolió el cuello.
5. A Julio le dolió el hombro.
6. A Ud. le dolió el codo.
7. A nosotros nos dolió el pecho.
8. A ti y a mí nos dolió la espalda.
9. A Uds. les dolieron las muñecas.
10. A Paco y a Luz les dolieron las rodillas.
11. A ti te dolió la pierna.
12. A Juan y a mí nos dolieron los tobillos.

Práctica B
1. Eduardo, ¿qué te parece
   …? Le faltan …
2. …¿qué le parece …?
   Me importa …
3. … ¿que les parece …?
   No nos interesa.
4. … ¿qué te parecen …?
   Me encantan.
5. … ¿qué le parece …?
   Le falta …
6. … ¿qué les parece …?
   Nos gusta …
7. … ¿qué le parece …?
   Le falta …
8. … ¿qué les parece …?
   No nos gusta …

Práctica C
1. … ¿qué te pareció …?
   Le faltaron …
2. … ¿qué le pareció …?
   Me importó …
3. … ¿qué les pareció …?
   No nos interesó.
4. … ¿qué te parecieron …?
   Me encantaron.
5. … ¿qué le pareció …?
   Le faltó …
6. … ¿qué les pareció …?
   Nos gustó …
7. … ¿qué le pareció …?
   Le faltó …
8. … ¿qué les pareció …
   No nos gustó …

Práctica D
Answers will vary.

Practice Sheet 11–8

Workbook Exs. G–J

 15 Tape Manual Ex. 1C

 16 Refrán

 17 Canción

Quiz 11–6

B **¿Qué le parece?** Victoria quiere saber lo que varias personas piensan de ciertos (*certain*) programas y películas. Pregunta y contesta según el modelo.

> Sra. Vidal / la nueva telenovela en el Canal 7 / faltarle personajes interesantes
>
> ESTUDIANTE A *Sra. Vidal, ¿qué le parece la nueva telenovela en el Canal 7?*
>
> ESTUDIANTE B *Le faltan personajes interesantes.*

1. Eduardo / la última película del director italiano Bondini / faltarle los subtítulos en español
2. Dra. Vázquez / el documental sobre su clínica / importar mucho
3. chicos / la entrevista con Carlos Salsa / no interesar
4. Teresa / los premios del programa de concurso / encantar
5. Sr. Moreno / el argumento de la película / faltarle un buen personaje principal
6. Mario y Judit / esa película doblada / gustar más la versión original
7. profesora Aguirre / la historia de ese desastre / faltarle más información
8. señoritas / el programa deportivo / no gustar el locutor

C **¿Y qué les pareció?** Repite la práctica B, pero esta vez en el pretérito. Sigue el modelo.

> Sra. Vidal / la nueva telenovela en el Canal 7 / faltarle personajes interesantes
>
> ESTUDIANTE A *Sra. Vidal, ¿qué le pareció la nueva telenovela en el Canal 7?*
>
> ESTUDIANTE B *Le faltaron personajes interesantes.*

D **Hablemos de ti.**
1. ¿A veces te falta algo cuando regresas de la escuela? ¿Qué clase de cosas te olvidas de llevar a casa? ¿Qué haces cuando te falta algo?
2. ¿Para qué cosas te falta tiempo? ¿Y para cuáles te falta dinero?
3. ¿Qué te importa hacer bien? ¿Qué no te importa hacer bien? ¿Por qué?
4. ¿Qué materias te interesan más? ¿Y cuáles no te interesan? ¿Por qué?
5. ¿Te duele algo ahora? ¿Tienes muchos resfriados? Cuando tienes un resfriado, ¿qué te duele? ¿Cuándo fue la última vez que te dolió algo?

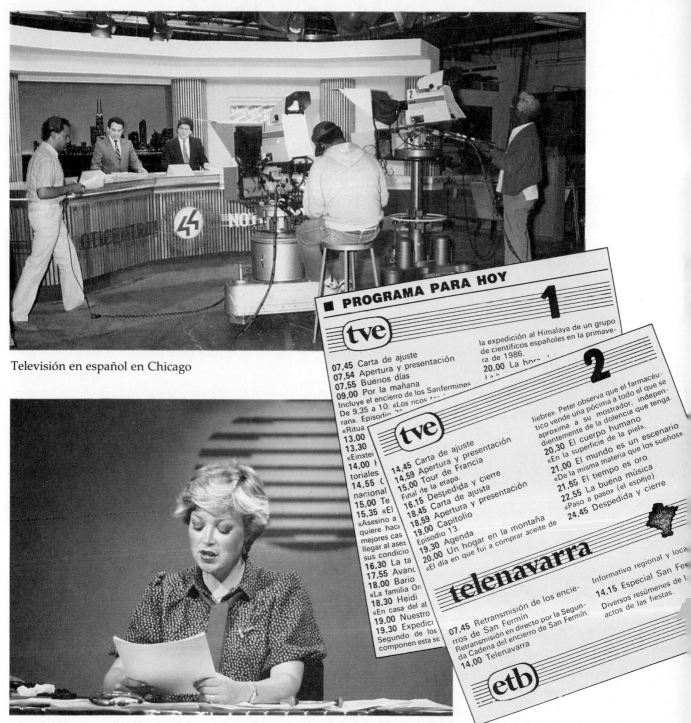

Televisión en español en Chicago

Un programa de noticias en México

■ PROGRAMA PARA HOY

1

tve

07,45 Carta de ajuste
07,54 Apertura y presentación
07,55 Buenos días
09,00 Por la mañana
Incluye el encierro de los Sanfermines
De 9,35 a 10: «Los ricos ta...
ran». Episodio 7...
«Ritua...
13,00
13,30
«Einstei...
14,00 ...
toriales
14,55 ...
nacional
15,00 Te...
15,35 «El...
«Asesino a...
quiere hac...
mejores cas...
llegar al ases...
sus condicio...
16,30 La ta...
17,55 Avanc...
18,00 Bario...
«La familia On...
18,30 Heidi
«En casa del al...
19,00 Nuestro...
19,30 Expedici...
Segundo de los...
componen esta se...

la expedición al Himalaya de un grupo de científicos españoles en la primavera de 1986.
20,00 La hora...

2

tve

14,45 Carta de ajuste
14,59 Apertura y presentación
15,00 Tour de Francia
Final de la etapa.
16,15 Despedida y cierre
18,45 Carta de ajuste
18,59 Apertura y presentación
19,00 Capitolio
Episodio 13.
19,30 Agenda
20,00 Un hogar en la montaña
«El día en que fui a comprar aceite de

liebre». Peter observa que el farmacéutico vende una pócima a todo el que se aproxima a su mostrador, independientemente de la dolencia que tenga.
20,30 El cuerpo humano
«En la superficie de la piel».
21,00 El mundo es un escenario
«De la misma materia que los sueños».
21,55 El tiempo es oro
22,55 La buena música
«Paso a paso» (el espejo)
24,45 Despedida y cierre

telenavarra

07,45 Retransmisión de los encierros de San Fermín
Retransmisión en directo por la Segunda Cadena del encierro de San Fermín.
14,00 Telenavarra

Informativo regional y loca...
14,15 Especial San Fe...
Diversos resúmenes de l...
actos de las fiestas.

etb

APLICACIONES Discretionary

Notes: Answers to the **Repaso** and **Tema** appear in the Teacher Notes.

REPASO

Notes: Review of:
1. *gustar* with prepositional pronouns
   gustar and similar verbs
   toda clase de
2. *conocer*
   personal *a*
   de meaning "on" / "in"
3. adverbs
   verb + *a* / *en*
   sino and *sino que*
4. preterite of *ver*
   personal *a*
   preterite of *pedir*
   indirect object pronouns
5. preterite of *decir*
   indirect object pronouns
   saber + infinitive
   adverbs of time
   ir a + infinitive
   prepositional pronouns

Mira con cuidado las frases modelo. Luego cambia las frases que siguen al español según los modelos.

Enrichment: You may want to use the model sentences in the **Repaso** for dictation.

1. *A Federico le gusta toda clase de programas.*
   (I love all kinds of plots.)
   (They're interested in all kinds of documentaries.)
   (We need all kinds of singers.)

2. *Conoces a todos los personajes de la telenovela.*
   (I know all the players on the team.)
   (We know all the announcers on that program.)
   (She knows all the ushers in that theater.)

3. *A veces no asisten a las funciones con sus padres sino conmigo.*
   (She doesn't usually go to the clinic with her mother but alone.)
   (Fortunately you (fam.) aren't participating in the games with our tennis players but with me.)
   (They probably aren't entering the store with those packages, but rather leaving.)

4. *Anoche vi a una escritora famosa en la librería y le pedí la hora.*
   (Last week you (fam.) saw a foreign director at the theater and asked him for an interview.)
   (Yesterday we saw our local team at the club and asked them (= equipo) for a photo.)
   (This morning they saw the new manager (fem.) at the box office and asked her for a schedule.)

5. *Nos dijo: "Yo sé manejar el coche y muy pronto voy a hacer un viaje con Uds."*
   (I said to him: "We know how to use the tape recorder and tomorrow we're going to tape a concert for you (fam.).")
   (He said to me: "She knows how to use the lawn mower and this afternoon she's going to mow the lawn for me.")
   (You (fam.) said to me: "They know how to roast meat and tonight they're going to have a barbecue with us.")

TEMA

Transparency 39

Notes: Time allowing, ask volunteers to present their **Tema** sentences to the class.

Escribe las frases en español.

1. Bernardo loves all kinds of movies.

2. He knows all the ticket sellers in town (<u>ciudad</u>).

3. He usually doesn't go to the movies with friends, but alone.

4. Yesterday he saw his favorite actress in the street and asked her for her autograph.

5. He said to her: "I know how to use a camera and someday I'm going to shoot a film with you (<u>formal</u>)."

REDACCIÓN

Ahora escoge uno de los siguientes temas para escribir tu propio diálogo o párrafo.

1. Expand the *Tema* by writing a paragraph about the kinds of movies Bernardo likes. What type of person do you think Bernardo is? What does he want to be when he grows up?
2. Make up an interview with a famous movie director or movie star about his or her new film. For example, who are the main characters? Is the plot simple or complicated? Where does the story take place?
3. Create a dialogue between two friends who are discussing a foreign movie that they recently saw.

COMPRUEBA TU PROGRESO   CAPÍTULO 11   Discretionary

Notes: Answers to the **Comprueba** appear in the Teacher Notes.

A   El pasado

Contesta cada pregunta con una frase completa.

¿Cuándo va a dormirse Teresita?
Ya se durmió.
¿Cuándo van a servir el café?
Ya lo sirvieron.

1. ¿Cuándo van Uds. a pedir el autógrafo?
2. ¿Cuándo va ella a repetir el pronóstico del tiempo?
3. ¿Cuándo va Ud. a hervir el agua para el café? (¡Cuidado! *El agua* es un sustantivo femenino.)
4. ¿Cuándo vas a reírte de mis chistes?
5. ¿Cuándo vas a servir los camarones?
6. ¿Cuándo van a vestirse las niñas?
7. ¿Cuándo vas a pedir el postre?

B   Todos vinieron

Pregunta y contesta con el pretérito del verbo *venir*. Sigue el modelo.

cómo / (tú) / en avión
ESTUDIANTE A   *¿Cómo viniste?*
ESTUDIANTE B   *Vine en avión.*

1. cuándo / (él) / el sábado pasado
2. por qué / (tú) / por la función
3. de dónde / ellos / de la estación
4. cómo / Uds. / en tren
5. a qué hora / (él) / a las 9 de la mañana
6. con quién / (ella) / con sus padres
7. por qué / Uds. / por tu cumpleaños

C   Pero, sino, sino que

Completa cada frase con *pero, sino* o *sino que*.

1. Me gustan los concursos _____ prefiero los deportes.
2. La función no tiene lugar a las 4:00 _____ a las 5:30.
3. No quiero ser locutora _____ estrella de cine.
4. Esto no es un huracán _____ parece una tormenta fuerte.
5. No es una película doblada _____ entiendo todo.

6. El trueno no viene antes del relámpago _____ después.
7. Bostezamos mucho _____ no nos aburrimos.

D   ¿Saber o conocer?

Completa cada frase con la forma correcta del presente de *saber* o *conocer*.

1. Carlos _____ hablar por señas.
2. ¡Cállate! Tú _____ que no debes discutir ahora.
3. Ana y Tomás _____ bien la ciudad de Londres.
4. (Yo) _____ a la directora de la telenovela.
5. (Yo) no _____ cuándo ocurrió el terremoto.
6. (Nosotras) no _____ a todos los jugadores.
7. Ella no _____ quién lo trajo.
8. ¿_____ (tú) la música de Andrés Segovia?

E   ¡Qué buena eres!

Usa las frases entre paréntesis para contestar las preguntas. Usa frases completas.

1. ¿A quién le agradecemos las entradas? (a la directora)
2. ¿A qué estrellas de cine reconoces en este programa?   (sólo a Pepe Culebra)
3. ¿Para quién traduces?   (para mi médico que no entiende el idioma)
4. ¿Qué reglas de tráfico conoces?   (muchas)
5. ¿A quiénes les agradeces las flores? (a mis admiradores)
6. ¿A quién reconoces en la foto?   (a mi padre)
7. ¿Qué me ofreces?   (un premio)

F   A mí y a ti

Haz frases según el modelo.

a mí / gustar / los programas deportivos
A mí me gustan los programas deportivos.

1. a nosotros / no importar / el público
2. a Uds. / faltar / un termómetro
3. a ti / interesar / los argumentos complicados
4. a mí / encantar / las versiones originales
5. a Ud. / no parecer / ser muy serio
6. a la directora / faltar / una actriz

VOCABULARIO DEL CAPÍTULO 11

Sustantivos
el acomodador, la
   acomodadora
el admirador, la admiradora
el argumento
el autógrafo
el/la cantante
el concurso
el desastre
el director, la directora
el documental
la entrevista
la estrella de cine
el éxito
la fila
el fracaso
la función, *pl.* las funciones
el grado
el huracán, *pl.* los huracanes
la información
el intervalo
el/la joven, *pl.* los/las jóvenes
el locutor, la locutora
la película doblada
el personaje
el premio
el programa de concursos
el pronóstico del tiempo
el público
el relámpago
el subtítulo
la taquilla
el taquillero, la taquillera
la telenovela
la temperatura
el termómetro
el terremoto
la tormenta
el trueno

Adjetivos
ciego, -a
complicado, -a
despierto, -a
dormido, -a
extranjero, -a
principal
rodeado, -a (de)
sencillo, -a
sordo, -a

Verbos
aburrir(se)
agradecer (c → zc)
bostezar
conocer (c → zc) *(to meet)*
discutir (de)
entrevistar
filmar
grabar
indicar
interesar
ocurrir
ofrecer (c → zc)

parecer (c → zc) *(to seem to be, to
   look like)*
reconocer (c → zc)
reírse de (e → i)
sentarse (e → ie)
traducir (c → zc)
dije/dijiste/dijo
traje/trajiste/trajo

Preposiciones
por *(on)*
sino
sino que + *verb*

Expresiones
al principio
¡cállate!
en versión original
hablar por señas
hacer el papel de
otra cosa
otra persona
tener éxito
tener lugar
toda clase de

CAPÍTULO 12

PRÓLOGO CULTURAL

¡CON SALSA!

What would you say is the music of the United States? If you said rock, jazz, or country and western, you would be right, but did you know that the *conga* and the *norteño* could also be added to the list?

The rhythms, dances, songs, and instruments of Latin America (especially the Caribbean) have been vital in the development of the music of this country. In the American Southwest, a unique mixture of folk music from Mexico, Europe, and the United States has been developing for more than a hundred years. Many instruments, such as the *bajo sexto*, a twelve-string guitar, and the *guitarrón*, an acoustic bass guitar, came from Mexico. The United States contributed its folk and country music, and the Germans and Eastern Europeans brought with them the accordion and the polka rhythms that developed into the *norteño*. In the 1920s, the Argentinian *tango* became very popular here. Later, so did Cuba's *rumba* and *conga*, and, more recently, the *salsa*, the big-band music of the Caribbean that found new life in cities like New York and Miami.

In 1958, Richie Valens (born Ricardo Valenzuela) brought together Mexican folk and American rock music in his hit song "La Bamba," a Mexican folk tune from the 1700s that he set to a modern rock beat. It was the first song sung entirely in Spanish to become a hit in the United States. Among the many Spanish-language songs that have gained popularity, either in the original Spanish or in English-language versions, are "Guantanamera," "Cielito lindo," "Perfidia," "Bésame mucho," "Eres tú," and "El Cóndor pasa."

PALABRAS NUEVAS I

Essential

¡Bravo!

If students ask: Other related words you may want to present: *la sinfonía*, symphony; *el instrumento de cuerda, de metal, de percusión, de viento*, string, brass, percussion, wind instrument.

la orquesta

—el contrabajo

el trombón
pl. los trombones

la tuba

el violoncelo

el oboe

el tambor

la flauta

el saxofón
pl. los saxofones

¡Bravo!

¡Bravo!

el director
la directora

¡Bravo!

la trompeta

aplaudir

el clarinete

el violín
pl. los violines

el coro

el bailarín
pl. los bailarines

la bailarina

CONTEXTO COMUNICATIVO

 2

1 MARTA   ¡Caramba! ¿Dónde está mi clarinete?

    MANUEL   ¿Por qué **gritas** tanto? ¿No puedes hablar en voz más baja?

    MARTA   Tengo **un ensayo** en media hora y no encuentro mi clarinete.

    MANUEL   ¿Y éste? ¿No es tuyo?

    MARTA   No, es de Rogelio. Es **parecido al** mío.

    MANUEL   Pues úsalo para tu ensayo. Rogelio está enfermo hoy.

gritar   *to shout*

el ensayo   *rehearsal*

parecido, -a (a)   *like, similar (to)*

Variaciones:

■ parecido → más nuevo que el

2 PEDRO   La nueva directora **demuestra** que tiene mucho **talento.**

    LUCÍA   Tienes razón. Cuando ella **dirige,*** todos **los músicos** prestan atención.

■ tiene mucho talento → sabe mucho sobre la música

demostrar (o → ue)   *to show, to demonstrate, to prove*

el talento   *talent*

dirigir (yo dirijo, tú diriges) *to direct, to conduct, to lead*

el músico, la música   *musician*

---

* Like verbs that end in *-ger (escoger, recoger),* verbs that end in *-gir* have a spelling change. In the present-tense *yo* form, *g → j.* And, since the stem for the present subjunctive comes from the present-tense *yo* form, *g → j* in the subjunctive: *que yo dirija, que tú dirijas,* etc.

3 ANDRÉS ¿Quién es ese hombre que está al lado del director?

   BÁRBARA Creo que es **el compositor**.

   ANDRÉS Por eso el público está **aplaudiendo tanto**.

   ■ creo que → **sin duda**
   ■ creo que → estoy segura de que
   ■ el público está → todos están

el compositor, la compositora
   composer

aplaudiendo (from **aplaudir**)
   applauding

tanto adv. *so much*

sin duda *without a doubt, undoubtedly*

4 MARIO ¿Qué es ese ruido? ¡Me **hace daño a** los oídos!

   LUISA Son los chicos con el violoncelo. **Ensayan** para el concierto de mañana.

   ■ ensayan → están **ensayando**

hacer daño (a) *to hurt, to harm*

ensayar *to rehearse*

ensayando *rehearsing*

5 EDUARDO ¿Cuál es **la diferencia** entre el oboe y la flauta?

   CARMEN Son **instrumentos** muy **diferentes**. **El sonido** del oboe es más **suave**.

   ■ la flauta → el clarinete
   ■ diferentes → distintos

la diferencia *difference*

el instrumento *instrument*

diferente = distinto, -a

el sonido *sound*

suave *soft*

PRÁCTICA

Enrichment: Before students begin Ex. A, you may want to lead a class discussion about playing musical instruments: *¿Quién toca un instrumento musical? ¿Qué tocas? ¿Cuántos años hace que tocas? ¿Cuántas veces a la semana ensayas?*

Práctica A
1. ¿Qué instrumento toca Elisa? La tuba.
2. ¿... Juan? El violoncelo.
3. ¿... Arturo? El contrabajo.
4. ¿... Raquel? El violín.
5. ¿... Laura? El clarinete.
6. ¿... Bernardo? El saxofón.
7. ¿... Anita? El trombón.
8. ¿... Óscar? El tambor.
9. ¿... Mariana? La flauta.

A **En la orquesta.** ¿Qué instrumentos tocan estas personas? Pregunta y contesta según el dibujo.

   ESTUDIANTE A *¿Qué instrumento toca Federico?*
   ESTUDIANTE B *El oboe.*

Federico   1. Elisa   2. Juan   3. Arturo   4. Raquel
6. Bernardo   5. Laura   7. Anita   8. Óscar   9. Mariana

B El periódico de la escuela. Imagina que escribes para el periódico de tu escuela. Escoge la palabra correcta de la lista para completar cada frase.

bailarina	coro	director	sonido
compositora	diferencia	ensayo	talento

1. La _____ principal de esa compañía ensaya ocho horas cada día.
2. El _____ del violín es muy agradable.
3. Todos los músicos llegaron a tiempo al _____.
4. ¿Cuál es la _____ entre una banda y una orquesta?
5. La música que escribió esa joven _____ demuestra que tiene mucho _____.
6. ¡Qué bien cantó el _____ de la iglesia!
7. El _____ de nuestra orquesta es muy enérgico.

Práctica B
1. bailarina
2. sonido
3. ensayo
4. diferencia
5. compositora / talento
6. coro
7. director

C En el concierto. Imagina que asististe a un concierto anoche. Escribe un párrafo de varias frases para describirlo. Escoge palabras y expresiones de cada columna.

el/la cantante	aplaudir	al principio
el concierto	cantar	anoche
el coro	dirigir	a las ocho
el/la director(a)	disfrutar de	a menudo
los músicos	divertirse	¡Bravo!
la orquesta	durar	alrededor de dos horas
el público	empezar	mucho
	gritar	muy bien
	tocar	varias canciones alemanas

Práctica C
Answers will vary.

Notes: You may want to assign Ex. C as written homework. Check students' work for correct spelling, punctuation, and capitalization.

D Hablemos de ti.

1. ¿Tiene tu escuela una banda o una orquesta? ¿Cuántos músicos hay en ella? ¿Cuándo ensayan? ¿Cuándo tocan? ¿Tocan toda clase de música?
2. ¿Tocas algún instrumento musical? ¿Cuál? ¿Cuántas horas tocas cada día? ¿Piensas ser músico(a) algún día? ¿Por qué sí o por qué no?
3. Si tocas un instrumento, ¿tocas en una banda u orquesta? ¿Cómo se llama el director o la directora? ¿Es muy estricto(a)? ¿Les enseña mucho a Uds.?
4. Si no tocas un instrumento musical, ¿te gustaría tocar alguno? ¿Cuál? ¿Por qué? ¿Qué instrumento te gusta oír más? ¿Por qué?
5. ¿Quién es tu compositor(a) de canciones favorito(a)? ¿Quién es tu cantante favorito? ¿Por qué te gusta tanto?

Práctica D
Answers will vary.

Practice Sheet 12–1

Workbook Exs. A–B

Tape Manual Exs. 1–2 3

Quiz 12–1

APLICACIONES

Dos mariachis[1] 4 5 Pronunciación

Culture: You may want to point out that approximately 10 percent of Colorado's population is of Hispanic origin.

Ricardo y David, dos jóvenes de Colorado, tratan de formar una banda de mariachis.

RICARDO Entonces, ¿aquí es donde ensayan?

DAVID Sí. Es el garaje del Sr. Robles. Lo podemos usar por las
5 tardes. ¿Trajiste tu instrumento?

RICARDO Por supuesto. Está en el coche. Mi guitarrón[2] no es tan pequeño como tu trompeta.

DAVID Pero sin duda tiene el sonido que nuestra banda necesita.

10 RICARDO ¿De quién fue la idea de hacer este grupo?

DAVID De José, nuestro violinista. Lo vas a conocer esta tarde. Es un poco tímido, pero es muy simpático. Es también nuestro mejor cantante y sabe cientos de canciones. Su familia es de México.

15 RICARDO Como la mía. ¡Esto es estupendo! Cuando nos mudamos aquí pensé: Ricardo, ya no vas a escuchar ni corridos[3] ni norteños.[4] Y ahora voy a tocar la misma música que antes.

DAVID Hablando de corridos, quiero que escuches el arreglo[5]
20 que hice para "La Adelita."[6]

RICARDO ¡"La Adelita"! ¡Todo el mundo conoce "La Adelita"!

DAVID Pero no como la vamos a tocar nosotros. Escucha y después me dices lo que piensas.

Tocando la guitarra
en Madrid, España

---

[1]**el mariachi** *Mexican street musician* [2]**el guitarrón** *oversized guitar used in the mariachi bands* [3]**el corrido** *Mexican song that tells a story* [4]**el norteño** *type of melody from the north of Mexico* [6]**arreglo** *arrangement* [6]**"La Adelita"** *a popular Mexican* corrido

Preguntas

Contesta según el diálogo.

1. Según lo que aprendiste en el diálogo, ¿puedes decir cómo es una banda de mariachis?   2. ¿Qué instrumentos tocan Ricardo y David? 3. Usa las palabras exactas de Ricardo para contar lo que pensó cuando se mudó a los Estados Unidos.   4. ¿De qué clases de música mexicana discuten los chicos? Da una definición de ellas.   5. ¿Qué clase de canción es "La Adelita"? ¿Crees que estos mariachis van a tocar "La Adelita" como la toca todo el mundo? ¿Por qué?

Mariachis en Austin, Texas

Participación

Work with a partner to make up a dialogue. Discuss the instruments you or your friends play. Do you play in a band? Do you rehearse often? What is the director or music teacher like?

PALABRAS NUEVAS II

Essential

Vamos a la exposición

🔊 6

Transparency 41

CONTEXTO VISUAL

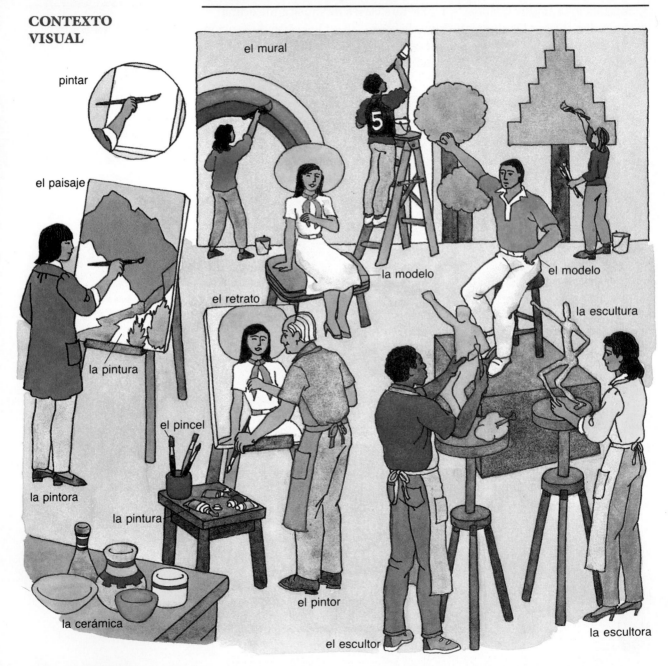

pintar

el paisaje

la pintura

la pintora

el pincel

la pintura

la cerámica

el mural

la modelo

el retrato

el modelo

la escultura

el pintor

el escultor

la escultora

CONTEXTO COMUNICATIVO 7

1 FELIPE ¡Qué interesante es **la colección** de pinturas en esta **galería** de arte!

EMILIA Sí, ¿verdad? ¿**Te fijaste en** esos murales **junto a** la salida?

FELIPE Sí. Parecen interesantísimos. ¿Quién los pintó?

EMILIA Osvaldo Guayasamín, un gran pintor ecuatoriano.

Variaciones:

■ pinturas → cuadros
■ junto a → al lado de
■ pintor → **artista**

la colección, pl. **las colecciones**	*collection*
la galería	*gallery*
fijarse en	*to notice, to pay attention to*
junto a = al lado de	
el/la artista	*artist*

2 MARÍA ¿Dónde están las **obras** de Arreguín, el artista mexicano?

MIGUEL **En el fondo** de la galería. **Sigue** derecho por allí.

MARÍA ¿Sabes si todavía **sigue pintando** paisajes y animales que parecen ser tan **abstractos**?

MIGUEL Sí, pero ahora pinta también a personas.

■ obras → pinturas
■ en el fondo → en **el centro**

la obra	*work*
en el fondo	*at the back, in the background*
seguir (e → i)	*to follow; to go on, to keep on, to continue*
sigue pintando (from **seguir**)	*is still painting*
abstracto, -a	*abstract*
el centro	here: *center, middle*

Un cuadro de Alfredo Arreguín

PRÁCTICA

A **En el estudio.** Usa las expresiones de la derecha para explicar dónde están todas las cosas. Pregunta y contesta según el dibujo.

Práctica A

Answers may vary.

1. ¿Dónde está la escultura abstracta?
   Está en el centro del dibujo.
2. ¿… están las pinturas?
   Están debajo de la silla.
3. ¿… está el modelo?
   Está junto a la escultura.
4. ¿… está el cuadro abstracto?
   Está a la derecha.
5. ¿… está la colección de cerámica?
   Está en el fondo.
6. ¿… está el mural?
   Está a la izquierda.
7. ¿… están los pinceles?
   Están junto a las pinturas.

la artista

ESTUDIANTE A   *¿Dónde está la artista?*
ESTUDIANTE B   *Está fuera del dibujo.*

1. la escultura abstracta	en el fondo
2. las pinturas	junto a las pinturas
3. el modelo	en el centro del dibujo
4. el cuadro abstracto	fuera del dibujo
5. la colección de cerámica	a la derecha
6. el mural	a la izquierda
7. los pinceles	debajo de la silla
	junto a la escultura

B En el museo. Imagina que visitaste un museo de arte. ¿Qué dijo la gente? Escoge la palabra correcta para completar las frases.

1. Me gustó *(la dirección / la colección / el pincel)* de monedas viejas.
2. ¿Te fijaste en la *(balanza / exposición / biblioteca)* de cerámica?
3. Quiero que mires el *(coro / retrato / compositor)* de la hija de Picasso.
4. Me interesan estas *(artistas / escultoras / esculturas)* de papel.
5. Nunca entiendo las *(pinturas / flautas / modelos)* abstractas.
6. Prefiero que veamos los *(coros / murales / directores)* en el fondo del museo.
7. La colección del museo incluye muchas obras de arte *(sordas / abstractas / suaves)*.
8. Hay una exposición de los *(cuadros / pinceles / pintores)* de la pintora mexicana Frida Kahlo.
9. Ahora vamos a comprar *(unos carteles / unas escultoras / unos sonidos)* en la tienda del museo.

Práctica B
1. la colección
2. exposición
3. retrato
4. esculturas
5. pinturas
6. murales
7. abstractas
8. cuadros
9 unos carteles

C Hablemos de ti.

1. ¿Te gusta pintar o dibujar? ¿Por qué? ¿Hay otras actividades artísticas que te gusta hacer? ¿Cuáles?
2. ¿Hay un museo en tu ciudad? ¿Qué clase de museo es? ¿Tiene muchas galerías? ¿Lo visitas a veces? ¿Qué te gusta ver cuando vas allí?
3. ¿Qué clase de arte prefieres? ¿El arte moderno, clásico o abstracto?
4. ¿En qué te fijas cuando miras un cuadro abstracto? ¿Por qué? ¿Te gusta más la pintura o la escultura? ¿Por qué? ¿Te gustaría ser pintor(a) o escultor(a)?
5. ¿Quién es tu pintor(a) preferido(a)? ¿De dónde es? ¿Qué clase de cuadros pinta (retratos, paisajes, murales, cuadros abstractos)? Si no tienes pintor(a) favorito(a), ¿qué pintores conoces? ¿Qué pintan ellos?

Práctica C
Answers will vary.

Practice Sheet 12–2

Workbook Exs. C–D

Tape Manual Exs. 3–4 8

Refrán 9

Quiz 12–2

Una pintora en San Miguel, El Salvador

ACTIVIDAD

El arte público Imagine that your class has been asked to make *una obra de arte* for the hall or entrance of your school. With two or three students, discuss what kind of *obra de arte* you would choose. You might consider these questions:

> ¿Va a ser una escultura grande, una pintura o un mural? ¿Por qué? Si es una pintura, ¿va a ser un retrato o algo abstracto? ¿Va a mostrar actividades de la escuela? ¿Cuáles?

Afterward, discuss the ideas as a class and see if you can reach an agreement as to what you would create.

Pintando un mural en Chicago, Illinois

ESTUDIO DE PALABRAS

Palabras con varios sentidos

As in English, there are many words in Spanish that have more than one meaning.

| la cartera | *(female) letter carrier* | la cartera | *wallet* |
| la clase | *class* | la clase | *kind, type* |

Often the meanings of these words are closely related.

| la música | *(female) musician* | la música | *music* |
| la pintura | *painting* | la pintura | *paint* |

What two meanings does the word *centro* have in these sentences?

1. Los bailarines ensayan en un teatro del *centro*.
2. La escultura está en el *centro* de la fuente.

Usa cada una de estas palabras dos veces en la misma frase.

| cuarto | lata | sobre |
| fuerte | nada | tienda |

1. ¡Qué _____! No puedo abrir la _____.
2. Dice que _____ muy bien, pero no es verdad. En el agua no sabe hacer _____.
3. Tiene una voz muy _____ y por eso canta tan _____.
4. Tu _____ está en el _____ piso.
5. El _____ está _____ la mesa.
6. Si queremos ir de camping tenemos que ir a la _____ para comprar una _____ de acampar.

Palabras con varios sentidos
1. downtown
2. middle, center

1. lata
2. nada
3. fuerte
4. cuarto
5. sobre
6. tienda

EXPLICACIONES I Essential

El presente progresivo

We use the present indicative tense to express an action that always or usually happens, that is happening now, or that will probably happen soon.

Dirijo la orquesta. $\left\{\begin{array}{l}\textit{I \textbf{direct} the orchestra (always / usually).}\\ \textit{I'm \textbf{directing} the orchestra (now / tomorrow).}\end{array}\right.$

When we want to emphasize that an action is happening right now, we use the present progressive tense.

Estoy dirigiendo la orquesta.   *I'm **directing** the orchestra (now).*

The present progressive consists of a present-tense form of *estar* + a present participle. To form the present participle, we drop the ending of the infinitive and add *-ando* to the stem of *-ar* verbs and *-iendo* to the stem of *-er* and *-ir* verbs.

camin**ar** → camin**ando**
corr**er** → corr**iendo**
viv**ir**   → viv**iendo**

Here are all of the forms of the present progressive of *bailar*.

$\left.\begin{array}{l}\text{estoy}\\ \text{estás}\\ \text{está}\end{array}\right\}$ bailando $\left.\begin{array}{l}\text{estamos}\\ \text{estáis}\\ \text{están}\end{array}\right\}$ bailando

1   When we use an object pronoun or a reflexive pronoun with the present progressive, we can either put the pronoun before the form of *estar* or we can attach it to the present participle.

$\left.\begin{array}{l}\text{¿Por qué \textbf{me estás gritando}?}\\ \text{¿Por qué \textbf{estás gritándome}?}\end{array}\right\}$ *Why are you **shouting at me**?*

Note that when we attach a pronoun to the present participle, we must use a written accent mark.

Notes: Refer to mini-dialogues 3 and 4 on p. 400 for examples of present progressive forms.

◆ **OBJECTIVES:**

TO DESCRIBE ACTIONS AND EVENTS THAT ARE HAPPENING NOW

TO EXPLAIN WHY PEOPLE ARE DOING THINGS

TO MAKE EXCUSES

TO COME TO PEOPLE'S DEFENSE

Reteach / Extra Help: You may want to bring in pictures from magazines, newspapers, or ads that show people in action. Ask *¿Qué está(n) haciendo?* as you show the pictures and elicit present progressive forms.

PRÁCTICA

Práctica A
1. Está pintando un paisaje.
2. Están bailando en el patio.
3. Está navegando en el velero.
4. Está tocando el clarinete.
5. Están nadando …
6. Está caminando …
7. Están montando en bicicleta …
8. Están jugando al tenis …
9. Están patinando ….

A **En el campamento.** ¿Qué están haciendo estos chicos? Sigue el modelo.

un pollo
Está cocinando un pollo.

1. un paisaje   2. en el patio   3. en el velero

4. el clarinete   5. en el lago   6. por las montañas

7. por el sendero   8. en la cancha de   9. sobre ruedas
la escuela

Práctica B
1. ¿Qué hace esa mujer?
Está vendiendo entradas.
2. ¿Qué hacen …?
Están dirigiendo a la gente …
3. ¿Qué hace esa niña?
Está corriendo por el pasillo.
4. ¿Qué hacemos?
Estamos escogiendo los mejores asientos.
5. ¿Qué hace …?
Está comiendo …
6. ¿Qué haces?
Estoy abriendo la … .
7. ¿Qué hace …?
Está aplaudiendo.
8. ¿Qué hacemos?
Estamos saliendo de aquí.

B **¡Contigo no vuelvo más al cine!** Fernando lleva a su hermanita al cine y ella le hace muchas preguntas. Pregunta y contesta según el modelo.

esos muchachos / hacer cola
ESTUDIANTE A *¿Qué hacen esos muchachos?*
ESTUDIANTE B *Están haciendo cola.*

1. esa mujer / vender entradas
2. los acomodadores / dirigir a la gente a sus asientos
3. esa niña / correr por el pasillo
4. (nosotros) / escoger los mejores asientos
5. esa señora / comer palomitas
6. (tú) / abrir la caja de dulces
7. el público / aplaudir
8. (nosotros) / salir de aquí

C **¿Por qué?**   Vuelve a hacer la Práctica B. El (la) Estudiante A debe añadir cada vez la pregunta ¿Por qué? El (la) Estudiante B puede dar cualquier (any) respuesta apropiada. Por ejemplo:

> esos muchachos / hacer cola
> ESTUDIANTE A   *¿Qué hacen esos muchachos?*
> ESTUDIANTE B   *Están haciendo cola.*
> ESTUDIANTE A   *¿Por qué?*
> ESTUDIANTE B   *Porque quieren comprar entradas / ver la película, etc.*

D **¿Me puedes ayudar?**   Imagina que quieres que alguien te ayude, pero todo el mundo siempre está ocupado. Pregunta y contesta según el modelo, escogiendo la respuesta de la lista de la derecha.

> arreglar la lámpara / bañarse
> ESTUDIANTE A   *¿Me puedes ayudar a arreglar la lámpara?*
> ESTUDIANTE B   *Ahora no. Estoy bañándome.*
> o: *Ahora no. Me estoy bañando.*

1. grabar este programa
2. poner mi cuarto en orden
3. lavar el coche
4. planchar la ropa
5. cortar el césped
6. llenar este formulario
7. traducir esto
8. envolver este paquete

ducharse
acostarse
limpiarse los zapatos
limarse las uñas
afeitarse
maquillarse
cepillarse los dientes
lavarse el pelo

E **La exposición.**   La clase tiene que preparar una exposición de arte. Hoy todos se reúnen (meet) para empezar sus tareas. La profesora no está, y llama por teléfono para averiguar qué están haciendo todos. Pregunta y contesta según el modelo.

> Armando / escoger las pinturas
> ESTUDIANTE A   *¿Armando va a escoger las pinturas?*
> ESTUDIANTE B   *Ya las está escogiendo.*
> o: *Ya está escogiéndolas.*

1. Alicia / pintar la escalera
2. Rogelio / grabar la música
3. Ramón / preparar el programa
4. tú / averiguar el precio de las pinturas
5. Uds. / escribir a máquina las etiquetas
6. Ignacio / hacer los carteles
7. Mateo y Gustavo / colocar los retratos en la pared
8. Uds. / tirar las cajas vacías

Práctica C
Identical to B with addition of ¿Por qué? and any logical reply.

Notes: You may want to ask students to do Exs. D and E first with the pronoun before the conjugated form of estar; then ask them to redo the exercise attaching the pronouns to the present participles.

Práctica D
Answers will vary but will follow the model: ¿Me puedes ayudar a …? Ahora no. Estoy —ándome (or: Me estoy —ando).

Práctica E
1. ¿Alicia va a pintar …? Ya la está pintando. (or: Ya está pintándola.)
2. ¿Rogelio va a …? Ya la está grabando. (or: Ya está grabándola.)
3. ¿Ramón va a …? Ya lo está preparando. (or: Ya está preparándolo.)
4. ¿Tú vas a …? Ya lo estoy averiguando. (or: Ya estoy averiguándolo.)
5. ¿Uds. van a …? Ya las estamos escribiendo a máquina. (or: Ya estamos escribiéndolas a máquina.)
6. ¿Ignacio va a …? Ya los está haciendo. (or: Ya está haciéndolos.)
7. ¿Mateo y Gustavo van a …? Ya los están colocando. (or: Ya están colocándolos.)
8. ¿Uds. van a …? Ya las estamos tirando. (or: Ya estamos tirándolas.)

El presente progresivo: Continuación

◆ **OBJECTIVE:**

**TO DESCRIBE
THINGS THAT ARE
HAPPENING NOW**

Notes: Point out that the
present participle of *ir* is *yendo*;
however, verbs of motion, like *ir*
and *venir* are not often used in
the present progressive tense.

Some *-er* and *-ir* verbs have slightly irregular present participles.

1 When the stem of an *-er* or *-ir* verb ends in a vowel, the *i* of *-iendo* usually changes to *y*.

caer → cayendo   incluir → incluyendo   oír → oyendo
creer → creyendo   leer → leyendo   traer → trayendo

¿Qué **estás leyendo**?   *What **are you reading**?*
Ya **están trayendo** la sopa.   *They're bringing the soup now.*

2 Any *-ir* verb that has the stem change *e* → *i* or *o* → *u* in the *Ud. / él / ella* and *Uds. / ellos / ellas* forms of the preterite has the same change in the present participle. Note that the irregular verbs *decir* and *venir* follow this pattern. Remember that their preterite forms have an *i*: *dije / dijiste*, etc., and *vino / viniste*, etc.

e → i
decir → diciendo   seguir → siguiendo
divertirse → divirtiéndose   sentirse → sintiéndose
hervir → hirviendo   servir → sirviendo
pedir → pidiendo   venir → viniendo
preferir → prefiriendo   vestir → vistiendo
repetir → repitiendo   vestirse → vistiéndose

Todavía **estoy vistiéndome**.   *I'm still **getting dressed**.*
¿Qué **está diciéndote**?   *What **is she telling you**?*

o → u

dormir(se) → $\begin{cases} \text{durmiendo} \\ \text{durmiéndose} \end{cases}$ morirse → muriéndose

Juan **se está durmiendo**.   *Juan **is falling asleep**.*
Estamos **muriéndonos** de sed.   *We're **dying** of thirst.*

3 With *reír(se)* and *sonreír*, we drop the stem vowel *e* and add *-iendo*.

reír(se) → $\begin{cases} \text{riendo} \\ \text{riéndose} \end{cases}$ sonreír → sonriendo

PRÁCTICA

A **¿Qué está pasando?** Muchas personas están en un restaurante. Haz frases según el modelo para indicar lo que están haciendo.

> El camarero / traernos servilletas
> *El camarero nos está trayendo servilletas.*
> o: *El camarero está trayéndonos servilletas.*

1. los jóvenes / pedir hamburguesas
2. esa camarera / servir arroz con pollo
3. ese camarero / hervir agua para el té
4. el cajero / sonreír a los niños
5. Patricia / morirse de hambre
6. el papá de Patricia / leer el menú
7. ese señor / reírse de todo lo que dice su esposa
8. el hermanito de Patricia / dormirse en la silla
9. el gato del dueño / seguirlo
10. (yo) / divertirse
11. (nosotros) / decirle al dueño que todo está sabroso
12. tú / no oír nada de lo que / (yo) decirte

B **Hablemos de ti.**

1. ¿Qué actividad importante estás haciendo estos días? ¿Por qué es importante?
2. ¿Qué estás estudiando en tu clase de historia? ¿Y en tus otras clases?
3. ¿Qué estás leyendo en tu clase de inglés?
4. ¿Qué estás haciendo ahora mismo?
5. ¿Qué materia estás estudiando ahora mismo? ¿Te interesa? ¿Es la primera vez que estudias esto, o lo estás repasando? ¿Estás aprendiendo mucho?

ACTIVIDAD

Charada With a partner, prepare a game of charades. Write down six actions on separate slips of paper. For example:

> Estoy tocando la flauta.
> Estoy pintando una pared.
> Estoy durmiendo.

Get together with another pair of students and take turns pantomiming the actions you wrote down while the others try to guess what the actions are. For example: *¿Estás tocando la flauta? ¿Estás pintando una pared?*, etc.

Práctica A
1. ... están pidiendo ...
2. ... está sirviendo ...
3. ... está hirviendo ...
4. ... está sonriendo ...
5. ... está muriéndose (*or:* se está muriendo) ...
6. ... está leyendo ...
7. ... está riéndose (*or:* se está riendo) ...
8. ... está durmiéndose (*or:* se está durmiendo) ...
9. ... está siguiéndolo (*or:* lo está siguiendo) ...
10. ... estoy divirtiéndome (*or:* me estoy divirtiendo)
11. Le estamos diciendo (*or:* Estamos diciéndole) ...
12. ... no estás oyendo nada de lo que estoy diciéndote (*or:* de lo que te estoy diciendo)

Práctica B
Answers will vary.

Practice Sheet 12–4

Workbook Exs. E–F

Tape Manual Ex. 6 11

Quiz 12–4

APLICACIONES

Discretionary

📼 12

La danza[1]

Notes: You may want to assign the **Antes de leer** questions as written homework.

ANTES DE LEER

1. ¿Qué hay que hacer para ser artista (pintor, escultor, escritor, actor, bailarín, etc.)?
2. ¿En qué son parecidas la vida diaria (*daily*) de los bailarines y la (*that*) de los atletas?
3. En tu opinión, ¿cuál es más importante para tener éxito, el talento, el trabajo o la suerte? ¿Por qué?

Notes: Make are students understand these cognates that have not been glossed: *suficiente*, sufficient / enough; *la dedicación*, dedication; *las responsabilidades*, responsibilities.

Blanche Hampton

¿Qué necesitas para ser bailarín o bailarina profesional? Al principio hay que demostrar gran talento. Sin duda eso es muy importante. Pero el talento solo no es suficiente. A ese talento debes añadirle trabajo, trabajo y más trabajo. Debes entrenarte[2] como un atleta: hacer ejercicio, seguir una dieta
5 sana, practicar todos los días y siempre tener mucho cuidado con el cuerpo. Después de todo, el cuerpo es el instrumento de la danza.

Blanche Hampton tiene dieciséis años y es bailarina de ballet. Es hija de madre cubana y padre estadounidense. Su familia vive en Tampa, Florida. Durante tres años, Blanche tomó clases de verano en la "School of Ameri-
10 can Ballet" en Nueva York, una de las mejores escuelas de danza del país. Como premio a su dedicación y talento, Blanche recibió una beca[3] para ser estudiante regular de esta escuela.

Blanche es muy joven todavía, pero su vida ya está llena de responsabilidades y de trabajo. Su día comienza como el de cualquier[4] otra chica de
15 dieciséis años. Va a la escuela, estudia para exámenes, hace la tarea . . . Pero su día no termina ahí.[5] Blanche también toma más de quince horas de clases de ballet por semana. A todo esto hay que añadir ensayos de cuatro o cinco horas cada semana cuando ella se está preparando para la presentación de un ballet. Como puedes ver, la vida de Blanche no es fácil.
20 Blanche vive ahora en Nueva York, muy lejos de su familia. La vida en esta gran ciudad le da un poco de miedo y frecuentemente se siente sola. Pero ella sabe que éste es el precio que tiene que pagar si quiere llegar a ser[6] una gran bailarina.

---

[1]**la danza** *dance*   [2]**entrenarse** *to train*   [3]**la beca** *scholarship*
[4]**el de cualquier** *that of any*   [5]**ahí** *there*   [6]**llegar a ser** *to become*

Preguntas

Contesta según la lectura.

1. ¿Quién es Blanche Hampton?
2. ¿Cuál es la diferencia entre la vida de Blanche y la de otras chicas de dieciséis años?
3. ¿Cómo es la vida de Blanche? Por ejemplo, en tu opinión, ¿tiene Blanche tiempo para ir a fiestas o para salir con un novio?
4. ¿Por qué crees que se siente sola y le da miedo vivir en Nueva York?
5. ¿Qué más necesita Blanche para llegar a ser una gran bailarina?

El Ballet Folklórico de México

EXPLICACIONES II Essential

Notes: Mini-dialogue 2 on p. 405 contains examples of *seguir*.

◆ **OBJECTIVES:**

TO DESCRIBE ONGOING ACTIVITIES

TO DESCRIBE THINGS THAT DON'T CHANGE

TO EXPRESS BOREDOM

El verbo *seguir*

The verb *seguir*, "to follow, to continue," is an $e \rightarrow i$ stem-changing verb. Here are all of the forms of *seguir* in the present tense.

INFINITIVO: **seguir**

	SINGULAR	PLURAL
	sigo	seguimos
	sigues	seguís
	sigue	siguen

El ensayo **sigue** hasta las 10:00. *The rehearsal **will continue** until 10:00.*
Las obras para el coro **siguen** *The works for chorus **follow** the*
al intervalo. *intermission.*

1 The command forms of *seguir* are *sigue (no sigas) / siga / sigan*.

   Sigue hasta la esquina y dobla a la *Continue to the corner and*
   izquierda. *turn left.*
   Sigan a la acomodadora, por favor. *Follow the usher, please.*

2 When we use *seguir* meaning "to follow," we often use *a* before the direct object, even when it is not a person.

   Los truenos siguen **a** los relámpagos. *Thunder **follows** the lightning.*

3 In the preterite, *seguir* is like other *-ir* stem-changing verbs. The *e* → *i* in the *Ud.* / *él* / *ella* and *Uds.* / *ellos* / *ellas* forms.

Reteach / Extra Help:
Reinforce the present-tense forms of *seguir* by asking questions such as: *Cuando bailas, ¿sigues tú o sigue tu compañero(a)? Cuando vas al cine, ¿sigues pensando en la película después de salir del teatro? ¿Seguimos practicando la pronunciación en esta clase?*

SINGULAR	PLURAL
seguí	seguimos
seguiste	seguisteis
siguió	siguieron

¿**Seguiste** a los otros?
Los admiradores **siguieron** al bailarín después de la función.

Did you follow the others?
The fans followed the dancer after the show.

4 We use *seguir* + present participle to indicate that an action that began in the past is still continuing or that it occurs regularly. When we use *seguir* this way, it means "to keep on, to go on, or to continue (doing something)."

Sigo pensando en la película.
¿**Seguiste mirando** la tele después de las noticias?
Le dije "Cállate!" pero **siguió hablando.**
Miré el reloj y **seguí leyendo** el periódico.

I keep thinking about the film.
Did you continue watching TV after the news?
I told her "Be quiet!" but she went on talking.
I looked at the clock and went on reading the newspaper.

Un concierto en Caracas, Venezuela

Andrés Segovia, famoso
músico español

Práctica A
1. ¿Y su papá? Sigue pintando
retratos.
2. ¿Y Uds.? Seguimos viviendo
…
3. ¿Y Ana? Sigue corriendo …
4. ¿Y su tío Felipe? Sigue
tocando …
5. ¿Y Ud., señora? Sigo
dirigiendo …
6. ¿Y Miguel? Sigue
trabajando …
7. ¿Y tú, Beatriz? Sigo
estudiando …
8. ¿Y el Sr. González? Sigue
gritando …

Reteach / Review: Before
students begin Ex. B, you may
want to do a quick choral drill
with the five active preterite
forms of *seguir.*

Práctica B
1. ¿Qué hicieron Uds.?
Seguimos hablando …
2. ¿… hicieron …? Siguieron
cenando.
3. ¿… hizo Ud. ¿Seguí
pintando …
4. ¿… hicieron …? Siguieron
durmiendo …
5. ¿…hicieron …? Seguimos
levantando …
6. ¿… hizo … ¿Siguió
discutiendo con …
7. ¿… hizo? Siguió haciendo
…
8. ¿… hiciste …? … seguí
tocando …

PRÁCTICA

A   La visita del Sr. Suárez.   El año pasado el Sr. Suárez se mudó a otra
ciudad. Acaba de regresar para visitar a sus amigos y quiere saber lo
que pasa. Pregunta y contesta según el modelo.

> ¿su mamá? / escribir novelas
> ESTUDIANTE A   *¿Y su mamá?*
> ESTUDIANTE B   *Sigue escribiendo novelas.*

1. ¿su papá? / pintar retratos
2. ¿Uds.? / vivir junto a la escuela
3. ¿Ana? / correr en el parque todos los días
4. ¿su tío Felipe? / tocar el saxofón
5. ¿Ud., señora? / dirigir la orquesta
6. ¿Miguel? / trabajar en el garaje
7. ¿tú, Beatriz? / estudiar escultura
8. ¿el Sr. González? / gritar a todos los chicos

B   La noche en que se apagaron las luces.   ¿Qué hizo cada uno esa
noche? Pregunta y contesta según el modelo.

> ¿Ud.? / asar pollo a la parrilla
> ESTUDIANTE A   *¿Qué hizo Ud.?*
> ESTUDIANTE B   *Seguí asando pollo a la parrilla.*

1. ¿Uds.? / hablar por teléfono
2. ¿Jorge y Mario? / cenar
3. ¿Ud.? / pintar el techo
4. ¿tus padres? / dormir
5. ¿Pablo y tú? / levantar pesas
6. ¿Elena? / discutir con Eva
7. ¿Silvia? / hacer ejercicio
8. ¿tú? / tocar el tambor

La posición de los adjetivos

You know that in Spanish a descriptive adjective usually follows the noun.

la montaña **verde**	*the green mountain*
un escultor **famoso**	*a famous sculptor*

But when the adjective describes a natural characteristic of the noun, the adjective goes before.

un **peligroso huracán**	*u dangerous hurricane*
la **blanca nieve**	*the white snow*

◆ OBJECTIVE:

TO GIVE COMPLETE OR PRECISE DESCRIPTIONS

Notes: Refer to mini-dialogue 1 on p. 405 for a sentence that contains two adjectives describing a noun.

Reteach / Extra Help:
Reinforce the position of adjectives by asking volunteers to suggest additional examples. Or you may want to use magazine and / or newspaper cutouts to elicit descriptive adjectives. Ask questions such as *¿Cómo es ____? Es un hombre grande, ¿verdad?*

1. Remember that these six adjectives drop the final *-o* before a masculine singular noun.

un **buen** artista	**ningún** talento	el **primer** ensayo
un **mal** pintor	**algún** sonido	el **tercer** contrabajo

The adjective *grande* becomes *gran* before any singular noun, either masculine or feminine.

un **gran** coro	una **gran** orquesta

2. Some adjectives change meaning depending on whether we use them before or after the noun.

un hombre **grande**	*a large man*
un **gran** hombre	*a great man*
la chica **pobre**	*the poor (penniless) girl*
la **pobre** chica	*the poor (pitiful) girl*
el coche **nuevo**	*the new (brand new) car*
el **nuevo** coche	*the new (different) car*
un amigo **viejo**	*an old (elderly) friend*
un **viejo** amigo	*an old (of long standing) friend*

3. When two or more adjectives describe a noun, we can place them after the noun, joined by the word *y*.

un niño **alto y pálido**	*a tall, pale boy*
un sonido **suave y bello**	*a soft, beautiful sound*

But if one of the adjectives usually comes before the noun, it remains there and the second adjective *follows* the noun.

una **gran** pintora **chilena**	*a great Chilean painter*
muchas esculturas **abstractas**	*many abstract sculptures*

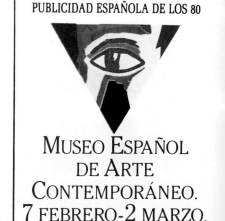

PUBLICIDAD ESPAÑOLA DE LOS 80

MUSEO ESPAÑOL
DE ARTE
CONTEMPORÁNEO.
7 FEBRERO-2 MARZO.

A **¿Dónde lo pongo?** Daniel está tomando una clase de composición y su profesor quiere que practique los adjetivos. Indica dónde debe ponerlos. Sigue el modelo.

> Fue un *día* que nunca voy a olvidar. (grande)
> *Fue un gran día que nunca voy a olvidar.*

1. Teresa es una *chica* que no tiene dinero. (pobre)
2. Estoy seguro que ese *hombre* pesa más de 200 kilos. (grande)
3. ¡Llega el *momento!* Van a entregar los premios. (grande)
4. ¿Tienes mi *dirección?* (nuevo)
5. Busca los guantes en la *maleta.* (grande)
6. Es un *hombre* que siempre pide monedas a la gente. (pobre)
7. Los *zapatos* siempre son incómodos. (nuevos)
8. Esa *mujer* acaba de romperse el tobillo. (pobre)
9. Hace muchos años que conocemos al director. Es un *amigo* nuestro. (viejo)

B **Una visita a los artistas.** Alguien está describiendo el estudio de unos artistas. Completa las frases con la forma correcta de los dos adjetivos. En cada frase uno de los adjetivos va delante del sustantivo y el otro sigue al sustantivo.

> Ella siempre usa pinceles. (diferentes / muchos)
> *Ella siempre usa muchos pinceles diferentes.*

1. Aquí trabaja una artista. (bueno / español)
2. ¿Viste dibujos? (algún / abstracto)
3. Felipe es un escultor. (grande / moderno)
4. Ese pintor siempre se sienta en el fondo. (extranjero / joven)
5. Me fijé en esas pinturas. (dos / parecido)
6. Ella es la modelo de la clase. (alto / único)
7. Ese pintor usa colores. (mucho / suave)
8. En este lugar trabajaron escultores. (famosos / varios)

(abajo, derecha) Pablo Picasso

AYUNTAMIENTO DE BARCELONA
MUSEO PICASSO **LAS MENINAS**

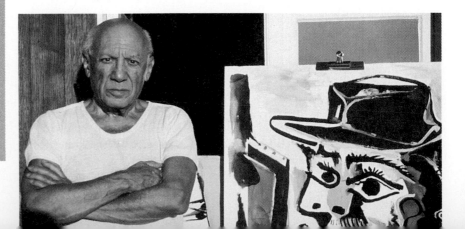

C Hablemos de ti.

Compara tu vida de hoy con tu vida durante los últimos dos o tres años.

1. ¿Sigues practicando los mismos deportes? ¿Cuáles son? ¿Por qué sí o por qué no? Si no, ¿qué deporte practicas ahora?
2. ¿Sigues visitando los mismos lugares? ¿Por qué sí o por qué no? ¿Cuáles visitas ahora?
3. ¿Te siguen gustando las mismas materias? ¿Cuáles son? ¿Sigues sacando las mismas notas? ¿O sacas notas mejores o peores? ¿Te sigue gustando estudiar español?
4. ¿Sigues aprendiendo mucho en la escuela? Por ejemplo, ¿qué aprendiste esta semana?
5. ¿Sigues mirando los mismos programas de televisión? ¿Por qué sí o por qué no? ¿Cuáles miras ahora?
6. ¿Sigues admirando a los mismos actores y cantantes? Si no, ¿a quiénes admiras ahora?
7. ¿Te siguen interesando los mismos pasatiempos? ¿Por qué sí o por qué no?

Práctica C
Answers will vary.

Practice Sheet 12–6

Worbook Exs. G–J

Tape Manual Ex. 8   14

Refrán   15

Canción   16

Quiz 12 6

En Barcelona, España

Notes: Answers to the **Repaso** and **Tema** appear in the Teacher Notes.

REPASO

Notes: Review of:
1. noun phrases with *de*
   possession with *de*
   present progressive
   position of adjectives
2. use of subject pronouns for
   clarity or emphasis
   present progressive
   noun phrases with *de*
   possession with *de*
3. present progressive
4. present subjunctive with
   implied commands
5. *seguir* + present participle

Enrichment: You may want
to use the model sentences in
the **Repaso** for dictation.

Mira con cuidado las frases modelo. Luego cambia las frases que siguen al español según los modelos.

1. *El coro de la escuela está ensayando una canción nueva.*
   (Mrs. González's students are reading a great novel.)
   (The band director is conducting a fantastic concert.)
   (The painter's son is painting an elegant portrait.)

2. *Ella está tocando las obras de Albéniz y él está grabando la música.*
   (The musicians are demonstrating the sounds of the instruments and the composer (fem.) is opening the piano.)
   (I'm signing the traveler's checks and my brother is counting the bills.)
   (Teresa is buying that nail polish and I'm looking at the perfumes.)

3. *Estamos pidiendo un libro que muestra cómo dibujar hojas.*
   (We're enclosing a notice that explains how to obtain information.)
   (They're choosing a magazine that demonstrates how to cut hair.)
   (I'm taking out a book that describes how to make ceramics.)

4. *La Sra. González me recomienda más tarde que tenga cuidado con los espejos.*
   (My parents always tell me not to hurt others.)
   (Our coach (masc.) usually recommends that we lift weights with the team.)
   (I ask you (pl.) again to pay attention for an hour.)

5. *Cuando empieza la entrevista, siguen aplaudiendo.*
   (When the accident occurred, he continued sleeping.)
   (When the players leave, I keep on shouting.)
   (When the rain began, I went on rehearsing.)

Un mural de David Alfaro Siqueiros en México

TEMA

Escribe las frases en español.

1. Mr. Pérez's class is painting a large mural.

2. Lucía is opening the cans of paint and Jorge is mixing colors.

3. María is reading a book that explains how to paint murals

4. Mr. Pérez tells us again to be careful with the paint.

5. When the class ends, we keep on pointing.

REDACCIÓN

Ahora escoge uno de los siguientes temas para escribir tu propio diálogo o párrafo.

1. Imagine that the mural that the students were planning to paint for the school is now completed. Describe it. What does it look like? What school landmarks or events did the students include?

2. Write a paragraph about an artist or performer whom you admire.

3. Create a dialogue between two people who are visiting an art museum.

Aplicaciones **423**

COMPRUEBA TU PROGRESO   CAPÍTULO 12   Discretionary

Notes: Answers to the **Comprueba** appear in the Teacher Notes.

A   ¿Qué están haciendo?
Haz frases según el modelo.

el chico / leer / el poema
El chico está leyendo el poema.

1. la gente / aplaudir / a los músicos
2. ella / pedir / otro saxofón
3. los músicos / devolver / los instrumentos
4. yo / tocar / el violoncelo
5. el director / dirigir / la orquesta
6. tú / limpiar / tu trompeta
7. el coro / ensayar / una canción diferente
8. nosotros / cantar / en el coro

B   Estoy haciéndolo ahora mismo
Contesta según el modelo.

¿Ya limpiaste el cuarto?
Estoy limpiándolo ahora mismo.

1. ¿Ya recogieron Uds. los cuadros?
2. ¿Ya escribió Irene el recado?
3. ¿Ya ensayaste la nueva obra?
4. ¿Ya terminaron Uds. el mural?
5. ¿Ya arregló Cristina tu guitarra?
6. ¿Ya oíste ese chisme?
7. ¿Ya pidieron ellos los anuncios?

C   ¿Cómo terminan?
Escoge la terminación (*ending*) correcta para cada
frase. Las terminaciones están en la columna de la
derecha.

1. Mi hermano no puede bajar de peso . . .
2. Después del ensayo, los músicos . . .
3. Me acuesto tarde todas las noches . . .
4. Para hacer buenos retratos . . .
5. Después de varios minutos, el público . . .
6. David se cayó y . . .
7. Cuando suena el despertador . . .

a. todavía sigue gritando.
b. tienes que seguir dibujando todos los días.
c. porque sigo mirando la televisión después de
   las noticias.
d. siguen practicando para el concierto.
e. lo apago y sigo durmiendo.
f. sigue aplaudiendo a los músicos.
g. porque sigue comiendo comida con muchas
   calorías.

D   El verbo *seguir*
Completa las frases con la forma correcta del
verbo *seguir* en el pretérito.

1. (Nosotros) _____ al coro hasta la puerta.
2. (yo) Te _____ hasta la galería de arte.
3. Mis perros me _____ cuando salí de casa.
4. El ensayo _____ hasta la medianoche.
5. ¿Por qué no _____ (tú) derecho por esa calle?
6. El público _____ a los artistas para pedirles
   autógrafos.

E   Hablan los músicos
Usa la forma correcta de cada adjetivo y ponla en
el lugar correcto, o antes o después de la palabra
en cursiva.

1. Ayer volví a tocar con mi *banda*.   (viejo)
2. ¿Sabes que Roberto grabó un *disco*?   (nuevo)
3. Es un *músico*. No puede comprar buenos
   instrumentos.   (pobre)
4. El concierto fue un *éxito*.   (grande)
5. Ésas son *canciones*. ¿Por qué no tocamos
   otras?   (viejo)
6. En esa tienda venden *instrumentos* muy
   baratos.   (nuevo)
7. El concierto de ese *compositor* fue un
   fracaso.   (pobre)
8. Necesitamos un *armario* para nuestros
   instrumentos.   (grande)

Activity Masters   Chapter 12 Test   [📼] Listening Comprehension Test

Workbook Review: Chapters 9–12   Cumulative Test: Chapters 9–12

VOCABULARIO DEL CAPÍTULO 12

Sustantivos
el/la artista
  el bailarín, *pl.* los bailarines; la
    bailarina
  el centro *(center, middle)*
  la cerámica
  el clarinete
  la colección, *pl.* las colecciones
  el compositor, la compositora
  el contrabajo
  el coro
  la diferencia
  el director, la directora
    (conductor)
  el ensayo
  el escultor, la escultora
  la escultura
  la flauta
  la galería
  el instrumento
el/la modelo
  el mural
  el músico, la música
  el oboe
  la obra
  la orquesta
  el paisaje *(landscape)*
  el pincel
  el pintor, la pintora
  la pintura *(paint; painting)*
  el retrato
  el saxofón, *pl.* los saxofones
  el sonido
  el talento
  el tambor
  el trombón, *pl.* los trombones
  la trompeta
  la tuba
  el violín, *pl.* los violines
  el violoncelo

Adverbio
tanto

Preposición
junto a

Expresiones
¡bravo!
en el fondo
hacer daño a
seguir + *present participle*
sin duda

Adjetivos
abstracto, -a
diferente
parecido, -a
suave

Verbos
aplaudir
demostrar (o → ue)
dirigir (j)
ensayar
fijarse en
gritar
pintar
seguir (e → i)

PRÓLOGO CULTURAL

EL CUERPO HABLA

If you have ever watched a conversation between native Spanish speakers, you know that gestures are almost as essential to them as words. Some gestures actually stand for words. For example, when Spanish speakers place an index finger just below one eye, they are saying *¡ojo!*, "watch out!" It's a silent way of warning you that someone or something can't be trusted. When they tap a cheek with their fingers, they're saying *cara*, part of the expression *¡qué cara tiene!*, which means that someone should be ashamed but isn't.

Sometimes their gestures and those of English speakers look the same, but their meanings may be quite different. For example, the gesture Spanish speakers use to mean "come here"—a hand held palm down with the fingers waving up and down—can easily be mistaken for "good-by" or even "go away" by an English speaker.

Gestures are conscious acts, but most body language consists of things we are not aware of doing. For example, if you are angry or impatient, your face and body will most likely reveal it.

One important difference in the unconscious body language of Spanish speakers and English speakers is that Spaniards and Latin Americans usually stand close to one another, even if they have just met. English speakers tend to stay about twice as far apart, and they may feel uncomfortable if a stranger stands any closer. Remember this the next time you talk to someone from a Spanish-speaking country. It will help you realize that they are not "invading" your space. And, if you can reach a compromise, they may realize that you are not standoffish.

427

PALABRAS NUEVAS I

Essential

 1

Transparency 43

CONTEXTO VISUAL

Amor y familia

If students ask: Other related words you may want to present: *la luna de miel,* honeymoon; *la fiesta de bodas,* wedding reception.

la boda

el novio

la novia

los novios

el bautizo

llorar   el bebé

regalar

desenvolver

* Couples are *novios* from the time they start dating each other regularly until they get married. After that they become *esposos.*

CONTEXTO COMUNICATIVO 2

1 CECILIA   Tengo las fotos de la fiesta de tus **bisabuelos.**

DIEGO   Fue una fiesta **inolvidable,** ¿verdad?

CECILIA   Mira, en esta foto tú **tocabas** el piano **mientras** yo **cantaba.**

Variaciones:
- bisabuelos → tíos
- inolvidable → maravillosa

el bisabuelo, la bisabuela *great-grandfather, great-grandmother*

los bisabuelos *great-grandparents*

inolvidable *unforgettable*

(yo) tocaba, (tú) tocabas (from **tocar**) *was / were playing*

mientras *while*

(yo) cantaba, (tú) cantabas (from **cantar**) *was / were singing*

2 JORGE   Tu **cuñado** Guillermo **se parece** mucho **a** su hermano.

JULIA   Sí, son **iguales:** altos y morenos.

JORGE   Bueno, iguales no, pero muy parecidos.

- cuñado → primo
- morenos → guapos

el cuñado, la cuñada *brother-in-law, sister-in-law*

parecerse a (c → zc) *to look like, to resemble*

igual *the same, alike*

3 SILVIA   ¿**Recuerdas** cuando **nació** Diego?

ANTONIO   Claro que sí. Y unos días después **nos reunimos*** con tus **parientes.** Su **madrina** hizo pasteles y todos tomamos **sidra.**

SILVIA   Y Diego nunca lloró durante la fiesta. **Era** un niño muy paciente.

ANTONIO   Pero ahora las cosas son distintas.

- cuando nació → el día del **nacimiento** de Diego
- nos reunimos → celebramos
- madrina → **padrino**
- sidra → **sangría**†

recordar (o → ue) *to remember*

nacer (c → zc) *to be born*

reunirse (yo me reúno, tu te reúnes) *to meet, to get together*

el pariente, la parienta *relative*

la madrina *godmother*

la sidra *cider*

era (from **ser**) *I / he / she was; you (formal) were*

el nacimiento *birth*

el padrino *godfather*

los padrinos *godparents*

la sangría *sangria*

---

* *Reunirse* has an accent on the *u* in all the present-tense forms except the *nosotros* and *vosotros* forms.

† *Sangría* is a popular summer punch made of wine, fruit, fruit juices, and carbonated water.

4	ALBERTO	**Tengo celos de** mi novia.	**tener celos de** *to be jealous of*
	NICOLAS	¿Por qué? ¿Crees que está **enamorada de** otro?	**enamorado, -a (de)** *in love (with)*
	ALBERTO	No, pero tiene muchos amigos y casi nunca la veo.	

- otro → otra persona
- la veo → estamos juntos

5	MARÍA	Tú tienes dos hermanos, ¿verdad?	
	MARCO	Sí, Mario, el mayor, está **casado con** una bailarina uruguaya.	**casado, -a (con)** *married (to)*
	MARÍA	¿Y el otro?	
	MARCO	Guillermo estudia arte y todavía está **soltero.**	**soltero, -a** *single, unmarried*

- está casado → **se casó** el año pasado
- bailarina → compositora

casarse con *to marry, to get married to*

6	MARÍA	Y cuéntame, ¿cómo es tu cuñada?	
	MARCO	Es una bailarina excelente pero me parece muy antipática.	
	MARÍA	Sin duda tu hermano la **quiere.**	**querer** here: *to love*
	MARCO	Sí. **El amor** es ciego, ¿no?	**el amor** *love*

- la quiere → está enamorado de ella

| 7 | JULIA | ¡Qué **sorpresa**! ¿Cuándo llegaste? | **la sorpresa** *surprise* |
| | JOSÉ | Esta tarde. Vine porque Anita **cumple** 16 **años** y quiero **felicitarla.** | **cumplir años** *to have a birthday, to turn* (+ age) |

- Anita cumple 16 años → es el cumpleaños de Anita

felicitar *to congratulate*

| 8 | MARIANA | Ahora que tenemos una hija mi **suegro** nos visita más frecuentemente que antes. Es muy **cariñoso con** ella. | **el suegro, la suegra** *father-in-law, mother-in-law* |
| | MANUEL | Sí, veo que es un hombre **feliz** cuando está con sus **nietos.** | **los suegros** *in-laws* |

- suegro → padre
- es un hombre feliz → está muy contento

cariñoso, -a (con) *affectionate (with)*
feliz, pl. **felices** *happy*
el nieto, la nieta *grandson, granddaughter*
los nietos *grandchildren*

EN OTRAS PARTES

felicitar

También se dice *la criatura, el tierno / la tierna* y *el nene / la nena*. En Chile, Bolivia, el Ecuador y el Perú se dice también *la guagua*.

En España se dice también *dar la enhorabuena*.

PRÁCTICA

A Los parientes.   Rogelio tiene una familia grande. Completa las frases según el dibujo.

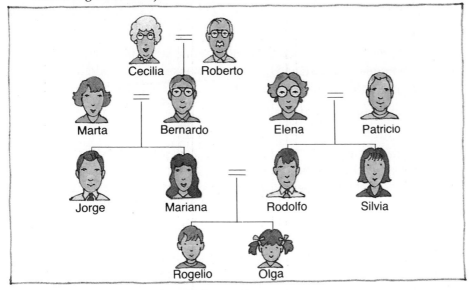

1. Elena es _____ de Mariana.
2. Mariana es _____ de Cecilia.
3. Cecilia y Roberto son _____ de Olga.
4. Olga es _____ de Jorge.
5. Jorge es _____ de Rodolfo.
6. Rodolfo es _____ de Silvia.
7. Silvia es _____ de Patricio.
8. Patricio es _____ de Olga.
9. Bernardo es _____ de Rodolfo.

Práctica A
1. la suegra
2. la nieta
3. los bisabuelos
4. la sobrina
5. el cuñado
6. el hermano
7. la hija
8. el abuelo
9. el suegro

Reteach / Review: After students have completed Ex. A either orally or in writing, you may want to ask them to create their own family tree or to invent an imaginary one.

B Una fiesta inolvidable. Josefina se casó con Juan la semana pasada. Después de la boda, los parientes de ella les dieron una fiesta. Usa el pretérito de los siguientes verbos para completar el párrafo.

agradecer casarse felicitar nacer sacar
aplaudir cumplir años irse regalar ser
bailar desenvolver llorar reunirse servir

En febrero Juan _____ 26 _____ y Josefina 24. Los dos _____ el mismo mes pero en diferentes años. El sábado pasado Juan y Josefina _____ en la iglesia del barrio. _____ una boda maravillosa. Cuando salimos de la iglesia (nosotros) _____ en la casa de la novia. Todo el mundo
5 _____ a los novios. Los parientes de la novia _____ una cena muy sabrosa. Después de cortar el pastel, los novios _____ el vals *(waltz)*. Todos _____. El fotógrafo _____ fotos de los novios junto a los parientes y amigos. Durante la fiesta Josefina y Juan _____ los regalos y _____ a todos los invitados. Sólo la tía Mariana les _____ dinero.
10 Exactamente a las doce los novios _____ de la fiesta. La madre de Josefina _____ mucho.

C Fiesta de Navidad. Cada Navidad, toda la familia Alegría se reúne en la granja de los abuelos. Usa la forma correcta del adjetivo apropiado para completar las frases.

cariñoso enamorado igual parecido
casado feliz inolvidable soltero

1. Esta Navidad va a ser diferente e _____. ¡Mi bisabuelo cumple 90 años el 25 de diciembre!
2. Éste es el único lugar donde yo soy completamente _____.
3. Mi primo Enrique está casado, pero tiene tres hermanos _____.
4. Mi hermana Sonia y su novio están muy _____. Piensan casarse pronto.
5. Todos dicen que la voz de Mónica es muy _____ a la mía.
6. Casi todas mis hermanas están _____ y tienen varios hijos.
7. Mi cuñada Ester quiere mucho a su bebé y es muy _____ con él.
8. Papá y mi tío Alberto son altos y pelirrojos. Todo el mundo dice que son _____.

D Hablemos de ti.

1. ¿Vas a veces a bodas? ¿Qué haces cuando asistes a una boda? En la última boda a la cual (*which*) asististe, ¿quiénes se casaron? ¿Cuándo ocurrió? ¿Dónde? ¿Disfrutaste de ella? ¿Qué les regalaste a los novios?
2. ¿A qué pariente te pareces más? ¿Te pareces a tu padre o a tu madre? ¿Tienes hermanos(as)? ¿Son Uds. parecidos o diferentes?
3. ¿Qué hace tu familia cuando alguien cumple años? ¿Qué te gusta hacer en tu cumpleaños?
4. ¿Eres cariñoso(a)? ¿A veces tienes celos de la gente? ¿Por qué?
5. ¿Piensas casarte o crees que vas a quedarte soltero(a)?
6. ¿Cuándo naciste? ¿Conoces a alguien que nació el mismo día que tú?

Práctica D
Answers will vary.

Practice Sheet 13–1

Workbook Exs. A–B

Tape Manual Exs. 1–2 3

Quiz 13–1

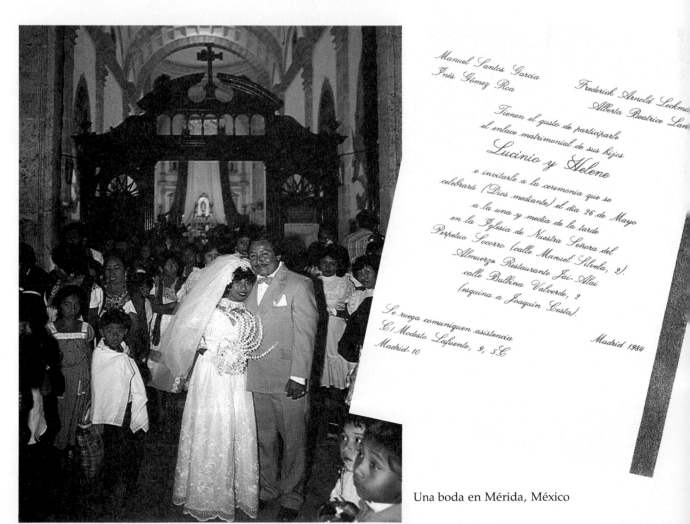

Una boda en Mérida, México

APLICACIONES Discretionary

 4 5 Pronunciación

La boda de mi hermana

Dos amigas se reúnen en un café.

MÓNICA Hola, Raquel, ¿qué hay?

RAQUEL Mira, acabo de recoger las fotos de la boda de Eva y Raúl. ¿Las quieres ver?

5 **MÓNICA** ¡Por supuesto!

RAQUEL Aquí está mi hermana poniéndose el vestido. Estaba[1] muy nerviosa ese día.

MÓNICA El vestido es fantástico. ¿Dónde lo encontró?

RAQUEL Nuestra bisabuela lo hizo. Es el mismo vestido que

10 llevaron la abuela y mamá cuando ellas se casaron. Mira, aquí están Eva y Raúl en la iglesia.

MÓNICA ¡Pobrecito! Parece muy pálido.

RAQUEL Sí, pero hacen una pareja[2] muy bonita, ¿verdad?

MÓNICA Tienes razón. ¿Y quién es toda esta gente?

15 **RAQUEL** Ésta es una foto de los recién casados[3] con todos los parientes. No falta nadie.

MÓNICA ¿Quién es este anciano?[4]

RAQUEL El bisabuelo de Raúl. Acaba de cumplir 88 años.

MÓNICA ¡Imagínate! ¡Cuatro generaciones juntas!

---

[1]**estaba** (from **estar**) *was*   [2]**la pareja** *couple*   [3]**el/la recién casado(a)** *newlywed*   [4]**el/la anciano(a)** *elderly gentleman/woman*

Preguntas

Contesta según el diálogo.

1. ¿Quiénes son Eva y Raúl?   2. Cuenta la historia del vestido que llevaba la novia.   3. ¿Tienes tú algo muy viejo de tus abuelos o bisabuelos? ¿Qué es?   4. En tu opinión, ¿fue la boda de Eva y Raúl muy grande? ¿Por qué?   5. ¿Cómo estaba Eva ese día? Y Raúl, ¿cómo estaba él?   6. ¿Cuántos años tiene el bisabuelo de Raúl?

Participación

Work with a partner to make up a dialogue about an event that one of you attended and the other one didn't. It might be a birthday party, a baptism, a wedding, a bar mitzvah, etc. Discuss what happened.

Diálogo
1. Los novios; la hermana y el cuñado de Raquel.
2. Su bisabuela lo hizo y su abuela y mamá lo llevaron cuando ellas se casaron.
3. Answers will vary.
4. Answers will vary, but probably: Sí, porque todos los parientes estaban allí.
5. Eva estaba nerviosa. Raúl estaba pálido.
6. Tiene ochenta y ocho años.

Reteach / Extra Help: Before students prepare their **Participación** dialogues, you may want to elicit questions that would arise in a conversation about an event. For example: *¿Cuándo fue? ¿Cuántas personas asistieron? ¿Qué sirvieron de comida? ¿Lo pasaste bien? ¿Por qué?*

Una boda en Caracas, Venezuela

PALABRAS NUEVAS II

Essential

¡Pórtate bien!

Transparency 44

CONTEXTO VISUAL

If students ask: Other related words you may want to present: *la pareja,* couple; *el carretón,* wagon; *la cerca,* fence.

la vecina

el vecino

CONTEXTO COMUNICATIVO

 7

Reteach / Review: Point out that *caer bien / mal* follows the same pattern as *gustar, encantar, doler*, and so on.

1 LAURA ¡Ese chico **me cae tan mal**!

CARLOS ¿Por qué?

LAURA **Se porta** mal, es muy **mal educado** y siempre **me toma el pelo.**

Variaciones:

- me cae tan mal → me **molesta** muchísimo
- se porta mal → no se porta bien
- me toma el pelo → **mete la pata**
- me toma el pelo → se ríe de mí

caerle bien / mal (a uno) *to make a good / bad impression (on someone); to like / not like (someone)*

portarse *to behave*

bien / mal educado, -a *polite / impolite, rude*

tomarle el pelo (a uno) *to pull someone's leg*

molestar *to bother*

meter la pata *to put one's foot in it, to goof*

2 PABLO ¿Me **permites** llevarte a casa?

DIANA Gracias, pero **no te molestes**. Queda muy lejos de aquí.

PABLO A mí no me importa, ¡de veras!

- me permites → puedo
- te molestes → es necesario
- queda muy lejos → tengo una **cita** con el dentista
  a mí no me importa, ¡de veras! → está bien

permitir *to let, to allow, to permit*

no te molestes *don't bother*

la cita *appointment, date*

Palabras Nuevas II **437**

3 ESPERANZA   ¿Te cae bien Ana?

    ALEJANDRO   Sí, pero a veces hace cosas **desagradables.** Por ejemplo, sabes que siempre **masca** chicle. Pues, ayer fuimos al parque y tiró su chicle en el césped. ¡Sin envolverlo!

    ESPERANZA   ¡Qué barbaridad!

- cosas desagradables → cosas que me molestan
- siempre masca → nunca **deja de** mascar

desagradable   *disagreeable, unpleasant*
mascar   *to chew*

dejar de + inf.   *to stop (doing something)*

4 CARLOS   **¿Qué te parece si** damos un paseo por aquí?

    BEATRIZ   No **se puede.** ¿No ves el letrero? Dice: "**Se prohibe** caminar por el césped."

- damos un paseo por → nos sentamos
  caminar por → sentarse en

¿qué te parece si + verb?   *how about (doing something)?*
se puede   *it is allowed; you can*
se prohibe   *it is forbidden*

5 CLAUDIA   El hijo de Rosita es muy bien educado.

    CARLOS   Es verdad. Siempre se porta bien y casi nunca **se pelea con** sus hermanos.

- se pelea con → tiene celos de
- casi nunca se pelea → siempre **comparte** sus cosas
- casi nunca se pelea con → siempre **cuida** a

pelearse con   *to quarrel, to fight (with)*

compartir   *to share*
cuidar   here: *to take care of*

Reteach / Extra Help: In connection with mini-dialogue 4, you may want to reinforce the expressions *se puede* and *se prohibe* by eliciting classroom do's and don'ts. For example: *Se puede hacer preguntas. Se prohibe hablar inglés.*

Estudiantes en Puerto Rico

6 LUCÍA   Recuerda que mamá te dijo que no hables mucho para no meter la pata.

PEDRITO   Ya sé. También dijo que no debo quitarme los zapatos **en público.**

LUCÍA   Y que después de la función **te despidas de** los abuelos y de todos **los mayores.**

■ te despidas de → saludes a
   y de todos → y a todos

en público   *in public*
despedirse de (e → i)   *to say good-by to*
los mayores   *grownups*

Reteach / Review: Point out that *despedirse* in mini-dialogue 6 is conjugated like *pedir.*

7 MARÍA   Necesito una nueva flauta.

MARIO   Ve a la Casa Odeón entonces. Hay una gran liquidación

MARÍA   **¿Por dónde** queda?

MARIO   **Por** la Segunda Avenida, al lado del Mercado del Sol. Anteayer compré una trompeta allí por muy poco dinero.

■ flauta → guitarra
■ al lado del → enfrente del
■ al lado del → junto al

¿por dónde?   *where, whereabouts*
por   *here: along*

PRÁCTICA

A   ¿Quién le cae bien?   A Bernardo le caen bien algunas personas y otras no. ¿Qué clases de personas le caen bien? Contesta según los modelos.

     la gente mal educada
     La gente mal educada le cae mal.

     los chicos bien educados
     Los chicos bien educados le caen bien.

1. la gente que se pelea con todo el mundo
2. Manuel, que siempre comparte sus cosas
3. la prima que masca chicle con la boca abierta
4. el vecino que pide prestadas cosas y se olvida de devolverlas
5. las personas que no hablan durante una película
6. los amigos que no prestan atención cuando él habla
7. la parienta que es optimista
8. su madrina que es cariñosa
9. los mayores que no le permiten hacer lo que quiere
10. su cuñada, que mete la pata a menudo
11. los niños que no saben portarse bien
12. los novios que tienen celos

Práctica A
1. … le cae mal.
2. … le cae bien.
3. … le cae mal.
4. … le cae mal.
5. … le caen bien.
6. … le caen mal.
7. … le cae bien.
8. … le cae bien.
9. … le caen mal.
10. … le cae mal.
11. … le caen mal.
12. … le caen mal.

Enrichment: After students have completed Ex. A either orally or in writing, you may want to ask them to create two or three sentences describing the kinds of people they like and dislike.

Práctica B
quiero
me caen
regalarles
Recuerda
Me estás tomando
te parece si
Me gustaría
me importa

B **¿Qué les vamos a regalar?** Jorge y su hermana Julia van a una boda. Completa el diálogo con las siguientes palabras.

me importa	quiero		me gustaría	me caen
regalarles	me estás tomando		recuerda	te parece si

JULIA   A Susana y Horacio los ____ mucho.

JORGE   A mí también ____ muy bien.

JULIA   Entonces vamos a ____ algo especial.

JORGE   ____ que Susana quiere cosas para la casa.

5   JULIA   Es una buena idea. ¿Crees que necesitan una aspiradora?

JORGE   ____ el pelo, ¿verdad? Una buena aspiradora es carísima.

JULIA   Entonces, ¿qué ____ les compramos unas ollas o una manta?

JORGE   Mira, Julia, ésos son regalos que dan los parientes. Sólo somos sus amigos. ____ gastar menos dinero.

10   JULIA   A mí no ____ gastar dinero para comprarles un buen regalo a mis amigos.

JORGE   Tienes razón. Vamos a comprarles una plancha.

JULIA   ¡Qué amigo tan tacaño que eres!

Práctica C
Answers will vary. Probable
choices are:
1. Damos la mano a
2. Damos la mano a /
   Abrazamos a
3. Nos reímos de
4. Nos peleamos con / Nos
   quejamos de
5. Besamos a / Abrazamos a
6. Damos la mano a /
   Abrazamos a / Besamos a /
   Felicitamos a
7. Agradecemos a
8. Nos reímos de
9. Damos la mano a /
   Abrazamos a / Besamos a /
   Felicitamos a
10. Nos quejamos de / Nos
    peleamos con
11. Agradecemos a
12. Nos peleamos con / Nos
    quejamos de
13. Nos quejamos de / Nos
    peleamos con

C **Acciones apropiadas.** ¿Qué hacemos en las siguientes situaciones? Usa los verbos y expresiones de la lista para hacer frases. Sigue el modelo.

abrazar a	besar a	felicitar a	quejarse de
agradecer a	dar la mano a	pelearse con	reírse de

nuestros parientes favoritos

Besamos
Abrazamos } *a nuestros parientes favoritos.*

1. los padres de nuestros amigos cuando nos vemos
2. nuestros viejos amigos cuando nos reunimos después de no vernos por mucho tiempo
3. un locutor de televisión que mete la pata
4. alguien que no deja de molestarnos
5. nuestros abuelos cuando nos despedimos de ellos
6. los novios después de la boda
7. alguien que recuerda que hoy es nuestro cumpleaños
8. alguien que sigue empujando una puerta en que el letrero dice "se prohibe entrar"
9. el padre del bebé que nació anoche
10. alguien que nunca comparte ninguna de sus cosas
11. alguien que nos ofrece algo
12. alguien que no nos permite hacer lo que tenemos que hacer
13. alguien que nunca recuerda que tiene una cita con nosotros

D Hablemos de ti.

1. ¿Cuáles son tres cosas que hace la gente que te molestan? ¿Por qué?
2. ¿Conoces a muchos ancianos? ¿Tienes parientes o amigos ancianos? ¿Es interesante hablar con ellos? ¿Por qué? En tu opinión, ¿cuántos años hay que tener para ser un(a) anciano(a)?
3. ¿Abrazas y besas a tus parientes? ¿Y a tus amigos? ¿Cuándo? ¿Tienes padrinos? ¿Se ven Uds. a menudo? ¿Son parientes o amigos de tu familia?
4. ¿Conoces a alguna familia extranjera? ¿Se abrazan y se besan más a menudo que tu familia? ¿Por qué? ¿Qué otras diferencias hay entre las dos familias?
5. ¿Te molesta compartir tus cosas? ¿Con quién prefieres hacerlo? ¿Qué clase de cosas compartes a menudo?

Práctica D
Answers will vary.

Practice Sheet 13–2

Workbook Exs. C–D

Tape Manual Exs. 3–4 🔲 8

Refrán 🔲 9

Quiz 13–2

ACTIVIDAD

¡Qué mal educado(a) es!   Work with a partner to create a description of two of the most obnoxious and irritating people in the world. Tell what they are like, and the kinds of things they do to get on your nerves. For example:

Él nunca deja de hablar, y lo que dice le molesta a todo el mundo.
Ella come con la boca abierta y se ríe de cosas tontas.

Reteach / Review: You may want to expand on the **Actividad** by asking students to suggest ways in which these irritating people could improve their manners. For example: *Él nunca deja de hablar, y lo que dice le molesta a todo el mundo. Debe pensar antes de hablar.*

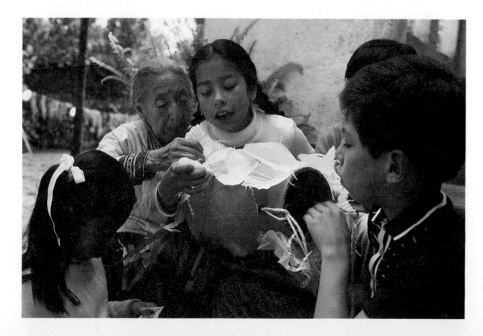

Haciendo una piñata en México

Palabras Nuevas II   **441**

ESTUDIO DE PALABRAS

The negative prefix *des-* often corresponds to the English prefixes *dis-* or *un-*. It makes a word mean the opposite of its original meaning. For example:

*des*agradable	*disagreeable*	*des*envolver	*to unwrap*
*des*enchufar	*to unplug*	*des*ordenado	*untidy*

What do you think these words mean?

desigual	deshacer	desafortunadamente
desconocido	deshonesto	descolorar

Familias de palabras
unequal
unknown
to undo
dishonest
unfortunately
to discolor

Antónimos
Cambia las palabras en cursiva por un antónimo.

Antónimos
1. casada
2. parecidos a / iguales a
3. deja de
4. empujar
5. Se puede
6. (te) rías
7. Nació

1. Ester todavía está *soltera*.
2. Anita y Carlos son *diferentes de* sus padres.
3. Carlos, *empieza a* trabajar.
4. Tienes que *tirar de* la puerta para abrirla.
5. *Se prohibe* nadar.
6. No *llores* tanto.
7. *Se murió* en octubre.

Familias de palabras
1. el nacimiento
2. el padrino
3. abrazar
4. casado
5. la madrina
6. besar
7. cariñoso
8. parecido
9. inolvidable
10. el recuerdo

Familias de palabras
Escribe una palabra relacionada con cada palabra de la lista.

1. nacer	3. brazo	5. madre	7. cariño	9. olvidar
2. padre	4. casarse	6. beso	8. parecer	10. recordar

Un bautizo en Madrid, España

EXPLICACIONES I

El imperfecto de los verbos que terminan en *-ar*

In Spanish, when we talk about things that happened in the past, we distinguish between two different kinds of actions. One kind began and ended at a definite time. These are completed actions, and we use the preterite to talk about them.

Ana **cantó.**   *Ana sang.*

The other kind are past actions without any indication of their beginning or end. We use the imperfect tense to describe them.

Ana **cantaba.**   *Ana was singing.*

We also use the imperfect to talk about actions that occurred regularly in the past. In English we often say "used to" or "would" to express this idea.

Ana **cantaba** mientras **cocinaba.** { *Ana **used to sing** while **she was cooking.*** { *Ana **would sing** while **she was cooking.***

Celebrando la Navidad en Texas

◆ **OBJECTIVES:**

TO REMINISCE

TO DESCRIBE HOW THINGS USED TO BE

TO TELL WHAT WAS HAPPENING OVER A PERIOD OF TIME

TO SHOW SURPRISE

Notes: Refer to mini-dialogues 1 and 3 on p. 429 for examples of verbs in the imperfect tense.

Make sure students understand that the imperfect of all *-ar* verbs is formed by adding the same endings to the stem of the infinitive. Stress the fact that *-ar* verbs with stem changes in other tenses (*despertar, acostar, jugar*, for example) do not have these changes in the imperfect.

1 All -*ar* verbs are regular in the imperfect. Notice the accent on the *nosotros* form.

INFINITIVO **hablar**

	SINGULAR		PLURAL
1	(yo) habl**aba**	(nosotros) (nosotras) }	habl**ábamos**
2	(tú) habl**abas**	(vosotros) (vosotras) }	habl**abais**
3	Ud. (él) } habl**aba** (ella)	Uds. (ellos) } habl**aban** (ellas)	

Since the *yo* form is the same as the *Ud.* / *él* / *ella* form, we often use the subject pronouns to avoid confusion.

2 Expressions that indicate that an action occurred over a period of time often cue us to use the imperfect. Some of these are *generalmente, cada noche (día,* etc.), *todas las noches (las tardes,* etc.), *durante, siempre, a menudo,* and *frecuentemente.*

PRÁCTICA

A No todos trabajaban. Algunos estaban ocupadísimos preparando el gran baile de fin de año. Pero otros, como siempre, no trabajaban. Sigue el modelo.

> César / limpiar los estantes / Javier / bañarse
> *Mientras César limpiaba los estantes, Javier se bañaba.*

1. Raúl / saludar a los invitados / Laura / probarse el vestido
2. tú / secar los vasos / Marta y Francisco / abrazarse
3. nosotros / asar la carne / Ángela / maquillarse
4. ellos / preparar la sangría / tú / pelearse con Eva
5. Julio / planchar los manteles / Uds. / quejarse del trabajo
6. tú / ensayar las canciones / ellos / gritarles a los músicos
7. nosotros / cortar los pasteles / ella / tomarle el pelo a Silvia
8. yo / decorar la sala / ella / descansar
9. nosotros / colocar las decoraciones / Rebeca / mirar por la ventana
10. ellas / contar las servilletas / Marco / limarse las uñas

B **¡Qué sorpresa!** ¿Qué pasa? Nadie está como estaba antes. Sigue el modelo.

> Roberto / pelearse con todo el mundo / nadie
> ESTUDIANTE A *¡Imagínate! Roberto se peleó con todo el mundo anoche.*
> ESTUDIANTE B *¿De veras? Antes nunca se peleaba con nadie.*

1. Ernesto / recordar mi santo / nada
2. Mariana / besar a Eugenio / nadie
3. Santiago / regalar flores a su suegra / flores a ella
4. Pilar / mascar chicle / chicle
5. Juanito / molestar a todos los mayores en la fiesta / nadie
6. Susana / olvidar nuestra cita / nada
7. Samuel / quejarse de los vecinos / nadie
8. Mónica / fijarse en mi nueva chaqueta / nada
9. Mauricio / preparar sangría / nada
10. mi cuñado / disfrutar de esa película / las películas dobladas

Práctica B
1. ¡Imagínate! Ernesto recordó mi santo anoche. ¿De veras? Antes nunca recordaba nada.
2. … besó a Eugenio anoche … besaba a nadie.
3. … regaló … regalaba flores a ella.
4. … mascó … mascaba chicle.
5. … molestó … molestaba a nadie.
6. … olvidó … olvidaba nada.
7. … se quejó … se quejaba de nadie.
8. … se fijó … se fijaba en nada.
9. … preparó … preparaba nada.
10. … disfrutó … disfrutaba de las películas dobladas.

C **Nos cuenta el bisabuelo . . .** El bisabuelo de Ricardo siempre le cuenta cómo era la vida cuando él era joven. Completa su cuento con la forma correcta de cada verbo en el imperfecto.

Cuando yo *(ser)* niño, nuestro pueblo *(ser)* muy distinto. Nadie *(cerrar)* nunca las puertas con llave y los niños *(quedarse)* en casa y *(ayudar)* a sus padres. (Nosotros) *(disfrutar)* de cosas sencillas. Por ejemplo, (nosotros) *(celebrar)* las fiestas con mejores desfiles y mucho más ruido que ahora. (Nosotros) *(nadar)* en un río cerca de aquí y, por supuesto,
5 nunca *(mirar)* la televisión ni *(escuchar)* la radio.

Los niños siempre *(escuchar)* a sus padres y *(prestar)* atención a los mayores. Todo el mundo *(respetar)* todas las reglas y también (nosotros) *(respetar)* a nuestros profesores. Todos (nosotros) *(estudiar)*
10 mucho y *(sacar)* buenas notas. Muchos jóvenes *(casarse)* alrededor de los 18 años, pero nadie *(besar)* a nadie en público.

Los domingos, después de regresar de la iglesia, (nosotros) *(cenar)* en casa o en la casa de unos parientes nuestros. Luego, todo el mundo *(caminar)* al parque, donde *(jugar)* y *(escuchar)* a la banda.
15 Nuestros padres nos *(comprar)* globos de muchos colores y cacahuates o frutas frescas: sandía o naranjas de un bello color verde o duraznos de un color y sabor increíbles. Más tarde, cuando yo *(ser)* mayor, yo *(tocar)* la trompeta en esa banda.

(Ser) una vida sana y feliz, llena de cosas sencillas pero inolvidables.

Notes: Before students begin Ex. C, you may want to point out *era*, an imperfect-tense form of *ser*, in mini-dialogue 3 on p. 429. The imperfect of irregular verbs *ir*, *ser*, and *ver* is introduced in Chap. 15.

Práctica C
era / era / cerraba
se quedaban / ayudaban
disfrutábamos
celebrábamos
nadábamos
mirábamos / escuchábamos
escuchaban / prestaban
respetaba
respetábamos / estudiábamos
sacábamos / se casaban
besaba
cenábamos
caminaba / jugaba / escuchaba
compraban
era
tocaba
Era

D Hablemos de ti.

1. ¿Antes te gustaban cosas que ahora no te gustan? ¿Cuáles? ¿Y no te gustaban cosas que ahora te gustan? ¿Cuáles?
2. ¿Tocabas un instrumento que ya no tocas? ¿Cuál? ¿Por qué dejaste de tocarlo?
3. ¿Antes coleccionabas cosas que ya no coleccionas? ¿Qué cosas?
4. ¿El año pasado mirabas más televisión que ahora, o menos? ¿Por qué?
5. ¿Te molestan muchas cosas? ¿Cuáles? ¿Son las mismas cosas que te molestaban antes?
6. ¿Antes te asustaban cosas que ya no te asustan? ¿Cuáles?

Celebrando un cumpleaños
en Buenos Aires, Argentina

ACTIVIDAD

Antes, yo . . .   Think up a tall tale about what you or someone else used to do. Use any *-ar* verb that you know. Then get together in groups of three or four, tell your stories, and choose the most outrageous ones. Feats of the past might include:

Yo enseñaba inglés en Buenos Aires.
Mi madre trabajaba en la televisión como directora de un programa deportivo.

APLICACIONES   Discretionary

La boda   Transparency 45

Julio y Raquel acaban de casarse. Los parientes celebran la boda con los novios. ¿Qué pasa ahora?

Julio's parents discuss whether or not they should say something to the two children who are fighting. Create a dialogue in which Julio's father asks his wife to tell the children to behave. You might want to use these words or phrases:

Notes: Sample dialogues for the **¿Qué pasa?** appear in the Teacher Notes.

desagradable	mal educado, -a	mientras	portarse bien
empujar	meter la pata	pelearse (con)	¿qué te parece si . . . ?

EXPLICACIONES II Essential

Los usos de *por*

◆ **OBJECTIVES:**

TO DESCRIBE HOW YOU DO CERTAIN THINGS

TO GIVE DIRECTIONS

TO DESCRIBE A ROUTE YOU TAKE

TO TELL HOW MUCH YOU PAID FOR SOMETHING

TO EXPLAIN WHY YOU DID SOMETHING

The word *por* has many different meanings. Here are some of them:

1   "For," "during," or "in" + time period:

   Voy a dormir **por** una semana.   *I'm going to sleep **for** a week.*
   Se reúnen mañana **por** la   *They meet tomorrow (**in the**)*
   tarde.   *afternoon.*

2   "By" or "by means of":

   Mandé la carta **por** vía aérea.   *I sent the letter **by** air mail.*

3   "Through," "along," or "around":

   Salieron **por** esta puerta.   *They left **through** this door.*
   Caminaba **por** el puente.   *I walked **along** the bridge.*
   Yo jugaba **por** aquí.   *I used to play **around** here.*

Un almuerzo especial en Popayán, Colombia

4 "Because of" or "on account of":

Me caí **por** mala suerte.   *I fell **because of** bad luck.*

With this meaning we often use *por* with an infinitive:

Ernesto les cayó mal a sus   *Ernesto made a bad impression on his*
profesores **por** llegar tarde.   *teachers **because of** being late.*

5 "A" or "per":

La cena costó 30 dólares **por**   *The dinner cost 30 dollars **per***
persona.   *person.*

6 "Tor," meaning "in exchange for":

Pagué 5.000 pesos **por** el reloj.   *I paid 5,000 pesos **for** the watch.*

7 "For," meaning "to get, to pick up":

Fui **por** la sidra.   *I went **for** the cider.*
Voy **por** ti a las tres.*   *I'll come **for** you at three.*

8 "For," meaning "in place of":

Yo la felicité **por** él.   *I congratulated her **for** him.*

Reteach / Extra Help: Before students begin the **Práctica** on pp. 449–451, you may want to ask volunteers to suggest additional examples for each of the eight uses of *por* described in **Explicaciones II.**

PRÁCTICA

A El viaje de Isabel. Isabel acaba de visitar a unos parientes en México. Pregunta y contesta según el modelo.

recibir la invitación de tu familia / teléfono
ESTUDIANTE A   *¿Cómo recibiste la invitación de tu familia?*
ESTUDIANTE B   *Por teléfono.*

1. anunciarles tu llegada a ellos / telegrama
2. averiguar el horario de vuelos / teléfono
3. hacer la reservación / teléfono
4. recibir el boleto / mensajero
5. averiguar la noticia del nacimiento de tu sobrina / una llamada de larga distancia
6. agradecerles a tus parientes su invitación / carta
7. mandarles ese paquete grande a tus padres / vía aérea

Práctica A
1. … les anunciaste … / Por telegrama.
2. … averiguaste … / Por teléfono.
3. … hiciste … / Por teléfono.
4. … recibiste … / Por mensajero.
5. … averiguaste … / Por una llamada de larga distancia.
6. … les agradeciste … / Por carta.
7. … les mandaste … / Por vía aérea.

* Note that in Spanish we often use *ir* where in English we use "to come." Spanish speakers use *venir* from the speaker's point of view. If someone is coming with you, toward you, or to the place where you are, you use *venir*. Otherwise the verb is *ir*.

Práctica B

1. e   4. d
2. f   5. c
3. b   6. a

B   **El arete de la bisabuela.**   Cuando Lupe vuelve de la escuela, le falta un arete que le regaló su bisabuela. Sus padres le preguntan por dónde fue. En la columna de la derecha busca una respuesta apropiada para cada pregunta.

1. ¿Por dónde saliste de la escuela?
2. ¿Por qué calle caminaste?
3. ¿Por dónde cruzaste la calle?
4. ¿Por dónde seguiste después?
5. ¿Por dónde entraste en la casa?
6. ¿Por dónde fuiste después?

a. por el pasillo hasta mi dormitorio
b. por el paso de peatones
c. por la puerta de la cocina
d. por la misma calle, todo derecho
e. por la entrada principal
f. por la avenida Colón

Práctica C

1. ¿... por el sacapuntas?
   ... lo cambié por otro.
2. ¿... por el cortacésped?
   ... lo cambié por otro.
3. ¿... por la tostadora?
   ... la cambié por otra.
4. ¿... por el lavaplatos?
   ... lo cambié por otro.
5. ¿... por el proyector?
   ... lo cambié por otro.
6. ¿... por la calculadora?
   ... la cambié por otra.
7. ¿... por la aspiradora?
   ... la cambié por otra.
8. ¿... por la máquina de escribir?
   ... la cambié por otra.
9. ¿... por el secador?
   ... lo cambié por otro.

C   **No se hacen las cosas como antes.**   Varias personas compraron aparatos *(appliances)* pero ninguno de ellos funcionaba. Pregunta y contesta según el modelo.

ESTUDIANTE A   *¿Pagaste mucho por el televisor?*
ESTUDIANTE B   *Sí, pero no funcionaba.*
Por eso lo cambié por otro.

1.
2.
3.
4.
5.
6.
7.
8.
9.

D ¿Por qué? Los niños que viven al lado de la Sra. Mendoza siempre le hacen muchas preguntas. En la columna de la derecha busca las respuestas que ella les da a las preguntas de sus vecinos.

1. ¿Por qué tiene Ud. sueño?
2. ¿Por qué la felicitó esa señora?
3. ¿Por qué le gusta ese restaurante?
4. ¿Por qué está Ud. haciendo ejercicio?
5. ¿Por qué lleva Ud. el pelo tan corto?
6. ¿Por qué se está poniendo un suéter?
7. ¿Por qué está Ud. riendo?
8. ¿Por qué le duelen los tobillos?

a. Por el chiste que me contó Teresa.
b. Por la moda.
c. Por el frío.
d. Por los mariscos deliciosos.
e. Por trabajar demasiado.
f. Por participar en la carrera de anteayer
g. Por la salud.
h. Por el bautizo de mi nieto.

Práctica D
1. e   5. b
2. h   6. c
3. d   7. a
4. g   8. f

E ¿Por qué haces tantas preguntas? Susana es muy curiosa. Siempre quiere saber por qué va y viene la gente. Pregunta y contesta según el modelo.

(tú) / ir a la cafetería / una hamburguesa
ESTUDIANTE A   *¿Por qué fuiste a la cafetería?*
ESTUDIANTE B   *Fui por una hamburguesa.*

1. Elena / regresar a casa / sus llaves
2. los hermanos López / venir a nuestro ensayo / sus trombones
3. David / correr a la taquilla / las entradas
4. (tú) / ir a la tienda / una secadora nueva
5. tus padres / volver a la recepción / sus pasaportes
6. Uds. / volver a la cancha de tenis / las raquetas
7. las profesoras / ir a la oficina / sus cheques
8. Víctor y Elena / ir al correo / un formulario y unos sellos

Práctica E
1. … regresó Elena … Regresó por sus llaves.
2. … vinieron los hermanos López … Vinieron por sus trombones.
3. … corrió David … Corrió por las entradas.
4. … fuiste … Fui por una secadora nueva.
5. … volvieron tus padres … Volvieron por sus pasaportes.
6. … volvieron Uds. … Volvimos por las raquetas.
7. … fueron las profesoras … Fueron por sus cheques.
8. … fueron Víctor y Elena … Fueron por un formulario y unos sellos.

F Hablemos de ti.
1. ¿Adónde fueron tú y tu familia de vacaciones el año pasado? ¿Por cuánto tiempo? ¿Adónde vas a ir este verano? ¿Sabes por cuánto tiempo?
2. ¿Por qué vas a la playa o a la piscina? ¿Por el agua o por el sol? ¿O vas por otra cosa?
3. ¿Más o menos cuántas horas por día miras la televisión? ¿Y por semana? ¿Cuántas horas por día asistes a clases? ¿Cuántas horas por día haces la tarea? ¿Cuántas horas por semana practicas deportes?
4. Explica por dónde vas para llegar a la escuela.
5. Cuando vas a la tienda de comestibles, ¿por qué cosas vas?

Práctica F
Answers will vary.

Practice Sheet 13–5

Workbook Exs. G–J

Tape Manual Exs. 7–8 🔲 11

Refrán 🔲 12

Canción 🔲 13

Quiz 13–4

APLICACIONES

REPASO

Notes: Review of:
1. preterite of reflexive verbs
2. preterite of -ar and -er verbs
   por vs. *para*
   para + infinitive
3. imperfect of -ar verbs
   reflexive verbs
4. imperfect of -ar verbs
5. imperfect of -ar verbs
   possession with *de* + prepositional pronoun for emphasis

Enrichment: The model sentences in the **Repaso** are suitable for dictation.

Mira con cuidado las frases modelo. Luego cambia las frases que siguen al español, según los modelos.

1. *Raquel y Ana se mudaron hoy.*
   (Juan and Pedro got together the day before yesterday.)
   (I got bored last night.)
   (We said good-by this afternoon.)

2. *Los padrinos manejaron por seis horas para llegar al bautizo.*
   (They worked for ten minutes to unwrap the box.)
   (She rehearsed for eight months to win that contest.)
   (I read for three days to finish the book.)

3. *Mientras los niños se peleaban, los vecinos se saludaban.*
   (While the grandchildren were shouting at each other, the relatives were sitting down.)
   (While the parents were going to bed, the baby was waking up.)
   (While you (fam.) were shaving, I was weighing myself.)

4. *Mientras apagábamos los faros, la bisabuela examinaba el parquímetro.*
   (While I was pushing the car, Mom was honking the horn.)
   (While we were looking at the traffic ticket, the old man was parking cars.)
   (While María was filling the tank, I was cleaning the windshield.)

5. *Durante la clase, mientras el profesor pintaba, los estudiantes admiraban las pinturas de ellos.*
   (During the concert, while the musicians were playing, the composer was reviewing his song.)
   (In the kitchen, while we were cooking, they were recommending their guacamole.)
   (After the accident, while we were waiting, the mechanic was repairing her car.)

Primera comunión
en México

TEMA

Transparency 46

Notes: Students may work in pairs to prepare their **Tema** sentences. Ask volunteers to present their sentences to the class and to write them on the board.

Escribe las frases en español.

1. Patricia and Jorge got married yesterday.

2. Uncle Eduardo traveled for two days to come to the wedding.

3. While the bride and groom were kissing, the in-laws were embracing each other.

4. While Patricia was cutting the cake, the photographer was taking pictures.

5. During the party, while the young people were dancing, the grownups were remembering their weddings.

REDACCIÓN

Reteach / Review: You may want to encourage students who choose topic 2 of the **Redacción** to use the subjunctive as much as possible.

Ahora escoge uno de los siguientes temas para escribir tu propio diálogo o párrafo.

1. Expand the story in the *Tema* by writing a paragraph about the wedding and the two families. What are they like? How old are the bride and groom? When were they born? Where do they work? Where are they going to live?

2. Write a dialogue in which a parent tells a young child how he or she should behave at a wedding.

3. Write a paragraph describing a relative or a neighbor. Do you like the person? What is he or she like? Does he or she do things that annoy you?

Aplicaciones **453**

COMPRUEBA TU PROGRESO   CAPÍTULO 13   Discretionary

Notes: Answers to the **Comprueba** appear in the Teacher Notes.

A   La familia
Completa cada frase con la palabra correcta.

bisabuela	novio	parientes
nieto	padrino	suegra

1. Raúl, mi mejor amigo, es el _____ de mi hijo.
2. El hijo de mi hijo es mi _____.
3. Mi _____ tiene noventa años, pero parece mucho más joven.
4. Yo tengo muchos _____.
5. La madre de mi esposa es mi _____.
6. El _____ de Elena le regaló un anillo hermoso cuando se casaron.

B   ¿Qué verbo?
Completa cada frase con la forma correcta del verbo apropiado de la lista.

besar	empujar
compartir	molestar
dar la mano	nacer
dejar de	regalar
despedirse	tener celos

1. Yo _____ al bebé en la cara cuando llora.
2. Cuando alguien me presenta a una persona, le _____.
3. Cuando era niño aprendí a _____ mis cosas con otros.
4. Luis tiene muchas amigas, y yo _____ de él.
5. Cuando enciendo el televisor, ellos _____ estudiar.
6. A mí me _____ los niños cuando gritan.
7. El bebé _____ ayer y la madre se siente muy feliz.
8. Cuando _____ de mis hermanos, los abrazo.
9. Si el coche no tiene gasolina, lo _____.
10. Mi prima cumplió años ayer y yo le _____ una pulsera.

C   ¿Qué pasaba?
Escribe cada frase en el imperfecto.

1. La madrina felicita al padrino.

2. Yo plancho mientras tú pasas la aspiradora.
3. Los ruidos fuertes asustan a todos.
4. El padre está muy nervioso mientras espera el nacimiento de su hijo.
5. Uds. cuentan el dinero en la caja.
6. Mandamos las cartas por vía aérea.
7. El anciano compra libros para su nieto.

D   Todas las mañanas
Cambia al imperfecto. Por ejemplo:

Canté en la iglesia.   (cada domingo)
Cada domingo yo cantaba en la iglesia.

1. Los abuelos bostezaron.   (cada dos minutos)
2. El actor sordo habló por señas.   (siempre)
3. Jorge llamó por teléfono a su novia.   (todos los días)
4. Andrea saludó al profesor.   (cada mañana)
5. Practicamos para el concierto.   (por la tarde)
6. Ellos nadaron en el club.   (los martes)
7. Tomé el autobús a las 9.   (todos los días)

E   ¡Por eso!
Lee cada diálogo. Luego escribe una frase con *por*. Sigue el modelo.

Teresa, ¿por qué vas al mercado?
Necesito mariscos.
Teresa va al mercado por mariscos.

1. Yolanda, ¿vendiste el coche?
   Sí, recibí doscientos dólares.
2. Javier, ¿por qué vas al sótano?
   Creo que la escoba está allí.
3. ¿Por qué no hay partido hoy?
   Porque está lloviendo.
4. Benjamín, ¿cómo le diste las noticias a Elena?
   Le mandé un telegrama.
5. Susana, ¿piensas dar un paseo?
   Sí, voy al parque.
6. ¿Por qué sacó malas notas Dolores?
   Porque estudió poco.
7. Jorge, ¿vas frecuentemente a la piscina?
   Cada semana voy dos veces.

Activity Masters   Chapter 13 Test   Listening Comprehension Test

VOCABULARIO DEL CAPÍTULO 13

Sustantivos
el amor
el anciano, la anciana
el bautizo
el bebé
el bisabuelo, la bisabuela
la boda
la cita
el cuñado, la cuñada
el chicle
la madrina
los mayores
el nacimiento
el nieto, la nieta
el novio, la novia *(bride / groom)*
el padrino
el pariente, la parienta
la sangría
la sidra
la sorpresa
el suegro, la suegra
el vecino, la vecina

Adjetivos
cariñoso, -a (con)
casado, -a (con)
desagradable
enamorado, -a (de)
feliz, *pl.* felices
igual
inolvidable
soltero, -a

Verbos
abrazar
besar
casarse (con)
compartir
cuidar *(to take care of)*
dejar de + *inf.* *(to stop)*
desenvolver (o → ue)
despedirse (e → i) (de)
empujar
felicitar
llorar
mascar
molestar
nacer (c → zc)
parecerse (c → zc) a
pelearse con
permitir
querer *(to love)*
recordar (o → ue)
regalar
reunirse
tirar (de) *(to pull)*
era

Preposición
por *(along)*

Conjunción
mientras

Expresiones
bien / mal educado, -a
caerle bien / mal (a uno)
cumplir años
dar la mano a
en público
meter la pata
no te molestes
¿por dónde?
portarse bien / mal
¿qué te parece si + *verb?*
se prohibe
se puede
tener celos de
tomarle el pelo (a uno)

PRÓLOGO CULTURAL

LA CIUDAD PERDIDA DE LOS INCAS

For almost four centuries Peru's Machu Picchu was a lost city. Abandoned sometime in the 1500s, it was not seen again until Hiram Bingham, a North American explorer, went looking for it in 1911.

Machu Picchu is perched on a ridge between two mountaintops 2,400 meters above a river valley. Protected by sheer cliffs, the city is virtually unapproachable on three sides.

Altogether, Machu Picchu covers about thirteen square kilometers, much of it broad terraces that were created along the mountainside for farming. Its two hundred small buildings follow the natural contours of the ridge.

Almost everything in Machu Picchu was made of stone. A typical building had only a few small windows and a single doorway. Even in the temples and palaces, people had to pass through an open courtyard to go from one room to another.

The walls in Machu Picchu are famous for two reasons: the enormous size of the stones and the fact that they were so perfectly shaped that no mortar was needed to hold them together. What is even more surprising is that the stones were cut and shaped with hard reeds, then smoothed by grinding their edges with smaller stones.

No one knows when Machu Picchu was built or exactly who lived there. It is fairly certain, however, that it was the last stronghold of the Incan kings after the Spanish conquered the royal city of Cuzco. Once the last king died, the workers and farmers had no reason to remain. They returned to the more fertile land of the valleys, and Machu Picchu became lost in the clouds.

PALABRAS NUEVAS I

Essential

Un tesoro antiguo

If students ask: Other related words you may want to present: *el cobre*, copper; *las piedras preciosas*, precious gems; *el plástico*, plastic.

el arqueólogo

la estatua

la arqueóloga

el tesoro

el agodón

el oro

el papel

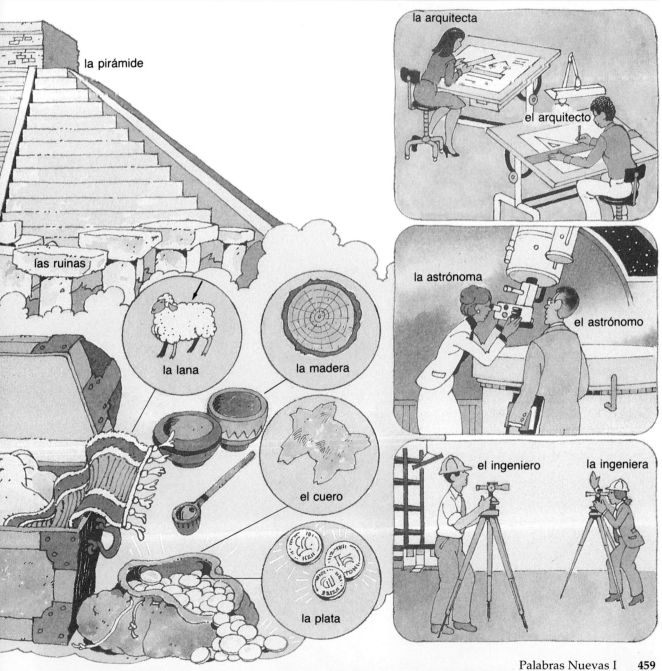

la pirámide

las ruinas

la lana

la madera

el cuero

la plata

la arquitecta

el arquitecto

la astrónoma

el astrónomo

el ingeniero

la ingeniera

1 ESTER **Los templos** de **los mayas** son **verdaderas** obras de arte.

JORGE ¿Sabes qué usaban para **construir**los?*

ESTER Creo que usaban **piedra.**

- templos → edificios
- mayas → **incas**
- verdaderas → formidables

2 SILVIA **La civilización** de los mayas es muy **antigua,** ¿no?

MARCOS Sí. Mira esas pirámides.

SILVIA ¡Qué **asombrosas**! Me gustaría saber en qué **siglo** las construyeron.

Variaciones:

- los mayas → **los aztecas**
- asombrosas → **impresionantes**

el templo *temple*

los mayas *Mayans (Indians of Mexico and Guatemala)*

verdadero, -a *real, true*

construir (yo construyo, tú construyes) *to build, to construct*

la piedra here: *stone*

los incas *Incas (Indians of Peru and Bolivia)*

la civilización, pl. **las civilizaciones** *civilization*

antiguo, -a *old, ancient*

asombroso, -a *amazing, astonishing*

el siglo *century*

los aztecas *Aztecs (Indians of Mexico and parts of Central America)*

impresionante *impressive*

* *Construir* follows the pattern of *incluir*. In the present tense, the *i* → *y* in all except the *nosotros* and *vosotros* forms:

constr**uyo**	constr**uimos**
constr**uyes**	constr**uís**
constr**uye**	constr**uyen**

This also occurs in the *Ud. / él / ella* and *Uds. / ellos / ellas* forms of the preterite (*construyó / construyeron*) and in the present participle (*construyendo*).

Ruinas mayas en Chichén Itzá, México

3 GLORIA   Los arqueólogos encontraron cuartos **secretos** en estas ruinas incas.

GERARDO   ¡Qué interesante! ¿**Había** algo en ellos?

GLORIA   Sí. Había **objetos de** oro y también ropa de lana muy parecida a la ropa que hacen ahora en este pueblo.

GERARDO   Me gustaría trabajar **de** arqueólogo.

- encontraron → **descubrieron**
- de oro → de plata
- hacen → **producen***

4 ALICIA   ¿Sabes algo de **la religión** de los mayas?

ÁNGEL   Era una religión muy complicada, con muchos **dioses.** El sol y la luna **tenían** un **significado** especial para ellos.

- complicada → interesante
- el sol y la luna → las estrellas

5 JORGE   Estas fotos son del terremoto de México.

JOSEFINA   **¡Qué horror!**

JORGE   Sí. La gente trató de **huir**† pero muchas personas quedaron **enterradas** debajo de los edificios que cayeron.

- fotos → diapositivas
- huir → **escaparse**

* In the preterite of *producir*, $c \rightarrow j$ in all six forms:

produje	produjimos
produjiste	produjisteis
produjo	produjeron

† *Huir* also follows the $i \rightarrow y$ pattern of *incluir* and *construir*.

secreto, -a *secret*

había (from **haber**) *there was, there were*

el objeto *object*

de + material *made of*

de here: *as a(n)*

descubrir *to discover*

producir (yo produzco, tú produces) *to produce*

la religión, pl. **las religiones** *religion*

el dios, la diosa *god, goddess*

tenían (imperfect of **tener**) *(they) had*

el significado *meaning*

¡qué horror! *how awful!*

huir (de) (yo huyo, tú huyes) *to flee (from)*

enterrado, -a *buried*

escaparse *to escape, to run away*

Culture: In connection with mini-dialogue 5, you may want to point out that earthquakes occur frequently in Latin America. In September of 1985 an earthquake struck central and south-western Mexico, killing over 7,000 people. (See the **Lectura** on pp. 477–478.)

En el Museo Nacional de Antropología en México

PRÁCTICA

Práctica A

1. ¿De qué es esta silla? Es de madera.
2. ¿De qué es este suéter? Es de lana.
3. ¿De qué es esta pirámide? Es de piedra.
4. ¿De qué es este tenedor? Es de plata.
5. ¿De qué es este avión? Es de papel.
6. ¿De qué es este collar? Es de oro.
7. ¿De qué son estas sandalias? Son de cuero.
8. ¿De qué es este pastel? Es de manzanas.
9. ¿De qué es esta camiseta? Es de algodón.

A **¿De qué es esto?**   El profesor de ciencias quiere que los estudiantes digan de qué están hechas las cosas que él les muestra. Sigue los modelos.

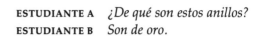

ESTUDIANTE A   *¿De qué es este anillo?*
ESTUDIANTE B   *Es de oro.*

ESTUDIANTE A   *¿De qué son estos anillos?*
ESTUDIANTE B   *Son de oro.*

1.   2.   3.

4.   5.   6.

7.   8.   9.

Enrichment: After students have completed Ex. A, they may work in pairs to ask each other *¿De qué es?* referring to articles of clothing or jewelry or other objects they may have with them.

Práctica B
descubrió
antiguos
construyeron
enterrado
diosa
civilizaciones
secretos

B **El tesoro secreto.**   Pilar habla de su abuelo con Julio. Escoge la palabra correcta para completar cada una de las siguientes frases.

PILAR   Mi abuelo es arqueólogo. Él *(construyó / descubrió / produjo)* muchos templos y pirámides en las montañas en Guatemala.

JULIO   Esos templos son muy *(antiguos / verdaderos / suaves)*, ¿verdad?

PILAR   ¡Por supuesto! Los *(quemaron / incluyeron / construyeron)* los
5   mayas muchos siglos antes de la llegada de los españoles. Mi abuelito encontró también un tesoro que estaba *(enterrado / estrecho / anticuado)* debajo de un templo.

JULIO   ¡Qué emocionante!

PILAR   Sí. Había un objeto pequeño de plata y una estatua
10   impresionante de una *(arqueóloga / ruina / diosa)* de los mayas.

JULIO   ¡Es asombroso, Pilar! ¡Qué interesante! A mí me interesan mucho las *(ingenieras / astrónomas / civilizaciones)* antiguas.

PILAR   ¿Ah sí? Pues, todavía hay tesoros *(nuevos / secretos / casados)* en muchos lugares.

15 JULIO   Sí, lo sé. ¡Ojalá que los descubra yo algún día!

C Aquí hay algo sobre ruinas. Usa palabras de la lista para completar el siguiente artículo.

algodón	enterrada	impresionantes	pirámides	significado
dioses	había	papeles	religión	verdadero

Un grupo de arqueólogos descubrió _____ ruinas aztecas en Honduras el año pasado. Encontraron asombrosas _____ y una gran ciudad que todavía estaba _____. Ahora un equipo de arquitectos e ingenieros estudia la clase de edificios que _____ en esa ciudad. En
5 uno de los templos encontraron _____ antiguos con dibujos fabulosos. El grupo está tratando de descubrir el _____ de estos dibujos. Los astrónomos dicen que los habitantes tenían una _____ muy complicada con muchos _____ como el sol y la luna.

D Hablemos de ti.
1. ¿Conoces algunas ruinas antiguas? ¿De qué país? ¿Qué sabes de ellas?
2. ¿Sabes algo de las ruinas antiguas del Perú o de México? ¿Qué sabes de ellas? ¿Te gustaría visitarlas? ¿Por qué?
3. ¿Sabes algo de las antiguas religiones de la América del Norte? ¿Conoces el nombre de algún dios o diosa de esas religiones?
4. ¿Tienes algún objeto de oro o de plata? ¿Qué es? ¿Es muy viejo? Descríbelo.
5. ¿Llevas algo que está hecho de cuero? ¿De lana? ¿De algodón? Descríbelo.   Practice Sheet 14–1   Workbook Exs. A–B

     3 Tape Manual Exs. 1–2   Quiz 14–1

ACTIVIDAD

La pirámide de papel Play this archaeological word game with two or three other students. One person starts by saying, ''Encontré un tesoro. Había . . .'' and then a noun plus an adjective or descriptive phrase that begins with the same letter as the last noun. The treasures can consist of likely or unlikely things. For example:

Había una pirámide de papel.
Había unos elefantes enterrados.
Había una cuchara de cuero.

Práctica C
impresionantes
pirámides
enterrada
había
papeles
significado
religión
dioses

Notes: You may want to assign Ex. C as written homework, asking students to write out the entire paragraph. Check students' work for correct spelling, punctuation, and capitalization.

Práctica D
Answers will vary.

Una antigua estatua de piedra en México

APLICACIONES Discretionary

Quiero ser arqueóloga

 4

5 Pronunciación

Durante una excursión a unas famosas ruinas mayas, dos estudiantes hablan sobre lo que ven.

MARTÍN Según la guía, cada pirámide es un templo dedicado a un dios o diosa. Esta pirámide es el templo de Chac, el
5 dios de la lluvia.

LUPE Creo que estás equivocado. Aquél es el templo de Chac. Éste es el templo del sol.

MARTÍN ¿Cómo lo sabes?

LUPE Porque es la pirámide más grande y el sol fue el dios
10 principal. Leí sobre eso en la guía.

MARTÍN ¿Crees que todavía hay alguien enterrado en estas pirámides?

LUPE No sé si en éstas, pero en algunas hay gente enterrada.*

MARTÍN Es asombroso cómo construyeron estos templos de
15 piedra sin equipos[1] modernos.

LUPE También les sorprende[2] a los arquitectos, ingenieros y astrónomos de hoy día.[3] A mí me interesan muchísimo las historias que se pueden descubrir en ciudades antiguas. Por eso quiero ser arqueóloga.

---

[1]**el equipo** here: *equipment*   [2]**sorprender** *to surprise*   [3]**de hoy día** *of today*

* Although Mayan pyramids served primarily as temples, many, such as the *Templo del sol*, were also tombs.

Preguntas
Contesta según el diálogo.

1. ¿Qué significado tenían las pirámides de los mayas?   2. Sabes que había pirámides dedicadas al sol y a la lluvia. ¿Qué otros dioses crees que había en la religión maya?   3. ¿Qué es asombroso para los arquitectos e ingenieros que estudian las pirámides mayas? ¿Qué otras cosas produjeron algunas civilizaciones antiguas que tú encuentras asombrosas?   4. ¿Qué quiere ser Lupe? ¿Por qué? ¿Qué quieres ser tú? ¿Por qué?   5. ¿Te gustaría visitar las ruinas de alguna civilización antigua? ¿Cuál? ¿Por qué?

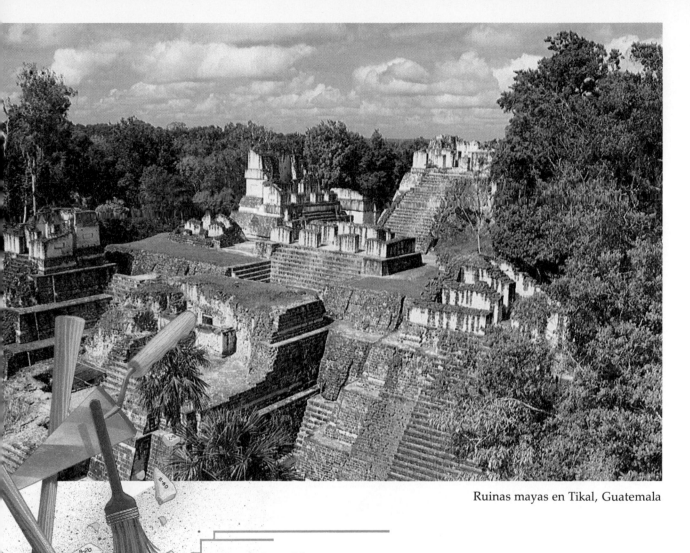

Ruinas mayas en Tikal, Guatemala

Participación

Work with a partner. Imagine that you're exploring a mysterious ancient city that has just been discovered. Tell what buildings and objects you found, what they were made of, and what you think the people used them for. You might draw a labeled map or diagram of the buildings. Here are some words you may want to use:

el algodón	la estatua	la piedra
la cerámica	la lana	la pintura
el cuarto	el mural	la pirámide
el dios, la diosa	el objeto	la plata
la escultura	el oro	el templo

PALABRAS NUEVAS II

Essential

CONTEXTO VISUAL

Las noticias

el humo

el héroe

la heroína

el bombero

la bombera

el periodista

la periodista

el diario

La Prensa

Todavía buscan a los ladrones

el titular

el artículo

el ladrón

la ladrona

Liquidación de ropa de invierno en el almacén Goya

¡Todo baratísimo!

el anuncio

Enrichment: After presenting the **Contexto comunicativo** on pp. 467–468, you may want to reinforce the new expression *darse cuenta de* by asking students when or how they realized certain things about themselves or others. For example: *¿Cuándo te diste cuenta de que deseabas ser ____? ¿Cómo te diste cuenta de que ____ era tu mejor amigo(a)?*

CONTEXTO COMUNICATIVO 7

1 PERIODISTA   ¿Cómo **te diste cuenta de** que había un **incendio?***

     CARLOS   Por el humo que entraba en mi cuarto.

     PERIODISTA   ¿Llegó el incendio a tu apartamento?

     CARLOS   No, no **se quemó** nada allí. Pero el incendio **destruyó†** gran parte del edificio.

     PERIODISTA   ¿Saben cuál fue **la causa**?

     CARLOS   No, todavía no lo saben.

Variaciones:
- de que había un → del
- del edificio → de la planta baja

darse cuenta de	*to realize*
el incendio	*fire*
quemarse	*to burn (up), to burn (down)*
destruir (yo destruyo, tú destruyes)	*to destroy*
la causa	*cause*

2 JULIO   Luisa, ¿por qué hay tanta gente en la calle?

     LUISA   Es por un **robo**.

     JULIO   No me digas. ¿Qué pasó?

     LUISA   No sé exactamente. **De repente** la gente empezó a gritar y un hombre se escapó. La policía lo siguió, pero no lo **hallaron**.

- por un robo → **a causa de** un robo
- hallaron → encontraron

el robo	*robbery*
de repente	*suddenly*
hallar	= encontrar
a causa de	*because of*

3 REBECA   ¡Qué horror, Roberto! ¿Recuerdas el accidente que vimos anteayer? Pues la mujer que manejaba el coche verde está **muerta**.

     ROBERTO   Ya lo sé. ¡Qué suerte que **salvaron** al bebé que estaba en el coche!

     REBECA   Sí. Fue un **acto** muy **heroico**.

- ¡qué horror! → ¡qué barbaridad!
- salvaron → descubrieron

muerto, -a	*dead*
salvar	*to save*
el acto	*act*
heroico, -a	*heroic*

---

* *El fuego* is a general term for fire. *Un incendio* is a fire that destroys things.
† *Destruir* follows the *i → y* pattern of *incluir, construir, huir*.

4 ELISA	Señora, escribo para **la sección** de noticias locales de nuestro diario. ¿Puede decirme algo sobre el robo en su casa?	**la sección,** pl. **las secciones** *section*
SRA. RUIZ	Me **robaron** muchas joyas: un collar de oro y varios anillos y aretes. Pero el policía me dijo que espera **capturar** a los ladrones muy pronto.	**robar** *to steal, to rob* **capturar** *to catch, to capture*

■ diario → periódico
■ oro → plata

5 PERIODISTA	Dra. Alas, ¿qué piensa Ud. que pasará* en el próximo siglo?	
DRA. ALAS	En mi **opinión,** nuestro **mundo** será mejor. Trabajaremos sólo tres o cuatro días por semana, viviremos en edificios cómodos y modernos y comeremos sólo comida sana como las verduras y frutas frescas, mariscos frescos, **etcétera.**	**la opinión,** pl. **las opiniones** *opinion* **el mundo** *world* **etcétera** *etc., and so on*

■ próximo siglo → siglo XXI
■ nuestro mundo → nuestra vida

* The endings -*á* and -*emos* that appear in this dialogue attached to the infinitive signify the future tense: *pasará* = will happen.

En Quito, Ecuador

PRÁCTICA

A Un incendio. Mira el dibujo. Usa la forma correcta de la palabra apropiada de la lista para completar las frases.

artículo   heroína   ladrón   robar
bombero   humo   periodista sección
causa   incendio   quemarse   titular

1. ¡Qué horror! Hay un _____ grande en el edificio de la esquina.
2. ¡Qué barbaridad! Mira cómo _____ ese apartamento.
3. Mira el _____ que sale de las ventanas. ¡Qué olor tan desagradable!
4. El _____ sobre el incendio está en la siguiente página. Dice que nadie sabe la _____ del incendio.
5. Un _____ entrevista a las personas en la calle.
6. Un _____ le _____ el bolso a esa mujer.
7. Los _____ están tratando de apagar el incendio.
8. El _____ dice "Gran incendio destruye edificio de apartamentos. Tres personas muertas."
9. La bombera que salvó a esa niña es una verdadera _____.

* *Véase* is the polite command form of *verse*. Its English equivalent is "see," but literally it is a very polite "let (something) be seen."

Práctica A
1. incendio
2. se quema
3. humo
4. artículo / causa
5. periodista
6. ladrón / robó
7. bomberos
8. titular
9. heroína

Práctica B
1. robó / se escapó / capturó
2. destruyó / salvó / descubrieron
3. entrevistó / se dio cuenta / contó / huyó
4. construyeron / descubrió (*or:* halló) / hallamos (*or:* descubrimos)

B **Las noticias.** Imagina que éstas son noticias del diario de tu ciudad. Escoge verbos de cada lista para completar cada noticia. Usa el pretérito.

ROBO DE UNA ESTATUA ANTIGUA

escaparse   portarse   robar   capturar   salvar

1. El lunes, una mujer _____ una estatua de plata de un mostrador de la Joyería Esmeralda. La ladrona _____, pero un cliente que estaba en la tienda de joyas la describió a la policía. En menos de una hora, la policía la _____.

INCENDIO EN EL BARRIO DE LA PALOMA

producir   salvar   destruir   huir   descubrir

2. El incendio _____ tres pisos del edificio. En un acto heroico, un niño _____ a su hermanito. Los bomberos no _____ la causa del incendio.

LLEGA DOLORES MILONGA A LA CIUDAD

capturar   contar   entrevistar   huir   darse cuenta

3. El periodista Enrique Parra _____ a la estrella de cine Dolores Milonga. Cuando Parra _____ del anillo grande en la mano de la estrella, ella le _____ de su boda secreta del mes pasado. Después, Milonga _____ de sus admiradores y se fue al hotel.

DESCUBREN TEMPLO DEL SOL

descubrir   hallar   construir   capturar   producir

4. "Creemos que los incas _____ este templo en el siglo XV," dice el grupo de arqueólogos que lo _____. "Nosotros _____ muchos objetos asombrosos enterrados en la sección más importante del templo. Sin duda su significado nos dará nueva información sobre la religión de esta civilización antigua."

C La entrevista. Imagina que viste un robo. Inventa respuestas a las preguntas que te hace un periodista.

1. Buenos días, señor(ita). ¿Puedo hacerle algunas preguntas sobre el robo?
2. ¿Cuándo se dio cuenta Ud. de que pasaba algo?
3. ¿Dónde estaba Ud. en ese momento?
4. ¿A qué hora ocurrió?
5. ¿Qué vio Ud. exactamente?
6. ¿Puede Ud. describir al ladrón?
7. Cuando se escapó el ladrón, ¿por dónde se fue?
8. ¿Quién llamó a la policía?
9. ¿Cuándo llegó la policía?
10. ¿Qué hizo la policía?

Práctica C
Answers will vary.

D Hablemos de ti.
1. ¿Cuál fue el último incendio que viste por la televisión? ¿Cuándo ocurrió? ¿Qué se quemó? Descríbelo.
2. ¿Cuál fue el último robo importante que ocurrió en tu ciudad? ¿Qué robaron? ¿Qué pasó? ¿Capturaron a los ladrones?
3. ¿Generalmente lees el diario? ¿Leíste el diario de ayer? ¿Qué sección del diario te interesa más? ¿Por qué? ¿Te interesan más las noticias internacionales, las nacionales o las locales? ¿Por qué?

Práctica D
Answers will vary.

Practice Sheet 14–2

Workbook Exs. C–D

Tape Manual Exs. 3–4 🔲 8

Refrán 🔲 9

Quiz 14–2

El periodista Frank Soler en Miami, Florida

ESTUDIO DE PALABRAS

Familias de palabras
Completa cada frase con una palabra relacionada con la palabra en cursiva.

1. Los titulares del periódico dicen "Joven *salvavidas* _____ a ocho personas."
2. Hay varios _____ extranjeros que trabajan para este *periódico*.
3. Dicen que *robaron* más de un millón de dólares de la casa de cambio. Fue un _____ asombroso.
4. Encontraron tres personas _____ en las ruinas del edificio. Dos personas más *murieron* en el hospital.
5. El *héroe* de esta historia capturó tres leones. ¡Qué acto tan _____!
6. Van a poner un _____ grande en el diario para *anunciar* la nueva obra de teatro.
7. Este bombero es un _____ héroe, *¿verdad?*

Sinónimos
Cambia la palabra en cursiva por un sinónimo.

1. Los arqueólogos *encontraron* tres estatuas de plata.
2. Los niños *se escaparon* por la ventana.
3. Esos arquitectos *hacen* muchas casas de madera.

Antónimos
Cambia las palabras en cursiva por un antónimo.

1. Esa compañía va a *construir* tres casas.
2. Esta sección es muy *moderna*.

EXPLICACIONES I

El imperfecto de los verbos que terminan en *-er* e *-ir*

You have learned how to form the imperfect tense of *-ar* verbs. Here are all of the imperfect forms of *-er* and *-ir* verbs. Note that they take the same set of endings.

APRENDER		VIVIR	
aprendía	aprendíamos	vivía	vivíamos
aprendías	aprendíais	vivías	vivíais
aprendía	aprendían	vivía	vivían

Yo **aprendía** algo cada día.   I ⎰ *was learning* ⎱ *something every day.*
                                    ⎱ *would learn* ⎰
                                    used to learn

Él **vivía** en España también.   He ⎰ *was living* ⎱ *in Spain too.*
                                     used to live

Notice that the *yo* and *Ud. / él / ella* forms are identical, just as they are with *-ar* verbs (*yo hablaba, Ud. / él / ella hablaba*).

1   Almost all verbs are regular in the imperfect.*

> Siempre **pedían** dulces.
> Los domingos yo **dormía** hasta las nueve.
> **Venían** a visitarme.
> Cuando **hacía frío me ponía** una chaqueta de lana.

> *They were always asking for candy.*
> *On Sundays I used to sleep until 9:00.*
> *They used to come to visit me.*
> *When it was cold I used to put on a wool jacket.*

2   The irregular present-tense verb form *hay* comes from the verb *haber*. The imperfect form of *haber* is *había* ("there was, there were"). Like *hay*, it is used only in the singular.

> **Había** un tesoro en la pirámide.
> **Había** muchas asombrosas civilizaciones antiguas.

> *There was a treasure in the pyramid.*
> *There were many amazing ancient civilizations.*

* Only *ir, ser,* and *ver* are irregular. You will learn their imperfect forms in Chapter 15.

Notes: Mini-dialogues 3 and 4 on p. 461 contain examples of *-er* verbs in the imperfect.

◆ **OBJECTIVES:**

TO DESCRIBE WHAT WAS HAPPENING OVER A PERIOD OF TIME

TO TELL HOW THINGS USED TO BE

TO REMINISCE

Reteach / Extra Help: You may want to reinforce the imperfect forms of *-er* and *-ir* verbs by eliciting sentences describing things that students used to do (or didn't used to do) in Spanish class. Write these verbs on the board: *escribir, leer, perder, tener / hacer tarea, divertirse, reir, repetir, saber,* and have volunteers make sentences with them.

PRÁCTICA

Práctica A

1. encendía
2. construía
3. discutía
4. envolvía
5. escribía
6. traducía
7. dormía / se sentía
8. descubría / había

A **¿Qué hacían?** Mientras un grupo de arqueólogos bolivianos trabajaba en las ruinas de un templo, ocurrió un pequeño terremoto. Escoge el verbo apropiado de la lista para decir lo que hacía cada persona cuando ocurrió el terremoto.

construir	discutir	encender	escribir	sentirse
descubrir	dormir	envolver	haber	traducir

1. Diego _____ una linterna para examinar los dibujos en la pared.
2. Eva _____ un modelo del templo.
3. Judit _____ en voz fuerte con Tomás sobre la religión inca.
4. Raúl _____ unos objetos para mandarlos al museo en La Paz.
5. Marta _____ a máquina un artículo para una revista española.
6. Inés _____ el artículo de Marta al inglés.
7. Juan _____ en el saco de dormir porque no _____ bien.
8. Eduardo _____ un pasillo secreto donde _____ objetos de plata en el suelo.

Práctica B

Answers will vary but will include these verb forms:

1. hacía / hacíamos
2. leía / leíamos
3. perdía / perdíamos
4. me divertía / nos divertíamos
5. me reunía / nos reuníamos
6. debía / debíamos
7. me aburría / nos aburríamos
8. construía / construíamos
9. tenía / teníamos
10. ponía / poníamos
11. recibía / recibíamos
12. tenía que levantarme / teníamos que levantarnos

B **¿Y Uds.?** Pedro habla con unos compañeros sobre lo que hacían el año pasado. Puedes dar cualquier (*any*) respuesta apropiada. Por ejemplo:

aprender mucho en la clase de ciencias

ESTUDIANTE A *Yo aprendía mucho en la clase de ciencias.*

ESTUDIANTE B *Nosotros también aprendíamos mucho*
Nosotros aprendíamos muy poco ⎫ *en la clase de*
Nosotros no aprendíamos nada ⎭ *ciencias.*

1. hacer mucha tarea los fines de semana
2. leer cuentos divertidos en la clase de inglés
3. perder casi todos los partidos de . . .
4. divertirse mucho en la clase de . . .
5. reunirse con (*nombre*) los sábados por la noche
6. deber volver a casa después de las clases
7. aburrirse mucho en la clase de . . .
8. construir aviones de papel en la clase de . . .
9. tener muchos resfriados
10. poner la mesa todos los días antes de la cena
11. recibir muchas cosas por correo
12. tener que levantarse a las . . .

C Cuando tenía cinco años . . .   Julio y sus amigos hablan de cuando tenían cinco años. Di lo que hacían. Escoge una frase de la derecha para hacer frases completas. Sigue el modelo.

Práctica C
Answers will vary.

> Sara
> *Sara construía barcos de papel.*

1. Juan
2. Mario y tú
3. María y Carmen
4. Jorge y yo
5. (tú)
6. Uds.
7. los hermanos López
8. yo

caerse a menudo
nunca poder acostarse tarde
construir barcos de papel
hacer pasteles de tierra y agua
leer libros de cuentos para niños
nunca compartir nada con nadie
repetir todo lo que decía la gente
romper los globos de los otros niños
saber contar hasta cien
tener celos de su hermanita
vestirse con la ropa de mamá
hacer miles de preguntas

D Hablemos de ti.

1. Cuando tenías cinco años, ¿ya sabías leer? ¿Sabías los días de la semana? ¿Y los nombres de los meses? ¿Sabías contar hasta diez en español?
2. Cuando tenías ocho años, ¿qué hacías por la noche? ¿Y durante los fines de semana? ¿Te acostabas temprano? ¿A qué hora, más o menos? ¿Te aburrías mucho? ¿Te divertías mucho? ¿Qué hacías para divertirte? ¿Dónde vivías?
3. Cuando tenías doce años, ¿qué hacías para divertirte? ¿Qué hacías durante las vacaciones de verano?
4. ¿Qué no podías hacer que puedes hacer ahora?
5. ¿Qué hacías que no debías hacer?
6. ¿Qué comida tenías que comer que no te gustaba?
7. Cuando tenías cinco años, ¿qué querías ser? ¿Piloto? ¿Auxiliar de vuelo? ¿Bombero(a)? ¿Estrella de cine? Y ahora, ¿qué quieres ser?

Práctica D
Answers will vary.

Practice Sheet 14–3

Workbook Exs. E–F

Tape Manual Exs. 5–6   10

Quiz 14–3

En el templo de Quetzalcóatl
en Teotihuacán, México

ACTIVIDAD

Somos arqueólogos   Each person should write down the names of two different objects or things on separate pieces of paper, and put them into a bag. Form teams of two or three students. Each team picks four slips of paper from the bag, and the objects named on them are the remains they have found of a lost civilization. Using these clues, make up a brief description of what these people were like and what they used to do. For example, if your words are *el templo, el anillo, el tenedor, la piscina,* you might come up with a description such as this:

> Visitaban sus templos frecuentemente y tenían que bañarse en una piscina grande antes de entrar en el templo. Llevaban muchas joyas de oro y comían con hermosos tenedores de plata.

Now get together with another group and tell about your lost civilizations. Use your imagination and have fun.

Una arqueóloga en Tenochtitlán, México

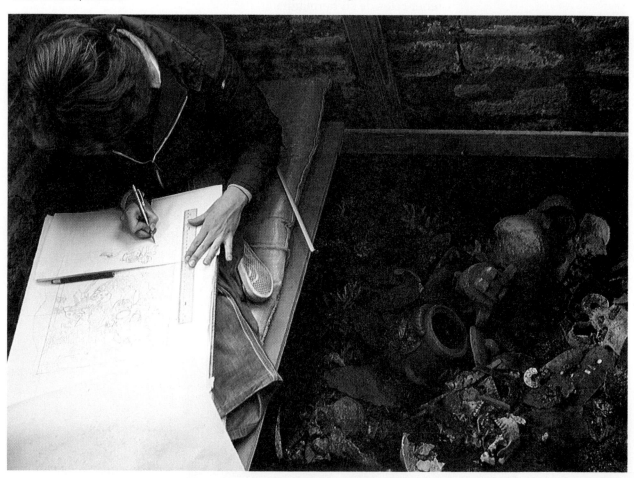

APLICACIONES Discretionary

El terremoto de México 11

Hay cuentos de los tiempos antiguos que hoy nos parecen fantásticos. Pero en esos tiempos los cuentos servían para explicarle a la gente las cosas que no comprendía. Una tribu[1] colombiana, por ejemplo, para explicar los terremotos, decía que había un dios que llevaba el mundo sobre los hombros.
5 Cuando un hombre estaba cansado, el dios ponía el mundo sobre el otro y . . . ¡Uy! La tierra temblaba.[2]

Hoy sabemos que el movimiento de grandes masas de roca[3] debajo de la tierra produce los terremotos. En el otoño de 1985 los sismólogos, que estudian la tierra donde ocurren los terremotos, ya sabían que uno estaba por[4]
10 ocurrir en México, pero no sabían ni el momento ni el lugar exacto. El pronóstico era correcto. El 19 de septiembre un terrible terremoto destruyó escuelas, edificios de apartamentos, hoteles y hospitales en la capital.

Miles de personas murieron y el desastre costó muchos millones de dólares. Pero durante este desastre ocurrieron muchos actos heroicos. Hom-
15 bres, mujeres y niños ayudaban a las víctimas, tratando de sacar a personas enterradas debajo de las ruinas. Era muy peligroso para ellos, pero nadie se

---

[1]**la tribu** *tribe*   [2]**temblar** *to tremble*   [3]**la masa de roca** *rock mass*   [4]**estar por** + inf.   *to be about to*

El terremoto de 1965 en México

quejaba y todo el mundo trabajaba día y noche. De todas partes del mundo llegaban personas con ropa, comida, medicinas y dinero para ayudar a la gente mexicana.

20   Ahora sabemos mucho más sobre cómo construir edificios en un lugar donde ocurren terremotos. Quizás a la gente del futuro le parecerá increíble que pudiera[5] ocurrir un desastre tan terrible. Pero la amistad[6] que mostró la gente del mundo no será un cuento fantástico, sino una historia verdadera.

---

[5]**pudiera** (from **poder**)   *could*   [6]**la amistad**   *friendship*

Preguntas

1. ¿Para qué usaba los cuentos la gente en tiempos antiguos?
2. ¿Conoces algún otro cuento sobre el tiempo, el viento, la lluvia o el cielo? ¿Le puedes contar la historia a la clase?
3. ¿Cómo explicaba la tribu de Colombia los terremotos?
4. ¿Qué es un terremoto?
5. ¿Qué no puede indicar un pronóstico de los sismólogos?
6. El terremoto del 19 de septiembre fue un verdadero desastre. Describe qué ocurrió.
7. ¿Sabes qué hacer si hay un terremoto donde tú vives? ¿Qué debes hacer?
8. ¿Qué debes hacer si viene un huracán? ¿Qué debes hacer y no hacer si hay relámpagos durante una tormenta?
9. ¿Puedes describirle a la clase un accidente o un desastre natural que viste o que conoces? ¿Cuándo y dónde ocurrió? ¿Qué pasó?

Culture: You may want students to do research on other natural disasters that have occurred in Latin America during the last two decades: for example, the 1972 earthquake in Managua, Nicaragua; the 1976 earthquake in Guatemala; the 1986 quake in El Salvador; the volcanic eruption in Colombia in 1985; Hurricane Fifi, which devastated northern Honduras in 1974.

Preguntas

1. Para explicar las cosas que no entendía.
2. Answers will vary.
3. Decían que un dios llevaba el mundo sobre los hombros. Cuando un hombre estaba cansado, ponía el mundo sobre el otro y la tierra temblaba.
4. Es el movimiento de grandes masas de roca debajo de la tierra.
5. El momento o el lugar exacto en que va a ocurrir un terremoto.
6. Destruyó escuelas, edificios de apartamentos, hoteles y hospitales. Muchas personas murieron.
7–9. Answers will vary.

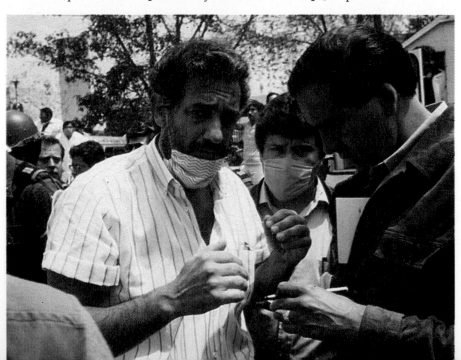

Plácido Domingo después del terremoto de México

EXPLICACIONES II Essential

El futuro

Notes: Point out the future-tense verb forms in mini-dialogue 5, p. 468.

You have learned two ways to talk about future events. One way is by using the present tense followed by a time expression.

Salgo mañana.   *I'll leave tomorrow.*

The other way is by using *ir a* + infinitive.

Voy a poner un anuncio en el diario.   *I'm going to put an ad in the paper.*

We use both of these constructions to talk about events that will take place in the near future.

◆ **OBJECTIVES:**

TO TALK ABOUT THE FUTURE

TO DESCRIBE FUTURE PLANS

TO NAG SOMEONE

TO PUT SOMEONE OFF

1 Spanish also has a future tense. For most verbs the stem for the future tense is the infinitive.

Compraré un anillo de oro.   *I'll buy a gold ring.*
En el próximo siglo la gente **vivirá** en la luna.   *In the next century people **will live** on the moon.*

Here are all of the forms of *hablar, aprender,* and *vivir* in the future tense.

HABLAR		APRENDER		VIVIR	
hablaré	hablar**emos**	aprenderé	aprender**emos**	viviré	vivir**emos**
hablarás	hablar**éis**	aprenderás	aprender**éis**	vivirás	vivir**éis**
hablará	hablar**án**	aprenderá	aprender**án**	vivirá	vivir**án**

All three types of verbs take the same endings. Note that there is an accent mark on all except the *nosotros* form.

2 Some verbs that are irregular in other tenses are regular in the future. For example:

IR	El año próximo **iremos** a Tampa.	*Next year **we'll go** to Tampa.*
SER	Algún día **serás** famoso.	*Some day **you'll be** famous.*
ESTAR	**Estaré** en casa a las diez.	*I'll be home at ten.*

PRÁCTICA

Práctica A
1. Eva jugará …
2. Ud. visitará …
3. Uds. entrarán …
4. Tú y tus amigos darán …
5. Tus primos comprarán …
6. Tomarás …
7. Ellas irán …
8. Comerá …
9. Participaremos …
10. Ganaré …

A En la feria. Unos amigos hablan sobre lo que quiere hacer cada uno en la feria. Sigue el modelo.

> (yo) / montar en las motos
> *Montaré en las motos.*

1. Eva / jugar a todos los juegos
2. Ud. / visitar todas las atracciones
3. Uds. / entrar en la casa de los fantasmas
4. tú y tus amigos / dar una vuelta en la rueda de feria
5. tus primos / comprar globos
6. (tú) / tomar muchas bebidas frías
7. ellas / ir a la casa de los espejos
8. (él) / comer varias bolsas de palomitas
9. (nosotros) / participar en unos concursos
10. (yo) / ganar premios en todos los puestos

Práctica B
1. ¿Qué será Andrés? Será policía. Capturará ladrones.
2. ¿Qué serán Miguel y tú? Seremos ingenieros. Construiremos puentes.
3. ¿Qué serán tus hermanas? Serán … Descubrirán huesos antiguos y …
4. ¿Qué serás? Seré … Estudiaré las estrellas.
5. ¿Qué serán Uds.? Seremos … Dirigiremos bandas u orquestas.
6. ¿Qué será Ángela? Será … Escribirá canciones folklóricas.
7. ¿Qué será tu hermano? Será … Entrevistará a gente famosa.
8. ¿Qué será Raquel? Será … Cuidará a la gente enferma.
9. Answers will vary but will include *seré.*

B ¿Qué serás? Di lo que serán las siguientes personas. Luego escoge de la lista de la derecha para decir lo que harán *(will do)* las personas. Pregunta y contesta según el modelo.

> Sonia / bombera
> **ESTUDIANTE A** *¿Qué será Sonia?*
> **ESTUDIANTE B** *Será bombera. Salvará a la gente de los incendios.*

1. Andrés / policía
2. Miguel y tú / ingenieros
3. tus hermanas / arqueólogas
4. (tú) / astrónomo(a)
5. Uds. / conductores
6. Ángela / compositora
7. tu hermano / periodista
8. Raquel / médica
9. Y tú, ¿qué serás?

dirigir bandas u orquestas
cuidar a la gente enferma
capturar ladrones
descubrir huesos antiguos y
   monedas de oro viejas
entrevistar a gente famosa
estudiar las estrellas
construir puentes
salvar a la gente de los incendios
escribir canciones folklóricas

Una especialista en terremotos en México

C ¡Qué impaciente eres!   Imagina que quieres saber si las siguientes personas ya terminaron de hacer ciertas (*certain*) cosas. Pregunta y contesta según el modelo.

> (tú) / terminar el libro sobre los aztecas / mañana
> ESTUDIANTE A   *¿Ya terminaste el libro sobre los aztecas?*
> ESTUDIANTE B   *Todavía no. Lo terminaré mañana.*

1. (tú) / llamar a Ana / durante el intervalo
2. Uds. / escribir el anuncio del espectáculo / mañana
3. Carlos / desenvolver los paquetes / pronto
4. ellas / arreglar la máquina de escribir / más tarde
5. (tú) / escoger el tema para tu composición / esta tarde
6. Uds. / comprar las bufandas de lana / pronto
7. Clara / recoger la madera para el fuego / antes del almuerzo
8. Ud. / leer el artículo de ese astrónomo / esta noche
9. (tú) / averiguar la información que necesitabas / la semana próxima

D Lo que pasará.   Imagina que en el siglo XV, un maya les cuenta una historia a sus hijos y describe un viaje al siglo XX. Cambia los verbos en cursiva del presente al futuro.

El mundo *es* muy distinto, hijos. Todo *parece* asombroso. No *construyen* hermosas pirámides como las nuestras sino edificios altísimos, de cien pisos y más. ¡La gente *vive* en el cielo! En la tierra, *ves* miles de hombres y mujeres. *Van* de un lugar a otro en cajas con 5 ruedas. Por la noche *se sientan* en casa y *miran* cajas pequeñas. En esas cajas *viven* muchas personas pequeñas que *hablan* a la gente pero que no la *oyen*. ¡*Es* una civilización increíble!

Los jóvenes no *aprenden* de sus padres y parientes cómo hacer las cosas. *Asisten* a una escuela. No *leen* las estrellas sino libros. Y no 10 *escriben* con piedras sino con máquinas.

¿Por qué se ríen Uds., hijitos? ¿Les parece graciosa mi historia? La *termino* en seguida. Pero primero les *cuento* la cosa más impresionante: ¡algunas personas *viajan* en pájaros grandes hasta la luna!

E Hablemos de ti.
1. ¿Dónde crees que estarás en el año 2000? ¿Por qué? ¿Estudiarás o trabajarás? ¿Dónde trabajarás? ¿Qué estudiarás?
2. ¿Crees que usarás el español en tu trabajo o en tu vida de todos los días? Explica por qué.
3. ¿Crees que viajarás mucho? ¿Adónde? ¿Por qué? ¿Qué esperas hacer?
4. En tu opinión, ¿cómo será el mundo en el año 2050?

APLICACIONES Discretionary

Notes: Answers to the **Repaso** and **Tema** appear in the Teacher Notes.

REPASO

Notes: Review of:
1. imperfect of *-ar* and *-ir* verbs
2. imperfect of *-er* and *-ir* verbs
   uses of *de*
3. adverbs of frequency
   imperfect
   position of adjectives
4. present subjunctive of *-ar* verbs following *querer/esperar/pedir*
   de + profession
5. future of regular verbs
   ser + profession

Enrichment: You may want to use the model sentences in the **Repaso** for dictation.

Mira con cuidado las frases modelo. Luego cambia las frases que siguen al español según los modelos.

1. *Cada noche hablábamos de las noticias.*
   (Every month I used to attend a race.)
   (Every Christmas they wrote to the newspaper.)
   (Every Sunday she used to participate in contests.)

2. *Él envolvía paquetes que incluían docenas de sorpresas maravillosas.*
   (They used to build pyramids that had walls of real gold.)
   (He used to produce ads that offered treasures of ancient religions.)
   (We were reading an article that included headlines about unforgettable disasters.)

3. *Siempre servías verduras y postres congelados.*
   (Sometimes I found impressive pyramids and temples.)
   (They frequently destroyed important paintings and statues.)
   (He would almost always recognize heroic acts and causes.)

4. *Mi madre quiere que yo trabaje de arquitecta.*
   (We hope you (fam.) *work as an engineer.)*
   (I want her to work as a journalist.)
   (He asks that we work as firefighters (m.)*.)*

5. *Pero creo que seré bombera. Apagaré incendios.*
   (But we say we'll be journalists. We'll write articles.)
   (But María says she'll be an engineer. She'll build bridges.)
   (But they think they'll be astronomers. They'll study stars.)

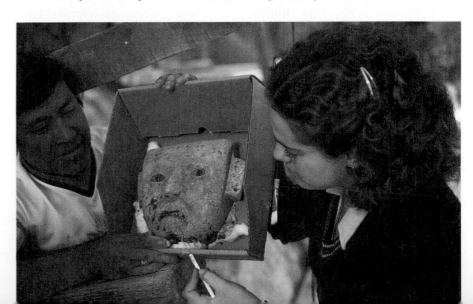

Jóvenes arqueólogos en México

TEMA

Transparency 49

Reteach / Extra Help: Before students begin the **Redacción,** you may want to lead a brief discussion about the pattern of most news stories. Refer students who choose topic 3 back to Ex. B on p. 470 and point out that the headline and lead paragraph in most items answer the questions *¿Quién?* *¿Qué pasó?, ¿Dónde?, ¿Cuándo?,* and *¿Por qué?*

Escribe las frases en español.

1. Every summer the Morales family fled (from) the city.

2. They used to visit places where there were ruins of ancient civilizations.

3. Sometimes they would discover amazing objects and places.

4. The Moraleses hope Mateo works as an archeologist.

5. But Mateo says he'll be an artist. He'll paint landscapes.

REDACCIÓN

Ahora escoge uno de los siguientes temas para escribir tu propio diálogo o párrafo.

1. Create a set of talk balloons for pictures 1 through 5.

2. Expand the story in the *Tema* by writing a paragraph about pictures 1 through 3. Tell what the Morales family used to do when they visited the ruins. What was their day like? Where did they sleep and eat? Did they enjoy themselves?

3. Write a paragraph about a real or imaginary heroic act. You might want to write it as a newspaper article, with a headline, lead paragraph, and a description of the event.

Aplicaciones 483

Notes: Answers to the **Comprueba** appear in the Teacher Notes.

A Busca la palabra
Completa las siguientes frases.

1. Una persona que roba a la gente es un . . .
2. Una persona que ayuda a apagar incendios es un . . .
3. Una persona que estudia las estrellas es un . . .
4. Una persona que escribe para los diarios trabaja de . . .
5. Cuando hay un incendio, generalmente lo que vemos primero es el . . .
6. Hay cien años en un . . .
7. La casa de un dios o diosa es un . . .
8. En los diarios, lo que está en letras grandes al principio de una noticia es un . . .

B Lo que hacían antes
Completa las frases con la forma correcta del imperfecto.

1. Claudia _____ celos de su hermano menor. *(tener)*
2. (Nosotras) _____ rápidamente porque nunca _____ mucho tiempo. *(comer / tener)*
3. A menudo (nosotros) _____ con nuestros padrinos. *(reunirse)*
4. (Yo) _____ muy triste mientras _____ que _____ un incendio en la montaña. *(sentirse / leer / haber)*
5. ¿_____ (tú) en el Perú? *(vivir)*
6. Yo _____ que (nosotros) _____ encontrar un tesoro enterrado. *(pensar / poder)*
7. Yo siempre _____ todo en orden antes de salir de la oficina. *(poner)*
8. Los arqueólogos _____ objetos de hueso y de madera. *(descubrir)*

C Los hermanos
Daniel y Ramón son hermanos, pero son muy diferentes. Cuando Daniel era niño siempre se portaba bien, pero Ramón no. Escribe seis frases y di qué hacía cada uno. Usa palabras y expresiones de las tres columnas.

Daniel	empujar	sus lecciones
Ramón	compartir	de su hermano
	entender	sus cosas
	comer	con la boca
	huir	abierta
	tener celos	a sus amigos
		cuando alguien
		lo llamaba

D Todos podemos cambiar
Cambia las frases según el modelo.

Todos los días hablo con María. (hoy / no)
Hoy no hablaré con María.

1. Generalmente desayunamos en la cocina. (hoy / en el comedor)
2. Siempre llevo blusa y jeans a la escuela. (mañana / un vestido)
3. Siempre regresamos a casa alrededor de las siete y media. (esta noche / más temprano)
4. Hoy llegamos a la escuela con tres minutos de retraso. (mañana / a tiempo)
5. Antes yo compartía mi comida. (hoy / no . . . nada)
6. Siempre comemos en la cafetería. (hoy / en el jardín)
7. Ayer corrí por el parque. (esta tarde / por la playa)
8. Yo bebía refrescos. (ahora / agua)

E ¿Quién lo va a hacer?
Contesta las siguientes preguntas con frases completas. Usa el futuro.

1. ¿Quién irá al bautizo de Juan Carlos? (yo)
2. ¿Quién se dará cuenta de que ese vaso está roto? (tu mamá)
3. ¿Quién se escapará? (el ladrón)
4. ¿Qué se quemará? (la casa)
5. ¿Quién salvará a los niños? (tú)
6. ¿Quiénes huirán? (nosotros)
7. ¿Quiénes se quedarán? (Clara y Miguel)
8. ¿Quiénes escribirán esos artículos? (los periodistas extranjeros)

Activity Masters   Chapter 14 Test   Listening Comprehension Test

VOCABULARIO DEL CAPÍTULO 14

Sustantivos
el acto
el algodón
el anuncio
el arqueólogo, la arqueóloga
el arquitecto, la arquitecta
el artículo
el astrónomo, la astrónoma
los aztecas
el bombero, la bombera
la causa
la civilización, *pl.* las
    civilizaciones
el cuero
el diario
el dios, la diosa
la estatua
el héroe, la heroína
el humo
los incas
el incendio
el ingeniero, la ingeniera
el ladrón, la ladrona
la lana
la madera
los mayas
el mundo
el objeto
la opinión, *pl.* las opiniones
el oro
el papel
el/la periodista
la piedra *(stone)*
la pirámide
la plata
la religión, *pl.* las religiones
el robo
las ruinas
la sección, *pl.* las secciones

el siglo
el significado
el templo
el tesoro
el titular

Adjetivos
antiguo, -a
asombroso, -a
enterrado, -a
heroico, -a
impresionante
muerto, -a
secreto, -a
verdadero, -a

Verbos
capturar
construir
descubrir
destruir
escaparse
haber
hallar
huir de
producir (c → zc)
quemarse
robar
salvar
había

Preposición
de *(as a(n))*

Expresiones
a causa de
darse cuenta de
de + *material*
de repente
etcétera
¡qué horror!

PRÓLOGO CULTURAL

ANIMALES DE LA AMÉRICA DEL SUR

W hat is the strangest animal in South America? There is no way to answer that question, because there are simply too many to choose from. Even if you were to limit your search to a single kind of animal—frogs, for example—you would still find it exceedingly difficult to choose. *Las ranas sudamericanas* have an astounding variety of shapes, colors, and characteristics. Some spend their entire lives in trees, and one kind of frog dines on rats as large as itself.

Among bats *(murciélagos),* the vampire bat is certainly unusual, but so is the Mexican bulldog bat, which swoops down over the water and grabs small fish with its hind legs. Among fish, the piranha, with its powerful jaws and razor-sharp teeth, is probably the most feared animal in the rivers of South America, but the electric eel *(anguila eléctrica),* which is really a fish, is much more unusual. To stun or kill its prey, it produces electric pulses up to 650 volts.

There are also many unusual candidates among the mammals. The sloth, aptly called *el perezoso,* spends its life hanging upside down from branches, and travels only slightly faster than a snail. The giant anteater *(oso hormiguero)* eats as many as 30,000 ants and termites every day, catching them with its long, sticky tongue.

It is not surprising that there are so many unusual animals in South America. After all, the continent offers a vast range of living conditions, from deserts to rain forests, and from lowland savannas to towering mountains. Nearly a quarter of all the world's known types of animals live in South America—and no one knows how many more are still to be discovered.

CONTEXTO VISUAL

¡Qué aventura!

el helicóptero

el volcán
pl. los volcanes

el desierto

el loro

la selva

la arena

el jaguar

la canoa

la tortuga

CONTEXTO COMUNICATIVO 2

1 INÉS   Pepe, ¿quieres **acompañarme** en mi **expedición** en canoa?

    PEPE   ¿Yo? No soy **bastante** valiente ni bastante loco para hacer eso.

Variaciones:
- acompañarme → venir conmigo
- en mi expedición → a **explorar** el río

acompañar *to go/come with, to accompany*

la expedición, pl. **las expediciones** *expedition*

bastante here: adj. & adv. *enough*

explorar *to explore*

Enrichment: After presenting the **Contexto comunicativo,** you may want to reinforce some of the new vocabulary by asking questions. For mini-dialogue 1: *¿Eres bastante valiente para darle de comer a un jaguar? ¿Y a una tortuga?* For 2: *¿Con qué soñabas cuando eras niño(a)? ¿Con qué sueñas ahora?* for 3: *¿Cuándo fue la última vez que te quedaste sin dinero?*

2 EVA   ¿Qué te parece si **hacemos una expedición** a la selva?

LAURA   ¡Magnífico! Cuando era niña **soñaba con** explorar lugares **misteriosos.**

EVA   Y yo soñaba con ser **antropóloga.** ¿Quieres ser mi **ayudante?**

- soñaba con explorar → mi **sueño** era descubrir
- lugares → **sitios**
- antropóloga → **exploradora**

hacer una expedición *to go on an expedition*

soñar (o → ue) con *to dream about / of*

misterioso, -a *mysterious*

el antropólogo, la antropóloga *anthropologist*

el/la ayudante *helper, assistant*

el sueño *dream*

el sitio *site, place*

el explorador, la exploradora *explorer*

3 ÁNGEL   ¿Cómo fue tu expedición, Diana?

DIANA   Así, así. **El clima** era muy **húmedo,** y la mochila estaba llena de **demasiados** objetos pesados.

ÁNGEL   Bueno, **por lo menos** no **te quedaste sin** comida, ¿verdad?

DIANA   No, pero la próxima vez seré más **práctica.** No llevaré tantas cosas.

- no te quedaste sin → no te faltó
- práctica → lista

el clima *climate*

húmedo, -a *humid, damp*

demasiado, -a *too much, too many*

por lo menos *at least*

quedarse sin *to run out of, to be left without*

práctico, -a *practical*

4 RITA   Anoche yo **iba** por la calle cuando de repente **hubo** un ruido fuerte y alguien gritó.

LUIS   ¡Ay, qué horror! ¿Y qué hiciste?

RITA   Grité: **"¡Socorro!"**

LUIS   Sí . . . ¿y entonces?

RITA   Y entonces me desperté.

- iba → caminaba
- ¿y qué hiciste? → ¿y qué ocurrió?
- ¡socorro! → ¡ayúdenme!

(yo) iba, (tú) ibas (imperfect of **ir**) *I was going, you were going*

hubo (preterite of **haber**) *there was, there were*

¡socorro! *'help!*

EN OTRAS PARTES

También se dice la *cotorra* y *el papagayo*.

Práctica A

1. Pedro buscaba agua cuando de repente gritó … ¡Socorro! ¡Un tigre!
2. Eduardo y Luisa cruzaban el río … gritaron … ¡Un caimán!
3. Tú subías al árbol … gritaste … ¡Una serpiente!
4. Mónica y yo dábamos un paseo … gritamos … ¡Un león!
5. Mi hermanito remaba en la canoa … gritó … ¡Una tortuga!
6. Ud. exploraba esos nuevos sitios … gritó … ¡Una araña!
7. Uds. huían de las hormigas … gritaron … ¡Un jaguar!
8. Yo empujaba el camión … grité … ¡Un rinoceronte!

PRÁCTICA

A No soy muy valiente.   Unos turistas y su guía hacían una expedición por la selva cuando de repente vieron animales que los asustaron. Al verlos, ¿qué hicieron? Pregunta y contesta según el modelo.

Lupe / caminar por el sendero

ESTUDIANTE A *Lupe caminaba por el sendero cuando de repente gritó . . .*

ESTUDIANTE B *¡Socorro! ¡Un leopardo!*

1. Pedro / buscar agua

2. Eduardo y Luisa / cruzar el río

3. tú / subir al árbol

4. Mónica y yo / dar un paseo

5. mi hermanito / remar en la canoa

6. Ud. / explorar esos nuevos sitios

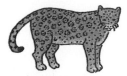

7. Uds. / huir de las hormigas

8. yo / empujar el camión

B En la selva.   Alejandro nos cuenta sobre su expedición a la selva. Completa el párrafo con las palabras correctas.

En mis últimas vacaciones hice una expedición a la selva de Yucatán. *(Acompañé / Exploré / Capturé)* a una antropóloga, amiga de mis padres. Yo fui su *(loro / ayudante / arena)*.

   La selva es un sitio *(distraído / perezoso / misterioso)*, ¿no crees?
5 También puede ser peligroso. ¡Especialmente durante la noche! No recomiendo que *(empujes / sueñes con / te quedes sin)* pilas para la linterna. También tienes que *(fijarte en / soñar con / tener celos de)* cada sonido que oyes.

   Todos los días *(explorábamos / salvábamos / hallábamos)* el río. El clima
10 era muy *(secreto / práctico / húmedo)*, especialmente después de una tormenta. Y había muchas tormentas grandes mientras estábamos allí.

   Tenía muchas aventuras emocionantes durante la expedición. Algunas fueron verdaderas, otras no. Por ejemplo, un día capturé *(un jaguar / un loro / una jaula)* de muchos colores. Ahora lo tengo en casa y
15 ya está aprendiendo a hablar un poco. Y también, una noche, capturé un jaguar. Pero eso era en *(un volcán / un sueño / una tortuga)*.

   Aprendí una cosa durante mi viaje: es mucho trabajo llevar una mochila pesada. No es *(práctico / húmedo / misterioso)* llevar *(bastantes / demasiadas / pocas)* cosas a la selva.

Práctica B
acompañé
ayudante
misterioso
te quedes sin
fijarte en
explorábamos
húmedo
un loro
un sueño
práctico
demasiadas

C En el desierto.   Completa el siguiente párrafo con las palabras de la lista.

la arena	una expedición	me quedaba sin	seco	soñé con
el clima	exploramos	por lo menos	un sitio	un volcán

La semana pasada hicimos ____ al desierto. ____ allí es muy ____. Hace calor durante el día y hace frío por la noche. No fue difícil encontrar ____ para dormir, pero yo no soy muy valiente y esa noche ____ serpientes y arañas debajo de mi saco de dormir y
5 también que ____ agua.

   Durante el día el desierto es maravilloso. Se pueden ver cactos con bellísimas flores y también muchos animales del mismo color que ____ del desierto. Un día nuestro guía nos indicó humo blanco que subía al cielo. Nos contó que subía de ____ que estaba lejos, cerca de
10 las montañas. Me gustaría volver otra vez y pasar ____ dos semanas allí.

Práctica C
una expedición / el clima / seco
un sitio
soñé con
me quedaba sin
la arena
un volcán
por lo menos

D Hablemos de ti.

1. ¿Te gustaría hacer una expedición a la selva? ¿Y al desierto? ¿Por qué? ¿Qué te gustaría hacer allí?
2. ¿Eres valiente? ¿Qué clase de cosas te asustan? ¿Tienes miedo de algunos animales? ¿De cuáles?
3. ¿Te gustaría explorar sitios misteriosos? ¿Cuáles? ¿Por qué? ¿Te gusta especialmente alguna película o novela de aventuras misteriosas o peligrosas? Cuéntala.
4. ¿Cómo te gustaría hacer una expedición, en helicóptero, en canoa, en camión, a pie, o a caballo? ¿Por qué?

ACTIVIDAD

La compañía de aventuras   With a partner, write a radio or magazine ad for a travel company that offers exciting tours.

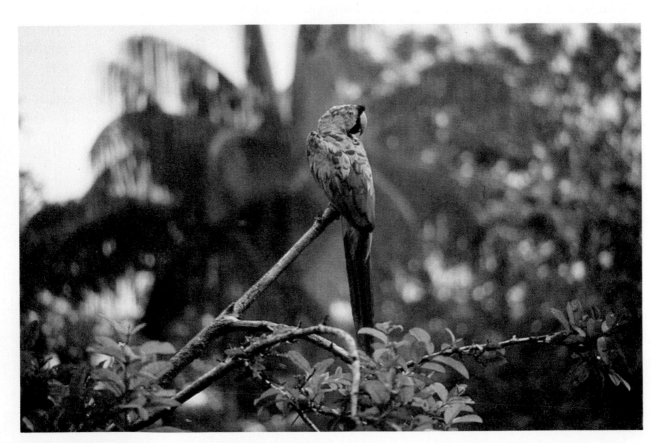

En la selva de Colombia

APLICACIONES

Discretionary

La Pirámide del Jaguar

 4

 5 Pronunciación

Notes: Make sure students understand the meaning of *sabelotodo*, (know-it-all).

RODOLFO ¿Dónde estabas anoche? Te llamé alrededor de las ocho.

CLAUDIA Es que no estaba nadie en casa. Todos fuimos al cine.

RODOLFO ¿Qué vieron?

5 CLAUDIA *La pirámide del jaguar.* ¿La conoces?

RODOLFO No, ¿de qué se trata?[1]

CLAUDIA ¡Ay, tienes que verla! Es impresionante. Se trata de dos exploradores que buscan unas ruinas donde hay un tesoro enterrado.

10 RODOLFO ¿Y por qué dices que es tan impresionante?

CLAUDIA Porque tiene lugar en un sitio muy misterioso en medio de[2] la selva. Hay unos jaguares que cuidan el tesoro.

RODOLFO Sí, pero, ¿qué pasa en la película?

15 CLAUDIA Pues, un hombre y una mujer tratan de entrar en las ruinas para robar el tesoro.

RODOLFO No me digas que un jaguar los ataca.[3] El hombre valiente lucha contra[4] él mientras la mujer grita ''¡socorro!'' y de repente aparece[5] un hombre

20 misterioso que los salva.

CLAUDIA Ay, Rodolfo, no te puedo contar nada. ¡Eres un sabelotodo!

---

[1]**tratarse** *to be about* [2]**en medio de** *in the middle of* [3]**atacar** *to attack*
[4]**luchar contra** *to fight with* [5]**aparecer** *to appear*

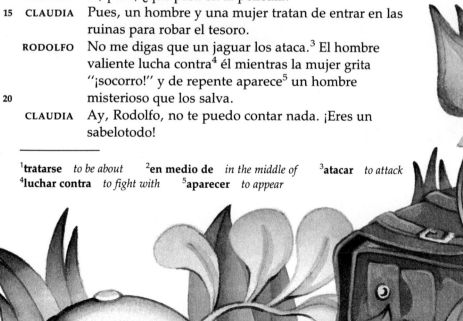

Preguntas

Contesta según el diálogo.

1. ¿Dónde estaba Claudia cuando Rodolfo la llamó? ¿Con quién?
2. ¿Qué película vieron esa noche? Descríbela.   3. ¿Por qué exploran el hombre y la mujer esas ruinas?   4. ¿Puedes adivinar *(guess)* cómo termina la película? Cuéntalo.   5. ¿Por qué le dice Claudia a Rodolfo que no puede contarle nada a él?   6. ¿Conoces algunas películas parecidas a ésta? ¿Cuáles son sus títulos? ¿Cómo son los personajes? ¿Generalmente tiene éxito esta clase de película? ¿Por qué?

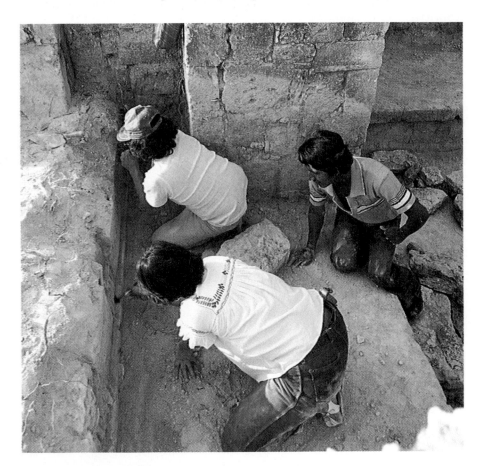

Arqueólogos en Yucatán, México

Participación

Work with a partner to make up a dialogue in which each of you tries to convince the other to see a certain film. What kind of film is it? Who are the leading actors? Do you know who directed it? What is the film about?

PALABRAS NUEVAS II

Essential

 CONTEXTO VISUAL

Me gustaría ser . . .

la universidad

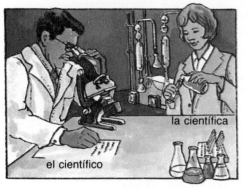

la científica

el científico

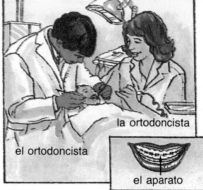

la ortodoncista

el ortodoncista

el aparato

el farmacéutico

la farmacéutica

la abogada

el abogado

el hombre de negocios

la mujer de negocios

la secretaria

el secretario

el millonario

la millonaria

CONTEXTO
COMUNICATIVO 🔊 7

1 DANIEL Teresa, ¿qué piensas hacer después de terminar el colegio?

TERESA Quisiera estudiar **derecho**. ¿Y tú?

DANIEL Espero **ganar** bastante dinero para ir a la universidad.

Variaciones:
■ después de terminar el colegio → para **ganarte la vida**
■ derecho → para ser **programadora de computadoras**
■ ganar → **ahorrar**

el derecho *law*
ganar *here: to earn*

ganarse la vida *to earn a living*
el programador / la programadora (de computadoras) *computer programmer*
ahorrar *to save*

2 VÍCTOR Ayer me ofrecieron un trabajo en una agencia de viajes. Tengo que darles una respuesta **para** mañana. ¿Qué me **aconsejas**?

DIANA ¡**Acépta**lo! Creo que es muy bueno tener un trabajo antes de **graduarse.***

■ darles una respuesta → **decidir**
■ me aconsejas → debo hacer
  ¡acéptalo! → ¿a mí me pides **consejos**?

para + time expression *by*
aconsejar *to advise*
aceptar *to accept*
graduarse (yo me gradúo, tú te gradúas) *to graduate*
decidir *to decide*

el consejo *piece of advice; pl., advice*

3 CLARA Mi **jefe** es un hombre de negocios muy **capaz** y con mucha **ambición**.

JULIO Sé que es muy capaz, pero ¿por qué dices que tiene ambición?

CLARA Me dijo que quiere tener su **propio negocio** algún día.

■ tiene ambición → es **ambicioso**
■ quiere tener → va a abrir
■ propio negocio → propia compañía

el jefe, la jefa *boss*
capaz, pl. **capaces** *capable, able*
la ambición, pl. **las ambiciones** *ambition*

propio, -a *own*
el negocio *business*

ambicioso, -a *ambitious*

---

* Like *continuar*, the present tense of *graduarse* has a written accent mark on the *u* in all except the *nosotros* and *vosotros* forms: *me gradúo, te gradúas, se gradúa, nos graduamos, os graduáis, se gradúan.*

4 ISABEL   Me van a pagar un buen **sueldo** en el nuevo trabajo. Probablemente lo gastaré todo en ropa nueva.

VICTORIA   No seas tonta, Isabel. No gastes más de **la mitad** y ahorra **el resto.** Y recuerda que todavía me **debes** diez dólares.

ISABEL   Te agradezco los consejos, Victoria.

■ no seas tonta → ¡qué barbaridad!

el sueldo   *salary*

la mitad   *half*
el resto   *rest, remainder*
deber   here: *to owe*

EN OTRAS PARTES

También se dice *los frenos* o *frenillos*.

También se dice *las leyes.*

PRÁCTICA

A   Las profesiones.   Para escoger una profesión es necesario saber qué te interesa. Pregunta y contesta según el modelo.

> dirigir una orquesta
> ESTUDIANTE A   *¿Te interesa dirigir una orquesta?*
> ESTUDIANTE B   *Sí, quisiera ser director(a) de orquesta.*

1. estudiar las estrellas
2. preparar y vender medicinas, etcétera
3. arreglarle a la gente los dientes
4. construir carreteras o puentes
5. escribir programas de computadoras
6. hacer expediciones a sitios que nadie conoce bien
7. discutir de derecho internacional
8. tener tu propio negocio
9. contestar el teléfono, recibir recados y escribir a máquina
10. estudiar las ciencias

Práctica A
Questions will follow the model.
1. ¿Te interesa estudiar las estrellas?
   Sí, quisiera ser astrónomo(a).
2. farmacéutico(a)
3. ortodoncista
4. ingeniero(a)
5. programador(a)
6. explorador(a)
7. abogado(a)
8. hombre / mujer de negocios
9. secretario(a)
10. científico(a)

Reteach / Review: After students do Ex. A, you may want to ask them to suggest similar questions and answers for additional professions, such as: *bailarín / bailarina, ingeniero(a), periodista, arquitecto(a), antropólogo(a), mecánico(a), médico(a).*

B En la universidad. Imagina que algunos amigos tuyos ya están en la universidad o ya saben qué profesión les interesa. Completa las frases.

1. Varios de mis amigos *(llegan / se gradúan)* de la universidad este año.
2. Más o menos *(la mitad / el sueldo)* piensa seguir estudiando.
3. *(La ambición / El resto)* de ellos prefiere encontrar un trabajo para empezar a ganarse la vida.
4. Patricio estaba fuerte en biología. Ahora es un *(científico / derecho)*.
5. Juana siguió *(los consejos / los derechos)* de sus profesores y ahora estudia para ser farmacéutica.
6. Victoria tiene mucha *(arena / ambición)*. Ella sueña con ser *(mujer de negocios / acomodadora)* y tener su propia tienda. Espera ser la *(jefa / dependiente)* de muchas personas.
7. Marcos piensa estudiar derecho. Quiere ser *(abogado / aparato)*.
8. A Ricardo le encantan las ciencias. Ya trabaja como *(ayudante / aparato)* de uno de los profesores.
9. Anita está muy fuerte en matemáticas y por eso va a ser una *(programadora de computadoras / millonaria)* muy capaz. Muy pronto va a ganar un *(sueldo / sueño)* muy bueno.

Una clase de computadoras en Maracaibo, Venezuela

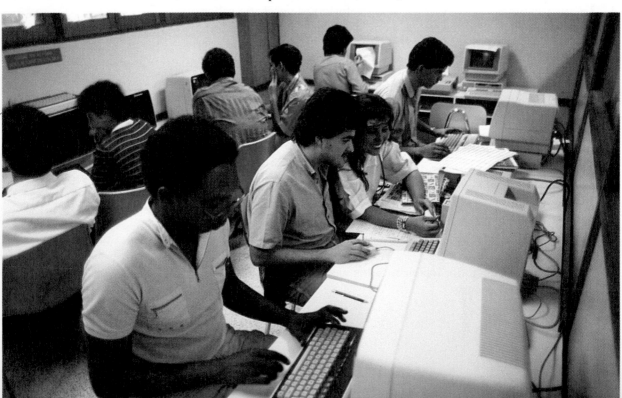

C **Estudio y trabajo.** Lee esta historia de alguien que afortunadamente cambió de idea. Completa cada frase con la palabra correcta.

Felicia siempre *(se quedaba sin / soñaba con)* ser arquitecta, pero cuando tenía 18 años *(dejó de asistir / siguió asistiendo)* a la escuela. No trabajaba ni estudiaba. Sus padres no estaban contentos y Felicia muy pronto *(se graduó / se quedó)* sin dinero. Su amiga Olga *(iba / caminaba)* a la
5 universidad. Un día, Felicia *(debió / acompañó)* a Olga a la universidad para buscar trabajo allí. La universidad le *(ofreció / aconsejó)* un trabajo como secretaria. El sueldo no *(ahorraba / era)* muy bueno, pero Felicia *(exploró / aceptó)* el trabajo porque podía estudiar gratis. *(Empezó / Ofreció)* a estudiar, y siete años después *(se fue / se graduó)*. Ahora *(se*
10 *gana / se aburre)* la vida como arquitecta.

Práctica C
soñaba con
dejó de asistir
se quedó / iba
acompañó
ofreció
era
aceptó
Empezó
se graduó
se gana

.D **Hablemos de ti.**
1. Después de graduarte, ¿piensas ir en seguida a la universidad o empezar a trabajar? ¿Por qué? ¿Qué quieres estudiar o dónde quieres trabajar? ¿Por qué?
2. ¿Qué profesión te interesa más ahora? ¿Por qué?
3. ¿Tienes mucha o poca ambición? ¿Te gustaría ser jefe(a) de muchas personas? ¿Por qué? ¿Te gustaría tener tu propio negocio? ¿Por qué?
4. ¿Prefieres recibir un buen sueldo o estar contento en tu trabajo? ¿Por qué?
5. Imagina que de repente recibes un millón de dólares. Ahora que eres millonario(a), ¿qué vas a hacer? ¿Vas a gastar o ahorrar el dinero? Si ahorras más o menos la mitad, ¿cómo gastarás el resto?

Práctica D
Answers will vary.

Practice Sheet 15–2

Workbook Exs. C–D

Tape Manual Exs. 3–4 8

Refrán 9

Quiz 15–2

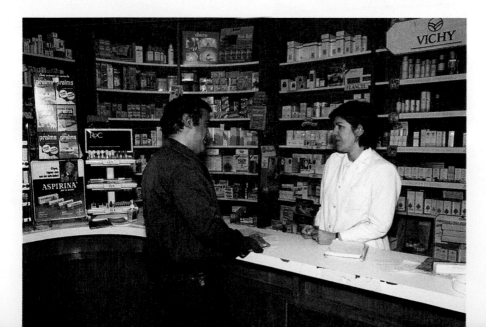

Una farmacia en Madrid, España

ESTUDIO DE PALABRAS

Sinónimos
1. sitio   2. socorro

Sinónimos

Cambia las palabras en cursiva por un sinónimo.
1. Ése no es un buen *lugar* para buscar tesoros enterrados.
2. *¡Ayúdame!* No sé nadar.

Familias de palabras I
1. el explorador, la exploradora
2. los consejos
3. el sueño
4. el / la ayudante

Familias de palabras I

¿Qué sustantivo conoces que corresponda a cada verbo?
1. explorar   2. aconsejar   3. soñar   4. ayudar

Familias de palabras II
1. científico
2. millonaria
3. farmacéutica
4. sueña

Familias de palabras II

Completa las frases con una palabra relacionada con la palabra en cursiva.
1. Mi hermano está muy fuerte en las *ciencias*. Quiere ser _____.
2. La dueña de estos almacenes es _____. El año pasado ganó más de dos *millones* de dólares.
3. ¿Conoces a la nueva _____ que trabaja en la *farmacia* de la esquina?
4. Raquel _____ con ser astrónoma. Su *sueño* es descubrir una estrella nueva.

Palabras con varios sentidos
1. I have ... dream
2. I'm ... sleepy
3. won
4. were supposed to (*or:* should have) / earned
5. owed

Palabras con varios sentidos

Explica el sentido de las palabras *sueño, ganar* y *deber* en las siguientes frases.
1. Cada noche *tengo* el mismo *sueño*.
2. *Tengo* mucho *sueño*. Voy a acostarme.
3. Nuestro equipo de tenis acaba de *ganar* el campeonato.
4. *Debíamos* ahorrar el dinero que *ganábamos*.
5. Todavía le *debían* la mitad de su sueldo.

EXPLICACIONES I

Essential

El imperfecto de *ir*, *ser* y *ver*

Ir, *ser*, and *ver* are the only verbs that are irregular in the imperfect.

INFINITIVO: **ir**

SINGULAR			PLURAL		
1	(yo)	**iba**	(nosotros) (nosotras)	}	**íbamos**
2	(tú)	**ibas**	(vosotros) (vosotras)	}	**ibais**
3	Ud. (él) (ella) }	**iba**	Uds. (ellos) (ellas) }		**iban**

Juan siempre llegaba tarde al trabajo y **se iba** temprano.

*Juan always arrived late to work and **left** early.*

We can also use the imperfect of *ir* + *a* + infinitive to say what someone "was going to do."

Íbamos a acompañar a Luisa.

*We **were going to go** with Luisa.*

Notes: Mini-dialogues 2, 3, and 4 on p. 489 contain examples of *ir* and *ser* in the imperfect.

◆ **OBJECTIVES:**

TO DISCUSS PLANS THAT DIDN'T WORK OUT

TO EXPLAIN WHY YOU DIDN'T DO SOMETHING

TO MAKE EXCUSES

TO DESCRIBE YOURSELF WHEN YOU WERE YOUNGER

TO TELL HOW THINGS USED TO BE

Enrichment: Reinforce the imperfect of *ir* + *a* + infinitive by eliciting or suggesting excuses such as: *Iba a llamarte anoche pero volví muy tarde a casa. _____ iba a comprar refrescos para todos pero se quedó sin dinero.*

Una antropóloga en México

Reteach / Extra Help: You may want to reinforce the forms of *ir, ser,* and *ver* in the imperfect before students begin the **Práctica** on pp. 502–503. Ask questions such as: *¿Te ibas de la escuela al mediodía cuando estabas en primer grado? ¿Se conocían tu y _____ cuando eran niños? ¿Me veías más frecuentemente el año pasado que éste?*

Notes: You may want to point out to students that the verb *ver* has an accent mark on the *i* in all forms of the imperfect.

INFINITIVO: **ser**

SINGULAR		PLURAL	
1	(yo) **era**	(nosotros) (nosotras) } **éramos**	
2	(tú) **eras**	(vosotros) (vosotras) } **erais**	
3	Ud. (él) (ella) } **era**	Uds. (ellos) (ellas) } **eran**	

Cuando **éramos** niños, vivíamos en un rancho.

*When **we were** children we lived on a ranch.*

INFINITIVO: **ver**

SINGULAR		PLURAL	
1	(yo) **veía**	(nosotros) (nosotras) } **veíamos**	
2	(tú) **veías**	(vosotros) (vosotras) } **veíais**	
3	Ud. (él) (ella) } **veía**	Uds. (ellos) (ellas) } **veían**	

Yo siempre **veía** al mismo dependiente en esa tienda.

*I always **used to see** the same salesclerk in that store.*

PRÁCTICA

Práctica A
1. era
2. era

A Los viejos tiempos. La bisabuela de Jaime le cuenta cómo era la vida cuando ella era niña. Haz frases con la forma correcta de *ser* en el imperfecto. Sigue el modelo.

mi padre / gerente de la estación de trenes
Mi padre era gerente de la estación de trenes.

1. mi madre / secretaria del único hombre de negocios del pueblo
2. mi hermana mayor / novia de un millonario

3. yo / muy atlética
4. mi hermana y yo / no muy parecidas
5. mi hermano y todos sus amigos / estudiantes de derecho
6. mi hermano / mucho mayor que yo
7. nuestros padres / muy cariñosos y pacientes
8. nuestra casa / de madera y bastante pequeña
9. la vida / más fácil que la vida de hoy
10. todos nosotros / muy felices

3. era
4. no éramos
5. eran
6. era
7. eran
8. era
9. era
10. éramos

B **¿Qué iban a hacer?** ¿Qué querían hacer estas personas y por qué no podían hacerlo? Pregunta y contesta según el modelo.

Raúl y Julia / volver al parador / no tener bastante tiempo
ESTUDIANTE A *¿Qué iban a hacer Raúl y Julia?*
ESTUDIANTE B *Iban a volver al parador pero no tenían bastante tiempo.*

1. (tú) / comprar un loro / no tener bastante dinero
2. Cecilia / navegar en canoa / no poder alquilar una
3. Bernardo y Leonor / aprender a manejar / los frenos no funcionar
4. Marcos y tú / participar en una regata / estar enfermos
5. Uds. / reparar el techo / siempre llover
6. (tú) / pintar un paisaje / siempre estar demasiado nublado
7. el primo de Luz / construir estantes / no hallar bastante madera
8. Ud. / hacer unos guantes para mi nieto / no encontrar la clase de lana que / querer

C **¿Qué veían?** Unos ancianos describen lo que veían cuando iban de vacaciones cuando eran niños. Usa palabras o expresiones de cada columna para hacer frases completas. Sigue el modelo.

Ana
A menudo Ana iba al rancho donde veía mucho ganado.

1. yo	al campo	muchos esquiadores
2. Gloria y Emilio	a la ciudad	exposiciones de arte abstracto
3. (nosotros)	al desierto	mucho ganado
4. Ud.	al lago	peces de todos los colores
5. Raimundo	a la montaña	muy pocos árboles
6. Beatriz y yo	a la playa	serpientes muy peligrosas
7. Uds.	al rancho	castillos de arena
8. (tú)	a la selva	flores por los senderos
		miles de loros en los árboles
		canoas y veleros

Práctica B
1. ¿Qué ibas a hacer?
   Iba a comprar un loro pero no tenía bastante dinero.
2. ¿Qué iba a hacer Cecilia?
   Iba a navegar en canoa pero no podía alquilar una.
3. ¿Qué iban a hacer …?
   Iban a aprender a manejar pero los frenos no funcionaban.
4. ¿Qué iban a hacer …?
   Íbamos a participar en una regata pero estábamos enfermos.
5. ¿Qué iban a hacer Uds?
   Íbamos a reparar el techo pero siempre llovía.
6. ¿Qué ibas a hacer?
   Yo iba a pintar un paisaje pero siempre estaba demasiado nublado.
7. ¿Qué iba a hacer …?
   Iba a construir estantes pero no hallaba bastante madera.
8. ¿Qué iba a hacer Ud.?
   Yo iba a hacer unos guantes para mi nieto pero no encontraba la clase de lana que quería.

Práctica C
Answers will vary.
1. iba / veía
2. iban / veían
3. íbamos / veíamos
4. iba / veía
5. iba / veía
6. íbamos / veíamos
7. iban / veían
8. ibas / veías

Otros usos del imperfecto

◆ **OBJECTIVES:**

TO DESCRIBE PAST ACTIONS OR EVENTS

TO TELL WHAT TIME IT WAS WHEN SOMETHING HAPPENED

TO TALK ABOUT YOUR CHILDHOOD

Notes: You may want to refer back to mini-dialogues 2, 3, and 4 on p. 489 for some uses of the imperfect.

Reteach / Extra Help: You may want to reinforce the different uses of the imperfect with a chain drill: *María tenía once años cuando empezó en esta escuela. ¿Cuántos años tenías tú? Eran las cinco cuando me desperté esta mañana. ¿Qué hora era cuando te despertaste tú? Cuando Juan era niño, le gustaba jugar en la arena. ¿Qué hacían tú y tus amigos?*

You have been using the imperfect to describe continuing or regularly occurring actions in the past. Here are some other very common uses.

1 We use the imperfect to give background information or to tell what was going on when something else happened.

Llovía mucho cuando **llegamos** a la playa.
It was raining a lot when we arrived at the beach.

Juana **estudiaba** cuando **sonó** el teléfono.
Juana was studying when the telephone rang.

Descubrieron el tesoro mientras **exploraban** la selva.
They discovered the treasure while they were exploring the jungle.

Anoche **había** mucho tráfico en la carretera.	*Last night **there was** a lot of traffic on the highway.*
Hubo un accidente.	*There was an accident.*
Hubo un accidente porque **había** tanto tráfico.	*There was an accident because **there was** so much traffic.*

Note that we use the imperfect to describe the action that was in progress. We use the preterite to describe the action that occurred while the other one was in progress.

2 We use the imperfect to tell time in the past.

Era la una de la mañana.	*It was one o'clock in the morning.*
Eran las cinco cuando despegó el avión.	*It was five o'clock when the plane took off.*

3 We use the imperfect to tell how old somebody was or to talk about a period in somebody's life.

Cuando yo **tenía dos años** nos mudamos a California.	*When I was two years old, we moved to California.*
Cuando él **era** niño **lloraba** mucho.	*When he was a child, he cried a lot.*

4 We also use the imperfect to describe a physical, mental, or emotional state.

Apagué la calefacción porque **hacía** demasiado **calor.**	*I turned off the heat because it was too hot.*
No comí porque **no tenía hambre.**	*I didn't eat because I wasn't hungry.*
Luis **no quería** acompañarnos al concierto.	*Luis didn't want to go with us to the concert.*
Mi madrina **tenía** ojos azules.	*My godmother had blue eyes.*

5 Here is a summary of the uses of the preterite and imperfect tenses.

PRETERITE	IMPERFECT
Specific action or event that had a definite beginning and end.	1. Continuous activity or condition with no indication of beginning or end.
	2. Activity or event that took place regularly.
	3. Information about what was going on when something else happened.
	4. Telling time in the past.
	5. Telling what someone's age was or about a period in someone's life.
	6. Describing past physical, mental, or emotional states.

PRÁCTICA

Práctica A
1. (a) Miraba las noticias.
   (b) Anunció que un huracán venía.
2. (a) Comíamos.
   (b) Oímos truenos.
3. (a) Escuchaba discos.
   (b) Se cayó por la ventana.
4. (a) Nos peleábamos.
   (b) Gritó ''¡socorro!''
5. (a) Salía corriendo de la casa.
   (b) El helicóptero aterrizó junto al garaje.
6. (a) Llorábamos.
   (b) Los fotógrafos llegaron.

Reteach / Review: After students complete Ex. A either orally or in writing, you may want to ask volunteers to restate each of the six sentences by reversing the clauses so that each sentence begins with *cuando*. Make sure students understand that the meaning does not change if the clause with *cuando* + preterite appears at the beginning of the sentence.

A Durante la tormenta. Juana le cuenta a su primo por teléfono que ayer hubo una tormenta muy fuerte. Pero la línea del teléfono todavía no funciona bien y su primo no oye todo lo que Juana le dice. Sigue el modelo.

> Mirábamos la tele cuando Javier volvió a casa.
> (a) ¿Qué hacían Uds.?   (b) ¿Qué hizo Javier?
>   *Mirábamos la tele.*   *Volvió a casa.*

1. Mi padre miraba las noticias cuando el locutor anunció que un huracán venía.
   (a) ¿Qué hacía tu padre?   (b) ¿Qué hizo el locutor?

2. Mi hermana y yo comíamos cuando oímos truenos.
   (a) ¿Qué hacían Uds.?   (b) ¿Qué oyeron?

3. Laura escuchaba discos cuando el árbol se cayó por la ventana.
   (a) ¿Qué hacía Laura?   (b) ¿Qué le pasó al árbol?

4. Susana y yo nos peleábamos cuando papá gritó ''¡Socorro!''
   (a) ¿Qué hacían Uds.?   (b) ¿Qué hizo tu papá?

5. Mamá salía corriendo de la casa cuando el helicóptero aterrizó junto al garaje.
   (a) ¿Qué hacía tu mamá?   (b) ¿Qué pasó?

6. Todos llorábamos cuando los fotógrafos llegaron.
   (a) ¿Qué hacían?   (b) ¿Quiénes llegaron?

Práctica B
1. ¿Qué hora era cuando la policía capturó al ladrón? Eran las ocho y cuarto.
2. ¿… apagaron las luces? Eran las cuatro.

B ¿Qué hora era? ¿A qué hora ocurrieron estas cosas? Pregunta y contesta según el modelo.

quemarse / el Teatro Juárez
ESTUDIANTE A *¿Qué hora era cuando se quemó el Teatro Juárez?*
ESTUDIANTE B *Eran las 6.*

1. la policía / capturar al ladrón   2. (ellos) / apagar las luces

3. terminar / el concurso
de violín

4. morir / la directora del coro

5. caerse / el puente

6. empezar / el campeonato
de fútbol

7. chocar / los trenes

8. los ayudantes / venir a
buscar sus cheques

9. ocurrir / el terremoto

3. ¿… terminó el concurso de
violín? Eran las once menos
veinte.
4. ¿… murió la directora del
coro? Eran las nueve y
veinte.
5. ¿… se cayó el puente? Eran
las dos menos diez.
6. ¿… empezó el campeonato
de fútbol? Eran las tres.
7. ¿… chocaron los trenes?
Eran las cinco y veinticinco.
8. ¿… los ayudantes vinieron a
buscar sus cheques? Eran
las dos.
9. ¿… ocurrió el terremoto?
Eran las ocho menos cuarto.

C **Cuando íbamos de vacaciones.** Eugenia, una chica argentina,
describe los veranos de su familia. Completa el párrafo con la forma
correcta del imperfecto o del pretérito.

Cuando (yo) *(ser)* niña, mi familia *(pasar)* las vacaciones en la playa
cada verano. En enero y febrero siempre *(hacer)* tanto calor que todo el
mundo *(ir)* allí. Mi familia siempre *(ir)* a un pueblo en el sur, pero un
año (nosotros) *(ir)* a Mar de Plata mientras mi padre *(quedarse)* en
5 Buenos Aires.

Esa vez, mi madre, mis hermanos y yo *(tomar)* el tren a la playa.
¡Qué aventura *(ser)* para nosotros! Durante el viaje mis hermanos
(tocar) la guitarra y *(cantar)* y yo *(jugar)* a los naipes con mamá. En el
tren *(haber)* mucha gente con animales, canastas grandes de comida y
10 bebés que *(llorar)* sin parar. Recuerdo que una vez (ellos) *(parar)* el tren
porque *(haber)* unas vacas en la vía y a causa de eso (nosotros) *(llegar)*
con casi una hora de retraso.

En aquellos años mucha gente *(ir)* de vacaciones por tres meses,
pero nosotros no *(quedarse)* tanto tiempo. Ese verano en Mar de Plata
15 (nosotros) *(vivir)* en una casa con muchas puertas y ventanas, donde
el viento del mar *(entrar)* todo el día. Recuerdo que generalmente
(nosotros) no *(necesitar)* llevar más que un traje de baño. ¡Qué buenos
tiempos *(ser)* aquéllos!

Práctica C
era / pasaba
hacía
iba / iba
fuimos / se quedó
tomamos
fue
tocaban / cantaban / jugaba
había
lloraban / pararon
había (*or:* hubo) / llegamos
iba
nos quedábamos
vivimos
entraba
necesitábamos
eran

D Cuenta. Usa el imperfecto y el pretérito para contar algo que hacías cuando eras niño(a) y algo que hiciste anoche. Usa los verbos de la lista. Por ejemplo: *cantar.*

> *Cuando era niño(a) cantaba en un coro.*
> *Anoche canté en una fiesta.*

beber	dormir	ir	leer	pensar	soñar con
comer	estudiar	jugar	mirar	ser	ver

E Hablemos de ti.
1. ¿A qué escuela ibas cuando eras pequeño(a)? ¿Cómo era tu primera escuela? ¿Por cuántos años fuiste a esa escuela? ¿A cuántas escuelas distintas fuiste? ¿Por qué?
2. ¿Cómo era tu primer(a) profesor(a)?
3. ¿Qué programas veías en la televisión cuando eras pequeño(a)? ¿Veías muchas películas? ¿Qué clase de películas preferías? ¿Ibas al cine? ¿Con quién?
4. Describe una fiesta de familia importante que recuerdas: un cumpleaños, una boda, un bautizo, etcétera. ¿Cuándo fue? ¿A qué hora fue? ¿En qué lugar fue? ¿Quiénes eran los invitados? ¿Qué había para comer? ¿Y para beber?

ACTIVIDAD

Las noticias. Look through a newspaper and cut out three photographs showing events or people in the news. Get together in small groups and take turns telling what was happening when the photographer took the picture.

Un incendio en Chicago

APLICACIONES

Notes: Sample dialogues for the **¿Qué pasa?** appear in the Teacher Notes.

Ganándose la vida   Transparency 52

Todo el mundo tiene que trabajar para ganarse la vida. ¿Qué hay en la planta baja? ¿Quién trabaja allí? ¿Qué hace ella? ¿Quiénes trabajan en los otros pisos? ¿Qué hacen ellos?

Raúl, a university student, is applying for a part-time job. Create a dialogue between him and the interviewer. You may want to use the following words or expressions.

Notes: Remind students that Raúl and the interviewer should address each other as *Ud.*

ahorrar	ganarse la vida	ser capaz
escribir a máquina	graduarse	ser práctico, -a
ganar	por lo menos	tener ambición

Aplicaciones   **509**

EXPLICACIONES II Essential

Notes: Mini-dialogues 1 on p. 488 and 1 and 2 on p. 496 contain examples of some uses of *para*.

◆ **OBJECTIVES:**

TO ASK FOR AND GIVE SUGGESTIONS OR ADVICE

TO TELL WHAT YOU WANT SOMEONE TO DO

TO PREPARE A LIST OF CHORES

TO ASK A FAVOR

Reteach / Extra Help: Reinforce the uses of *para* by asking volunteers to suggest additional examples for each of the five meanings.

Los usos de *para*

Here are some common uses of *para*:

1 "For" (intention):

Mis consejos son **para** Luisa.   *My advice is (intended) **for** Luisa.*

2 "To" or "in order to" (purpose):

Trabajo **para** ganarme la vida.   *I work **(in order) to** earn a living.*

3 "For" (destination):

Mañana salimos **para** Chile.   *Tomorrow we leave **for** Chile.*

4 "By" or "for" a certain time:

Lee el artículo **para** mañana.   *Read the article **for** tomorrow.*
Necesito el resto **para** el martes.   *I need the rest **by** Tuesday.*

5 "For," meaning "considering the fact that" or "compared with":

Para una niña de seis años,   ***For** a six-year-old child, Marta*
Marta es muy capaz.   *is very capable.*

En el lago Titicaca, entre Bolivia y el Perú

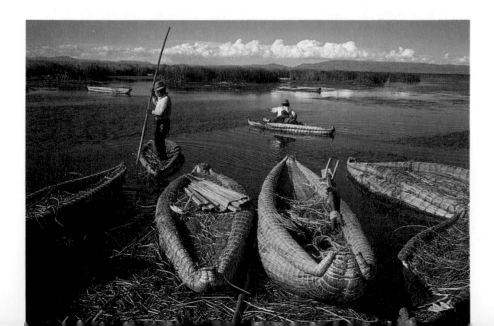

PRÁCTICA

A ¿Para quién? Imagina que trabajas en una librería y ayudas a tus clientes a decidir qué libros deben regalar. Escoge el libro más apropiado para cada persona. Pregunta y contesta según el modelo.

Práctica A
1. Busco algo para una abogada.
   ¿Por qué no le compra *El derecho comercial*?
2. … un antropólogo.
   ¿… *La civilización antigua de los aztecas*?

un millonario
ESTUDIANTE A *Busco algo para un millonario.*
ESTUDIANTE B *¿Por qué no le compra* Cómo gastar dinero y ahorrarlo al mismo tiempo?

1. una abogada	5. un ortodoncista
2. un antropólogo	6. una mujer de negocios
3. una secretaria	7. un explorador
4. una programadora	8. una farmacéutica

3. …una secretaria.
   ¿… *Cómo escribir a máquina 100 palabras por minuto*?
4. … una programadora.
   ¿… *La computadora del siglo XXI*?
5. … un ortodoncista.
   ¿… *Sonríe sin miedo*?
6. … una mujer de negocios.
   ¿… *Los clientes siempre tienen razón*?
7. … un explorador.
   ¿… *Hernando de Soto, descubridor del Misisipí*?
8. … una farmacéutica.
   ¿… *Pastillas nuevas para el resfriado*?

Práctica B

Quiero que empiecen el dibujo de la patinadora para esta tarde.

Quiero que coloquen las esculturas en el patio para mañana.

Quiero que repasen los apuntes sobre Velázquez para el viernes.

Quiero que visiten la galería de arte moderno para este fin de semana.

Quiero que comiencen la biografía de Goya para la semana próxima.

Quiero que compren pinceles nuevos para el lunes.

Quiero que estudien para la prueba sobre el arte abstracto para el miércoles.

Quiero que escojan el tema del mural para el fin del mes.

B ¿Para cuándo?   La profesora de arte les da un horario a sus estudiantes. ¿Para cuándo quiere que hagan cada tarea? Sigue el modelo.

Quiero que terminen el retrato de los bailarines para hoy.

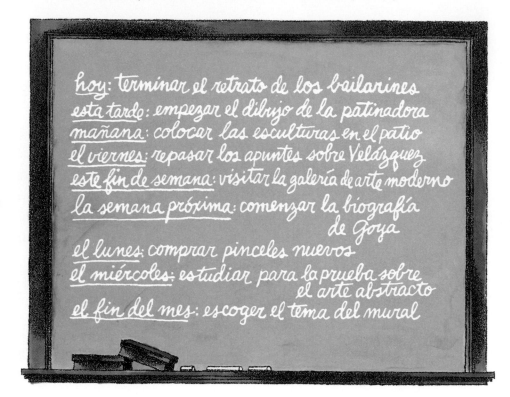

hoy: terminar el retrato de los bailarines
esta tarde: empezar el dibujo de la patinadora
mañana: colocar las esculturas en el patio
el viernes: repasar los apuntes sobre Velázquez
este fin de semana: visitar la galería de arte moderno
la semana próxima: comenzar la biografía de Goya
el lunes: comprar pinceles nuevos
el miércoles: estudiar para la prueba sobre el arte abstracto
el fin del mes: escoger el tema del mural

Práctica C

1. g. Por favor, ¿puedes ir por el banco para cobrar este cheque?
2. d
3. f
4. h
5. c
6. a
7. b
8. e

C Por favor.   Cuando Pilar sale de casa su mamá siempre le pide que haga algo para ella. ¿Por qué quiere su mamá que vaya por esos lugares? Sigue el modelo.

la cancha de tenis
Por favor, ¿puedes ir por la cancha de tenis para buscar mi raqueta?

1. el banco
2. la tienda de ropa
3. la tienda de comestibles
4. la peluquería
5. el correo
6. la farmacia
7. la estación de servicio
8. la biblioteca

a. recoger mi medicina
b. llenar el tanque
c. mandar esta carta certificada
d. devolver estos pantalones
e. sacar una novela policíaca
f. comprar una docena de huevos
g. cobrar este cheque
h. averiguar la hora de mi cita
i. buscar mi raqueta

D ¿Por o para? Completa las siguientes frases con *para* o *por*.

1. ¿_____ cuándo lo necesitas? Lo necesito _____ mañana _____ la tarde.
2. Este anciano tiene _____ lo menos 85 años pero va a la oficina cinco días _____ semana.
3. Será difícil _____ mí pagar a Mariana lo que le debo.
4. Luis vino _____ la casa _____ pedirme consejos.
5. Decidí hacer una expedición _____ las islas _____ varios días _____ ver los volcanes.
6. Quisiera comprar algo práctico _____ un hombre de negocios que va a viajar _____ el África.
7. ¿_____ dónde entró el ladrón? _____ la ventana del baño.
8. Antes de salir _____ el aeropuerto, ¿por qué no llamas a tu tía _____ teléfono?
9. _____ un joven de diecisiete años, Jorge es muy ambicioso.
10. El chico se lastimó _____ no mirar _____ dónde caminaba.

E Hablemos de ti.

1. Cuando vas a la escuela, ¿por dónde vas? Y cuando regresas, ¿vas por los mismos lugares?
2. ¿Trabajaste durante el verano pasado? ¿Dónde? ¿Para quién? ¿Por cuánto tiempo? ¿Trabajas ahora? ¿Cuánto dinero ganas por hora o por semana?
3. ¿Te gusta hacer cosas para tus amigos? ¿Qué clase de cosas haces para ellos?
4. Escoge un objeto y explica para qué es. Por ejemplo: un taxi es para llevar gente de una parte de la ciudad a otra.

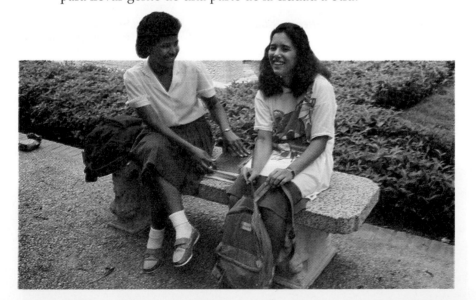

Práctica D
1. Para / para / por
2. por / por
3. para
4. por / para
5. por / por / para
6. para / por
7. Por / por
8. para / por
9. Para
10. por / por

Práctica E
Answers will vary.

Practice Sheet 15–6

Workbook Exs. G–J

Tape Manual Exs. 8–9 🔲 12

Refrán 🔲 13

Canción 🔲 14

Quiz 15–5

En una plaza en Ponce, Puerto Rico

APLICACIONES

Notes: Answers to the **Repaso** and **Tema** appear in the Teacher Notes.

REPASO

Notes: Review of:
1. preterite of *hacer* / *dar* / *ir*
   expressions with *hacer* / *dar* / *ir*
   prepositional phrases with
   por and *en*
2. adverbs of frequency
   imperfect
   para + infinitive
3. time expressions
   imperfect
   preterite of *ver*
   imperfect vs. preterite
   imperfect of *ser* / *estar*
   absolute superlatives
4. imperfect
   demonstrative adjectives
   ya no
   indirect object pronouns
5. preterite
   adjective agreement
   meanings of *en*

Enrichment: You may want
to use the model sentences in
the **Repaso** for dictation.

Mira con cuidado las frases modelo. Luego cambia las frases que siguen al español, según los modelos.

1. *El verano pasado hicimos un viaje por Venezuela.*
   (Last week I went for a walk through the city.)
   (Last October he went fishing in the sea.)
   (Last winter I had a barbecue in the mountains.)

2. *A veces pedían helicópteros nuevos para visitar los sitios.*
   (We usually rented young horses to go up the volcano.)
   (Sometimes there wasn't enough cotton to make bandages.)
   (She always wore comfortable sandals to cross the desert.)

3. *Ayer caminábamos por el parque cuando vimos unos loros. ¡Eran bellísimos!*
   (This morning I was running next to the lake when I saw a jaguar. It was terribly dangerous!)
   (Last week she was traveling through the desert when she saw the anthropologists. They were extremely thin!)
   (Last night we were looking through the window when we saw the ambulance. We were (estar) terribly worried!)

4. *"Había muchos millonarios en este barrio, pero ya no," me dijo el guía.*
   ("I used to know a lot of scientists at that university, but not anymore," the assistant told them.)
   ("There used to be too many flies in this restaurant, but not anymore," the manager told her.)
   ("I used to see several patients at that clinic, but not anymore," the orthodontist told him.)

5. *Ahorró varios dólares pero gastó la mayoría del dinero en regalos.*
   (She earned a lot of money but bought most of her clothes on sale.)
   (We got enough schedules and asked for a one-way ticket at the ticket window.)
   (I cashed several checks and spent half of my salary on food.)

Un jaguar en Colombia

TEMA

Escribe las frases en español.

1. Last year I went on an expedition through the jungle.

2. We generally used small canoes to explore the river.

3. One day we were going along the river when we saw a turtle. It was extremely large!

4. "We used to see more turtles in this place, but not anymore," the explorer told us.

5. We took some pictures and made the rest of the trip by helicopter.

REDACCIÓN

Ahora escoge uno de los siguientes temas para escribir tu propio diálogo o párrafo.

1. Create a set of talk balloons for pictures 1 through 5 from the point of view of one of the other members of the expedition.

2. Write a paragraph about a trip you took. Where did you go and with whom? For how many days? What did you do and see? Would you like to do it again?

3. Write a paragraph about an important event that took place when you were a child. What happened? How old were you then? When and where did the event take place?

Notes: Answers to the **Comprueba** appear in the Teacher Notes.

A   En la selva

Usa palabras de la siguiente lista para completar el párrafo.

arqueólogos	expedición	húmedo
canoas	explorar	loros
capaz	helicóptero	práctico

El verano pasado un grupo de _____ de la universidad hizo una _____ a la selva. Todos soñaban con descubrir y _____ el sitio de una civilización antigua. Primero viajaron en _____. El piloto era un hombre muy _____ y conocía muy bien la selva. Después navegaron por el río en _____. En los árboles veían monos, serpientes y bellos _____ de muchos colores. El clima era muy _____. Llovía todos los días. Pero todo el mundo era muy _____. Llevaba botas e impermeable.

B   La expedición

Haz frases en el imperfecto.

1. ¿Quién (*ser*) la exploradora en el cuento?
2. Cada día los ayudantes (*ir*) a la selva.
3. A menúdo (nosotros) (*ver*) algo misterioso.
4. ¿(*Ir*) (tú) frecuentemente a Machu Picchu?
5. Todos los días (ellos) (*ver*) muchos animales diferentes en la selva.
6. (*Haber*) jaguares pero generalmente (*ser*) muy viejos y flacos.
7. Yo (*ver*) tortugas en la arena.

C   ¿El imperfecto o el pretérito?

Completa las frases con el pretérito o el imperfecto de los verbos entre paréntesis.

1. Yo siempre (*manejar*) por la noche.
2. Anoche (*haber*) un partido en la universidad.
3. Todos los días (yo) (*ir*) en tren porque no (*haber*) mucha gente.
4. Mi madre me (*acompañar*) cada vez que (yo) (*ir*) de compras.
5. El año pasado (tú) (*explorar*) ese sitio, ¿no?
6. Por mucho tiempo mis nietos (*soñar*) con ser arquitectos.

7. Todos los jugadores (*reunirse*) anteayer para hacer planes.
8. Cuando (yo) (*ser*) niña, nunca (*tener*) celos.
9. (*Ser*) las siete de la mañana cuando (nosotros) (*oír*) el ruido del helicóptero.

D   ¿Qué quieren ser?

Indica si las siguientes frases son verdaderas o falsas. Si son falsas, corrígelas (*correct them*).

1. Hay que estudiar derecho si quieres ser arquitecto.
2. La persona que prepara las medicinas que receta el médico es el farmacéutico.
3. Ana quiere ser jefa porque le interesa estudiar las civilizaciones antiguas.
4. Los abogados tienen que pasar muchas horas en el laboratorio.
5. Una dentista que pone aparatos en los dientes es una ortodoncista.
6. Mario quiere tener mucho dinero, y por eso sueña con ser ayudante.

E   ¿Por o para?

Completa las frases. Usa *por* o *para*.

1. ¿Por qué fuiste al estadio? ¡_____ aceptar el gran premio!
2. Necesitas trabajar _____ ganarte la vida.
3. ¿Estudias mucho _____ ambición o sólo _____ ganar dinero?
4. ¿Necesitas el resto de las cintas _____ hoy o _____ mañana?
5. Necesitas practicar mucho _____ ser capaz de hacer eso.
6. ¿Puedes ir a la tienda _____ mí? Tengo mucho trabajo _____ mañana.
7. Durante el viaje _____ España tomamos un tren _____ Sevilla.
8. _____ cruzar el río era necesario ir _____ el puente.
9. _____ una persona que no es muy práctica en su propio negocio, puede aconsejar bastante bien a los otros. Me dio consejos muy buenos _____ ahorrar dinero.

Activity Masters   Chapter 15 Test   🔲 Listening Comprehension Test

VOCABULARIO DEL CAPÍTULO 15

Sustantivos
el abogado, la abogada
la ambición, *pl.* las ambiciones
el antropólogo, la antropóloga
el aparato
la arena
el/la ayudante
la canoa
el científico, la científica
el clima
el consejo
el derecho
el desierto
la expedición, *pl.* las
    expediciones
el explorador, la exploradora
el farmacéutico, la farmacéutica
el helicóptero
el hombre de negocios
el jaguar
el jefe, la jefa
el loro
el millonario, la millonaria
la mitad
la mujer de negocios
el negocio
el/la ortodoncista
el programador / la programadora
    (de computadoras)
el resto
el secretario, la secretaria
la selva
el sitio
el sueldo
el sueño
la tortuga
la universidad
el volcán, *pl.* los volcanes

Adjetivos
ambicioso, -a
bastante *(enough)*
capaz, *pl.* capaces
demasiado, -a
húmedo, -a
misterioso, -a
práctico, -a
propio, -a

Adverbio
bastante *(enough)*

Preposición
para *(by)*

Verbos
aceptar
acompañar
aconsejar
ahorrar
deber *(to owe)*
decidir
explorar
ganar *(to earn)*
graduarse
soñar (o → ue) con
hubo

Expresiones
ganarse la vida
hacer una expedición
por lo menos
quedarse sin
¡socorro!

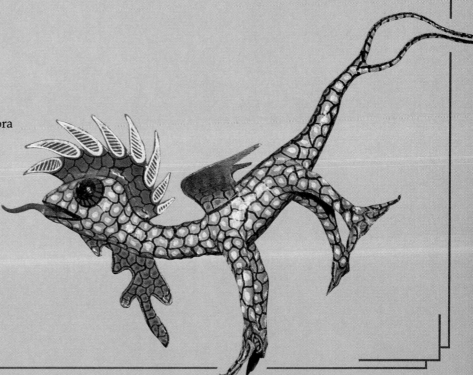

PRÓLOGO CULTURAL

¡QUE TENGAS BUENA SUERTE!

Do you carry a silver dollar or wear your birthstone? Do you avoid walking under ladders or putting a hat on a bed? You probably don't pay much attention to the superstition that associates black cats with bad luck. But people once believed that evil spirits sometimes disguised themselves that way, and it was definitely bad luck to own one. In parts of Latin America, however, though it may be considered bad luck if a black cat crosses your path, it is good luck if someone gives you a black cat.

What are some other tokens of good luck in Latin America? A horseshoe *(una herradura)*—but only if it has seven nail holes—or finding a four-leaf clover *(un trébol de cuatro hojas)* is considered as lucky there as it is in the United States. Other good omens include accidentally spilling wine on a tablecloth or drinking the last drop from a bottle of wine. *Capicúas*, numbers that read the same from left to right or from right to left—for example, 24642—are especially lucky. In Spain, if the bus ticket you buy in the morning has a *capicúa*, you're bound to have a good day, and a lottery ticket with a *capicúa* is considered a sure thing.

Sometimes you have to work a little for your luck. When two people say the same thing at the same time, one of them may be lucky. In Argentina when this occurs, the good luck goes to the first person to touch the other one's elbow. In Nicaragua, the luck belongs to the first one to say *"Suerte para mí."*

On the other hand, whatever the superstition, most people everywhere will usually agree with the old saying, *la suerte es ciega.*

PALABRAS NUEVAS I

Essential

Transparency 54

¿Crees o dudas?

If students ask: Other related words you may want to present: *despreocupado, -a,* carefree; *furioso, -a,* angry; *cuidadoso, -a,* careful; *descuidado, -a,* careless.

CONTEXTO VISUAL

supersticioso, -a

obstinado, -a

tener vergüenza

orgulloso, -a

enojado, -a

CONTEXTO COMUNICATIVO

1 MATEO ¡Qué niño!
ANITA ¿Por qué **te enojas** con él?
MATEO Porque **miente** tanto.
ANITA **Vamos,** Mateo. **Ten paciencia** con él.

Variaciones:
- miente tanto → dice tantas **mentiras**
- miente tanto → siempre **está de mal humor**
- miente tanto → cree en demasiadas **supersticiones**
- ten paciencia → sé paciente

enojarse (con) *to be / get angry (at)*

mentir (e → ie) *to lie*

vamos here: *come on*

tener paciencia *to be patient*

la mentira *lie*

estar de buen / mal humor *to be in a good / bad mood*

la superstición, pl. **las supersticiones** *superstition*

---

2 SILVIA   ¿Cómo está mi mamá hoy, doctor? ¿**Sufre** mucho?

    DOCTOR   Está mucho mejor, Silvia. No **te preocupes.**

    SILVIA   ¿Cuándo sale del hospital?

    DOCTOR   **Dentro de** una semana.

  ■ te preocupes → hay problemas

sufrir   *to suffer*

preocuparse (por)   *to worry (about)*

dentro de   here: *within*

---

3 PABLO   **Dudo** que ganemos el partido del viernes.

    NORMA   ¿Qué pasa ahora?

    PABLO   **Temo** que Rodolfo no pueda jugar. Se lastimó la rodilla.

    NORMA   **Siento** que Uds. tengan tantos problemas.

  ■ la rodilla → el tobillo
  ■ tantos problemas → tanta mala suerte

dudar   *to doubt*

temer   *to fear, to be afraid*

sentir (e → ie)   *to be sorry*

---

4 ANA   **Me alegro de** que mi hijo saque tan buenas notas.

    OLGA   Sí, debes estar muy orgullosa de él.

    ANA   No lo puedo **negar.** Estoy muy feliz.

  ■ no lo puedo negar → no puedo decir que no
  ■ feliz → contenta

alegrarse (de)   *to be happy (about)*

negar (e → ie)   *to deny*

---

5 ELISA   ¿Te importa que Carlos venga al centro con nosotros?

    MARIO   No, al contrario. Él es muy amable y parece tener un gran **sentido del humor.**

    ELISA   Sí. Es una **lástima** que sólo se quede tres días aquí.

  ■ importa → molesta
  ■ venga al centro con nosotros → nos acompañe

el sentido del humor   *sense of humor*

la lástima   *shame, pity*

6 ANITA ¿Laura? Me **sorprende** verte aquí. Creía que estabas **de viaje** en Florida.

LAURA Con sólo cuatro días de vacaciones, **no valía la pena** viajar tan lejos.

- me sorprende → **qué alegría**
- me sorprende → qué sorpresa
- me sorprende → no esperaba
- estabas de viaje en → viajabas por

sorprender *to surprise*
de viaje *on a trip*
valer la pena *to be worth the effort, to be worth it*

¡qué alegría! *how nice! how marvelous!*

PRÁCTICA

Práctica A
1. No tiene sentido del humor.
2. Dice una mentira.
3. No tiene sentido del humor.
4. No está segura.
5. Es supersticioso.
6. Está de buen humor.
7. Dice una mentira.
8. No está segura.

Reteach / Extra Help: After students do Ex. A, you may want to assign it as written homework, asking students to make up their own sentences to illustrate each of the five expressions.

A **¿Qué es?** Raúl y Clara están en el hotel de su tío y hablan de la gente que conocen allí. Escoge una de las siguientes frases para describir a cada persona.

Dice una mentira.
Es supersticioso(a).
Está de buen humor.

No está seguro(a).
No tiene sentido del humor.

1. Es una lástima que al cartero no le gusten los chistes.
2. El tío de Domingo dice que tiene 35 años, pero tiene 42.
3. El salvavidas no quiere que le tomemos el pelo.
4. La Srta. Mendoza no sabe si vale la pena quedarse en este hotel.
5. El gerente nunca abre el paraguas dentro de una habitación.
6. El niño de los Valdés está sonriendo a todo el mundo.
7. Graciela dice que limpió las habitaciones, pero no lo hizo.
8. Esa señora no sabe dónde dejó la llave de su maleta.

Tres jóvenes venezolanos en Caracas

B Me enojo mucho cuando . . .   Habla con un(a) compañero(a) sobre cómo te sientes cuando ocurren algunas cosas. Por ejemplo:

> me enojo mucho
> ESTUDIANTE A *Me enojo mucho cuando llego tarde al cine.*
> ESTUDIANTE B *Pues yo me enojo cuando pierdo mis llaves.*

Reteach / Review: Before students begin Ex. B, you may want to remind them that *doler* functions like *gustar*.

Práctica B
Answers will vary.

1. estoy contento(a)	dar una vuelta en (el carrusel, etcétera)
2. estoy de mal humor	
3. tengo vergüenza	dolerme (los oídos, etcétera)
4. me preocupo mucho	estar a dieta
5. me siento orgulloso(a)	estar con gente (que no conozco, etcétera)
6. estoy de buen humor	
7. me alegro	estar de viaje / de compras
8. me sorprende mucho	ganar (un premio, etcétera)
9. sufro mucho	llegar a tiempo / tarde a (una función, etcétera)
10. me enojo mucho	
11. siento mucho	mentir a (mis amigos, etcétera)
12. me quejo	nadar en (el mar, etcétera)
	perder (un partido, etcétera)
	sentirme bien / mal

C Bienvenida, Lucía.   Cuando Lucía volvió de sus vacaciones, encontró una nota de María, la joven con quien comparte un apartamento. Usa las siguientes palabras y expresiones para completar la nota.

Práctica C
¡Qué alegría!
dudo
te preocupes
te sientas
valía la pena
Ten paciencia
niega
enojada
Me alegro de

dudo	niega	te sientas
enojada	qué alegría	ten paciencia
me alegro de	te preocupes	valía la pena

Lucía:

¡ ____! Por fin regresas. Espero estar aquí cuando llegues, pero tenemos mucho trabajo en la oficina, y ____ que pueda volver a tiempo. Pero no ____. Mañana es sábado y vamos a tener todo el día
5 para hablar. Espero que ____ mejor después de tus vacaciones y que tengas muchas cosas que contarme. Tengo ganas de viajar también, pero no voy a poder hacerlo antes de noviembre. Cuando le dije a mi jefe que quería ir de vacaciones a la playa, me dijo que no ____ ir a la playa en el verano porque siempre está llena de gente. "¿Ud. cree que
10 es mejor ir en el invierno?" le pregunté. "____," me dijo. "Pronto vas a tener tus vacaciones." Él ____ que me prometió dos semanas de vacaciones en agosto. ¡Imagínate! Estoy tan ____ que pienso buscar otro trabajo.

____ tenerte aquí otra vez. Nos vemos esta noche.

15 María

D Hablemos de ti.

1. ¿Eres supersticioso(a)? ¿Por qué sí o por qué no? ¿En qué supersticiones crees?
2. ¿Te preocupas por muchas cosas? ¿Por cuáles? ¿Te preocupas por otras personas? ¿Por quiénes? ¿Por qué?
3. ¿Tienes paciencia con otras personas? ¿Cuándo eres impaciente? ¿Cuándo te enojas? ¿Con quiénes te enojas?
4. ¿Eres obstinado(a)? ¿Cuándo eres obstinado(a)? ¿Eres obstinado(a) cuando discutes? ¿Sigues discutiendo aun *(even)* cuando sabes que no tienes razón?
5. ¿De qué estás orgulloso(a)?
6. En tu opinión, ¿qué cosas valen la pena en la vida? ¿Y qué cosas no valen la pena? ¿Por qué?

ACTIVIDAD

¿Quién sabe? Write down two or three situations that people will respond to with expressions of feeling, such as *Gerardo sigue negando que mintió* or *Me voy a casar mañana.*

Then, in small groups, take turns reading your sentences. After each one, the others should break out in appropriate expressions of grief, amazement, irritation, and so on. Here are some expressions you might use:

¿De veras?	¡Por supuesto!	¡Qué lástima!
¡Felicidades!	¡Qué alegría!	¡Qué lata!
¡Increíble!	¡Qué alivio!	¡Qué suerte!
Lo siento.	¡Qué bueno!	¡Qué susto!
¡No me digas!	¡Qué chistoso!	¿Quién sabe?
No vale la pena.	¿Qué importa?	¡Socorro!

Dos amigas en Puerto Rico

DIÁLOGO

APLICACIONES

Discretionary

No creo en las supersticiones

4

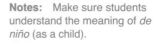

5 Pronunciación

Notes: Make sure students understand the meaning of *de niño* (as a child).

Bernardo y Margarita hablan mientras salen de la escuela.

BERNARDO ¡No camines por debajo de esa escalera![1] Trae mala suerte.

MARGARITA ¡Qué supersticioso eres!

BERNARDO No me creas si no quieres. Pero esta mañana un gato negro cruzó delante de mí, y cuando la Profesora Silva me hizo preguntas en clase yo no sabía las respuestas.

MARGARITA Vamos, Bernardo. ¿No tienes vergüenza? No podías responder porque hablabas con Juan y no prestabas atención.

BERNARDO ¡Yo siempre presto atención! Por eso siempre gano cuando jugamos al ajedrez.

MARGARITA ¡Mientes! Tú ganas porque aprendiste de niño a jugar. Oye, ¿jugamos un partido mañana?

BERNARDO ¡Estás loca! Mañana es martes 13.

MARGARITA ¡No me digas que crees en eso también!

BERNARDO Recuerda el dicho,[2] "El martes ni te cases ni te embarques."[3] Tú sabes que el martes es día de mala suerte. Y si es martes 13, ¡peor!*

---

[1]**la escalera** here: *ladder* [2]**el dicho** *saying* [3]**embarcarse** *to set sail*

* In Hispanic countries it is Tuesday—not Friday—the thirteenth that is considered to be unlucky.

Preguntas

1. ¿Por dónde no quiere Bernardo que camine Margarita? ¿Por qué?
2. Según Bernardo, ¿por qué no podía contestar las preguntas que le hizo la profesora? ¿Y según Margarita? ¿Qué crees tú?   3. ¿Por qué no quiere Bernardo jugar al ajedrez al día siguiente?   4. ¿Cuál es el dicho que repite Bernardo? ¿Conoces algunos otros dichos o refranes (*proverbs*) en español? ¿Cuáles?   5. ¿Cuáles son los equivalentes de estos dichos y refranes en inglés? "Las paredes oyen." "Escoba nueva barre bien." "Más vale tarde que nunca." "Ver para creer." "Querer es poder." "Más vale pájaro en mano que ciento volando."

Participación

Working with a partner, make up a dialogue about one or two superstitions you know of.

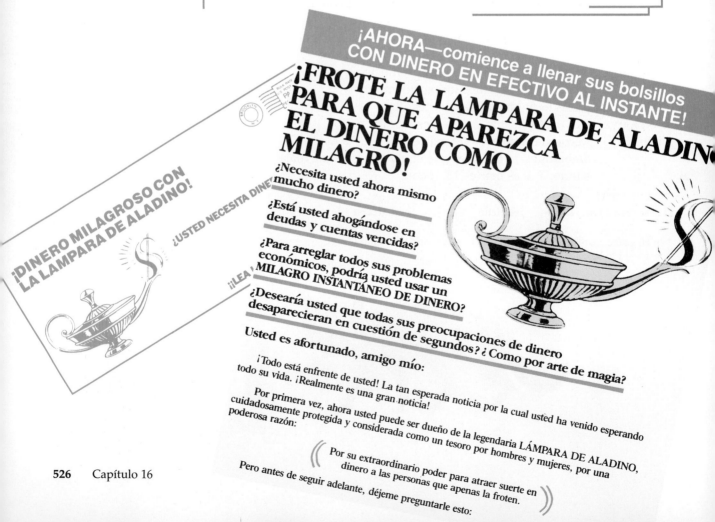

¡AHORA—comience a llenar sus bolsillos CON DINERO EN EFECTIVO AL INSTANTE!

¡FROTE LA LÁMPARA DE ALADINO PARA QUE APAREZCA EL DINERO COMO MILAGRO!

¿Necesita usted ahora mismo mucho dinero?

¿Está usted ahogándose en deudas y cuentas vencidas?

¿Para arreglar todos sus problemas económicos, podría usted usar un MILAGRO INSTANTÁNEO DE DINERO?

¿Desearía usted que todas sus preocupaciones de dinero desaparecieran en cuestión de segundos? ¿Como por arte de magia?

Usted es afortunado, amigo mío:

¡Todo está enfrente de usted! La tan esperada noticia por la cual usted ha venido esperando todo su vida. ¡Realmente es una gran noticia!

Por primera vez, ahora usted puede ser dueño de la legendaria LÁMPARA DE ALADINO, cuidadosamente protegida y considerada como un tesoro por hombres y mujeres, por una poderosa razón:

Por su extraordinario poder para atraer suerte en dinero a las personas que apenas la froten.

Pero antes de seguir adelante, déjeme preguntarle esto:

¡DINERO MILAGROSO CON LA LÁMPARA DE ALADINO!

¿USTED NECESITA DINE

¡¡LEA

PALABRAS NUEVAS II

Essential

📼 6

Transparency 55

CONTEXTO VISUAL

En el aeropuerto

If students ask: Other related words you may want to present: *la cabina,* cockpit; *caer,* to crash; *la caída,* crash.

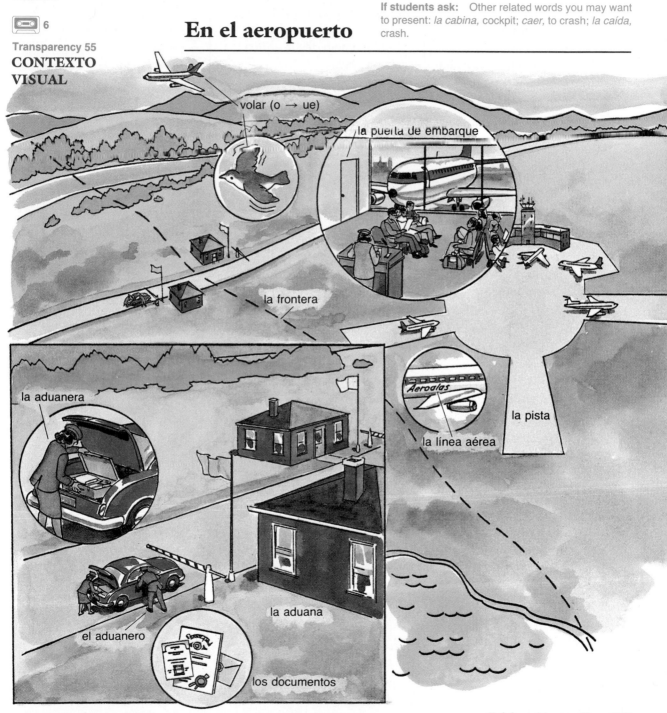

volar (o → ue)

la puerta de embarque

la frontera

la aduanera

la línea aérea

la pista

el aduanero

la aduana

los documentos

1   ALICIA   Nicolás, trata de obtener boletos para un vuelo **sin escala.**

      NICOLÁS   Ya lo **intenté,** Alicia. El único vuelo desde aquí a Buenos Aires **hace escala** en Dallas.

Variaciones:
- trata de → intenta
- trata de obtener → espero que obtengas

la escala	*stopover*
sin escala	*nonstop*
intentar = tratar de	
hacer escala	*to make a stopover (planes)*

2   ADUANERA   ¿Tiene Ud. algo que **declarar,** señor?

      SR. ORÚS   Sólo unos regalos para mis hijos.

      ADUANERA   ¿Le importa abrir las maletas? Debo **registrar** su equipaje.

- hijos → parientes
- ¿le importa . . . ? → tenga la bondad de
- registrar su equipaje → registrarlas

declarar	*to declare (at customs)*
registrar	*to check, to inspect*

3   INÉS   Guillermo me dijo que perdiste tu pasaporte, **¿es cierto?**

      PEDRO   Sí. Lo busqué **por todas partes** pero no lo encontré.

- cierto → **verdad**
- encontré → hallé

cierto, -a	*certain*
es cierto	*it's true*
(por / en) todas partes	*everywhere*
es verdad	*it's true*

4   EMILIA   Ahora dicen que el avión va a salir con retraso.

      ALBERTO   ¿Cuánto es **la demora**?

      EMILIA   Es **posible** que pasemos todo el día aquí.

      ALBERTO   ¡Pero eso es **imposible**! ¡Tenemos que estar en Madrid antes de las ocho!

      EMILIA   No te enojes, Alberto. Eso no cambiará nada.

- con retraso → tarde
- posible → **probable**
- te enojes → vale la pena enojarse

la demora	*delay*
posible	*possible*
imposible	*impossible*
probable	*probable*

5 SILVIA   Es **improbable** que veamos a Carlos esta noche.

SIMÓN   ¿Por qué lo dices?

SILVIA   Él está muy **extraño** estos días. Nunca hace lo que promete.

- es improbable → no creo
- nunca hace lo que promete → cambia de idea
  continuamente

improbable *improbable*

extraño, -a *strange*

continuamente *continually*

PRÁCTICA

A   **En la agencia de viajes.**   El Sr. Ortiz va a la agencia de viajes para comprar un boleto a Barranquilla, Colombia. Lee las preguntas y busca las respuestas en la columna de la derecha.

1. Quiero ir a Barranquilla, pero no sé si debo ir en avión o en barco. ¿Qué recomienda?
2. ¿Qué línea aérea va a Barranquilla?
3. Ése es un vuelo sin escala, ¿verdad?
4. ¿Tiene un asiento junto a la ventanilla?
5. ¿Y allí en la aduana registran las maletas?
6. ¿Tengo que declarar la cámara?
7. ¿A qué hora tengo que estar en la puerta de embarque?

a. Sí, queda uno.
b. A las 3:45.
c. Sólo si es nueva.
d. Es mejor que vuele, señor.
e. Lo siento, pero hace escala en Bogotá por 25 minutos.
f. Aero-Colombia tiene un vuelo a las 4:30.
g. Sólo si tiene algo que declarar.

Práctica A
1. d
2. f
3. e
4. a
5. g
6. c
7. b

En el aeropuerto de Santiago, Chile

Práctica B
1. escala / imposible
2. extraño
3. posible
4. pista
5. improbable
6. demoras
7. registren

B **¡Tengo prisa!** Leonardo siempre tiene prisa, por eso prefiere volar. Se siente muy nervioso si hay una demora. Escoge la palabra o frase correcta.

1. Intenté comprar boletos sin *(vergüenza / escala)* pero fue *(posible / imposible)*.
2. Me parece *(extraño / expreso)* que ninguna línea aérea vuele directamente desde aquí hasta Medellín.
3. Date prisa, Marta, o es *(posible / imposible)* que el avión salga sin nosotros.
4. Espero que no pasemos mucho tiempo en la *(demora / pista)* antes de despegar.
5. Con tanta nieve y hielo, es *(cierto / improbable)* que el avión despegue pronto.
6. Después de tantas *(líneas aéreas / demoras)*, estoy seguro de que vamos a llegar muy tarde.
7. ¿Es posible que los aduaneros *(registren / declaren)* mi bolso?

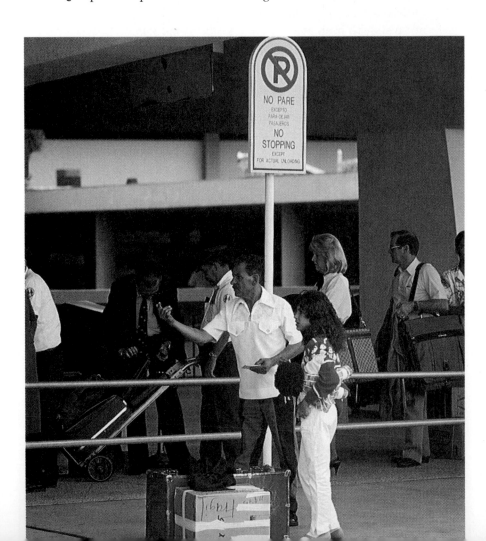

En el aeropuerto de
San Juan, Puerto Rico

C Hablemos de ti.

1. ¿Vives cerca de una frontera? ¿Cuál? ¿Qué documentos necesitas generalmente para cruzar una frontera?
2. ¿Qué documentos de identificación tienes? ¿Para qué son? ¿Tienes pasaporte?
3. La última vez que fuiste de vacaciones, ¿cruzaste una frontera? ¿Cuál? ¿Había una aduana? ¿Qué te pidieron?
4. ¿Te gusta volar? ¿O prefieres viajar en coche, en tren o en autobús? ¿Por qué?
5. Imagina que vuelas entre Nueva York y Los Ángeles, y que la línea aérea te ofrece hacer escala en otra ciudad. ¿Qué ciudad te gustaría visitar? ¿Por qué?
6. ¿Te enojas cuando hay demoras o tienes mucha paciencia? ¿Qué clase de demora te molesta más? ¿Qué haces cuando hay una demora?

ESTUDIO DE PALABRAS

In Spanish the prefix *in-* often means "not": *in* + *cómodo* = "uncomfortable" or "not comfortable." Just as in English, *in-* becomes *im-* before words beginning with *b* or *p*: *imposible, improbable, impaciente*. The prefix *in-* / *im-* corresponds to these English prefixes: *un-* (unhappy), *im-* (impossible), *ir-* (irregular), or *il-* (illogical). What do you think these words mean?

inactivo   incapaz   infeliz   insuficiente   impagable

Sinónimos

Cambia las palabras en cursiva por sinónimos.
1. Miguel no *tiene miedo de* los gatos negros.
2. ¿Es *cierto* que hay una demora de dos horas?
3. *Trataré* de alquilar un coche.

Antónimos

Cambia las palabras en cursiva por antónimos.
1. Es *probable* que Juan llame.
2. Él nunca *dice la verdad*.
3. Es *imposible* volar cuando hace mal tiempo.

Familias de palabras

Escribe frases usando verbos parecidos a cada una de estas palabras.

1. sorpresa	3. alegría	5. enojado
2. mentira	4. preocupado	6. vuelo

Práctica C
Answers will vary.

Practice Sheet 16–2

Workbook Exs. C–D

Tape Manual Exs. 3–4   8

Refrán   9

Quiz 16–2

Enrichment: In connection with the **Estudio de palabras**, you may want to elicit the meanings of these unfamiliar cognates: *ilegal, imperfecto, incompleto, inapropiado* (illegal, imperfect, incomplete, inappropriate).

Estudio de palabras
inactive / incapable / unhappy / insufficient / unpayable

Sinónimos
1. teme
2. verdad
3. Intentaré

Antónimos
1. improbable
2. miente
3. posible

Familia de palabras
Sentences will vary.
1. sorprender   4. preocuparse
2. mentir   5. enojarse
3. alegrarse de   6. volar

EXPLICACIONES I Essential

Notes: Mini-dialogues 3, 4, and 5 on p. 521 contain examples of the subjunctive after verbs and expressions of emotion.

◆ **OBJECTIVES:**

TO EXPRESS REGRET, FEAR, AND WORRY

TO EXPRESS PRIDE, PLEASURE, AND SURPRISE

TO EXPRESS ANNOYANCE OR ANGER

TO SAY THAT SOMETHING BOTHERS YOU

El subjuntivo con expresiones de emoción

You have been using the subjunctive after verbs or expressions of wishing, wanting, and hoping and when we ask, insist, or recommend that someone do something. We also use the subjunctive after verbs and expressions that indicate emotions such as regret, fear, surprise, anger, or pleasure.

Siento que trabajes hoy.	*I'm sorry you're working* today.
Temo que ellos se enojen.	*I'm afraid they'll get angry.*
Me alegro de que Uds. vengan a la boda.	*I'm glad you're coming* to the *wedding.*

1 Remember that sentences with the subjunctive usually have two parts with two different subjects. When there is only one subject we usually use the infinitive.

Siento llegar tan tarde.	*I'm sorry to arrive* so late.
Se alegran de ir al bautismo.	*They're happy about going* to the *baptism.*

2 Many expressions of emotion are formed with *estar* + adjective. For example:

$$estar \begin{cases} contento \\ enojado \\ orgulloso \\ preocupado \end{cases} + \begin{cases} de\ que + subjunctive \\ de + infinitive \end{cases}$$

Estoy contento de que estés aquí.	*I'm happy you're* here.
Estoy contento de estar aquí.	*I'm happy to be* here.
Estamos orgullosos de que ella saque tan buenas notas.	*We're proud she's getting* such good grades.
Estamos orgullosos de sacar tan buenas notas.	*We're proud about getting* such good grades.

3 Other verbs of emotion that you know are *importar* "to mind," *molestar* "to bother," and *sorprender* "to surprise." Note that they all take an indirect object pronoun.

> **Nos sorprende que** Gloria **se case.**
> **¿Te importa que** lo **invitemos?**
> **A ella le molesta que masques** chicle.

> *We're surprised Gloria is getting married.*
> *Do you mind if we invite him?*
> *It bothers her that you chew gum.*

PRÁCTICA

A **Una carta de Diana.** Diana está de vacaciones en Colombia y le está escribiendo una carta a su compañero Ricardo en los Estados Unidos. Completa su carta escogiendo las expresiones correctas.

Querido Ricardo:

Hace tres semanas que estamos en Cartagena. Vivimos en casa de mis tíos. Me gusta Colombia y los colombianos son todos muy simpáticos, pero *(me molesta / me alegro de)* que hablen tan rápidamente. También
5 *(siento / me sorprende)* que mucha gente extranjera viva aquí. No lo sabía.

Como sabes, mañana es mi cumpleaños. *(Estoy enojada / Estoy orgullosa)* de que Jorge, mi primo favorito, no pueda estar aquí para la gran fiesta. Se fue a Venezuela en un viaje de negocios. *(Temo / Me*
10 *alegro de)* que él no regrese hasta el mes próximo. También *(siento / me sorprende)* que tú tampoco puedas estar aquí para ayudarme a celebrar.

Oye, ¿cómo está María? *(Estoy contenta de / Estoy preocupada de)* que no responda a mis cartas. *(Espero / Temo)* que no le pase nada malo.

Bueno, Ricardo, espero que me contestes pronto.

Tu amiga,

Diana

Estudiantes en Cartagena, Colombia

Explicaciones I   **533**

Práctica B
Answers will vary. Verb forms
as follows:
1. piense
2. siga
3. saque
4. me tome
5. comparta
6. me felicite
7. se quede
8. me regale
9. no me permitan
10. hable

B **¿Qué sientes?** Escoge las expresiones de la lista para decir qué sientes en las siguientes situaciones. Por ejemplo:

me alegro de   siento   (no) me sorprende
temo   (no) me importa (no) me molesta

> Tu mejor amigo tiene un coche nuevo.
> *Me alegro de*
> *Me sorprende* } *que mi mejor amigo tenga un coche nuevo.*
> *No me importa*

1. El profesor no piensa darnos un examen hoy.
2. El público sigue hablando durante la película.
3. Tu amigo saca mejores notas que tú.
4. Un amigo tuyo te toma el pelo.
5. Un amigo tuyo no comparte nada contigo.
6. Nadie te felicita el día de tu cumpleaños.
7. El padre de tu amigo se queda sin trabajo.
8. Tu novio(a) te regala algo muy caro.
9. Tus padres no te permiten salir de noche cuando hay escuela.
10. Tu novio(a) habla continuamente de otros(as) chicos(as).

Práctica C
1. Creo que aquella auxiliar de vuelo se enoja con esas mujeres. Pues me sorprende que se enoje.
2. sirve / que sirva
3. parece / que parezca
4. permite / permita
5. recomiendan / recomienden
6. parece / parezca
7. pierde / pierda
8. dura / dure
9. tiene / tenga
10. aterriza / aterrice

C **Antes de despegar.** Varios viajeros están hablando en la sala de espera de un aeropuerto. Sigue el modelo usando las expresiones de la lista.

me alegro de que   me sorprende que
me molesta que   estoy preocupado(a) de que

> (ellos) / dar películas en este vuelo
> ESTUDIANTE A   *Creo que dan películas en este vuelo.*
> ESTUDIANTE B   *Pues me alegro de que den películas.*

1. aquella auxiliar de vuelo / enojarse con esas mujeres
2. esta línea aérea / servir comidas sabrosas
3. el piloto / parecer distraído
4. esta línea aérea / permitir colocar maletas debajo del asiento
5. todos los agentes de viajes / recomendar esta línea aérea
6. el cielo / parecer oscuro
7. esta línea aérea / nunca perder el equipaje
8. el vuelo / durar más de cuatro horas
9. la pista / tener hielo
10. el avión / aterrizar alrededor de las cinco

D Opiniones. Con un(a) compañero(a), da tu opinión sobre los siguientes temas. Usa expresiones de la lista. Por ejemplo:

estoy orgulloso(a) de que   temo que
estoy enojado(a) de que   me molesta que
estoy contento(a) de que   me sorprende que

la escuela

ESTUDIANTE A   *Estoy contento de que pinten el gimnasio.*
ESTUDIANTE B   *Me sorprende que la cafetería no sirva comida más sabrosa.*

1. la clase de _____
2. el equipo de _____
3. las vacaciones
4. los fines de semana
5. los amigos
6. la ciudad o pueblo
7. las películas
8. la música
9. la televisión

E De vacaciones. La familia González va a pasar las vacaciones en la casa de sus primos. Ahora la familia está en el aeropuerto esperando que despegue el avión. Todo el mundo está hablando. Sigue el modelo.

Pedro / sentir / no poder ir con nosotros
Yo / sentir / él / tener que quedarse solo
ESTUDIANTE A   *Pedro siente no poder ir con nosotros.*
ESTUDIANTE B   *Yo siento que él tenga que quedarse solo.*

1. (Yo) / alegrarse de / estar de vacaciones
   Yo / alegrarse de / (nosotros) / ver a nuestros primos
2. A Virginia / molestarle / llevar tanto equipaje
   A mí / molestarme / las maletas / pesar tanto
3. Molestarme / esperar en esta sala de espera sucia
   A mí / molestarme / el avión / salir con dos horas de retraso
4. (Yo) / alegrarse de / poder llevar al perro
   Yo / alegrarse de / el perro / portarse bien
5. Sorprenderme / ver a tanta gente aquí
   A mí / sorprenderme / la ciudad / no construir un aeropuerto más grande
6. Papá / sentir / tener sólo una semana de vacaciones
   Yo / sentir / él / volver solo
7. Mamá / temer / viajar en avión
   A mí / molestarme / el avión / hacer dos escalas

Práctica D
Answers will vary.

Enrichment: Additional topics for Ex. D: *las supersticiones, los profesores, los coches deportivos, las bandas de rock, los animales pequeños, el español.*

Práctica E
1. Me alegro de estar de vacaciones.
   Yo me alegro de que veamos a nuestros primos.
2. A Virginia le molesta llevar tanto equipaje.
   A mí me molesta que las maletas pesen tanto.
3. Me molesta esperar en esta sala … A mí me molesta que el avión salga …
4. Me alegro de poder llevar al perro. Yo me alegro de que el perro se porte bien.
5. Me sorprende ver a tanta gente aquí. A mí me sorprende que la ciudad no construya …
6. Papá siente tener … Yo siento que él vuelva solo.
7. Mamá teme viajar en avión. A mí me molesta que el avión haga dos escalas.

Todas las vacaciones del mundo.

El subjuntivo con expresiones de duda

◆ **OBJECTIVES:**

TO DENY THINGS

TO EXPRESS DOUBT OR UNCERTAINTY

TO EXPRESS CERTAINTY OR CONVICTION

Notes: Point out the use of the subjunctive after *dudar* in mini-dialogue 3 on p. 521.

Reteach / Extra Help: You may want to reinforce the subjunctive-indicative contrast by writing *dudar, no creer, negar, no estar seguro* in one column on the board and *no dudar, creer, no negar, estar seguro* in another column. Ask questions and have volunteers choose one of the expressions to use in their answers: *¿Será Ronald Reagan presidente el año próximo? ¿Estudiará _____ español el año que viene? ¿Se van a ver tú y _____ durante el verano? ¿Vale la pena preocuparte por los exámenes?*

We also use the subjunctive after verbs and expressions that indicate doubt, denial, or uncertainty.

Dudo que David hable bien el español.
I doubt that David speaks Spanish well.

No creo que empecemos mañana.
I don't think we'll begin tomorrow.

Niego que él mienta.
I deny that he's lying.

No estamos seguros de que ellos se casen este año.
We're not sure they'll get married this year.

1 We always use the subjunctive after these verbs and expressions, even when there is no change of subject.

Dudo que (yo) **hable** bien el español.
I doubt that I speak Spanish well.

No creo que empiece mañana.
I don't think I'll begin tomorrow.

Ella niega que mienta.
She denies that she's lying.

No están seguros de que se casen este año.
They're not sure they'll get married this year.

2 However, when the verb or expression expresses certainty (or a lack of doubt, disbelief, or denial), we use the indicative mood.

No dudo que el viaje **vale** la pena.
I don't doubt that the trip is worth the effort.

Creo que empezamos mañana.
I think we'll begin tomorrow.

No niego que él **miente.**
I don't deny he's lying.

Estamos seguros de que ellos se casan este año.
We're sure they'll get married this year.

Práctica A
1. ... no cree que ... quiera ...
2. ... duda que ... sufra ...
3. ... no está seguro de que ... se mejore ...
4. ... duda que ... ahorre ...
5. ... niega que ... robe ...
6. ... no creen que ... mienta
7. ... duda que ... pueda ...
8. ... niega que ... intente ...
9. ... niega que ... sueñe ...
10. ... niega que ... tenga ...

PRÁCTICA

A Es muy sencillo. Yolanda y Armando no están de acuerdo sobre lo que está ocurriendo en su telenovela favorita, *Corazón de oro.* Cambia según el modelo.

> Rosa sabe que Rafael le debe mucho dinero a su jefe. (dudar)
> *No. Rosa duda que Rafael le deba mucho dinero a su jefe.*

1. El hijo de Rosa cree que su madre quiere a Rafael. (no creer)
2. El vecino piensa que su hijo sufre del corazón. (dudar)
3. El médico dice que el niño se mejora. (no estar seguro de)

4. La familia cree que Rafael ahorra mucho dinero para pagar al médico. (dudar)
5. La hermana de Rafael está segura de que él roba coches. (negar)
6. Los amigos de Rafael saben que él miente mucho. (no creer)
7. El abogado dice que Rafael puede cruzar la frontera. (dudar)
8. La abuela de Rafael dice que su nieto intenta escaparse. (negar)
9. Rosa dice que continuamente sueña con ser rica. (negar)
10. Todo el mundo dice que Rosa tiene vergüenza. (negar)

B **¿Por qué discutes tanto?** Cuando Armando y Yolanda miran la televisión nunca están de acuerdo sobre lo que pasa en los programas. Usa las expresiones para hacer frases según el modelo.

> Creo / Pues yo no creo
> No dudo / Pues yo dudo
> Es verdad / En mi opinión, no es verdad
> Estoy seguro(a) de / Yo no estoy seguro(a) de

> Esa mujer / ganar el premio
> ESTUDIANTE A *No dudo que esa mujer va a ganar el premio.*
> ESTUDIANTE B *Pues yo dudo que ella gane el premio.*

1. Dolores Martín / cantar
2. los ladrones / robar la plata
3. los novios / decidir graduarse de la universidad
4. Montoya / esquiar bien
5. Quijote / besar a Dulcinea
6. el policía / hallar al arqueólogo dentro de una semana
7. el héroe / salvar a los jóvenes
8. el millonario / regalarles las joyas a sus parientes
9. el explorador / compartir el tesoro con sus ayudantes
10. el piloto / estar de mal humor

C **Hablemos de ti.**
1. ¿Te preocupas por los exámenes? ¿Por qué? ¿Por qué otras cosas te preocupas? ¿De qué te alegras?
2. ¿Te enojas con la gente que no hace lo que promete? ¿Con qué otras personas te enojas?
3. ¿Te molesta que la gente diga que no le importan tus problemas? ¿A ti te importan los problemas de otras personas? ¿Qué haces para ayudarlas?
4. ¿Qué cosas te sorprenden? Por ejemplo, ¿te sorprende que algunas personas mientan? ¿Por qué dicen mentiras?

Práctica B
1. ... va a cantar.
   ... que cante.
2. ... van a robar ...
   ... que roben ...
3. ... van a decidir ...
   ... que decidan ...
4. ... va a esquiar ...
   ... que esquíe ...
5. ... va a besar ...
   ... que bese ...
6. ... va a hallar ...
   ... que halle ...
7. ... va a salvar ...
   ... que salve ...
8. ... va a regalarles ...
   ... que les regale ...
9. ... va a compartir ...
   ... que comparta ...
10. ... va a estar ...
    ... que esté ...

Práctica C
Answers will vary.

Practice Sheet 16–4

Workbook Exs. E–F

Tape Manual Ex. 7 [cassette] 11

Quiz 16–4

APLICACIONES Discretionary

Un secreto del desierto 12

Antes de leer
1–3. Answers will vary.

ANTES DE LEER

Contesta estas preguntas.
1. ¿Conoces algunas enormes obras de arte antiguas? ¿Cuáles? ¿Por qué fueron hechas?
2. ¿Conoces algún dibujo hecho por una persona ciega?
3. ¿Crees que es posible hacer algo tan grande que no se pueda ver?

Notes: You may want to assign the **Antes de leer** questions as written homework.
  Make sure students understand these words that have not been glossed: *forman*, form; *figuras*, figures; *geométricas*, geometric; *plantas*, plants; *proporciones*, proportions; *la tierra*, (here) ground; *planetas*, planets; *calcular*, to calculate; *la posición*, position.

¿Quiénes hicieron los enormes dibujos que se encuentran[1] en el desierto del Perú? Es probable que nunca encontremos las respuestas a todas las preguntas sobre lo que llamamos "las líneas de Nazca." Las líneas forman dos clases de dibujos: figuras geométricas y dibujos de plantas o animales, 5 todas en proporciones enormes. Por ejemplo, hay un dibujo de un mono que es más grande que un campo[2] de fútbol. Hay también una araña de cincuenta metros de largo.[3] Hace muchos siglos que esos dibujos extraños están allí. Pero sólo podemos verlos desde un avión. Desde la tierra, parecen líneas sin ningún significado. ¿Quién hizo estas líneas, y por qué? ¿Y 10 cómo podían hacerlas sin ver lo que hacían? Es muy misterioso.

Un libro popular presenta la teoría[4] de que visitantes de otros planetas llegaron a este lugar e hicieron los dibujos geométricos para indicar a sus naves espaciales[5] dónde aterrizar. Según esta teoría, los habitantes de esa parte del Perú creyeron que los visitantes eran dioses. Cuando los visitantes regresaron a su planeta la gente de Nazca dibujó los animales para llamar otra vez a sus "dioses."

Pero los astrónomos y antropólogos no creen en esta teoría. Según ellos, las líneas geométricas probablemente servían para calcular la posición del sol y de las estrellas durante el año. Pero todavía no pueden explicar los 20 dibujos de animales y de plantas. Quizás es verdad que eran recados para los dioses, pero no dioses con naves espaciales, sino dioses de la naturaleza[6] como el dios del sol.

---

[1]**encontrarse**   *to be found*   [2]**el campo**   here: *field*   [3]**de cincuenta metros de largo** *50 meters long*   [4]**la teoría**   *theory*   [5]**la nave espacial**   *space ship*   [6]**la naturaleza** *nature*

Líneas de Nazca en el Perú

Preguntas

1. ¿Por qué nos sorprenden las líneas de Nazca?
2. Descríbelas.
3. ¿De dónde se pueden ver los dibujos?
4. ¿Cómo son los dibujos del mono y de la araña?
5. Explica, con otras palabras, la teoría en la lectura.
6. ¿Qué creen los científicos sobre las líneas geométricas?
7. ¿Qué piensas tú de estos dibujos? ¿Tienes tú alguna teoría sobre ellos? ¿Puedes inventar una?

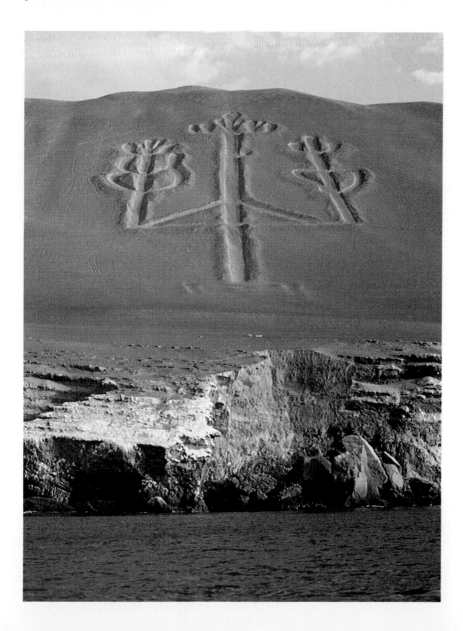

Cerca de Nazca, Perú

EXPLICACIONES II

Notes: Refer to mini-dialogues 5 on p. 521, 4 on p. 528, and 5 on p. 529 for examples of the subjunctive after impersonal expressions.

El subjuntivo con expresiones impersonales

◆ **OBJECTIVES:**

TO EXPRESS OPINIONS

TO GIVE ADVICE

TO TELL WHAT MAY OR MAY NOT HAPPEN

Another common use of the subjunctive is after certain impersonal expressions that give an indirect command or that indicate opinion, emotion, doubt, possibility, or denial. Some impersonal expressions you know that require the subjunctive are:

Es difícil	Es mejor
Es importante	Es necesario
Es imposible	Es posible
Es improbable	Es probable
Es (una) lástima	Es triste

No es necesario que César **responda.**	*It isn't necessary for César to answer.*
Es una lástima que no puedas acompañarnos.	*It's too bad you can't come with us.*
Es posible que visitemos las ruinas mañana.	*It's possible that we'll visit the ruins tomorrow.*
Es imposible que ellos duerman aquí.	*It's impossible for them to sleep here.*

1 We use the indicative with impersonal expressions that express certainty.

Es verdad que él tiene mucha **paciencia.**	*It's true that he's very patient.*
Es cierto que el vuelo **llega** tarde.	*It's true that the flight will arrive late.*

But we use the subjunctive with impersonal expressions that show uncertainty.

No es verdad que ella crea en fantasmas.	*It's not true that she believes in ghosts.*
No es cierto que el *aduanero* **registre** el *equipaje.*	*It's not true that the customs officer will check the luggage.*

2 When there is no change of subject, we use the infinitive.

Es difícil dormir con ese ruido.	*It's hard to sleep with that noise.*
Es imposible llegar a tiempo.	*It's impossible to arrive on time.*
No es necesario llevar eso.	*It's not necessary to take that.*

PRÁCTICA

A Consejos del director. El director del colegio quiere que los estudiantes se porten mejor y les da unos consejos. Sigue el modelo.

> María / no estudiar / es importante
> ESTUDIANTE A *María no estudia.*
> ESTUDIANTE B *Es importante que estudie.*

1. Roberto / nunca tomar apuntes / es mejor
2. Estela y Marta / nunca prestar atención / es importante
3. Laura / no escribir a máquina / es necesario
4. Luz / nunca compartir la computadora / es mejor
5. Pedro y Carmen / nunca participar en los partidos / es importante
6. Gustavo / no respetar las reglas / es necesario
7. Armando y Javier / no intentar llegar a tiempo / es importante
8. Victoria / nunca seguir los consejos de la profesora / es mejor

B A las montañas. Unos amigos piensan ir de excursión a las montañas mañana. Usa expresiones de la lista para preguntar y contestar. Por ejemplo:

| (no) es difícil | es una lástima | es posible |
| es imposible | es necesario | es probable |

> nosotros / caminar mucho
> ESTUDIANTE A *¿Vamos a caminar mucho?*
> ESTUDIANTE B *Es probable que caminemos mucho.*

1. Julio / llevar su radio
2. (nosotros) / encontrar animales peligrosos
3. (nosotros) / hallar el sendero hasta el campamento
4. tus amigos / visitar nuestro campamento
5. Graciela y Andrés / subir a la montaña
6. todos (nosotros) / poder dormir
7. (nosotros) / despertarse temprano
8. llover mañana

Práctica A
1. Roberto nunca toma apuntes.
   Es mejor que tome apuntes.
2. Estela y Marta nunca prestan atención.
   Es importante que presten atención.
3. Laura no escribe a máquina.
   Es necesario que escriba a máquina.
4. Luz nunca comparte la computadora.
   Es mejor que comparta la computadora.
5. Pedro y Carmen nunca participan en los partidos.
   Es importante que participen …
6. Gustavo no respeta las reglas.
   Es necesario que respete …
7. Armando y Javier no intentan llegar a tiempo.
   Es importante que intenten …
8. Victoria nunca sigue los consejos de la profesora.
   Es mejor que siga …

Práctica B
1. ¿Julio va a llevar su radio?
   … que lleve …
2. ¿Vamos a encontrar …?
   … que encontremos …
3. ¿Vamos a hallar …?
   … que hallemos …
4. ¿Tus amigos van a visitar …?
   … que visiten …
5. ¿Graciela y Andrés van a subir …?
   … que suban …
6. ¿Todos vamos a poder dormir?
   … que podamos …
7. ¿Vamos a despertarnos temprano?
   … que nos despertemos …
8. ¿Va a llover mañana?
   … que llueva …

Ruinas de Sacsahuamán, en el Perú

Práctica C
Answers will vary.

Reteach / Extra Help: If your
class finds Ex. C difficult, ask
volunteers to model the first few
items. Remind students to use
the indicative with *es cierto*.

C **¿Cierto o no?** Usa las expresiones *(no) es cierto* o *(no) es posible* para dar tu opinión en cada una de las frases. Usa el indicativo o el subjuntivo según la expresión.

1. Los gatos negros traen mala suerte.
2. Viven animales extraños en la luna.
3. Las estrellas nos aconsejan.
4. La tierra da vueltas alrededor del sol.
5. Los animales entienden lo que la gente dice.
6. La mayoría de las personas tienen vergüenza a veces.
7. La gente puede discutir sin pelearse.
8. La gente puede vivir varias semanas sin beber nada.
9. El número 13 trae mala suerte.

Práctica D
recibir
espero
diga / mandes
quieras
nadar
conozcan
encontrar
visitemos
hallemos
viven
pueden / pensar
tengas

D **¡Una carta de mi novia!** Roberto acaba de recibir una carta de Susana. Complétala usando el infinitivo, el presente del indicativo o del subjuntivo de los verbos entre paréntesis.

Playa Azul, 25 de mayo

Querido Roberto:

¿Por qué no me escribes? ¡Es tan emocionante *(recibir)* tus cartas! Todos los días (yo) *(esperar)* al cartero y siempre es triste que él me *(decir)* que no hay nada para mí. Es necesario que (tú) me *(mandar)* los
5 libros que te pedí. No tengo nada bueno para leer.

Es una lástima que (tú) no *(querer)* venir a visitarme. Es muy bonito aquí. Paso los días en la playa. Es maravilloso *(nadar)* en agua tan clara y azul. Es importante que los visitantes *(conocer)* a los muchachos de aquí, porque ellos saben dónde es posible *(encontrar)* playas bonitas
10 que no estén llenas de gente.

Es posible que Teresa y yo *(visitar)* una casa vieja donde dicen que hay fantasmas. Claro que no es probable que (nosotras) *(hallar)* fantasmas allí. Pero no dudo que *(vivir)* fantasmas en la pensión donde estoy. Todas las noches oigo ruidos extraños en el pasillo, y
15 cuando abro la puerta, ¡no hay nada! Es verdad que esos ruidos *(poder)* ser de ratones, pero es más interesante *(pensar)* que son fantasmas. Crees que estoy loca, ¿verdad? Pues es posible que (tú) *(tener)* razón. ¡Escríbeme!

Te mando un beso.

20 Susana

E Hablemos de ti.

1. ¿Es emocionante volar en avión? ¿Dar una vuelta en la montaña rusa? ¿Por qué?
2. ¿Es fácil para ti hablar con gente que no conoces bien? ¿Por qué?
3. ¿Es importante decir siempre la verdad? ¿Por qué?
4. ¿Es necesario que tú comas por lo menos tres veces por día y que duermas ocho horas? ¿Por qué?
5. ¿Es agradable no hacer nada? ¿Por qué?
6. ¿Es probable que viajes a algún lugar interesante este año? ¿Adónde? ¿Con quién irás?

Práctica E
Answers will vary.

Practice Sheet 16–5

Workbook Exs. G–J

Tape Manual Exs. 8–9 🔲 13

Refrán 🔲 14

Canción 🔲 15

Quiz 16–5

ACTIVIDAD

¡El subjuntivo ganador!   Get together in groups of three or five students. Write down the impersonal expressions that require the subjunctive on separate slips of paper. Choose one person to be the leader; the others should form two teams. The leader then picks a slip of paper and reads the expression aloud. The first team to say a correct sentence using the expression gets a point. After five expressions, the team with the most points wins the round and a new leader is chosen.

Notes: You may want to do the **Actividad** as a whole-class activity. Prepare a slip of paper with an impersonal expression for each student, put the slips into a paper bag, and ask students to pull one out. Then divide the class into teams. Give everyone a chance to say a sentence. The team with the most points wins the game.

Una fiesta de estudiantes en España

APLICACIONES   Discretionary

Notes: Answers to the **Repaso** and **Tema** appear in the Teacher Notes.

REPASO

Notes: Review of:
1. impersonal expressions
    + subjunctive
2. verbs of doubt / emotion
    + subjunctive
3. use of subjunctive /
    indicative after *(no) creer /*
    (no) dudar
4. expressions of emotion
    + subjunctive
    prepositional pronouns
5. exclamations with *¡qué!*
    verbs of emotion
    + subjunctive
    direct object pronouns

Enrichment: You may want
to use the model sentences in
the **Repaso** for dictation.

Mira con cuidado las frases modelo. Luego cambia las frases que siguen al español según los modelos.

1. *Es necesario que Claudia regrese a casa.*
    (It's possible that you (fam.) will travel to Costa Rica.)
    (It's important that you (pl.) pay Francisco.)
    (It's probable that we'll sail to Mallorca.)

2. *Pero Elena siente que ellos vengan tarde a la cita.*
    (But I doubt we'll arrive at the border soon.)
    (But Mrs. López doesn't think you (fam.) will return home early.)
    (But they're sorry I won't come back to the inn again.)

3. *Yo creo que ella miente mucho, pero ellos dudan que ella diga mentiras.*
    (We think he plays well, but we doubt he'll win the game.)
    (He doesn't deny that you (formal) teach well, but he doesn't think you're patient.)
    (I don't deny she paints well, but I don't think she understands art.)

4. *Estoy triste de que la clase continúe sin ella.*
    (We're proud that you (formal) will work with us.)
    (He's angry that I'll start without him.)
    (They're happy that we'll run with them.)

5. *¡Qué mala suerte! Nos preocupamos de que nuestros primos nos visiten.*
    (What a surprise! I'm happy my godparents will accompany me.)
    (What a shame! They're worried that their grandchildren won't find them.)
    (What a relief! She's happy that no one recognizes her.)

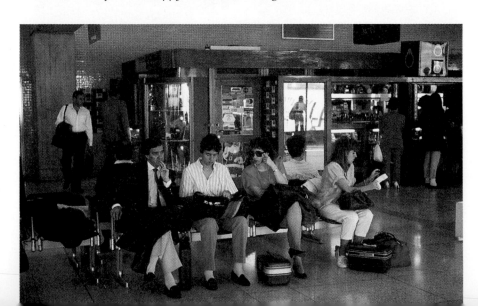

En el aeropuerto de
Caracas, Venezuela

TEMA

Transparency 56

Reteach / Extra Help: Before students begin work on the **Tema** sentences, you may want to show transparency 56 and ask students to work in pairs to talk about the cartoon strip.

Escribe las frases en español.

1. It's necessary for Diego and Miguel to fly to Caracas.

2. But Diego fears they'll arrive at the airport late.

3. Diego thinks the plane will leave on time, but Miguel doubts that he is right.

4. Diego is worried that the plane will take off without them.

5. What a relief! Diego is happy that his friend wakes him up.

REDACCIÓN

Enrichment: In connection with the **Redacción,** if many of your students have never traveled, you may want to tell the class about your own travel experiences, or suggest that students may choose to write about the travel experiences of someone they know.

Ahora escoge uno de los siguientes temas para escribir tu propio diálogo o párrafo.

1. Expand the *Tema* by writing a paragraph about pictures one through four. At what time do Diego and Miguel leave the house? How do they get to the airport? Why is Diego afraid they will be late?

2. Have you ever traveled to another country? If so, write a paragraph about your experience. How did you travel? Did you need documents, such as a passport? Did you have to go through customs? Did you make any stops before you reached your destination? What did you think of the trip?

3. Write a dialogue between a passenger and a customs official.

COMPRUEBA TU PROGRESO   CAPÍTULO 16   Discretionary

Notes: Answers to the **Comprueba** appear in the Teacher Notes.

A   El aeropuerto
Completa cada frase con la forma correcta de la palabra apropiada.

aduana   escala   puerta de embarque
declarar   frontera   registrar
demora   pista   viaje

1. El avión va a despegar. Está en la _____.
2. Otros aviones esperan. Hay una _____ grande.
3. La gente que llega en el vuelo desde Colombia pasa por la _____ para _____ lo que compró allá.
4. El agente _____ las maletas.
5. Los pasajeros suben al avión por la _____.
6. Fue un vuelo corto. No hizo ninguna _____.
7. La familia López está de _____ en el Perú.

B   ¿Qué crees tú?
Escoge la forma correcta del verbo.

1. Dudo que él _____ mucho.
   a. sufre   b. sufra
2. Mamá no cree que (yo) _____ mucho.
   a. ayudo   b. ayude
3. Pepe cree que (nosotros) _____ bien.
   a. cocinamos   b. cocinemos
4. No creo que el avión _____ a tiempo.
   a. aterriza   b. aterrice
5. ¿Niegas que Juan _____ bastante dinero?
   a. ahorra   b. ahorre
6. ¿Dudas que _____ a manejar?
   a. aprendo   b. aprenda
7. No dudo que _____ sed.
   a. tienes   b. tengas
8. Marta no niega que ella _____ la historia.
   a. cree   b. crea
9. No estoy seguro de que Pepe nos _____.
   a. espera   b. espere

C   Me alegro de que vengas
Cambia las frases al subjuntivo según el modelo.

Olga teme llorar. (yo)
Olga teme que yo llore.

1. Me enoja gastar tanto dinero.   (nosotros)
2. Es importante tener un sentido del humor. (tú)
3. ¿Te alegras de recibir un sueldo tan grande? (nosotros)
4. A Jorge no le molesta pedir consejos.   (ellas)
5. Me sorprende descubrir eso.   (él)
6. Nos alegramos de pasar la tarde aquí.   (María)
7. Temo no comprender nada.   (Uds.)
8. Sentimos no poder conocer a tus suegros. (ellos)

D   Me alegro, pero también dudo
Forma frases según el modelo.

Viajan en coche cama.   (él / negar)
Él niega que viajen en coche cama.

1. Entienden el significado de eso.   (el profesor / no estar seguro)
2. Me enojo con Andrés.   (ellos / dudar)
3. Compartimos el trabajo.   (tú / alegrarse de)
4. No empiezas a las nueve.   (el jefe / sentir)
5. Nuestro equipo siempre gana.   (nosotros / dudar)
6. La aduanera registra el equipaje.   (Laura / no creer)

E   ¿Es importante?
Haz frases según el modelo.

¿Es importante estudiar mucho?   (nosotros)
¿Es importante que estudiemos mucho?

1. Es imposible volver a intentar.   (yo)
2. Es necesario terminar tan temprano.   (tú)
3. Es una lástima deber tanto dinero.   (él)
4. Es mejor no mentir.   (ellos)
5. Es importante asistir al espectáculo. (nosotros)
6. Es posible traer las joyas.   (Ud.)

Activity Masters   Chapter 16 Test   ⌷☐◻ Listening Comprehension Test
Workbook Review: Chapters 13–16   Cumulative Test: Chapters 13–16

VOCABULARIO DEL CAPÍTULO 16

Sustantivos
la aduana
el aduanero, la aduanera
la demora
el documento
la escala
la frontera
la lástima
la línea aérea
la mentira
la pista
la puerta de embarque
el sentido del humor
la superstición, *pl.* las
    supersticiones

Adjetivos
cierto, -a
enojado, -a
extraño, -a
imposible
improbable
obstinado, -a
orgulloso, -a
posible
probable
supersticioso, -a

Adverbio
continuamente

Preposición
dentro de *(within)*

Verbos
alegrarse (de)
declarar
dudar
enojar(se) (con)
intentar
mentir (e → ie)
negar (e → ie)
preocuparse (por)
registrar
sentir (e → ie)
sorprender
sufrir
temer
volar (o → ue)

Expresiones
de viaje
es cierto
es verdad
estar de buen / mal humor
hacer escala
(por / en) todas partes
¡qué alegría!
sin escala
tener paciencia
tener vergüenza
valer la pena
vamos *(come on)*

APÉNDICE:
SI UDS. QUIEREN

On the following pages you will find a few additional structures that you will learn more about next year. To learn them now will certainly help you in any outside reading you do, and, of course, Spanish speakers use them often in conversation just as you use their English equivalents.

El presente perfecto   Can be taught after Chapter 11.

In English we form this tense by using *have* or *has* with the past participle of a verb: *he has gone, they've eaten, have you looked?* In Spanish we use the present tense of the verb *haber* with a past participle. To form the past participle, we add *-ado* to the stem of most *-ar* verbs and *-ido* to the stem of most *-er* / *-ir* verbs:

-AR	-ER	-IR
hablar → hablado	comer → comido	salir → salido
mirar → mirado	tener → tenido	dormir → dormido
dar → dado	querer → querido	recibir → recibido
llevar → llevado	ser → sido	ir → ido

Here are the present perfect forms of *hablar*, *comer*, and *salir*:

SINGULAR		PLURAL	
1 **he**	hablado comido salido	**hemos**	hablado comido salido
2 **has**	hablado comido salido	**habéis**	hablado comido salido
3 **ha**	hablado comido salido	**han**	hablado comido salido

Ya **hemos comido.**	*We've already eaten.*
No **ha llegado** todavía.	*He hasn't arrived yet.*

Many past participles are also used as adjectives. One irregular one that you know is the past participle of *hacer: hecho* ("made, done").

PRÁCTICA

¿Qué han hecho? Con un(a) compañero(a), di lo que estas personas han hecho este año. Sigue el modelo.

(tú) / ganar todos los partidos de bolos
ESTUDIANTE A *¿Qué has hecho este año?*
ESTUDIANTE B *He ganado todos los partidos de bolos.*

1. el (la) profesor(a) de español / trabajar mucho
2. los estudiantes / aprender mucho
3. el equipo de *(deporte)* / perder varios partidos
4. (nosotros) / disfrutar de la clase de *(materia)*
5. *(nombre de un chico)* / sacar buenas notas en *(materia)*
6. *(nombre de dos chicas)* / salir bien en todas las pruebas de *(materia)*
7. (tú) / llegar a tiempo (o tarde) a la escuela todos los días
8. tú y *(nombre)* / comer en la cafetería cada día

Práctica
1. ¿Qué ha hecho …? Ha trabajado …
2. ¿Qué han hecho …? Han aprendido …
3. ¿Qué ha hecho …? Ha perdido …
4. ¿Qué hemos hecho? Hemos (*or:* han) disfrutado …
5. ¿Qué ha hecho …? Ha sacado …
6. ¿Qué han hecho …? Han salido …
7. ¿Qué has hecho? He llegado …
8. ¿Qué han hecho …? Hemos comido …

El pluscuamperfecto

We use the pluperfect tense to describe an action in the past that occurred before another action in the past. Its English equivalent is *had* + past participle: *he had gone, they'd eaten, had you looked?* To form the pluperfect, we use the imperfect forms of *haber* plus the past participle:

	SINGULAR			PLURAL	
1	había	hablado comido salido		**habíamos**	hablado comido salido
2	habías	hablado comido salido		habíais	hablado comido salido
3	había	hablado comido salido		habían	hablado comido salido

Note that object pronouns and reflexive pronouns come right before the form of *haber*.

¿Se habían acostado cuando llegaste?

Had they gone to bed when you arrived?

¿No te habíamos dado la dirección correcta?

Hadn't we given you the correct address?

PRÁCTICA

¿Por qué? Explica por qué estas personas no hicieron ciertas cosas. Sigue el modelo.

(tú) / nadar / esta mañana

ESTUDIANTE A *¿Por qué no nadaste?*
ESTUDIANTE B *Porque ya había nadado esta mañana.*

1. Federico / ir al cine con nosotros / dos veces esta semana
2. los chicos / limpiar su dormitorio / la semana pasada
3. (nosotros) / correr ayer por la tarde / ayer por la mañana
4. (tú) / almorzar conmigo / más temprano
5. (ellos) / hacer un asado el domingo / el sábado
6. el profesor de historia / mostrar sus diapositivas / ayer
7. Uds. / escoger la película / la última vez
8. ella / venir con nosotros / sola en autobús
9. (yo) / ensayar con Uds. / dos veces esta semana

Práctica
1. ¿Por qué no fue Federico al cine con nosotros? Porque ya había ido dos veces esta semana.
2. ¿Por qué no limpiaron los chicos …? Porque ya habían limpiado …
3. ¿Por qué no corrimos …? Porque ya habían (or: habíamos) corrido …
4. ¿Por qué no almorzaste …? Porque ya había almorzado …
5. ¿Por qué no hicieron …? Porque ya habían hecho …
6. ¿Por qué no mostró …? Porque ya había mostrado …
7. ¿Por qué no escogieron Uds. …? Porque ya habíamos escogido …
8. ¿Por qué no vino ella …? Porque ya había venido …
9. ¿Por qué no ensayé …? Porque ya habías ensayado …

El imperfecto progresivo

Can be taught after Chapter 14.

You have learned to use the present progressive tense to express an action or event that is taking place right now. To describe something that was taking place at a certain time in the past, we use the imperfect progressive. We form this tense by using the imperfect forms of *estar* or *seguir* and the present participle.

Cuando me desperté **estaba lloviendo** mucho.   *When I woke up **it was raining hard**.*

Cuando llegué, **seguían buscando** su tarea.   *When I arrived, **they went on looking for** their homework.*

Remember that object pronouns can come before the main verb or can be attached to the present participle. If we attach them to the participle, we must add an accent mark to keep to stress on the correct syllable.

Él { **me estaba hablando.**
    { **estaba hablándome.**   *He **was talking to me**.*

PRÁCTICA

¿Qué estaban haciendo?   Con un(a) compañero(a), pregunta y contesta según el modelo.

> tus padres cuando llegaste anoche / mirar la tele
> **ESTUDIANTE A**   *¿Qué estaban haciendo tus padres cuando llegaste anoche?*
> **ESTUDIANTE B**   *Estaban mirando la tele.*

1. la profesora de química cuando entraste / leer una historia
2. Uds. cuando empezó la tormenta / sacar los platos del lavaplatos
3. los nadadores cuando llegó la salvavidas / gritar "¡socorro!"
4. (tú) cuando oíste las noticias / cortar el césped
5. tu mamá cuando sonó el teléfono / poner la mesa
6. los otros cuando llegó la cajera / buscar a la gerente
7. (tú) cuando apagaron las luces / pedir la cuenta
8. Juanita y tú cuando ella se cortó la mano / envolver regalos

Práctica
1. ¿Qué estaba haciendo la profesora …?
   Estaba leyendo una historia.
2. ¿Qué estaban haciendo Uds. …?
   Estábamos sacando …
3. ¿Qué estaban haciendo …?
   Estaban gritando …
4. ¿Qué estabas haciendo …?
   Estaba cortando …
5. ¿Qué estaba haciendo …?
   Estaba poniendo …
6. ¿Qué estaba haciendo …?
   Estaban buscando …
7. ¿Qué estabas haciendo …?
   Estaba pidiendo …
8. ¿Qué estaban haciendo …?
   Estábamos envolviendo …

Uso del complemento directo con el complemento indirecto

When we use a direct and an indirect object pronoun together, we always put the indirect object pronoun right before the direct object pronoun.

¿Quién **te** presta **la cámara?**	*Who's lending **you the camera?***
Luz **me la** presta.	*Luz is lending **it to me.***
¿Quién **les** enseña **español?**	*Who's teaching **you Spanish?***
El Sr. Díaz **nos lo** enseña.	*Mr. Díaz is teaching **it to us.***

When the indirect object pronoun *le* or *les* would come before the direct object pronouns *lo, la, los,* or *las,* the *le* or *les* becomes *se.*

¿**Le** vas a decir **el chisme a Juan?**	*Are you going to tell **Juan the gossip?***
Se lo digo ahora.	*I'm telling **it to him** now.*
¿**Les** mostraron **las preguntas?**	*Did they show **them the questions?***
Se las muestran ahora.	*They're showing **them to them** now.*

When we attach two object pronouns to an infinitive or present participle, we must add an accent mark to preserve the original stress.

Luz piensa **prestármela.**	*Luz plans **to lend it to me.***
Estoy **diciéndoselo.**	*I'm **telling it to him.***

PRÁCTICA

¿Quién los puede ayudar?   Con un(a) compañero(a), di quién va a ayudar a esta gente. Sigue el modelo.

Ramón necesita tijeras (dar / yo)
ESTUDIANTE A *Ramón necesita tijeras. ¿Quién va a dárselas?*
ESTUDIANTE B *Yo se las doy.*

1. Mariana necesita un sujetapapeles. (dar / Sofía)
2. Raimundo y Rodolfo necesitan hojas de papel. (dar / nosotros)
3. Lucía necesita un libro. (prestar / Rosa)
4. Necesito un borrador. (prestar / yo)
5. Mario y yo necesitamos una grapadora. (prestar / la Srta. López)
6. Teresa necesita una silla. (ir a buscar / yo)
7. Necesito cuadernos. (comprar / nosotros)
8. Uds. necesitan unas tizas. (dar / él)

El condicional

We use the conditional in Spanish to tell what we *would* do.

Me gustaría ir pero no puedo.	*I'd like to go but I can't.*
No comeríamos en ese café.	*We wouldn't eat in that café.*
Dijo que **llegaría** temprano.	*He said he'd arrive early.*

As with the future, we form the conditional of most verbs by adding the appropriate endings to the infinitive. The endings are the same as those for the imperfect of -*er* / -*ir* verbs, and in the conditional we use them with -*ar* verbs too. Note that there is an accent on all of the forms.

CANTAR		COMER		VIVIR	
cantaría	cantaríamos	comería	comeríamos	viviría	viviríamos
cantarías	cantaríais	comerías	comeríais	vivirías	viviríais
cantaría	cantarían	comería	comerían	viviría	vivirían

PRÁCTICA

Sé paciente, por favor. Algunas personas siempre quieren que hagas cosas en seguida. Sigue el modelo.

(ellos) apagar las lámparas / apagarlas después
ESTUDIANTE A   *¿No han apagado las lámparas?*
ESTUDIANTE B   *Prometieron que las apagarían después.*

1. (tú) limpiar el horno / limpiarlo más tarde
2. (él) planchar las camisas / plancharlas esta noche
3. (ella) secar la ropa / secarla después del almuerzo
4. (ellos) encender el aire acondicionado / encenderlo en un momento
5. (tú) hallar el abrelatas / buscarlo después
6. (Uds.) comprar detergente / comprarlo esta tarde
7. (ellas) barrer el suelo / barrerlo antes de salir
8. (Alberto y tú) calentar la sopa / calentarla después de limpiar estas ollas y sartenes

VERBOS

Regular Verbs

cantar

PRESENT INDICATIVE	canto, cantas, canta; cantamos, cantáis, cantan
PRESENT SUBJUNCTIVE	cante, cantes, cante; cantemos, cantéis, canten
PRETERITE	canté, cantaste, cantó; cantamos, cantasteis, cantaron
IMPERFECT	cantaba, cantabas, cantaba; cantábamos, cantabais, cantaban
FUTURE	cantaré, cantarás, cantará; cantaremos, canteréis, cantarán
COMMANDS	canta, no cantes; (no) cante Ud.; (no) canten Uds.
PRESENT PARTICIPLE	cantando

aprender

PRESENT INDICATIVE	aprendo, aprendes, aprende; aprendemos, aprendéis, aprenden
PRESENT SUBJUNCTIVE	aprenda, aprendas, aprenda; aprendamos, aprendáis, aprendan
PRETERITE	aprendí, aprendiste, aprendió; aprendimos, aprendisteis, aprendieron
IMPERFECT	aprendía, aprendías, aprendía; aprendíamos, aprendíais, aprendían
FUTURE	aprenderé, aprenderás, aprenderá; aprenderemos, aprenderéis, aprenderán
COMMANDS	aprende, no aprendas; (no) aprenda Ud.; (no) aprendan Uds.
PRESENT PARTICIPLE	aprendiendo

vivir

PRESENT INDICATIVE	vivo, vives, vive; vivimos, vivís, viven
PRESENT SUBJUNCTIVE	viva, vivas, viva; vivamos, viváis, vivan
PRETERITE	viví, viviste, vivió; vivimos, vivisteis, vivieron
IMPERFECT	vivía, vivías, vivía; vivíamos, vivíais, vivían
FUTURE	viviré, vivirás, vivirá; viviremos, viviréis, vivirán
COMMANDS	vive, no vivas; (no) viva Ud.; (no) vivan Uds.
PRESENT PARTICIPLE	viviendo

Reflexive Verbs

lavarse

PRESENT INDICATIVE	me lavo, te lavas, se lava; nos lavamos, os laváis, se lavan
PRESENT SUBJUNCTIVE	me lave, te laves, se lave; nos lavemos, os lavéis, se laven
PRETERITE	me lavé, te lavaste, se lavó; nos lavamos, os lavasteis, se lavan
IMPERFECT	me lavaba, te lavabas, se lavaba; nos lavábamos, os lavabais, se lavaban
FUTURE	me lavaré, te lavarás, se lavará; nos lavaremos, os lavaréis, se lavarán
COMMANDS	lávate, no te laves; lávese Ud., no se lave Ud.; lávense Uds., no se laven Uds.
PRESENT PARTICIPLE	lavándose

Stem-changing Verbs

acostar (o → ue)

PRESENT INDICATIVE	acuesto, acuestas, acuesta; acostamos, acostáis, acuestan
PRESENT SUBJUNCTIVE	acueste, acuestes, acueste; acostemos, acostéis, acuesten
PRETERITE	acosté, acostaste, acostó; acostamos, acostasteis, acostaron
IMPERFECT	acostaba
FUTURE	acostaré
COMMANDS	acuesta, no acuestes; (no) acueste Ud.; (no) acuesten Uds.
PRESENT PARTICIPLE	acostando

Verbs like **acostar: contar, costar, demostrar, encontrar, mostrar, probar, recordar, sonar, soñar, volar**

acostarse (o → ue)   See *acostar* and Reflexive Verbs.

almorzar (o → ue)

PRESENT INDICATIVE	almuerzo, almuerzas, almuerza; almorzamos, almorzáis, almuerzan
PRESENT SUBJUNCTIVE	almuerce, almuerces, almuerce; almorcemos, almorcéis, almuercen
PRETERITE	almorcé, almorzaste, almorzó; almorzamos, almorzasteis, almorzaron
IMPERFECT	almorzaba
FUTURE	almorzaré
COMMANDS	almuerza, no almuerces; (no) almuerce Ud.; (no) almuercen Uds.
PRESENT PARTICIPLE	almorzando

calentar (e → ie)

PRESENT INDICATIVE	caliento, calientas, calienta; calentamos, calentáis, calientan
PRESENT SUBJUNCTIVE	caliente, calientes, caliente; calentemos, calentéis, calienten
PRETERITE	calenté
IMPERFECT	calentaba
FUTURE	calentaré
COMMANDS	calienta, no calientes; (no) caliente Ud.; (no) calienten Uds.
PRESENT PARTICIPLE	calentando

Verbs like **calentar: cerrar, despertar, pensar, recomendar**

colgar (o → ue)

PRESENT INDICATIVE	cuelgo, cuelgas, cuelga; colgamos, colgáis, cuelgan
PRESENT SUBJUNCTIVE	cuelgue, cuelgues, cuelgue; colguemos, colguéis, cuelguen
PRETERITE	colgué, colgaste, colgó; colgamos, colgasteis, colgaron
IMPERFECT	colgaba
FUTURE	colgaré
COMMANDS	cuelga, no cuelgues; (no) cuelgue Ud.; (no) cuelguen Uds.
PRESENT PARTICIPLE	colgando

Verbs like **colgar: descolgar**

comenzar (e → ie)

PRESENT INDICATIVE	comienzo, comienzas, comienza; comenzamos, comenzáis, comienzan
PRESENT SUBJUNCTIVE	comience, comiences, comience; comencemos, comencéis, comiencen
PRETERITE	comencé, comenzaste, comenzó; comenzamos, comenzasteis, comenzaron

comenzar *(cont'd.)*

IMPERFECT	comenzaba
FUTURE	comenzaré
COMMANDS	comienza, no comiences; (no) comience Ud.; (no) comiencen Uds.
PRESENT PARTICIPLE	comenzando

Verbs like **comenzar: empezar**

despedirse (e → i)   See *pedir* and Reflexive Verbs.

despertarse (e → ie)   See *calentar* and Reflexive Verbs.

divertirse (e → ie)   See *hervir* and Reflexive Verbs.

dormir (o → ue)

PRESENT INDICATIVE	duermo, duermes, duerme; dormimos, dormís, duermen
PRESENT SUBJUNCTIVE	duerma, duermas, duerma; durmamos, durmáis, duerman
PRETERITE	dormí, dormiste, durmió; dormimos, dormisteis, durmieron
IMPERFECT	dormía
FUTURE	dormiré
COMMANDS	duerme, no duermas; (no) duerma Ud.; (no) duerman Uds.
PRESENT PARTICIPLE	durmiendo

Verbs like **dormir: morir**

dormirse (o → ue)   See *dormir* and Reflexive Verbs.

encender (e → ie)

PRESENT INDICATIVE	enciendo, enciendes, enciende; encendemos, encendéis, encienden
PRESENT SUBJUNCTIVE	encienda, enciendas, encienda; encendamos, encendáis, enciendan
PRETERITE	encendí
IMPERFECT	encendía
FUTURE	encenderé
COMMANDS	enciende, no enciendas; (no) encienda Ud.; (no) enciendan Uds.
PRESENT PARTICIPLE	encendiendo

Verbs like **encender: entender, perder**

hervir (e → ie)

PRESENT INDICATIVE	hiervo, hierves, hierve; hervimos, hervís, hierven
PRESENT SUBJUNCTIVE	hierva, hiervas, hierva; hirvamos, hirváis, hiervan
PRETERITE	herví, herviste, hirvió; hervimos, hervisteis, hirvieron
IMPERFECT	hervía
FUTURE	herviré
COMMANDS	hierve, no hiervas; (no) hierva Ud.; (no) hiervan Uds.
PRESENT PARTICIPLE	hirviendo

Verbs like **hervir: mentir, preferir, sentir**

jugar (u → ue)

PRESENT INDICATIVE	juego, juegas, juega; jugamos, jugáis, juegan
PRESENT SUBJUNCTIVE	juegue, juegues, juegue; juguemos, juguéis, jueguen
PRETERITE	jugué, jugaste, jugó; jugamos, jugasteis, jugaron
IMPERFECT	jugaba
FUTURE	jugaré

jugar *(cont'd.)* | COMMANDS | juega, no juegues; (no) juegue Ud.; (no) jueguen Uds.
| PRESENT PARTICIPLE | jugando

llover (o → ue) | PRESENT INDICATIVE | llueve
| PRESENT SUBJUNCTIVE | llueva
| PRETERITE | llovió
| IMPERFECT | llovía
| FUTURE | lloverá
| PRESENT PARTICIPLE | lloviendo

morirse See *dormir* and Reflexive Verbs.

negar (e → ie) | PRESENT INDICATIVE | niego, niegas, niega; negamos, negáis, niegan
| PRESENT SUBJUNCTIVE | niegue, niegues, niegue; neguemos, neguéis, nieguen
| PRETERITE | negué, negaste, negó; negamos, negasteis, negaron
| IMPERFECT | negaba
| FUTURE | negaré
| COMMANDS | niega, no niegues; (no) niegue Ud.; (no) nieguen Uds.
| PRESENT PARTICIPLE | negando

nevar (e → ie) | PRESENT INDICATIVE | nieva
| PRESENT SUBJUNCTIVE | nieve
| PRETERITE | nevó
| IMPERFECT | nevaba
| FUTURE | nevará
| PRESENT PARTICIPLE | nevando

pedir (e → i) | PRESENT INDICATIVE | pido, pides, pide; pedimos, pedís, piden
| PRESENT SUBJUNCTIVE | pida, pidas, pida; pidamos, pidáis, pidan
| PRETERITE | pedí, pediste, pidió; pedimos, pedisteis, pidieron
| IMPERFECT | pedía
| FUTURE | pediré
| COMMANDS | pide, no pidas; (no) pida Ud.; (no) pidan Uds.
| PRESENT PARTICIPLE | pidiendo

Verbs like **pedir: repetir, servir, vestir**

poder (o → ue) See Irregular Verbs.

probarse (o → ue) See *acostar* and Reflexive Verbs.

querer (e → ie) See Irregular Verbs.

reír (e → i) See Irregular Verbs.

reírse (e → i) See Irregular Verbs and Reflexive Verbs.

seguir (e → i) | PRESENT INDICATIVE | sigo, sigues, sigue; seguimos, seguís, siguen
| PRESENT SUBJUNCTIVE | siga, sigas, siga; sigamos, sigáis, sigan
| PRETERITE | seguí, seguiste, siguió; seguimos, seguisteis, siguieron

seguir *(cont'd.)*

IMPERFECT	seguía
FUTURE	seguiré
COMMANDS	sigue, no sigas; (no) siga Ud.; (no) sigan Uds.
PRESENT PARTICIPLE	siguiendo

sentarse (e → ie)   See *calentar* and Reflexive Verbs.

sentirse (e → ie)   See *hervir* and Reflexive Verbs.

sonreír (e → i)   See Irregular Verbs.

vestirse (e → i)   See *pedir* and Reflexive Verbs.

volver (o → ue)

PRESENT INDICATIVE	vuelvo, vuelves, vuelve; volvemos, volvéis, vuelven
PRESENT SUBJUNCTIVE	vuelva, vuelvas, vuelva; volvamos, volváis, vuelvan
PRETERITE	volví, volviste, volvió; volvimos, volvisteis, volvieron
IMPERFECT	volvía
FUTURE	volveré
COMMANDS	vuelve, no vuelvas; (no) vuelva Ud.; (no) vuelvan Uds.
PRESENT PARTICIPLE	volviendo

Verbs like **volver: desenvolver, devolver, doler, envolver**

Verbs with Spelling Changes

abrazar (z → c)

PRESENT INDICATIVE	abrazo, abrazas, abraza; abrazamos, abrazáis, abrazan
PRESENT SUBJUNCTIVE	abrace, abraces, abrace; abracemos, abracéis, abracen
PRETERITE	abracé, abrazaste, abrazó; abrazamos, abrazasteis, abrazaron
IMPERFECT	abrazaba
FUTURE	abrazaré
COMMANDS	abraza, no abraces; (no) abrace Ud.; (no) abracen Uds.
PRESENT PARTICIPLE	abrazando

Verbs like **abrazar: aterrizar, bostezar, cruzar**

almorzar (z → c)   See Stem-Changing Verbs.

apagar (g → gu)

PRESENT INDICATIVE	apago, apagas, apaga; apagamos, apagáis, apagan
PRESENT SUBJUNCTIVE	apague, apagues, apague; apaguemos, apaguéis, apaguen
PRETERITE	apagué, apagaste, apagó; apagamos, apagasteis, apagaron
IMPERFECT	apagaba
FUTURE	apagaré
COMMANDS	apaga, no apagues; (no) apague Ud.; (no) apaguen Uds.
PRESENT PARTICIPLE	apagando

Verbs like **apagar: despegar, entregar, llegar, navegar, pagar**

arrancar (c → qu)

PRESENT INDICATIVE	arranco, arrancas, arranca; arrancamos, arrancáis, arrancan
PRESENT SUBJUNCTIVE	arranque, arranques, arranque; arranquemos, arranquéis, arranquen

arrancar *(cont'd.)*	PRETERITE	arranqué, arrancaste, arrancó; arrancamos, arrancasteis, arrancaron
	IMPERFECT	arrancaba
	FUTURE	arrancaré
	COMMANDS	arranca, no arranques; (no) arranque Ud.; (no) arranquen Uds.
	PRESENT PARTICIPLE	arrancando

Verbs like **arrancar: buscar, colocar, chocar, explicar, indicar, marcar, mascar, practicar, sacar, secar, tocar**

averiguar (u → ü)	PRESENT INDICATIVE	averiguo, averiguas, averigua; averiguamos, averiguáis, averiguan
	PRESENT SUBJUNCTIVE	averigüe, averigües, averigüe; averigüemos, averigüéis, averigüen
	PRETERITE	averigüé, averiguaste, averiguó; averiguamos, averiguasteis, averiguaron
	IMPERFECT	averiguaba
	FUTURE	averiguaré
	COMMANDS	averigua, no averigües; (no) averigüe Ud.; (no) averigüen Uds.
	PRESENT PARTICIPLE	averiguando

colgar (g → gu) See Stem-Changing Verbs.

comenzar (z → c) See Stem-Changing Verbs.

continuar (u → ú)	PRESENT INDICATIVE	continúo, continúas, continúa; continuamos, continuáis, continúan
	PRESENT SUBJUNCTIVE	continúe, continúes, continúe; continuemos, continuéis, continúen
	PRETERITE	continué, continuaste, continuó; continuamos, continuasteis, continuaron
	IMPERFECT	continuaba
	FUTURE	continuaré
	COMMANDS	continúa, no continúes; (no) continúe Ud.; (no) continúen Uds.
	PRESENT PARTICIPLE	continuando

creer (i → y)	PRESENT INDICATIVE	creo, crees, cree; creemos, creéis, creen
	PRESENT SUBJUNCTIVE	crea, creas, crea; creamos, creáis, crean
	PRETERITE	creí, creíste, creyó; creímos, creísteis, creyeron
	IMPERFECT	creía
	FUTURE	creeré
	COMMANDS	cree, no creas; (no) crea Ud.; (no) crean Uds.
	PRESENT PARTICIPLE	creyendo

Verbs like **creer: leer**

descolgar (g → gu) See Stem-Changing Verbs.

dirigir (g → j)	PRESENT INDICATIVE	dirijo, diriges, dirige; dirigimos, dirigís, dirigen
	PRESENT SUBJUNCTIVE	dirija, dirijas, dirija; dirijamos, dirijáis, dirijan
	PRETERITE	dirigí, dirigiste, dirigió; dirigimos, dirigisteis, dirigieron
	IMPERFECT	dirigía

dirigir *(cont'd.)*

FUTURE	dirigiré
COMMANDS	dirige,no dirijas; (no) dirija Ud.; (no) dirijan Uds.
PRESENT PARTICIPLE	dirigiendo

empezar (z → c)   See Stem-Changing Verbs.

escoger (g → j)

PRESENT INDICATIVE	escojo, escoges, escoge; escogemos, escogéis, escogen
PRESENT SUBJUNCTIVE	escoja, escojas, escoja; escojamos, escojáis, escojan
PRETERITE	escogí, escogiste, escogió; escogimos, escogisteis, escogieron
IMPERFECT	escogía
FUTURE	escogeré
COMMANDS	escoge, no escojas; (no) escoja Ud.; (no) escojan Uds.
PRESENT PARTICIPLE	escogiendo

Verbs like **escoger:** recoger

esquiar (i → í)

PRESENT INDICATIVE	esquío, esquías, esquía; esquiamos, esquiáis, esquían
PRESENT SUBJUNCTIVE	esquíe, esquíes, esquíe; esquiemos, esquiéis, esquíen
PRETERITE	esquié, esquiaste, esquió; esquiamos, esquiasteis, esquiaron
IMPERFECT	esquiaba
FUTURE	esquiaré
COMMANDS	esquía, no esquíes; (no) esquíe Ud.; (no) esquíen Uds.
PRESENT PARTICIPLE	esquiando

graduarse (u → ú)   See *continuar* and Reflexive Verbs.

jugar (g → gu)   See Stem-Changing Verbs.

negar (g → gu)   See Stem-Changing Verbs.

reunirse (u → ú)

PRESENT INDICATIVE	me reúno, te reúnes, se reúne; nos reunimos, os reunís, se reúnen
PRESENT SUBJUNCTIVE	me reúna, te reúnas, se reúna; nos reunamos, os reunáis, se reúnan
PRETERITE	me reuní, te reuniste, se reunió; nos reunimos, os reunisteis, se reunieron
IMPERFECT	me reunía
FUTURE	me reuniré
COMMANDS	reúnete, no te reúnas; reúnase Ud., no se reúna Ud.; reúnanse Uds., no se reúnan Uds.
PRESENT PARTICIPLE	reuniéndose

Irregular Verbs

caer

PRESENT INDICATIVE	caigo, caes, cae; caemos, caéis, caen
PRESENT SUBJUNCTIVE	caiga, caigas, caiga; caigamos, caigáis, caigan
PRETERITE	caí, caíste, cayó; caímos, caísteis, cayeron
IMPERFECT	caía
FUTURE	caeré

caer *(cont'd.)*

COMMANDS	cae, no caigas; (no) caiga Ud.; (no) caigan Uds.
PRESENT PARTICIPLE	cayendo

caerse   See *caer* and Reflexive Verbs.

conocer

PRESENT INDICATIVE	conozco, conoces, conoce; conocemos, conocéis, conocen
PRESENT SUBJUNCTIVE	conozca, conozcas, conozca; conozcamos, conozcáis, conozcan
PRETERITE	conocí, conociste, conoció; conocimos, conocisteis, conocieron
IMPERFECT	conocía
FUTURE	conoceré
COMMANDS	conoce, no conozcas; (no) conozca Ud.; (no) conozcan Uds.
PRESENT PARTICIPLE	conociendo

Verbs like **conocer: agradecer, nacer, ofrecer, parecer, reconocer**

construir

PRESENT INDICATIVE	construyo, construyes, construye; construimos, construís, construyen
PRESENT SUBJUNCTIVE	construya, construyas, construya; construyamos, construyáis, construyan
PRETERITE	construí, construiste, construyó; construimos, construisteis, construyeron
IMPERFECT	construía
FUTURE	construiré
COMMANDS	construye, no construyas; (no) construya Ud.; (no) construyan Uds.
PRESENT PARTICIPLE	construyendo

Verbs like **construir: destruir, huir, incluir**

dar

PRESENT INDICATIVE	doy, das, da; damos, dais, dan
PRESENT SUBJUNCTIVE	dé, des, dé; demos, deis, den
PRETERITE	di, diste, dio; dimos, disteis, dieron
IMPERFECT	daba
FUTURE	daré
COMMANDS	da, no des; (no) dé Ud.; (no) den Uds.
PRESENT PARTICIPLE	dando

decir

PRESENT INDICATIVE	digo, dices, dice; decimos, decís, dicen
PRESENT SUBJUNCTIVE	diga, digas, diga; digamos, digáis, digan
PRETERITE	dije, dijiste, dijo; dijimos, dijisteis, dijeron
IMPERFECT	decía
FUTURE	diré, dirás, dirá; diremos, diréis, dirán
COMMANDS	di, no digas; (no) diga Ud.; (no) digan Uds.
PRESENT PARTICIPLE	diciendo

estar

PRESENT INDICATIVE	estoy, estás, está; estamos, estáis, están
PRESENT SUBJUNCTIVE	esté, estés, esté; estemos, estéis, estén
PRETERITE	estuve, estuviste, estuvo; estuvimos, estuvisteis, estuvieron
IMPERFECT	estaba
FUTURE	estaré
COMMANDS	está, no estés; (no) esté Ud.; (no) estén Uds.
PRESENT PARTICIPLE	estando

haber		
	PRESENT INDICATIVE	he, has, ha; hemos, habéis, han
	PRESENT SUBJUNCTIVE	haya, hayas, haya; hayamos, hayáis, hayan
	PRETERITE	hube, hubiste, hubo; hubimos, hubisteis, hubieron
	IMPERFECT	había
	FUTURE	habré, habrás, habrá; habremos, habréis, habrán
	PRESENT PARTICIPLE	habiendo

hacer		
	PRESENT INDICATIVE	hago, haces, hace; hacemos, hacéis, hacen
	PRESENT SUBJUNCTIVE	haga, hagas, haga; hagamos, hagáis, hagan
	PRETERITE	hice, hiciste, hizo; hicimos, hicisteis, hicieron
	IMPERFECT	hacía
	FUTURE	haré, harás, hará; haremos, haréis, harán
	COMMANDS	haz, no hagas; (no) haga Ud.; (no) hagan Uds.
	PRESENT PARTICIPLE	haciendo

ir		
	PRESENT INDICATIVE	voy, vas, va; vamos, vais, van
	PRESENT SUBJUNCTIVE	vaya, vayas, vaya; vayamos, vayáis, vayan
	PRETERITE	fui, fuiste, fue; fuimos, fuisteis, fueron
	IMPERFECT	iba, ibas, iba; íbamos, ibais, iban
	FUTURE	iré
	COMMANDS	ve, no vayas; (no) vaya Ud.; (no) vayan Uds.
	PRESENT PARTICIPLE	yendo

irse   See *ir* and Reflexive Verbs.

oír		
	PRESENT INDICATIVE	oigo, oyes, oye; oímos, oís, oyen
	PRESENT SUBJUNCTIVE	oiga, oigas, oiga; oigamos, oigáis, oigan
	PRETERITE	oí, oíste, oyó; oímos, oísteis, oyeron
	IMPERFECT	oía
	FUTURE	oiré
	COMMANDS	oye, no oigas; (no) oiga Ud.; (no) oigan Uds.
	PRESENT PARTICIPLE	oyendo

parecerse   See *conocer* and Reflexive Verbs.

poder		
	PRESENT INDICATIVE	puedo, puedes, puede; podemos, podéis, pueden
	PRESENT SUBJUNCTIVE	pueda, puedas, pueda; podamos, podáis, puedan
	PRETERITE	pude, pudiste, pudo; pudimos, pudisteis, pudieron
	IMPERFECT	podía
	FUTURE	podré, podrás, podrá; podremos, podréis, podrán
	PRESENT PARTICIPLE	pudiendo

poner		
	PRESENT INDICATIVE	pongo, pones, pone; ponemos, ponéis, ponen
	PRESENT SUBJUNCTIVE	ponga, pongas, ponga; pongamos, pongáis, pongan
	PRETERITE	puse, pusiste, puso; pusimos, pusisteis, pusieron
	IMPERFECT	ponía
	FUTURE	pondré, pondrás, pondrá; pondremos, pondréis, pondrán
	COMMANDS	pon, no pongas; (no) ponga Ud.; (no) pongan Uds.
	PRESENT PARTICIPLE	poniendo

ponerse   See *poner* and Reflexive Verbs.

producir

PRESENT INDICATIVE	produzco, produces, produce; producimos, producís, producen
PRESENT SUBJUNCTIVE	produzca, produzcas, produzca; produzcamos, produzcáis, produzcan
PRETERITE	produje, produjiste, produjo; produjimos, produjisteis, produjeron
IMPERFECT	producía
FUTURE	produciré
COMMANDS	produce, no produzcas; (no) produzca Ud.; (no) produzcan Uds.
PRESENT PARTICIPLE	produciendo

Verbs like **producir**: traducir

querer

PRESENT INDICATIVE	quiero, quieres, quiere; queremos, queréis, quieren
PRESENT SUBJUNCTIVE	quiera, quieras, quiera; queramos, queráis, quieran
PRETERITE	quise, quisiste, quiso; quisimos, quisisteis, quisieron
IMPERFECT	quería
FUTURE	querré, querrás, querrá; querremos, querréis, querrán
COMMANDS	quiere, no quieras; (no) quiera Ud.; (no) quieran Uds.
PRESENT PARTICIPLE	queriendo

reír

PRESENT INDICATIVE	río, ríes, ríe; reímos, reís, ríen
PRESENT SUBJUNCTIVE	ría, rías, ría; riamos, riáis, rían
PRETERITE	reí, reíste, rió; reímos, reísteis, rieron
IMPERFECT	reía
FUTURE	reiré
COMMANDS	ríe, no rías; (no) ría Ud.; (no) rían Uds.
PRESENT PARTICIPLE	riendo

Verbs like **reír: sonreír**

reírse   See *reír* and Reflexive Verbs.

saber

PRESENT INDICATIVE	sé, sabes, sabe; sabemos, sabéis, saben
PRESENT SUBJUNCTIVE	sepa, sepas, sepa; sepamos, sepáis, sepan
PRETERITE	supe, supiste, supo; supimos, supisteis, supieron
IMPERFECT	sabía
FUTURE	sabré, sabrás, sabrá; sabremos, sabréis, sabrán
COMMANDS	sabe, no sepas; (no) sepa Ud.; (no) sepan Uds.
PRESENT PARTICIPLE	sabiendo

salir

PRESENT INDICATIVE	salgo, sales, sale; salimos, salís, salen
PRESENT SUBJUNCTIVE	salga, salgas, salga; salgamos, salgáis, salgan
PRETERITE	salí, saliste, salió; salimos, salisteis, salieron
IMPERFECT	salía
FUTURE	saldré, saldrás, saldrá; saldremos, saldréis, saldrán
COMMANDS	sal, no salgas; (no) salga Ud.; (no) salgan Uds.
PRESENT PARTICIPLE	saliendo

ser

PRESENT INDICATIVE	soy, eres, es; somos, sois, son
PRESENT SUBJUNCTIVE	sea, seas, sea; seamos, seáis, sean

ser *(cont'd.)*

PRETERITE	fui, fuiste, fue; fuimos, fuisteis, fueron
IMPERFECT	era, eras, era; éramos, erais, eran
FUTURE	seré
COMMANDS	sé, no seas; (no) sea Ud.; (no) sean Uds.
PRESENT PARTICIPLE	siendo

tener

PRESENT INDICATIVE	tengo, tienes, tiene; tenemos, tenéis, tienen
PRESENT SUBJUNCTIVE	tenga, tengas, tenga; tengamos, tengáis, tengan
PRETERITE	tuve, tuviste, tuvo; tuvimos, tuvisteis, tuvieron
IMPERFECT	tenía
FUTURE	tendré, tendrás, tendrá; tendremos, tendréis, tendrán
COMMANDS	ten, no tengas; (no) tenga Ud.; (no) tengan Uds.
PRESENT PARTICIPLE	teniendo

Verbs like **tener: obtener**

traer

PRESENT INDICATIVE	traigo, traes, trae; traemos, traéis, traen
PRESENT SUBJUNCTIVE	traiga, traigas, traiga; traigamos, traigáis, traigan
PRETERITE	traje, trajiste, trajo; trajimos, trajisteis, trajeron
IMPERFECT	traía
FUTURE	traeré
COMMANDS	trae, no traigas; (no) traiga Ud.; (no) traigan Uds.
PRESENT PARTICIPLE	trayendo

venir

PRESENT INDICATIVE	vengo, vienes, viene; venimos, venís, vienen
PRESENT SUBJUNCTIVE	venga, vengas, venga; vengamos, vengáis, vengan
PRETERITE	vine, viniste, vino; vinimos, vinisteis, vinieron
IMPERFECT	venía
FUTURE	vendré, vendrás, vendrá; vendremos, vendréis, vendrán
COMMANDS	ven, no vengas; (no) venga Ud.; (no) vengan Uds.
PRESENT PARTICIPLE	viniendo

ver

PRESENT INDICATIVE	veo, ves, ve; vemos, veis, ven
PRESENT SUBJUNCTIVE	vea, veas, vea; veamos, veáis, vean
PRETERITE	vi, viste, vio; vimos, visteis, vieron
IMPERFECT	veía, veías, veía; veíamos, veíais, veían
FUTURE	veré
COMMANDS	ve, no veas; (no) vea Ud.; (no) vean Uds.
PRESENT PARTICIPLE	viendo

VOCABULARIO ESPAÑOL-INGLÉS

The *Vocabulario español-inglés* contains all active vocabulary from *PASOS Y PUENTES* and *VOCES Y VISTAS*.

A dash (—) represents the main entry word. For example, **el — mineral** following **el agua** means **el agua mineral**.

The number following each entry indicates the chapter in which the word or expression is first introduced. Two numbers indicate that it is introduced in one chapter and elaborated upon in a later chapter. A Roman numeral (I) indicates that the word was presented in *VOCES Y VISTAS*.

The following abbreviations are used: *adj.* (adjective), *adv.* (adverb), *dir. obj.* (direct object), *f.* (feminine), *fam.* (familiar), *ind. obj.* (indirect object), *inf.* (infinitive), *m.* (masculine), *prep.* (preposition), *pl.* (plural), *pron.* (pronoun), *sing.* (singular).

a, al at; to; *as sign of dir. obj.* (I)
 — **menudo** often (I)
 — **pie** on foot (I)
 — **tiempo** on time (I)
 — **veces** sometimes (I)
abierto, -a open (I)
el abogado, la abogada lawyer (15)
abrazar to embrace, to hug (13)
el abrelatas, *pl.* **abrelatas** can opener (4)
el abrigo overcoat (I)
abril April (I)
abrir to open (I)
abstracto, -a abstract (12)
el abuelo, la abuela grandfather, grandmother (I)
los abuelos grandfathers; grandparents (I)
aburrido, -a bored; boring (I)
aburrir to bore (11)
 —se to be bored, to get bored (11)
acabar de + *inf.* to have just *(done something)* (I)
acampar: la tienda de — tent (4)
el accidente accident (8)
el aceite oil (4)
la aceituna olive (4)
el acelerador accelerator (8)
acelerar to speed up, to accelerate (8)
el acento accent mark (I)
aceptar to accept (15)

el acomodador, la acomodadora usher (11)
acompañar to go / come with, to accompany (15)
acondicionado: el aire — air conditioning (2)
aconsejar to advise (15)
acostar (o → ue) to put *(someone)* to bed (I)
 —se to go to bed (I)
la actividad activity (4)
activo, -a active, energetic (5)
el acto act (14)
el actor, la actriz, *f. pl.* **actrices** actor, actress (I)
acuerdo:
 de — right! okay! all right! (5)
 estar de — to agree (I)
adentro inside (I)
adiós good-by (I)
el admirador, la admiradora fan (11)
admirar to admire (1)
¿adónde? (to) where? (I)
la aduana customs (16)
el aduanero, la aduanera customs official (16)
aérea:
 la línea — airline (16)
 vía — air mail (10)
el aeropuerto airport (I)
afeitar(se) to shave (7)
 la crema de — shaving cream (7)

 la maquinilla de — razor (7)
el aficionado, la aficionada (a) fan (of) (I)
afortunadamente fortunately (3)
el África *f.* Africa (I)
afuera outside (I)
la agencia de viajes travel agency (I)
el/la agente de viajes travel agent (I)
agosto August (I)
agradable pleasant (I)
agradecer (c → zc) to thank *(someone)* for, to appreciate (11)
el agua *f.* water (I)
 el — mineral mineral water (I)
el aguacate avocado (9)
¡ah, sí! yes! (I)
ahora now (I)
 — mismo right away, right now (2)
ahorrar to save (15)
el aire acondicionado air conditioning (2)
el ajedrez chess (I)
el ajo garlic (4)
alegrarse (de) to be happy (about) (16)
alegría: ¡qué —! how nice! how marvelous! (16)
alemán (*pl.* **alemanes), alemana** German (I)
el alemán German *(language)* (I)

Alemania Germany (I)
la alfombra rug (I)
el álgebra algebra (I)
algo something, anything (I)
   tomar — to have something to drink (I)
el algodón cotton (14)
alguien someone, somebody, anyone (I)
algún, alguna some, any, a (I)
alguno, -a, -os, -as *pron.* some, any, one (I)
alivio: ¡qué —! what a relief! (3)
el almacén, *pl.* **almacenes** department store (I)
la almohada pillow (I)
almorzar (o → ue) to eat lunch, to have lunch (2)
el almuerzo lunch (I)
¿aló? hello? *(on phone)* (I)
alquilar to rent (2)
alrededor de around, about (7)
alto, -a tall (I)
   en voz —a in a loud voice, out loud (10)
el alumno, la alumna pupil (I)
allá (over) there (I)
allí there (I)
   por — around there, over there, that way (8)
amable kind, nice (I)
amarillo, -a yellow (I)
la ambición, *pl.* **ambiciones** ambition (15)
ambicioso, -a ambitious (15)
la ambulancia ambulance (9)
la América Central / del Norte / del Sur / Latina Central / North / South / Latin America (I)
americano, -a American (I)
el amigo, la amiga friend (I)
el amor love (13)
anaranjado, -a orange (I)
el anciano, la anciana old man, old woman (13)
ancho, -a wide (7)
el andén, *pl.* **andenes** *(railway)* platform (6)
el anillo ring (I)
   animados: los dibujos — movie cartoons (I)
el animal animal (I)
   el — doméstico pet (I)
anoche last night (I)
anteayer the day before yesterday (5)

los anteojos eyeglasses (I)
   los — de sol sunglasses (I)
antes before (that), first (3)
   — de before (I)
   — de + *inf.* before *(doing something)* (I)
anticuado, -a old-fashioned (7)
antiguo, -a old, ancient (14)
antipático, -a unpleasant, not nice (I)
el antropólogo, la antropóloga anthropologist (15)
anunciar to announce (6)
el anuncio advertisement, ad (14)
   el — comercial commercial (I)
añadir to add (2)
el año year (I)
   ¿cuántos —s tienes? how old are you? (I)
   cumplir . . . —s to have a birthday, to turn (+ *age*) (13)
   el — escolar school year (1)
   el día de fin de — New Year's Eve (I)
   los quince —s fifteenth birthday (party) (I)
   tener . . . —s to be . . . years old (I)
el Año Nuevo New Year's Day (I)
apagar to put out, to turn off *(a fire, light, etc.)* (4)
el aparato braces *(for teeth)* (15)
el apartado postal post office box (10)
el apartamento apartment (I)
el apellido last name, surname (I)
aplaudir to applaud (12)
aprender to learn (I)
   — a + *inf.* to learn how (to) (I)
   — de memoria to memorize (I)
el apunte note (1)
aquel, aquella; aquellos, aquellas *adj.* that; those (2)
aquél, aquélla; aquéllos, aquéllas *pron.* that one; those (2)
aquello *neuter pron.* that (2)
aquí here (I)
   — lo (la / los / las) tiene(s) here it is, here they are (I)
   — tienes / tiene Ud. here is; here are (I)
   por — around here, over here, this way (8)
la araña spider (4)
el árbol tree (I)
la arena sand (15)

el arete earring (I)
argentino, -a Argentine (6)
el argumento plot (11)
el armario closet (I)
el arqueólogo, la arqueóloga archaeologist (14)
el arquitecto, la arquitecta architect (14)
   arrancar to start *(car)* (8)
   arreglar to fix, to repair (I)
el arroz rice (I)
el arte art (I)
el artículo article (14)
el/la artista artist (12)
   asado, -a roasted (4)
el asado barbecue (4)
   hacer un — to have a barbecue (4)
   asar to roast (4)
   — a la parrilla to barbecue, to grill (4)
el ascensor elevator (I)
   así, así so-so (I)
el asiento seat (I)
   asistir a to attend (I)
   asombroso, -a amazing, astonishing (14)
la aspiradora vacuum cleaner (2)
   pasar la — to vacuum (2)
el astrónomo, la astrónoma astronomer (14)
   asustado, -a frightened, scared (3)
   asustar to frighten, to scare (3)
   atar(se) to tie (7)
la atención: prestar — to pay attention (1)
   aterrizar to land (I)
el/la atleta athlete (I)
   atlético, -a athletic (I)
la atracción, *pl.* **atracciones** *(amusement park)* ride, attraction (3)
   aumentar: — de peso to gain weight (9)
   ausente absent (I)
el autobús, *pl.* **autobuses** bus (I)
el autógrafo autograph (11)
el autor, la autora author (1)
el/la auxiliar de vuelo flight attendant (I)
la avenida avenue (I)
la aventura adventure (I)
   averiguar to find out (10)
el avión, *pl.* **aviones** plane (I)
el aviso notice; warning (10)
   ayer yesterday (I)

el/la **ayudante** helper, assistant (15)
  ayudar (a + *inf.*) to help (I)
los **aztecas** Aztecs (14)
el **azúcar** sugar (I)
  azul blue (I)

  bailar to dance (I)
el **bailarín (***pl.* **bailarines), la**
    bailarina dancer (12)
el **baile** dance (I)
  bajar to come down, to go down
    (I)
    — **de** to get off or out of
      (*vehicles*) (I)
    — **de peso** to lose weight (9)
  bajo, -a short (I)
    en voz —a in a soft voice, softly
      (10)
    la planta —a ground floor (I)
la **balanza** scale (9)
el **balcón,** *pl.* **balcones** balcony (I)
el **balón,** *pl.* **balones** ball (I)
el **banco** bank (I)
la **banda** band (*musical*) (3)
la **bandera** flag (I)
  bañar to bathe (*someone*) (I)
    —**se** to take a bath (I)
el **baño** bathroom (I)
    el traje de — bathing suit (I)
  barato, -a cheap, inexpensive (I)
la **barba** beard (7)
  barbaridad: ¡qué —! good grief!
    how awful! (5)
el **barco** boat (I)
  barrer to sweep (2)
el **barrio** neighborhood (I)
el **básquetbol** basketball (I)
  bastante rather, fairly, kind of (I);
    enough (15)
la **basura** garbage (2)
el **basurero** garbage can (2)
  batir to beat (2)
el **baúl** (*car*) trunk (8)
el **bautizo** baptism (13)
el **bebé** baby (13)
  beber to drink (I)
la **bebida** drink, beverage (I)
el **béisbol** baseball (I)
  bellísimo, -a very beautiful (I)
  bello, -a beautiful (I)
  besar to kiss (13)
el **beso** kiss (10)
la **biblioteca** library (I)
el **bibliotecario, la bibliotecaria**
    librarian (1)

la **bicicleta** bicycle (I)
  montar en — to ride a bicycle
    (I)
  bien well, good (I)
    está — okay, all right (I)
  bienvenido, -a welcome (I)
el **bigote** mustache (7)
  bilingüe bilingual (I)
el **billete** bill (*money*) (6)
la **biografía** biography (1)
la **biología** biology (I)
el **bisabuelo, la bisabuela** great-
    grandfather, great-
    grandmother (13)
el **bistec** steak (I)
  blanco, -a white (I)
la **blusa** blouse (I)
la **boca** mouth (I)
la **bocina** (*car*) horn (8)
  tocar la — to honk the horn (8)
la **boda** wedding (13)
el **boleto** ticket (I)
el **bolígrafo** (ballpoint) pen (I)
  boliviano, -a Bolivian (6)
los **bolos: jugar a los —** to bowl (3)
la **bolsa** bag (3)
el **bolsillo** pocket (6)
el **bolso** purse (I)
el **bombero, la bombera** firefighter
    (14)
la **bombilla** lightbulb (2)
  bondad: tenga la — de + *inf.* will
    you...? (10)
  bonito, -a pretty, good-looking (I)
el **borrador** (blackboard) eraser (I)
  borrar to erase (I)
  bostezar to yawn (11)
la **bota** boot (I)
la **botella** bottle (I)
el **Brasil** Brazil (I)
  brasileño, -a Brazilian (6)
  ¡bravo! bravo! (12)
el **brazo** arm (I)
  bucear to scuba dive (5)
  bueno (buen), -a good (I)
    —**as noches** good evening,
      good night (I)
    —**as tardes** good afternoon,
      good evening (I)
    bueno, . . . well . . . (I)
    ¡bueno! okay, fine (I)
    —**os días** good morning (I)
    ¡buen provecho! enjoy your
      meal (4)
    hace buen tiempo it's nice (out)
      (I)

    ¡qué —! great! (I)
la **bufanda** scarf, muffler (I)
el **burrito** burrito (I)
  buscar to look for (I)
    ir / venir a — to go / come get,
      to pick up (10)
el **buzón,** *pl.* **buzones** mailbox (10)

el **caballo** horse (I)
  montar a — to ride horseback (5)
la **cabeza** head (I)
la **cabina telefónica** phone booth (I)
el **cacahuate** peanut (3)
la **cacerola** pan, saucepan (2)
el **cacharro** jalopy (8)
  cada each, every (I)
  caer to fall (10)
    —**se** to fall down (10)
    — **bien / mal a** to make a good /
      bad impression (*on someone*);
      to like / not like (*someone*) (13)
el **café** café; coffee (I)
    el — con leche coffee with
      cream (I)
la **cafetería** cafeteria (I)
el **caimán,** *pl.* **caimanes** alligator (I)
la **caja** box (I); cash register (7)
el **cajero, la cajera** cashier (7)
el **calcetín,** *pl.* **calcetines** sock (I)
la **calculadora** calculator (1)
la **calefacción** heating system, heat
    (2)
el **calendario** calendar (I)
  calentar (e → ie) to heat (4)
  caliente hot (I)
el **calor:**
    hace — it's hot (out) (I)
    tener — to be hot (*person*) (I)
las **calorías** calories (9)
  ¡cállate! be quiet! (11)
la **calle** street (I)
    el cruce (de —s) intersection (8)
la **cama** bed (I)
    el coche — sleeping car (6)
la **cámara** camera (I)
el **camarero, la camarera** waiter,
    waitress (I)
el **camarón,** *pl.* **camarones** shrimp
    (9)
  cambiar to change, to exchange
    (I)
    — **de idea** to change one's
      mind (3)
el **cambio: la casa de —** currency
    exchange (6)

caminar to walk (I)

el camino road (I)

el camión, *pl.* camiones truck (I)

la camisa shirt (I)

la camiseta t-shirt (I)

el campamento campground (4)

el campeón (*pl.* campeones), la campeona champion (5)

el campeonato championship (5)

el campesino, la campesina farm worker (4)

camping: ir de — to go camping (4)

el campo country, countryside (I)

canadiense Canadian (I)

el canal TV channel (I)

la canasta basket (3)

la canción, *pl.* canciones song (I)

la cancha de tenis tennis court (5)

la canoa canoe (15)

cansado, -a tired (I)

el/la cantante singer (11)

cantar to sing (I)

capaz, *pl.* capaces capable, able (15)

la capital capital (I)

el capítulo chapter (I)

el capó (*car*) hood (8)

capturar to catch, to capture (14)

la cara face (I)

costar un ojo de la — to cost an arm and a leg (7)

¡caramba! gosh! gee! (I)

el Caribe Caribbean (I)

el cariño affection (10)

con — affectionately (10)

cariñoso, -a (con) affectionate (with) (13)

carísimo, -a very expensive (I)

el carnaval carnival, Mardi Gras (I)

la carne meat (I)

el carné membership card, ID card (5)

la carnicería butcher shop (I)

caro, -a expensive (I)

la carrera race (5)

la carretera highway (8)

el carril lane (8)

el carrusel carrousel, merry-go-round (3)

la carta letter (I)

el cartel poster (I)

la cartera wallet (I)

el cartero, la cartera mail carrier (10)

la casa house (I)

a — (*to one's*) home (I)

en — at home (I)

la — de cambio currency exchange (6)

la — de los espejos house of mirrors (3)

la — de los fantasmas house of horrors (3)

casado, -a (con) married (to) (13)

casarse (con) to marry, to get married (to) (13)

casi almost (I)

el caso: un — de urgencia emergency (case) (9)

castaño, -a chestnut (*color*) (7)

el castillo castle (6)

catorce fourteen (I)

la causa cause (14)

a — de because of (14)

la cebolla onion (I)

la cebra zebra (I)

la celebración, *pl.* celebraciones celebration (I)

celebrar to celebrate (I)

celos: tener — de to be jealous of (13)

la cena dinner, supper, evening meal (I)

cenar to have dinner (4)

el centavo cent (I)

el centro downtown (I); center, middle (12)

centroamericano, -a Central American (I)

cepillar (el pelo) to brush (someone's hair) (I)

—se (los dientes, el pelo) to brush one's (teeth, hair) (I)

el cepillo de dientes toothbrush (I)

la cerámica ceramics (12)

cerca de near, close to (I)

el cerdo pig (I)

la chuleta de — pork chop (I)

el cereal cereal (9)

la cereza cherry (9)

cero zero (I)

cerrado, -a closed (I)

cerrar (e → ie) to close (I)

certificado, -a registered (10)

el césped lawn (2)

ciego, -a blind (11)

el cielo sky (I)

cien one hundred (I)

ciencia ficción: de — *adj.* science fiction (I)

las ciencias science (I)

el científico, la científica scientist (15)

ciento uno, -a; ciento dos; etc. 101; 102; etc. (I)

cierto, -a certain (16)

es — it's true (16)

cinco five (I)

cincuenta fifty (I)

el cine movies; movie theater (I)

la estrella de — movie star (11)

la cinta tape (I)

el cinturón, *pl.* cinturones belt (I)

el — de seguridad, *pl.* cinturones de seguridad seatbelt (8)

la cita appointment, date (13)

la ciudad city (I)

la civilización, *pl.* civilizaciones civilization (14)

el clarinete clarinet (12)

claro, -a bright, clear (6)

— (que sí) of course (I)

— que no of course not (I)

la clase (de) class; kind, type (I)

el compañero, la compañera de — classmate (I)

de primera (segunda) — first-(second-)class (6)

toda — de all kinds of (11)

clásico, -a classical (I)

el/la cliente customer (I)

el clima climate (15)

la clínica clinic (9)

el club, *pl.* clubes club (5)

cobrar:

— un cheque to cash a check (6)

la llamada por — collect call (10)

cocido, -a: bien / medio / poco — well-done / medium / rare (4)

la cocina kitchen (I)

cocinar to cook (I)

el coco coconut (9)

el coche car (I)

el — cama, *pl.* —s cama sleeping car (6)

el — comedor, *pl.* —s comedor dining car (6)

el — deportivo sports car (8)

el código postal zip code (10)

el codo elbow (9)

la col cabbage (9)

cola: hacer — to stand in line (I)

la colección, *pl.* colecciones collection (12)

coleccionar to collect (I)

el colegio high school (I)

el — **particular** private school (1)

colgar (o → ue) to hang up (10)

la **colina** hill (4)

colocar to put, to place (6)

colombiano, -a Colombian (6)

el **color** color (I)

¿**de qué** —? what color? (I)

en —**es** in color (I)

el **collar** necklace (I)

el **comedor** dining room (I)

el coche — dining car (6)

comenzar (e → ie) (a + *inf.*) to begin, to start (6)

comer to eat (I)

dar de — **a** to feed (I)

comercial *see* **anuncio**

los **comestibles** groceries (I)

cómico, -a comic (I)

la **comida** food; meal (I)

como like, as (2)

cómo how (I)

¿— **es** . . . ? what's . . . like? (I)

¡— **no!** of course! (I)

¿— **te llamas?** what's your name? (I)

la **cómoda** dresser (I)

cómodo, -a comfortable (I)

el **compañero, la compañera de clase** classmate (I)

la **compañía** company (10)

compartir to share (13)

completamente completely (3)

complicado, -a complicated (11)

la **composición,** *pl.* **composiciones** composition (1)

el **compositor, la compositora** composer (12)

comprar to buy (I)

compras: de — shopping (I)

comprender to understand (I)

la **computadora** computer (I)

el programador / la programadora de —**s** computer programmer (15)

con with (I)

— **cariño** affectionately (10)

— **cuidado** carefully (8)

— **mucho gusto** gladly, with pleasure (I)

— **permiso** excuse me (I)

— **(+** *time* **+ de) retraso** late (6)

el **concierto** concert (I)

el **concurso** contest, competition (11)

el programa de —**s** quiz show (11)

el **conductor, la conductora** driver (8)

congelado, -a frozen (4)

conmigo with me (I)

conocer (c → zc) to know, to be acquainted with (I); to meet, to get to know (11)

conocido, -a: muy — well-known (I)

el **consejo** piece of advice; *pl.* advice (15)

construir to build, to construct (14)

contado: pagar al — to pay cash (6)

contar (o → ue) to count, to tell (I)

contento, -a happy (I)

contestar to answer (I)

contigo with you (*fam.*) (I)

continuamente continually (16)

continuar to continue (I)

contra against, versus (5)

el **contrabajo** bass (12)

contrario: al — on the contrary (I)

el **corazón** heart (I)

la **corbata** tie (I)

el **cordero** lamb (I)

la chuleta de — lamb chop (I)

el **cordón,** *pl.* **cordones** cord (2)

los cordones de los zapatos shoelaces (7)

el **coro** chorus, choir (12)

correcto, -a correct (I)

el **correo** post office (I); mail (10)

por — by mail (10)

correr to run (I)

la **corrida (de toros)** bullfight (I)

el **cortacésped** lawn mower (2)

cortar to cut; to mow (2)

—**(se) el pelo / las uñas** to cut (one's) hair / nails (7)

la **cortina** curtain (2)

corto, -a short (I)

la **cosa** thing (I)

otra — something else, anything else (11)

costar (o → ue) to cost (I)

— **un ojo de la cara** to cost an arm and a leg (7)

costarricense Costa Rican (1)

el **crédito: la tarjeta de** — credit card (6)

creer to think, to believe (I)

creo que no I don't think so (I)

creo que sí I think so (I)

la **crema de afeitar** shaving cream (7)

el **cruce (de calles)** intersection (8)

cruzar to cross (6)

el **cuaderno** notebook (I)

la **cuadra** (city) block (8)

el **cuadro** painting (3)

¿**cuál, -es?** what?; which one(s)? (I)

¿— **es la fecha de hoy?** what's the date today? (I)

cuando when (I)

¿**cuándo?** when? (I)

¿**cuanto?** how much? (I)

¿— **dura?** how long does (*something*) last? (I)

¿— **tiempo?** how long? (I)

¿**cuántos, -as?** how many? (I)

¿— **años tienes?** how old are you? (I)

cuarenta forty (I)

cuarto:

menos — quarter to (I)

y — quarter after, quarter past (I)

cuarto, -a fourth (5)

el **cuarto** room (I)

cuatro four (I)

cuatrocientos, -as four hundred (I)

cubano, -a Cuban (I)

la **cuchara** spoon (I)

la **cucharita** teaspoon (2)

el **cuchillo** knife (I)

el **cuello** neck (9)

la **cuenta** check (*in restaurant*) (I)

darse — **de** to realize (14)

el **cuento** story (I)

el **cuero** leather (14)

el **cuerpo** body (I)

cuidado:

¡—! watch out! be careful! (I)

con — carefully (8)

tener — to be careful (I)

cuidar to take care of (13)

— **a los niños** to baby-sit (I)

el **cumpleaños** birthday (I)

¡**feliz** —! happy birthday! (2)

cumplir . . . **años** to have a birthday, to turn (+ *age*) (13)

el **cuñado, la cuñada** brother-in-law, sister-in-law (13)

el **champú** shampoo (I)

la **chaqueta** jacket (I)

el **cheque** check (6)

cobrar un — to cash a check (6)

el — **de viajero** traveler's check (6)

el **chicle** chewing gum (13)
el **chico, la chica** boy, girl (I)
el **chile** chili pepper (I)
   el **— con carne** chili con carne (I)
   el **— relleno** stuffed pepper (I)
   chileno, -a Chilean (6)
el **chisme** piece of gossip; *pl.* gossip (10)
el **chiste** joke (I)
   chistoso, -a funny (I)
   chocar (con) to hit (*something*), to bump (into), to crash into (8)
el **chocolate** chocolate, hot chocolate (I)
la **chuleta de cerdo / cordero** pork / lamb chop (I)
los **churros** churros (I)

las **damas** checkers (I)
   daño: hacer — a to hurt, to harm (12)
   dar to give (I)
   — de comer a to feed (I)
   — la mano a to shake hands (with) (13)
   — la vuelta to turn around, to go around (8)
   — miedo a to frighten, to scare (I)
   — un paseo to go for a walk / ride (3)
   — una película / un programa to show a movie / a program (I)
   — una vuelta to take a ride (3)
   —se cuenta de to realize (14)
   —se prisa to hurry (7)
   de (del) from; of; *possessive* —'s, —s'; about (I); by (1); as a(n) (14)
   antes — before (I)
   — camping camping (4)
   — compras shopping (I)
   — ida one-way (6)
   — ida y vuelta round-trip (6)
   — + *material* made of (14)
   — moda fashionable (7)
   — nada you're welcome (I)
   — pesca fishing (4)
   — postre for dessert (I)
   — prisa in a hurry, quickly, fast (I)
   — profesión by profession (6)

— propina for a tip (I)
¿— qué color? what color? (I)
¿— quién? whose? (I)
— repente suddenly (14)
— vacaciones on vacation (I)
— veras really (I)
debajo de under (I)
deber should, ought to (I); to owe (15)
débil weak (I)
decidir to decide (15)
décimo, -a tenth (5)
decir to say, to tell (I)
   ¿cómo se dice . . .? how do you say . . . ? (I)
   — que sí / no to say yes / no (I)
   ¡no me digas! you don't say! (I)
   ¿qué quiere — . . . ? what does . . . mean? (I)
declarar to declare (*at customs*) (16)
la **decoración,** *pl.* **decoraciones** decoration (I)
decorar to decorate (I)
el **dedo** finger (I)
dejar to leave (behind) (I)
   — de + *inf.* to stop (*doing something*) (13)
delante de in front of (I)
delgado, -a thin (I)
delicioso, -a delicious (I)
demasiado *adv.* too; too much (I); *adj.* too much, too many (15)
la **demora** delay (16)
demostrar (o → ue) to demonstrate, to show, to prove (12)
dentífrica: la pasta — toothpaste (I)
el/la **dentista** dentist (I)
dentro de inside (of) (I); within (16)
el **departamento** department (7)
el **dependiente, la dependienta** salesclerk (7)
el **deporte** sport (I)
   deportivo, -a *adj.* sports (5)
derecha: a la — (de) to the right (of) (I)
derecho: (todo) — straight ahead (8)
el **derecho** law (15)
desagradable disagreeable, unpleasant (13)
el **desastre** disaster (11)
desayunar to eat breakfast (4)
el **desayuno** breakfast (I)

descansar to rest (I)
descolgar (o → ue) to pick up (*phone*) (10)
descompuesto, -a (*machines*) broken, out of order (2)
describir to describe (I)
descubrir to discover (14)
desde from (I)
desear: ¿qué desea Ud.? may I help you? (I)
desenchufar to unplug (2)
desenvolver (o → ue) to unwrap (13)
el **desfile** parade (I)
el **desierto** desert (15)
el **desodorante** deodorant (I)
el **desorden** disorder, mess (2)
desordenado, -a messy (2)
despacio slowly (I)
despedirse (e → i) (de) to say good-by (to) (13)
despegar to take off (*planes*) (I)
el **despertador** alarm clock (I)
despertar (e → ie) to wake (*someone*) up (I)
   —se to wake up (I)
despierto, -a awake (11)
después afterwards, later (I)
   — de after (I)
   — de + *inf.* after (*doing something*) (I)
destruir to destroy (14)
el **detergente** detergent (2)
detrás de behind (I)
devolver (o → ue) to return (*something*), to give back, to take back (7)
el **día** day (I)
   el — de fiesta, *pl.* **días de fiesta** holiday (I)
   el — de fin de año New Year's Eve (I)
   el plato del — special of the day (9)
   todos los —s every day (I)
el **diablo** devil (I)
la **diapositiva** slide, transparency (1)
el **diario** newspaper (14)
dibujar to draw (I)
el **dibujo** drawing (I)
   los —s animados movie cartoons (I)
el **diccionario** dictionary (1)
diciembre December (I)
diecinueve nineteen (I)

dieciocho eighteen (I)

dieciséis sixteen (I)

dieccisiete seventeen (I)

los **dientes** teeth (I)

el **cepillo de** — toothbrush (I)

la **dieta** diet (9)

estar a — to be on a diet (9)

diez ten (I)

la **diferencia** difference (12)

diferente different (12)

difícil hard, difficult (I)

el **dinero** money (I)

el **dios, la diosa** god, goddess (14)

la **dirección,** *pl.* **direcciones** address (I)

el **director, la directora** (school) principal (1); director (11); conductor (12)

dirigir (j) to direct, to conduct, to lead (12)

el **disco** record (I)

discúlpeme excuse me, pardon me, I beg your pardon (I)

discutir (de) to argue (about), to discuss (11)

el **disfraz,** *pl.* **disfraces** costume, disguise (I)

la **fiesta de disfraces** costume party (I)

disfrutar de to enjoy (I)

la **distancia: de larga** — long-distance (10)

distinto, -a (de) different (from) (7)

distraído, -a absent-minded (8)

diversiones: el parque de — amusement park (3)

divertido, -a amusing, entertaining (I)

divertirse (e → ie) to have fun, to have a good time (I)

doblada: la película — dubbed film (11)

doblar to turn (8)

doble: la habitación — double room (6)

doce twelve (I)

la **docena (de)** dozen (I)

el **doctor, la doctora** doctor *(as title)* (I)

el **documental** documentary (11)

el **documento** document (16)

el **dólar** dollar (I)

doler (o → ue) to hurt, to ache (I)

doméstico: el animal — pet (I)

domingo Sunday (I)

el — on Sunday (I)

dominicano, -a Dominican (1)

¿dónde? where? (I)

¿a—? (to) where? (I)

¿de —? from where? (I)

dormido, -a asleep (11)

dormir (o → ue) to sleep (I)

—se to fall asleep, to go to sleep (I)

el **saco de** — sleeping bag (4)

el **dormitorio** bedroom (I)

dos two (I)

doscientos, -as two hundred (I)

la **ducha** shower (I)

ducharse to take a shower (I)

duda: sin — without a doubt, undoubtedly (12)

dudar to doubt (16)

el **dueño, la dueña** owner (6)

los **dulces** candy (I)

durante during (I)

durar to last (I)

el **durazno** peach (9)

e and (I)

ecuatoriano, -a Ecuadorian (6)

el **edificio** building (I)

la **educación física** physical education (I)

educado, -a: bien / mal — polite / impolite, rude (13)

ejemplo: por — for example (4)

ejercicio: hacer — to exercise (9)

el **m.** *sing.* the (I)

él he; him, it *after prep.* (I)

eléctrico, -a electric (2)

el **elefante** elephant (I)

elegante elegant (7)

ella she; her, it *after prep.* (I)

ellos, ellas they; them *after prep.* (I)

embarque: la puerta de — boarding gate (16)

emocionante exciting, thrilling (I)

la **empanada** meat pie (I)

el **empate** tie *(in a game)* (5)

empezar (a + inf.) (e → ie) to begin, to start (I)

empujar to push (13)

en in; at; on (I)

— + *vehicle* by (I)

— casa at home (I)

— seguida right away, immediately (I)

— venta for sale (I)

enamorado, -a (de) in love (with) (13)

encantar to love (I)

encender (e → ie) to light, to turn on (4)

encontrar (o → ue) to find (I)

enchufar to plug in (2)

el **enchufe** plug; outlet (2)

enérgico, -a energetic (I)

enero January (I)

el **enfermero, la enfermera** nurse (I)

enfermo, -a sick (I)

enfrente de across from, opposite (I)

enojado, -a angry (16)

enojar(se) (con) to be / get angry (at) (16)

enorme enormous, huge (I)

la **ensalada** salad (I)

ensayar to rehearse (12)

el **ensayo** rehearsal (12)

enseñar to teach (I)

entender (e → ie) to understand (3)

enterrado, -a buried (14)

entonces then, so (I)

la **entrada** ticket; entrance (I)

entrar (en) to go in, to come in, to enter (I)

entre between (I)

entregar to deliver (10)

el **entrenador, la entrenadora** coach (5)

la **entrevista** interview (11)

entrevistar to interview (11)

envolver (o → ue) to wrap (10)

el **equipaje** luggage (6)

el **equipo** team (I)

el — **local** home team (5)

equivocado, -a wrong (10)

esa *see* **ese**

la **escala** stopover (16)

hacer — to make a stopover *(planes)* (16)

sin — nonstop (16)

la **escalera** staircase (I)

la — **mecánica** escalator (7)

escaparse to escape, to run away (14)

la **escoba** broom (2)

escoger (j) to choose (2)

escolar: el año — school year (I)

escribir to write (I)

¿cómo se escribe . . . ? how do you spell . . . ? (I)

— a máquina to type (1)

la **máquina de** — typewriter (1)

el **escritor, la escritora** writer,
    author (I)
el **escritorio** desk (I)
  escuchar to listen (to) (I)
la **escuela** school (I)
el **escultor, la escultora** sculptor (12)
la **escultura** sculpture (12)
  ese, -a; -os, -as *adj.* that; those (I)
  ése, ésa; ésos, ésas *pron.* that one;
    those (2)
el **esmalte de uñas** nail polish (7)
  eso *neuter pron.* that (2)
    por — that's why (I)
la **espalda** back (9)
  España Spain (I)
  español, -a Spanish (I)
el **español** Spanish *(language)* (I)
los **espárragos** asparagus (9)
  especial special (I)
  especialmente especially (3)
el **espectáculo** show, performance (3)
el **espejo** mirror (I)
    la casa de los —s house of
      mirrors (3)
    espera: la sala de — waiting room
      (9)
    esperar to wait (for); to hope, to
      expect (I)
    ¡espero que sí / no! I hope so /
      not! (I)
las **espinacas** spinach (9)
el **esposo, la esposa** husband, wife (I)
el **esquí** ski; skiing (5)
    el — acuático water skiing (5)
el **esquiador, la esquiadora** skier (5)
  esquiar to ski (I)
la **esquina** street corner (I)
    a la vuelta de la — around the
      corner (I)
  esta *see* **este**
la **estación,** *pl.* **estaciones** season;
    station (I)
    la — de servicio, *pl.* **estaciones
      de servicio** service station (8)
el **estacionamiento** parking lot (8)
  estacionar to park (8)
el **estadio** stadium (I)
los **Estados Unidos** United States (I)
el **estante** shelf (I)
  estar to be (I)
    está bien okay, all right (I)
    — de acuerdo to agree (I)
la **estatua** statue (14)
  este, -a; -os, -as, *adj.* this; these (I)
    esta noche tonight (I)

  éste, ésta; éstos, éstas *pron.* this
    one; these (2)
el **este** east (I)
  esto *neuter pron.* this (2)
el **estómago** stomach (I)
  estornudar to sneeze (9)
  estrecho, -a narrow (7)
la **estrella** star (I)
    la — de cine movie star (11)
  estricto, -a strict (5)
el/la **estudiante** student (I)
  estudiar to study (I)
    estudio: la sala de — study hall
      (I)
la **estufa** stove (I)
  estupendo, -a fantastic, great (I)
  etcétera etc. (14)
la **etiqueta** tag, price tag, label (7)
  Europa Europe (I)
  exactamente exactly (3)
el **examen,** *pl.* **exámenes** test, exam
    (I)
  examinar to examine (I)
  excelente excellent (I)
la **excursión: ir de —** to go on a
    short trip or excursion (3)
la **excusa** excuse (I)
el **éxito** success (11)
    tener — to be successful (11)
la **expedición,** *pl.* **expediciones**
    expedition (15)
    hacer una — to go on an
      expedition (15)
  explicar to explain (1)
el **explorador, la exploradora**
    explorer (15)
  explorar to explore (15)
la **exposición,** *pl.* **exposiciones**
    exhibit (3)
  expreso express (6)
  extranjero, -a foreign (11)
  extraño, -a strange (16)

  fabuloso, -a fabulous (I)
  fácil easy (I)
la **falda** skirt (I)
  faltar to need, to be missing or
    lacking *(something)* (I)
la **familia** family (I)
  famoso, -a famous (3)
el **fantasma** ghost (I)
    la casa de los —s house of
      horrors (3)
  fantástico, -a fantastic (I)

el **farmacéutico, la farmacéutica**
    pharmacist (15)
la **farmacia** pharmacy, drugstore (I)
el **faro** headlight (8)
  favor: por — please (I)
  favorito, -a favorite (I)
  febrero February (I)
la **fecha** date (I)
  ¡felicidades! congratulations! (I)
  ¡felicitaciones! congratulations! (I)
  felicitar to congratulate (13)
  feliz, *pl.* **felices** happy (13)
    ¡ — cumpleaños! happy birth-
      day! (2)
  feo, -a ugly (I)
la **feria** fair (3)
    la rueda de — Ferris wheel (3)
la **fiebre** fever (I)
la **fiesta** holiday; party (I)
    el día de — holiday (I)
    la — de disfraces costume
      party (I)
  fijarse en to notice, to pay
    attention to (12)
la **fila** row (11)
  filmar to film (11)
el **fin:**
    el día de — de año New Year's
      Eve (I)
    el — de semana, *pl.* **fines de
      semana** weekend (I)
    por — at last, finally (3)
la **firma** signature (10)
  firmar to sign (6)
la **física** physics (I)
    físico, -a: la educación —a
      physical education (I)
  flaco, -a *(animals)* skinny (3)
el **flan** flan, baked custard (I)
la **flauta** flute (12)
    flojo, -a: estar — en to be poor in
      (I)
la **flor** flower (I)
    folklórico, -a *adj.* folk (I)
el **fondo: en el —** at the back, in the
    background (12)
  formidable terrific (I)
el **formulario** form (10)
la **foto** photo (I)
el **fotógrafo, la fotógrafa** photo-
    grapher (I)
el **fracaso** failure (11)
    francés *(pl.* **franceses), francesa**
      French (I)
el **francés** French *(language)* (I)

Francia France (I)
la **frase** sentence, phrase (I)
frecuentemente frequently (3)
el **fregadero** sink (2)
el **freno** brake (8)
la **fresa** strawberry (9)
fresco, -a fresh (4)
el **fresco: hace —** it's cool (out) (I)
los **frijoles** beans (I)
frío, -a cold (I)
el **frío:**
 hace — it's cold (out) (I)
 tener — to be cold *(person)* (I)
 frito, -a fried (I)
 las papas —as French fries (I)
la **frontera** border (10)
la **fruta** fruit (I)
el **fuego** fire (4)
 los — artificiales fireworks (I)
la **fuente** fountain (I)
 fuera de outside (of) (I)
 fuerte strong (I); loud (5)
 estar — en to be good in (I)
la **función,** *pl.* **funciones** show (11)
 funcionar *(machines)* to work, to run (2)
la **funda** pillowcase (I)
el **fútbol** soccer (I)
 el **— americano** football (I)

la **galería** gallery (12)
la **galleta** cracker (4)
la **gallina** hen (I)
el **gallo** rooster (I)
el **ganado** cattle (4)
 ganador, -a winning (5)
el **ganador, la ganadora** winner (5)
 ganar to win (I); to earn (15)
 —se la vida to earn a living (15)
 ganas *see* **tener**
la **ganga** bargain (7)
el **garaje** garage (I)
la **garganta** throat (I)
la **gasolina** gas (8)
 gastar to spend (7)
el **gato** cat (I)
el **gazpacho** gazpacho (I)
 generalmente generally, usually (I)
 generoso, -a generous (I)
la **gente** people (I)
 lleno, -a de — crowded (I)
la **geometría** geometry (I)
el/la **gerente** manager (I)
 gimnasia: hacer — to do gymnastics (5)

el **gimnasio** gymnasium (I)
el **globo** balloon (3)
el **golf** golf (I)
el **Golfo de México** Gulf of Mexico (I)
 gordo, -a fat (I)
la **grabadora** tape recorder (I)
 grabar to record (11)
 gracias thank you, thanks (I)
 muchas — thanks a lot (I)
 gracioso, -a funny, comic (3)
el **grado** degree (11)
 graduarse to graduate (15)
el **gramo** gram (I)
 gran, *pl.* **grandes** great (I)
 grande large (I)
la **granja** farm (I)
el **granjero, la granjera** farmer (I)
la **grapa** staple (1)
la **grapadora** stapler (1)
 gratis, *pl.* **gratis** free (3)
la **gripe** flu (I)
 gris, *pl.* **grises** gray (I)
 gritar to shout (12)
el **grupo** group (I)
el **guacamole** guacamole (9)
el **guante** glove (I)
 guapo, -a handsome, good-looking (I)
el **guardián, la guardiana (de zoológico)** (zoo)keeper (I)
 guatemalteco, -a Guatemalan (1)
la **guía** guidebook (I)
 la **— telefónica** phone book (I)
el/la **guía** guide (I)
los **guisantes** peas (I)
la **guitarra** guitar (I)
 gustar to like (I)
 me gustaría I'd like (3)
 gusto:
 con mucho — gladly, with pleasure (I)
 mucho — pleased to meet you (I)

haber (hay / había / hubo) there is / are; there was / were (I, 14, 15)
la **habitación,** *pl.* **habitaciones** room (6)
 la **— doble** double room (6)
 la **— individual** single room (6)
el/la **habitante** inhabitant (1)
 hablar to speak, to talk (I)

 — por señas to talk in sign language (11)
 — por teléfono to talk on the phone (I)
 hace:
 — + *time* **+ que** for + *time* (I)
 See also **calor, fresco, frío, sol, tiempo, viento**
 hacer to do; to make (I)
 — cola to stand in line (I)
 — daño a to hurt, to harm (12)
 — ejercicio to exercise (9)
 — el papel de to play the role of (11)
 — la maleta to pack a suitcase (I)
 — un asado to have a barbecue (4)
 — una expedición to go an expedition (15)
 — un picnic to have a picnic (3)
 — una pregunta to ask a question (1)
 — un viaje to take a trip (I)
 hallar to find (14)
 hambre: tener — to be hungry (I)
la **hamburguesa** hamburger (I)
 hasta until (I); to, out to, as far as (5)
 — la vista see you later (I)
 — luego see you later (I)
 — mañana see you tomorrow (I)
 — pronto see you soon (I)
 hay there is, there are (I)
 — que + *inf.* we (you, one) must, it's necessary (I)
 no — de qué you're welcome (I)
 ¿qué —? what's new? (10)
 hecho, -a made (7)
la **heladería** ice cream parlor (3)
el **helado** ice cream (I)
el **helicóptero** helicóptero (15)
el **hermanito, la hermanita** little brother, little sister (I)
el **hermano, la hermana** brother, sister (I)
los **hermanos** brothers; brother(s) and sister(s) (I)
 hermoso, -a beautiful (I)
el **héroe, la heroína** hero, heroine (14)
 heroico, -a heroic (14)
 hervir (e → ie) to boil (4)
el **hielo** ice (3)
la **hierba** grass (I)

el hijo, la hija son, daughter (I)

los hijos sons; son(s) and daughter(s) (I)

el hipopótamo hippopotamus (I)

la historia history (I); story (1)

    histórico, -a historic (6)

la hoja leaf (I)

    la — de papel, *pl.* **—s de papel** piece of paper (I)

    hola hello, hi (I)

el hombre man (I)

    el — de negocios businessman (15)

el hombro shoulder (9)

    hondureño, -a Honduran (1)

la hora hour (I)

    ¿a qué —? (at) what time? (I)

    la media — half an hour (I)

    ¿qué — es? what time is it? (I)

el horario schedule (I)

la hormiga ant (4)

el horno oven (2)

    horror: ¡qué —! how awful! (14)

el hospital hospital (I)

el hotel hotel (I)

    hoy today (I)

    — no not today (I)

    hubo *see* **haber**

el hueso bone (9)

el huevo egg (I)

    huir (de) to flee (from) (14)

    húmedo, -a humid, damp (15)

el humo smoke (14)

el humor:

    el sentido del — sense of humor (16)

    estar de buen / mal — to be in a good / bad mood (16)

el huracán, *pl.* **huracanes** hurricane (11)

    ida:

    de — one-way (6)

    de — y vuelta round-trip (6)

la idea idea (2)

    cambiar de — to change one's mind (3)

el idioma language (1)

la iglesia church (I)

    igual the same, alike (13)

la iguana iguana (I)

    ¡imagínate! imagine! (I)

    impaciente impatient (8)

el impermeable raincoat (1)

importante important (I)

importar to matter to, to be important to, to mind (I)

    ¿qué —? so what? (I)

imposible impossible (16)

impresionante impressive (14)

improbable improbable (16)

el impuesto tax (7)

los incas Incas (14)

el incendio fire (14)

    incluir to include, to enclose (10)

    incómodo, -a uncomfortable (I)

    increíble incredible (5)

    indicar to indicate, to show (11)

    individual: la habitación — single room (6)

la información information (11)

el ingeniero, la ingeniera engineer (14)

    Inglaterra England (I)

    inglés *(pl.* **ingleses), inglesa** English (I)

el inglés English *(language)* (I)

    inolvidable unforgettable (13)

el inspector, la inspectora *(train)* conductor (6)

el instructor, la instructora instructor (8)

el instrumento instrument (12)

    inteligente intelligent (I)

    intentar to try (16)

    interesante interesting (I)

    interesar to interest (11)

el intervalo intermission (11)

el invierno winter (I)

la invitación, *pl.* **invitaciones** invitation (I)

el invitado, la invitada guest (I)

    invitar to invite (I)

la inyección, *pl.* **inyecciones** shot (I)

    poner una — to give a shot (I)

    ir to go (I)

    — a + *inf.* going to + *verb* (I)

    — a buscar to go get, to pick up (10)

    —se to leave, to go away (7)

la isla island (5)

    Italia Italy (I)

    italiano, -a Italian (I)

el italiano Italian *(language)* (I)

    izquierda: a la — (de) to the left (of) (I)

el jabón, *pl.* **jabones** soap (I)

el jaguar jaguar (15)

el jai alai jai alai (5)

el jamón ham (I)

el jardín, *pl.* **jardines** garden (I)

la jaula cage (I)

los jeans jeans (I)

el jefe, la jefa boss (15)

la jirafa giraffe (I)

    joven, *pl.* **jóvenes** young (I)

el/la joven, *pl.* **los/las jóvenes** young person (11)

las joyas jewels (I)

el juego game (I)

    jueves Thursday (I)

    el — on Thursday (I)

el jugador, la jugadora player (I)

    jugar (u → ue) to play (I)

    — a(l) to play *(sports or games)* (I)

el jugo (de) juice (I)

    julio July (I)

    junio June (I)

    junto a next to (12)

    juntos, -as together (I)

el kilo kilo (I)

    la the *f. sing.;* you *f. formal,* her, it *dir. obj.* (I)

el labio lip (7)

    el lápiz de —s lipstick (7)

el laboratorio laboratory (I)

    lado: al — de next to, beside (I)

el ladrón, la ladrona thief (14)

el lago lake (I)

la lámpara lamp (I)

la lana wool (14)

la langosta lobster (9)

el lápiz, *pl.* **lápices** pencil (I)

    el — de labios lipstick (7)

    largo, -a long (I)

    de —a distancia long-distance (10)

    las the *f. pl.;* you *f. pl.,* them *f. dir. obj.* (I)

la lástima shame, pity (16)

    ¡qué —! that's too bad, that's a shame (I)

    lastimarse to hurt *(a part of one's body)* (9)

la lata can (4)

    ¡qué —! what a drag! what a bore! (3)

latinoamericano, -a Latin American (I)
la lavadora washing machine (2)
el lavaplatos dishwasher (2)
lavar to wash (I)
   —se (la cara, las manos, el pelo) to wash (one's face, hands, hair) (I)
le (to / for) you *formal,* him, her *ind. obj.* (I)
la lección, *pl.* **lecciones** lesson (I)
la leche milk (I)
   el café con — coffee with cream (I)
la lechuga lettuce (I)
leer to read (I)
lejos de far from (I)
la lengua language (I)
lentamente slowly (10)
lento, -a slow (I)
el león, *pl.* **leones** lion (I)
el leopardo leopard (I)
les (to / for) you *pl.,* them *ind. obj.* (I)
el letrero sign (7)
el levantador / la levantadora de pesas weightlifter (5)
levantar to lift, to raise (I)
   — pesas to lift weights (5)
   —se to get up (I)
libre free, not busy (I)
la librería bookstore (I)
el libro book (I)
la lima de uñas nail file (7)
limar(se) las uñas to file nails (7)
el limón, *pl.* **limones** lemon (I)
la limonada lemonade (I)
limpiar to clean (I)
   —(se) los zapatos / los anteojos to clean (one's) shoes / eyeglasses (7)
limpio, -a clean (I)
la línea line (I)
   la — aérea airline (16)
la linterna flashlight (4)
la liquidación, *pl.* **liquidaciones** (clearance) sale (7)
listo, -a smart, clever (I)
el litro liter (I)
lo you *m. formal,* him, it *dir. obj.* (I)
   — que what (I)
   — siento I'm sorry (I)
local local (6)
   el equipo — home team (5)
loco, -a crazy (I)

el locutor, la locutora announcer (11)
el loro parrot (15)
los the *m. pl.;* you, them *dir. obj.* (I)
luego then, láter (I)
   hasta — see you later (I)
el lugar place (3)
   tener — to take place (11)
la luna moon (I)
lunes Monday (I)
   el — on Monday (I)
la luz, *pl.* **luces** light (2)

la llama llama (I)
la llamada call (10)
   la — por cobrar collect call (10)
llamar to call (I)
   ¿cómo te llamas? what's your name? (I)
   — por teléfono to phone (I)
   —se to be called, to be named (I)
la llanta tire (8)
la llave key (I)
la llegada arrival (6)
llegar to arrive (I)
llenar to fill (up) (8); to fill out / in (10)
lleno, -a full (I)
   — de gente crowded (I)
llevar to wear; to carry (I); to take (4)
llorar to cry (13)
llover (o → ue) to rain (I)
   llueve it's raining (I)
la lluvia rain (I)

la madera wood (14)
la madre mother (I)
la madrina godmother (13)
magnífico, -a magnificent (I)
el maíz corn (I)
mal not well, badly (I)
la maleta suitcase (I)
   hacer la — to pack a suitcase (I)
malo (mal), -a bad (I)
la mamá mom (I)
mandar to send (I)
manejar to drive (8)
   el permiso de — driver's license (8)
la mano hand (I)
   dar la — a to shake hands (with) (13)

la manta blanket (I)
el mantel tablecloth (I)
la mantequilla butter (I)
la manzana apple (I)
mañana tomorrow (I)
   hasta — see you tomorrow (I)
la mañana morning (I)
   de la — in the morning; A.M. (I)
   por la — in the morning (I)
el mapa map (I)
el maquillaje makeup (7)
maquillar(se) to put makeup on (7)
la máquina:
   escribir a — to type (1)
   la — de escribir typewriter (1)
la maquinilla de afeitar razor (7)
el mar sea (I)
   maravilla: ¡qué —! how marvelous! great! (3)
maravilloso, -a marvelous, wonderful (6)
la marca brand (7)
marcar to dial (10)
los mariscos seafood, shellfish (9)
marrón, *pl.* **marrones** brown (I)
martes Tuesday (I)
   el — on Tuesday (I)
marzo March (I)
más plus; more (I)
   el / la / los / las — + *adj.* the most *+ adj.,* the *+ adj. +* -est (I)
   — + *adj.* (**+ que**) more *+ adj.* (+ than), *adj. +* -er (I)
   — de + *number* more than (I)
   — o menos more or less (I)
mascar to chew (13)
la máscara mask (I)
las matemáticas mathematics (I)
la materia school subject (I)
   máximo, -a: la velocidad —a speed limit (8)
los mayas Mayans (14)
mayo May (I)
la mayonesa mayonnaise (9)
mayor older (I)
los mayores grownups (13)
la mayoría de most (of), the majority of (7)
me me *dir. obj.;* (to / for) me *ind. obj.;* myself (I)
   mecánico, -a: la escalera —a escalator (7)
el mecánico, la mecánica mechanic (8)

media:
   la — **hora** half an hour (I)
   y — half-past; and a half (I)
la **medianoche** midnight (I)
la **medicina** medicine (9)
el **médico, la médica** doctor (I)
   medio cocido, -a *(meat)* medium (4)
el **mediodía** noon (I)
   al — at noon (I)
   mejor better (I)
   el / la — the best (I)
mejorarse to get better, to improve (9)
memoria: aprender de — to memorize (I)
menor younger (I)
menos minus; + *number (in time telling)* (minutes) to (I)
   el / la / los / las — + *adj.* the least + *adj.* (I)
   más o — more or less (I)
   — + *adj.* + **que** less + *adj.* + than (I)
   — **de** + *number* less than, fewer than (I)
   por lo — at least (15)
el **mensajero, la mensajera** messenger (10)
mentir (e → ie) to lie (16)
la **mentira** lie (16)
el **menú** menu (I)
   menudo: a — often (I)
el **mercado** market (I)
la **mermelada** jelly, preserves (I)
el **mes** month (I)
la **mesa** table (I)
   poner la — to set the table (I)
   meter: — **la pata** to put one's foot in it, to goof (13)
el **metro** subway (I)
mexicano, -a Mexican (I)
mezclar to mix (2)
mi, mis my (I)
mí me *after prep.* (I)
miedo:
   dar — **a** to frighten, to scare (I)
   tener — **(de)** to be afraid (of) (I)
la **miel** honey (9)
mientras while (13)
miércoles Wednesday (I)
   el — on Wednesday (I)
mil one thousand (I)
   miles (de) thousands (of) (7)
el **milagro** miracle (5)
el **millón (de)**, *pl.* **millones** million (1)

el **millonario, la millonaria** millionaire (15)
el **minuto** minute (I)
mío, -a my, (of) mine (8)
el **mío, la mía, los míos, las mías** mine (8)
mirar to look (at), to watch (I)
mismo, -a same (1)
   ahora — right away, right now (2)
misterioso, -a mysterious (15)
la **mitad** half (15)
la **mochila** knapsack, backpack (I)
la **moda** fashion (7)
   de — fashionable, in fashion (7)
el/la **modelo** model (12)
mojado, -a wet (4)
molestar to bother (13)
   no te molestes don't bother (13)
un **momento** just a moment (I)
la **moneda** coin (I)
el **mono** monkey (I)
la **montaña** mountain (I)
   la — **rusa** roller coaster (3)
montar:
   — **a caballo** to ride horseback (5)
   — **en bicicleta** to ride a bicycle (I)
morado, -a purple (I)
moreno, -a dark, brunette (I)
morirse (o → ue) to die (9)
la **mosca** fly (4)
el **mosquito** mosquito (4)
la **mostaza** mustard (4)
el **mostrador** (display) counter (7)
mostrar (o → ue) to show (I)
la **moto** motorcycle (I)
el **motor** motor (8)
el **muchacho, la muchacha** boy, girl (I)
mucho a lot, much (I)
mucho, -a, -os, -as much, many, a lot of; very (I)
   — **gusto** pleased to meet you (I)
mudarse to move (10)
los **muebles** furniture (I)
muerto, -a dead (14)
la **mujer** woman (I)
   la — **de negocios** businesswoman (15)
la **muleta** crutch (9)
la **multa** fine; (traffic) ticket (8)
   poner una — to give a ticket (8)
el **mundo** world (14)
   todo el — everybody, everyone (I)

la **muñeca** wrist (9)
el **mural** mural (12)
el **museo** museum (I)
la **música** music (I)
   musical musical (I)
el **músico, la música** musician (12)
muy very (I)

nacer (c → zc) to be born (13)
el **nacimiento** birth (13)
   nada nothing, not anything (I)
   de — you're welcome (I)
el **nadador, la nadadora** swimmer (5)
   nadar to swim (I)
   nadie no one, nobody, not anyone (I)
los **naipes** cards (I)
la **naranja** orange (I)
la **naranjada** orangeade (I)
la **nariz** nose (I)
la **natación** swimming (5)
   navegar to sail (5)
la **Navidad** Christmas (I)
   necesario, -a necessary (I)
   necesitar to need (I)
   negar (e → ie) to deny (16)
el **negocio** business (15)
   el hombre / la mujer de —**s** businessman, businesswoman (15)
   negro, -a black (I)
   nervioso, -a nervous (8)
   nevar to snow (I)
   nieva it's snowing (I)
   ni . . . ni neither . . . nor, not . . . or
   no . . . — not even (6)
   nicaragüense Nicaraguan (1)
el **nieto, la nieta** grandson, granddaughter (13)
los **nietos** grandchildren (13)
la **nieve** snow (I)
   ningún, ninguna *adj.* no, not any (I)
   ninguno, -a *pron.* none, (not) any (I)
el **niño, la niña** little boy, little girl (I)
los **niños** little boys; boys and girls; children (I)
   cuidar a los — to baby-sit (I)
no no; not (I)
   ¡cómo —**!** of course (I)
   ¿—**?** don't you? aren't I? etc. (I)

la noche night (I)
    de la — at night, in the evening; P.M. (I)
    esta — tonight (I)
    por la — in the evening, at night (I)
el nombre name (I)
el noreste northeast (1)
el noroeste northwest (1)
el norte north (I)
    norteamericano, -a North American (I)
nos us *dir. obj.*; (to / for) us *ind. obj.*; ourselves (I); each other (7)
nosotros, -as we; us *after prep.* (I)
la nota grade (I)
la noticia piece of news, news item (10); *pl.* news (I)
novecientos, -as nine hundred (I)
la novela novel (I)
noveno, -a ninth (5)
noventa ninety (I)
noviembre November (I)
el novio, la novia boyfriend, girl-friend (I); bride, groom (13)
los novios bride and groom (13)
la nube cloud (I)
    nublado: está — it's cloudy (I)
nuestro, -a our (I); our, (of) ours (8)
el nuestro, la nuestra, los nuestros, las nuestras ours (8)
nueve nine (I)
nuevo, -a new (I)
el número number (I); *(shoe)* size (7)
    el — de teléfono phone number (I)
nunca never (I)

o or (I)
    — . . . — either . . . or (10)
el objeto object (14)
el oboe oboe (12)
la obra work (12)
    la — de teatro play (I)
obstinado, -a obstinate, stubborn (16)
obtener to get, to obtain (8)
el océano ocean (I)
octavo, -a eighth (5)
octubre October (I)
ocupado, -a busy; occupied (I)
ocurrir to happen, to occur (11)
ochenta eighty (I)

ocho eight (I)
ochocientos, -as eight hundred (I)
el oeste west (I)
    del — western (I)
la oficina office (I)
ofrecer (c → zc) to offer (11)
el oído (inner) ear (I)
oír to hear (I)
¡ojalá! I hope so! let's hope so! (I)
el ojo eye (I)
    costar un — de la cara to cost an arm and a leg (7)
la ola wave (I)
el olor odor, smell (4)
olvidar to forget *(something)* (3)
    —se (de + *inf.*) to forget (to) (I)
la olla pot (2)
once eleven (I)
el operador, la operadora operator (10)
la opinión, *pl.* opiniones opinion (14)
optimista optimistic (I)
el orden order (2)
    poner en — to straighten up / out (2)
ordenado, -a neat (2)
la oreja ear (I)
orgulloso, -a proud (16)
origen: de — of . . . origin (I)
original: en versión — in a foreign language (11)
el oro gold (14)
la orquesta orchestra (12)
el/la ortodoncista orthodontist (15)
oscuro, -a dark (6)
el oso bear (I)
el otoño autumn, fall (I)
otro, -a other, another (I)
    otra cosa / persona something / someone else (11)
    otra vez again (I)
la oveja sheep (I)
¡oye! listen! hey! (I)

la paciencia: tener — to be patient (16)
paciente patient (8)
el/la paciente patient (9)
el padre father (I)
los padres parents, mother and father (I)
el padrino godfather; *pl.* godparents (13)
la paella paella (I)

pagar to pay (for) (I)
    — + *sum of money* + por to pay + *sum of money* + for (I)
    — al contado to pay cash (6)
la página page (I)
el país country (I)
el paisaje landscape (4, 12)
el pájaro bird (I)
la palabra word (I)
pálido, -a pale (9)
las palomitas popcorn (3)
el pan bread (I)
    el — tostado toast (I)
la panadería bakery (I)
panameño -a Panamanian (1)
los pantalones pants (I)
la pantalla screen (1)
las pantimedias pantyhose (I)
el pañuelo handkerchief (I)
el papá dad (I)
la papa potato (I)
    las —s fritas French fries (I)
la papaya papaya (9)
el papel paper (14)
    hacer el — de to play the role of (11)
    la hoja de — piece of paper (I)
la papelera wastebasket (I)
el paquete package (10)
para for (I); by + *time* (15)
    — + *inf.* to, in order to (I)
el parabrisas, *pl.* parabrisas windshield (8)
el parachoques, *pl.* parachoques bumper (8)
el parador inn *(run by Spanish government)* (6)
el paraguas umbrella (I)
paraguayo, -a Paraguayan (6)
parar to stop (3)
parecer (c → zc) to seem *(to someone)* (I); to seem to be, to look like (11)
    —se (c → zc) a to look like, to resemble (13)
    ¿no te parece? don't you think so? (15)
    ¿qué te parece . . . ? how do you like . . . ? what do you think of . . . ? (I)
    ¿qué te parece si + *verb*? how about *(doing something)*? (13)
parecido, -a (a) like, similar to (12)
la pared wall (I)

el **pariente, la parienta** relative (13)
el **parque** park (I)
    el **— de diversiones** amusement park (3)
el **parquímetro** parking meter (8)
la **parrilla** grill (4)
la **parte** part (1)
    de mi — from me, for me (10)
    ¿de — de quién? who's calling? (10)
    por / en todas —s everywhere (16)
    participar to participate, to take part (5)
    particular: el colegio — private school (1)
el **partido (de +** *sport***)** game, match (I)
    pasado, -a last; past (I)
el **pasajero, la pasajera** passenger (6)
el **pasaporte** passport (I)
    pasar to spend *(time)* (I); to happen (2)
    — la aspiradora to vacuum (2)
el **pasatiempo** pastime, hobby (I)
el **paseo: dar un —** to go for a walk / ride (3)
el **pasillo** hall (2)
el **paso de peatones** crosswalk (8)
la **pasta dentífrica** toothpaste (I)
el **pastel** cake, pastry (I)
la **pastilla** pill (9)
la **pata: meter —** to put one's foot in it, to goof (13)
el **patín,** *pl.* **patines (de ruedas)** (roller) skate (3)
el **patinador, la patinadora** skater (5)
    patinar to skate (3)
    — sobre hielo to ice-skate (3)
    — sobre ruedas to roller-skate (3)
el **patio** courtyard (I)
el **pato** duck (I)
el **pavo** turkey (I)
el **peatón,** *pl.* **peatones** pedestrian (8)
    el paso de —es crosswalk (8)
el **pecho** chest (9)
    pedir (e → i) to ask for, to order, to request (I)
    — prestado, -a (a) to borrow (from) (I)
    peinar to comb someone's hair (I)
    —se to comb one's hair (I)

el **peine** comb (I)
    pelearse (con) to quarrel, to fight (with) (13)
la **película** movie, film (I)
    la — doblada dubbed film (11)
    peligroso, -a dangerous (8)
    pelirrojo, -a red-haired (I)
el **pelo** hair (I)
    tomarle el — a to pull someone's leg (13)
la **pelota** ball (I)
la **peluquería** barber / beauty shop (7)
el **peluquero, la peluquera** barber, hairdresser (7)
la **pena: valer la —** to be worth the effort, to be worth it (16)
    pensar (e → ie) to think (I)
    — + *inf.* to plan, to intend (I)
    — de to think of, to have an opinion about (I)
    — en to think about (I)
la **pensión,** *pl.* **pensiones** boardinghouse (6)
    peor worse (I)
    el / la — worst (I)
    pequeño, -a small, little (I)
la **pera** pear (9)
    perdedor, -a losing (5)
    perder (e → ie) to lose (I)
    ¡perdón! pardon me (I)
    perezoso, -a lazy (I)
    perfecto, -a perfect (I)
el **perfume** perfume (7)
el **periódico** newspaper (I)
el/la **periodista** journalist, reporter (14)
    permiso:
    con — excuse me (I)
    el — de manejar driver's license (8)
    permitir to let, to allow, to permit (13)
    pero but (I)
el **perro** dog (I)
    el — caliente hot dog (4)
la **persona** person (I)
    otra — someone else, no one else (11)
el **personaje** character (11)
    peruano, -a Peruvian (6)
    pesado, -a heavy (4)
    pesar(se) to weigh (oneself) (9)
las **pesas** weights (5)
    pesca: ir de — to go fishing (4)
el **pescado** fish *(cooked)* (I)
la **peseta** peseta (I)

    pesimista pessimistic (I)
el **peso** peso (I); weight (9)
    aumentar / bajar de — to gain / lose weight (9)
el **pez,** *pl.* **peces** fish *(live)* (I)
el **piano** piano (I)
    picante spicy, hot (I)
el **picnic** picnic (3)
    hacer un — to have a picnic (3)
el **pie** foot (I)
    a — on foot (I)
la **piedra** rock (4); stone (14)
la **pierna** leg (I)
la **pila** *(flashlight)* battery (4)
el/la **piloto** pilot (I)
la **pimienta** pepper (4)
el **pincel** paintbrush (12)
    pintar to paint (12)
el **pintor, la pintora** painter (12)
la **pintura** paint, painting (12)
la **piña** pineapple (9)
la **piñata** pinata (I)
la **pirámide** pyramid (14)
los **Pirineos** Pyrenees Mts. (I)
la **piscina** swimming pool (I)
el **piso** floor, story (I)
    el primer (segundo, tercer) — second (third, fourth) floor (I)
la **pista** runway (16)
la **pizarra** chalkboard (I)
la **placa** license plate (8)
el **plan** plan (I)
la **plancha** iron (2)
    planchar to iron (2)
el **plano** street map (6)
la **planta baja** ground floor (I)
la **plata** silver (14)
el **plátano** banana (I)
el **platillo** saucer (I)
el **plato** dish; plate (I)
    el — del día special of the day (9)
    quitar los — to clear the table (I)
la **playa** beach (I)
la **plaza** town square, plaza (I)
    pobre poor (I)
    ¡pobrecito, -a! poor thing! (I)
un **poco (de)** a little (I)
    — cocido, -a rare *(meat)* (4)
    pocos, -as a few, not many (I)
    poder (o → ue) can, to be able to (I)
    se puede it is allowed, you can (13)
el **poema** poem (I)

el/la **poeta** poet (I)
el/la **policía** police officer (I)
policíaco, -a *adj.* detective,
 mystery (I)
el **pollo** chicken (I)
poner to put, to place (I)
 — en orden to straighten up /
 out (2)
 — la mesa to set the table (I)
 —se to put on *(clothes)* (I)
 — una inyección to give a shot
 (I)
 — una multa to give a ticket (8)
popular popular (I)
por through, across (I); for (9);
 along (13); per (13)
 — allí around there, over there,
 that way (8)
 — aquí around here, over here,
 this way (8)
 — eso that's why (I)
 — favor please (I)
 — fin at last, finally (3)
 — la mañana in the morning (I)
 — la noche in the evening, at
 night (I)
 — la radio / tele on the radio /
 TV (11)
 — la tarde in the afternoon (I)
 — lo menos at least (15)
 ¿— qué? why? (I)
 ¡— supuesto! of course (I)
 — teléfono on the phone (I)
porque because (I)
portarse bien / mal to behave well /
 badly (13)
portugués (*pl.* **portugueses**),
 portuguesa Portuguese (I)
el **portugués** Portuguese *(language)*
 (I)
posible possible (16)
postal:
 el apartado — post office box
 (10)
 el código — zip code (10)
 la tarjeta — post card (I)
el **postre** dessert (I)
 de — for dessert (I)
practicar to practice (I)
práctico, -a practical (15)
el **precio** price (7)
preferido, -a favorite (I)
preferir (e → ie) to prefer (I)
la **pregunta** question (I)
 hacer una — to ask a question
 (1)

preguntar to ask (I)
el **premio** prize (11)
preocupado, -a worried (I)
preocuparse (por) to worry
 (about) (16)
preparado, -a prepared, ready (I)
preparar to prepare (I)
presentar to introduce (I)
presente *adj.* present (I)
prestado, -a: pedir — (a) to
 borrow (from) (I)
prestar to lend (I)
 — atención to pay attention (1)
la **primavera** spring (I)
primero (primer), -a first (I)
 el — piso second floor (I)
el **primo, la prima** cousin (I)
principal main, leading (11)
el **principio: al —** at first (11)
prisa:
 darse — to hurry (7)
 de — in a hurry, quickly, fast
 (I)
 tener — to be in a hurry (8)
privado, -a private (I)
probable probable (16)
probablemente probably (3)
probar (o → ue) to taste (4)
 —se to try on (7)
el **problema** problem (I)
producir (c → zc) to produce (14)
la **profesión,** *pl.* **profesiones**
 profession (6)
 de — by profession (6)
el **profesor, la profesora** teacher (I)
el **programa** program (I)
 el — de concursos quiz show
 (11)
el **programador / la programadora
 (de computadoras)**
 (computer) programmer (15)
prohibir: se prohibe it is
 forbidden (13)
prometer to promise (4)
el **pronóstico del tiempo** weather
 forecast (11)
pronto soon (I)
 hasta — see you soon (I)
la **propina** tip (I)
 de — for a tip (I)
propio, -a own (15)
provecho: ¡buen —! enjoy your
 meal (4)
próximo, -a next (I)
el **proyector** projector (I)
la **prueba** test (I)

público, -a public (1)
el **público** audience (11)
 en — in public (13)
el **pueblo** town (4)
el **puente** bridge (I)
la **puerta** door (I)
 la — de embarque boarding
 gate (16)
puertorriqueño, -a Puerto Rican
 (I)
pues well (I)
el **puesto** booth, stand (3)
la **pulsera** bracelet (I)
el **pupitre** student desk (I)

que that; who; than (I) *see also*
 hay, tener
 lo — what (I)
qué what? (I)
 no hay de — you're welcome (I)
 ¿por —? why? (I)
 **¡— + *adj.!* how + *adj.!* (I)
 **¡— + *noun!* what a(n) + *noun!*
 (I)
 ¿— desea Ud.? can I help you?
 (I)
 ¿— importa? so what? (I)
 ¿— tal? how's it going? (I)
quedar to fit, to look good on (7);
 to be located (8)
 —se to stay, to remain (I)
 —se sin to run out of, to be left
 without (I)
quejarse (de) to complain (about)
 (7)
quemado, -a burned (2)
quemar to burn (2)
 —se to burn up, to burn down
 (14)
querer (e → ie) to want (I); to
 love (13)
 ¿qué quiere decir . . . ? what
 does . . . mean? (I)
 **¿quiere(n) + *inf.?* will you . . . ?
 (6)
 quisiera I'd like (I)
querido, -a dear (10)
el **queso** cheese (I)
¿quién, —es? who? whom? (I)
 ¿a —? whom? to whom? (I)
 ¿de parte de —? who's calling?
 (10)
 ¿de —? whose? (I)
la **química** chemistry (I)
quince fifteen (I)

la **quinceañera** fifteen-year-old girl (I)

los **quince años** fifteenth birthday (party) (I)

quinientos, -as five hundred (I)

quinto, -a fifth (5)

quisiera *see* **querer**

quitar:

— **los platos** to clear the table (I)

—**se** to take off *(clothes)* (I)

quizás maybe, perhaps (1)

la **radio** radio *(broadcast)* (I)

por la — on the radio (11)

el **radio** radio *(set)* (I)

la **rana** frog (4)

el **rancho** ranch (4)

rápidamente fast, rapidly (I)

rápido, -a fast (I)

la **raqueta** racket (5)

el **ratón,** *pl.* **ratones** mouse (4)

razón:

no tener — to be wrong (I)

tener — to be right (I)

el **recado** message (10)

la **recepción,** *pl.* **recepciones** reception desk (6)

la **receta** prescription (I)

recetar to prescribe (9)

recibir to receive, to get (I)

el **recibo** receipt (10)

recoger (j) to pick up (2); to pick (4)

recomendar (e → ie) to recommend, to advise (9)

reconocer (c → zc) to recognize (11)

recordar (o → ue) to remember (13)

el **recuerdo** souvenir (I)

el **refresco** soda, pop (I)

el **refrigerador** refrigerator (I)

regalar to give a present (13)

el **regalo** present, gift (I)

la **regata** boat race (5)

registrar to check, to inspect (16)

el **registro** *(hotel)* register (6)

la **regla** rule, law (8)

regresar to return, to go back, to come back (I)

la **reina** queen (I)

reír (e → i) to laugh (5)

—**se (de)** to laugh (at) (11)

el **relámpago** lightning (11)

la **religión,** *pl.* **religiones** religion (14)

el **reloj** clock (I)

relleno: el chile — stuffed pepper (I)

remar to row (3)

el **remitente** return address (10)

repasar to review (I)

el **repaso** review (1)

repente: de — suddenly (14)

repetir (e → i) to repeat (I)

la **reservación,** *pl.* **reservaciones** reservation (I)

el **resfriado** cold (I)

respetar to respect, to obey (8)

responder (a) to answer (10)

la **respuesta** answer (I)

el **restaurante** restaurant (I)

el **resto** rest, remainder (15)

retraso: con (+ *time* + **de**) — late (6)

el **retrato** portrait (12)

reunirse to meet, to get together (13)

la **revista** magazine (I)

el **rey** king (I)

rico, -a rich (I)

el **rinoceronte** rhinoceros (I)

el **río** river (I)

robar to steal, to rob (14)

el **robo** robbery (14)

el **rock** rock *(music)* (I)

rodeado, -a (de) surrounded (by) (11)

la **rodilla** knee (9)

rojo, -a red (I)

romántico, -a romantic (I)

romper to break (I)

romperse to break *(a bone)* (9)

la **ropa** clothing, clothes (I)

rosado, -a pink (7)

roto, -a broken (9)

rubio, -a blond (I)

la **rueda** wheel (3)

patinar sobre —**s** to roller-skate (3)

el **patín de** —**s,** *pl.* **patines de** —**s** roller-skate (3)

la — **de feria** Ferris wheel (3)

la silla de —**s** wheelchair (9)

el **ruido** noise (I)

las **ruinas** ruins (14)

rusa: la montaña — roller coaster (3)

sábado Saturday (I)

el — on Saturday (I)

la **sábana** sheet (I)

saber to know (I)

— + *inf.* to know how to (I)

(no) lo sé I (don't) know that (I)

el **sabor** taste (4)

sabroso, -a delicious, tasty, flavorful (4)

el **sacapuntas,** *pl.* **sacapuntas** pencil sharpener (1)

sacar to take out, to remove (I)

— **fotos** to take pictures (I)

— **una buena / mala nota** to get a good / bad grade (I)

el **saco de dormir** sleeping bag (4)

la **sal** salt (4)

la **sala** living room (I)

la — **de espera** waiting room (9)

la — **de estudio** study hall (1)

la **salchicha** sausage (4)

la **salida** exit (I); departure (6)

salir (de) to leave, to go out, to come out (I)

— **bien / mal en** to do well / badly on *(tests)* (I)

la **salud** health (9)

saludar to greet, to say hello / good-by (10)

¡saludos! greetings! (I)

salvadoreño, -a Salvadoran (1)

salvar to save (14)

el **salvavidas** life preserver (5)

el/la **salvavidas** lifeguard (5)

las **sandalias** sandals (I)

la **sandía** watermelon (4)

el **sandwich** sandwich (I)

la **sangría** sangria (13)

sano, -a healthy (9)

el **santo** saint's day (I)

la **sartén,** *pl.* **sartenes** frying pan (2)

el **saxofón,** *pl.* **saxofones** saxophone (12)

se yourself *formal,* himself, herself, itself, yourselves, themselves (I); each other (7)

el **secador** hair dryer (7)

la **secadora** (clothes) dryer (2)

secar to dry (2)

la **sección,** *pl.* **secciones** section (14)

seco, -a dry (4)

el **secretario, la secretaria** secretary (15)

secreto, -a secret (14)

sed: tener — to be thirsty (I)

la **seda dental** dental floss (I)

seguida: en — right away, immediately (I)

seguir (e → i) to follow (12)
  — + *present participle* to go on, to keep on, to continue + *verb* + -ing (12)

según according to (I)

segundo, -a second (I)
  el — piso third floor (I)

el segundo second (I)

la seguridad: el cinturón de — seatbelt (8)

seguro, -a sure (I)

seis six (I)

seiscientos, -as six hundred (I)

el sello stamp (I)

la selva jungle (15)

el semáforo traffic light (8)

la semana week (I)
  el fin de — weekend (I)

sencillo, -a simple (11)

el sendero path (4)

sentarse (e → ie) to sit down (11)

el sentido del humor sense of humor (16)

sentir (e → ie) to be sorry (16)
  —se to feel (9)

la señal de tráfico, *pl.* **señales de tráfico** traffic sign (8)

las señas: hablar por — to talk in sign language (11)

el señor (Sr.) Mr.; sir (I)

la señora (Sra.) Mrs.; ma'am (I)

la señorita (Srta.) Miss; ma'am (I)

septiembre September (I)

séptimo, -a seventh (5)

ser to be (I)

serio, -a serious (I)

la serpiente snake (I)

la servilleta napkin (I)

servir (e → i) to serve (I)

sesenta sixty (I)

setecientos, -as seven hundred (I)

setenta seventy (I)

sexto, -a sixth (5)

si if (I)

sí yes (I)

la sidra cider (13)

siempre always (I)

siento: lo — I'm sorry (I)

siete seven (I)

el siglo century (14)

el significado meaning (14)

siguiente next, following (1)

¡silencio! silence! be quiet! (1)

la silla chair (I)

la — de ruedas wheelchair (9)

el sillón, *pl.* **sillones** armchair (I)

simpático, -a nice, pleasant (I)

sin without (I)
  — duda without a doubt, undoubtedly (12)

sino *(after negative)* but, but rather (11)
  — que + *verb (after negative)* but, but rather (11)

el sitio place, site (15)

sobre on; about (I); over (6)

el sobre envelope (10)

el sobrino, la sobrina nephew, niece (I)

los sobrinos nephews; niece(s) and nephew(s) (I)

¡socorro! help! (15)

el sofá sofá (I)

el sol sun (I)
  hace — it's sunny (I)
  los anteojos de — sunglasses (I)
  tomar el — to sunbathe (1)

solo, -a alone (I)

sólo only (I)

soltero, -a single, unmarried (13)

el sombrero hat (I)

la sombrilla beach umbrella (I)

sonar (o → ue) to ring (10)

el sonido sound (12)

son las + *number* it's . . . o'clock (I)

sonreír (e → i) to smile (5)

soñar (con) to dream (about) (15)

la sopa soup (I)

sordo, -a deaf (11)

sorprender to surprise (16)

la sorpresa surprise (13)

el sótano basement (2)

su, sus his, her, your *formal,* their (I)

suave soft (12)

subir to go up, to come up (I)
  — a to get on or in *(vehicles)* (I)

el subtítulo subtitle (11)

sucio, -a dirty (I)

sudamericano, -a South American (I)

el suegro, la suegra father-in-law, mother-in-law (13)

el sueldo salary (15)

el suelo floor (2)

sueño: tener — to be sleepy (I)

el sueño dream (15)

suerte:
  ¡qué (mala) —! what (bad) luck! (I)

tener (mala) — to be (un)lucky (I)

el suéter sweater (I)

sufrir to suffer (16)

el sujetapapeles, *pl.* **sujetapapeles** paper clip (1)

el supermercado supermarket (I)

la superstición, *pl.* **supersticiones** superstition (16)

supersticioso, -a superstitious (16)

supuesto: por — of course (I)

el sur south (I)

el sureste southeast (1)

el suroeste southwest (1)

susto: ¡qué —! what a scare! (3)

suyo, -a your, (of) yours; his, of his; her, (of) hers (8)

el suyo, la suya, los suyos, las suyas yours, his, hers, theirs (8)

tacaño, -a stingy (I)

el taco taco (I)

tal:
  ¿qué —? how's it going? (I)
  — vez maybe, perhaps (I)

el talento talent (12)

la talla *(garment)* size (7)

también too, also (I)

el tambor drum (12)

tampoco neither, not either (I, 6)

tan so, as (I)
  — + *adj. / adv.* **+ como** as + *adj. / adv.* + as (3)

el tanque gas tank (8)

el tanteo score (5)

tanto *adv.* so much (12)

tanto, -a so much, so many (3)
  — + *noun* **+ como** as much / many + *noun* + as (3)

la taquilla box office (11)

el taquillero, la taquillera ticket seller (11)

tardar en + *inf.* to take + *time* + *verb* (6)

tarde late (I)

la tarde afternoon (I)
  de la — in the afternoon or early evening; P.M. (I)
  por la — in the afternoon (I)

la tarea homework (I)

la tarjeta:
  la — de crédito credit card (6)
  la — postal post card (I)

el **taxi** taxi (I)
la **taza** cup (I)
te you *fam. dir. obj.;* (to / for) you *fam. ind. obj.* (I)
el **té** tea (I)
el **teatro** theater (I)
    la **obra de —** play (I)
    telefónico, -a:
        la **cabina —**a phone booth (I)
        la **guía —**a phone book (I)
el **techo** roof; ceiling (2)
el **teléfono** telephone (I)
    el **número de —** phone number (I)
    hablar por — to talk on the phone (I)
    llamar por — to phone (I)
el **telegrama** telegram (10)
la **telenovela** soap opera (11)
la **televisión (tele)** television (TV) (I)
    por la — on television (11)
el **televisor** TV set (I)
el **tema** topic, subject (1)
temer to fear, to be afraid (16)
la **temperatura** temperature (11)
el **templo** temple (14)
temprano early (I)
el **tenedor** fork (I)
tener to have (I)
    — fiebre / gripe to have a fever / the flu (I)
    — ganas de + *inf.* to feel like *(doing something)* (I)
    — que *inf.* to have to (I)
    ¿qué tienes / tiene Ud.? what's wrong with you? (9)
    See also **año, calor, celos, cuidado, éxito, frío, hambre, lugar, miedo, paciencia, prisa, razón, sed, sueño, suerte, vergüenza**
el **tenis** tennis (I)
    la **cancha de —** tennis court (5)
    los **zapatos de —** tennis shoes (5)
el/la **tenista** tennis player (5)
tercero (tercer), -a third (I)
    el **— piso** fourth floor (I)
terminar to end, to finish (I)
el **termómetro** thermometer (11)
el **terremoto** earthquake (11)
terror: de — *adj.* horror (I)
el **tesoro** treasure (14)
ti you *fam. after prep.* (I)
la **tía** aunt (I)

el **tiempo** weather; time (I)
    a — on time (I)
    ¿cuánto —? how long? (I)
    hace buen / mal — it's nice / bad (out) (I)
    ¿qué — hace? what's the weather like? what's it like out? (I)
la **tienda** store (I)
    la **— de acampar** tent (4)
    la **— de (ropa, discos, etc.)** (clothing, record, etc.) store (I)
la **tierra** earth, soil (I)
el **tigre** tiger (I)
las **tijeras** scissors (7)
tímido, -a shy, timid (3)
el **tío, la tía** uncle, aunt (I)
los **tíos** uncles; aunt(s) and uncle(s) (I)
tirar to throw, to throw away (2)
    — (de) to pull (13)
el **titular** headline (14)
el **título** title (I)
la **tiza** chalk (I)
la **toalla** towel (I)
el **tobillo** ankle (9)
el **tocadiscos,** *pl.* **tocadiscos** record player (I)
tocar to play *(musical instruments / records)* (I)
    — la bocina to honk the horn (8)
todavía still (I)
    no . . . — not yet (1)
    — no not yet (1)
todo *pron.* everything (I)
todo, -a, -os, -as every; all; the whole (I)
    (por / en) todas partes everywhere (16)
    toda clase de all kinds of (11)
    (—) derecho straight ahead (8)
    todo el mundo everybody, everyone (I)
    todos los días every day (I)
tomar to take; to drink (I)
    — algo to have something to drink (I)
    — el sol to sunbathe (I)
    —le el pelo a to pull someone's leg (13)
el **tomate** tomato (I)
el **tono** tone, dial tone (10)
tonto, -a dumb, foolish (I)

el **torero, la torera** bullfighter (I)
la **tormenta** storm (11)
el **toro** bull (I)
la **toronja** grapefruit (9)
la **tortilla** tortilla (4)
    la **— española** Spanish omelet (I)
la **tortuga** turtle (15)
    toser to cough (9)
    tostado: el pan — toast (I)
la **tostadora** toaster (2)
trabajar to work (I)
el **trabajo** job; work (I)
traducir (c → zc) to translate (11)
traer to bring (I)
el **tráfico** traffic (8)
    la **señal de —,** *pl.* **señales de —** traffic sign (8)
el **traje** suit (I)
    el **— de baño** bathing suit (I)
tratar de + *inf.* to try (to) (I)
trece thirteen (I)
treinta thirty (I)
    — y uno (un); — y dos; etc. 31; 32; etc. (I)
el **tren** train (I)
tres three (I)
trescientos, -as three hundred (I)
triste unhappy, sad (I)
el **trombón,** *pl.* **trombones** trombone (12)
la **trompeta** trumpet (12)
el **trueno** thunder, thunderclap (11)
tu, tus your (I)
tú you *fam.* (I)
la **tuba** tuba (12)
el/la **turista** tourist (I)
tuyo, -a your, (of) yours (8)
el **tuyo, la tuya, los tuyos, las tuyas** yours (8)

u or (I)
¡uf! ugh! phew! (I)
último, -a last (5)
un, una a, an, one (I)
    a la una at 1:00 (I)
único, -a only (I)
    el **hijo —, la hija—** only child (I)
el **uniforme** uniform (1)
la **universidad** university (15)
uno one (I)
unos, -as some, a few (I)
la **uña** nail (7)
    el **esmalte de —s** nail polish (7)

la lima de —s nail file (7)
limar(se) las —s to file nails (7)
la urgencia: un caso de — emergency (case) (9)
uruguayo, -a Uruguayan (6)
usar to use (I)
usted (Ud.) you *formal sing.* (I)
ustedes (Uds.) you *pl.* (I)
las uvas grapes (9)

la vaca cow (I)
las vacaciones vacation (I)
  de — on vacation (I)
vacío, -a empty (I)
el vagón, *pl.* **vagones** train car (6)
valer la pena to be worth the effort, to be worth it (16)
valiente brave, courageous (3)
el valle valley (4)
vámonos let's leave, let's go (I)
vamos come on (16)
  — a + *inf.* let's + *verb* (I)
varios, -as several (I)
el vaso glass (I)
el vecino, la vecina neighbor (13)
veinte twenty (I)
  veintiuno (veintiún); veintidós; etc. 21; 22; etc. (I)
el velero sailboat (5)
la velocidad máxima speed limit (8)
la venda bandage (9)
el vendedor, la vendedora salesclerk (I)
vender to sell (I)
  — a + *(amount of money)* to sell for . . . (I)
venezolano, -a Venezuelan (6)
venir to come (I)
  — a buscar to come get, to pick up (10)
la venta sale (I)
  en — for sale (I)
la ventana window (I)
la ventanilla little window (I); ticket window (6); car window (8)
ver to see (I)
el verano summer (I)
veras: de — really (I)
la verdad truth (I)

es — it's true (16)
¿—? isn't that so? right? (I)
verdadero, -a real, true (14)
verde green (I)
la verdura vegetable (I)
vergüenza: tener — to be embarrassed, to be ashamed (16)
la versión: en — original in a foreign language (11)
el vestido dress (I)
vestido, -a de dressed as (I)
vestir (e → i) to dress *(someone)* (I)
  —se to get dressed (I)
el veterinario, la veterinaria veterinarian (I)
la vez, *pl.* **veces** time (I)
  a veces sometimes (I)
  dos veces twice (I)
  otra — again (I)
  por primera (segunda, etc.) — for the first (second, etc.) time (5)
  tal — maybe, perhaps (I)
  una — once (I)
la vía train track (6)
  por — aérea by air mail (10)
viajar to travel (I)
el viaje trip (I)
  la agencia de —s travel agency (I)
  el/la agente de —s travel agent (I)
  de — on a trip (16)
  hacer un — to take a trip (I)
el viajero, la viajera traveler (6)
  el cheque de — traveler's check (6)
la vida life (1)
  ganarse la — to earn a living (15)
viejo, -a old (I)
el viento: hace — it's windy (I)
viernes Friday (I)
  el — on Friday (I)
el vinagre vinegar (4)
el vino wine (I)
el violín, *pl.* **violines** violin (12)
el violoncelo cello (12)
la visita visit (I)
el/la visitante visitor (5)

visitar to visit (I)
vista:
  con — a(l) with a view of (I)
  hasta la — see you later (I)
la vitrina store window (7)
vivir to live (I)
el volante steering wheel (8)
volar (o → ue) to fly (16)
el volcán, *pl.* **volcanes** volcano (15)
el volibol volleyball (I)
volver (o → ue) to return, to go back, to come back (I)
  — a + *inf.* to *(do something)* again, to re- + *verb* (10)
la voz, *pl.* **voces** voice (5)
  en — alta in a loud voice, out loud (10)
  en — baja softly, in a soft voice (10)
el vuelo flight (I)
  el/la auxiliar de — flight attendant (I)
la vuelta:
  a la — de la esquina around the corner (I)
  dar la — to turn around, to go around (8)
  dar una — to take a ride (3)
  de ida y — round-trip (6)

y and (I)
  — + *number (in time telling)* (minutes) past (I)
  — media half-past; and a half (I)
ya already (I); now (9)
  — no not anymore (I)
yo I (I)
el yogur yogurt (I)

la zanahoria carrot (I)
el zapato shoe (I)
  los cordones de los — shoelaces (7)
  los —s de tenis tennis shoes (5)
el zoológico zoo (I)
  el guardián, la guardiana de — zookeeper (I)

ENGLISH-SPANISH VOCABULARY

The *English-Spanish Vocabulary* contains all active vocabulary from *PASOS Y PUENTES* and *VOCES Y VISTAS*.

A dash (—) represents the main entry word. For example, — **from** following **across** means **across from.**

The number following each entry indicates the chapter in *PASOS Y PUENTES* in which the word or expression is first introduced. Two numbers indicate that it is introduced in one chapter and elaborated upon in a later chapter. A Roman numeral (I) indicates that the word was presented in *VOCES Y VISTAS*.

a, an un, una (I); algún, alguna (I)
able capaz, *pl.* capaces (15)
　to be — poder (o → ue) (I)
about sobre; de (I); alrededor de (7)
　how — *(doing something)?* ¿qué te parece si + *verb?* (13)
absent ausente (I)
absent-minded distraído, -a (8)
abstract abstracto, -a (12)
to accelerate acelerar (8)
accelerator el acelerador (8)
accent mark el acento (I)
to accept aceptar (15)
accident el accidente (8)
to accompany acompañar (15)
according to según (I)
to ache doler (o → ue) (I)
acquainted: to be — with conocer (I)
across por (I)
　— from enfrente de (I)
act el acto (14)
active activo, -a (s)
activity la actividad (4)
actor, actress el actor, la actriz, *f. pl.* actrices (I)
ad el anuncio (14)
to add añadir (2)
address la dirección, *pl.* direcciones (I)
　return — el remitente (10)
to admire admirar (1)
adventure la aventura (I)
advertisement el anuncio (14)
advice los consejos (15)

piece of — el consejo (15)
to advise recomendar (e → ie) (9); aconsejar (15)
affection el cariño (10)
affectionate (with) cariñoso, -a (con) (13)
affectionately con cariño (10)
afraid: to be — (of) tener miedo (de) (I); temer (16)
Africa el África (I)
after después de (+ *noun / inf.*) (I)
afternoon la tarde (I)
　good — buenas tardes (I)
　in the — de la tarde; por la tarde (I)
afterwards después (I)
again otra vez (I)
　to *(do something)* **—** volver (o → ue) a + *inf.* (10)
against contra (5)
agency: travel — la agencia de viajes (I)
agent: travel — el / la agente de viajes (I)
to agree estar de acuerdo (I)
ahead: straight — (todo) derecho (8)
air conditioning el aire acondiciona-do (2)
airline la línea aérea (16)
air mail vía aérea (10)
airplane el avión, *pl.* aviones (I)
airport el aeropuerto (I)
alarm clock el despertador (I)
algebra el álgebra (I)
alike igual (13)

all todo, -a (I)
alligator el caimán, *pl.* caimanes (I)
to allow permitir (13)
　allowed: it is — se puede (13)
all right está bien (I); de acuerdo (5)
almost casi (I)
alone solo, -a (I)
along por (13)
already ya (I)
also también (I)
always siempre (I)
A.M. de la mañana (I)
amazing asombroso, -a (14)
ambition la ambición, *pl.* ambiciones (15)
ambitious ambicioso, -a (15)
ambulance la ambulancia (9)
American americano, -a (I)
amusement park el parque de diversiones (3)
amusing divertido, -a (I)
ancient antiguo, -a (14)
and y; e (I)
angry enojado, -a (16)
　to be / get — (at) enojar(se) (con) (16)
animal el animal (I)
ankle el tobillo (9)
to announce anunciar (6)
announcer el locutor, la locutora (11)
another otro, -a (I)
answer la respuesta (I)
to answer contestar (I); responder (a) (10)

ant la hormiga (4)

anthropologist el antropólogo, la antropóloga (15)

any *adj.* algún, alguna; *pron.* alguno, -a, -os, -as (I)

   not — *adj.* (no . . .) ningún, ninguna; *pron.* (no . . .) ninguno, -a, -os, -as (I)

anymore: not — ya no (I)

anyone alguien (I)

   not — (no . . .) nadie (I)

anything algo (I)

   — else (no . . .) otra cosa (11)

   not — (no . . ,) nada (I)

apartment el apartamento (I)

to **applaud** aplaudir (12)

apple la manzana (I)

   — juice el jugo de manzana (I)

appointment la cita (13)

to **appreciate** agradecer (c → zc) (11)

April abril (I)

archaeologist el arqueólogo, la arqueóloga (14)

architect el arquitecto, la arquitecta (14)

Argentina la Argentina (I)

Argentine argentino, -a (6)

to **argue** discutir (11)

arm el brazo (I)

   to cost an — and a leg costar un ojo de la cara (7)

armchair el sillón, *pl.* sillones (I)

around alrededor de (7)

   — here / there por aquí / allí (8)

   — the corner a la vuelta de la esquina (I)

   to turn — dar la vuelta (8)

arrival la llegada (6)

to **arrive** llegar (I)

art el arte (I)

   — exhibit la exposición de arte, *pl.* exposiciones de arte (3)

article el artículo (14)

artist el / la artista (12)

as tan (I); como (2)

   — + adj. / adv. + — tan + adj. / adv. + como (3)

   — a(n) de (14)

   — much / many — tanto, -a + noun + como (3)

ashamed: to be — tener vergüenza (16)

to **ask** preguntar (I)

   to — a question hacer una pregunta (1)

   to — for pedir (e → i) (I)

asleep dormido, -a (11)

   to fall — dormirse (o → ue) (I)

asparagus los aspárragos (9)

assistant el / la ayudante (15)

astonishing asombroso, -a (14)

astronomer el astrónomo, la astrónoma (14)

at a(l) (I)

   — home en casa (I)

   — last por fin (3)

   — least por lo menos (15)

athlete el / la atleta (I)

athletic atlético, -a (I)

to **attend** asistir a (I)

attendant *see* **flight attendant**

attention: to pay — (to) prestar atención (a) (1); fijarse (en) (12)

attraction la atracción, *pl.* atracciones (3)

audience el público (11)

August agosto (I)

aunt la tía (I)

   —(s) and uncle(s) los tíos (I)

author el escritor, la escritora (I); el autor, la autora (1)

autograph el autógrafo (11)

autumn el otoño (I)

avenue la avenida (I)

avocado el aguacate (9)

awake despierto, -a (11)

away:

   to go — irse (7)

   to run — escaparse (14)

   to throw — tirar (2)

awful: how —! ¡qué barbaridad! (5); qué horror! (14)

Aztecs los aztecas (14)

baby el bebé (13)

to **baby-sit** cuidar a los niños (I)

back la espalda (9)

   at the — en el fondo (12)

back:

   to come / go — volver (o → ue); regresar (I)

   to give / take — devolver (o → ue) (7)

background: in the — en el fondo (12)

backpack la mochila (I)

bad malo (mal), -a (I)

   —ly mal (I)

   it's — out hace mal tiempo (I)

   that's too — ¡qué lástima! (I)

bag la bolsa (3)

sleeping — el saco de dormir (4)

bakery la panadería (I)

balcony el balcón, *pl.* balcones (I)

ball la pelota; el balón, *pl.* balones (I)

balloon el globo (3)

banana el plátano (I)

band *(musical)* la banda (3)

bandage la venda (9)

bank el banco (I)

baptism el bautizo (13)

barbecue el asado (4)

   to have a — hacer un asado (4)

to **barbecue** asar a la parrilla (4)

barber el peluquero, la peluquera (7)

   — shop la peluquería (7)

bargain la ganga (7)

baseball el béisbol (I)

basement el sótano (2)

basket la canasta (3)

basketball el básquetbol (I)

bass el contrabajo (12)

bath: to take a — bañarse (I)

to **bathe (someone)** bañar (I)

bathing suit el traje de baño (I)

bathroom el baño (I)

battery *(flashlight)* la pila (4)

to **be** ser; estar (I)

   to — (located) estar (I); quedar (8)

beach la playa (I)

   — umbrella la sombrilla (I)

beans los frijoles (I)

bear el oso (I)

beard la barba (7)

to **beat** batir (2)

beautiful hermoso, -a; bello, -a (I)

beauty shop la peluquería (7)

because porque (I)

   — of por (13); a causa de (14)

bed la cama (I)

   to go to — acostarse (o → ue) (I)

   to put someone to — acostar (o → ue) (I)

bedroom el dormitorio (I)

before antes de + *noun / inf.* (I)

   — (that) antes (3)

to **begin** empezar (e → ie) (a + *inf.*) (I); comenzar (e → ie) (a + *inf.*) (6)

to **behave well / badly** portarse bien / mal (13)

behind detrás de (I)

to **believe** creer (I)

belt el cinturón, *pl.* cinturones (I)

beside al lado de (I)

best: the — + noun + in el/la mejor + *noun* + de(l) (I)

better mejor (I)
  to get — mejorarse (9)
between entre (I)
beverage la bebida (I)
bicycle la bicicleta (I)
  to ride a — montar en bicicleta (I)
big grande (I)
bilingual bilingüe (I)
bill *(money)* el billete (6)
biography la biografía (1)
biology la biología (I)
bird el pájaro (I)
birth el nacimiento (13)
birthday el cumpleaños (I)
  fifteenth — los quince años (I)
  happy — ¡feliz cumpleaños! (2)
  to have a — cumplir años (13)
black negro, -a (I)
blanket la manta (I)
blind ciego, -a (11)
block *(city)* la cuadra (8)
blond rubio, -a (I)
blouse la blusa (I)
blue azul (I)
boarding gate la puerta de embarque (16)
boardinghouse la pensión, *pl.* pensiones (6)
boat el barco (I)
  — race la regata (5)
body el cuerpo (I)
to boil hervir (e → ie) (4)
Bolivian boliviano, -a (6)
bone el hueso (9)
book el libro (I)
  phone — la guía telefónica (I)
bookstore la librería (I)
boot la bota (I)
booth el puesto (3)
  phone — la cabina telefónica (I)
border la frontera (16)
bore: what a —! ¡qué lata! (3)
to bore aburrir (11)
bored aburrido, -a *(estar)* (I)
  to be / get — aburrirse (11)
boring aburrido, -a *(ser)* (I)
born: to be — nacer (c → zc) (13)
to borrow (from) pedir prestado, -a (a) (I)
boss el jefe, la jefa (15)
to bother molestar (13)
  don't — no te molestes (13)
bottle la botella (I)
to bowl jugar a los bolos (3)
box la caja (I)
  — office la taquilla (11)

post office — el apartado postal (10)
boy el muchacho; el chico (I)
  little — el niño (I)
boyfriend el novio (I)
bracelet la pulsera (I)
braces *(for teeth)* el aparato (15)
brake el freno (8)
brand la marca (7)
brave valiente (3)
bravo! ¡bravo! (12)
Brazil el Brasil (I)
Brazilian brasileño, -a (6)
bread el pan (I)
to break romper (I)
  to — *(a bone)* romperse (9)
breakfast el desayuno (I)
  to have — desayunar (4)
bride la novia (13)
  — and groom los novios (13)
bridge el puente (I)
bright claro, -a (6)
to bring traer (I)
broken descompuesto, -a (2); roto, -a (9)
broom la escoba (2)
brother el hermano (I)
  —in-law el cuñado (13)
  —(s) and sister(s) los hermanos (I)
  little — el hermanito (I)
brown marrón, *pl.* marrones (I)
brunette moreno, -a (I)
brush el pincel (12)
to brush (someone's hair) cepillar (el pelo) (I)
  — (one's teeth / hair) cepillarse (los dientes / el pelo) (I)
to build construir (14)
building el edificio (I)
bull el toro (I)
bullfight la corrida (de toros) (I)
bullfighter el torero, la torera (I)
to bump (into) chocar (con) (8)
bumper el parachoques, *pl.* parachoques (8)
buried enterrado, -a (14)
to burn quemar (I)
  to — up / down quemarse (14)
burned quemado, -a (2)
burrito el burrito (I)
bus el autobús, *pl.* autobuses (I)
business el negocio (15)
businessman / businesswoman el hombre / la mujer de negocios (15)

busy ocupado, -a (I)
  not — libre (I)
but pero (I); *(after negative)* sino (11); sino que + *verb* (11)
  — rather sino (11); sino que + *verb* (11)
butcher shop la carnicería (I)
butter la mantequilla (I)
to buy comprar (I)
by en + *vehicle* (I); de (1); por (13); para + *time* (15)

cabbage la col (9)
café el café (I)
cafeteria la cafetería (I)
cage la jaula (I)
cake el pastel (I)
calculator la calculadora (1)
calendar el calendario (I)
call la llamada (10)
  collect — la llamada por cobrar (10)
to call llamar (I)
  to — on the phone llamar por teléfono (I)
  who's —ing? ¿de parte de quién? (10)
called: to be — llamarse (I)
calories las calorías (9)
camera la cámara (I)
campground el campamento (4)
camping: to go — ir de camping (4)
can poder (o → ue) (I)
  — I help you? ¿qué desea Ud.? (I)
  you — se puede (13)
can la lata (4)
can opener el abrelatas, *pl.* abrelatas (4)
  garbage — el basurero (2)
Canada el Canadá (I)
Canadian canadiense (I)
candy los dulces (I)
canoe la canoa (15)
capable capaz, *pl.* capaces (15)
capital la capital (I)
to capture capturar (14)
car el coche (I); *(train)* el vagón; *pl.* vagones (6)
  dining — el coche comedor, *pl.* coches comedor (6)
  sleeping — el coche cama, *pl.* coches cama (6)
  sports — el coche deportivo (8)
card:
  credit — la tarjeta de crédito (6)

ID — el carné (5)
membership — el carné (5)
cards los naipes (I)
care: to take — of cuidar (13)
careful:
   be —! ¡cuidado! (I)
   to be — tener cuidado (I)
carefully con cuidado (8)
Caribbean el Caribe (I)
carnival el carnaval (I)
carrot la zanahoria (I)
carrousel el carrusel (3)
to carry llevar (I)
cartoons los dibujos animados (I)
case: emergency — un caso de urgencia (9)
cash:
   — register la caja (7)
   to pay — pagar al contado (6)
to cash a check cobrar un cheque (6)
cashier el cajero, la cajera (7)
castle el castillo (6)
cat el gato (I)
to catch capturar (14)
cattle el ganado (4)
cause la causa (14)
ceiling el techo (2)
to celebrate celebrar (I)
celebration la celebración, *pl.* celebraciones (I)
cello el violoncelo (12)
cent(avo) el centavo (I)
center el centro (12)
Central America la América Central (I)
Central American centroamericano, -a (I)
century el siglo (14)
ceramics la cerámica (12)
cereal el cereal (9)
certain cierto, -a (16)
chair la silla (I)
chalk la tiza (I)
chalkboard la pizarra (I)
champion el campeón (*pl.* campeones), la campeona (5)
championship el campeonato (5)
to change cambiar (I)
   to — one's mind cambiar de idea (3)
channel el canal (I)
chapter el capítulo (I)
character el personaje (11)
cheap barato, -a (I)
check (*in restaurant*) la cuenta (I); (*bank*) el cheque (6)

to cash a — cobrar un cheque (6)
traveler's — el cheque de viajero (6)
to check registrar (16)
checkers las damas (I)
cheese el queso (I)
chemistry la química (I)
cherry la cereza (9)
chess el ajedrez (I)
chest el pecho (9)
chestnut (*color*) castaño, -a (7)
to chew mascar (13)
chewing gum el chicle (13)
chicken el pollo (I)
child el niño, la niña (I)
children (*boys and girls*) los niños; (*sons and daughters*) los hijos (I)
Chilean chileno, -a (6)
chili (pepper) el chile (I)
chili con carne el chile con carne (I)
chocolate el chocolate (I)
   hot — el chocolate (I)
choir el coro (12)
to choose escoger (j) (2)
chop la chuleta (I)
   lamb / pork — la chuleta de cordero / cerdo (I)
chorus el coro (12)
Christmas la Navidad (I)
church la iglesia (I)
churros los churros (I)
cider la sidra (13)
city la ciudad (I)
civilization la civilización, *pl.* civilizaciones (14)
clarinet el clarinete (12)
class la clase (de) (I)
   first- / second- — de primera / segunda clase (6)
classical clásico, -a (I)
classmate el compañero, la compañera de clase (I)
clean limpio, -a (I)
to clean limpiar (I)
   to — (one's) shoes / eyeglasses limpiar(se) los zapatos / los anteojos (7)
clear claro, -a (6)
to clear the table quitar los platos (I)
clearance sale la liquidación, *pl.* liquidaciones (7)
clever listo, -a (I)
climate el clima (15)
clinic la clínica (9)
clock el reloj (I)
   alarm — el despertador (I)
to close cerrar (e → ie) (I)

close to cerca de (I)
closed cerrado, -a (I)
closet el armario (I)
clothes, clothing la ropa (I)
cloud la nube (I)
cloudy: it's — está nublado (I)
club el club, *pl.* clubes (5)
coach el entrenador, la entrenadora (5)
coat el abrigo; la chaqueta (I)
coconut el coco (9)
coffee el café (I)
   — with cream el café con leche (I)
coin la moneda (I)
cold frío, -a (I)
   it's — (out) hace frío (I)
   to be — (*people***)** tener frío (I)
cold el resfriado (I)
collect call la llamada por cobrar (10)
to collect coleccionar (I)
collection la colección, *pl.* colecciones (12)
Colombian colombiano, -a (6)
color el color (I)
   in — en colores (I)
   what —? ¿de qué color? (I)
comb el peine (I)
to comb someone's hair peinar (I)
   to — one's hair peinarse (I)
to come venir (I)
   — on vamos (16)
   to — back volver (o → ue); regresar (I)
   to — down bajar (I)
   to — get venir a buscar (10)
   to — in entrar (en) (I)
   to — out salir (de) (I)
   to — up subir (I)
   to — with acompañar (15)
comedy (*film*) la película cómica (I)
comfortable cómodo, -a (I)
comic cómico, -a (I); gracioso, -a (3)
commercial el anuncio comercial (I)
company la compañía (10)
competition el concurso (11)
to complain (about) quejarse (de) (7)
completely completamente (3)
complicated complicado, -a (11)
composer el compositor, la compositora (12)
composition la composición, *pl.* composiciones (1)
computer la computadora (I)
   — programmer el programador / la programadora de computadoras (15)

concert el concierto (I)

to **conduct** dirigir (j) (12)

conductor *(train)* el inspector, la inspectora (6); *(orchestra)* el director, la directora (12)

to **congratulate** felicitar (13)

congratulations! ¡felicidades!; ¡felicitaciones! (I)

to **construct** construir (14)

contest el concurso (11)

continually continuamente (16)

to **continue** continuar (I); seguir (e → i) + *present participle* (12)

contrary: on the — al contrario (I)

to **cook** cocinar (I)

cool: it's — (out) hace fresco (I)

cord el cordón, *pl.* cordones (2)

corn el maíz (I)

corner la esquina (I)

    around the — a la vuelta de la esquina (I)

correct correcto, -a (I)

to **cost** costar (o → ue) (I)

    to **— an arm and a leg** costar un ojo de la cara (7)

Costa Rican costarricense (1)

costume el disfraz, *pl.* disfraces (I)

    — party la fiesta de disfraces (I)

cotton el algodón (14)

to **cough** toser (9)

to **count** contar (o → ue) (I)

counter el mostrador (7)

country el país (I)

country(side) el campo (I)

courageous valiente (3)

court: tennis — la cancha de tenis (5)

courtyard el patio (I)

cousin el primo, la prima (I)

cow la vaca (I)

cracker la galleta (4)

to **crash (into)** chocar (con) (8)

crazy loco, -a (I)

cream:

    coffee with — el café con leche (I)

    shaving — la crema de afeitar (7)

credit card la tarjeta de crédito (6)

to **cross** cruzar (6)

crosswalk el paso de peatones (8)

crowded lleno, -a de gente (I)

crutch la muleta (9)

to **cry** llorar (13)

Cuban cubano, -a (I)

cup la taza (I)

currency exchange la casa de cambio (6)

---

curtain la cortina (2)

custard el flan (I)

customer el / la cliente (I)

customs la aduana (16)

    — official el aduanero, la aduanera (16)

to **cut** cortar (2)

    to **— (one's) hair / nails** cortar(se) el pelo / las uñas (7)

dad el papá (I)

damp húmedo, -a (15)

dance el baile (I)

to **dance** bailar (I)

dancer el bailarín *(pl.* bailarines), la bailarina (12)

dangerous peligroso, -a (8)

dark oscuro, -a (6)

    — glasses los anteojos de sol (I)

    —(-haired) moreno, -a (I)

date la fecha (I); la cita (13)

    what's the — today? ¿cuál es la fecha de hoy? (I)

daughter la hija (I)

day el día (I)

    — before yesterday anteayer (5)

    every — todos los días (I)

    special of the — el plato del día (9)

dead muerto, -a (14)

deaf sordo, -a (11)

dear querido, -a (10)

December diciembre (I)

to **decide** decidir (15)

to **declare** *(at customs)* declarar (16)

to **decorate** decorar (I)

decoration la decoración, *pl.* decoraciones (I)

degree el grado (11)

delay la demora (16)

delicious delicioso, -a (I); sabroso, -a (4)

to **deliver** entregar (10)

to **demonstrate** demostrar (o → ue) (12)

dental floss la seda dental (I)

dentist el / la dentista (I)

to **deny** negar (e → ie) (16)

deodorant el desodorante (I)

department el departamento (7)

    — store el almacén, *pl.* almacenes (I)

departure la salida (6)

---

to **describe** describir (I)

desert el desierto (15)

desk el escritorio (I)

    reception — la recepción, *pl.* recepciones (6)

    student — el pupitre (I)

dessert el postre (I)

    for — de postre (I)

to **destroy** destruir (14)

detective *adj.* policíaco, -a (I)

detergent el detergente (2)

devil el diablo (I)

to **dial** marcar (10)

dial tone el tono (10)

dictionary el diccionario (1)

to **die** morirse (o → ue) (9)

diet la dieta (9)

    to be on a — estar a dieta (9)

difference la diferencia (12)

different (from) distinto, -a (de) (7); diferente (12)

difficult difícil (I)

dining car el coche comedor, *pl.* coches comedor (6)

dining room el comedor (I)

dinner la cena (I)

    to have — cenar (4)

to **direct** dirigir (j) (12)

director el director, la directora (11)

dirty sucio, -a (I)

disagreeable desagradable (13)

disaster el desastre (11)

to **discover** descubrir (14)

to **discuss** discutir (11)

disguise el disfraz, *pl.* disfraces (I)

dish el plato (I)

dishwasher el lavaplatos (2)

disorder el desorden (2)

dive: to scuba — bucear (5)

to **do** hacer (I)

    to — well / badly on *(tests)* salir bien / mal en (I)

doctor el médico, la médica; el doctor (Dr.), la doctora (Dra.) *(as title)* (I)

document el documento (16)

documentary el documental (11)

dog el perro (I)

dollar el dólar (I)

Dominican dominicano, -a (1)

Dominican Republic la República Dominicana (I)

door la puerta (I)

double room la habitación doble (6)

doubt: without a — sin duda (12)

to doubt dudar (16)
down:
    to come / go — bajar (I)
    to fall — caerse (10)
    to sit — sentarse (e → ie) (11)
downtown el centro (I)
dozen la docena (de) (I)
drag: what a —! ¡qué lata! (3)
to draw dibujar (I)
drawing el dibujo (I)
dream el sueño (15)
to dream (about) soñar (o → ue) (con)
    (15)
dress el vestido (I)
to dress (someone) vestir (e → i) (I)
    to get —ed vestirse (e → i) (I)
dressed as vestido, -a de (I)
dresser la cómoda (I)
drink la bebida (I)
to drink beber; tomar (I)
    to have something to — tomar
    algo (I)
to drive manejar (8)
driver el conductor, la conductora
    (8)
    —'s license el permiso de mane-
    jar (8)
drugstore la farmacia (I)
drum el tambor (12)
dry seco, -a (4)
to dry secar (2)
dryer la secadora (2)
    hair — el secador (7)
dubbed film la película doblada (11)
duck el pato (I)
dumb tonto, -a (I)
during durante (I)

each cada (I)
    — other nos (7); se (7)
ear la oreja (I)
    (inner) — el oído (I)
early temprano (I)
to earn ganar (15)
    to — a living ganarse la vida (15)
earring el arete (I)
earth la tierra (I)
earthquake el terremoto (11)
east el este (I)
easy fácil (I)
to eat comer (I)
    to — breakfast desayunar (4)
    to — dinner cenar (4)
    to — lunch almorzar (o → ue) (2)
Ecuador el Ecuador (I)

Ecuadorian ecuatoriano, -a (6)
effort: to be worth the — valer la
    pena (16)
egg el huevo (I)
eight ocho (I)
eighteen dieciocho (I)
eighth octavo, -a (5)
eight hundred ochocientos, -as (I)
eighty ochenta (I)
either:
    not — (ni . . .) tampoco (I)
    — . . . or o . . . o (10)
elbow el codo (9)
electric eléctrico, -a (2)
elegant elegante (7)
elephant el elefante (I)
elevator el ascensor (I)
eleven once (I)
else: someone / something — otra
    persona / cosa (11)
embarrassed: to be — tener ver-
    güenza (16)
to embrace abrazar (13)
emergency (case) un caso de
    urgencia (9)
empty vacío, -a (I)
to enclose incluir (10)
to end terminar (I)
energetic enérgico, -a (I); activo, -a
    (5)
engineer el ingeniero, la ingeniera
    (14)
England Inglaterra (I)
English inglés (*pl.* ingleses), inglesa
    (I)
English *(language)* el inglés (I)
to enjoy disfrutar de (I)
    — your meal ¡buen provecho! (4)
enormous enorme (I)
enough bastante (15)
to enter entrar (en) (I)
entertaining divertido, -a (I)
entrance la entrada (I)
envelope el sobre (10)
to erase borrar (I)
eraser el borrador (I)
escalator la escalera mecánica (7)
to escape escaparse (14)
especially especialmente (3)
etc. etcétera (14)
Europe Europa (I)
even: not — no . . . ni (6)
evening: good — buenas tardes /
    buenas noches (I)
every todo, -a; cada (I)
    — day todos los días (I)

everybody / everyone todo el
    mundo (I)
everything todo (I)
everywhere (por / en) todas partes
    (16)
exactly exactamente (3)
exam el examen, *pl.* exámenes (I)
to examine examinar (I)
example: for — por ejemplo (4)
excellent excelente (I)
exchange: currency — la casa de
    cambio (6)
to exchange cambiar (I)
exciting emocionante (I)
excursion: to go on an — ir de
    excursión (3)
excuse la excusa (I)
excuse me con permiso; discúlpeme
    (I)
to exercise hacer ejercicio (9)
exhibit la exposición, *pl.* exposicio-
    nes (3)
exit la salida (I)
to expect esperar (I)
expedition la expedición, *pl.*
    expediciones (15)
    to go on an — hacer una
    expedición (15)
expensive caro, -a (I)
    very — carísimo, -a (I)
to explain explicar (1)
to explore explorar (15)
explorer el explorador, la
    exploradora (15)
express *adj.* expreso (6)
eye el ojo (I)
eyeglasses los anteojos (I)

fabulous fabuloso, -a (I)
face la cara (I)
failure el fracaso (11)
fair la feria (3)
fairly bastante (I)
fall el otoño (I)
to fall caer (10)
    to — asleep dormirse (o → ue) (I)
    to — down caerse (10)
family la familia (I)
famous famoso, -a (3)
fan el admirador, la admiradora (11)
    — (of) el aficionado, la aficionada
    (a) (I)
fantastic estupendo, -a; fantástico,
    -a (I)
far from lejos de (I)

farm la granja (I)
— **worker** el campesino, la campesina (4)
farmer el granjero, la granjera (I)
fashion la moda (7)
fashionable de moda (7)
fast *adj.* rápido, -a; *adv.* rápidamente; de prisa (I)
fat gordo, -a (I)
father el padre (I)
—**-in-law** el suegro (13)
favorite favorito, -a; preferido, -a (I)
to **fear** temer (16)
February febrero (I)
to **feed** dar de comer a(l) (I)
to **feel** sentirse (e → ie) (9)
to — **like** *(doing something)* tener ganas de + *inf.* (I)
Ferris wheel la rueda de feria (3)
fever la fiebre (I)
to have a — tener fiebre (I)
few pocos, -as (I)
a — unos, -as (I)
—**er (than)** menos (que / de) (I)
fifteen quince (I)
fifteenth birthday los quince años (I)
fifteen-year-old girl la quinceañera (I)
fifth quinto, -a (5)
fifty cincuenta (I)
to **fight (with)** pelearse (con) (13)
to **file (one's) nails** limar(se) las uñas (7)
to **fill (up / out / in)** llenar (8, 10)
film la película (I)
dubbed — la película doblada (11)
to **film** filmar (11)
finally por fin (3)
to **find** encontrar (o → ue) (I); hallar (14)
to — **out** averiguar (10)
fine ¡bueno! (I)
fine la multa (8)
finger el dedo (I)
to **finish** terminar (I)
fire el fuego (4); el incendio (14)
—**fighter** el bombero, la bombera (14)
fireworks los fuegos artificiales (I)
first primero (primer), -a; el primero *in dates* (I); antes (3)
at — al principio (11)
— **-class** de primera clase (6)
— **floor** la planta baja (I)

fish *(live)* el pez, *pl.* peces; *(cooked)* el pescado (I)
fishing: to go — ir de pesca (4)
to **fit** quedar (7)
five cinco (I)
— **hundred** quinientos, -as (I)
to **fix** arreglar (I)
flag la bandera (I)
flan el flan (I)
flashlight la linterna (4)
— **battery** la pila (4)
flavorful sabroso, -a (4)
to **flee (from)** huir (de) (14)
flight el vuelo (I)
— **attendant** el / la auxiliar de vuelo (I)
floor el piso (I); el suelo (2)
ground — la planta baja (I)
second (third / fourth) — el primer (segundo / tercer) piso (I)
flower la flor (I)
flu la gripe (I)
to have the — tener gripe (I)
flute la flauta (12)
fly la mosca (4)
to **fly** volar (o → ue) (16)
folk *adj.* folklórico, -a (I)
to **follow** seguir (e → i) (12)
following siguiente (1)
food la comida (I)
foot el pie (I)
on — a pie (I)
to put one's — **in it** meter la pata (13)
football el fútbol americano (I)
for para (I); por (9)
— **example** por ejemplo (4)
— **sale** en venta (I)
forbidden: it is — se prohíbe (13)
forecast: weather — el pronóstico del tiempo (11)
foreign extranjero, -a (11)
in a — **language** en versión original (11)
to **forget** *(something)* olvidar (3)
to — **(to)** olvidarse (de + *inf.*) (I)
fork el tenedor (I)
form el formulario (10)
fortunately afortunadamente (3)
forty cuarenta (I)
fountain la fuente (I)
four cuatro (I)
— **hundred** cuatrocientos, -as (I)
fourteen catorce (I)
fourth cuarto, -a (5)

— **floor** el tercer piso (I)
France Francia (I)
free *(not busy)* libre (I); *(no charge)* gratis, *pl.* gratis (3)
French francés *(pl. franceses),* francesa (I)
French *(language)* el francés (I)
French fries las papas fritas (I)
frequently frecuentemente (3)
fresh fresco, -a (4)
Friday viernes (I)
on — el viernes (I)
fried frito, -a (I)
friend el amigo, la amiga (I)
to **frighten** dar miedo a (I); asustar (3)
frightened asustado, -a (3)
frog la rana (4)
from de(l); desde (I)
— **me** de mi parte (10)
front: in — **of** delante de (I)
frozen congelado, -a (4)
fruit la fruta (I)
frying pan la sartén, *pl.* sartenes (2)
full lleno, -a (I)
fun: to have — divertirse (e → ie) (I)
funny chistoso, -a (I); gracioso, -a (3)
furniture los muebles (I)

to **gain weight** aumentar de peso (9)
gallery la galería (12)
game el partido (de + *sport*); el juego (I)
garage el garaje (I)
garbage la basura (2)
— **can** el basurero (2)
garden el jardín, *pl.* jardines (I)
garlic el ajo (4)
gas la gasolina (8)
— **tank** el tanque (8)
gate: boarding — la puerta de embarque (16)
gazpacho el gazpacho (I)
gee! ¡caramba! (I)
generally generalmente (I)
generous generoso, -a (I)
geometry la geometría (I)
German alemán *(pl. alemanes),* alemana (I)
German *(language)* el alemán (I)
Germany Alemania (I)
to **get** recibir (I); obtener (8)
to — **a good / bad grade** sacar una buena / mala nota (I)
to — **better** mejorarse (9)

to — bored aburrirse (11)
to come — venir a buscar (10)
to — dressed vestirse (e → i) (I)
to go — ir a buscar (10)
to — married (to) casarse (con) (13)
to — off /out of *(vehicles)* bajar de (I)
to — on / in *(vehicles)* subir a (I)
to — together reunirse (13)
to — to know conocer (c → zc) (11)
to — up levantarse (I)
ghost el fantasma (I)
gift el regalo (I)
giraffe la jirafa (I)
girl la muchacha; la chica (I)
   little — la niña (I)
girlfriend la novia (I)
to give dar (I)
   to — a present regalar (13)
   to — back devolver (o → ue) (7)
   to — someone a shot poner una inyección (I)
   to — a ticket poner una multa (8)
gladly con mucho gusto (I)
glass el vaso (I)
glasses los anteojos (I)
   dark —es los anteojos de sol (I)
glove el guante (I)
to go ir (I)
   —ing to + *verb* ir a + *inf.* (I)
   how's it —ing? ¿qué tal? (I)
   to — around dar la vuelta (8)
   to — away irse (7)
   to — back volver (o → ue); regresar (I)
   to — down bajar (I)
   to — for a ride / walk dar un paseo (3)
   to — get ir a buscar (10)
   to — in(to) entrar (en) (I)
   to — on + *verb* + **-ing** seguir (e → i) + *present participle* (12)
   to — out salir (de) (I)
   to — to bed acostarse (o → ue) (I)
   to — to sleep dormirse (o → ue) (I)
   to — up subir (I)
   to — with acompañar (15)
   what's —ing on? ¿qué pasa? (I)
god, goddess el dios, la diosa (14)
godfather, godmother el padrino, la madrina (13)
godparents los padrinos (13)
gold el oro (14)

golf el golf (I)
good bien (I); *adj.* bueno (buen), -a (I)
   — afternoon buenas tardes (I)
   — evening buenas tardes / buenas noches (I)
   — grief! ¡qué barbaridad! (5)
   — morning buenos días (I)
   — night buenas noches (I)
   to be — in estar fuerte en (I)
   to have a — time divertirse (e → ie) (I)
   to look — on quedar (7)
good-by adiós (I)
   to say — (to) saludar (a) (10); despedirse (e → i) (de) (13)
good-looking bonito, -a; guapo, -a (I)
to goof meter la pata (13)
gosh! ¡caramba! (I)
gossip los chismes (10)
   (piece of) — el chisme (10)
grade la nota (I)
   to get a good / bad — sacar una buena / mala nota (I)
to graduate graduarse (15)
gram el gramo (I)
grandchildren los nietos (13)
granddaughter la nieta (13)
grandfather el abuelo (I)
grandmother la abuela (I)
grandparents los abuelos (I)
grandson el nieto (13)
grapefruit la toronja (9)
grapes las uvas (9)
grass la hierba (I)
   to cut the — cortar el césped (2)
gray gris, *pl.* grises (I)
great gran; fantástico (I)
   —! ¡qué bueno! (I); ¡qué maravilla! (3)
great-grandfather el bisabuelo (13)
great-grandmother la bisabuela (13)
great-grandparents los bisabuelos (13)
green verde (I)
to greet saludar (10)
greetings! ¡saludos! (I)
grief: good —! ¡qué barbaridad! (5)
grill la parrilla (4)
to grill asar a la parrilla (4)
groceries los comestibles (I)
groom el novio (13)
ground floor la planta baja (I)
group el grupo (I)
grownups los mayores (13)

guacamole guacamole (9)
Guatemalan guatemalteco, -a (1)
guest el invitado, la invitada (I)
guide el / la guía (I)
guidebook la guía (I)
guitar la guitarra (I)
Gulf of Mexico el Golfo de México (I)
gum: chewing — el chicle (13)
gym(nasium) el gimnasio (I)
gymnastics: to do — hacer gimnasia (5)

hair el pelo (I)
   — dryer el secador (7)
   See also **to brush, to comb**
hairdresser el peluquero, la peluquera (7)
half la mitad (15)
   and a — y media (I)
   — an hour la media hora (I)
   — -past y media (I)
hall el pasillo (2)
   study — la sala de estudio (1)
ham el jamón (I)
hamburger la hamburguesa (I)
hand la mano (I)
   to shake —s (with) dar la mano a (13)
handkerchief el pañuelo (I)
handsome guapo, -a (I)
to hang up colgar (o → ue) (10)
to happen pasar (2); ocurrir (11)
happy contento, -a (I); feliz, *pl.* felices (13)
   — birthday! ¡feliz cumpleaños! (2)
   to be — (about) alegrarse (de) (16)
hard difícil (I)
to harm hacer daño a (12)
hat el sombrero (I)
to have tener (I)
   to — a barbecue hacer un asado (4)
   to — a birthday cumplir años (13)
   to — a fever / the flu tener fiebre / gripe (I)
   to — a good time / fun divertirse (e → ie) (I)
   to — a picnic hacer un picnic (3)
   to — dinner cenar (4)
   to — lunch almorzar (o → ue) (2)
   to — just *(done something)* acabar de + *inf.* (I)
   to — something to drink tomar algo (I)
   to — to tener que + *inf.* (I)

he él (I)
head la cabeza (I)
headlight el faro (8)
headline el titular (14)
health la salud (9)
healthy sano, -a (9)
to hear oír (I)
heart el corazón (I)
heat la calefacción (2)
to heat calentar (e → ie) (4)
heating system la calefacción (2)
heavy pesado, -a (4)
helicopter el helicóptero (15)
hello ¡hola!; ¿aló? *(on phone)* (I)
   to say — saludar (10)
help! ¡socorro! (15)
to help ayudar (a + *inf.*) (I)
   may I — you? ¿qué desea Ud.? (I)
helper el / la ayudante (15)
hen la gallina (I)
her su, sus *poss. adj.;* ella *after prep.;*
   la *dir. obj.* (I); suyo, -a *poss. adj.*
   (8)
   to / for — le (I)
here aquí (I)
   around — por aquí (8)
   — is / — are aquí tienes / tiene
   Ud. (I)
   — it is / — they are aquí lo (la,
   los, las) tiene(s) (I)
   over — por aquí (8)
hero, heroine, el héroe, la heroína
   (14)
heroic heroico, -a (14)
hers *pron.* el suyo, la suya, los
   suyos, las suyas (8)
   of — *adj.* suyo, -a (8)
herself se (I)
hey! ¡oye! (I)
hi ¡hola! (I)
high school el colegio (I)
highway la carretera (8)
hill la colina (4)
him él *after prep.;* lo *dir. obj.* (I)
   to / for — le (I)
himself se (I)
hippopotamus el hipopótamo (I)
his su, sus (I); suyo, -a (8); *pron.* el
   suyo, la suya, los suyos, las
   suyas (8)
   of — *adj.* suyo, -a (8)
historic histórico, -a (6)
history la historia (I)
to hit *(something)* chocar (con) (8)
hobby el pasatiempo (I)

holiday la fiesta; el día de fiesta, *pl.*
   días de fiesta (I)
home la casa (I)
   at — en casa (I)
   — team el equipo local (5)
   (to one's) — a casa (I)
homework la tarea (I)
Honduran hondureño, -a (1)
honey la miel (9)
to honk (the horn) tocar la bocina (8)
hood *(car)* el capó (8)
to hope esperar (I)
   I — not espero que no (I)
   I — so ¡ojalá!; espero que sí (I)
   let's — so ¡ojalá! (I)
horn la bocina (8)
horror *adj.* de terror (I)
   house of —s la casa de los
   fantasmas (3)
horse el caballo (I)
horseback: to ride — montar a
   caballo (5)
hospital el hospital (I)
hot caliente; *(spicy)* picante (I)
   — dog el perro caliente (4)
   it's — (out) hace calor (I)
   to be — *(people)* tener calor (I)
hotel el hotel (I)
hour la hora (I)
   half an — la media hora (I)
house la casa (I)
   — of horrors la casa de los
   fantasmas (3)
   — of mirrors la casa de los
   espejos (3)
how? ¿cómo? (I)
   — + *adj.!* ¡qué + *adj.!* (I)
   — about *(doing something)?* ¿qué te
   parece si + *verb*? (13)
   — are you? ¿cómo estás / está
   Ud.? (I)
   — do you like . . . ? ¿qué te
   parece . . . ? (I)
   — long? ¿cuánto tiempo? (I)
   — long (does something) last?
   ¿cuánto dura? (I)
   — many? ¿cuántos, -as? (I)
   — much? ¿cuánto? (I)
   — old are you? ¿cuántos años
   tienes? (I)
   —'s it going? ¿qué tal? (I)
   to know — (to) saber + *inf.* (I)
   to learn — (to) aprender a + *inf.* (I)
to hug abrazar (13)
huge enorme (I)

humid húmedo, -a (15)
humor: sense of — el sentido del
   humor (16)
hundred cien (I); *see also* **two, three,**
   etc.
   101; 102; etc. ciento uno, -a;
   ciento dos; etc. (I)
hungry: to be — tener hambre (I)
hurricane el huracán, *pl.* huracanes
   (11)
hurry:
   in a — de prisa (I)
   to be in a — tener prisa (8)
to hurry darse prisa (7)
to hurt doler (o → ue) (I); hacer daño a
   (12)
   to — (a part of one's body) lastimarse (9)
husband el esposo (I)

I yo (I)
ice el hielo (3)
ice cream el helado (I)
   — parlor la heladería (3)
idea la idea (2)
identification el documento (16)
   — card el carné (5)
if si (I)
iguana la iguana (I)
imagine! ¡imagínate! (I)
immediately en seguida (I)
impatient impaciente (8)
impolite mal educado, -a (13)
important importante (I)
   to be — to importar (I)
impossible imposible (16)
impression: to make a good / bad
   — *(on someone)* caer bien / mal a
   (13)
impressive impresionante (14)
improbable improbable (16)
to improve mejorarse (9)
in en (I)
   — order to para + *inf.* (I)
Incas los incas (14)
to include incluir (10)
incredible increíble (5)
to indicate indicar (11)
inexpensive barato, -a (I)
information la información (11)
inhabitant el / la habitante (1)
in-laws los suegros (13)
inn *(run by Spanish government)* el
   parador (6)

inside adentro (I)
— **(of)** dentro de (I)
to **inspect** registrar (16)
instructor el instructor, la
instructora (8)
instrument el instrumento (12)
intelligent inteligente (I)
to **intend to** pensar (e → ie) + *inf.* (I)
to **interest** interesar (11)
interesting interesante (I)
intermission el intervalo (11)
intersection el cruce (de calles) (8)
interview la entrevista (11)
to **interview** entrevistar (11)
into en (I)
to **introduce** presentar (I)
invitation la invitación, *pl.*
invitaciones (I)
to **invite** invitar (I)
iron la plancha (2)
to **iron** planchar (2)
island la isla (5)
it él, ella; lo, la *dir. obj.* (I)
Italian italiano, -a (I)
Italian *(language)* el italiano (I)
Italy Italia (I)
itself se (I)

jacket la chaqueta (I)
jaguar el jaguar (15)
jai alai el jai alai (5)
jalopy el cacharro (8)
January enero (I)
jealous: to be — of tener celos de (13)
jeans los jeans (I)
jelly la mermelada (I)
jewels, jewelry las joyas (I)
job el trabajo (I)
joke el chiste (I)
journalist el / la periodista (14)
juice el jugo (de) (I)
July julio (I)
June junio (I)
jungle la selva (15)
just: to have — *(done something)*
acabar de + *inf.*(I)

to **keep on** + *verb* + **-ing** seguir
(e → i) + *present participle* (12)
key la llave (I)
kilo el kilo (I)
kind *adj.* amable (I)
kind la clase (de) (I)
all —s of toda clase de (11)

kind of *adv.* bastante (I)
king el rey (I)
kiss el beso (10)
to **kiss** besar (13)
kitchen la cocina (I)
knapsack la mochila (I)
knee la rodilla (9)
knife el cuchillo (I)
to **know** saber; conocer (I)
I (don't) — that (no) lo sé (I)
to — how to saber + *inf.* (I)

label la etiqueta (7)
laboratory el laboratorio (I)
to **lack** faltar (I)
lake el lago (I)
lamb el cordero (I)
— **chop** la chuleta de cordero (I)
lamp la lámpara (I)
to **land** aterrizar (I)
landscape el paisaje (4, 12)
lane el carril (8)
language la lengua (I); el idioma (1)
to talk in sign — hablar por señas
(11)
large grande (I)
last pasado, -a (I); último, -a (5)
at — por fin (3)
— **name** el apellido (I)
— **night** anoche (I)
to **last** durar (I)
late tarde (I); con (+ *time* + de)
retraso (6)
later más tarde; después; luego (I)
see you — hasta luego; hasta la
vista (I)
Latin America la América Latina (I)
Latin American latinoamericano, -a
(I)
to **laugh** reír (e → i) (5)
to — at reírse (e → i) de (11)
law la regla (8); el derecho (15)
lawn el césped (2)
— **mower** el cortacésped (2)
lawyer el abogado, la abogada (15)
lazy perezoso, -a (I)
to **lead** dirigir (j) (12)
leading principal (11)
leaf la hoja (I)
to **learn** aprender (I)
to — how (to) aprender a + *inf.* (I)
least:
at — por lo menos (15)
the — + *adj.* el / la / los / las
menos + *adj.* (I)

leather el cuero (14)
to **leave** salir (de) (I); irse (7)
to — behind dejar (I)
left:
to be — without quedarse sin
(15)
to the — (of) a la izquierda (de)
(I)
leg la pierna (I)
to cost an arm and a — costar un
ojo de la cara (7)
to pull someone's — tomarle el
pelo a (13)
lemon el limón, *pl.* limones (I)
lemonade la limonada (I)
to **lend** prestar (I)
leopard el leopardo (I)
less:
— **+** *adj.* **+ than** menos + *adj.* +
que (I)
— **than +** *number* menos de +
number (I)
more or — más o menos (I)
lesson la lección, *pl.* lecciones (I)
to **let** permitir (13)
let's vamos a + *inf.* (I)
— **leave!** ¡vámonos! (I)
letter la carta (I)
lettuce la lechuga (I)
librarian el bibliotecario, la
bibliotecaria (1)
library la biblioteca (I)
license:
driver's — el permiso de manejar
(8)
— **plate** la placa (8)
lie la mentira (16)
to **lie** mentir (e → ie) (16)
life la vida (1)
— **preserver** el salvavidas (5)
lifeguard el / la salvavidas (5)
to **lift** levantar (I)
to — weights levantar pesas (5)
light la luz, *pl.* luces (2)
traffic — el semáforo (8)
to **light** encender (e → ie) (4)
lightbulb la bombilla (2)
lightning el relámpago (11)
like *adv. / prep.* como (2); *adj.*
parecido, -a (a) (12)
to feel — *(doing something)* tener
ganas de + *inf.* (I)
to look — parecer(se) (c → zc) (a)
(11, 13)
what's *(someone / something)* **—?**
¿cómo es . . .? (I)

like *(cont'd.)*
  what's the weather —? ¿qué tiempo hace? (I)
to like gustar (I)
  how do you — . . .? ¿qué te parece . . .? (I)
  I'd — quisiera (I); me gustaría (3)
  to — / not — *(someone)* caer bien / mal a (13)
  limit: speed — la velocidad máxima (8)
line la línea (I)
  to stand in — hacer cola (I)
lion el león, *pl.* leones (I)
lip el labio (7)
lipstick el lápiz de labios (7)
to listen (to) escuchar (I)
  —! ¡oye! (I)
liter el litro (I)
little pequeño, -a (I)
  a — un poco (de) (I)
to live vivir (I)
  living: to earn a — ganarse la vida (15)
  living room la sala (I)
llama la llama (I)
lobster la langosta (9)
local local (6)
located: to be — estar (I); quedar (8)
long largo, -a (I)
  how —? ¿cuánto tiempo? (I)
  — distance de larga distancia (10)
to look:
  to — (at) mirar (I)
  to — for buscar (I)
  to — good on quedar (7)
  to — like parecer(se) (c → zc) (a) (11, 13)
to lose perder (e → ie) (I)
  to — weight bajar de peso (9)
losing perdedor, -a (5)
lot:
  a — mucho (I)
  a — of muchos, -as (I)
loud fuerte (5)
  in a — voice en voz alta (10)
  out — en voz alta (10)
love el amor (13)
  in — (with) enamorado, -a (de) (13)
to love encantar (I); querer (e → ie) (13)
low: in a — voice en voz baja (10)
lucky: to be — tener suerte (I)
luggage el equipaje (6)
lunch el almuerzo (I)
  to eat — almorzar (o → ue) (2)

ma'am señora / señorita (I)
made hecho, -a (7)
  — of de + *material* (14)
magazine la revista (I)
magnificent magnífico, -a (I)
mail el correo (10)
  air — vía aérea (10)
  by — por correo (10)
mailbox el buzón, *pl.* buzones (10)
mail carrier el cartero, la cartera (10)
main principal (11)
majority of la mayoría de (7)
to make hacer (I)
makeup el maquillaje (7)
  to put — on maquillar(se) (7)
man el hombre (I)
  old — el anciano (13)
manager el / la gerente (I)
many muchos, -as (I)
  as — + *noun* + as tantos, -as + *noun* + como (3)
  how —? ¿cuántos, -as? (I)
  not — pocos, -as (I)
  too — demasiado, -a (15)
map el mapa (I)
  street — el plano (6)
March marzo (I)
Mardi Gras el carnaval (I)
market el mercado (I)
married:
  — (to) casado, -a (con) (13)
  to get — (to) casarse (con) (13)
to marry casarse (con) (13)
marvelous maravilloso, -a (6)
  how —! ¡qué maravilla! (3); ¡qué alegría! (16)
mask la máscara (I)
match el partido (de + *sport*) (I)
mathematics las matemáticas (I)
to matter to importar (I)
May mayo (I)
may I help you? ¿qué desea Ud.? (I)
Mayans los mayas (14)
maybe tal vez (I); quizás (1)
mayonnaise la mayonesa (9)
me mí *after prep.*; me (I)
  from / for — de mi parte (10)
  to / for — me (I)
  with — conmigo (I)
meal la comida (I)
  enjoy your — ¡buen provecho! (4)
mean: what does . . . —? ¿qué quiere decir? (I)
meaning el significado (14)
meat la carne (I)
  — pie la empanada (I)

mechanic el mecánico, la mecánica (8)
medicine la medicina (9)
medium *(meat)* medio cocido, -a (4)
to meet conocer (c → zc) (11); reunirse (13)
  pleased to — you mucho gusto (I)
membership card el carné (5)
to memorize aprender de memoria (I)
menu el menú (I)
merry-go-round el carrusel (3)
mess el desorden (2)
message el recado (10)
messenger el mensajero, la mensajera (10)
messy desordenado, -a (2)
meter: parking — el parquímetro (8)
Mexican mexicano, -a (I)
Mexico México (I)
middle el centro (12)
midnight la medianoche (I)
milk la leche (I)
million millón (de), *pl.* millones (de) (1)
millionaire el millonario, la millonaria (15)
mind: to change one's — cambiar de idea (3)
to mind importar (I)
mine, el mío, la mía, los míos, las mías (8)
  of — *adj.* mío, -a (8)
mineral water el agua mineral (I)
minus menos (I)
minute el minuto (I)
miracle el milagro (5)
mirror el espejo (I)
  house of —s la casa de los espejos (3)
Miss (la) señorita (Srta.) (I)
missing: to be — something faltar (I)
to mix mezclar (2)
model el / la modelo (12)
mom la mamá (I)
Monday lunes (I)
  on — el lunes (I)
money el dinero (I)
monkey el mono (I)
month el mes (I)
mood: to be in a good / bad — estar de buen / mal humor (16)
moon la luna (I)
more más (I)
  — or less más o menos (I)
  — + *adj.* + than más + *adj.* + que (I)

— than + *number* más de + *number* (I)
morning la mañana (I)
  good — buenos días (I)
  in the — de la mañana; por la mañana (I)
  yesterday — ayer por la mañana (I)
mosquito el mosquito (4)
most: the — + *adj.* el / la / los / las más + *adj.* (I)
  — (of) la mayoría de (7)
mother la madre (I)
  and father los padres (I)
  — in law la suegra (13)
motor el motor (8)
motorcycle la moto (I)
mountain la montaña (I)
mouse el ratón, *pl.* ratones (4)
mouth la boca (I)
to **move** mudarse (10)
movie la película (I)
  —s el cine (I)
  — star la estrella de cine (11)
  — theater el cine (I)
to **mow** cortar (2)
Mr. (el) señor (Sr.) (I)
Mrs. (la) señora (Sra.) (I)
much mucho (I)
  as — + *noun* + **as** tanto, -a + *noun* + como (3)
  how —? ¿cuánto? (I)
  so — *adj.* tanto, -a (3); *adv.* tanto (12)
  too — *adv.* demasiado (I); *adj.* demasiado, -a (15)
muffler la bufanda (I)
mural el mural (12)
museum el museo (I)
music la música (I)
musical *adj.* musical (I)
musician el músico, la música (12)
must: we / you / one — hay que + *inf.* (I)
mustache el bigote (7)
mustard la mostaza (4)
my mi, mis (I); mío, -a, -os, -as (8)
myself me (I)
mysterious misterioso, -a (15)

nail la uña (7)
  — file la lima de uñas (7)
  — polish el esmalte de uñas (7)
  to file —s limar(se) las uñas (7)
name el nombre (I)

brand — la marca (7)
last — el apellido (I)
my — is me llamo (I)
  what's your—? ¿cómo te llamas? (I)
named: to be — llamarse (I)
napkin la servilleta (I)
narrow estrecho, -a (7)
near cerca de (I)
neat ordenado, -a (2)
necessary necesario, -a (I)
  it's — (to) hay que + *inf.*; es necesario (I)
neck el cuello (9)
necklace el collar (I)
to **need** necesitar; faltar (I)
neighbor el vecino, la vecina (13)
neighborhood el barrio (I)
neither (ni . . .) tampoco (I, 6)
  — . . . nor (no . . .) ni . . . ni (6)
nephew el sobrino (I)
nervous nervioso, -a (8)
never (no . . .) nunca (I)
new nuevo, -a (I)
  what's —? ¿qué hay? (10)
New Year's Day el Año Nuevo (I)
New Year's Eve el día de fin de año (I)
news las noticias (I)
  — item la noticia (10)
newspaper el periódico (I); el diario (14)
next próximo, -a (I); siguiente (1)
  — to al lado de (I); junto a (12)
Nicaraguan nicaragüense (1)
nice simpático, -a; amable (I)
  how —! ¡qué alegría! (16)
  it's — out hace buen tiempo (I)
  not — antipático, -a (I)
niece la sobrina (I)
  —(s) and nephew(s) los sobrinos (I)
night la noche (I)
  at — de la noche; por la noche (I)
  good — buenas noches (I)
  last — anoche (I)
nine nueve (I)
  — hundred novecientos, -as (I)
nineteen diecinueve (I)
ninety noventa (I)
ninth noveno, -a (5)
no no; *adj.* (no . . .) ningún, ninguna (I)
  — one (no . . .) nadie (I)
  — one else (no . . .) otra persona (11)
nobody (no . . .) nadie (I)

noise el ruido (I)
none ninguno, -a (I)
nonstop sin escala (16)
noon el mediodía (I)
  at — al mediodía (I)
nor: neither . . . — (no . . .) ni . . . ni (6)
north el norte (I)
North America la América del Norte (I)
North American norteamericano, -a (I)
northeast el noreste (1)
northwest el noroeste (1)
nose la nariz (I)
not no (I)
  — any *adj.* (no . . .) ningún, ninguna (I); *pron.* (no . . .) ninguno, -a (I)
  — anyone (no . . .) nadie (I)
  — even no . . . ni (6)
  — many pocos, -as (I)
  — well mal (I)
  — yet todavía no (no . . . todavía) (1)
note el apunte (1)
notebook el cuaderno (I)
nothing (no . . .) nada (I)
notice el aviso (10)
to **notice** fijarse en (12)
novel la novela (I)
November noviembre (I)
now ahora (I); ya (9)
  right — ahora mismo (2)
number el número (I)
nurse el enfermero, la enfermera (I)

to **obey** respetar (8)
object el objeto (14)
oboe el oboe (12)
obstinate obstinado, -a (16)
to **obtain** obtener (8)
occupied ocupado, -a (I)
to **occur** ocurrir (11)
ocean el océano (I)
o'clock:
  it's 1 — es la una (I)
  it's 2 —, 3 —, etc. son las dos, tres, etc. (I)
October octubre (I)
odor el olor (4)
of de(l) (I)
of course ¡cómo no!; ¡por supuesto!; ¡claro (que sí)! (I)
  — not ¡claro que no! (I)

off:
    to get — *(vehicles)* bajar de (I)
    to take — *(planes)* despegar;
      (clothes) quitarse (I)
    to turn — apagar (4)
to offer ofrecer (c → zc) (11)
    office la oficina (I)
    box — la taquilla (11)
often a menudo (I)
oh! ¡ah! (I)
    —, yes ¡ah, sí! (I)
oil el aceite (4)
okay ¡bueno!; está bien (I); de
    acuerdo (5)
old viejo, -a (I); antiguo, -a (14)
    how — are you? ¿cuántos años
      tienes? (I)
    — man / woman el anciano, la
      anciana (13)
older mayor (I)
old-fashioned anticuado, -a (7)
olive la aceituna (4)
omelet: Spanish — la tortilla
    española (I)
on en; sobre (I)
    — foot a pie (I)
    — the phone por teléfono (I)
    — the radio / TV por la radio / la
      tele (11)
    — time a tiempo (I)
    — vacation de vacaciones (I)
    to turn — encender (e → ie) (4)
once una vez (I)
one uno; *pron.* alguno, -a (I)
    at — o'clock a la una (I)
    — hundred cien (I)
    — thousand mil (I)
    — -way de ida (6)
    which —(s)? ¿cuál(es)? (I)
onion la cebolla (I)
only *adj.* único, -a; *adv.* sólo (I)
open abierto, -a (I)
to open abrir (I)
    opera: soap — la telenovela (11)
    operator el operador, la operadora
      (10)
    opinion la opinión, *pl.* opiniones
      (14)
    to have an — about pensar
      (e → ie) de (I)
    opposite enfrente de (I)
    optimistic optimista (I)
    or o; u (I)
      either . . . — o . . . o (10)
      not . . . — (no . . .) ni . . . ni (6)
    orange *adj.* anaranjado, -a (I)

orange la naranja (I)
    — juice el jugo de naranja (I)
orangeade la naranjada (I)
orchestra la orquesta (12)
order el orden (2)
    in — to para + *inf.* (I)
    out of — descompuesto, -a (2)
to order pedir (e → i) (I)
origin: of . . . — de origen . . . (I)
orthodontist el / la ortodoncista (15)
other otro, -a (I)
    each — nos (7); se (7)
ought to deber + *inf.* (I)
our nuestro, -a (I, 8)
ours el nuestro, la nuestra, los
    nuestros, las nuestras (8)
    of — *adj.* nuestro, -a (8)
out:
    it's cool (cold / hot) — hace fresco
      (frío / calor) (I)
    it's nice (bad) — hace buen (mal)
      tiempo (I)
    — loud en voz alta (10)
    — of order descompuesto, -a (2)
    to come / go — salir de (I)
    to get — of *(vehicles)* bajar de (I)
    to put — *(fire, light, etc.)* apagar
      (4)
    to run — of quedarse sin (15)
outing: to go on an — ir de ex-
    cursión (3)
outlet el enchufe (2)
outside afuera (I)
    — (of) fuera de (I)
oven el horno (2)
over sobre (6)
    — here / there por aquí / allí (8)
    — there allá (I)
overcoat el abrigo (I)
to owe deber (15)
own propio, -a (15)
owner el dueño, la dueña (6)

to pack a suitcase hacer la maleta (I)
package el paquete (10)
paella la paella (I)
page la página (I)
paint la pintura (12)
to paint pintar (12)
    paintbrush el pincel (12)
    painter el pintor, la pintora (12)
    painting el cuadro (3); la pintura
      (12)
pale pálido, -a (9)
pan la cacerola (2)

frying — la sartén; *pl.* sartenes (2)
Panama Panamá (I)
Panamanian panameño, -a (1)
pants los pantalones (I)
pantyhose las pantimedias (I)
papaya la papaya (9)
paper el papel (14)
    — clip el sujetapapeles, *pl.*
      sujetapapeles (1)
    piece of — la hoja de papel, *pl.*
      hojas de papel (I)
parade el desfile (I)
Paraguay el Paraguay (I)
Paraguayan paraguayo, -a (6)
pardon me perdón; discúlpeme (I)
parents los padres (I)
park el parque (I)
    amusement — el parque de
      diversiones (3)
to park estacionar (8)
    parking:
    lot el estacionamiento (8)
    — meter el parquímetro (8)
parrot el loro (15)
part la parte (1)
    to take — participar (5)
to participate participar (5)
    party la fiesta (I)
    passenger el pasajero, la pasajera
      (6)
    passport el pasaporte (I)
    past pasado, -a (I)
    pastime el pasatiempo (I)
    pastry el pastel (I)
    path el sendero (4)
    patient el / la paciente (9)
    patient paciente (8)
    to be — tener paciencia (16)
to pay (for) pagar (I)
    to — attention (to) prestar
      atención (a) (1); fijarse (en) (12)
    to — + *sum of money* + for
      pagar + *sum of money* + por (I)
    to — cash pagar al contado (6)
peach el durazno (9)
peanut el cacahuate (3)
pear la pera (9)
peas los guisantes (I)
pedestrian el peatón, *pl.* peatones
    (8)
pen el bolígrafo (I)
pencil el lápiz, *pl.* lapices (I)
    — sharpener el sacapuntas, *pl.*
      sacapuntas (1)
people la gente (I)
    young — los / las jóvenes (11)

pepper la pimienta (4)
  chili — el chile (I)
  stuffed — el chile relleno (I)
per por (13)
perfect perfecto, -a (I)
performance el espectáculo (3)
perfume el perfume (7)
perhaps tal vez (I); quizás (1)
to **permit** permitir (13)
person la persona (I)
  young — el / la joven, *pl.* los / las
    jóvenes (11)
Peru el Perú (I)
Peruvian peruano, -a (6)
peseta la peseta (I)
peso el peso (I)
pessimistic pesimista (I)
pet el animal doméstico (I)
pharmacist el farmacéutico, la
  farmacéutica (15)
pharmacy la farmacia (I)
phew! ¡uf! (I)
phone el teléfono (I)
  on the — por teléfono (I)
  — book la guía telefónica (I)
  — booth la cabina telefónica (I)
  — number el número de teléfono
    (I)
to **phone** llamar por teléfono (I)
photo la foto (I)
photographer el fotógrafo, la
  fotógrafa (I)
physical education la educación
  física (I)
physics la física (I)
piano el piano (I)
to **pick** recoger (j) (4)
  to — up recoger (j) (2); ir / venir a
    buscar (10); *(phone)* descolgar
    (o → ue) (10)
picnic el picnic (3)
  to have a — hacer un picnic (3)
picture: to take —s sacar fotos (I)
piece:
  — of gossip el chisme (10)
  — of news la noticia (10)
  — of paper la hoja de papel, *pl.*
    hojas de papel (I)
pig el cerdo (I)
pill la pastilla (9)
pillow la almohada (I)
pillowcase la funda (I)
pilot el / la piloto (I)
piñata la piñata (I)
pineapple la piña (9)
pink rosado, -a (7)

pity la lástima (16)
place el lugar (3); el sitio (15)
  to take — tener lugar (11)
to **place** poner (I); colocar (6)
plan el plan (I)
to **plan to** pensar (e → ie) + *inf.* (I)
plane el avión, *pl.* aviones (I)
plate el plato (I)
  license — la placa (8)
platform *(railway)* el andén, *pl.*
  andenes (6)
play la obra de teatro (I)
to **play** jugar (u → ue); tocar *(musical
  instruments, records)* (I)
  to — the role of hacer el papel de
    (11)
  to — *(sports, games)* jugar a(l) (I)
player el jugador, la jugadora (I)
  tennis — el / la tenista (5)
plaza la plaza (I)
pleasant simpático, -a; agradable (I)
please por favor (I)
pleased to meet you mucho gusto
  (I)
pleasure: with — con mucho gusto
  (I)
plot el argumento (11)
plug el enchufe (2)
to **plug in** enchufar (2)
plus más (I)
P.M. de la tarde / noche (I)
pocket el bolsillo (6)
poem el poema (I)
poet el / la poeta (I)
police officer el / la policía (I)
polish: nail — el esmalte de uñas
  (7)
polite bien educado, -a (13)
poor pobre (I)
  — thing! ¡pobrecito, -a! (I)
  to be — in estar flojo, -a en (I)
pop el refresco (I)
popcorn las palomitas (3)
popular popular (I)
pork chop la chuleta de cerdo (I)
portrait el retrato (12)
Portuguese portugués *(pl.* portugueses), portuguesa (I)
Portuguese *(language)* el portugués
  (I)
possible posible (16)
post card la tarjeta postal (I)
post office el correo (I)
  — box el apartado postal (10)
poster el cartel (I)
pot la olla (2)

potato la papa (I)
practical práctico, -a (15)
to **practice** practicar (I)
to **prefer** preferir (e → ie) (I)
to **prepare** preparar (I)
  prepared preparado, -a (I)
to **prescribe** recetar (9)
prescription la receta (I)
present *adj.* presente (I)
present el regalo (I)
  to give a — regalar (13)
preserves la mermelada (I)
pretty bonito, -a (I)
price el precio (7)
  — tag la etiqueta (7)
principal *(school)* el director, la
  directora (1)
private privado, -a (I)
  — school el colegio particular (1)
prize el premio (11)
probable probable (16)
probably probablemente (3)
problem el problema (I)
to **produce** producir (c → zc) (14)
profession la profesión, *pl.*
  profesiones (6)
  by — de profesión (6)
program el programa (I)
programmer el programador / la
  programadora (de computadoras) (15)
projector el proyector (1)
to **promise** prometer (4)
proud orgulloso, -a (16)
to **prove** demostrar (o → ue) (12)
public público, -a (1)
  in — en público (13)
Puerto Rican puertorriqueño, -a (I)
to **pull** tirar (de) (13)
  to — someone's leg tomarle el
    pelo a (13)
pupil el alumno, la alumna (I)
purple morado, -a (I)
purse el bolso (I)
to **push** empujar (13)
to **put** poner (I); colocar (6)
  to — makeup on maquillar(se) (7)
  to — on *(clothes)* ponerse (I)
  to — one's foot in it meter la pata
    (13)
  to — out *(fire, light, etc.)* apagar (4)
  to — (someone) to bed acostar
    (o → ue) (I)
pyramid la pirámide (14)
Pyrenees Mts. los Pirineos (I)

to quarrel (with) pelearse (con) (13)
quarter:
  — **after / past** y cuarto (I)
  — **to** menos cuarto (I)
queen la reina (I)
question la pregunta (I)
  to ask a — hacer una pregunta (1)
quickly de prisa (I)
quiet: be — ¡silencio! (1); ¡cállate! (11)
quiz show el programa de concursos (11)

race la carrera (5)
  boat — la regata (5)
racket la raqueta (5)
radio *(broadcast)* la radio; *(set)* el radio (I)
  on the — por la radio (11)
rain la lluvia (I)
to rain llover (o → ue) (I)
  it's —ing llueve (I)
raincoat el impermeable (I)
to raise levantar (I)
ranch el rancho (4)
rapidly rápidamente (I)
rare *(meat)* poco cocido, -a (4)
rather bastante (I)
  but — sino (11); sino que + *verb* (11)
razor la maquinilla de afeitar (7)
to read leer (I)
ready preparado, -a (I)
real verdadero, -a (14)
to realize darse cuenta de (14)
really de veras (I)
to receive recibir (I); obtener (8)
receipt el recibo (10)
reception desk la recepción, *pl.* recepciones (6)
to recognize reconocer (c → zc) (11)
to recommend recomendar (e → ie) (9)
record el disco (I)
  — **player** el tocadiscos, *pl.* tocadiscos (I)
to record grabar (11)
red rojo, -a (I)
  — **-haired** pelirrojo, -a (I)
refrigerator el refrigerador (I)
register *(hotel)* el registro (6)
  cash — la caja (7)
registered certificado, -a (10)
rehearsal el ensayo (12)

to rehearse ensayar (12)
relative el pariente, la parienta (13)
relief: what a —! ¡qué alivio! (3)
religion la religión, *pl.* religiones (14)
to remain quedarse (I)
remainder el resto (15)
to remember recordar (o → ue) (13)
to remove sacar (I)
to rent alquilar (2)
to repair arreglar (I)
to repeat repetir (e → i) (I)
reporter el / la periodista (14)
to request pedir (e → i) (I)
to resemble parecerse (c → zc) a (13)
reservation la reservación, *pl.* reservaciones (I)
to respect respetar (8)
rest el resto (15)
to rest descansar (I)
restaurant el restaurante (I)
to return volver (o → ue); regresar (I); *(something)* devolver (o → ue) (7)
return address el remitente (10)
review el repaso (1)
to review repasar (I)
rhinoceros el rinoceronte (I)
rice el arroz (I)
rich rico, -a (I)
ride *(amusement park)* la atracción, *pl.* atracciones (3)
  to go for a — dar un paseo (3)
  to take a — dar una vuelta (3)
to ride:
  to — **a bicycle** montar en bicicleta (I)
  to — **horseback** montar a caballo (5)
right:
  all — está bien (I)
  —! de acuerdo (5)
  —? ¿verdad? (I)
  — **away** en seguida (I); ahora mismo (2)
  to be — tener razón (I)
  to the — **(of)** a la derecha (de) (I)
ring el anillo (I)
to ring sonar (o → ue) (10)
river el río (I)
road el camino (I)
to roast asar (4)
roasted asado, -a (4)
to rob robar (14)
robbery el robo (14)
rock la piedra (4); *(music)* el rock (I)

role: to play the — **of** hacer el papel de (11)
roller coaster la montaña rusa (3)
roller skate el patín de rueda, *pl.* patines de ruedas (3)
romantic romántico, -a (I)
roof el techo (2)
room el cuarto (I); la habitación, *pl.* habitaciones (6)
  single / double — la habitación individual / doble (6)
rooster el gallo (I)
round-trip de ida y vuelta (6)
row la fila (11)
to row remar (3)
rude mal educado, -a (13)
rug la alfombra (I)
ruins las ruinas (14)
rule la regla (8)
to run correr (I); *(machine)* funcionar (2)
  to — **away** escaparse (14)
  to — **out of** quedarse sin (15)
  to — **the vacuum cleaner** pasar la aspiradora (2)
runway la pista (16)

sad triste (I)
to sail navegar (5)
sailboat el velero (5)
saint's day el santo (I)
salad la ensalada (I)
salary el sueldo (15)
sale la venta (I); *(clearance)* la liquidación, *pl.* liquidaciones (7)
  for — en venta (I)
salesclerk el vendedor, la vendedora (I); el dependiente, la dependienta (7)
salt la sal (4)
Salvadoran salvadoreño, -a (1)
same mismo, -a (1)
  the — igual (13)
sand la arena (15)
sandals las sandalias (I)
sandwich el sandwich (I)
sangria la sangría (13)
Saturday sábado (I)
  on — el sábado (I)
saucepan la cacerola (2)
saucer el platillo (I)
sausage la salchicha (4)
to save salvar (14); ahorrar (15)
saxophone el saxofón, *pl.* saxofones (12)
to say decir (I)

how do you — . . . ? ¿cómo se dice . . . ? (I)

to — good-by (to) saludar (a) (10); despedirse (e → i) (de) (13)

to — hello saludar (10)

to — yes / no decir que sí / no (I)

you don't — ¡no me digas! (I)

scale la balanza (9)

scare: what a —! ¡qué susto! (3)

to scare dar miedo a (I); asustar (3)

scared asustado, -a (3)

to be — (of) tener miedo (de) (I)

scarf la bufanda (I)

schedule el horario (I)

school la escuela (I)

high — el colegio (I)

private — el colegio particular (1)

— year el año escolar (1)

science las ciencias (I)

— fiction adj. de ciencia ficción (I)

scientist el científico, la científica (15)

scissors las tijeras (7)

score el tanteo (5)

screen la pantalla (1)

to scuba dive bucear (5)

sculptor el escultor, la escultora (12)

sculpture la escultura (12)

sea el mar (I)

seafood los mariscos (9)

season la estación, pl. estaciones (I)

seat el asiento (I)

seatbelt el cinturón de seguridad, pl. cinturones de seguridad (8)

second el segundo (I); segundo, -a (I)

— class de segunda clase (6)

— floor el primer piso (I)

secret secreto, -a (14)

secretary el secretario, la secretaria (15)

section la sección, pl. secciones (14)

to see ver (I)

— you later hasta luego; hasta la vista (I)

— you soon hasta pronto (I)

— you tomorrow hasta mañana (I)

to seem (to someone) parecer (c → zc) (I)

to — to be parecer (c → zc) (11)

to sell vender (I)

to — for + sum of money vender a + sum of money (I)

to send mandar (I)

sense of humor el sentido del humor (16)

sentence la frase (I)

September septiembre (I)

serious serio, -a (I)

to serve servir (e → i) (I)

service station la estación de servicio, pl. estaciones de servicio (8)

to set the table poner la mesa (I)

seven siete (I)

— hundred setecientos, -as (I)

seventeen diecisiete (I)

seventh séptimo, -a (5)

seventy setenta (I)

several varios, -as (I)

to shake hands (with) dar la mano a (13)

shame la lástima (16)

that's a — ¡que lástima! (I)

shampoo el champú (I)

to share compartir (13)

to shave afeitar(se) (7)

shaving cream la crema de afeitar (7)

she ella (I)

sheep la oveja (I)

sheet la sábana (I)

shelf el estante (I)

shellfish los mariscos (9)

shirt la camisa (I)

shoe el zapato (I)

— laces los cordones de los zapatos (7)

— size el número (7)

tennis —s los zapatos de tenis (5)

shopping de compras (I)

short bajo, -a; corto, -a (I)

shot la inyección, pl. inyecciones (I)

to give someone a — poner una inyección (I)

should deber + inf. (I)

shoulder el hombro (9)

to shout gritar (12)

show el espectáculo (3); la función, pl. funciones (11)

quiz — el programa de concursos (11)

to show mostrar (o → ue) (I); indicar (11); demostrar (o → ue) (12)

to — a movie / a program dar una película / un programa (I)

shower la ducha (I)

to take a — ducharse (I)

shrimp el camarón, pl. camarones (9)

shy tímido, -a (3)

sick enfermo, -a (I)

sign el letrero (7)

traffic — la señal de tráfico (8)

sign language: to talk in — hablar por señas (11)

to sign firmar (6)

signature la firma (10)

silence! ¡silencio! (1)

silver la plata (14)

similar (to) parecido, -a (a) (12)

simple sencillo, -a (11)

to sing cantar (I)

singer el / la cantante (11)

single soltero, -a (13)

— room la habitación individual (6)

sink el fregadero (2)

sir señor (I)

sister la hermana (I)

little — la hermanita (I)

—-in-law la cuñada (13)

to sit down sentarse (e → ie) (11)

site el sitio (15)

six seis (I)

— hundred seiscientos, -as (I)

sixteen dieciséis (I)

sixth sexto, -a (5)

sixty sesenta (I)

size (garment) la talla (7); (shoes) el número (7)

skate el patín, pl. los patines (3)

roller — el patín de ruedas, pl. los patines de ruedas (3)

to skate patinar (3)

to ice-— patinar sobre hielo (3)

to roller-— patinar sobre ruedas (3)

skater el patinador, la patinadora (5)

ski el esquí (5)

to ski esquiar (I)

skier el esquiador, la esquiadora (5)

skiing el esquí (5)

water — el esquí acuático (5)

skinny (animals) flaco, -a (3)

skirt la falda (I)

sky el cielo (I)

to sleep dormir (o → ue) (I)

to go to — dormirse (o → ue) (I)

sleeping bag el saco de dormir (4)

sleeping car el coche cama, pl. coches cama (6)

sleepy: to be — tener sueño (I)

slide transparency la diapositiva (1)

slow lento, -a (I)

—ly despacio (I); lentamente (10)

small pequeño, -a (I)

smart listo, -a (I)
smell el olor (4)
to **smile** sonreír (e → ie) (5)
smoke el humo (14)
snake la serpiente (I)
to **sneeze** estornudar (9)
snow la nieve (I)
to **snow** nevar (e → ie) (I)
   it's —ing nieva (I)
so *conj.* entonces (I); *adv.* tan (I)
   don't you think —? ¿no te parece? (5)
   I don't think — creo que no (I)
   I hope — ¡ojalá!; espero que sí (I)
   I think — creo que sí (I)
   let's hope — ¡ojalá! (I)
   — much *adv.* tanto (12)
   — much / many tanto, -a (3)
   — what? ¿qué importa? (I)
soap el jabón, *pl.* jabones (I)
   — opera la telenovela (11)
soccer el fútbol (I)
sock el calcetín, *pl.* calcetines (I)
soda el refresco (I)
sofa el sofá (I)
soft suave (12)
   in a — voice en voz baja (10)
   —ly en voz baja (10)
soil la tierra (I)
some unos, -as; algún, alguna; *pron.* alguno, -a, -os, -as (I)
somebody / someone alguien (I)
   — else otra persona (11)
something algo (I)
   — else otra cosa (11)
   to have — to drink tomar algo (I)
sometimes a veces (I)
son el hijo (I)
   —(s) and daughter(s) los hijos (I)
song la canción, *pl.* canciones (I)
soon pronto (I)
   see you — hasta pronto (I)
sorry:
   I'm — lo siento (I)
   to be — sentir (e → ie) (16)
so-so así, así (I)
sound el sonido (12)
soup la sopa (I)
south el sur (I)
South America la América del Sur (I)
South American sudamericano, -a (I)
southeast el sureste (1)
southwest el suroeste (1)
souvenir el recuerdo (I)

Spain España (I)
Spanish español, -a (I)
Spanish *(language)* el español (I)
to **speak** hablar (I)
special *adj.* especial (I)
special of the day el plato del día (9)
speed limit la velocidad máxima (8)
to **speed up** acelerar (8)
spell: how do you — . . . ? ¿cómo se escribe . . . ? (I)
to **spend** gastar (7); *(time)* pasar (I)
spicy picante (I)
spider la araña (4)
spinach las espinacas (9)
spoon la cuchara (I)
sport el deporte (I)
sports *adj.* deportivo, -a (5)
   — car el coche deportivo (8)
spring la primavera (I)
stadium el estadio (I)
stairs la escalera (I)
stamp el sello (I)
stand el puesto (3)
to **stand in line** hacer cola (I)
staple la grapa (1)
stapler la grapadora (1)
star la estrella (I)
   movie — la estrella de cine (11)
to **start** empezar (e → ie) (a → *inf.*) (I); comenzar (e → ie) (a + *inf.*) (6); *(car)* arrancar (8)
station la estación, *pl.* estaciones (I)
statue la estatua (14)
to **stay** quedarse (I)
steak el bistec (I)
to **steal** robar (14)
steering wheel el volante (8)
still todavía (I)
   to be — + *verb* + -ing seguir (e → i) + *present participle* (12)
stingy tacaño, -a (I)
stomach el estómago (I)
stone la piedra (14)
to **stop** parar (3)
   to — *(doing something)* dejar de + *inf.* (13)
stopover la escala (16)
   to make a — hacer escala (16)
store la tienda (de) (I)
   department — el almacén, *pl.* almacenes (I)
   — window la vitrina (7)
storm la tormenta (11)
story el cuento (I); la historia (1)
stove la estufa (I)
straight ahead (todo) derecho (8)

to **straighten up / out** poner en orden (2)
strange extraño, -a (16)
strawberry la fresa (9)
street la calle (I)
   — corner la esquina (I)
   — map el plano (6)
strict estricto, -a (5)
strong fuerte (I)
stubborn obstinado, -a (16)
student el / la estudiante (I)
to **study** estudiar (I)
study hall la sala de estudio (1)
stuffed pepper el chile relleno (I)
stupid tonto, -a (I)
subject el tema (1); *(in school)* la materia (I)
subtitle el subtítulo (11)
subway el metro (I)
success el éxito (11)
successful: to be — tener éxito (11)
suddenly de repente (14)
to **suffer** sufrir (16)
sugar el azúcar (I)
suit el traje (I)
   bathing — el traje de baño (I)
suitcase la maleta (I)
   to pack a — hacer la maleta (I)
summer el verano (I)
sun el sol (I)
to **sunbathe** tomar el sol (I)
Sunday domingo (I)
   on — el domingo (I)
sunglasses los anteojos de sol (I)
sunny: it's — hace sol (I)
supermarket el supermercado (I)
superstition la superstición, *pl.* supersticiones (16)
superstitious supersticioso, -a (16)
supper la cena (I)
sure seguro, -a (I)
surprise la sorpresa (13)
to **surprise** sorprender (16)
surrounded (by) rodeado, -a (de) (11)
sweater el suéter (I)
to **sweep** barrer (2)
to **swim** nadar (I)
swimmer el nadador, la nadadora (5)
swimming la natación (5)
   — pool la piscina (I)

table la mesa (I)
   to clear the — quitar los platos (I)
   to set the — poner la mesa (I)

tablecloth el mantel (I)
taco el taco (I)
tag la etiqueta (7)
to **take** tomar (I); llevar (4)
    to — + *time* + *verb* tardar en + *inf.* (6)
    to — a bath bañarse (I)
    to — a ride dar una vuelta (3)
    to — a shower ducharse (I)
    to — a trip hacer un viaje (I)
    to — a walk / ride dar un paseo (3)
    to — back devolver (o → ue) (7)
    to — care of cuidar (13)
    to — off *(planes)* despegar; *(clothes)* quitarse (I)
    to — out sacar (I)
    to — part participar (5)
    to — pictures sacar fotos (I)
    to — place tener lugar (11)
talent el talento (12)
to **talk** hablar (I)
    to — in sign language hablar por señas (11)
tall alto, -a (I)
tank el tanque (8)
tape la cinta (I)
    — recorder la grabadora (I)
to **tape** grabar (11)
taste el sabor (4)
to **taste** probar (o → ue) (4)
tasty sabroso, -a (4)
tax el impuesto (7)
taxi el taxi (I)
tea el té (I)
to **teach** enseñar (I)
teacher el profesor, la profesora (I)
team el equipo (I)
    home — el equipo local (5)
teaspoon la cucharita (2)
teeth los dientes (I)
    to brush one's — cepillarse los dientes (I)
telegram el telegrama (10)
telephone *see* **phone**
television la televisión (tele) (I)
    on — por la televisión (11)
    — channel el canal (I)
    — set el televisor (I)
to **tell** decir; contar (o → ue) (I)
temperature la temperatura (11)
temple el templo (14)
ten diez (I)
tennis el tenis (I)
    — court la cancha de tenis (5)
    — player el / la tenista (5)

    — shoes los zapatos de tenis (5)
tent la tienda de acampar (4)
tenth décimo, -a (5)
terrific formidable (I)
test el examen, *pl.* exámenes; la prueba (I)
than que (I)
to **thank (someone) for** agradecer (c → zc) (11)
thanks, thank you gracias (I)
    — a lot muchas gracias (I)
that *adj.* ese, -a (I); aquel, aquella (2); *neuter prons.* eso (2); aquello (2), *conj.* que (I)
    — one ése, ésa (2); aquél, aquélla (2)
    —'s why por eso (I)
    — way por allí (8)
the el, la, los, las (I)
theater el teatro (I)
    movie — el cine (I)
their su, sus (I); suyo, -a (8)
theirs el suyo, la suya, los suyos, las suyas (8)
    of — *adj.* suyo, -a (8)
them ellos, ellas *after prep.*; los, las *dir. obj.* (I)
    to / for — les (I)
themselves se (I)
then entonces; luego (I)
there allí (I)
    around — por allí (8)
    over — allá (I); por allí (8)
    — is / are hay (I)
    — was / were había (14); hubo (15)
thermometer el termómetro (11)
these *adj.* estos, -as (I); *pron.* éstos, éstas (2)
they ellos, ellas (I)
thief el ladrón, la ladrona (14)
thin delgado, -a (I)
thing la cosa (I)
to **think** creer; pensar (e → ie) (I)
    don't you — so? ¿no te parece? (5)
    I don't — so creo que no (I)
    I — so creo que sí (I)
    to — about pensar en (I)
    to — of pensar de (I)
    what do you — of . . . ? ¿qué te parece . . . ? (I)
third tercero (tercer), -a (I)
    — floor el segundo piso (I)
thirsty: to be — tener sed (I)
thirteen trece (I)

thirty treinta (I)
    31; 32; etc. treinta y uno (un); treinta y dos; etc. (I)
this *adj.* este, -a (I); *neuter pron.* esto (2)
    — one *pron.* éste, ésta (2)
    — way por aquí (8)
those *adjs.* esos, -as (I); aquellos, aquellas (2); *prons.* ésos, ésas (2); aquéllos, aquéllas (2)
thousand mil (I, 7)
three tres (I)
    —hundred trescientos, -as (I)
thrilling emocionante (I)
throat la garganta (I)
through por (I)
to **throw (away)** tirar (2)
thunder, thunderclap el trueno (11)
Thursday jueves (I)
    on — el jueves (I)
ticket *(entrance)* la entrada; *(travel)* el boleto (I); *(traffic)* la multa (8)
    — seller el taquillero, la taquillera (11)
    — window la ventanilla (6)
tie la corbata (I); *(in a game)* el empate (5)
to **tie** atar(se) (7)
tiger el tigre (I)
time el tiempo; la vez, *pl.* veces (I)
    (at) what —? ¿a qué hora? (I)
    for the first (second, etc.) — por primera (segunda, etc.) vez (5)
    on — a tiempo (I)
    to have a good — divertirse (e → ie) (I)
    what — is it? ¿qué hora es? (I)
timid tímido, -a (3)
tip la propina (I)
    for a — de propina (I)
tire la llanta (8)
tired cansado, -a (I)
title el título (I)
to a(l) (I); hasta (5)
    (in order) — para + *inf.* (I)
    minutes — *(in time-telling)* menos + *number* (I)
    — where? ¿adónde? (I)
toast el pan tostado (I)
toaster la tostadora (2)
today hoy (I)
    not — hoy no (I)
together juntos, -as (I)
    to get — reunirse (13)
tomato el tomate (I)
tomorrow mañana (I)
    see you — hasta mañana (I)

tone el tono (10)
tonight esta noche (I)
too también; demasiado (I)
  — **many** *adj.* demasiado, -a (15)
  — **much** *adv.* demasiado (I); *adj.*
    demasiado, -a (15)
toothbrush el cepillo de dientes (I)
toothpaste la pasta dentífrica (I)
topic el tema (1)
tortilla la tortilla (4)
tourist el / la turista (I)
towel la toalla (I)
town el pueblo (4)
  — **square** la plaza (I)
track *(train)* la vía (6)
traffic el tráfico (8)
  — **light** el semáforo (8)
  — **sign** la señal de tráfico (8)
  — **ticket** la multa (8)
train el tren (I)
  — **car** el vagón, *pl.* vagones (6)
  — **track** la vía (6)
to **translate** traducir (c → zc) (11)
transparency la diapositiva (1)
to **travel** viajar (I)
travel agency la agencia de viajes (I)
travel agent el / la agente de viajes (I)
traveler el viajero, la viajera (6)
  —**'s check** el cheque de viajero (6)
treasure el tesoro (14)
tree el árbol (I)
trip el viaje (I)
  on a — de viaje (16)
  to go on a short — ir de excursión (3)
  to take a — hacer un viaje (I)
trombone el trombón, *pl.*
    trombones (12)
truck el camión, *pl.* camiones (I)
true verdadero, -a (14)
  it's — es verdad (16); es cierto (16)
trumpet la trompeta (12)
trunk *(car)* el baúl (8)
truth la verdad (I)
to **try (to)** tratar (de + *inf.*) (I); intentar
    (16)
  to — **on** probarse (o → ue) (7)
t-shirt la camiseta (I)
tuba la tuba (12)
Tuesday martes (I)
  on — el martes (I)
turkey el pavo (I)
to **turn** doblar (8)
  to — + *age* cumplir años (13)
  to — **around** dar la vuelta (8)
  to — **off** apagar (4)
  to — **on** encender (e → ie) (4)

turtle la tortuga (15)
TV la tele (I)
twelve doce (I)
twenty veinte (I)
  21; 22; etc. veintiuno (veintiún);
    veintidós; etc. (I)
twice dos veces (I)
two dos (I)
  — **hundred** doscientos, -as (I)
type la clase (de) (I)
to **type** escribir a máquina (1)
typewriter la máquina de escribir (1)

ugh! ¡uf! (I)
ugly feo, -a (I)
umbrella el paraguas (I)
  beach — la sombrilla (I)
uncle el tío (I)
uncomfortable incómodo, -a (I)
under debajo de (I)
to **understand** comprender (I);
    entender (e → ie) (3)
undoubtedly sin duda (12)
unforgettable inolvidable (13)
uniform el uniforme (1)
United States los Estados Unidos (I)
university la universidad (15)
unlucky: to be — tener mala suerte (I)
unmarried soltero, -a (13)
unpleasant antipático, -a (I); desa-
    gradable (13)
to **unplug** desenchufar (2)
until hasta (I)
to **unwrap** desenvolver (o → ue) (13)
up:
  to come / go — subir (I)
  to get — levantarse (I)
Uruguay el Uruguay (I)
Uruguayan uruguayo, -a (6)
us nosotros, -as *after prep.;* nos (I)
  to / for — nos (I)
to **use** usar (I)
  used to *imperfect tense* (13)
usher el acomodador, la
    acomodadora (11)
usually generalmente (I)

vacation las vacaciones (I)
  on — de vacaciones (I)
to **vacuum** pasar la aspiradora (2)
vacuum cleaner la aspiradora (2)
valley el valle (4)
vegetable la verdura (I)

Venezuelan venezolano, -a (6)
versus contra (5)
very *adj.* mucho, -a; *adv.* muy (I)
veterinarian el veterinario, la
    veterinaria (I)
view: with a — **of** con vista a(l) (I)
vinegar el vinagre (4)
violin el violín, *pl.* violines (12)
visit la visita (I)
to **visit** visitar (I)
visitor el / la visitante (5)
voice la voz, *pl.* voces (5)
volcano el volcán, *pl.* volcanes
volleyball el volibol (I)

to **wait (for)** esperar (I)
waiter, waitress el camarero, la
    camarera (I)
waiting room la sala de espera (9)
to **wake up** despertarse (e → ie) (I)
  to — *(someone)* despertar (e → ie) (I)
walk: to go for / take a — dar un
    paseo (3)
to **walk** ir a pie; caminar (I)
wall la pared (I)
wallet la cartera (I)
to **want** querer (e → ie) (I)
warning la noticia (10)
to **wash** lavar (I)
  to — **(one's face, hands, hair)**
    lavarse (la cara, las manos, el
    pelo) (I)
washing machine la lavadora (2)
wastebasket la papelera (I)
to **watch** mirar (I)
  — **out!** ¡cuidado! (I)
water el agua *f.* (I)
  — **skiing** el esquí acuático (5)
watermelon la sandía (4)
wave la ola (I)
way: this / that — por aquí / allí (8)
we nosotros, -as (I)
weak débil (I)
to **wear** llevar (I)
weather el tiempo (I)
  — **forecast** el pronóstico del
    tiempo (11)
  what's the — **like?** ¿qué tiempo
    hace? (I)
wedding la boda (13)
Wednesday miércoles (I)
  on — el miércoles (I)
week la semana (I)
weekend el fin de semana, *pl.* fines
    de semana (I)

to weigh (oneself) pesar(se) (9)
  weight el peso (9)
    to gain / lose — aumentar / bajar de peso (9)
  weightlifter el levantador / la levantadora de pesas (5)
  weights las pesas (5)
welcome bienvenido, -a (I)
  you're — de nada; no hay de qué (I)
well bien; pues; bueno (I)
  — **done** *(meat)* bien cocido, -a (4)
  not — mal (I)
  —**-known** muy conocido, -a (I)
west el oeste (I)
western *adj.* del oeste (I)
wet mojado, -a (4)
what lo que (I)
  so —? ¿qué importa? (I)
  —? ¿qué? (I); ¿cuál? (I)
  — **a(n)** + *noun!* ¡qué + *noun!* (I)
  —**'s** *(someone / something)* **like?** ¿cómo es . . . ? (I)
  —**'s your name?** ¿cómo te llamas? (I)
wheel la rueda (3)
  Ferris — la rueda de feria (3)
  steering — el volante (8)
wheelchair la silla de ruedas (9)
when ¿cuándo?; cuando (I)
where ¿dónde?; donde; ¿por dónde? (13)
  from —? ¿de dónde? (I)
  (to) —? ¿adónde? (I)
which, which one(s)? ¿cuál(es)? (I)
while mientras (13)
white blanco, -a (I)
who que; ¿quién(es)? (I)
whole: the — todo, -a (I)
whom? ¿a quién(es)? (I)
  for —? ¿para quién(es)? (I)
  to —? ¿a quién(es)? (I)
  with —? ¿con quién(es)? (I)
whose? ¿de quién(es)? (I)
why? ¿por qué? (I)
  that's — por eso (I)

wide ancho, -a (7)
wife la esposa (I)
will you . . . ? ¿quiere(n) + *inf.?* (6); tenga la bondad de + *inf.* (10)
to win ganar (I)
windshield el parabrisas, *pl.* parabrisas (8)
window la ventana; *(in vehicles)* la ventanilla (I, 8)
  store — la vitrina (7)
  ticket — la ventanilla (6)
windy: it's — hace viento (I)
wine el vino (I)
winner el ganador, la ganadora (5)
winning ganador, -a (5)
winter el invierno (I)
with con (I)
  — **me** conmigo (I)
  — **you** *fam.* contigo (I)
within dentro de (16)
without sin (I)
  — **a doubt** sin duda (12)
woman la mujer (I)
  old — la anciana (13)
wonderful maravilloso, -a (6)
wood la madera (14)
wool la lana (14)
word la palabra (I)
work el trabajo (I); la obra (12)
to work trabajar (I); *(machines)* funcionar (2)
  worker: farm — el campesino, la campesina (4)
world el mundo (14)
worried preocupado, -as (I)
to worry (about) preocuparse (por) (16)
worse peor (I)
worst: the — + *noun* + **in** el / la peor + *noun* + de(l) (I)
worth: to be — **it / the effort** valer la pena (16)
would *imperfect tense* (13)
to wrap envolver (o → ue) (10)
wrist la muñeca (9)
to write escribir (I)

writer el escritor, la escritora (I)
wrong equivocado, -a (10)
  to be — no tener razón (I)
  what's — **with you?** ¿qué tienes / tiene Ud.? (9)

to yawn bostezar (11)
  year el año (I)
  school — el año escolar (1)
  to be . . . —s old tener . . . años (I)
yellow amarillo, -a (I)
yes sí (I)
yesterday ayer (I)
  the day before — anteayer (5)
  — **morning** ayer por la mañana (I)
yogurt el yogur (I)
you *fam.* tú; *formal* usted (Ud.); *pl.* ustedes (Uds.); ti *after prep.;* lo, la *sing. formal dir. obj.;* los, las *pl. dir. obj.;* te *fam. dir. obj.* (I)
  to / for — *formal* le; *pl.* les; *fam.* te (I)
  with — *fam.* contigo (I)
young joven, *pl.* jóvenes (I)
younger menor (I)
your tu, tus *fam.;* su, sus *formal & pl.* (I); tuyo, -a (8); suyo, -a (8)
you're welcome *see* **welcome**
yours el tuyo / suyo, la tuya / suya, los tuyos / suyos, las tuyas / suyas (8)
  of — *adj.* tuyo, -a (8); suyo, -a (8)
yourself te *fam.;* se *(formal)* (I)
yourselves se (I)

zebra la cebra (I)
zero cero (I)
zip code el código postal (10)
zoo el zoológico (I)
zookeeper el guardián, la guardiana (de zoológico) (I)

INDEX

Most new structures are first presented in conversational contexts and explained later. Bold-face numbers refer to pages where structures are explained or highlighted. Light-face numbers refer to pages where they are initially presented, reviewed, or elaborated upon.

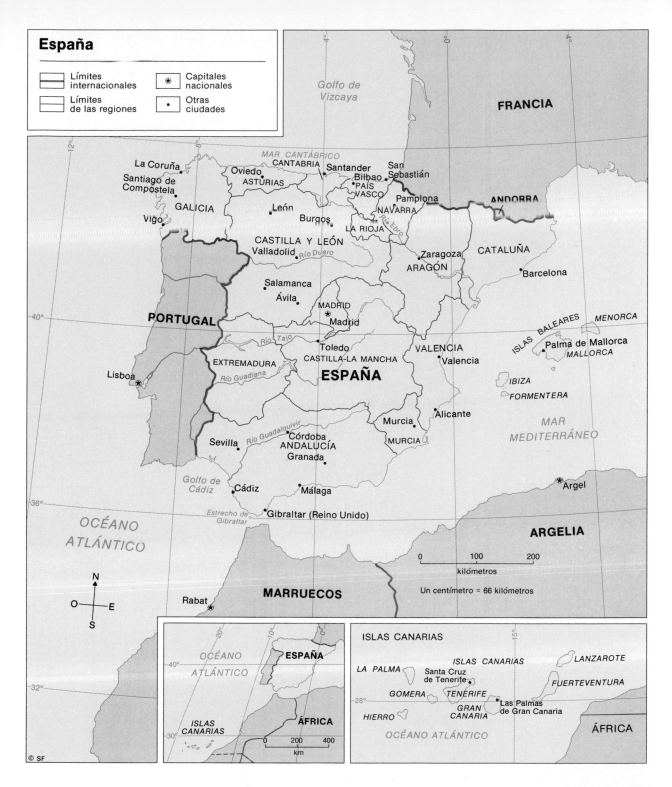

España

Límites
internacionales

Límites
de las regiones

⊛ **Capitales**
nacionales

• **Otras**
ciudades

*Golfo de
Vizcaya*

FRANCIA

MAR CANTÁBRICO

La Coruña

Santiago de
Compostela

GALICIA

Vigo

Oviedo

ASTURIAS

CANTABRIA

Santander

Bilbao

**PAÍS
VASCO**

San
Sebastián

NAVARRA

Pamplona

ANDORRA

León

Burgos

LA RIOJA

Río Ebro

CASTILLA Y LEÓN

Valladolid

Río Duero

Zaragoza

ARAGÓN

CATALUÑA

Barcelona

Salamanca

Ávila

MADRID

⊛

Madrid

PORTUGAL

Río Tajo

Toledo

CASTILLA-LA MANCHA

VALENCIA

Valencia

ISLAS BALEARES

MENORCA

Palma de Mallorca

MALLORCA

EXTREMADURA

Río Guadiana

ESPAÑA

IBIZA

FORMENTERA

Lisboa

⊛

Murcia

Alicante

*MAR
MEDITERRÁNEO*

MURCIA

Sevilla

Córdoba

ANDALUCÍA

Granada

Río Guadalquivir

**OCÉANO
ATLÁNTICO**

*Golfo de
Cádiz*

Cádiz

Málaga

Argel

⊛

N
O — E
S

MARRUECOS

*Estrecho de
Gibraltar*

Gibraltar (Reino Unido)

ARGELIA

0   100   200
kilómetros

Un centímetro = 66 kilómetros

Rabat ⊛

© SF

*OCÉANO
ATLÁNTICO*

ESPAÑA

*ISLAS
CANARIAS*

ÁFRICA

0   200   400
km

ISLAS CANARIAS

ISLAS CANARIAS

LA PALMA

Santa Cruz
de Tenerife

LANZAROTE

FUERTEVENTURA

GOMERA

TENERIFE

Las Palmas
de Gran Canaria

HIERRO

*GRAN
CANARIA*

ÁFRICA

OCÉANO ATLÁNTICO

Mapas   **607**

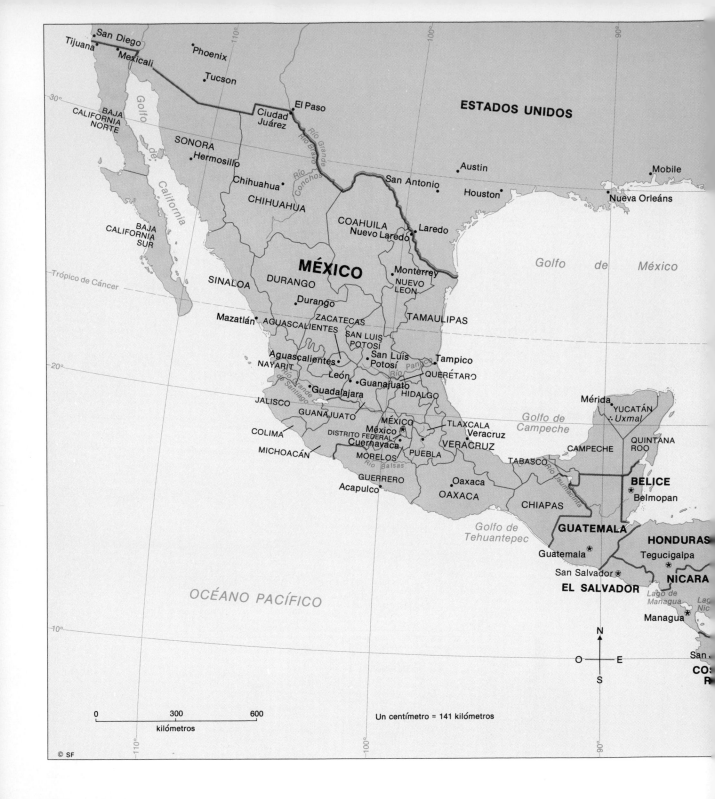

Tijuana
San Diego
Mexicali
Phoenix
Tucson
El Paso
Ciudad Juárez

ESTADOS UNIDOS

BAJA CALIFORNIA NORTE
Golfo de California
SONORA
Hermosillo
Chihuahua
CHIHUAHUA

30°

Río Grande
Río Bravo
Río Conchos

Austin
San Antonio
Houston
Mobile
Nueva Orleáns

BAJA CALIFORNIA SUR

COAHUILA
Nuevo Laredo
Laredo

MÉXICO

Golfo de México

Trópico de Cáncer

SINALOA
DURANGO
Durango
Monterrey
NUEVO LEON

Mazatlán
ZACATECAS
AGUASCALIENTES
SAN LUIS POTOSÍ
San Luis Potosí
Tampico
QUERÉTARO
Río Pánuco

TAMAULIPAS

20°

Aguascalientes
NAYARIT
León
Guanajuato
HIDALGO
Río Grande de Santiago

JALISCO
GUANAJUATO
MÉXICO
México
TLAXCALA
Veracruz
VERACRUZ
Mérida
Uxmal
YUCATÁN
Golfo de Campeche

Guadalajara
Río Lerma

COLIMA
DISTRITO FEDERAL
Cuernavaca
PUEBLA
MICHOACÁN
MORELOS
Río Balsas
GUERRERO
Acapulco
Oaxaca
OAXACA
CHIAPAS
TABASCO
Río Usumacinta
CAMPECHE
QUINTANA ROO

BELICE
Belmopan

Golfo de Tehuantepec

GUATEMALA
Guatemala
San Salvador
EL SALVADOR

HONDURAS
Tegucigalpa

NICARA

Lago de Managua
Lago Nic

OCÉANO PACÍFICO

Managua

10°

N
O E
S

San
COS
R

0   300   600
kilómetros

Un centímetro = 141 kilómetros

© SF

608   Mapas

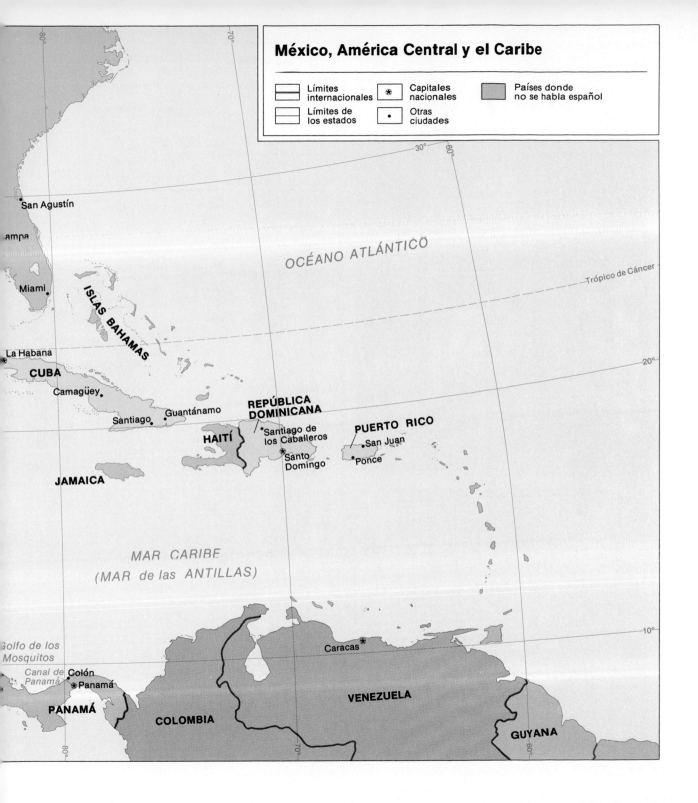

México, América Central y el Caribe

Límites internacionales
Límites de los estados
Capitales nacionales
Otras ciudades
Países donde no se habla español

San Agustín

Tampa

OCÉANO ATLÁNTICO

Miami

Trópico de Cáncer

ISLAS BAHAMAS

La Habana

CUBA

20°

Camagüey

Santiago
Guantánamo

REPÚBLICA DOMINICANA

PUERTO RICO

HAITÍ

Santiago de los Caballeros
San Juan

Santo Domingo
Ponce

JAMAICA

MAR CARIBE
(MAR de las ANTILLAS)

Golfo de los Mosquitos

Caracas

Canal de Panamá
Colón
Panamá

VENEZUELA

10°

PANAMÁ

COLOMBIA

GUYANA

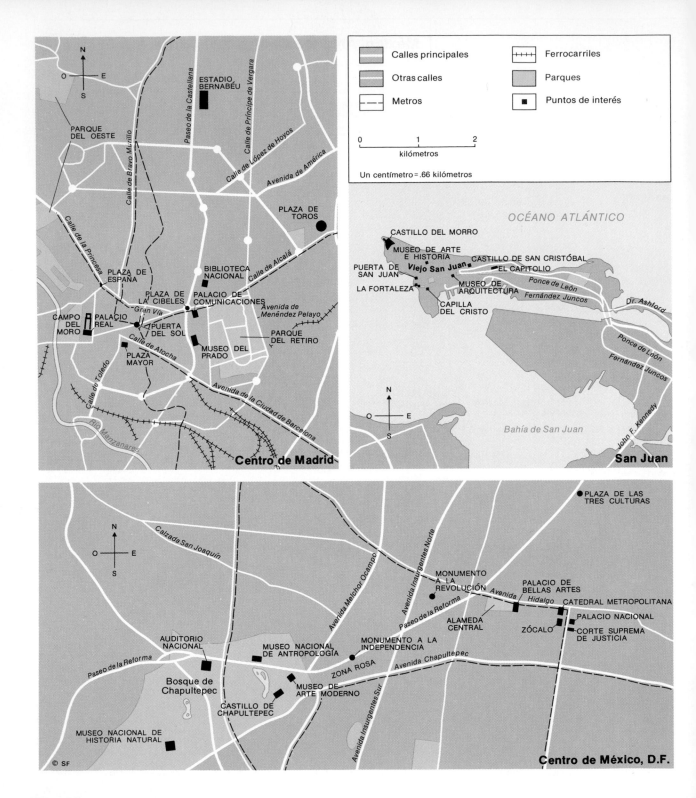

Centro de Madrid

N
O — E
S

PARQUE DEL OESTE

Calle de Bravo Murillo

Paseo de la Castellana

ESTADIO BERNABÉU

Calle de Príncipe de Vergara

Calle de López de Hoyos

Avenida de América

PLAZA DE TOROS

Calle de la Princesa

PLAZA DE ESPAÑA

BIBLIOTECA NACIONAL

Calle de Alcalá

PLAZA DE LA CIBELES

PALACIO DE COMUNICACIONES

Avenida de Menéndez Pelayo

Gran Vía

CAMPO DEL MORO

PALACIO REAL

PUERTA DEL SOL

Calle de Atocha

MUSEO DEL PRADO

PARQUE DEL RETIRO

PLAZA MAYOR

Calle de Toledo

Avenida de la Ciudad de Barcelona

Río Manzanares

	Calles principales		Ferrocarriles
	Otras calles		Parques
	Metros		Puntos de interés

0   1   2
kilómetros

Un centímetro = .66 kilómetros

San Juan

OCÉANO ATLÁNTICO

CASTILLO DEL MORRO

MUSEO DE ARTE E HISTORIA

CASTILLO DE SAN CRISTÓBAL

EL CAPITOLIO

PUERTA DE SAN JUAN

Viejo San Juan

Ponce de León

Dr. Ashford

LA FORTALEZA

MUSEO DE ARQUITECTURA

Fernández Juncos

CAPILLA DEL CRISTO

Ponce de León

Fernández Juncos

N
O — E
S

Bahía de San Juan

John F. Kennedy

Centro de México, D.F.

N
O — E
S

Calzada San Joaquín

PLAZA DE LAS TRES CULTURAS

Avenida Melchor Ocampo

Avenida Insurgentes Norte

MONUMENTO A LA REVOLUCIÓN

Paseo de la Reforma

Avenida Hidalgo

PALACIO DE BELLAS ARTES

CATEDRAL METROPOLITANA

AUDITORIO NACIONAL

MUSEO NACIONAL DE ANTROPOLOGÍA

MONUMENTO A LA INDEPENDENCIA

ALAMEDA CENTRAL

PALACIO NACIONAL

ZÓCALO

CORTE SUPREMA DE JUSTICIA

Paseo de la Reforma

ZONA ROSA

MUSEO DE ARTE MODERNO

Avenida Chapultepec

Bosque de Chapultepec

CASTILLO DE CHAPULTEPEC

Avenida Insurgentes Sur

MUSEO NACIONAL DE HISTORIA NATURAL

© SF

610   Mapas

ACKNOWLEDGMENTS

Illustrations

Illustrations by Steve Boswick, James Buckley, Aldo Castillo, Donald Charles, Len Ebert, Linda Kelen, Carl Kock, Yoshi Miyake, Mike Muir, Rob Porazinski, Dan Siculan, Suzanne Snider, Ed Taber, Justin Wager, Don Wilson, and John Youssi

Photos

Positions of photographs are shown in abbreviated form as follows: topt(t), bottom(b), center(c), left(l), right(r), insert(INS). Unless otherwise acknowledged, all photos are the property of Scott, Foresman and Company. Cover, Stuart Cohen; ii–iii, iv–v, John Moore; vi, Stuart Cohen; ix, Peter Menzel; x, xii–xiii, xiv, xvi–xvii, Robert Frerck/Odyssey Productions, Chicago; 1, Stuart Cohen; 12, Peter Menzel; 16tl, Robert Frerck/Odyssey Productions, Chicago; 16tr, Stuart Cohen; 16b, 17l, Joseph F. Viesti; 17r, Robert Frerck/Click/Chicago Ltd.; 21t, Mike Mazzaschi/Stock Boston; 21b, K. Benser/Leo de Wys; 23tl, William Dyckes; 23tr, Stuart Cohen; 23b, Larry Mangino/The Image Works; 25, David R. Frazier Photolibrary; 26, Tor Eigeland/Susan Griggs Agency; 27, William Dyckes; 28–29, Robert Frerck/Odyssey Productions, Chicago; 33t, Owen Franken; 33INS: tr, cl, Owen Franken; cc, Stuart Cohen; cl, bl, Owen Franken; bc, Stuart Cohen; br, Owen Franken; 35, Stuart Cohen; 37, 46, Robert Frerck/Odyssey Productions, Chicago; 48, Stuart Cohen; 53l, Owen Franken; 53INS, Stuart Cohen; 53r, 55, Robert Frerck/Odyssey Productions, Chicago; 57, Stuart Cohen; 58l, 58r, Robert Frerck/Odyssey Productions, Chicago; 61, Courtesy of The Newberry Library, Chicago; 62–63, 68, Robert Frerck/Odyssey Productions, Chicago; 69tr, Lee Foster; 69c, Stuart Cohen; 69b, Owen Franken; 71t, Stuart Cohen; 71b, Peter Menzel; 74, Robert Frerck/Odyssey Productions, Chicago; 76, José Carrillo/Click/Chicago Ltd.; 81, Robert Frerck/Odyssey Productions, Chicago; 84t, Gerald Marella/D. Donne Bryant; 84b, Stuart Cohen; 85, Robert Frerck/Odyssey Productions, Chicago; 89, Peter Menzel; 91, South American Pictures; 92l, 92r, Joseph F. Viesti; 95, Franz Altschuler; 96–97, Mike Yamashita (© 1986); 100, Robert Frerck/Odyssey Productions, Chicago; 101, Peter Menzel; 103, Bob Daemmrich; 108l, Stuart Cohen; 108r, William Dyckes; 111, Stuart Cohen; 112, Owen Franken; 113, 117, Robert Frerck/Odyssey Productions, Chicago; 119, Stuart Cohen; 122, Mark Antman/The Image Works; 123, Peter Menzel; 125, 126, Robert Frerck/Odyssey Productions, Chicago; 129, Eugenia Fawcett; 130–131, Tom Hopkins; 134, Robert Frerck/Odyssey Productions, Chicago; 135, South American Pictures; 138, Artstreet; 139, Stuart Cohen; 142, Loren McIntyre; 144, Bob and Ira Spring; 145l, Victor Englebert; 145r, 146l, Stuart Cohen; 146r, Mark Antman/The Image Works; 153, Brian Seed/Click/Chicago Ltd.; 155l, Milt & Joan Mann/Cameramann International, Ltd.; 155r, Stuart Cohen; 156c, Joseph F. Viesti; 156r, Robert Frerck/Odyssey Productions, Chicago; 159, Victor Englebert; 160l, Joseph F. Viesti; 160r, Stuart Cohen; 163, Dwayne Newton; 164–165, Stuart Cohen; 168, David Ryan/D. Donne Bryant; 170l, 170r, Focus On Sports; 171, Joseph F. Viesti; 172–173l, Duomo Photography Inc.; 173r, Stuart Cohen; 178, 180, Robert Frerck/Odyssey Productions, Chicago; 181, Focus On Sports; 182, John Apolinski/Hillstrom Stock Photos; 187, M. Timothy O'Keefe/Tom Stack & Associates; 188l, Focus On Sports; 188c, Paul J. Sutton/Duomo Photography Inc.; 188r, South American Pictures; 191, John Henebry; 192, Adam J. Stoltman/Duomo Photography Inc.; 195, Courtesy of the Artisan Shop, Cuyahoga Falls, Ohio; 196–197, Loren McIntyre; 202l, Susan Dobinsky; 202r, Robert Frerck/Odyssey Productions, Chicago; 204, Stuart Cohen; 205, South American Pictures; 208l, Peter Menzel; 208r, Robert Frerck/Odyssey Productions, Chicago; 210, Robert Freed/D. Donne Bryant; 216, Artstreet; 217, Robert Frerck/Odyssey Productions, Chicago; 218, Joseph F. Viesti; 219, Peter Menzel; 219r, 226, Joseph F. Viesti; 229, Collection of Santiago and Roseanne Mendoza; 230–231, (© 1983) Stephanie Maze/Woodfin Camp & Associates; 236tl, Joseph F. Viesti; 236 tr, Kennedy/TexaStock; 239, Milt & Joan Mann/Cameramann International, Ltd.; 241, Beryl Goldberg; 246, Robert Frerck/Odyssey Productions, Chicago; 247, David R. Frazier Photolibrary; 248l, Joseph F. Viesti; 248r, Stuart Cohen; 256, Milt & Joan Mann/Cameramann International, Ltd.; 258, Joseph F. Viesti; 260, John Henebry; 263, From the collection of Peter and Roberta Markman. Photo by Joan Benedetti for the Craft & Folk Art Museum Exhibition, "Masks in Motion," 1984; 264–265, Peter Menzel; 269, Stuart Cohen; 270l, 270r, Robert Frerck/Odyssey Productions, Chicago; 271, Peter Menzel; 272, Larry Mangino/The Image Works; 273, Frerck/Click/Chicago Ltd.; 276, Stuart Cohen; 277, Robert Frerck/Odyssey Productions, Chicago; 280, Artstreet; 281, Stuart Cohen; 284l, David Ryan/D. Donne Bryant; 284r, Artstreet; 285, Larry Mangino/The Image Works; 287, Paul Dix/Reflejo; 292, 296–297, 300, Robert Frerck/Odyssey Productions, Chicago; 302, Joseph F. Viesti; 303, David Phillips; 305, Larry Kolvoord/TexaStock; 309, Robert Frerck/Odyssey

Productions, Chicago; 313, Owen Franken; 315, Robert Frerck/Odyssey Productions, Chicago; 319, Stuart Cohen; 324, Joseph F. Viesti; 327, Courtesy: Cortland-Leyten Gallery; 328–329, William Dyckes; 332, Milt & Joan Mann/Cameramann International, Ltd.; 335, David R. Frazier Photolibrary; 337, Joseph F. Viesti; 343, Charmayne McGee; 348, Beryl Goldberg; 350, Peter Menzel; 353, Stuart Cohen; 355, Don and Pat Valenti; 357, Beryl Goldberg; 358, Owen Franken; 361, Aldo Castillo; 362–363, Horst Munzig/Susan Greggs Agency; 369, Black Star; 373, Larry Mangino/The Image Works; 375(all), The Bettmann Archive; 376, South American Pictures; 379, Peter Menzel; 381, Robert Frerck/Odyssey Productions, Chicago; 382, Larry Mangino/The Image Works; 387l, Stuart Cohen; 387r, William Dyckes; 391b, Peter Menzel; 395, D. Donne Bryant; 396–397, Milt & Joan Mann/ Cameramann International, Ltd.; 402, Stuart Cohen; 403, Bob Daemmrich; 405, Alfredo Arrequín; 407, Sheryl McNee/Click/ Chicago Ltd.; 408, Artstreet; 414, *The Tampa Tribune;* 415, Robert Frerck/Odyssey Productions, Chicago; 417, Joseph F. Viesti; 418, Menaud/Figaro/Gamma-Liaison; 420, Roberto Otero/Black Star; 421, Peter Menzel; 422, Stuart Cohen; 425, Jackie Foryst/ Bruce Coleman Inc.; 426–427, Robert Frerck/Odyssey Productions, Chicago; 433, Peter Menzel; 435, 438, Stuart Cohen; 441, Robert Frerck/Odyssey Productions, Chicago; 442, Peter Menzel; 443, David Kennedy/TexaStock; 446, Milt & Joan Mann/ Cameramann International, Ltd.; 448, Inge Morath/Magnum Photos; 452, Stephanie Maze/Woodfin Camp & Associates; 455, Norma Morrison; 456–457, Dom Nebbia/Click/Chicago Ltd.; 460, J. Alex Langley/DPI; 461, Norman Prince; 463, Tessing Design Inc.; 465, Norman Prince; 468, Stuart Cohen; 471, Ken Hawkins/Sygma; 475, Robert Frerck/Odyssey Productions, Chicago; 476, Andrew Rakoczy/Bruce Coleman Inc.; 477, Barbara Laing/Black Star; 478, R. Neveu/Gamma-Liaison; 480, 482, Peter Menzel; 485, Robert Frerck/Odyssey Productions, Chicago; 486–487, Loren McIntyre; 492, Wolfgang Kaehler; 494, Peter Menzel; 498, Milt & Joan Mann/Cameramann International, Ltd.; 499, Beryl Goldberg; 501, Robert Frerck/Odyssey Productions, Chicago; 508, Manolo Rodríguez; 510, Victor Englebert; 513, Robert Frerck/Odyssey Productions, Chicago; 514, Loren McIntyre; 517, Eugenia Fawcett; 522, Milt & Joan Mann/Cameramann International, Ltd.; 524, Owen Franken; 529, David Phillips; 530, David R. Frazier Photolibrary; 533, Owen Franken; 538, Robert Frerck/Odyssey Productions, Chicago; 539, J. C. Carton/Bruce Coleman Inc.; 541, Chip & Rosa Maria Peterson; 543, 544, Stuart Cohen; 547, Courtesy: Cortland-Leyten Gallery.

TEACHER NOTES

TEACHER NOTES